THE

100

BEST

STOCKS

YOU CAN BUY

2001

John Slatter

Adams Media Corporation
Holbrook, Massachusetts

Dedication

To my sister and brother:
Ruth Backus
Bill Slatter

Acknowledgments

Writing a book is far easier than finding a publisher. My first book, *Safe Investing*, didn't find a home until I latched on to my dutiful agent, Edythea Ginis Selman. Edy knows how to find a publisher, and she knows how to convince the editor that I am worth paying a living wage.

My publisher, Adams Media, has treated me like a king. That could be because the editor is Edward Walters, an easy guy to do business with.

Published by
Adams Media Corporation
260 Center Street, Holbrook, MA 02343
www.adamsmedia.com

ISBN: 1-58062-425-1

Printed in Canada.

J I H G F E D C B

This book is not designed or intended to provide or replace professional investment advice. Readers should invest with care, including seeking specific professional advice, since investments by nature involve significant risk and can result in financial losses. The past performance of the investments reported in this book does not guarantee or predict future performance.

Cover design by Mike Stromberg.

This book is available at quantity discounts for bulk purchases.
For information, call 1-800-872-5627

Visit our exciting small business website: www.businesstown.com

Table of Contents

Part I

The Art and Science of Investing in Stocks

Preface

When I wrote the fourth edition of *The 100 Best Stocks You Can Buy*, I was warned by the editor that I might be called upon to update the book if investors in droves bought it. Apparently, that's what happened, so I was ordered back to my computer.

The editor didn't think this would be much of a chore, but he turned out to be wrong. Using the 1999 annual reports—and other information such as *Value Line*, newspaper and magazine articles, and Standard & Poor's reports—I found that about 80 percent of my write-ups were old news. In some instances I abandoned the entire text and started over.

Equally important, I added a batch of new stocks and dropped an equal number that I decided no longer interested me. Among the new stocks are such intriguing companies as Cintas, Cisco Systems, Costco Wholesale, Medtronic, and Texas Instruments

Adding new stocks means dropping old ones. One investor suggested that I give reasons for each stock being eliminated. Although this may seem sensible, I have elected not to comply. On the other hand, I see no reason to sell your shares of the stocks that do not appear in this edition. In most instances, switching from one stock to another doesn't work out. For one thing, every time you replace a stock, you have two commissions to pay. And don't forget the cash you have to ship to the IRS when you sell a stock that has risen in price.

In this edition, I have become somewhat more growth-oriented and aggressive. The number of stocks labeled *aggressive growth* has been climbing. This will probably surprise many of the people who know me well. They tend to regard me as a "value investor." They will be shocked that I am recommending such stocks as FDX, Washington REIT, and Intel.

And, for heaven's sake, don't fret when you can't find your favorite stock in my list of 100. Some of my own stocks are also missing, such as Indiana Energy, and Lakehead Pipeline. What it amounts to is this: There are more than a hundred great stocks. Nor is my list necessarily the best one.

On the other hand, my wife and I own over forty of the 100 stocks, which I guess makes us believers. It also makes us believers in the magic of common-stock investing.

It has now been over thirty years since I first joined the investment community. My philosophy over that span has not changed drastically, but there are a few fundamental truths that I cling to:

- You can't forecast the market, so quit trying.
- Common stocks are the only place to put your money. Everything else is inferior, such as real estate, bonds, coins, stamps, antiques, baseball cards, certificates of deposit, and money-market funds.

- Trading is the quickest way to the poorhouse. The only sensible strategy is to buy and hold.
- Don't bet the farm on one or two stocks. There are 3,000 stocks listed on the New York Stock Exchange. Surely you can find 15 or 20 that will help you become rich.
- Don't buy mutual funds. Why? They charge too much; they create unwanted tax liabilities; they are often inept. What's more, there are over 9,000 to choose from; many are managed by kids who are still in their twenties. Also, there is no way to know which ones are the best. Past history is of little help since managers move from one fund to another.
- Don't ask anyone for advice; make up your own mind. That way you won't have anyone to blame if you goof. And you will goof once in a while. But you don't have to be right too often to make a bundle. If the average stock returns 10 percent a year, here is how rich you'll be at age 65. If you invest $5,000 a year beginning at age 45, you'll have $286,375 at age 65. If you start at age 35, you'll have $822,470. It pays to start early. Here's proof. If you start at age 25 and invest only $2,000 a year, you'll reach age 65 with $885,185.

- Don't put off investing because you are saving for a car, saving for education, saving for a house, saving for a vacation. Put aside at least 10 percent of every paycheck. Even better, make it 15 or 20 percent. But don't do this unless you are prepared to reach retirement with stocks worth hundreds of thousands of dollars.
- Don't make the mistake of avoiding high-priced stocks such as IBM, Exxon, Intel, or GE. Investors often tell me, "I am just a small investor; I can't afford a high-priced stock. Don't you have something under $30 a share?" Rubbish. Buy 10, 20, or 30 shares if you can't afford 100.
- Don't buy a stock simply because my write-up appeals to you. Call the company and get a copy of the annual report. Study it as if your life depended on it. It does. If managing your own portfolio makes you nervous and fretful, call me at (802) 879-4154 and I'll give you some good reasons why the firm I am associated with (First Financial Investment Management) can do the chore for you. Our minimum account is $250,000. You can also reach me by e-mail: bluechip@ together.net

Why Invest in Stocks?

Investing is a complex business. But, then, so is medicine, engineering, chemistry, geology, law, gardening, philosophy, cooking, paleontology, dentistry, photography, history, accounting—you name it.

In fact, investing is so daunting and intimidating that many otherwise intelligent individuals avoid it. Instead, they stash their money in certificates of deposit (CDs), annuities, bonds, or mutual funds.

Apparently they can't face buying common stocks. This is too bad, because common stocks are precisely where the money is made. To be sure, you don't make money every day, every week, or even every year. But over the long term, you will make the most out of your investment dollars in stocks.

Look at the Facts

One persuasive study, for instance, contends that common stocks will make money for you in most years. This study, which was done by the brokerage firm Smith Barney, looked at the thirty-five one-year periods between 1960 and 1995.

The study computed total return, which adds together capital gains and dividends. Over that span, stocks (as represented by the Standard & Poor's 500 index) performed unsatisfactorily in only eight of those thirty-five years. In other words, you would have been better off in money-market funds during those eight years. That's not a bad track record. Common stocks would have been more successful in twenty-seven of those thirty-five years.

Investing for the Long Term

Investing, however, is not a one-year endeavor. Most investors start their programs in their forties and fifties, which means they could be investing over a twenty-, thirty-, or forty-year period.

If we look at the relative returns of different investments over five-year periods—rather than one-year periods—the results are even more encouraging. During the years from 1960 through 1994, there were thirty-one such periods. In only two of those five-year periods did the total return of the Standard & Poor's-based portfolio become negative.

Let's move ahead to all ten-year holding periods. There were twenty-six in that span. Exactly 100 percent worked out profitably. Equally important, the returns to the investor were impressive in all of these one-, five-, and ten-year periods. The one-year periods, for instance, gave you an average annual total return of 11.1 percent; for five-year periods, it was 10.5 percent, and for ten-year periods, it was 10.2 percent.

Based on this brokerage house study, then, we can say with a great deal of confidence that over a lifetime of investing, an investor will reap a total annual return of 10 percent or more.

If you compare this with the amount you could earn by owning CDs, annuities, government bonds, or any other conservative investment, the difference is considerable.

Some Profitable Comparisons

Let's see how that difference adds up. Suppose you invested $25,000 in a list of common stocks at the age of forty, and your portfolio built up at a 10 percent compound annual rate. By the time you reached sixty-five, your common stock nest egg would be worth $270,868.

On the other hand, let's say you had invested your money in government bonds, yielding 6 percent. The same $25,000 would be worth only $107,297, which is a difference of $163,571. Neither of these calculations has taken into account income taxes or brokerage commissions.

Now, let's look at the timid soul who invested $25,000 in CDs at age forty and averaged a return of 4 percent. By age sixty-five, that investment would be worth a paltry $66,646.

Why Doesn't Everyone Buy Common Stocks?

That's a good question, and I'm not sure I can provide you with a satisfactory answer. Part of the reason may be ignorance. Not everyone is willing to investigate the field of common stocks. These noninvestors may be too preoccupied with their jobs, sports, reading, gardening, travel, soap operas, hobbies, or whatever. Then there are the people who are heavily influenced by family members who have sold them on the idea that stocks are too speculative and better left to millionaires. (Of course, that's how many of these millionaires became millionaires.)

Even if you are convinced that I may be right about the potential of stocks, you are probably wondering how anyone can possibly figure out which stocks to buy, since there are tens of thousands to choose from. That, in essence, is the purpose of this book—and the subject of the chapter that follows.

A Real-Life Example

If you are a newcomer to the realm of investing, you may still doubt that you are capable of building a portfolio of stocks that will make you rich. You may be thinking, "Maybe it would be safer to stash my retirement money in certificates of deposit (CDs) and settle for a steady return of 5 percent."

Not all stocks are going to live up to their early promise, no matter how much time you devote to making a selection. On the other hand, even if you pick your stocks blindfolded, you will have some winners. Let's suppose that you want to invest $100,000 in 20 stocks, or $5,000 in each. Admittedly, some will work out and some won't.

Hypothetically, it does not seem unreasonable to project that 10 of these stocks will just plug along, making you neither rich nor poor. Suppose we assume that these 10 stocks will appreciate (rise in value) an average of only 7 percent per year over the next 10 or 20 years. Toss in a 2 percent annual dividend and the total return adds up to 9 percent per year. That is not exactly riches, since stocks over the last 75 years have averaged about 11 percent.

At any rate, here is what your $50,000 will be worth at the end of 10 years and 20 years:

$118,368 $280,221

Next, let's look at the three stocks that performed above your wildest dreams. They appreciated an average of 15 percent per year. Add in a modest annual dividend of only 1 percent, and you have a total return of 16 percent.

Assuming you invest $5,000 in each of these three stocks, here is how that $15,000 climbs over the next 10- and 20-year periods:

$66,172 $291,911

So far, so good. Now, for the bad news. Two of your stocks hit the skids and never recovered. Total results for the $10,000 invested in these losers is: Zero.

$00,000 $00,000

Finally, five of your 20 stocks do about average. They appreciate an average of 9 percent per year and have an average yearly dividend of 2 percent. That's a total return of 11 percent. Since you have five stocks in this category, your total investment in this sector is $25,000. Here is what you end up with 10 and 20 years from now:

$70,986 $201,558

If we add up these various results, the final figures make you look reasonably rich:

$255,525 $773,690

By contrast, had you acted in a cowardly manner and invested exclusively in CDs, you would have only the following at the end of the two periods:

$162,889 $265,330

One final note. If you figure in taxes, you look even better, since the capital gains (on your stocks) are taxed at a much lower rate than ordinary income (which applies to CDs). And, you wouldn't even have to worry about capital gains on your stocks if you elected not to sell them.

Picking the Right Stocks for You

Whenever I visit a bookstore, I make a mad dash to look at the books devoted to investing. I want to make sure they have ample copies of my latest books, including my introductory text, *Straight Talk About Stock Investing*, published by McGraw-Hill.

On a recent visit to a local bookstore, I actually saw a woman—she appeared to be in her mid-thirties—leafing through the 2000 edition of *The 100 Best Stocks You Can Buy*. Considering the huge number of investment books that were competing against my masterpiece, I was tempted to congratulate her for having such keen judgment.

But I didn't have to. She spoke first. "Aren't you John Slatter?" she said.

"How did you know?"

"You made a talk to our investment club a few weeks ago. My name is Rhodes—Glabella Rhodes. My husband and I are both in the investment club, trying to learn how to pick stocks so we can send our son Scott to college. I'm one of the few who didn't buy a book. I've felt guilty ever since."

"Maybe you should pay the supreme penalty and buy three copies: one for yourself, one for your husband, and one for Scott."

"Sounds like a good idea," she said. "But only if you explain to me how I can figure out which of these 100 stocks I should buy."

"What if your husband finds out you are talking to a strange man?"

"He wouldn't dare divorce me. I'm too good a cook. If you have a few spare minutes, why don't we find a vacant table and go over your strategy—if I'm not being too forward."

"Let me scoot out to my car and get my briefcase. I think I have a yellow legal pad and one of my trusty Hewlett-Packard 12C calculators. Can you believe I own four of them? No matter where I am, a Hewlett-Packard 12C is handy. The last one I got at a garage sale for a paltry $5— it had never been used."

"It sounds like you are a bargain-hunter. Is that how you got rich?"

"That's my secret. I'm so tight I don't even buy new cars."

When we found a suitable place to set up shop, I said, "I'm a fiend for developing methods of stock selection. I have scores of notebooks full of my back-testing. I have been doing research for over 30 years."

"What's back-testing?"

"Whenever I come up with a bright idea on how to pick stocks, I check out its history by consulting back issues of *Value Line* or the Standard & Poor's *Stock Guide*. My office is stuffed with these back issues.

"Most of the time, my strategies *don't* work out, at least not consistently. One idea that gave me some publicity involves picking the 10 high-yield Dow stocks. I devised that strategy in the spring of 1988, and it was later published in the *Wall Street Journal*."

"That sounds like the Dogs of the Dow."

"I know, but don't blame me for that. Those stocks are not dogs. At one time or another, IBM, Merck, GE, GM, J. P. Morgan, AT&T, DuPont, Chevron, Texaco, 3M, Exxon, and Caterpillar have been among the so-called dogs. In my mind, they are blue-chip stocks—the cream of American industry. But that's beside the point. This idea made me famous, but it is not an idea that had staying power. It has failed to work for the past several years. Strange at it may seem, I have never used it."

"I'm assuming you have ideas that *do* work."

"Despite the huge amount of time I have spent trying to find foolproof strategies—I have never found one—not one!"

"Wow! How can you have the nerve to write books if you don't know what you're doing?"

"My publisher forces me. He says investors are buying my books with great abandon—despite the fact that none of my systems works 100 percent of the time. Fortunately, they work part of the time, usually at least 65 percent of the time. If that sounds reasonable, I will tell you how to use them."

"I was hoping for 100 percent. But I guess I'll have to settle for 65 percent. Maybe you could introduce me to someone who could do 100 percent."

"Most of them can't even do 50 percent. That's why they usually fail to do as well as the market. And that includes mutual funds, bank trust departments, stock brokers, pension funds, and advisors. Picking stocks is clearly not that easy. That's why I rely on my simple strategies. Are you ready to learn how they work?"

"Go ahead."

"For the most part, I rely on the statistical information that can be found in the Standard & Poor's *Stock Guide*."

"The *Stock Guide?* That sounds familiar. Where can I get one?"

"You can call the company and sign up for a subscription. Their phone number is 1-800-221-5277. The *Stock Guide* is a monthly publication that lists thousands of stocks, giving you such things as the current dividend, the high and low price of the stock in recent years, a history of earnings per share, the stocks's financial strength rating, and so forth. If you want to look at a copy, check your local library. Also, every brokerage house has them. In fact, some stock brokers give free copies to good customers. If you buy your own, it might cost you $182 a year, perhaps less in the beginning."

"So, I need a *Stock Guide* to implement your strategies."

"Right. Now, let me give you an idea how to use it. To begin with, there are only four factors that I need. First, I want to know how strong the company is financially. There are several ways to determine this, such as examining the balance sheet to see how much debt the company has. *Value Line* also rates the company, giving it such ratings as A++, which is the best, down to B++ which is about average. The *Stock Guide's* ratings start at A+, and B+ is about average."

"Why not stick to stocks that are rated A+ and forget about those that are faltering?"

"Strange as it may seem, A+ does not necessarily guarantee you a winner. In 1999, for instance, Philip Morris was an A+ stock—and has been for many years. During 1999, the stock plunged over 50 percent. It was the worst-performing stock in the Dow Jones Industrial Average.

"In sharp contrast was Alcoa, which was rated B- at the beginning of that year. It soared over 100 percent in 1999 and was the best stock to own among the blue chips in the Dow Jones Industrial Average. So, as you can see, the S&P rating is not the whole story."

"I think I'm getting confused. Tell me more."

"I intend to. I never use just one factor. Instead, I use a combination. The next factor I use is the dividend yield. It's not infallible. In fact, a high yield may indicate that something is wrong. Once again, I point to Philip Morris, which had a high yield at the beginning of 1999—and it got a lot higher as the year wore on.

"Still another factor to examine is the price-earnings ratio, sometimes abbreviated to P/E ratio or multiple. You calculate it by dividing the price of the stock by the earnings per share in the most recent 12 months. Let's say a stock is selling for $75 and has earnings per share of $2.81. You divide $75 by $2.81, and get a P/E of 26.7. High multiples are generally characteristic of companies that are growing at a good clip, let's say 15 or 20 percent a year. On the other hand, a low P/E would be characteristic of a company with flat earnings, such as a public utility."

"So, am I to assume that a high P/E is what you should look for?" Mrs. Rhodes asked.

"Generally speaking, I prefer stocks that are not at either end of the spectrum. Stocks with high multiples—let's say 50 or 75—are often vulnerable to bad news. On the other hand, those with a low price-earnings ratios may be stuck in a rut and going nowhere."

"I think I get the picture."

"The next factor is called the payout ratio," I said. "It's a relationship between the earnings per share and the annual dividend. As an example, if a company earns $3.50 per share in a given year and pays out $2.65, the payout ratio would be 75.7 percent—a very high figure. It would be typical of a public utility, rather than a growth stock. I prefer companies that pay out less than 50 percent of earnings. For instance, if you look at IBM, Intel, Home Depot, or Hewlett-Packard, you will find all of them are stingy dividend payers."

"Why are they so stingy?" she asked.

"They need that cash to plow back into such things as research, advertising, or expansion. In the long run, a growing company translates into price appreciation."

"In other words, it helps me become a millionaire like you."

"I don't recall telling you I was a millionaire," I said.

"I notice you're driving a huge Cadillac, so I put two and two together. Now that you have explained your four factors, what do I do next?"

"The next step is to select a list of stocks that appeal to you—from among the 100 stocks described in my book. Pick at least 10 that fit your temperament—15 would be even better. Then, make up a table and grade each stock, using at least three factors. My favorite three are the S&P quality rating, the P/E ratio, and the payout ratio."

"I think you're going too fast—what do you mean by *grade*?"

"Let me show you what I mean. Here is a table that I drew up recently. It's a list of 15 stocks from the Dow Jones Industrial Average—the first 15 alphabetically. It shows how these stocks performed in 1999. For instance, Alcoa climbed over 100 percent, while Coca-Cola sagged over 13 percent.

"In grading these stocks, I give one point for the best score. For instance, if a stock is an A+, it gets a one. If there are several stocks rated A+, each one receives a one. In this table, there are four stocks with a one. That means that each A stock gets a five. If there had only been one stock with an A+, each A stock would be awarded a two. Thus, it depends on how many stocks in each category there are for you to be able to determine the correct score."

Mrs. Rhodes began shaking her head. "I think you have lost me. What about A-. There were no A- stocks in this table. Do you skip right over it?"

"Exactly. Each A stock is rated 5. Since there are only two of them, we go directly to B+ and give each one 7 points."

"In other words, the best stock gets one point, and the worst one gets 15. Right?"

	S&P	Pts	P/E Ratio	Pts	Payout Ratio	Pts	Total	Percent Change
Alcoa	B-	15	15.2	2	20.4%	3	20	+ 122.64%
Am. Express	B+	7	22.8	7	20.0	2	16	+62.20
AT&T	B+	7	21.5	6	37.5	8	21	+0.61
Boeing	B	10	NM	14	NM	14	34	+27.04
Caterpillar	B	10	10.3	1	16.8	6	17	+2.30
Citigroup	A+	1	17.7	3	25.7	5	9	+68.11
Coca-Cola	A+	1	44.7	12	40.0	9	22	-13.06
DuPont	B	10	35.6	10	94.0	13	33	+24.16
East. Kodak	B	10	NM	14	NM	14	38	-7.99
ExxonMobil	A	5	24.5	8	54.8	12	25	+10.18
Gen. Elect.	A+	1	37.8	11	51.9	11	23	+51.72
Gen. Motors	B	10	18.2	4	50.8	10	24	+16.99
Home Depot	A+	1	61.8	13	12.1	1	15	+68.53
Honeywell	B+	7	19.7	5	26.7	7	19	+30.20
Hewlett-Pack.	A	5	24.7	9	23.1	4	18	+66.52

5 Best Scores		5 Worst Scores	
Citigroup	+68.11%	Eastman Kodak	-7.99%
Home Depot	+ 68.53	Boeing	+27.04
Am. Express	+ 62.20	DuPont	+24.16
Caterpillar	+ 2.30	Exxon	+ 10.18
Hewlett-Packard	+ 66.52	Gen. Motors	+ 16.99
	+ 53.53%		+ 14.08%

"That's generally the way it works, unless there are several stocks rated B-. Then, there would be none with 15 points. Next, let's look at the P/E ratio. You will notice that two stocks don't have a price-earnings ratio. That's because it can't be calculated. You can't calculate the P/E if there are no earnings, or if the earnings figure is very small, such as $.10."

"I assume that a rating of NM means that stocks gets a poor score, such as 14 or 15."

"You seem to be catching on. Next, let's look at the payout ratio. The stock with the best score is Home Depot, since that company likes to plow back most of its earnings and only pays out 12.1 percent. By contrast, DuPont paid out 94 percent in 1999."

"It looks like you take all these scores and arrive at a total. Am I right?"

"That's all there is to it. Like golf, the lowest score is best. In this instance, Citigroup was the big winner. As it turned out, it was a good stock to own in 1999, since it advanced over 68 percent.

"You'll notice at the bottom of my table I have singled out the five stocks with the best scores. As a group, they rose 53.53 percent in 1999. At the other extreme, the five poorest were up only 14.08 percent."

"I thought you said this system only works 65 percent of the time. I don't think I'll show this scheme to my husband. He'll start using it and get so rich he will be able to afford to divorce me."

"I thought you said you were a good cook. Maybe you can still hang on to him."

For Busy Investors, a Strategy that Rarely Fails

As far as I know, I'm one of the few writers who gives readers the opportunity to call if they have any questions. That's why my telephone number is on the page opposite the inside back cover of this book. When you consider the tens of thousands of investors who read my books, very few actually call. And when they do, they are startled and surprised that I usually answer the phone myself—no secretary to screen out malcontents, deadbeats, and cranks.

One of the readers who called a few weeks ago was Horst Graben, a CPA from Wyoming.

"I liked your book, Mr. Slatter, and I read every word. In fact, I actually read it twice, since there are a lot of succulent morsels to digest."

"In other words," I said, "You are *not* calling to complain."

"Well, yes and no," he said. "With 100 stocks to pick from, I am having trouble deciding which ones to buy—and when to sell them if they falter."

I thought for a moment and then said, "Most investors find buying a lot easier than selling. Too often they let a stock sag down week after week, and suddenly they realize it's down 40 percent, and they grit their teeth, hoping it will start back up again. Usually, it doesn't."

"So what should I do?" Horst Graben asked.

"If you are going to manage your own portfolio, you have to be prepared to keep track of your stocks. That means you have to read quarterly and annual reports. It also means reading such publications as the *Wall Street Journal*, the *New York Times*, *Forbes*, *Barron's*, *Business Week*, *Fortune*, and *Better Investing*."

"I was afraid you would say that," he said. "The only problem I have is time . . . I'm particularly busy during tax season . . . I work seven days a week. And even during the rest of the year, I have journals to read and other business commitments. As you might have guessed, I'm a CPA with a busy practice. Reading all that investment stuff is out of the question."

"I can understand your plight, Mr. Graben. Most successful people are busy. That's why they're successful. They spend fifty or sixty hours a week making sure they stay successful."

"Are you telling me to forget about stocks and put my money in mutual funds or certificates of deposit?"

"Absolutely not," I assured him. "I have a systematic approach to stock selection that is made to order for people like you. However, I am reluctant to divulge this strategy unless you promise not to tell a soul about it—not even your wife. Are you prepared to do this?"

"Well, let me think. If you tell me how I can manage my investments without having to do a lot of research and study, you are insisting that I keep the strategy a secret. No one is to know. Okay, I agree."

"Now that I know I can trust you, here goes," I said. "It involves investing exclusively in the 30 stocks that make up the Dow Jones Industrial Average." Then I read him the current components of the index, including their ticker symbols:

Honeywell (HON)
Alcoa (AA)
AT&T (T)
Am. Express (AXP)
Boeing (BA)
Caterpillar (CAT)
Home Depot (HD)
Citigroup (C)
Coca-Cola (KO)
Disney, Walt (DIS)
DuPont (DD)
Eastman Kodak (EK)
ExxonMobil (XOM)
Gen'l Electric (GE)
General Motors (GM)
Intel (INTC)
Hewlett Pack.(HWP)
Int'l Bus. M. (IBM)
Int'l Paper (IP)
John. & John. (JNJ)
McDonald's (MCD)
Merck (MRK)
Minnesota Mining (MMM)
Morgan, J. P. (JPM)
Philip Morris (MO)
Procter & Gamble (PG)
Microsoft (MSFT)
SBC Comm. (SBC)
United Tech. (UTX)
Wal-Mart (WMT)

"That sounds like a great list," he said. "In other words, I concentrate on these 30 stocks, instead of the 100 in your book. Is that what you are saying?"

"Right. These are some of the world's greatest blue-chip stocks. Not all of them will be winners, but enough of them will so that you will end up a millionaire." Then, I went on to outline how to implement the Dow 30 strategy.

The reason the strategy rarely fails is because it entails investing exclusively in the 30 stocks that make up the Dow Jones Industrial Average. Most investors judge their results by this average. It follows that if you invest in all 30 stocks, your performance will approximate that of this well-known index.

Incidentally, if you forget the names of these 30 stocks, you can refresh your memory by consulting the *Wall Street Journal* any day of the week. Look in the third section (*Money and Investing*).

Are You Ready to Be Mediocre!

Buying these 30 stocks may seem like a simplistic and cowardly approach to investing, since you are guaranteed that you will be merely average—or mediocre. And who wants to be mediocre? Most mutual funds would be delighted to be mediocre. Only a small percentage have been average in the past. The vast majority have been **below** average.

Nothing Is Perfect

To be sure, this method of managing a portfolio has some shortcomings:

• You will miss out on such growth stocks and high-flyers as Yahoo!, America Online, Harley-Davidson, Pfizer, Illinois Tool Works, Interpublic, Cisco Systems, Dell, and Lucent.

• You may end up owning a few lackluster performers such as Texaco, Eastman Kodak, Bethlehem Steel, Woolworth, and International Paper. Three of those stocks, incidentally, are no longer in the index: Texaco, Bethlehem Steel, and Woolworth. Nor are Chevron or Westinghouse (now CBS). They were replaced in 1997 by Hewlett-Packard, Johnson & Johnson, Wal-Mart, and Travelers (now Citigroup). This move markedly improved the quality of the Dow Jones Industrial Average—it added four super growth stocks to the index. In 1999, moreover, four new stocks were added: Microsoft, SBC Communications, Home

Depot, and Intel, which improved the growth prospects of the index.

- You could achieve the same objective by investing in an index fund.

In Defense of My Strategy

In my view, the reasons why this strategy has merit can be summed up as follows. On the face of it, investing seems incredibly complex because of the thousands of alternatives. In the realm of mutual funds, for instance, there are 9,000 to choose from. What's more, there is no strategy that leads you to the best ones. Nor are lists gleaned from financial magazines particularly helpful.

If you elect to invest in stocks, the field is even more crowded. There are some 3,000 stocks listed on the New York Stock Exchange. If you venture into the over-the-counter market (or Nasdaq), the choices are vast, at least 5,000. And we haven't even mentioned the vast field of foreign equities.

That's why it makes sense to find a simple—yet effective—way to invest in common stocks. The 30 stocks in the Dow Jones Average give you a playing field that is not nearly as overwhelming or complex as the above alternatives. And these companies are well-managed and unlikely to disappear. They don't always thrive, but they have the size and financial strength to make a comeback. They can afford to cast aside inept CEOs and replace them with executives with proven track records.

Best of all, 30 stocks is a number that you can keep track of. They are not obscure and are well-covered by Wall Street analysts and the *Wall Street Journal,* as well as by such periodicals as *Barron's, Forbes,* and *Fortune.* If you concentrate your attention on these stocks, you can bypass the other 3,000 stocks. It makes sense that most investors can become familiar with these 30 stocks and be able to determine which ones are best, based on the ample information

available from the media, brokerage houses, investment manuals, and annual reports. What's more, all 30 stocks are discussed in the 2001 edition of *The 100 Best Stocks You Can Buy.*

Not every investor, of course, has sufficient funds to buy all 30 stocks. On the other hand, good diversification can be achieved by owning 15 or 20. In any event, there is no need to buy the entire portfolio on day one. If you set aside $5,000 a year and start at age 40, you can buy one stock each year. By the time you reach 65, you will own 25 stocks. From then on, sit back and live off the dividends. In many instances the dividends will increase every year, helping you keep pace with inflation.

The 30 stocks in the Dow are not always the same. In 1999, for instance, four new stocks were added and four were deleted. On average, about one stock is replaced each year. This is your cue to sell the stock that is tossed out, replacing it with new blood. Because of the low turnover, your taxes on capital gains are minimal, as are your brokerage charges.

Buying an index fund has become popular in recent years, as investors have observed that managed mutual funds don't often do as well. However, not everyone is satisfied to be average. If you invest in the 30 Dow stocks, you can use your ingenuity to pick the 15 or 20 with the best prospects, casting aside the ones that don't impress you.

A $100,000 Package to Consider

If you want to play a more active part in selecting your stocks, here is an approach that might appeal to you. Let's say you have $100,000 to invest. Set aside $10,000 in a money market fund. Invest the rest as follows:

Pick out the 10 stocks that you think are going to be big winners and invest $4,000 in each one for a total of $40,000. Next, pick the 10 that you think may also do better than average. Invest $3,000 in each for a total of $30,000. Finally, invest $2,000 in the 10 stocks that you think will be also-rans. That brings your overall total to $90,000 in stocks and $10,000 in cash.

You might ask: Why should I buy *any* of the last 10? The reason is that you are not that smart—nor is anyone else. You will be surprised that some of those "dogs" turn out ok.

This Strategy Saves You Money

Picking stocks can also save you money, as compared with mutual funds. The average fund charges 1.5 percent a year. By managing your own portfolio, you can avoid this expense ratio.

Many of the Dow stocks, incidentally, will permit you to buy stock directly from the company, thus sidestepping a commission broker. Once you own a few shares of such stocks as ExxonMobil or Procter & Gamble, you can purchase more by merely mailing in $500 or $1,000, which will be invested without a commission.

The DRIP (dividend reinvestment plan) has some shortcomings. For one thing, you can never be sure what price you will pay, since your check may not be invested for a week or more after you mail it in. The same is true when you decide to cash in some shares.

Even more troublesome are the tax consequences when you sell your shares.

To calculate your cost basis, you have to tabulate the price paid with each dividend and for each payment mailed in. If you haven't kept meticulous records, the chore might be daunting to say the least.

In a Nutshell

When I finished explaining my Dow 30 idea to Horst Graben, he said, "It sounds like an interesting idea. Let me try to summarize what you have said. As I see it, the idea of buying these 30 stocks is to make it easier for me to keep track of the stocks I plan to buy.

"It also assures me that I will be investing in many of the nation's leading companies, such as GE, Exxon, Merck, Procter & Gamble, and IBM. In other words, no speculating. Since I am busy taking care of clients, it gives me more time to devote to their welfare, and thus makes them happy with my services. Anything else?"

"I think you have the picture, Horst. And don't forget the tax implications. Since the stocks in the Dow stay pretty much the same year after year, you probably won't have to sell more than one or two stocks a year—and they're usually ones that haven't done well, so the tax bite won't be onerous.

"One final word. Remember your solemn promise not to mention this ingenious scheme to anyone!"

"You have my word as a CPA."

Some Thoughts on Analyzing Stocks

Ideally, a stock you plan to purchase should have all of the following characteristics:

- A rising trend of earnings, dividends, and book value per share.
- A balance sheet with less debt than other companies in its particular industry.
- An S&P rating of B+ or better.
- A P/E ratio no higher than average.
- A dividend yield that suits your particular needs.
- A stock that insiders are not selling in significant quantities.
- A below-average dividend payout ratio.
- A history of earnings and dividends not pockmarked by erratic ups and downs.
- Companies whose return on equity is 15 or better.
- A ratio of price to cash flow that is not too high when compared to other stocks in the same industry.

Where to Get Information

If you are going to concentrate your efforts on the 30 Dow stocks, you must do some reading. Most people don't want to own all 30 stocks. In addition, you will probably find some stocks not to your liking. Let's say you are opposed to tobacco—then you may want to omit Philip Morris from your portfolio. Or, you may think that traditional retailers, such as Sears, Roebuck, are not going to do well against such companies as Wal-Mart, Bed, Bath & Beyond, or Home Depot. Similarly, a cyclical company like International Paper might appear too stodgy for an aggressive investor.

Because the Dow stocks are large and prominent, there is no shortage of information about them. In any given day, the *Wall Street Journal* will have a story about one or two Dow stocks. The same might be said for the *New York Times*. If you are serious about doing your homework, it would be wise to clip out these articles and file them away for future reference. You will also see articles on these companies in such publications as *Barron's*, *Better Investing*, *Forbes*, *Business Week*, and *Fortune*.

There are two well-known advisory services that you won't want to ignore: Standard & Poor's publishes "tear sheets" on thousands of companies. Of course, your only interest will be in the 30 Dow stocks. These tear sheets are available in public libraries and brokerage houses.

And don't forget to check *Value Line Survey*. It reviews 1,700 companies on a regular basis. Every 13 weeks, your Dow Stocks are updated. This service costs over $500 a year, but is readily available in brokerage offices and libraries.

In this modern age, you may also be tempted to seek out information on the Internet. Here is a sampling of what you can check:

- www.briefing.com reports upgrades and downgrades on stocks by full-service brokers and gives a detailed report on the market three times daily. It also offers in-depth comments on several stocks during the day.
- www.hoovers.com provides profiles of thousands of companies, as well as financial data and links to company home pages.
- www.investorama.com provides more than 8,000 links to other investment Web sites.
- www.zacks.com provides consensus earnings predictions for the coming quarter, current year, and next year. It also shows whether company insiders are buying or selling.

The Four Essentials of Successful Investing

If you want to end up rich at age 65, here are the essential factors to bear in mind.

First, start young. Many people wait until age 50 before they realize what has happened. Before that, they spend their money on cars, houses, clothes, vacations, and boats. Assuming you have not reached 50 or so, here is why investing early pays huge dividends.

Let's assume you want to have $1 million by age 65. That may not be enough, but it's a lot more than most people have when they decide to retire from the world of commerce and frustration.

If you start at age 35 and can realize an annual return of 10 percent compounded, you will have to put aside $6,079 each year. If you delay until you are 45, it will mean you have to set aside $17,460 each year. If you start at age 55, the amount gets a little steep: $62,746!

Invest Mostly in Stocks, not Bonds

So far, you can see that it takes some commitment, even if you start early in life to save for the future. But if you are cowardly and buy bonds, certificates of deposit, or a money market fund, the task is infinitely tougher. Let's try the different ages again, but this time assuming a compound annual return of only 6 percent instead of 10 percent.

If you start at age 35 and want to have a million bucks at age 65, it will mean plunking $12,649 into a CD each year—that's a lot more than the first illustration, which required an annual payment of $6,079.

If you start at age 45, the annual contribution to your nest egg will have to be $27,185.

Finally, those who start their programs at age 55 and pick fixed-income vehicles will be forced to set aside $75,868 each year.

Don't be a Spendthrift

As you can see, saving money for your later years is not going to be easy, no matter when you start. An important ingredient of successful investing is discipline. Of course, it pays to earn an above-average salary. If you make $30,000 a year and have four children, you are not likely to end up rich. Sorry about that.

On the other hand, there are plenty of people who make great incomes, such as $100,000 or more, and still don't own any stocks. The reason: they can always find things to buy.

Successful investors not only make a good income, but they are thrifty shoppers. For instance, why do you need to buy a new car every two or three years? I happen to be rich, and I always buy used cars. Not rusted out jalopies, of course. Normally I buy Buicks that are three years old. My most recent purchase was a bit on the extravagant side, however. I recently splurged for a 1998 Cadillac.

If you want to find out how people get rich, you should get a copy of *The Millionaire Next Door*. It's by Thomas J. Stanley and William D. Danko. Both are Ph.Ds. Typically, millionaires don't look the part. They don't buy $1,000 suits or drive new cars. And they don't live in an exclusive neighborhood. They are extremely careful how they spend their money. And they invest in good-quality common stocks, and usually let them sit there—very infrequent trading.

Picking the Right Investments

The final factor is picking the right stocks or mutual funds. Surprisingly, this is the *least* important factor. That's because no one knows how to do it—at least not consistently. To be sure, there are mutual funds with good records. But those managers are rarely able to duplicate their performance year after year. The manager who scored big last year is likely to look like a dunce this year.

However, that shouldn't deter you from trying. It stands to reason that you will pick your share of winners if you do your homework and exercise patience. Finally, make sure you don't make any big bets. I have seen people who do this, but I prefer to own 20 or more stocks, with no more than 10 percent in any one industry. I probably sound like a broken record. That's because this simple approach does work. At least it has for me.

In brief, here are the 4 rules:

- Start to invest early in life.
- Invest in common stocks. Forget about fixed-income vehicles such as bonds.
- Invest enough to make it worthwhile, such as 10 percent of your income. You can only do this if you are thrifty.
- Study this book and do enough reading to make sure you are picking companies that have the potential to make you rich.

Basic Terminology

If you are new to the investment arena, you may have difficulty understanding parts of this book. To get you over the rough spots, I have listed some common expressions that appear frequently in books on investing. You will also encounter them in the *Wall Street Journal, Forbes, Business Week, Barron's,* and other periodicals devoted to investing.

This is not a glossary but merely a brief list of terms that are essential for understanding this book. If you would like a more complete glossary, refer to either of my previous books: *Safe Investing* (Simon & Schuster, 1991) or *Straight Talk About Stock Investing* (McGraw-Hill, 1995).

Analyst

In nearly every one of the one hundred articles, you will note that I refer to "analysts" and what they think about the prospects for a particular stock. Analysts are individuals who have special training in analyzing stocks. Typically, they have such advanced degrees as M.B.A.s or C.F.A.s. Many of them work for brokerage houses, but they may also be employed by banks, insurance companies, mutual funds, pension plans, or other institutions. Most analysts specialize in one or two industries. A good analyst can tell you nearly everything there is to know about a particular stock or the industry it's part of.

However, analysts can be dead wrong about the future action of a stock. The reason is surprises. Companies are constantly changing, which means they are acquiring, divesting, developing new products, restructuring, buying back their shares, and so forth. When they make a change and announce this change to Wall Street, the surprise can change the course of the stock. In short, analysts can be helpful, but don't bet the store on what they tell you.

Annual Report

If you own a common stock, you can be certain that you will receive a fancy annual report a couple of months after the close of the year. If the year ends December 31, look for your annual report in March or April. If the fiscal year ends some other time of the year, such as September 30, the annual report will appear in your mailbox two or three months later.

Not all investors read annual reports, but they might be better off if they did. Although most companies will not list their problems, you can usually get a pretty good idea how things are going. In particular, read the report by the president or CEO. It's usually one, two, or three pages long and is written in language you can understand.

If you want detailed information on the company's various businesses, the annual report will often overwhelm you with details that may be difficult to fathom. If you are really curious about what they are trying to say, feel free to call the investor contact. I have provided the name of this person in all one hundred stocks listed. Have a list of questions ready, and call during the person's lunch hour, leaving your name and phone number. This sneaky little strategy means the cost of the call back will be paid by the company, not you. By the way, don't assume you will be intimidated by the investor contact. Investor contacts are usually quite personable and helpful.

Asset Allocation

This is not the same as diversification. Rather, it refers to the strategy of allocating your investment funds among different types of investments, such as stocks, bonds, or money-market funds. In the long run, you will be better off with all of your assets concentrated in common stocks. In the short run, this may not be true, since the market occasionally has a sinking spell. A severe one, such as that of 1973–74, can cause your holdings to decline in value 20 percent or more. To protect against this, most investors spread their money around. They may, for instance, allocate 50 percent to stocks, 40 percent to bonds, and 10 percent to a money-market fund. A more realistic breakdown might be 70 percent in stocks, 25 percent in bonds, and 5 percent in a money-market fund.

Balance Sheet

All corporations issue at least two financial statements: the balance sheet and the income statement. Both are important. The balance sheet is a financial picture of the company on a specific date, such as December 31 or at the end of a quarter.

On the left side of the balance sheet are the company's assets, such as cash, current assets, inventories, accounts receivable, and buildings. On the right side are its liabilities, including accounts payable and long-term debt. Also on the right side is shareholders' equity. The right side of the balance sheet adds up to the same value as the left side, which is why it is called a balance sheet.

In most instances, corporations give you figures for the current year and the prior year. By examining the changes, you can get an idea of whether the company's finances are improving or deteriorating.

Bonds

Entire books have been written on the various kinds of bonds. A bond, unlike a stock, is not a form of ownership. A bond is a contractual agreement that means you have loaned money to some entity, and that entity has agreed to pay you a certain sum of money (interest) every six months until that bond matures. At that time, you will also get back the money you originally invested—no more, no less. Most bonds are issued in $1,000 denominations. The safest bonds are those issued by the U.S. government. Not since the War of 1812 has there been a default on government bonds. The two advantages of bonds are safety and income. If you wait until the maturity date, you will be assured of getting the face value of the bond. In the meantime, however, the bond will fluctuate, because of changes in interest rates or the creditworthiness of the corporation. Long-term bonds, moreover, fluctuate far more than short-term bonds. But enough about bonds. This book is about stocks.

Capital Gains

When you buy common stocks, you expect to make money in two ways: capital gains and dividends. Over an extended period of time, about half of your total return will come from each sector. If the stock rises in value and you sell it above your cost, you are enjoying a capital gain. The tax on long-term capital gains is less than it is on dividends—a maximum of 20 percent if the stock is held for 12 months.

Common Stocks

We might as well define what a common stock is, since this whole book is devoted to them. All publicly owned companies— those that trade their shares outside of a small group of executives or the founding family—are based on common stocks. A common stock is evidence of partial ownership in a corporation. Most of the stocks described in this book have millions of shares of their stock outstanding, and the really large ones may have in excess of 100 million shares. When you own common stock, there are no guarantees. If the company is successful, it will probably pay a dividend four times a year. These dividends may be raised periodically, perhaps once a year. If, however, the company has problems, it may cut or eliminate its dividend. This can happen even to a major company, such as IBM, Goodyear, or General Motors. As I said, there are no guarantees.

Investors who own common stock can sell their shares at any time. All you do is call your broker, and the trade is executed a few minutes later at the prevailing price— which fluctuates nearly every day, sometimes by a sixteenth of a point (a point is a dollar) or sometimes two or three points.

Current Ratio

The current ratio is calculated by dividing current assets by current liabilities. Current assets include any assets that will become cash within one year, including cash itself. Current liabilities are those that will be paid off within a year. A current ratio of 2 is considered ideal. Most companies these days have a current ratio of less than 2.

Diversification

Since investments are inherently risky, it pays to spread the risk by diversifying. If you don't, you may be too heavily invested in a stock or bond that turns sour. Even well-known stocks such as Alcoa, International Paper, Eastman Kodak, and American Express can experience occasional sinking spells.

To be on the safe side, don't invest more than 5 percent of your portfolio in any one stock. In addition, don't invest too heavily in any one sector of the economy. A good strategy is to divide stocks among twelve sectors: basic industries, capital goods/technology, capital goods, consumer growth, consumer cyclical, credit cyclical, financial, energy, transportation, utilities, and conglomerates.

Here's a rule of thumb that will keep you out of trouble: Invest at least 4 percent in each sector but not more than 12 percent. That means that you should own at least twelve stocks so that you have representation in all twelve sectors.

Dividends

Unlike bonds, common stocks may pay a dividend. Bonds pay interest. Most dividends are paid quarterly, but there is no set date that all corporations use. Some, for instance, may pay January 1, March 1, July 1, and September 1. Another company may pay February 10, May 10, August 10, and November 10. If you want to receive checks every month, you will have to make sure you buy stocks that pay dividends at different times of the year. The Standard & Poor's *Stock Guide* is a source for this information, as is the *Value Line Survey*. Most companies like to pay the same dividend every quarter until they can afford to increase it. Above all, they don't like to cut their dividends, since investors who depend on this income will sell their shares, and the stock will decline in price. If you use good judgment in selecting your stocks, you can expect that your companies will increase their dividends nearly every year.

Dividend Payout Ratio

If a company earns $4 per share in a given year and pays out $3 to its shareholders, it has a payout ratio of 75 percent. If it pays out only $1, the payout ratio is 25 percent. A low payout ratio is preferred, since it means that the company is plowing back its profits into future growth.

The Dividend Reinvestment Plan

Unless you are retired, you might like to reinvest your dividends in more shares. Many companies have a plan (also known as a DRIP) that will allow you to do this, and the charge for this service is often minimal. Most of these companies also allow you to mail in additional cash, which will be used to purchase new shares, again at minimal cost.

In recent years, a few companies have created "direct" dividend reinvestment plans. Unlike most plans, direct plans enable you to buy your initial shares directly from the company. To alert you to which companies have direct plans, I have inserted the word *direct*. Companies having such plans include ExxonMobil, McDonald's, Procter & Gamble, Merck, and Lilly. Incidentally, you can rarely buy just one share. Many companies have a minimum, such as $500.

This may sound like a good way to avoid paying brokerage commissions, but there are some drawbacks to bear in mind. For one thing, you can't time your purchases, since it may be a week or more before your purchase is made.

Even worse is calculating your cost basis for tax purposes. By the time you sell, you may have made scores of small investments in the same stock, each with a different cost basis. Make sure you keep a file for each company so that you can make these calculations when the time comes. Or, better still, don't sell.

Dollar Cost Averaging

Dollar cost averaging is a systematic way to invest money over a long period, such as 10, 15, or 20 years. It entails investing the same amount of money regularly, such as each month or each quarter. If you do this faithfully, you will be buying more stock when the price is lower, and less stock when the price is higher. This tends to smooth out the gyrations of the market. Dollar cost averaging is often used with a mutual fund, but it can just as easily be done with a company that has a dividend reinvestment plan (DRIP).

Income Statement

Most investors are more interested in the income statement than they are the balance sheet. They are particularly interested in the progress (or lack of it) in earnings per share. The income statement lists such items as net sales, cost of sales, interest expense, and gross profit. As with the balance sheet, it makes sense to compare this year's numbers with those of the prior year.

Investment Advisor

Investors who do not have the time or inclination to manage their own portfolios may elect to employ an investment advisor. Most advisors charge 1 percent a year. Thus, if you own stocks worth $300,000, your annual fee would be $3,000. Advisors differ from brokers, since they do not profit from changes. Brokers, by contrast, charge a commission on each transaction, which means they profit from changes in your portfolio. Advisors profit only when the value of your holdings increases. For instance, if the value of your portfolio increases to $500,000, the annual fee will be $5,000. You, of course, will be $200,000 richer.

Preferred Stock

The name sounds impressive. In actual practice, owning preferred stocks is about as exciting as watching your cat take a bath. A preferred stock is much like a bond. It pays the same dividend year in and year out. The yield is usually higher than a common stock. If the company issuing the preferred stock does well, you do not benefit. If it does poorly, however, you may suffer, since the dividend could be cut or eliminated. My advice is: Never, never buy a preferred stock.

Price–Earnings Ratio

This is a term that is extremely important. Don't make the mistake of overlooking it. Whole books have been written on the importance of the P/E ratio, which is sometimes referred to as "the P/E" or "the multiple."

The P/E ratio tells you whether a stock is cheap or expensive. It is calculated by dividing the price of the stock by the company's earnings per share over the most recent 12 months. For instance, if you refer to the *Stock Guide*, you will see that Leggett and Platt had earnings of $2.23. At the time, the stock was selling for $52. Divide that figure by $2.23 and you get a P/E of 23.32.

In most instances, a low P/E indicates a stock that Wall Street is not too excited about. If they like a stock, they will bid it up to the point where its P/E is quite high, let's say 25 or 30. Coca-Cola is such a stock. In this same *Stock Guide*, Coca-Cola had annual earnings per share of $1.59. Based on the price of the stock at that time (it was $75), that works out to a P/E ratio of 47.17. Of course, Coca-Cola is extremely well regarded by investors and is expected to do well in the future—but is it really worth 47 times earnings?

Stock Split

Corporations know that investors like to invest in lower-priced stocks. Thus, when the price of the stock gets to a certain level, which varies with the company, they will split the stock. For instance, if the stock is $75, they might split it three-for-one. Your original 100 shares now become 300 shares. Unfortunately, your 300 shares are worth exactly the same as your original 100 shares. What it amounts to is this: Splits please small investors, but they don't make them any richer. One company, Berkshire Hathaway, has never been split. It is now worth a huge amount per share: over $50,000. It also pays no dividend. The company is run by the legendary Warren Buffett. He has made a lot of people very wealthy without a stock split or dividend.

Yield

If your company pays a dividend, you can relate this dividend to the price of the stock in order to calculate the yield. A $50 stock that pays a $2 annual dividend (which amounts to 50 cents per quarter) will have a yield of 4 percent. You arrive at this figure by dividing $2 by $50. Actually, you don't have to make this calculation, since the yield is given to you in the stock tables of the *Wall Street Journal*. Here are some typical yields from mid-2000. Coca-Cola, 1.3 percent; ExxonMobil, 2.1 percent; General Electric, 1.0 percent; Illinois Tool Works, 1.2 percent; Kimberly-Clark, 1.8 percent; and Minnesota Mining and Manufacturing, 2.6 percent. Although the yield is of some importance, you should not judge a stock by its yield without looking at many other factors.

Closed-end Investment Company

A managed investment portfolio, similar to a mutual fund, which is generally traded on a stock exchange. The price fluctuates with supply and demand, not because of changes in the assets within the trust. An open-end investment trust, or mutual fund, changes in size as investors buy new shares or surrender their shares for cash. A closed-end trust, by contrast, does not permit new money to be invested, nor can shares be redeemed by the company. Thus the number of shares remains the same once the trust begins trading. One feature of the closed-end trust is worth mentioning: they often sell at a discount to their asset value. An open-end trust always sells at precisely its asset value.

Moving Average

Some investors use the moving average to time the market. The strategy is to buy a stock when it is selling above its moving average and selling when it falls below. A popular moving average is the 200-day version. A dotted line is drawn, taking the average price of the stock over the previous 200 days. The actual price of the stock is plotted on the same graph. Studies show that this method of timing the market does not work on a consistent basis.

Some Simple Formulas for Asset Allocation

Serious investors spend a lot of time deciding which stocks or mutual funds to buy. I can't quarrel with that. If you are going to invest $10,000 in Merck, Illinois Tool Works, Praxair, Leggett & Platt, or United Technologies, you shouldn't do it without some research and thought.

On the other hand, some financial gurus maintain that it is far more important to make an effort to achieve an effective approach to asset allocation. They believe that you should place your emphasis on how much of your portfolio is invested in such sectors as:

Government bonds
Corporate bonds
Municipal bonds
Convertible bonds
Preferred stocks
Large-capitalization domestic stocks
Small-capitalization domestic stocks
Foreign stocks
Foreign bonds
Certificates of deposit
Annuities
Money-market funds

There are probably a few other categories you could include in your portfolio, but I think that examining this list gives you an idea of what is meant by asset allocation.

To illustrate the importance of asset allocation, look at 1998. You may recall that the long bull market temporarily aborted in mid-July of that year. Prior to that time, the big blue chip stocks had been making heady progress. Beneath the surface, however, the small and medium-size stocks were already in their own bear market. Thus, if you had avoided these smaller companies in the first six months of 1998, you would have sidestepped the devastation that was taking place in this sector.

After mid-July, however, the big stocks—particularly the financial stocks such as J. P. Morgan, Travelers (now Citigroup), and American Express—took a real tumble. The best place to be during this period was in U.S. government bonds. Once again, we are talking about asset allocation and how it can help or hurt you.

My Approach to Asset Allocation

From the comments made so far, you can see that asset allocation, like everything else in the world of finance, can get rather complex and confusing. It is no wonder that many people don't delve into this arcane realm. That's where John Slatter comes to the rescue. My idea of investing is to make it simple. After all, there are just so many hours in the day. If you are still gainfully employed, you probably work eight hours a day making a living. In the evenings, you may spend a few hours a week reading journals and other material so that you don't get fired. Obviously, that doesn't leave much time for studying the stock market.

For my part, I don't invest in many small-cap stocks, foreign stocks, bonds, convertibles, preferred stocks, or most of the other stuff on my list. I prefer to invest mostly in big-cap stocks (such as Exxon, GE, Merck, IBM, Procter & Gamble, and Johnson & Johnson) and money-market funds (a safe alternative to cash).

This reduces my categories to two, not a dozen. All you have to do is decide what percentage of your portfolio is in stocks. The rest is in a money-market fund. Of course, the *percentage* is vitally important.

A Few Alternatives to Consider

Some people may be shocked that I am not concerned about foreign stocks. One firm I once worked for insisted that we strive to invest 20 percent of each investor's portfolio in foreign stocks, such as Schlumberger, Repsol, Royal Dutch Petroleum, British Telecommunications, or Elf Aquitaine.

I have no objection to such stocks, but I see no urgency to adhere to a rigid percentage. For one thing, foreign stocks are more difficult to research. Their annual reports are far less revealing than those put out by corporations here at home. They also have different and less informative accounting.

In any event, the United States has hundreds of great companies. We are the envy of the world when it comes to business. The Japanese—at least for a decade or two—tried to convince people otherwise. But they have spent that last several years wallowing in a serious recession.

As far as bonds are concerned, they don't have a particularly impressive record. Except for a year here or there, common stocks have always been a better place to be. What's more, the return on bonds today is not much better than the rate you can get on a money-market fund.

One more thing: bonds, even U.S. Treasuries, have an element of risk; they decline in value when interest rates go up. Long-term bonds, moreover, slide precipitously when rates shoot up.

I don't want to spend too much time discussing the shortcomings of the rest of the list. I would prefer to point out the virtues of major stocks, such as McDonald's, Wal-Mart, Hewlett-Packard, J. P. Morgan, AT&T, Chevron, Alcoa, Eli Lilly, Minnesota Mining, and Walt Disney.

Blue chip companies are not likely to go bankrupt. To be sure, they have their troubles, but they are big enough to hire a CEO who can bring them back to life. Among the thirty companies in the Dow Jones Industrial Average, for instance, such companies as IBM, Eastman Kodak, AT&T, Sears, Roebuck, United Technologies, and AlliedSignal were restructured in recent years by a few dynamic executives.

Major corporations are also found in most institutional portfolios such as mutual funds, pension plans, bank trust departments, and insurance companies. One reason they like these big-capitalization stocks is liquidity. Since institutions have huge amounts of cash to invest, they feel comfortable with these stocks. The reason: the number of shares outstanding is huge, which means they won't disturb the market when they buy or sell. By contrast, if they try to invest a million dollars in a tiny Nasdaq company, the stock will shoot up several points before they complete their investing. It could be just as disruptive when they try to get out. As a consequence, major companies are in demand and are not left to drift. On the other hand, there are thousands of small companies that no one ever heard of. The only investors who can push them up are individuals—not institutions.

Another reason I like big companies is because they can afford to hire top-notch executives and they have the resources to allocate to research and marketing. In addition, their new products, acquisitions, management changes, and strategies are discussed frequently in such publications as the *Wall Street Journal,* the *New York Times, Barron's, Fortune, Forbes,* and *Business Week,* all of which I subscribe to.

How Much Should You Invest in Stocks?

When it comes to deciding on the percentage you should devote to common stocks, there are several alternatives that should be considered. All have some merit, and none are perfect.

In fact, there is no such thing as a perfect formula for asset allocation. It depends on such factors as your age and your temperament. It might also depend on what you think the market is going to do. If it's about to soar, you would want to be fully invested. But if you think stocks are poised to fall off a cliff, you might prefer to seek the safety of a money-market fund.

Forget About Everything Else and Buy Only Stocks

Believe it or not, there are some investors who are convinced that common stocks—and common stocks alone—are the royal road to riches. A good friend of mine has never bought anything but stocks, and he's been doing it for many years. He even went through the severe bear market of 1973–1974, when stocks plunged over 40 percent. He wasn't exactly happy to see his stocks being ground to a pulp, but he hung on. Today, he is a millionaire many times over. He's now sixty years old, still a comparatively young investor. His name is David A. Seidenfeld, a businessman in Cleveland.

Dave got his start by listening to the late S. Allen Nathanson, a savvy investor who wrote a series of magazine articles on why common stocks are the best way to achieve great wealth. Dave Seidenfeld recently collected these essays and published them as a hardcover book, *Bullishly Speaking*, which is available in bookstores.

If you start investing early, such as in your forties, this method can work. If you systematically invest, setting aside ten or fifteen percent of your earnings each year and doing it through thick and thin, you won't need any bonds, money-market funds, or any of the other alternatives that financial magazines seem to think you must have. You will arrive at retirement with a large portfolio that will enable you to live off the dividends.

However, if you arrived late to the investment party—let's say in your late fifties or early sixties—you may not be able to sleep too well if you rely entirely on common stocks. After all, stocks have their shortcomings too. They tend to bounce around a lot, and they can cut their dividends when things turn bleak.

Some Options to Consider

If you are an ultraconservative investor, I suggest you invest only 55 percent of your portfolio in common stocks. To be sure, when the stock market is marching ahead, as it has in recent years, you won't be able to keep pace. But if it falters and heads south for a year or two, your cautious approach will keep you out of the clutches of insomnia. Frankly, I don't think such a timid approach is the best way to approach asset allocation. However, I worked for a firm a few years ago that used this formula on nearly everyone. As far as I know, there weren't too many people complaining.

A better way to handle the uncertainty is to invest 70 percent in stocks, with the rest in a money-market fund. Once you decide on a particular percentage, stick with it. Don't change it every time someone makes a market forecast. These market forecasts don't work often enough to pay any attention to them. To my knowledge, no professional investor has a consistent record in forecasting. Every once in a while, one of these pundits makes a correct call at a crucial turning point, and from that day on, every one listens intently to the pronouncements of this person—until the day the pronouncement is totally wrong. That day always comes.

My Favorite Formula for Asset Allocation

I think age is the key to asset allocation. The older you are, the less you should have in common stocks. If you are age 65, you should have 65 percent in common stocks, with the rest in a money-market fund. If you are younger than 65, add 1 percent per year to your common stock sector. As an example, if you are 60 years old, you will have 70 percent in stocks.

If you are older than 65, deduct 1 percent a year. Thus, if you are age 70, you will have only 60 percent in stock. When you reach 80, you will be 50–50. And if you are much younger than 65, let's say 45, you will have 85 percent in stocks.

If you are not sure what this all means, here is a table breaking down the two percentages by age:

Age	Stocks	Money-Market Funds
40	90%	10%
45	85	15
50	80	20
55	75	25
60	70	30
65	65	35
70	60	40
75	55	45
80	50	50
85	45	55

Part II
100 Best Stocks You Can Buy

The following table lists the 100 stocks discussed in this book. A brief description of the stock appears here.

The ticker symbol is given so that you can use the quote machine in your broker's office. Or, if you call your broker on the phone, it makes it easier if you know the ticker symbol, since your broker may not.

In the table, "Industry" refers to one of the company's main businesses. This is not always easy to express in one or two words.

For instance, United Technologies is involved in such industries as aircraft engines, elevators, and air conditioning equipment. To describe the company succinctly, I arbitrarily picked the designation "aircraft engines."

Similarly, General Electric presents an even more daunting problem since it owns NBC, makes appliances, aircraft engines, medical devices, and a host of other things.

The designation "Sector" indicates the broad economic industry group that the company operates in, such as Transportation, Capital Goods, Energy, Consumer Cyclicals, and so forth. As described elsewhere, a properly diversified portfolio should include at least one stock in each of the 12 sectors. However, I see no problem in having stocks in 9 or 10 sectors.

"Category" refers to one of the following: (1) Income (Income) (2) Growth and Income (Gro Inc) (3) Conservative Growth (Con Grow) or (4) Aggressive Growth (Aggr Gro). As above, it might make sense to have some representation in each category, even though you have a strong preference for only one.

I have not included the page numbers because of space limitations. In any event, it is easy enough to find a particular stock, since they appear alphabetically in the book.

Company	Symbol	Industry	Sector	Category
—A—				
Abbott Laboratories	ABT	Med Supplies	Cons Staples	Con Grow
Air Products	APD	Chemical	Basic Ind	Con Grow
Alcoa	AA	Metals	Basic Ind	Aggr Gro
American Express*	AXP	Credit Card	Financial	Aggr Gro
American Home Prod.	AHP	Drugs	Cons Staples	Con Gro
American Water Works	AWK	Water	Utilities	Gro Inc
AT&T Corp.	T	Telephone	Utilities	Con Grow
Avery Dennison*	AVY	Adhesives	Basic Ind	Con Grow
—B—				
Baldor Electric	BEZ	Elect Equip	Capital Goods	Gro Inc
Baxter Int'l*	BAX	Med Supplies	Cons Staples	Con Grow
Becton, Dickinson	BDX	Med Supplies	Cons Staples	Con Grow
Boeing*	BA	Aerospace	Capital Goods	Aggr Gro
BP, plc*	BP	Oil	Energy	Grow Inc
Bristol-Myers Squibb	BMY	Drugs	Cons Staples	Con Grow

Company	Symbol	Industry	Sector	Category
—C—				
Caterpillar*	CAT	Machinery	Capital Goods	Gro Inc
Cedar Fair	FUN	Entertain.	Cons Staples	Income
Chevron	CHV	Oil	Energy	Grow Inc
Chubb*	CB	Insurance	Financial	Con Grow
Cintas*	CTAS	Uniforms	Cons Cyclical	Aggr Gro
Cisco Systems*	CSCO	Computers	Cap Goods-Tech	Aggr Gro
Citigroup*	C	Bank, Ins.	Financial	Con Grow
Clayton Homes	CMH	Housing	Credit Cycl	Aggr Gro
Clorox	CLX	Household Pd	Cons Staples	Aggr Gro
Coca-Cola	KO	Beverages	Cons Staples	Con Grow
Colgate-Palmolive	CL	Household Pd	Cons Staples	Con Grow
Costco Wholesale*	COST	Wholesale	Cons Cyclical	Aggr Gro
—D—				
Delphi Automotive*	DPH	Automotive	Cons Cyclical	Con Grow
Disney, Walt	DIS	Entertain.	Cons Staples	Aggr Gro
Dover	DOV	Machinery	Capital Goods	Con Grow
Duke Energy	DUK	Elect. Util.	Utilities	Income
DuPont*	DD	Chemicals	Basic Ind.	Grow Inc
—E—				
Eastman Kodak*	EK	Photography	Cons Cycl	Con Grow
Edwards, A. G.	AGE	Stockbroker	Financial	Aggr Gro
Emerson Electric	EMR	Elect Equip	Capital Goods	Con Grow
Ethan Allen	ETH	Furniture	Credit Cycl	Aggr Gro
ExxonMobil	XOM	Oil	Energy	Grow Inc
—F—				
FedEx Corporation	FDX	Air Freight	Transportation	Aggr Gro
Ford Motor*	F	Automobile	Cons Cyclical	Grow Inc
FPL Group	FPL	Elect Util	Utilities	Income
—G—				
Gannett	GCI	Publishing	Cons Services	Con Grow
General Electric	GE	Elect Equip	Capital Goods	Con Grow
General Motors	GM	Automobile	Cons Cyclical	Grow Inc
Genuine Parts	GPC	Parts Distrib	Cons Cyclical	Gro Inc
Grainger, W. W.	GWW	Elect Equip	Cap Goods-Tech	Con Grow
—H—				
Hewlett-Packard	HWP	Computers	Cap Goods-Tech	Aggr Gro
Home Depot	HD	Retail	Credit Cycl	Aggr Gro
Honeywell Int'l	HON	Diversified	Conglomerates	Aggr Gro
Houghton Mifflin	HTN	Publishing	Con Services	Con Grow
—I—				
Illinois Tool Works	ITW	Machinery	Capital Goods	Con Grow
Intel	INTC	Computers	Cap Goods-Tech	Aggr Gro
Int'l Business Mach	IBM	Computers	Cap Goods-Tech	Aggr Gro
International Paper*	IP	Paper	Basic Ind	Gro Inc
—J—				
Jefferson-Pilot	JP	Insurance	Financial	Gro Inc
Johnson & Johnson	JNJ	Med Supplies	Cons Staples	Con Grow
—K—				
Kimberly-Clark	KMB	Tissues	Basic Ind	Gro Inc
Kimco Realty	KIM	REIT	Cons Cyclical	Income
—L—				
Leggett & Platt	LEG	Furn Compon	Credit Cycl	Con Grow
Lilly, Eli	LLY	Drugs	Cons Staples	Aggr Gro

Company	Symbol	Industry	Sector	Category
Lubrizol*	LZ	Oil Additives	Basic Ind	Income
Lucent Technologies	LU	Tel Equip	Cap Goods-Tech	Aggr Gro
—M—				
Marsh & McLennan*	MMC	Insurance	Financial	Grow Inc
McCormick & Co.	MKC	Spices	Cons Staples	Con Grow
McDonald's	MCD	Restaurant	Cons Services	Con Grow
McGraw-Hill	MHP	Publishing	Cons Services	Con Grow
Medtronic*	MDT	Med. Devices	Cap Goods-Tech	Aggr Gro
MDU Resources	MDU	G&E Utility	Utilities	Income
Merck	MRK	Drugs	Cons Staples	Con Grow
Microsoft	MSFT	Comp Soft	Cap Goods-Tech	Aggr Gro
Minnesota Mining	MMM	Diversified	Cap Goods-Tech	Gro Inc
Morgan, J. P.	JPM	Bank	Financial	Grow Inc
Motorola*	MOT	Electronics	Cap Goods-Tech	Aggr Gro
—N—				
National City	NCC	Bank	Financial	Income
New Plan Excel	NXL	REIT	Cons Cyclical	Income
Nicor Inc.	GAS	Natural Gas	Utilities	Income
Nordson	NDSN	Machinery	Capital Goods	Con Grow
—P—				
PACCAR Inc.	PCAR	Trucks	Cons Cyclical	Income
Pfizer	PFE	Drugs	Cons Staples	Aggr Gro
Philip Morris	MO	Tobacco	Cons Staples	Income
Piedmont Nat'l Gas*	PNY	Nat'l Gas	Utilities	Income
Pitney Bowes	PBI	Postage Mtrs	Cap Goods-Tech	Gro Inc
PPG Industries	PPG	Glass	Basic Ind	Con Grow
Praxair	PX	Indust Gases	Basic Ind	Con Grow
Procter & Gamble	PG	Household Pd	Cons Staples	Con Grow
—R—				
Royal Dutch Petroleum*	RD	Petroleum	Energy	Income
—S—				
SBC Communications*	SBC	Telephone	Utilities	Gro Inc
Stryker*	SYK	Medical Sup	Cons Staples	Aggr Gro
Sysco Corporation	SYY	Food Distribution	Cons Staples	Con Grow
—T—				
Texas Instruments*	TXN	Computers	Cap Goods-Tech	Aggr Gro
—U—				
United Parcel*	UPS	Package Delivery	Transportation	Aggr Gro
United Technologies	UTX	Aircraft Eng	Cap Goods-Tech	Con Grow
—V—				
Varian Medical*	VAR	Medical Devices	Cap Goods-Tech	Con Grow
Vulcan Materials	VMC	Construction	Credit Cyclical	Gro Inc
—W—				
Wachovia	WB	Bank	Financial	Gro Inc
Wal-Mart Stores	WMT	Retail	Cons Cyclical	Aggr Gro
Wash. Gas Light	WGL	Natural Gas	Utilities	Income
Washington Real Est.	WRE	REIT	Cons Cyclical	Income
Weingarten Realty	WRI	REIT	Cons Cyclical	Income
Wells Fargo*	WFC	Bank	Financial	Con Grow
Weyerhaeuser	WY	Forest Prod	Basic Ind	Gro Inc
Williams-Sonoma*	WSM	Retail	Cons Cyclical	Aggr Gro

*New in this edition.

Abbott Laboratories

100 Abbott Park Road □ Abbott Park, Illinois 60064-6048 □ Investor contact: John Thomas (847) 938-2655 □ Dividend reinvestment plan is available: (888) 332-2268 □ Web site: www.abbott.com □ Ticker symbol: ABT □ S&P rating: A+ □ Value Line financial strength rating: A++

In 1999, Abbott acquired U.S. comarketing rights to the drug Mobic, one of a new class of highly promising pain medications known generally as "Cox-2 inhibitors." Abbott sells the drug along with its maker, Germany's Boehringer Ingelheim GmbH. The Cox-2 drugs, so-called because they act on an enzyme called cyclooxygenas e-2, represent a potential breakthrough in the treatment of arthritis. Wall Street analysts say they will constitute a market of several billion dollars soon. That is because they treat pain as well as current drugs but hold the potential of doing so without causing severe gastrointestinal difficulties, such as bleeding ulcers, as current arthritis drugs do in some patients.

For Abbott, the deal with Boehringer is a major departure and is an example of things to come. The venture reflects the more aggressive style of its new chief executive, Miles D. White.

In interviews, Mr. White makes it clear that Abbott, which long has shunned pharmaceutical comarketing deals and largely avoided mergers, now will be more assertive in pursuing both. Apart from acquiring rights to Mobic, Abbott also began comarketing the Boehringer hypertension drug Micardis, also among a promising new class of drugs called angiotensin II receptor blockers.

Company Profile

Abbott Laboratories is one of the largest diversified health care manufacturers in the world, with 1999 revenues of $13.2 billion. The company's products are sold in more than 130 countries, with about 40 percent of sales derived from international operations.

Abbott's major business segments include Pharmaceuticals & Nutritionals (prescription drugs, medical nutritionals, and infant formulas) and Hospital & Laboratory Products (intravenous solutions, administrative sets, drug-delivery devices, and diagnostic equipment and reagents).

Although revenue growth in Abbott's infant formula and diagnostics businesses has slowed in recent years, new drugs (such as the antibiotic Clarithromycin), new indications (including the BPH claim for Hytrin), the launch of disease-specific medical nutritionals, and cost-cutting (diagnostics and hospital supplies) continue to boost the company's profits.

Brand names include Erythrocin, Similac, Isomil, and Selsun Blue. What's more, Ensure (an over-the-counter medical nutritional for adults) is an important cornerstone of the company's nutritional products franchise and one of the largest OTC health care and nutritional products sold in the United States.

Shortcomings to Bear in Mind

■ At the end of 1999, Abbott Laboratories abandoned its $7.3 billion acquisition of Alza Corporation because of antitrust opposition from the Federal Trade Commission (FTC). Analysts became convinced that the deal was imperiled when the companies said in September that they would sell Viadur, one of Alza's experimental treatments for prostate cancer, to satisfy antitrust concerns from the FTC. Abbott sells Lupron, a leading prostate cancer drug. According to Dr. Ernest Mario, Alza's CEO, "From the very beginning, the

FTC was concerned about what they called the monopoly Abbott had in prostate cancer treatments. We thought we had done enough by offering to sell Viadur, but we could never come to terms with them."

- In 1999, when many stocks, including most major drug stocks, were climbing to new highs, Abbott's shares languished, falling from a high of $53 early in the year to just below $30 in early 2000.

  Pushing the stock down were a number of developments. Abbott's troubles began when the Food and Drug Administration (FDA) found problems at one of the company's plants that makes test kits used by hospitals to inspect tumors and blood. To get back in the good graces of the FDA, Abbott had to stop selling certain types of kits and pay a $100 million fine—the biggest penalty ever levied by the FDA. One analyst said that Abbott's diagnostic-equipment segment would see its growth rate fall to the 3 percent level, or well below a more traditional 9 percent. In 1999, sales of these diagnostic products amounted to $3 billion, a sizable part of Abbott's total revenues of $13 billion.

- Nor was this the end of the company's mishaps. The FDA also barred Abbott from selling its anticlotting drug, Abbokinase, since Abbott failed to ensure that the product's main ingredients, kidney cells, were free of infection. Prior to this episode, the company's annual sales of Abbokinase amounted to $275 million.

- Like many drug companies, Abbott has to be concerned with drugs that lose their patent protection. When this happens, firms that specialize in generic drugs can flood the market with their copycat product at a small fraction of the cost of the branded item. In this realm, Abbott's major product for prostate

problems, Hytrin, was trying to cope with generic imitations. As a result, the sale of Hytrin could plunge to the $200 million level, from $465 million in 1999.

Reasons to Buy

- When you consider the above problems, it's no wonder that the shares of Abbott have taken a swan dive. Some analysts, those with a longer-term prospective, believe that Abbott will prove to be a rewarding holding, though perhaps not until late in 2000 or in the first half of 2001. According to one of these analysts, "If you look back over 30 or 40 years, Abbott stands out as a company with one of the most consistent returns in earnings, cash flow, and dividends. That suggests to us it will continue over time."

- The cornerstone of Abbott's neuroscience business is Depakote, a versatile agent for the treatment of epilepsy and bipolar disorder and the prevention of migraine headaches. In 1998, Depakote surpassed lithium, the long-standing market leader, to become the agent most prescribed by psychiatrists for treating patients who experience manic episodes associated with bipolar disorder (also known as manic depression).

- Abbott is broadening its product offerings in the area of pain management. Noteworthy is Actiq, the first product that specifically focuses on severe cancer pain.

- Another drug, Anzemet, which helps prevent postoperative nausea, also holds promise.

- Clarithromycin is the treatment of choice for the eradication of Helicobacter pylori (H. pylori), a bacterium that is believed to be responsible for about 90 percent of active or recurrent duodenal (small intestine) ulcers. Clarithromycin is prescribed in 85 percent of all antibiotic regimens for ulcers.

- Abbott's adult nutritional business, led by the Ensure brand, has been growing in international markets. Sales are strengthened by Abbott's presence in emerging markets where economic growth is spurring demand for quality health care.
- Abbott is focusing on global opportunities for its pediatric nutritional products, particularly the new, reformulated Similac infant formula. This product has been launched in more than 20 countries, including the United States.

The reformulation has made Similac closer than ever to breast milk. The new formulation is marketed as Improved Similac in the United States and as Similac Advance and other Similac trademarks in the rest of the world. It is the only infant formula with added nucleotide levels patterned after the potentially available nucleotides from breast milk. Nucleotides, the building blocks of DNA and RNA, are compounds found naturally in all cells and in breast milk. The new formula is the product of a seven-year research effort—the largest such program ever conducted by Abbott's nutritional research scientists.

- Abbott is the leader in rapid testing, in both hospitals and doctors's offices, with tests for strep, pregnancy, and a microbe that causes ulcers. The company's Determine line of tests are self-contained, low cost, and easy to use. Since its acquisition of MediSense, Inc. in 1996, the company's blood glucose monitoring systems have been well received by diabetic patients. Abbott is making substantial investments in commercial infrastructure and manufacturing capacity to support the growing demand for these products.
- Anesthesia is a cornerstone of Abbott's hospital pharmaceutical strategy. The company's worldwide leadership in anesthesia is providing the catalyst for growth in other hospital business segments, particularly outside the United States.

Abbott's inhalation anesthetic, sevoflurane (marketed as Ultane in the United States and Sevorane in other countries), had the most successful new hospital product launch in Abbott history. Anesthesiologists in 56 countries now use this versatile agent. Sevoflurane has broad applicability for both induction and maintenance of anesthesia in pediatric and adult patients. And because it allows patients to emerge from anesthesia rapidly and smoothly, it has helped the company penetrate the growing market for outpatient surgery. Sevoflurane has experienced steady growth since its introduction in 1994. It is the induction agent of choice for anesthesiologists who have administered it.

- Abbott Laboratories, already a major player in drugs for the treatment of AIDS, moved to strengthen its position further in mid-1999 with a $335-million alliance with Triangle Pharmaceuticals Inc. to produce new antiviral compounds. Abbott said it will develop and copromote products for the AIDS-causing HIV virus and for hepatitis B that are being developed by Triangle. Abbott already sells Norvir, generically called ritonavir, and is developing a highly promising new compound called ABT-378 that is in Phase III, the final stage of human trials. Arthur Higgins, Abbott's senior vice president of pharmaceutical operations, said the alliance with Triangle could "potentially launch at least one new antiviral each year over the next four years."
- At the end of 1999, Abbott reached an agreement to sell its agricultural products business, a strategic step that will allow the company to focus on the growth of its core health care business.

■ Abbott's president, Robert L. Parkinson, sees promising momentum in many parts of the company. He is particularly impressed with a 50-50 joint venture with Takeda Chemical of Japan. Abbott doesn't book sales from the Takeda undertaking, which in 1999 rose by 42 percent to $2.9 billion. On the other hand, Abbott does benefit from one-half of the venture's earnings. In 1999, Abbott's share of profits shot up 46 percent, to $390 million, or more than 10 percent of the company's total pretax earnings.

Total assets: $13,216 million
Current ratio: 1.36
Common shares outstanding: 1,521 million
Return on 1999 shareholders' equity: 36.5%

		1999	1998	1997	1996	1995	1994	1993	1992
Revenues (millions)		13131	12477	11883	11014	10012	9156	8408	7852
Net income (millions)		2586	2333	2094	1882	1689	1517	1399	1198
Earnings per share		1.66	1.51	1.34	1.21	1.06	.94	.85	.71
Dividends per share		.68	.60	.54	.48	.42	.38	.34	.30
Price	High	53.3	50.1	34.9	28.7	22.4	16.9	15.4	17.1
	Low	27.9	32.5	24.9	19.1	15.4	12.7	11.3	13.1

CONSERVATIVE GROWTH

Air Products and Chemicals, Inc.

7201 Hamilton Boulevard □ Allentown, Pennsylvania 18195-1501 □ Investor contact: Michael F. Hilton (610) 481-5775 □ Direct dividend reinvestment plan is available: (888) 694-9458 □ Web site: www.airproducts.com □ Listed: NYSE □ Fiscal year ends September 30 □ Ticker symbol: APD □ S&P rating: A □ Value Line financial strength rating: B++

In fiscal 2000, Air Products introduced its new CRYO-QUICK JUMBO CF Tunnel Freezer, specially designed to meet the processing needs of the case-ready meat market. The new freezing system, with special features to accommodate the size and weight of the product, enables food processors to rapidly chill and crust freeze the outer layer of the meat to increase both the speed and quality of subsequent slicing steps. This helps boost production, increase slicing rates, decrease waste as a result of fewer fines, and reduce the amount of time spent above 40°F for improved product safety.

Company Profile
Air Products and Chemicals, Inc., with operations in 30 countries and 1999 revenues in excess of $5 billion, is a leading supplier of industrial gases and related equipment, specialty and intermediate chemicals, as well as environmental and energy systems.

Air Products' industrial gas and chemical products are used by a diverse base of customers in manufacturing, process, and service industries.

In the environmental and energy businesses, Air Products and its affiliates own and operate facilities to reduce air and water pollution, dispose of solid waste, and generate electric power.

Industrial Gases
• APD is a world leader.
• Its products are essential in many manufacturing processes.

• Gases are produced by cryogenic, adsorption, and membrane technologies

• They are supplied by tankers, on-site plants, pipelines, and cylinders

• International sales, including the company's share of joint ventures, represent more than half of Air Products' gas revenues.

The markets served by Industrial Gases include chemical processing, metals, oil and gas production, electronics, research, food, glass, health care, and pulp and paper. Principal products are industrial gases—such as nitrogen, oxygen, hydrogen, argon, and helium—and various specialty, cutting, and welding gases.

Chemicals

• APD has a leadership position in over 80 percent of the markets served.

• Markets include a wide range of attractive, diversified end uses that reduce overall exposure to economic cycles.

• World-scale, state-of-the-art production facilities and process technology skills ensure consistent, low-cost products while enhancing long-term customer relationships.

• International sales, including exports to over 100 countries, represent almost 40 percent of APD's business.

The markets served by the Chemicals operation include adhesives, agriculture, furniture, automotive products, paints and coatings, textiles, paper, and building products. Its principal products are emulsions, polyvinyl alcohol, polyurethane and epoxy additives, surfactants, amines, and polyurethane intermediaries.

Environmental and Energy Systems

• Facilities, owned and operated with partners, dispose of solid waste, reduce air pollution, and generate electrical power.

• Strong positions are built by extending core skills developed in the industrial gas business.

• Forces driving this market are environmental regulations, demand for efficient sources of electrical power, utility deregulation, and privatization. Principal products are waste-to-energy plants, electric power services, and air pollution-control systems.

The markets served by Environmental and Energy Systems include solid waste disposal, electrical power generation, and air pollution reduction.

Equipment and Services

• Cryogenic and noncryogenic equipment is designed and manufactured for various gas-processing applications.

• Equipment is sold worldwide or manufactured for Air Products industrial gas business and its international network of joint ventures.

The markets served by Equipment and Services include chemicals, steel, oil and gas recovery, and power generation.

Shortcomings to Bear in Mind

■ Air Products has a rather leveraged balance sheet. Its common stock represents only 56 percent of capitalization. As a consequence, its coverage of long-term debt interest is only 4.9 times.

■ Air Products did not perform as expected in 1999, and the numbers make this story very clear. Excluding one-time items in both years, ADP's net income was $451 million, down from the prior year's $489 million. Earnings per share declined 6 percent to $2.09 on a diluted basis. Although there were some mitigating circumstance that caused the lackluster performance, the CEO, H. A. Wagner, confesses that "we did not perform well in 1999, and our management team didn't react quickly enough to fully mitigate these negative conditions as they occurred."

Mr. Wagner says, "We are implementing price increases as rapidly as possible to offset rising new material costs. And we've restructured some of our businesses by closing under-performing assets, improving operating efficiency, and reducing the workforce in targeted areas."

- Air Products had to record a $300-million after-tax charge in the second quarter of 2000 as a result of its failed joint attempt to acquire rival BOC Group, p.l.c. Its partner in the deal was Air Liquide SA of France. The two companies said they would withdraw their bid of $11 billion because couldn't meet the May 12 deadline, the date on which their offer expired.

Reasons to Buy

- Demand for industrial gas has been strong. This high demand is more than a cyclical phenomenon and is being fueled by new applications and new industrial gas production technology.
- Beyond its leadership in tonnage hydrogen, Air Products also has a substantial liquid hydrogen business. The National Aeronautics and Space Administration (NASA) is the world's largest customer of liquid hydrogen. The company has been serving NASA since the 1960s, when APD first began supplying hydrogen for the Apollo space program. Over the last 20 years, Air Products has safely and reliably provided hydrogen for NASA's space shuttle engine-testing program and all 85 shuttle launches.
- Today, some 60,000 customers in North America—once served by 80 different locations—are now managed from the company's Single-Point-Of-Contact Center, using state-of-the-art information technology systems. The number of error-free deliveries is improving, customer runouts are significantly lower, and APD's customers are increasingly positive about the changes made.

- Air Products is well positioned to benefit from increased demand from new plants being built in the chemical, paper, and other basic industries. In particular, the company is seeing an acceleration in bidding for new gas contracts in the electronics market and in gaseous hydrogen for oil refineries.
- Air Products' reputation for reliability and innovation has made the company a preferred supplier to the electronics industry. As the market leader in North America and Europe and a strong competitor in Asia through joint ventures, APD's global infrastructure assures its electronics customers that they can count on receiving the same high-quality products and services, regardless of where they are.
- Air Products continues to be among the lowest-cost, highest-quality manufacturers in the chemicals industry. To maintain that leadership, the company implemented a systematic process for setting productivity goals and monitoring progress throughout its operations.
- The chemical and process industries (CPI) market is the company's largest. At the forefront of the shift from "make" to "buy" hydrogen decisions, Air Products has over 50 hydrogen plants around the world, plus extensive pipeline systems in the United States, Europe, and Asia, to meet unprecedented demand from refiners for hydrogen needed to produce a cleaner slake of fuels and carbon monoxide and synthesis gas for petrochemical producers.
- Earnings and dividends have been advancing at a healthy clip. EPS climbed from 97 cents in 1989 to $2.09 in 1999, a compound annual growth rate of 8 percent. In the same ten-year stretch, dividends expanded from 32 cents to 70 cents, a growth rate of 8.1 percent.

Total assets: $8,236 million
Current ratio: 1.18
Common shares outstanding: 209 million
Return on 1999 shareholders' equity: 16.1%

	1999	1998	1997	1996	1995	1994	1993	1992
Revenues (millions)	5020	4919	4638	4008	3865	3485	3328	3217
Net income (millions)	451	489	429	416	368	264	268	235
Earnings per share	2.09	2.22	1.95	1.69	1.62	1.03	1.16	1.19
Dividends per share	.70	.64	.58	.54	.51	.48	.44	.42
Price High	49.3	45.3	44.8	35.3	29.8	25.2	24.3	24.8
Low	25.7	33.2	25.2	21.9	19.4	18.8	18.2	12.8

AGGRESSIVE GROWTH

Alcoa Inc.

Alcoa Corporate Center ◻ 201 Isabella Street at 7th Street Bridge ◻ Pittsburgh, Pennsylvania 15212-5858 ◻ Investor contact: Edgar M. Cheely, Jr. (412) 553-2231 ◻ Dividend reinvestment plan is available: (800) 317-4445 ◻ Web site: www.alcoa.com ◻ Listed: NYSE ◻ Ticker symbol: AA ◻ S&P rating: B ◻ Value Line financial strength rating: A

Alcoa began the twenty-first century with an unprecedented show of strength. In 1999, the company posted record revenues and earnings. Impressively, Alcoa's growth topped all 30 Dow companies (which includes such blue chips as IBM, GE, Wal-Mart, Microsoft, Intel, and Home Depot) by a wide margin, with a total return of 126 percent.

Company Profile

Alcoa (formerly Aluminum Company of America), founded in 1888, is the world's leading integrated producer of aluminum products. These products are used worldwide by packaging, transportation, building, and industrial customers. In addition to components and finished products, Alcoa produces alumina, alumina-based chemicals, as well as primary aluminum for a multitude of applications.

Alcoa's operations are broken down into the following segments:

The alumina and chemicals segment includes the production and sale of bauxite, alumina, and alumina chemicals.

Aluminum processing comprises the manufacturing and marketing of molten metal, ingot, and aluminum products that are flat-rolled, engineered, or finished.

The non-aluminum products segment includes the production and sale of electrical, ceramic, plastic, and composite materials products, manufacturing equipment, gold, separations systems, magnesium products, as well as steel and titanium forgings.

Since aluminum is expensive and has difficulty competing against steel—even though it has some admirable qualities—it might appear to be a rare element. Not so.

Aluminum is an abundant metal and, in fact, is the most abundant metal in the earth's crust. Of all the elements, only oxygen and silicon are more plentiful. Aluminum makes up 8 percent of the crust. It is found in the minerals of bauxite, mica, and cryolite, as well as in clay.

Until about a hundred years ago, aluminum was virtually a precious metal. Despite its abundance, it was very rare as a pure metal. The reason: it was so difficult to extract from its ore. This is because aluminum is a reactive metal, and it cannot be extracted by smelting with carbon.

To solve the enigma, displacement reactions were tried, but metals such as sodium or potassium had to be used, making the cost prohibitive. Electrolysis of the molten ore was tried, but the most plentiful ore, bauxite, contains aluminum oxide, which does not melt until it reaches 2050°C.

The solution to the problem of extracting aluminum from its ore was discovered by Charles Hall in the United States and by Paul Heroult in France—both working independently. The method now used to extract aluminum from its ore is called the Hall-Heroult process.

I won't bore you with the steps taken to effect this process. The important fact to remember is that it is far from cheap. Even so, it can be done economically enough to make aluminum the second most widely used metal. However, it is not likely to replace iron and steel any time soon. Iron makes up more than 90 percent of the metals used in the world.

The main cost in the Hall-Heroult process is electricity. So much energy is required that aluminum smelters have to be situated near a cheap source of power, normally hydro-electric.

The price of entry into the business is so high that it discourages most upstarts from taking the plunge.

On the other hand, this frustrating effort to produce commercial aluminum is worth the cost, since the white metal has a number of valuable attributes:

- It has a low density.
- It is highly resistant to corrosion.
- It is light weight—one-third the weight of steel.
- It is an excellent reflector of heat and light.
- It is nonmagnetic.
- It is easy to assemble.
- It is nontoxic.
- It can be made strong with alloys.
- It can be easily rolled into thin sheets.

- It has good electrical conductivity.
- It has good thermal conductivity.
- It doesn't rust.

Shortcomings to Bear in Mind

■ While Alcoa and Western rivals warily circle each other in their efforts to retain supremacy in the aluminum business, a relatively obscure but powerful competitor that operates extensively in the former Soviet Union has been increasing its control in a region responsible for much of the world's supply. Trans-World Group, a privately owned company based in London, is already the largest seller of aluminum ingots, the bulk form of processed aluminum. It has been concentrating its effort in Ukraine where it has formed an alliance with the government that could hurt the company's few remaining competitors. Ukraine is an important source of raw material for the huge smelters that underpinned the Russian aluminum industry. Those smelters have been responsible for much of the aluminum that has flooded world markets in recent years and depressed the price. Whether Trans-World's activities could change the balance of supply and demand in the global aluminum industry remains unclear. But they could potentially exert more effect on prices than the merger between Alcoa and Reynolds Metals.

■ There is substantial excess capacity in the aluminum industry worldwide. Aluminum also faces stiff competition from such materials as plastics, steel, glass, and ceramics. In recent years, for instance, plastic, in the form of polyethylene terephthalate (PET), has been displacing aluminum in the beverage can market. On the other hand, aluminum is gaining market share in passenger car applications, at the expense of steel.

Reasons to Buy

- When Canada's Alcan Aluminum Ltd., Pechiney of France, and Alusuisse Lonza Group Ltd of Switzerland announced a three-way merger to create what would be the world's biggest aluminum company, Alcoa responded with a $5.9 billion offer for Reynolds Metals. Together, Alcoa and Reynolds would have combined sales of $22 billion to the foreign trio's combined $21 billion. When the deal was approved in May 2000, Alcoa operated in more than 300 locations in 36 countries. Alcoa believes that the transactions could bolster its earnings in the first year following completion of the transaction. To accomplish this the company expects to achieve $200 million in pretax cost savings by the end of the second year, in addition to its ongoing $1.1 billion cost-reduction program.

  In order to approve the merger, the U.S. Department of Justice stipulated that Alcoa would have to sell Reynolds's 25 percent interest in a Washington smelter and all of Reynolds's alumina refineries. However, these assets, while significant, were not Alcoa's prime target. Alcoa was more interested in Reynolds's lucrative packaging and consumer business, which makes Reynolds Wrap and other household products.

  Meanwhile, the Alcan merger fell apart in April of 2000 under the weight of antitrust opposition by European regulators.

  "The new company will be better positioned to address the globalization of the metals industry and the new competitive landscape this is creating," said Alain J. P. Belda, Alcoa's president and CEO. "It will permit the greater efficiencies and cost reductions required by an environment that has seen the lowest prices in many years for our commodity products."

- Late in 1999, Alcoa and Hyundai Group Companies announced that they have entered into an agreement to purchase Aluminum of Korea, Ltd.'s (Koralu's) shares, which are now owned by Hyundai Group Companies. Koralu is Korea's largest aluminum flat-rolled products producer.

- In the spring of 2000, Alcoa invested $2.3 billion to buy Cordant Technologies in a move to further diversify beyond its aluminum-making business. Buying Cordant, based in Ogden, Utah, Alcoa is moving into the growing and profitable aerospace and industrial markets. It is Mr. Belda's goal of having Alcoa expand into a $40 billion company by 2004, from $16.3 billion in 1999. Cordant's largest market is industrial gas turbines that generate power. The company's other businesses consist of rocket-propulsion systems, fasteners, and super-alloy and titanium components used in jets.

- While the aluminum industry in general suffers through a protracted slump in aluminum prices, Alcoa has seen its profits rise. Part of that is due to the effects of recent acquisitions. But much of the improvement can be traced to a new corporate philosophy, called the "Alcoa Business System." Essentially, it calls for plants to produce more, produce it faster, and not let it sit on the docks for too long. The new production processes are "deceptively simple and seemingly obvious," says one analyst. But, on top of other cost-cutting efforts already in the works, they are helping Alcoa weather what otherwise might be a dismal year. As aluminum prices recover—either because of growing demand or because excess capacity is shuttered—Alcoa stands to see earnings jump dramatically. Analysts say that each penny increase in the LME price of aluminum boosts Alcoa's per-share earnings by about 12 cents. LME refers to the spot price of aluminum ingots on the London Metals Exchange. Normally, the prevailing world price of aluminum is an important determinant of aluminum companies' profits. From 1982 through 1995, Alcoa's earnings and the LME price moved in lock step. Since then, however, the LME price has dropped while Alcoa's earnings have held steady or drifted up. According to the company's chief financial officer, Richard Kelson, "We are breaking away from the LME pricing."

■ Aluminum usage in automobiles and light trucks has been climbing steadily. It's a new and potentially powerful trend, and Alcoa has played a major role in getting it started. As recently as 1990 there were no aluminum-structured passenger cars in production anywhere in the world. Aluminum shipments to the automotive sector grew by $400 million in 1998, fueled by acquisitions as well as by internal growth.

In North America, from 1996 to 1999, aluminum use in brakes, drive lines, chassis, and suspensions rose 46 percent; in steering systems, 47 percent; and closure panels, 65 percent. Aluminum use by automakers in North America, western Europe, and Japan over the next 10 years is expected to climb by 52 percent. Areas of growth include body parts, engine blocks, and safety systems.

■ The Mercedes-Benz S-Class is the newest production model from the German automaker to feature aluminum in body structure applications. Introduced at the 1999 Geneva Auto Show, the car went into full production in early 2000. Alcoa Automotive's Casting and Extrusion Finishing plant in Soest, Germany is producing several components for this path-breaking Mercedes, including an Alcoa Vacuum Die Cast sidewall component as well as extrusions for the front and rear roof frames and supporting cross members for the passenger compartment.

Total assets: $17,066 million
Current ratio: 1.60
Common shares outstanding: 368 million
Return on 1999 shareholders' equity: 17.2%

	1999	1998	1997	1996	1995	1994	1993	1992
Revenues (millions)	16323	15340	13319	13061	12500	9904	9056	9492
Net income (millions)	1054	859	759	555	796	193	67	196
Earnings per share	1.41	1.22	1.09	.79	1.11	.27	.10	.28
Dividends per share	.40	.38	.25	.33	.23	.20	.20	.20
Price High	41.7	20.3	22.4	16.6	15.1	11.3	9.8	10.1
Low	18.0	14.5	16.1	12.3	9.2	8.0	7.4	7.6

American Express Company

World Financial Center ❑ 200 Vesey Street ❑ New York, New York 10285-4805 ❑ Investor contact: Susan Korchak (212) 640-4953 ❑ Direct dividend reinvestment plan is available: (800) 842-7629 ❑ Web site: www.americanexpress.com ❑ Listed: NYSE ❑ Ticker symbol: AXP ❑ S&P rating: B+ ❑ Value Line financial strength rating: A

For 150 years, American Express has continuously transformed itself to meet changing customer needs. What began as a rough-and-tumble freight-forwarding company in 1850 later became a travel company then a card company and today a leading global financial and travel services company.

Company Profile

American Express is best known for its flagship charge card and travelers check products. It also offers travel-related services, financial advisory services, and international banking services. The company is the world's largest travel agency (tied with Japan Travel) and issuer of traveler's checks.

Continuing the reconfiguration it began with the spinoff of stockbroker Lehman Brothers, the company is focusing on its corporate travel and credit card businesses and has launched an online bank: American Express Membership Banking.

The company's growth strategy focuses on three principal themes:

• Expanding its international presence.

• Strengthening the charge card network.

• Broadening financial services offerings.

Travel Related Services

Travel Related Services (TRS) markets travelers checks and the American Express Card, including the Gold Card, the Platinum Card, the Corporate Card, and the Optima Card. TRS also offers business-expense management products and services, corporate and consumer travel products, tax preparation and business-planning services, magazine publishing, and merchant transaction processing.

American Express Financial Advisors

Financial Advisors provides financial products, including financial planning and advice, insurance and annuities, investment products such as mutual funds, limited partnerships, investment advisory services, trust and employee plan administration services, personal auto and homeowner's insurance, and retail securities brokerage services.

American Express Bank Ltd.

American Express Bank Ltd. offers products designed to meet the financial services needs of corporations, financial institutions, affluent individuals, and retail customers. Primary business lines are corporate banking and finance, correspondent banking, private banking, personal financial services, and global trading. The unit also operates the Travelers Check business.

Highlights of 1999

■ Financial performance that met or exceeded the company's long-term financial targets of 12 to 15 percent growth in earnings per share, return on equity of 18 to 20 percent, and at least an 8 percent increase in revenues. In fact, the company's double-digit increase in revenues in 1999 was the best performance of the decade.

■ Growth in cards in force in both the United States and internationally, continued success in adding new merchants who accept AXP cards, and a substantial increase in cardmember lending balances.

- The introduction of several significant new products—including Blue from American Express, the ultra-premium Centurion Card, Membership Banking, and American Express Brokerage. According to management, these new products "set new standards which distinguished American Express from the competition."

- Continued success at American Express Financial Advisors with strong growth in sales and assets under management, improved investment performance, and the launch of new initiatives to help retain and attract additional financial advisors.

- Solid international card and travel-related business results, including higher billed business and lending balances despite economic weakness in many regions of the world.

- Net income for 1999 was $2.48 billion, up 16 percent from $2.14 billion in 1998. On a diluted per-share basis, earnings were $5.42, up 17 percent over the prior year. Net revenues on a managed basis for the year totaled $19.5 billion, up 13 percent over 1998. Return on equity was an impressive 25.3 percent.

Shortcomings to Bear in Mind

- Although 1999 was a good year for AXP, it was far from perfect. The company had a number of disappointments, among them:
  - Overall expenses that rose at the same rate as revenue. According to management, "This arithmetic is sustainable, but not adequate."
  - A time-to-market for new products and services that is much better than in the past, "but still falls short of our standards."

- A difficult year at American Express Bank.
- Legal actions against American Express Financial Advisors that resulted in an agreement in principle to settle three class-action lawsuits related to the sales of insurance and annuity products. Management says, "We expect that the settlement will provide for approximately $215 million of benefits to more than two million class participants."

- Analysts have been impressed with the company's new Internet card, the "Blue" smart card, and its aggressive advertising campaign. However, it has diverted the public eye from such rivals as Visa USA and MasterCard International, which are actively developing their own Internet shopping strategies. On a more negative note, some analysts believe that it is still possible that the whole category could fall apart.

There is also another concern: the campaign's touting of Blue's security benefits may send the wrong signal—planting the seed that other American Express cards are somehow unsafe for shopping on the Internet. American Express, after all, isn't abandoning any of its other cards because of Blue. In response, Alfred F. Kelly, Jr., president of the American Express Consumer Card Services Group, says the Blue advertising campaign wasn't meant to diminish the unique functions of other American Express cards. But he concedes that a few customers may cancel other American Express cards now that they can have a Blue. But "I would rather be cannibalizing myself," says Mr. Kelly, "than have the competition do it."

Reasons to Buy

- Over the past decade, American Express has acquired about 70 accounting firms, including the largest independent accounting firms in Chicago and New York. American Express officials say the company is aiming to become "a national accounting practice."

With 55 offices in 18 states, including the biggest markets, it has already made a giant step toward that goal.

American Express Tax and Business Services is now the ninth-largest accounting firm in the United States, according to Bowman's *Accounting Report*. In late 1998, AXP bought Altschuler, Melvoin and Glasser, the largest non-Big Five accounting firm in Chicago. Before that, it acquired Goldstein Golub Kessler & Company, a New York-based accounting firm that was the nation's largest single-office CPA firm.

According to a company spokesman, "We have a goal to become one of the biggest tax advice firms in the United States. Our cardholders have been asking for tax services."

- American Express's Blue credit card has been a huge success. Demand for the card, which contains a computer chip to make buying products on the Internet easier, has been more than twice the expected rate. The card also offers such perks as no annual fee, a low fixed interest rate, and a link to the company's web site for online bill payment and other money-management software. What's more, the company launched a rewards program for Blue similar to the programs currently offered with its other cards.

- American Express' cumulative total return to shareholders has exceeded both the S&P Financials and the S&P 500 Index for the past five-year period. Including share price appreciation and reinvestment of dividends, an investment of $100 in American Express stock at year-end 1994 was worth $602.43 at year-end 1999, compared with $356.47 for the S&P Financials and $350.63 for the S&P 500.

- For the 15th year in a row, American Express Financial Advisors achieved impressive growth and record financial results. In addition to revenue and net increases of 17 percent and 14 percent, respectively, several key business indicators showed improvement as well.

The segment's total sales force increased 10 percent, to nearly 11,400. Assets owned, managed, or administered increased by nearly 24 percent and totaled $262.5 billion at the end of 1999. The total number of clients expanded by four percent during 1999. Nearly one-third of them are American Express Card members—and they have become a major source of new business.

- American Express launched significant new card products in international markets in 1999. Available by invitation only, the ultra-premium Centurion Card—which features a smart chip—was introduced in the United Kingdom. Also introduced were Platinum Cards in Thailand and Puerto Rico. The company issued a cobranded card with Manulife Financial in Canada, and offered an American Express Card to Suncorp Metway customers in Australia.

- American Express continues to build and strengthen relationships with banking partners. Global Network Services (GNS) now has 58 partnership arrangements in more than 60 countries. In 1999, 38 new GNS products were launched, including the Taishin Gold Card in Taiwan, the WOWOW Saison American Express Card in Japan, the Portuguese Engineering Association Card, and the HSBC Global Card in Brazil.

Total assets: $148,517 million
Common shares outstanding: 1,344 million
Return on 1999 shareholders' equity: 25.3%

	1999	1998	1997	1996	1995	1994	1993	1992
Revenues (millions)	21279	19026	17760	16237	15841	14282	14173	26961
Net income (millions)	2475	2201	1991	1739	1564	1380	1172	653
Earnings per share	1.81	1.59	1.38	1.30	1.04	.89	.77	.44
Dividends per share	.30	.30	.30	.30	.30	.30	.33	.33
Price High	56.3	39.5	30.5	20.1	15.0	11.0	12.2	8.5
Low	31.6	22.3	17.9	12.9	9.7	8.4	7.5	6.7

CONSERVATIVE GROWTH

American Home Products Corporation

Five Giralda Farms □ Madison, New Jersey 07940 □ Investor contact: Thomas G. Cavanagh (973) 660-5000 □ Dividend reinvestment plan is available: (800) 565-2067 □ Web site: www.ahp.com □ Listed: NYSE □ Ticker symbol: AHP □ S&P rating: B+ □ Value Line financial strength rating: A+

People who have to count sheep at night now have a sleeping pill they can take in the middle of the night without having to fret about being drowsy when they read the morning newspaper. Sonata, a prescription drug, was introduced by American Home Products in Europe in the spring of 1999; in the fall of that year it was launched in the United States.

Sleep experts say that Sonata is a significant improvement because of the flexibility it gives people who wake up three or four hours before the alarm clock starts ringing. "This is an advantage," said Richard Gelula, executive director of the National Sleep Foundation. "You can take the pill when you travel on a long plane trip and be able to safely drive yourself home." Sonata's effects last just four hours, so you can take it at 3 A.M., even if you've set your alarm for 7 A.M. By contrast, the effects of most sleeping medications last eight hours or more. Analysts expect Sonata to eventually reach annual sales of over $500 million.

Company Profile

American Home Products is a global leader in discovering and commercializing innovative and cost-effective health care products.

AHP's broad, growing lines of prescription drugs, vaccines, nutritionals, over-the-counter medications, and medical devices benefit health care worldwide. Among the company's leading products are such names as Triphasal, Norplant, Premarin, Cordarone, Redux, Naprelan, Orudis, Advil, Anacin, Dimetapp, Robitussin, Preparation H, Centrum vitamins, Primatene, SMA, Lodine, and Effexor.

Shortcomings to Bear in Mind

■ In the fall of 1999—in the latest in a string of embarrassing setbacks—American Home Products said it was recalling nearly 600,000 allergy kits and indicated it had known for more than a year that the product might become discolored before its expiration date and ought to be thrown away. The medicine's label warns users to discard it if discoloration occurs, but a spokesman said the company didn't recall it earlier because tests showed the drug remained effective even when discolored.

Few drug companies are facing the fusillade of bad news that has befallen AHP. In 1997, for instance, it had to recall its popular diet drugs Redux and Pondimin after they were linked to heart-valve problems. In early 1998, it withdrew its application for approval of Verdia, a new blood-pressure medication, because of regulators' concerns it could cause liver problems.

Shortly after that the company had to recall Duract, a painkiller that caused fatal liver problems in some long-term users.

- In 1999, the company suffered from some red ink. These results include after-tax charges associated with the antiobesity products litigation and the restructuring of the agricultural products business, and the suspension of shipments and voluntary market withdrawal of RotaShield.

- During 1999, the company began to pursue the divestiture of it agricultural products business. This business had a difficult year due, in large part, to poor conditions in the agricultural industry. However, historically, it has been a significant contributor to AHP. After divestiture of this operation, virtually the entire portfolio of American Home Products will consist of pharmaceutical, consumer health care, and animal health products.

Reasons to Buy

- American Home Products formed a biotechnology research alliance with Elan Corporation P.L.C. in the spring of 2000 to develop an Alzheimer's vaccine. The alliance will allow AHP and the Irish firm to collaborate in research, development, and marketing of an experimental therapy called AN-1792 to treat mild to moderate Alzheimer's and possibly prevent the onset of the affliction. Elan's preclinical research has shown that the therapy reduces and prevents the development of amyloid plaque, a substance associated with Alzheimer's.

- Besides Sonata, the company had other new product introductions in 1999: Rapamune, ReFacto, and Meningitec. Additionally, in February of 2000, the company received U.S. market clearance for Prevnar and European market clearance for Enbrel. Protonix also was approved in the United States in February 2000.

ReFacto, the first albumin-free formulated recombinant factor VIII product for the treatment of hemophilia A, achieved 1999 sales of more than $30 million. Approval in the United States is expected in 2000.

Rapamune Oral Solution, the first in a new class of agents developed for the prevention of organ rejection in kidney transplant patients, received market clearance in the United States in September 1999. Rapamune already is being used by more than 80 of the top 100 transplant centers in the United States.

Meningitec is the world's first conjugate vaccine against meningococcal Group C disease. Within two months after being approved in the United Kingdom, sales were nearly $50 million—considerably ahead of expectations.

Prevnar is a novel, seven-valent pneumococcal conjugate vaccine. A Centers for Disease Control and Prevention advisory committee voted to recommend Prevnar for routine use in all healthy children in identified groups ages two to five.

Protonix is indicated for the short-term treatment of erosive esophagitis. When its intravenous formulation is cleared and an additional research study is completed, it will be the first and only intravenous formulation of a proton pump inhibitor to be sold in the United States.

- Whitehall-Robins Healthcare continues to be a major force in the consumer health care segment, recording net sales of $2.4 billion in 1999. This represents an increase of 9 percent over the prior year, due primarily to strong performance by nutritional supplements—which include Centrum products and Caltrate—as well as by cough/cold/allergy products, including Robitussin and Dimetapp, and by Chap Stick.

In 1999, Whitehall-Robins introduced several new products in the nutritional supplements category, including Centrum Performance, Centrum Focused Formulas, and Caltrate+Soy. The division's flagship brand, Advil, introduced Children's Advil Chewables, extending the product's reach into the pediatric market.

The acquisition of Solgar Vitamin and Herb Company in 1998 also contributed to the growth of the company's consumer health care franchise in 1999. Solgar nutritional supplements continued to expand their position within the health care food store channel. Future growth potential for Solgar remains significant due to favorable demographic trends, licensing of new, proprietary formulas, and international expansion.

■ Premarin and its family of products are the most prescribed medications in the United States. Considering that Premarin has been on the market for nearly 60 years, this leadership position is particularly noteworthy. And now there are new opportunities to use Premarin as a springboard to expand the company's women's health care franchise.

Research provides increasing evidence of the potential consequences of estrogen deficiency on bone mineral density, cardiovascular health, and cognitive functioning. Wyeth-Ayerst, through its Women's Health Research Institute, is at the forefront of research in hormone replacement and estrogens. Currently, the company is pursuing Phase III studies of lower doses of Prempro to determine its benefits on bone and on menopausal symptoms.

Trimegestone, a new progestin for hormone replacement and contraception, is undergoing evaluations in combination with Premarin, as well as with 17 B-estradiol for hormone replacement and with ethinyl estradiol for contraception.

■ Another major focus of the Women's Health Research Institute is on tissue-selective estrogens. These estrogens target certain tissue systems, such as bone, creating the opportunity for highly selective drug candidates. TSE-424, a new generation selective estrogen receptor modulator, was chosen from a large number of candidate molecules because of its impressive tissue-selective profile. The main clinical goal for this selective estrogen product is to prevent osteoporosis.

■ Enbrel, the first FDA-approved biological treatment for rheumatoid arthritis (RA), is rapidly extending its reach. Discovered by Immunex Corporation, a majority-owned subsidiary of AHP, and comarketed in the United States by Wyeth-Ayerst and Immunex, Enbrel was approved by the FDA in 1998 for the treatment of moderate-to-severe RA in people who had not responded adequately to disease-modifying medicines.

In May 1999, a Supplemental Biologic License Application was approved to treat children and teenagers (ages four to 17) with juvenile rheumatoid arthritis, and in July 1999 a submission was made for disease modification in early RA (less than three years duration). In February 2000, Enbrel received approval in the European Union for the treatment of rheumatoid arthritis and juvenile rheumatoid arthritis.

Currently, there are a number of programs under way to study Enbrel in the treatment of other diseases which may be driven by tumor necrosis factor, including congestive heart failure and psoriasis as well as gastrointestinal disorders.

- Enbrel is the cornerstone product of American Home Products's musculoskeletal franchise. Also included in

this family of products is Synvisc, which supplements the synovial fluid around the knee joint to lubricate and to relieve pain in osteoarthritis. Synvisc was launched in 1997 and is a collaborative effort with Biomatrix.

Total assets: $23,906 million
Current ratio: 1.27
Common shares outstanding: 1,306 million
Return on 1999 shareholders equity: NM

		1999	1998	1997	1996	1995	1994	1993	1992
Revenues (millions)		13550	13463	14196	14088	13376	8966	8305	7874
Net income (millions)		(1227)	2474	2160	1883	1338	1528	1469	1371
Earnings per share		(.94)	1.85	1.67	1.48	1.10	1.24	1.18	1.09
Dividends per share		.91	.87	.86	.79	.76	.74	.72	.67
Price	High	70.3	58.8	42.4	33.3	25.0	16.8	17.3	21.1
	Low	36.5	37.8	28.5	23.5	15.4	13.8	13.9	15.8

GROWTH AND INCOME

American Water Works Company

1025 Laurel Oak Road ◻ P.O. Box 1770 ◻ Voorhees, New Jersey 08043 ◻ Investor contact: Thomas G. McKitrick (856) 346-8200 ◻ Dividend reinvestment program is available: (877) 987-9757 ◻ Web site: www.amwater.com ◻ Ticker symbol: AWK ◻ S&P rating: A ◻ Value Line financial strength rating: A

The water utility business is less competitive than other utility businesses. For one thing, it is not threatened by the competitive pressures weighing down the electric and telephone utility businesses.

Water is a relatively inexpensive commodity to obtain but a difficult one to transport, which makes competition in the industry less likely. Barriers to entry include the immense cost of infrastructure development and necessary proximity to a water supply.

Company Profile
In addition to being the most capital-intensive of all utilities, the water business in the United States is highly fragmented. Ninety percent of the country's estimated sixty thousand separate water systems serve fewer than three thousand people each and are finding it increasingly difficult to provide the capital required to

remain profitable and to provide adequate service. Thus, regional approaches are emerging as the preferred solution to the nation's water service challenges.

For its part, American Water Works Company, Inc. is a holding company of water utilities. Together with its 23 wholly owned water service companies, it represents the largest regulated water utility business in the United States.

Subsidiaries serve a population of about twelve million people in more than nine hundred communities in 23 states, from Pennsylvania and Tennessee in the East and Southeast to Indiana and California in the Midwest and West. AWK serves a total of 2.5 million customers.

American Water Works gets most of its water from lakes, rivers, and streams, but also taps wells and other utilities to produce more than two hundred and fifty billion gallons of water each year.

The American Water Works Service Company, a subsidiary, provides professional services to affiliated companies. These services include accounting, administration, communication, corporate secretarial, engineering, financial, human resources, information systems, operations, rates and review, risk management, and water quality. This arrangement, which provides these services at cost, affords affiliated companies professional and technical talent otherwise unavailable economically or on a timely basis.

Shortcomings to Bear in Mind

- The weather plays an important part in the fortunes of a typical water company. They do best during hot, dry summers, since this stimulates the use of water for showers, lawns, and gardens. However, if the weather is excessively dry, the government may step in and ration the use of water for car washing, gardens, and lawns.

  On the other hand, if the region is deluged with rain, there is far less reason for customers to water their lawns and gardens. They may even take fewer showers if the temperature is cool.

  American Water Works, for its part, is not as seriously hurt by a dry summer in one or two of its territories, assuming the weather is not severe in its other jurisdictions. Smaller water companies, by contrast, usually serve parts of a single state or city and are more vulnerable to droughts or other vagaries in the weather.

- A water utility—like all public utilities—is closely regulated by a state commission. Each state has its own commission, some of which are more politically motivated than others. They tend to settle rate cases by favoring the consumer, rather than the company. In recent years, most state commissions have reduced the amount they will permit the company to earn on common

equity. Typical awards are in the 11 or 12 percent range. If the company disagrees with the decision of the commission, it may go to court in hopes of overturning a harsh award. More often than not, the courts side with the politicians.

For its part, American Water Works has to cope with 23 different commissions, since it operates in 23 states. This has one disadvantage: it means keeping track of 23 commissions, trying to keep from offending them or incurring their wrath.

It has an important benefit, however. The company does not stake its whole livelihood on one commission, which may be unreasonable. What it amounts to is the protection of geographic diversification.

- Public utilities fret about interest rates. There are two reasons: For one thing, they borrow a lot of money, and high interest rates boost their costs. Secondly, they offer investors a good source of income. However, when interest rates rise, some investors may sell their utility shares and go elsewhere to take advantage of the higher interest rates. When this happens, the shares of the utility decline.

- Because of the large number of acquisitions completed in 1999, earnings in 2000 will be flat or perhaps down by two or three cents per share.

Reasons to Buy

- The water utility industry is extremely fragmented, but it is becoming less so as takeovers reduce their ranks. Even so, there are still more than 60,000 independent water systems. Most are owned by financially constrained local municipalities or private investors. The attraction of many of these smaller utilities to the larger water companies is the risk reduction they could provide through geographic diversification.

The smaller entities have another serious problem: Water utilities have had to spend large sums of money in recent years in order to bring their plant and equipment up to the standards mandated by the Safe Drinking Water Act, the Clean Air Act, and other regulations. In this realm, the larger investor-owned utilities are much better suited to tap the financial markets in order to raise the needed cash to solve regulatory mandates.

To meet today's standards of quality, reliability, and affordability requires ever-increasing technical expertise, financial resources, and operational efficiencies. In this environment, size and financial strength become essential elements in satisfying the water service needs of customers. Yet 90 percent of the water systems in the nation serve fewer than three thousand three hundred people each, and 97 percent serve fewer than ten thousand.

- There should be ample opportunities for growth. The Environmental Protection Agency predicts it will take $138.5 billion in restructuring during the next 20 years to update and maintain the nation's 55,000 water systems, almost all of which will need fixing up with in those two decades.
- American Water Works has been active on the acquisition front. In 1999, the company completed more than a dozen acquisitions, which further augments its strategy of geographic diversification and customer growth. Among these was SJW Corporation, a holding company with two subsidiaries, San Jose Water Company and SJW Land Company. San Jose Water Company provides drinking water to 216,000 customers in and around San Jose, California. It is the largest integrated water system regulated by the California Public Utilities Commission. To acquire this company,

AWK invested $390 million in cash and assumed $90 million in debt.

In October of 1999, American Water Works signed an agreement to acquire the water and wastewater utility assets of Citizens Utilities Company for $745 million in cash and the assumption of $90 million in debt. Citizens Utilities provides water service to some two hundred eighteen thousand customers and wastewater service to about 87,000 customers in Arizona, California, Illinois, Indiana, Ohio, and Pennsylvania.

Although these acquisitions will be dilutive to earnings per share in the 18 months after closing, they provide the foundation for long-term earnings growth, an action which is consistent with the company's commitment to the creation of shareholder value for years to come.

- One of the key characteristics of the consolidation of the water utility business is the demand for high water quality. Unlike any other utility service, water companies must protect the safety of their product because people drink it. Pollution of water sources, better testing technology, and government regulation are requiring additional water filtration, chemical treatment, and extensive water monitoring.

For many water systems, that means skyrocketing costs and greater technical expertise in the operation and monitoring of water treatment facilities. Assuring water quality today requires an ongoing investment in research, construction, testing, and monitoring.

A leader in the water business, American Water Works and its subsidiaries have long committed the capital and employee resources needed to maintain a high level of water quality across the 23-state system of water utilities.

Recently, new regulation and public concern have centered on naturally occurring parasite contaminants such as giardia and cryptosporidium. American Water Works has reacted in anticipation of these regulations with the incorporation of particle-count monitoring, improved disinfection, and upgraded filtration. In addition, with regulation targeting more stringent control of byproducts from the use of chlorine and other chemicals, process modification and alternative disinfectants are being introduced into existing facilities.

Another potential future treatment requirement is the removal of radon from some well water sources. American Water Works has tested every source of well water in its operations and is prepared to introduce either aeration or granular activated carbon filtration when needed.

- American Water Works has an impressive record of dividend increases—25 consecutive years. In the most recent 10-year period (1989-1999), dividends per share advanced from $.37 to $.86, a compound annual growth rate of 8.8 percent, which is far better than most public utilities.

Total assets: 5,778 million
Current ratio: .72
Common shares outstanding: 97 million
Return on 1999 Shareholders' equity: 11.0%

		1999	1998	1997	1996	1995	1994	1993	1992
Revenues (millions)		1261	1017	954	895	803	770	718	657
Net income (millions)		148	127	115	102	92	74	79	72
Earnings per share		1.53	1.54	1.45	1.31	1.26	1.17	1.15	1.04
Dividends per share		.86	.82	.78	.70	.64	.54	.50	.47
Price	High	34.8	33.8	29.7	22.0	19.6	16.1	16.1	14.2
	Low	20.5	25.3	19.9	17.8	13.4	12.6	12.3	10.3

CONSERVATIVE GROWTH

AT&T Corporation

32 Avenue of the Americas □ New York, New York 10013-2412 □ Investor contact: Connie Weaver (212) 387-5400 □ Dividend reinvestment plan is available (800) 348-8288 □ Web site: www.att.com □ Listed: NYSE □ Ticker symbol: T □ S&P rating: B+ □ Value Line financial strength rating: A++

In 2000, IBM and AT&T joined forces to provide wireless Internet access for large business customers in what analysts called the largest Web push to date. By the end of 2000, the two companies expect to develop a system to enable business customers to access the Web as well as corporate networks and databases over cell telephones, laptop computers, and hand-held devices.

The pact between the two Wall Street giants combined IBM software and services with AT&T's wireless Internet Protocol network. In the words of Gary Cohen, General Manager, IBM Global Telecommunications Industry, "E-business is going mobile. Over the next five years, more than 80 percent of new corporate applications will be designed for non-PC devices, such as wireless phones."

Company Profile

AT&T is among the world's communications leaders, providing voice, data, and video telecommunications services to large and small businesses, consumers, and government agencies. The company provides regional, domestic, international, local, and Internet communication transmission services, including cellular telephone and other wireless services.

Some History

A multitude of changes have transformed AT&T since the huge enterprise spun off its seven Baby Bells back in 1984. The regional companies have since reduced their number by mergers, including Bell Atlantic's takeover of NYNEX and GTE, and Southwestern Bell's acquisition of Pacific Telesis. Under its new name, SBC Communications, the company now includes another former Baby Bell, Ameritech, which provides local service in the Midwest.

AT&T took a big stride toward entering the local services market by acquiring Teleport Communications Group for $11.3 billion in stock.

In 1998 the company acquired Tele-Communications, Inc., (TCI), one of the nation's largest cable companies, in a stock transaction valued at a hefty $48 billion. C. Michael Armstrong, AT&T's chairman, made the risky move to buy TCI in an attempt to do an end-run around the local Bell phone companies, which have been slow to open their markets to rivals, including AT&T. TCI and its various partners potentially give AT&T access to one-third of American homes, enabling it to provide local telephone and Internet access on a mass scale.

AT&T Wireless Services operates on a TDMA (Time Division Multiple Access) digital technology platform. It serves 7.2 million subscribers.

AT&T WorldNet Internet access service has gone from a startup in March 1996 to a leading provider of online services, with nearly 1.3 million subscribers at the end of 1998.

In 1998 the company sold its Universal Card Services unit to Citicorp for $3.5 billion in cash. In March of 1998, AT&T sold its Solutions Customer Care business to Cincinnati Bell for $625 million in cash. These moves were part of an effort to focus only on businesses that fit AT&T's communications strategy.

In 1996, the company completed a plan to split into three separate publicly traded companies. The largest of the companies consists primarily of core long-distance operations and wireless services, as well as 25 percent of the Bell Laboratories unit, which designs and develops new products and carries out basic research. This company retains the widely recognized AT&T name. The company provides its long-distance services throughout the United States and internationally to virtually all nations and territories. Its wireless operations are the largest of any domestic carrier.

In 1996 AT&T spun off Lucent Technologies. Lucent's operations include telecommunications equipment manufacturing and the remaining 75 percent of Bell Laboratories. The spinoff of the third company, the NCR computer unit, completed the separation.

Shortcomings to Bear in Mind

■ There seems to be a brain drain at AT&T of late. About a dozen executives have left the company since Mr. Armstrong arrived in 1997. Some were driven by the desire to become a CEO of an Internet startup, such as Daniel H. Schulman who went with priceline.com. Inc., which gave him a $100-million multiyear compensation package. Others were impatient with AT&T's slow progress in transforming itself from a creaky old phone company into a dashing Internet player. For others, frictions with Mr. Armstrong have been as big a factor in their departures as the lure of exciting opportunities elsewhere. Michael Armstrong is admired by many for his strongman style, but to some executives who have worked for him he's overbearing and inflexible. He manages them too closely, they say, and prevents them from spending money they need to expand their businesses.

- When AT&T unveiled plans to bring local phone service to customers in their homes via its vast digital wireless system, the company hailed it as "the communications medium of the 21st century." But more than three years later, the plans, code-named "Project Angel," have yet to take flight. Project Angel—now known inside AT&T as "fixed wireless"—is a major part of the company's effort to bypass the copper phone networks of its Baby Bell rivals and grab a slice of the giant local phone-service market, with revenues of $100 billion a year.

- In May of 2000, the U.S. Court of Appeals for the District of Columbia affirmed the constitutionality of a federal law limiting the number of cable TV systems a single company may own. This dealt a blow to AT&T's big bet on cable as the means of reaching into millions of homes with telephone and high-speed Internet connections.

The ruling indicates that AT&T will face a tough choice in achieving federal approval of its latest cable purchase, MediaOne Group. It could sell MediaOne's 25 percent stake in Time Warner Entertainment, which owns cable systems in major cities such as New York. Its other option would be to spin off Liberty Media, a holding company with substantial stakes in video programming. Liberty trades as an AT&T tracking stock. "One of the rays of hope that AT&T was holding out for was that the court would rule that the cap was illegal," said Michael Goodman, an analyst with the Yankee Group in Boston.

Reasons to Buy

- In the nation's biggest initial public offering, AT&T agreed in the spring of 2000 to sell 360 million shares of its new wireless tracking stock (AT&T Wireless—its ticker symbol is AWE) for $29.50 each. That brought in $10.6 billion (less more than $300 million that was paid to investment bankers for underwriting the deal). AT&T Wireless unit is growing by more than 40 percent a year, with annual revenues of more than $8 billion.

- In April of 2000 a group of companies led by AT&T acquired a 39 percent voting stake in Net2Phone Inc., a fast-growing company that routes low-priced phone calls over the Internet. AT&T can save billions of dollars each year by using Net2Phone's Internet-based phone technology, said Kathleen Earley, president of the company's Data & Internet Services unit. She said that AT&T can avoid paying access fees to local phone service providers by using Net2Phone technology.

- For years, AT&T has chafed against its image as a slow-but-steady giant, watching enviously as startup ventures cash in on the explosive growth of wireless communications. To be sure, the company itself is a wireless leader. However, that fact has gotten lost against other realities—its declining share of the long-distance market and its escalating expenditures in deploying "broadband," or high-speed Internet access, over its cable properties.

In the spring of 2000, AT&T took a major step toward shaking off its moribund reputation. The company elected to sell stock that would track its cellular holdings. The sale of some 360 million shares brought into the company's coffers a tidy $13 billion—a huge IPO—in fact, the largest initial public offering in history.

Tracking stocks have become a popular means of raising corporate capital by offering investors a chance to buy the assets—and profits—of single, fast-growing divisions with mature companies.

- Late in 1999, AT&T reached an agreement with General Motors and Delphi Automotive Systems (a recent GM spin-off) to provide more than $550 million in data-transmission and Internet service over the next five years. Under the contract, AT&T's Solutions unit will provide the Internet and data backbone to line GM's and Delphi's global operations. Delphi has more than 170 manufacturing sites, 38 joint ventures, and 30 technical centers on six continents. For its part, General Motors has more than 1,100 locations in more than 40 countries. The agreement is intended to give GM a standardized worldwide data infrastructure, something the auto maker lacked before its pact with AT&T.

- In 1999 AT&T bought MediaOne Group, paying $58 billion. This move made the company the largest cable company in the nation. It gives AT&T access to 26 million American households and minority stakes in cable systems that have access to 34 million more. Starting in 2000, the company plans to use cable wires to deliver the entire menu of telecom products to consumers—not merely long distance, but also local telephone service, high-speed Internet access, and cable television. By delivering bundled services, AT&T believes it can offer lower prices and effectively compete with the local telephone companies that are gearing up to provide a similar array of services.

- In another stunning move in 1999, the company cut a deal with Microsoft to provide software for AT&T's cable boxes. Under the agreement, which included a $5 billion investment by Microsoft, AT&T will use Windows CE software in at least 2.5 million set-top boxes that will deliver digital television, telephone, and Internet service.

- AT&T, the number one domestic long-distance telephone company, and British Telecommunications PLC, the largest phone company in Great Britain, said their $10 billion global venture, Concert, had reached financial closure early in 2000. Concert combines the transborder assets and operations of AT&T and BT, including their international networks, all their international traffic, and their international products for business customers.

  In a statement, Sir Peter Bonfield, BT's CEO, said, "This is a new company for the new millennium addressing the massive growth in e-business in the Internet enabled global economy. Concert hits the ground running. David Dorman was appointed CEO last spring and has built a formidable management team which takes over full control today (January 5, 2000)." At the time of the announcement, management said that in 2000 Concert is expected to generate revenues of more than $7 billion and earnings before interest and taxes of about $700 million.

- AT&T and British Telecommunications PLC bought a stake in the Japan Telecom Company in the spring of 1999, adding a third partner to their $10-billion alliance and speeding their entry into the Japanese market. British Telecom bought 20 percent and AT&T 10 percent of Japan Telecom, the country's fourth-largest phone company, for about 150 billion yen ($1.3 billion). British Telecom and AT&T needed direct links to customers in the $111 billion Japanese market to compete with rivals like MCI Worldcom.

  Prior to the deal, AT&T already had a joint venture with 25 Japanese corporations, including KDD Corporation, Fujitsu Ltd. And Hitachi Ltd, to offer Internet access and other service to business. The venture, formed in 1984 and called AT&T Jens, was the country's first commercial Internet service provider.

■ A key element in the transformation of AT&T is its new CEO, C. Michael Armstrong, who took the reins in late 1997. Since then he has been making wholesale changes, beginning with the purchase of the cable giant, TCI, with plans to rebuild its creaking rural systems so that he can deliver telephone calls, video, and data all on the same wires. He formed a joint venture with British Telecom to combine international phone operations. He bought Teleport Communications Group, a phone company that serves big businesses in city centers and sold AT&T's credit card business to Citibank. He also signed long-term contracts with Citibank and later Banc One, among others, to manage their communications networks.

Armstrong brought in new managers to run AT&T's major businesses, designating outsiders to take over the consumer, commercial, and international telecom operations. He began cutting the company's bloated costs, leaving AT&T more or less debt-free—all while completing an 18,000-person middle management staff cut a year ahead of schedule.

■ In 1999, AT&T and Time Warner decided to team up to offer a package of telecommunications services via cable TV wires, moving closer to the day when customers get one bill for their television service, phones, and Internet access.

Combined with earlier moves—notably AT&T's purchase of Tele-Communications—this latest development allows AT&T to offer these services to 40 percent of U.S. households, or 35 million homes, within five years. Finally, the pact marks another big step by AT&T to get back into local phone service, which it left after being dismantled by the government in 1984.

Total assets: $169,406 million
Current ratio: .55
Common shares outstanding: 3,195 million
Return on 1999 shareholders' equity: 13.5%

		1999	1998	1997	1996	1995	1994	1993	1992
Revenues (millions)		62391	53223	51319	52184	79609	75094	67156	64904
Net income (millions)		5450	5235	4472	5608	1866	4879	4258	3807
Earnings per share		2.20	1.94	1.83	2.31	.79	2.09	2.10	1.91
Dividends per share		.88	.88	.88	.88	.88	.88	.88	.88
Price	High	64.1	52.7	42.7	45.9	45.7	38.1	43.3	35.4
	Low	41.5	32.3	20.5	22.2	31.8	31.5	33.5	24.4

Avery Dennison Corporation

150 North Orange Grove Boulevard ◻ Pasadena, California 91103-3596 ◻ Investor contact: Cynthia S. Guenther (626)-304-2204 ◻ Direct dividend reinvestment plan is available: (800) 756-8200 ◻ Web site: www.averydennison.com ◻ Listed: NYSE ◻ Ticker symbol: AVY ◻ S&P rating: A ◻ Value Line financial strength rating: A

If you're tired of licking stamps, you should try the Postal Service's self-adhesive stamps. Unlike the old stamps, the new ones adhere to the envelope without any coaxing. These stamps represent the first time the U.S. Postal Service has offered a stamp die-cut in the shape of the image. And because Avery has been die-cutting intricately shaped labels for decades, it has been able to make that possible for stamps, as well.

According to the annual report, "We even developed a special backing material so thin that it allows stamps to be dispensed through ATMs all over the world. And self-adhesive stamps are now so popular, they account for about 90 percent of stamp sales in the United States."

Company Profile

Avery Dennison is a global specialty chemical company, industrial, and consumer-products company. Its pioneering pressure-sensitive technology is an integral part of products found in virtually every major industry. The company was formed in 1990 with the merger of Avery International Corporation and Dennison Manufacturing Corporation.

The company's primary businesses are organized into two sectors under a decentralized management structure.

The Pressure-Sensitive Adhesives and Materials Sector manufactures adhesives and base materials for industrial and commercial applications.

The Consumer and Converted Products Sector manufactures self-adhesive products for the office and home—including desktop printer labels and cards, markers, and organization and presentation products—and a variety of self-adhesive industrial labels, fastening devices, self-adhesive industrial labels, fastening devices, self-adhesive postage stamps, battery tester labels, and other specialized label products for global markets.

The company employs more than sixteen thousand people in 200 manufacturing and sales facilities that produce and sell Avery Dennison products in 89 countries.

The company is best known for its Avery-brand office products, Fasson-brand self-adhesive base materials, peel-and-stick postage stamps, industrial and security labels, retail tag and labeling systems, self-adhesive tapes, and specialty chemicals. Well-known products include the United States Postal Service's self-adhesive stamps and Duracell's battery-testing labels.

Under the Avery Dennison and Fasson brands the company makes papers, films, and foils coated with adhesive and sold in rolls to printers. The company also makes school and office products (Avery, Marks-A-Lot, Hi-LITER) such as notebooks, three-ring binders, markers, fasteners, business forms, tickets, tags, and imprinting equipment.

Shortcomings to Bear in Mind

■ During 1999 there were several times when insiders, such as directors and officers, were selling shares in Avery Dennison. This is not necessarily an indication they are disenchanted with their holdings, but it is disconcerting, nonetheless.

■ According to one analyst, "Adverse currency translation and a weaker product mix may slightly restrict top-line improvement."

Reasons to Buy

■ Avery is benefiting from increasing demand for more informative labels on products, expanding use of PCs and printers, accelerating use of bar codes, and growth of consumer spending in developing countries.

■ The dividend has been increased for 24 consecutive years. In the last 10 years (1989–1999), dividends advanced from 27 cents to 99 cents, a compound annual growth rate of 13.9 percent. In the same period earnings per share expanded from 98 cents to $2.51, a growth rate of 9.9 percent.

■ Self-adhesive labels imprinted with bar codes have greatly increased the speed and accuracy of baggage sorting—as well as a multitude of other tasks. For instance, they're used for inventory control, product tracking, distribution, and logistics management. What's more, you'll find them everywhere: airports, hospitals, warehouses, retail stores, and packages ordered on the Internet.

■ The company's Fasson-brand materials set the industry standard for variable information printing applications. They ensure superior bar-coding, which translates into accurate scanning. Also, they stay stuck to a wide variety of surfaces, even in harsh environments.

■ In another sector, Avery Dennison automotive products decorate, seal, identify, and secure items throughout millions of automobiles. The automotive industry uses the company's specialty self-adhesive tapes instead of nuts, bolts, and other fasteners. What's more,

that industry uses Avery's labels to carry all kinds of important information— from part numbers to safety warnings— on components like air bags and radiator covers.

These products can also enhance a car's appearance, inside and out, with attractive exterior graphics, including decorative striping and interior laminates such as wood-grain films.

In addition, Avery Dennison Avloy Dry Paint film is changing the way the automotive industry thinks about finishing plastic-based car parts. Major manufacturers are using the company's performance films more and more as an alternative to spray-painting—on everything from side moldings to spoilers. And with good reason. Avery Dennison Avloy film looks great and is durable, cost-effective, and friendly to the environment.

■ Although Avery Dennison is well-known for its office products, the company is now expanding beyond the office with useful, creative, and fun products for making personalized items right at home. These include greeting cards, banners, posters, flyers, and T-shirts.

■ Even the wine industry is being attracted to Avery products. For wine label designers, the possibilities are endless. According to management, "Wineries love the production efficiencies—hundreds of domestic wineries are using pressure-sensitive labels already— and Avery Dennison is leading the way worldwide."

Avery Dennison's Decorating Technologies Division worked with E&J Gallo Winery to create a new Avery Dennison Clear ADvantage heat-transfer label for a new line of wines known as Wild Vines. Gallo selected the Avery Dennison labeling process because of its unique capability in achieving a frosted-bottle look.

- Nor has the company ignored the Internet. The Avery Web site enhanced consumer awareness and demand for Avery-brand products. The site, which drew several million hits in 1999, provides free Avery Wizard and Avery LabelPro software, which can be downloaded to create an instant base of new customers.
- The company now has a European Films Center in Gotha, Germany, the largest label film facility outside North America, to meet rapidly growing demand for Fasson pressure-sensitive label materials throughout Europe.
- The company's Fasson Roll Specialty business has achieved double-digit growth, creating innovative, customized solutions—such as dissolvable labels, holographic films, and unique wall-covering materials—that incorporate pressure-sensitive adhesive technology.
- South of the border, Avery has been aggressively pursuing its Latin American growth strategy—including the acquisition of a prominent pressure-sensitive materials business in Colombia and substantial majority ownership in its label materials operation in Argentina—significantly strengthening the company's market presence of its roll materials business in this expanding region.
- Across the Pacific, despite economic turmoil in some Asian nations, the company's label materials operation in Asia Pacific continues to grow, reflecting the rapid growth of consumer products markets in the region. Sales of the company's pressure-sensitive materials have been growing in China at a double-digit pace.
- In 1999 the company's Worldwide Ticketing Services business, according to Philip M. Neal, Avery's CEO, "continued to turn in a stellar performance, gaining market share as it consistently delivers double-digit sales and operating profit growth. Operating satellite imprinting centers in 22 countries, Worldwide Ticketing serves the apparel marketing industry with a sophisticated global data management system that provides both the convenience of local ticket printing and worldwide inventory tracking."
- Avery Dennison has joined with leading German maker of pens and markers Schwan-STABILO to distribute writing instruments in the United States and Canada in new Avery-brand packaging. STABILO features a complete line of innovative, high-quality writing instruments providing visibility for the Avery brand in this important office products category.
- In 1999 the company finalized the purchase of Stimsonite, a leading producer of reflective materials for the transportation and highway safety markets. The company also acquired Bear Rock Technologies, a leading software development company specializing in bar-coding applications, labeling solutions, and Web-enabled printing technologies. Bear Rock joins Avery's growing software business. Finally, the company created a joint venture between Avery Dennison and Hitachi Maxell, Ltd. to develop and sell cobranded office products in Japan under the powerful Avery and Maxell brand names.

Total assets: $2,143 million
Current ratio: 1.12
Common shares outstanding: 113 million
Return on 1999 shareholders' equity: 25%

	1999	1998	1997	1996	1995	1994	1993	1992
Revenues (millions)	3768	3460	3346	3222	3114	2857	2609	2623
Net income (millions)	258	223	205	174	143	109	83	80
Earnings per share	2.55	2.15	1.94	1.61	1.34	.99	.72	.67
Dividends per share	.99	.87	.72	.62	.56	.50	.45	.41
Price High	73.0	62.1	45.8	36.5	25.1	18.0	15.8	14.6
Low	39.4	39.4	33.4	23.8	16.6	13.3	12.6	11.6

GROWTH AND INCOME

Baldor Electric Company

5711 R. S. Boreham Jr. Street ▫ Fort Smith, Arkansas 72902-2400 ▫ Investor contact: John A. McFarland (501) 646-4711 ▫ Dividend reinvestment plan is available: (800) 509-5586 ▫ Web site: www.baldor.com ▫ Listed: NYSE ▫ Ticker symbol: BEZ ▫ S&P rating: A ▫ Value Line financial strength rating: B++

Baldor recently received two "Market Leadership Awards" from Frost & Sullivan, an internationally recognized market research firm. The "Product Innovation Award" is given to the company that demonstrates excellence in product innovation.

Baldor also received the "Customer Service Award" in recognition of superior customer service. Baldor was also honored as the "Marketer of the Year" by the Electrical Insulation Conference. This award is in recognition of Baldor's success from the introduction of ISR-Inverter Spike Resistant magnet wire in all one horsepower and larger AC three-phase motors.

Company Profile

With annual sales of less than $600 million, Baldor Electric Company is a pygmy among giants. Baldor makes electric motors that power pumps, fans, conveyor belts, and all the other automated components that keep modern factories humming. It competes successfully against much larger firms such as Reliance Electric, Emerson Electric, and General Electric. But what Baldor lacks in size, it more than makes up for in flexibility and profitability.

Baldor Electric designs and manufactures a broad product line to serve its customers' diverse needs. Industrial AC and DC electric motors, ranging from 1/50 through 800 horsepower, are the mainstay of the company's products.

Baldor's line of Standard-E motors are designed to meet the efficiency requirements of the Energy Policy Act. Baldor's premium efficient Super-E motors are widely recognized as offering some of the highest efficiencies. These higher efficiencies translate into lower operating costs to the motor end-user.

Baldor also offers customers a wide range of "definite-purpose" motors. Examples include Baldor's Washdown Duty motors, which are ideal for food processing and other wet environments. Baldor's Chemical Processing line of cast-iron motors are built for the harsh environment of mills and processing plants. Baldor Farm Duty motors meet the rugged outdoor requirements in the agricultural market. Also included are broad lines of brake motors, explosion-proof, C-Face, pump motors, and gear motors.

The fastest-growing segment of Baldor's product line is adjustable-speed drives. The company offers DC SCR controls, AC inverters and vector control, and a wide range of servo and positioning products. Baldor markets Matched Performance by offering customers matched motor and control packages with lab-tested performance.

Baldor recently introduced the Baldor SmartMotor, an integrated motor and adjustable-speed control. Now available from 1 to 10 horsepower, this breakthrough new product is easy to install and offers many performance advantages.

Shortcomings to Bear in Mind

Baldor's operations have experienced some softness of late. The company's top-line growth has slowed to a low single-digit pace. The causes were several. For one thing, the economic uncertainties in such regions as Asia and Latin America have cut back on demand. Even in the United States, the slowdown is evident, since some of the company's customers have been hurt by problems abroad.

Reasons to Buy

- Even though sales dipped about 2 percent in 1999—the first decline in eight years—the company has been taking solid steps to enhance sales. For instance, Baldor's new catalog includes over 350 new products, more than it has ever introduced at one time. What's more, the company has expanded its sales organization by opening new sales offices and adding additional warehouses and salespeople. Also, in 2000 Baldor was able to reduce its three-week lead times to two weeks—a strong competitive advantage.
- Baldor's new family of mini inverters received the coveted "Product of the Year" Gold Award for 1999 from *Plant Engineering* magazine. The *Plant Engineering* Product of the Year Awards were established to honor the most innovative and useful products introduced to the industrial plant engineering market each year.
- What sets Baldor apart, analysts believe, is its innovative approach to the business. For one thing, Baldor offers a broad selection of motors. What's more, it produces motors in small lot sizes that only fit the needs of a small group of customers. About one-third of what it sells are custom products.

Second, the company is a domestic manufacturer. Even so, Baldor's margins are about the same as most of its competitors. Some of these rivals, moreover, also include higher-margined mechanical transmissions linkage products. What's more, Baldor has the highest margins of any domestic industrial motor manufacturer. Analysts think part of the explanation relates to Baldor's fragmented customer base—it has over 8,000 customers. Additionally, the company sells only a modest volume into the consumer market where the customers are large and can exercise significant pricing leverage.

Third, Baldor doesn't have its own sales force. Instead, it relies on independent sales representatives who are paid on commission. Each of these agents has an exclusive territory and sells all of Baldor's products in that region. In addition, the mix of Baldor's business is more heavily weighted to distributor sales—50 percent of sales, compared with 33 percent for the industry. This is a plus factor because distributors tend to concentrate on the replacement market—it's more recession-resistant than the original-equipment realm.

- Baldor Electric spends thousands of hours every year talking with customers to see how the company is perceived. Baldor consistently receives high grades. In recent surveys, for instance, 82 percent of those interviewed named Baldor first when asked, "What motor line do you prefer?"

- Management's philosophy toward inventories is not typical. Although many efficiency experts argue that manufacturers should strive for just-in-time operations, Baldor has a mind of its own. Baldor believes that, given the nature of its customers, the benefits of having inventories on hand outweigh the costs. Quick delivery times are very important to Baldor's customers, especially the distributors. Therefore, having available products and being able to deliver nearly any motor in less than 24 hours helps the company to obtain sales. What's more, the margins on short-lead-time sales are also higher.

- Information is an important competitive advantage for Baldor. The company's CD-ROM electronic catalog, first introduced in 1994, is now in its fifth edition. It is used by over 30,000 customers. BEZ's Internet Web site, moreover, is visited daily by users around the world. In 1998, Baldor added 285 new motors and drives to its catalog. The company now offers more than 5,000 different products—far and away the industry's broadest line of stock motors and drives.

- In 2000, Baldor was first to introduce a new technology grease developed by ExxonMobil especially for electric motor bearings. This new grease has a lubrication life up to four times longer than other greases in temperatures as high as 350°F. It also exhibits greater durability to mechanical shearing forces and has superior resistance to washout, rust, and corrosion.

- The long-awaited move to factory automation is gaining momentum, which is good news for Baldor. Such core industries as pulp and paper, mining, and petrochemical, for instance, are devising new, more efficient methods of operation. These include applications perfect for Baldor's extensive line of high-performance drives, from logging and sawmilling to textiles and plastics.

- Electric motors and drives are used in virtually all industries. Take, for example, the high-precision, robotic positioning needs of medical equipment and semiconductor manufacturers. These represent new and fast-growing markets for Baldor servos, especially the company's new palm-size BSM 50 brushless servo motor.

- Baldor engineers have been working for several years on a line of commercial-duty motors. These motors are designed for use in commercial applications such as ventilation blowers used in shopping malls and fast-food restaurants where industrial motors are "too much" for the job. Baldor has also developed special flange-mount pump commercial motors. The company estimates the domestic market for these commercial motors to be as much as $400 million.

- Today, the industrial drives business is growing much faster than the motor business. In fact, within a couple of years, the company believes it will be as big as the entire industrial motor business. This nearly doubles BEZ's opportunities for growth domestically and abroad.

  Baldor high-performance drives are now being used in applications previously handled by fixed-speed motors. The result is far greater productivity, flexibility, and reduced operating costs.

- More than half of the company's capital equipment has been replaced during the past five years. Its work force is nonunion. The company relies on a vertically integrated manufacturing strategy to achieve solid quality control, producing most of the component parts that go into its motors, such as laminations, endplates, rotors, and conduit boxes.

■ Somewhat surprisingly, motor manufacturing is still a rather labor-intensive endeavor (final assembly is still done largely by hand). However, Baldor has invested heavily in modernizing its factories, using a concept called flexible-flow manufacturing. The essence of flexible flow, compared with the prior-batch system is this: in the past, the company might have produced hundreds and perhaps thousands of a particular motor model before switching production to another, thereby generating a potentially large (and unnecessary) finished goods inventory of each model. With flexible flow, production runs are much shorter—perhaps even tailored to a single order. Each worker puts together a complete motor from a tray of parts. The tray is tagged with a computer printout directing the assembler what kind of motor to build, how to assemble the parts, and test the complete motor.

As a result of the Baldor approach, lead times for custom motors been dramatically reduced and are running at about one-half of the competition.

■ The popularity of Baldor's Web site, www.baldor.com, continues to grow, with over 20,000 separate visits per month. *Plant Services* magazine named the company's Web site as one of the best at serving the needs of plant engineers. Baldor recently added a feature to give its distributors the ability to check inventory availability on any of the company's more than 5,000 stock products, such as motor efficiency data, dimension drawings, and Matched Performance curves. What's more, new products are highlighted as well as information on the company's training classes, trade shows, sales offices, and service centers. In addition, Baldor made it easy for someone to quickly locate the Baldor stocking distributors close to them by simply entering a zip code.

Total assets: $412 million
Current ratio: 3.41
Common shares outstanding: 36 million
Return on 1999 shareholders' equity: 16.4%

	1999	1998	1997	1996	1995	1994	1993	1992
Revenues (millions)	577	589	558	503	473	418	357	319
Net income (millions)	44	45	40	35	32	26	19	15
Earnings per share	1.19	1.17	1.09	.97	.84	.70	.52	.42
Dividends per share	.45	.40	.35	.29	.26	.21	.16	.14
Price High	21.7	27.2	23.8	18.8	19.9	13.6	12.3	9.4
Low	17.0	10.1	18.2	13.9	12.9	10.6	8.1	6.1

CONSERVATIVE GROWTH

Baxter International, Incorporated

One Baxter Parkway ❏ **Deerfield, Illinois 60015** ❏ **Investor contact: Neville Jeharajah (847)-948-2875**
❏ **Dividend reinvestment program is available: (800) 446-2617** ❏ **Web site: www.baxter.com** ❏ **Listed: NYSE**
❏ **Ticker symbol: BAX** ❏ **S&P rating: B** ❏ **Value Line financial strength rating: A**

Health care is one of the fastest-growing industries in the world. This growth is being fueled by a combination of factors, including a growing and aging population. On October 12, 1999, the world population exceeded six billion and is projected to double to 12 billion before the end of the 21st century.

The greatest population growth is in developing countries—places like China,

India, and Latin America. As the economic expansion continues in these countries, their spending on health care will increase.

In addition, the world population is aging. Globally, the average life span has jumped from 49.5 years in 1972 to more than 63 years today. As people get older, they usually require more health care. As these trends continue, the demand for the products, services, and therapies that Baxter provides will increase. With Baxter's significant global presence, the company is well positioned to meet the needs of patients in high-growth markets worldwide.

Company Profile

Baxter dates back to 1931 when it was the first producer of commercially prepared intravenous solutions. The company is now a leading producer of medical products and equipment, with an emphasis on products and technologies associated with the blood and circulatory system. Sales abroad accounted for 53 percent of revenues in 1999.

In 2000, the company spun off its CardioVascular business as a separate publicly traded company. As now constituted, Baxter operates three divisions:

I.V. Systems/Medical Products
1999 Sales: $2.5 billion

This division manufactures a range of products used to deliver fluids and drugs to patients. These products provide fluid replacement, nutrition therapy, pain management, antibiotic therapy, chemotherapy, and other therapies.

The company provides intravenous (IV) and irrigating solutions in flexible plastic containers; premixed liquid and frozen drugs for IV delivery; IV access systems and tubing sets; electronic IV infusion pumps; solutions, containers, and automated compounding systems for IV nutrition; IV anesthesia devices and inhalation agents; and ambulatory infusion systems.

In 1999, Baxter reclaimed the distribution rights for its inhalation agents in Canada and Western Europe from Pharmacia & Upjohn, Inc. It also acquired its IV business in Germany.

Baxter also began distributing Gensia Sicor's genetic propofol anesthetic. Late in 1999, Baxter announced the acquisition of several outpatient infusion pumps and related medical systems from Sabratek Corporation. Baxter also continues to expand its alliances with pharmaceutical companies to premix and package their drugs in Baxter IV solution containers.

Blood Therapies
1999 Sales: $2.2 billion

This segment produces therapeutic proteins from plasma and through recombinant methods to treat hemophilia, immune deficiencies, and other blood-related disorders. These include coagulation factors, immune globulins, albumin, wound-management products, and vaccines. Baxter also has a stake in blood-collection containers and automated blood-cell separation and collection systems. These products are used by hospitals, blood banks, and plasma-collection centers to collect and process blood components for therapeutic use or for processing into therapeutic products such as albumin. Therapeutic blood components are used to treat patients undergoing surgery, cancer therapy, and other critical therapies.

In November of 1999, Baxter announced plans to acquire North American Vaccine, Inc., further broadening its position in the vaccines market. Finally, Baxter's alliance with Cerus Corporation in the development of technologies to inactivate viral pathogens in collected blood components represents a significant area of potential future growth.

Renal

1999 Sales: $1.7 billion

The Renal segment provides a range of renal dialysis products and services to support people with kidney failure. The company is the world's leading manufacturer of products for peritoneal dialysis (PD), a home dialysis therapy. These products include PD solutions, container systems, and automated machines that cleanse patients' blood overnight while they sleep. Baxter also manufactures dialyzers and instrumentation for hemodialysis (HD). Baxter's Renal Therapy Services (RTS) operates dialysis clinics in 12 countries outside the United States, while Renal Management Strategies Inc. (RMS) works with U.S. nephrologists to provide a kidney-disease management program to health care payers.

In late 1999, Baxter announced that it was acquiring Althin Medical AB, a Swedish manufacturer of hemodialysis instruments and dialyzers. Also in 1999, the company entered into a joint venture with Gambro AB of Sweden to create Tandem Healthcare LLC. Tandem makes dialyzers—the filters through which blood is circulated to cleanse it during hemodialysis—for both Baxter and Gambro in Baxter's Mountain Home, Arkansas plant.

The company's RTS business continues to acquire dialysis clinics in Asia, Europe, and Latin America where it operates the clinics in partnership with local doctors. RTS entered the year 2000 with more than 160 clinics in Argentina, Brazil, China, Colombia, France, Indonesia, Korea, Malaysia, Singapore, Spain, Taiwan, and the United Kingdom.

Shortcomings to Bear in Mind

- Growth in earnings per share is rather lackluster. In the 1989–1999 period, earnings per share increased from $1.50 to $2.64, a compound annual growth rate of only 5.8 percent. In the same 10-year span, dividends edged up from $.56 to $1.16, a growth rate of 7.6 percent.

- According to management's comments in the 1999 annual report, "The company's primary markets are highly competitive and subject to substantial regulation. There has been consolidation in the company's customer base and by its competitors, which has resulted in pricing and share pressures. The company has experienced increases in its labor and material costs, which are partly influenced by general inflationary trends. Competitive market conditions have minimized inflation's impact on the selling prices of the company's products and services. Management expects these trends to continue."

Reasons to Buy

- As its name suggests, Baxter International is a global enterprise with more than half of sales coming from overseas. CEO Harry M. Jansen Kraemer, Jr. contends he has the Rx to improve all of its global operations. "Big companies are most efficient when they're most focused on what they do well," he says, listing research and development, manufacturing skills, and worldwide distribution as Baxter's strengths.

- As we enter the twenty-first century, the growing, aging population is creating unprecedented, explosive growth in medical conditions that occur more frequently and grow more acute with age. Baxter manufactures and markets products and services that are used to treat patients with many of these conditions, including cancer, trauma, hemophilia, immune deficiencies, infectious diseases, kidney disease, and other disorders.

The company also makes products that are used in the treatment of patients undergoing most surgical procedures. All of these conditions can cause severe physical, emotional, and financial burdens to patients and their families. Baxter's role is to help alleviate these burdens by developing innovative technologies that improve the patient's quality of life and medical outcome and lower the overall cost of patient care. The majority of Baxter's businesses are pioneers in their field, with more than 70 percent of sales coming from products with leading market positions.

- Cancer kills millions of people a year of all ages. More than half of all malignant cancers disable patients during their most productive years. For patients undergoing high-dose chemotherapy, Baxter makes automated blood-component collection systems that harvest "stem cells" from patients' blood for reinfusion to rebuild their immune systems.
- Injury or trauma is the leading cause of death for people under age 44. Many trauma victims receive Baxter products—IV solutions, plasma-volume expanders, blood-transfusion products, and other products for fluid replenishment and blood-volume stabilization.
- Infectious diseases continue to cause illness and death around the world. While some infectious diseases have been conquered in some regions through modern advances in antibiotics and vaccines, new diseases are constantly emerging. Lyme disease, AIDS, and new strains of influenza are all diseases that have emerged within the last 20 years. Baxter makes the leading vaccine for tick-borne encephalitis (TBE), a potentially fatal disease common in

portions of Europe and Asia. The company recently introduced its next-generation TBE vaccine, Ticovac. Baxter also is developing vaccines for influenza and Lyme disease.

- Baxter products are used in a variety of surgical applications. Most people undergoing surgery require IV access for solutions and medicines. Precise infusion requires sophisticated electronic infusion pumps to regulate flow. Baxter provides a broad range of anesthetic agents and delivery devices for general anesthesia. The company makes fibrin sealant to facilitate blood clotting and wound healing in surgery.
- Kidney disease continues to be a growing cause of illness and death around the world. Patients with end-stage renal disease (ESRD), or kidney failure, require dialysis or a kidney transplant to cleanse their blood of toxins, waste, and excess water normally removed by healthy kidneys. Baxter was a pioneer in dialysis and remains the world's leading provider of products for dialysis.
- In biosciences, Mr. Kraemer looks for revenues to climb by more than 20 percent a year. In 1999, they rose by 17 percent, to $2.2 billion. Major expansions are planned, especially for new therapies for treating hemophilia and for vaccines. Mr. Kraemer says, "We now have one-third of sales and probably 45 percent of operating earnings in bioscience products." He thinks Wall Street is "just beginning to recognize Baxter for bioscience."

Total assets: $9,644 million
Current ratio: 1.67
Common shares outstanding: 291 million
Return on 1999 shareholders' equity: 22%

	1999	1998	1997	1996	1995	1994	1993	1992
Revenues (millions)	6380	6599	6138	5438	5048	9324	8879	8471
Net income (millions)	779	731	652	575	485	596	539	561
Earnings per share	2.64	2.53	2.31	2.11	1.75	2.13	1.95	1.99
Dividends per share	1.16	1.16	1.13	1.17	1.11	1.03	1.00	.86
Price High	76.0	66.0	60.3	48.1	44.8	28.9	32.8	40.5
Low	56.8	48.5	39.9	39.8	26.8	21.6	20.0	30.5

CONSERVATIVE GROWTH

Becton Dickinson and Company

1 Becton Drive ◻ Franklin Lakes, New Jersey 07417-1880 ◻ Investor contact: Ronald Jasper (201) 847-7160 ◻ Direct dividend reinvestment plan is available: (800) 955-4743 ◻ Web site: www.bd.com ◻ Fiscal year ends September 30 ◻ Ticker symbol: BDX ◻ S&P rating: A ◻ Value Line financial strength rating: A

Becton Dickinson has the technology to help reduce the medical errors that have received attention of late. A U.S. government scientific panel found that about 75,000 hospital patients die each year from medical mistakes. Yet only 9 percent of the facilities have invested in equipment to address the problem.

For its part, BDX is offering two hand-held devices based on 3Com's Palm Computing technology. One tracks drugs from the initial order through their administration. The other serves a similar purpose for specimen collection, testing, and patient file management.

Company Profile

Becton Dickinson is the worldwide leader in flow cytometry analysis; evacuated blood collection systems; insulin injection systems for diabetes health care; and hypodermic needles, syringes, and prefillable drug delivery systems.

The company's $3.4 billion in 1999 revenues breaks down as follows: medical systems (56 percent of sales), pre-analytical solutions (15 percent), and bioscience diagnostic products (29 percent). About 49 percent of total sales are derived internationally.

BDX's products are ubiquitous in almost all health care settings. Becton's core business consists of some of the most basic tools used to deliver medical care in the United States (and internationally, to a large extent), so that the company carries a high name recognition in the health care community.

Shortcomings to Bear in Mind

- Nearly half of the company's sales come from abroad. This exposes Becton to the risks associated with foreign currency rates, which could create increased volatility in reported earnings. On the other hand, BDX has done a good job of managing foreign currency exposure, and the impact on earnings has typically been limited to only 1 or 2 percent.

- Recent tensions between India and Pakistan as well as India and China regarding nuclear testing could interfere with the company's aggressive expansion into these densely populated markets. This might come through domestic or U.N. economic sanctions. However, analysts believe that any sanctions would exclude companies providing medical supplies.

Reasons to Buy

- Becton, Dickinson has been growing at a solid pace. In the 1989–1999 period, earnings per share climbed from $.50 to $1.46, a compound annual growth rate of 11.3 percent—nor did earnings dip in any of those years. In the same 10-year span, dividends per share expanded from $.13 to $.34, a growth rate of 10.1 percent.

- The company has been repositioning the newly formed Bioscience/Diagnostics business towards faster-growing markets through new technologies. In the past, BDX has been strong in two markets: clinical microbiology and flow cytometry for clinical and research applications.

  In the microbiology market, the company is trying to leverage its strong market position by introducing new technology platforms. These include a new automated microbiology system as well as the new Probetec DNA analyzer.

  In flow cytometry, Becton Dickinson is trying to compete more broadly (both in research and clinical diagnostics), relying partly on acquisitions. For instance, the acquisition of Biometric Imaging (BMI) broadened the company's technology platform in cellular analysis. In addition, the purchase of Clontech Laboratories, a rapidly growing maker of reagents and tools used in the study of molecular biology (such as genomics), added research products for gene expression analysis.

- Domestic sales of insulin needles and syringes are expected to increase in the high-single digits during the next few years, fueled by the estimated five percent annual growth in the number of Americans suffering from diabetes, plus the trend toward multiple insulin injections. Recent scientific studies have shown that the use of multiple daily injections of insulin reduces the severity of the disease's longer-term deleterious effects. Becton, Dickinson, which accounts for about 90 percent of the domestic insulin syringe market, has entered into an arrangement with Eli Lilly, the largest domestic producer of insulin products, and Boehringer Mannheim, a major manufacturer of glucose monitoring devices, to provide information to diabetics regarding the best manner in which to control their disease. Over time, this program should accelerate the trend toward multiple daily insulin injections. The company is also reviewing a number of noninvasive techniques to monitor glucose levels in diabetics. This device could reach the market before the end of the decade and further enhance the company's overall position in the diabetic sector.

- Becton Dickinson recently was awarded a four-year contract from Novation (the nation's largest Group Purchase Organization, with annual purchases of more than $11 billion) to sole-source supply hypodermic needles and certain safety devices. An analyst with A. G. Edwards estimates that this could add about $20 million per year to sales starting in 2001.

  This further strengthens an already existing relationship, as BDX has been Novation's sole-source provider for I.V. catheters, blood collection, and microbiology products. Furthermore, Becton's foray into the pre-fillable saline-syringe market is a logical move. It should help the company capture additional sole-source-provider contracts in the injectionable product realm. According to A. G. Edwards, "This would add an element of convenience for health-care workers and reduce injectionable contamination concerns among patients."

- With a strong base of proprietary technology, Becton Dickinson holds a leading worldwide market position in peripheral vascular access devices for infusion therapy and is an important supplier of components and procedural kits for regional anesthesia.

- Becton holds a strong market position in hypodermic needles and syringes and pre-fillable systems and offers a wide array of safety products for medication delivery in many areas of the world.

- The company's use of computer-aided design and manufacturing technology enables Becton to bring quality products to market faster and at a lower cost. One such technology is stereo lithography, which uses a laser system to quickly create a three-dimensional physical object from a computer-aided design model. Engineers can use this extremely accurate model as a prototype, improving both the quality of the product design and the speed of the product development process.

- Becton Dickinson is developing several technologies that will reinvent the administration of medication, making it less invasive and enhancing the level of patient safety and compliance. The company's AccuSpray nasal system, a proprietary design based on its Hypak syringe technology, is being developed in conjunction with Aviron's Flu-Mist nasal vaccine for influenza. Currently in clinical trial, this system painlessly administers the annual flu shot and delivers a precise aerosol spray to the nasal mucosal tissue.

To deliver medication through the skin, transdermal patches eliminate the needle altogether and provide a sustained rate of drug delivery, eliminating many of the side effects of pills and tablets. BDX is collaborating with several pharmaceutical companies on promising applications and began Phase III clinical trials in early 2000.

- In the Medical Products and Pre-Analytical businesses, the primary source of acceleration is safety through the development of advanced protection products. The company is attempting to decrease the risk of needle-stick injuries to health care workers by incorporating safety features into needle-oriented products. These products include injection systems, infusion-therapy products, and sample-collection systems. Together, these businesses represent $1.8 billion, or just over half of the company's business. What's more, as the dominant player in each of these markets, Becton Dickinson stands to benefit most from a shift to safety products.

In the past, however, the market for these products has been limited. In the late 1980s, the Center for Disease Control (CDC) estimated that on an annual basis some 800,000 health care workers accidentally stick themselves with needles that had been used in patient treatment. Since that time, the company has developed a number of safety-needle devices that can protect health care workers from this type of injury.

So far, about 20 percent of the domestic market has converted to safety-engineered products. The company says that "within the next few years, we believe the market will be 85 percent converted. The primary impetus to date has been state legislation. This is now expanding to a national level via recent OSHA regulatory action and anticipated federal legislation that will effectively require the use of safety-engineered devices in all U.S. health care facilities. Similar activities, at an earlier stage, are also taking hold in Europe.

"Our first safety-engineered product, the Safety-Lok syringe, reached the market in 1998. We were in the lead at the time, and we have steadily enhanced our position so that we now have the most complete line in the industry: over 220 safety-engineered devices. In fact, BD is by far the leading patent holder and innovator for safety-engineered devices, a result of many years of diligent product development and steady investment."

■ BDX has been active on the acquisition front. In fiscal 1999, for instance, the company acquired 10 businesses for a total of $382 million in cash and 357,522 common shares. Most significant was the August, 1999 purchase of privately held Clontech Laboratories, Inc. for $201 million in cash. Clontech serves the life sciences market, providing reagents in the areas of gene-based drug discovery technology and molecular biology research.

Total assets: $4,437 million
Current ratio: 1.26
Common shares outstanding: 252 million
Return on 1999 shareholders' equity: 16.3%

	1999	1998	1997	1996	1995	1994	1993	1992
Revenues (millions)	3418	3117	2810	2770	2712	2560	2465	2365
Net income (millions)	386	360	315	283	252	227	213	201
Earnings per share	1.46	1.37	1.21	1.06	.90	.75	.68	.64
Dividends per share	.34	.29	.26	.23	.21	.19	.17	.15
Price High	44.2	49.6	27.8	22.8	19.0	12.5	10.2	10.5
Low	22.4	24.4	20.9	17.7	12.0	8.5	8.2	8.0

AGGRESSIVE GROWTH

The Boeing Company

Post Office Box 3707 MC 10-16 ❒ Seattle, Washington 98124-2207 ❒ Investor contact: Barbara Bodker (206) 655-2608 ❒ Dividend reinvestment plan is available: (888) 777-0923 ❒ Web site: www.boeing.com ❒ Listed: NYSE ❒ Ticker symbol: BA ❒ S&P rating: B ❒ Value Line financial strength rating: A

In May of 2000, the company named Michael Sears to the post of chief financial officer. He replaced Deborah Hopkins who left to take a position with Lucent Technologies. Mr. Sears, who was 52 when he became CFO, is seen as a logical choice, partly because his division (he was president of BA's defense unit) had consistently outpaced all other Boeing units in operating profit margins.

Mr. Sears had served most recently over the company's divisions making F/A-18 attack planes, missiles, and C-17 military transports. Before that, he was in charge of the Douglas Aircraft Company's commercial jet unit.

Company Profile
Founded 84 years ago by William E. Boeing, The Boeing Company is the leading aerospace company in the world, as measured by total revenues. The holder of 5,075 patents, Boeing is the world's largest manufacturer of commercial jetliners and military aircraft and provides related services worldwide.

Boeing is also NASA's largest contractor. The company's capabilities and related services include helicopters, electronic and defense systems, missiles, rocket engines, launch systems, and advanced information and communications systems. Boeing has customers in 145 countries.

Boeing's military aircraft include the F/A-18 Hornet strike fighter, the F-15E Eagle fighter-bomber, the C-17 Globemaster III transport, and the AH-64D Apache Longbow helicopter.

Boeing's space operations include communications satellites, Delta rockets, and the Space Shuttle (with Lockheed Martin). Finally, the company is also the prime contractor for the International Space Station.

Boeing's defense and space operations (about one-third of revenues) primarily makes the F-18 fighter jet for the U.S. Navy, the E-3 Airborne Warning and Control System (AWACS), the 767-based AWACS, and CH-47 helicopter. The company also has important development programs: the Joint Strike Fighter, the Airborne Laser, the F-22 fighter, and the expendable launch vehicle. Finally, the unit also makes Delta rockets, which are primarily used to carry commercial and military satellites.

Highlights of 1999

- Achieved total shareholder return of 29 percent, compared with 21 percent for the Standard & Poor's Index.
- Returned commercial airplane production to robust health, delivering a record 620 jetliners, with fewer people, less overtime, and dramatically improved on-time performance.
- Met or exceeded all companywide 1999 Value Scorecard goals, improving its overall performance and freeing up capital for growth.
- Won several strategically important major competitions while successfully expanding its service businesses—for commercial and military customers—with great potential for future growth.

Shortcomings to Bear in Mind

- In the spring of 2000, the company settled a 40-day strike by 13,400 union

engineers. The strike disrupted a financial resurgence that seemed to be progressing more smoothly in the months prior to the work stoppage, and it left bruised feelings among workers who had seemed to favor company goals. One analyst commented that he wondered "what management was thinking when it allowed the strike in the first place, particularly since they met all union demands."

- Boeing's fabled past was founded on the company's ability to produce innovative, state-of-the-art commercial aircraft. In the late 1950s, Boeing produced the 707, the world's first commercial major jetliner. In the late 1960s, the company invested heavily to develop the very successful 747, the world's first jumbo jet. As a result, for many years Boeing was able to post impressive earnings growth.

However, the commercial aircraft business has changed dramatically in recent years. Cost-conscious airlines now demand planes that can materially reduce operating costs, such as fuel, pilot training, and maintenance expenses. Understandably, commercial aircraft have become commodity items, vulnerable to cutthroat competition and deep price discounting. As a consequence, Boeing's commercial aircraft operation has seen its profit margins wither away from 10 percent in 1991 to 1 percent in 1998.

- The company is also feeling the heat from its archrival, Airbus, a four-nation European consortium. Historically, BA controlled 60 percent of the global commercial aircraft market. Unfortunately, its market share has been deteriorating and is now down to 53 percent, while Airbus has edged up to 47 percent.
- Boeing's CEO, Phil Condit, expects that the company will go ahead with development of a bigger 747 jumbo jet, setting the stage for a heated encounter with

rival Airbus Industrie. Mr. Condit also expects that Airbus ultimately will proceed with its own planned giant new airliner, the A-3XX, which is being proposed to major airlines. If built, Boeing's 747-x will have a range of 7,500 or more nautical miles and will seat 500. The Airbus super jumbo will have a range of 7,600 to 8,600 nautical miles and will seat even more, between 555 and 655.

Assuming both plane makers proceed with their projects, the next few years will bring a pitched battle for sales of new super jumbo jets. Without doubt, there will be risks involved for both companies. Airbus could suffer financially if it fails to sell enough of its planes to justify development costs of $10 billion or more. Boeing, meanwhile, risks losing its dominance of a most-profitable market share if the new Airbus craft turns out to be a big success.

Reasons to Buy

- Boeing will launch more than 40 satellites for the European telecommunications system Skybridge LP and has agreed to become a minority shareholder in the project. The launch agreement marks a particular coup for Boeing, which has been eager to place contracts with European-controlled buyers for its advanced Delta rocket line. The satellite launch leader is Arianespace SA of France. Under the launch agreement, Boeing will provide six launches for Skybridge, a planned 80-satellite system costing $4.8 billion. Pascale Sourisse, president and CEO of Skybridge, said the agreement is "certainly good for Boeing" and said that she is pleased to have a new major partner based in the United States. Ms. Sourisse wouldn't detail Boeing's ultimate ownership stake but described it as "very significant."

- As 1999 drew to a close, Boeing announced firm orders for 120 planes valued at about $8.5 billion. The total included a major order from General Electric's aircraft-leasing unit for big 747 and 767 airliners. The order from GE's aviation-services unit included 26 planes valued at about $2.5 billion. It is said to include five 747 jumbo jets and 15 two-engine 767 aircraft, along with at least six future purchase options. The other 100 orders were from more than 15 buyers and included a 50-plane order from International Lease Finance Corporation, a unit of New York insurance giant, American International Group. In 1999, Boeing had orders for a total of 380 aircraft. However, Airbus Industrie did better, with 420.

- Boeing is in the process of reviewing ways to streamline its purchasing processes for supplies, ranging from metal and wire used in airlines to paper clips and fax paper required for internal operations, according to company officials. "Boeing is looking to move into e-business and e-commerce, and we see opportunities in terms of working with our suppliers and our customers," said Scott Griffin, the company's new chief information offer. "We see this as a revenue-making tool."

  When Boeing needs to buy supplies, it releases a request for bids, collects and reviews each bid, and then negotiates final pricing and delivery with individual suppliers. In theory, an electronic marketplace would speed up and reduce the cost of this process.

- In 1996, Boeing paid about $3 billion to buy Rockwell International's space-business assets. Early in 2000, the company bought the satellite-making holdings of Hughes Electronics, a unit of General Motors, for $3.75 billion, a transaction that made Boeing the leading maker of commercial satellites.

Over the past few years, Boeing's space unit has committed to high-risk projects representing more than $20 billion in existing and future contracts. It is in the testing stages of a complex National Missile Defense system for intercepting inbound nuclear warheads, a remnant of the Reagan-era "Star Wars" thinking that could be worth as much as $10 billion to Boeing under existing and future Pentagon contracts.

Under another government contract valued initially at $5 billion, Boeing agreed to build a new constellation of advanced spy satellites. Also in the works are new lines of advanced rockets for military and commercial use, including a separate line launched from an ocean platform, at a time when demand for rockets has fallen. What's more, the company is at work on another Star Wars-style holdover—lasers capable of firing from the nose of 747 jumbo jets for knocking out enemy missiles.

■ Boeing is the nation's largest exporter, with nearly $27 billion in overseas sales in 1999. Since World War II, leaders in Washington and Europe have viewed civil aerospace as a strategic industry that provides thousands of high-paying jobs and helps amortize the high costs of military research.

■ Despite the fatal crash of a Boeing 767 flown by Egyptair, the world's airlines still consider Boeing jets to be safe and reliable.

■ In a ground-braking agreement with DHL Worldwide Express, valued at more than $2 billion, Boeing has been modifying 44 used jetliners; it then delivers and maintains them. The DHL deal reflects a push by Boeing to expand its presence in the financing, service, and leasing businesses, which have profit margins at least twice the slim margins on airliners the company makes. As part of the transaction, the jet maker agreed to buy the first 34 of the Boeing 757s from British Airways. Boeing's newly organized aviation-services unit has been converting the British Airways passenger jets to package-freight aircraft; it then sold them and leased various of the jets back to the air-carrier unit of DHL, a package-delivery provider. For its part, Boeing provides all maintenance services through subcontractors with maintenance shops.

To get into leasing and maintenance, Boeing modeled its strategy on successful initiatives by engine-maker General Electric and others. Boeing has had talks with several other major carriers aimed at similar contracts.

■ In 2000, Boeing and BF Goodrich Aerospace teamed up to exploit the $24-billion world market for airliner maintenance, repair, and overhaul. The move is part of Boeing's strategy to broaden its aircraft-making business into aviation-related services. Boeing decided not to set up its own airframe-maintenance network from scratch. With Goodrich, it can cooperate with firms already performing the work in various parts of the world.

Total assets: $36,147 million
Current ratio: 1.18
Common shares outstanding: 935 million
Return on 1999 shareholders' equity: 20.1%

	1999	1998	1997	1996	1995	1994	1993	1992
Revenues (millions)	57993	56154	45800	22681	19515	21924	25438	30184
Net income (millions)	2309	1120	632	976	393	856	1244	1554
Earnings per share	2.49	1.15	.63	1.42	.58	1.26	1.83	2.29
Dividends per share	.56	.56	.56	.55	.50	.50	.50	.50
Price High	48.5	56.3	60.5	53.8	40.0	25.1	22.4	27.3
Low	31.6	29.0	43.0	37.1	22.2	21.1	16.7	16.6

GROWTH AND INCOME

BP Amoco, p.l.c.

Britannic House, 1 Finsbury Circus ◻ **London EC2M 7BA,** ◻ **United Kingdom** ◻ **Investor contact:**
Ken Kaminski (216) 586-6220 ◻ **Dividend reinvestment program not available** ◻ **Web site: www.bp.com**
◻ **Listed: NYSE** ◻ **Ticker symbol: BPA** ◻ **S&P rating: Not rated** ◻ **Value Line financial strength rating: A++**

Beneath the Gulf of Mexico's surface and far from the shores of Texas—under a 2,000-foot layer of salt in waters 6,000 feet deep—BP has uncovered a vast new source of value. The discovery in 1999 of the Crazy Horse field was a technical triumph, and its estimated resources of one billion barrels of oil equivalent make it the largest deep-water Gulf discovery to date.

The company also announced in 1999 the discovery of three other significant deep-water Gulf fields: Holstein, Atlantis, and Mad Dog. Together, they could boost resources by an estimated one billion barrels of oil equivalent.

Company Profile

Formed from the merger of British Petroleum and Amoco (year-end 1998), BP Amoco p.l.c. is the holding company of the world's third-largest petroleum company. Its main activities are exploration and production of crude oil and natural gas and refining. It also has a stake in petrochemicals, natural gas, and solar power generation.

BP Amoco (name to be changed in April, 2001 to BP p.l.c.) produces oil in 19 countries and has proved reserves of 12.7

billion barrels of oil equivalent, including large reserves in Alaska and the North Sea. BP has well-established operations in Europe, North and South America, Australia, and Africa. The company is the largest U.S. oil and gas producer and one of the two top gas producers in Canada. The company owns more than 28,000 service stations throughout the world.

BP is second only to Royal Dutch in terms of total oil and gas production and reserves. The company is a major producer of petrochemicals, selling products to bulk, wholesale, and retail customers in more than 60 countries. Products include acetic acid, acrylonitrile, and polyethylene.

Shortcomings to Bear in Mind

- In the past 10 years (1989 to 1999), earnings per share were far from impressive, rising from $1.39 to $1.92, a compound annual growth rate of only 3.3 percent. In the same 10-year span, dividends per share edged up from $.98 to $1.31, a modest growth rate of 6.3 percent.
- Over the past few years, BP has plowed most of its Russia investment into a 10 percent stake in Sidanko, a onetime oil conglomerate that formerly owned

some of the most valuable energy assets in Russia, notably the Chernogorneft field in Siberia. More recently, production subsidiaries of Sidanko were pushed into bankruptcy and sold off under controversial circumstances, essentially leaving the parent company as an empty shell. A Russian company, Tyumen, bought Chernogorneft at a fraction of its value. BP and others have accused Tyumen, which is nearly half owned by the Russian government, of tampering with the courts to influence the bankruptcy proceedings and liquidation sales.

Reasons to Buy

- As 2000 got underway, BP Amoco, p.l.c. acquired ExxonMobil's 30 percent stake in their combined European gasoline business for $1.5 billion, ending a three-year venture so the newly created ExxonMobil could meet European regulators' merger conditions. At the same time, the two companies divided up the lubricants assets of the venture, which Mobil and the former British Petroleum formed in 1996 to better compete in Europe's tough refining and marketing environment.

    In dissolving the venture, BP picked up about 8,500 service stations in Europe, two British refineries, as well as refineries in France, the Netherlands, and Spain and stakes in French, Turkish, and German refineries.

- BP Amoco, p.l.c. will make a major investment to develop natural-gas reserves in Algeria, the company said in early 2000. The company said it would develop a $2.5-billion complex of natural gas fields, called In Salah, deep in the Sahara desert, in partnership with Algeria's state-owned energy company, Sonatrach. Gas deliveries to Europe will begin in 2003. The output rate of the In Salah fields is expected to quickly ratchet up to about 9 billion cubic meters a year.

    Richard Olver, BP Amoco, p.l.c.'s exploration chief, said the companies intend to meet the rapidly growing demand for gas in Southern Europe. PB said Italian utility Enel SpA already had contracted to take 4 billion cubic meters a year, and Edison SpA, also of Italy, had signed a letter of intent to take a similar amount. BP has a 65 percent stake in the venture and commensurate investment commitments with Sonatrach holding the remainder. The Algerian gas project fills a hole in BP Amoco's global gas business. The company already has significant natural gas businesses in the United Kingdom and the United States. The presence in Southern Europe will "put BP in a top-tier competitive position in gas with ExxonMobil and the Royal Dutch/Shell Group," said Rodney Schmidt, managing director at Petroleum Finance Company.

- In the spring of 2000, BP invested $4.73 billion to acquire Burmah Castrol p.l.c., a British lubricants company with worldwide operations. BP paid a steep premium of about 60 percent for Burmah. Even so, BP's management was convinced it was a fair price to pay for a company that has a brand as strong as Castrol in the worldwide lubricants market.

    Burmah's main asset is its best-selling Castrol motor oil, which will now become BP Amoco's leading lubricants brand. "Put simply, the combination will add millions of new customers worldwide and give BP access to emerging markets where we currently have a limited presence," said BP CEO Sir John Browne. "It will make Castrol products available to our own massive customer base worldwide, including commercial and industrial users. The result will powerfully strengthen our existing business and give us entry to new markets that offer immense potential for continuing growth."

BP said it expects to shed 1,700 jobs and save $260 million a year by 2003 as a result of the merger, and it planned to take a $390 million charge in 2000 to pay for the combination.

- With increasing quantities of feedstocks available from the North Sea, the company's Grangemouth refining and petrochemicals complex is becoming one of Europe's most integrated, technically advanced, and environmentally responsible sites.

  BP has already invested more than $2 billion in the complex since 1990. Current and planned projects to expand the petrochemical operations accounted for an additional $750 million of investment. The investment program involves improving the productivity of the crude processing plant, expansion of ethylene and ethanol production capacity, and construction of a new polyethylene and polypropylene plant. To support this expansion, a new combined heat and power plant was constructed at Grangemouth; it was commissioned in 2000.

  Designed to be the lowest-cost producer in Europe, the new polypropylene plant came on stream in early 2000, providing customers with the raw materials needed to produce a wide range of everyday goods, such as food packaging and car components.

- BP holds extensive leases in the federal waters of the Gulf of Mexico. It is one of the three largest acreage holders in the Gulf and the leading acreage holder in the Gulf's deep-water portion. Onshore, the company operates some 470 natural gas wells and 330 oil wells.

  The Houston region's offshore production currently totals about 240,000 barrels of oil equivalent a day. Production onshore in the region is more than 365,000 barrels of oil equivalent a day. These figures will rise sharply as offshore projects under development come on stream.

- In the spring of 2000, the federal government and three states suspended their lawsuit, which would have blocked BP's $30 billion acquisition of ARCO. The deal revolved around BP's willingness to sell one of its crown jewels of the deal, ARCO's large oil holdings in Alaska, to Phillips Petroleum for $7 billion. Once that had been agreed to, the Federal Trade Commission voted 5 to 0 to approve the ARCO acquisition.

- The company's solar energy business was transformed into BP Solarex in mid-1999 after BP purchased Enron's holdings in Solarex for $45 million. The new company has a 20 percent share of the global market and is one of the largest manufacturers of photovoltaic modules and systems, with plants in the United States, Spain, Australia, and India. In 1999, BP Solarex revenues totaled $179 million, and solar module production grew 28 percent. Many of the segment's successes in 1999 were based on advanced technology. One major project, Plug in the Sun, involves installing solar modules on 200 new service stations in 11 countries.

Total assets: $84,770 million
Current ratio: 1.01
Common shares outstanding: 19,484 million
Return on 1999 shareholders' equity: 14.4%

	1999	1998	1997	1996	1995	1994	1993	1992
Revenues (millions)	83566	68304	71274	76490	57047	50667	52425	50208
Net income (millions)	6196	4468	4628	4114	2070	2001	1062	947
Earnings per share	1.92	1.39	2.44	2.18	1.13	1.08	.59	.53
Dividends per share	1.31	1.45	1.32	1.08	.83	.52	.48	.63
Price High	62.6	8.7	46.5	35.9	26.0	21.3	16.3	16.6
Low	40.2	36.5	32.4	23.6	18.9	14.6	10.5	10.3

CONSERVATIVE GROWTH

Bristol-Myers Squibb Company

345 Park Avenue ☐ New York, New York 10154-0037 ☐ Listed: NYSE ☐ Investor contact: Tim Cost (212) 546-4103 ☐ Dividend reinvestment plan is available: (800) 356-2026 ☐ Web site: www.bms.com ☐ Ticker symbol: BMY ☐ S&P rating: A ☐ Value Line financial strength rating: A++

Bristol-Myers has an experimental drug that may become an important new weapon in the battle against high blood pressure—one of the major risk factors for heart attacks and strokes. Two studies presented at a special meeting of cardiologists showed that the new drug, called omapatrilat, proved significantly more effective in lowering blood pressure than two of the most widely used and best-selling medicines on the market.

"This is the most powerful oral drug that we've ever had available for high blood pressure," said Michael A. Weber, chairman of medicine at Brookdale University Hospital and Medical Center, Brooklyn, New York.

Company Profile

Bristol-Myers Squibb is a leading diversified health care and personal-care company. Its list of products includes ethical (prescription) drugs, over-the-counter preparations, diagnostics, infant formulas, orthopedic implants, as well as health-and-beauty aids.

Bristol-Myers is a global leader in chemotherapy drugs and ranks near the top in cardiovascular drugs and antibiotics. Heart drugs include Pravachol, a cholesterol-reducing agent, Capoten/Capozide and Monopril, which are antihypertensive preparations. Through a joint venture with Sanofi, SA, BMY produces Plavix, a platelet aggregation inhibitor for the prevention of stroke, heart attack, and vascular diseases; and Avapro, an angiotensin II receptor blocker that treats hypertension. Principal anticancer drugs consist of Taxol, Paraplatin, VePesid, and Platinol.

The company features a wide variety of anti-infective drugs, including Duricef/Ultracef, Cefzil, and Maxipime antibiotics; and Videx and Zerit AIDS therapeutics.

The company's nutritionals encompass infant formulas such as Enfamil and ProSobee, vitamins and nutritional supplements.

Beauty care items include Clairol, Ultress, Matrix Essentials, and Herbal Essence lines of hair care products, Nice 'n Easy and Clairesse hair colorings, Final Net hair spray, Vitalis hair preparation, and other products.

Shortcomings to Bear in Mind

■ Bristol-Myers Squibb withdrew its application for government approval of a promising blood pressure medication in April of 2000 after regulators asked for more information on the severe swelling the drug caused in some patients. The drug, Vanlev, had been expected to quickly become a blockbuster, with projected annual sales of $1 billion. Studies have shown the drug could be one of the most potent heart medications on the market. The problem is a condition called angioedema, which is swelling in the face, throat, lips, and tongue. The side effect occurred in 44 of the 7,000 patients who took Vanlev in clinical trials. The company said that it planned to continue clinical trials with the drug and expected to resubmit its application for approval early in 2001. However, initial sales of the drug will be delayed at least a year.

- In 1999, the company's biggest selling drug, the cholesterol-reducer, Pravachol, lost market share to Lipitor, a drug produced by Warner-Lambert. Even though the market for these drugs is growing briskly, Pravachol's sales grew only 1 percent in the fourth quarter of 1999.

- Taxol, BMY's important cancer drug, is obtained from the bark of yew trees found mainly in old-growth forests. It derives its ability—unique among cancer drugs—to block a cancer cell from dividing and growing. It does so by way of a clever defense mechanism that fir-like yew trees use to fend off fungal infections and other disease-causing germs.

  Like everything else, Taxol does not always act like a wonder drug. Some fast-dividing cancer cells can mutate into forms resistant to the drug. In some instances, patients with advanced cancer who initially benefit from Taxol cease to respond after several cycles of treatment because their cells become resistant, too. Despite conducting dozens of trials over the years, Bristol-Myers has been frustrated in its efforts to expand Taxol's effectiveness beyond certain breast, ovarian, and lung cancers.

- In the spring of 2000, a federal judge issued a ruling against Bristol-Myers Squibb that could clear the way for more generic competition in the market for the Taxol. In 1999, Taxol had worldwide sales of $1.5 billion. Taxol's growth potential attracted generic-drug companies, which are seeking regulatory approval to market Taxol in the generic form, paclitaxel. But BMY fought back, filing a patent-infringement suit against would-be generic contenders for Taxol.

- Analysts were pleased with BMY's pharmaceutical sales in 1999. In the final quarter of that year, for instance, ethical drug sales expanded by an impressive 23 percent. On the international front, however, the news was not as rosy. In the same period, sales overseas advanced by a modest 2 percent, hurt by the strong dollar and because some of the company's fastest-growing products are licensed from foreign companies and thus are only sold by Bristol-Myers in the United States.

- Bristol-Myers is well-known for aggressively developing and marketing drugs that it licenses from other companies or academic institutions, but its internal research efforts have lagged other top drug companies. Its two biggest products, Pravachol for lowering cholesterol and Taxol for cancer, are drugs that it licensed.

  Under new research chief Peter Ringrose, a former star research manager at Pfizer, the company plans to increase its scientific staff 50 percent to 6,000 workers by 2002. With this greater emphasis on research, BMY is hoping to reach its goal of tripling the number of new drugs approved to three a year by 2003, compared with the current rate of about one a year.

Reasons to Buy

■ Bristol-Myers Squibb has leading positions in many markets:

Pharmaceuticals

● Number one in chemotherapeutic cancer drugs, such as Taxol, in the world.

● Number one in AIDS Reverse Transcriptase Inhibitors (RTI) drugs in the world, led by Zerit.

● Number one drug for Type 2 diabetes in the United States: Glucophage.

Beauty Care

● Number one in total hair products in the United States and number two in the world, led by Clairol.

Consumer Medicines

● First and only approved nonprescription migraine treatment: Excedrin Migraine.

Nutritionals

● Number one in infant formula in the world: Enfamil.

Medical Devices

● Number one ostomy and advanced wound care products in the world: ConvaTec.

● The company has four strong businesses—pharmaceutical, nutritionals, consumer products, and medical devices—each of which fields a broad line of high-quality products. These products are first or second in sales in 10 of its 15 largest product lines.

● During the past two decades, the business environment in which Bristol-Myers Squibb operates has become increasingly complex. The company has responded in a number of ways. It has entered new therapeutic areas, made major commitments to R&D, expanded marketing, and added or divested businesses as needed, culminating in one of the largest events in the history of corporate America, the merger of Bristol-Myers and Squibb in 1989.

■ Bristol's nonpharmaceutical businesses, which include medical devices, nonprescription health and consumer products, should outpace the substantially larger pharmaceutical business in terms of sales and earnings growth over the next few years.

■ Bristol-Myers Squibb has paid a dividend to its shareholders for an unbroken 67 years—since becoming a public company in 1933. What's more, the company has increased the dividend each year since 1972.

■ Glucophage is a novel antidiabetic agent indicated for first-line or combination treatment of Type II diabetes. Type II diabetes is the most prevalent form. It affects over 13 million of the 14 million who suffer from diabetes. Glucophage is believed to work by increasing peripheral utilization of glucose (sugar), increasing the production of insulin, decreasing hepatic glucose production, and altering intestinal absorption of glucose. The advantage of Glucophage over standard diabetic therapy is its action outside the liver. Conventional antidiabetic agents work solely by increasing insulin production. They sometimes lead to excessive insulin levels and associated low blood glucose levels (hypoglycemia), a complication that Glucophage avoids.

■ Sustagen, a nutritious flavored milk-substitute for pre-school and school-age children and pregnant or lactating mothers, is particularly popular in Latin America and Asia. As Mead Johnson seeks to standardize the product's formulation, Sustagen has become a cornerstone of the division's efforts to globalize its business.

■ In 1998, the Food and Drug Administration (FDA) approved extra-strength Excedrin as the first over-the-counter medicine for migraines. The extra-strength version of the 20-year-old painkiller is potent enough to treat mild to moderate migraines, FDA officials said. The approval gives Bristol-Myers a competitive advantage in the nation's $4-billion pain-reliever market, analysts said. As many as 18 million suffer from migraine headaches that can last for 24 hours or more. Many of these people cannot afford prescription drugs or a visit to the doctor to obtain a prescription.

- In a new strategy designed to exploit the fast-moving advances in human gene science, Bristol-Myers, the world's number one maker of cancer drugs, is gearing up a major research initiative to usher in a new era of cancer care. The company's goal is to enhance the effectiveness of its existing drugs as well as those under development. This would be accomplished by tailoring all future treatment to an individual's unique genetic personality.

  To accomplish this, BMY has a major agreement with one of the premier gene-hunting companies, Millennium Pharmaceuticals, Inc. of Cambridge, Massachusetts, to determine the unique genetic makeup of tumors. Bristol-Myers plans to use Millennium's "molecular fingerprinting" to help identify which patients will respond best to which drugs. The new gene-based approach is being aggressively promoted by the National Cancer Institute and embraced by major cancer treatment centers and other drug makers.

- In the cancer research sector, Bristol-Myers said it is in the late-stage tests of a new colon and rectal cancer drug that is likely to have comparatively few side effects and could become the drug of choice for these diseases. In the longer term, the company is testing several ambitious new approaches, including what could be one of the first vaccines to prevent the reoccurrence of severe skin cancer. It also is nearing clinical testing of new genetic approaches to attacking cancer that would turn off signals from mutant genes that tell cancer cells to divide.

- Avapro and Plavix are both important additions to BMY's strong cardiovascular franchise that the company plans to develop aggressively. Resulting from the research staff of Sanofi, a leading French pharmaceutical company, these important drugs are being codeveloped and comarketed by Sanofi and Bristol-Myers. Avapro, the company's advanced antihypertensive medication, received initial approvals in the fall of 1997. But Bristol-Myers has already seen strong interest in this compound, which it believes is the best in its class. The reason is simple: With Avapro, physicians need not compromise efficacy by reducing dosage levels in an effort to reduce side effects in the treatment of hypertension. Avapro has tolerability similar to a placebo at all doses. Plavix, an antiplatelet agent, received approval from the U.S. Food and Drug Administration in November of 1997. It is used for the reduction of atherosclerotic events (myocardial infarction, stroke, and vascular deaths).

- In early 2000, Bristol-Myers announced that it was selling its Matrix Essentials hair care unit—a move that analysts said could signal the eventual divestiture of more operations as the company focuses on its core pharmaceutical business where profit margins are far more attractive. Matrix makes professional hair-care products sold exclusively through salons. In this realm, the company wants to put more emphasis on its Clairol hair care line.

Total assets: $17,114 million
Current ratio: 1.66
Common shares outstanding: 1,984 million
Return on 1999 equity: 48.2%

	1999	1998	1997	1996	1995	1994	1993	1992
Revenues (millions)	20222	18284	16701	15065	13767	11984	11413	11156
Net income (millions)	4167	3630	3205	2850	2600	2331	2269	2108
Earnings per share	2.06	1.80	1.61	1.42	1.28	1.15	1.10	1.02
Dividends per share	.86	.78	.76	.75	.74	.73	.72	.69
Price High	79.3	67.6	49.1	29.1	21.8	15.3	16.8	22.5
Low	57.3	44.2	26.6	19.5	14.4	12.5	12.7	15.0

GROWTH AND INCOME

Caterpillar Incorporated

100 N. E. Adams Street ◻ Peoria, Illinois 61629-7310 ◻ Investor contact: Laurie J. Huxtable (309) 675-4619 ◻ Direct dividend reinvestment plan is available: (800) 955-4749 ◻ Web site: www.CAT.com/investor ◻ Listed: NYSE ◻ Ticker symbol: CAT ◻ S&P rating: B ◻ Value Line financial strength rating: B++

Recently, Solar Turbines—a Caterpillar company—won the prestigious Malcolm Baldrige National Quality Award in the manufacturing category. Solar gas turbine engines and turbo-machinery systems are used on land and offshore in 85 nations for the production and pipelining of crude oil, petroleum products, and natural gas; for generating electricity and thermal energy used in a wide variety of industrial applications; and for a growing marine propulsion market.

Company Profile
Headquartered in Peoria, Illinois, Caterpillar is the world's largest manufacturer of construction and mining equipment, diesel and natural gas engines, and industrial gas turbines. It is a Fortune 50 industrial company with more than $26 billion in assets.

Caterpillar's broad product line ranges from the company's new line of compact construction equipment to hydraulic excavators, backhoe loaders, track-type tractors, forest products, off-highway trucks, agricultural tractors, diesel and natural gas engines, and industrial gas turbines. Cat products are used in the construction,

road-building, mining, forestry, energy, transportation, and material-handling industries.

Over the years, Caterpillar has earned a reputation for rugged machines that typically set industry standards for performance, durability, quality, and value. The company's goal is to remain the technological leader in its product lines. Today, thanks to accelerated design and testing, computer-based diagnostics and operations, and greatly improved materials, the company can deliver to customers new and better products sooner.

Caterpillar products are sold in nearly 200 countries. The company delivers superior service through it extensive worldwide network of 195 dealers, composed of 64 dealers in the United States and 131 abroad. Many of these dealers have relationships with their customers that have spanned at least two generations. More than 80 percent of Cat's sales are to repeat customers.

Caterpillar products and components are manufactured in 41 plants in the United States and 43 plants in Australia, Brazil, Canada, England, France, Germany, Hungary, India, Indonesia,

Italy, Japan, Mexico, The Netherlands, Northern Ireland, China, Poland, Russia, South Africa, and Sweden.

Caterpillar's commitment to customer service is demonstrated by the fastest parts delivery system in its industry. Caterpillar's customers can obtain replacement parts from their dealers usually upon request. If not, Caterpillar ships them anywhere in the world within 12 hours, often much sooner.

Caterpillar offers its customers an easy means of buying Cat equipment through its financial products subsidiary, Caterpillar Financial Services Corporation, a global enterprise with an $11.6 billion managed portfolio.

History

1925—Daniel Best and Benjamin Holt formed Caterpillar.

1950—The company began international expansion with the establishment of Caterpillar Tractor Co. Ltd. in Great Britain.

1953—The company solidified its commitment to engine market with the creation of separate division for engine customers.

1970s—The company introduced a broad range of new products that would become the forerunner of today's best-selling lines.

1987—$1.8 billion plant modernization program launched.

1990s—The company organized into closer-to-the-customer business units with greater financial accountability; profits to $1 billion for the first time in company history (1995); growth initiatives launched in electric power generation, compact construction equipment, agriculture; company sales double over six-year period (1993–1998) during which the company achieved six consecutive years of record sales and revenues; profit hit consecutive record highs for five years (1993–1997).

Shortcomings to Bear in Mind

- In 1999, the company experienced weak demand for its larger machines and large engines in key industry segments of mining and oil and gas. In addition, demand was weak in several key geographic regions. However, according to Glen A. Barton, Cat's Chairman and CEO, "we continue to benefit from our growing product, services and geographic diversity. Truck engine sales are a bright spot—both sales and our share of the industry hit all-time highs—and revenues from Financial Products are up significantly."

  The year was also affected by sales volume that was hurt by a reduction in dealer inventories and lower commodity prices. In addition, foreign profits suffered from the impact of a stronger U.S. dollar.

  Finally, rising interest expenses more than offset the company's share-repurchase program.

- Sales of Caterpillar diesel engines rose 5 percent in 1999 to $6.85 billion, up from $6.5 billion the year before. That was a welcome bright spot in a year when overall sales fell 6.2 percent to $19.7 billion.

  However, one of the largest markets for Cat diesel engines is in over-the-road trucks. In 2000, makers of those behemoths have been putting on the brakes. Of the 335,600 heavy-duty trucks made in the United States in 1999, a large number didn't sell. Consequently, inventories are high. In 2000, moreover, heavy-duty truck sales may fall 15 or 20 percent, which means Caterpillar could be selling far fewer diesel engines.

Reasons to Buy

- Growth. That single word better than any other explains Caterpillar. In recent years, Caterpillar has dramatically increased its global presence through expanded facility locations. According to Mr. Barton, "We have furthered our industry leadership through major growth initiatives, including joint ventures, acquisitions, new and improved products, and the addition of innumerable services."

- A growing family of diverse service organizations complements the company's global leadership in machines and engines and will help fuel growth.
- Caterpillar Financial Services has 20 offices in 14 countries to support the sale of Cat equipment around the world. Plans are to expand into Asia-Pacific, Brazil, Poland, and the Czech Republic.
- A new subsidiary, Caterpillar Redistribution Services, helps Cat dealers sell used Cat equipment while providing customers with Caterpillar's unmatched product support.
- Caterpillar Logistics Services provides logistics services, including managing inventories and distribution for other companies' products. Sales have grown 70 percent since 1994, with promising growth still ahead.
- As opportunities abound, the company anticipates that sales will exceed $30 billion before the end of the new decade. The growth will come in two primary areas: new products and expansion into new markets. Increasingly, the company uses acquisitions and joint ventures as a means to grow in both areas. Since 1991, Caterpillar has entered into 38 acquisitions or joint ventures that range from partial to 100 percent ownership.
- In the realm of new products, here is a summary of its progress:
- Engines: To meet the world's growing demand for new ways to provide power, Caterpillar's engine business is expanding its capabilities in electric power generation, fuel systems, and distributed power. New initiatives include acquisition of German engine manufacturer MaK and formation of a joint venture with the United Kingdom's F. G. Wilson, a world leader in generator set packaging. Sales of electric power generation products and systems could triple in the next few years, the company believes.
- Agriculture: As farms grow larger and the agriculture industry becomes more high tech, Caterpillar strengthened its commitment to farmers. As a result of the company's more aggressive agriculture strategy, Caterpillar formed a joint venture with Claas, a German combine/harvester manufacturer, and is broadening its ag tractor product line.
- Forestry: The growing forestry industry is looking for more productive machines that respect the environment. Caterpillar's renewed commitment to the forestry industry has seen the acquisition of a Swedish forest products group along with investment in the first Caterpillar facility dedicated solely to the manufacture of forest products.
- Compact machines: The $3.6-billion compact machines industry is growing at an 11 percent clip and represents a significant opportunity for Caterpillar to expand its customer base. In this realm, a number of new product families show promise: mini hydraulic excavators, compact wheel loaders, skid steer loaders, and a comprehensive range of nearly 60 work tools designed to enhance versatility.
- According the company, more than 80 percent of the people in the world live in developing countries. In these regions, there is limited access to water, electricity, and transportation. Currently, sales of Caterpillar products into these regions account for only about 23 percent of total company sales. That percent will grow as Asia, Central Europe, and the Commonwealth of Independent States, in particular, continue to invest

in developing highways, bridges, and waterways necessary to sustain economic growth.

- Over the last five years, Caterpillar grew by 88 facilities, acquired 20 companies, and formed 17 joint ventures. The company introduced 244 new or improved products.
- In 1998, the company acquired the assets of Perkins Engines, extending Cat's global position as a full-line producer of diesel and gas reciprocating engines. It also acquired Veratech Holdings B.V., owner of a leading bucket and work tool specialist in The Netherlands.

- In the company's 1999 annual report, Mr. Barton said, "We are moving aggressively to become a 'high velocity' company—significantly shortening the time between a customer's order and the delivery of a machine or engine, improving processes throughout the value chain. We'll use the Internet to help Caterpillar and our dealers become even more responsive to customer needs. A corporate Web site with virtual dealer storefronts is in place. All this helps customers and dealers and will increase our asset turnover, freeing up capital we can use to invest or reward shareholders."

Total assets: $26,635 million
Current ratio: 1.43
Common shares outstanding: 354 million
Return on 1999 shareholders' equity: 17.9%

		1999	1998	1997	1996	1995	1994	1993	1992
Revenues (millions)		19702	20977	18925	16522	16072	14328	11615	10194
Net income (millions)		946	1513	1665	1361	1136	955	681	def.
Earnings per share		2.63	4.11	4.37	3.54	2.86	2.35	1.68	def.
Dividends per share		1.25	1.15	.95	.78	.60	.32	.15	.15
Price	High	66.4	60.8	61.6	40.5	37.6	30.3	23.3	15.5
	Low	42.0	39.1	36.3	27.0	24.1	22.2	13.5	10.3

INCOME

Cedar Fair, L. P.

One Cedar Point Drive ◻ Sandusky, Ohio 44871-5006 ◻ Investor contact: Brain C. Witherow (419) 627-2173 ◻ Dividend reinvestment plan is available: (800) 278-4352 ◻ Web site: www.cedarfair.com ◻ Listed: NYSE ◻ Ticker symbol: FUN ◻ S&P rating: Not rated ◻ Value Line financial strength rating: B+

In 2000, Cedar Point unveiled yet another roller coaster, the Millennium Force, which is higher than a football field is long—310 feet. If you care to ride this monster, you will drop at an 80-degree angle and careen down the tracks at 92 miles per hour. The Millennium Force has generated tremendous interest among parkgoers, the news media, and within the amusement park industry.

A million rides are likely in 2000, according to Richard L. Kinzel, Cedar

Fair's CEO—and he was one of the first to ride the $25-million Millennium Force.

Company Profile

Cedar Fair, L. P. owns and operates five amusement parks, two major water parks, three resort hotels, several year-round restaurants, a marina, and an RV campground. The company's parks attract more than 10 million visitors a year.

Cedar Fair prides itself on the growth of its roller coasters. Cedar Point alone boasts 14—more than any other park in the world. All told, Cedar Fair parks have 38 roller coasters, including some of the tallest, steepest, and highest-rated coasters ever built.

Cedar Fair's Five Parks

Cedar Point, which is located on Lake Erie between Cleveland and Toledo, is one of the largest amusement parks in the United States; it serves a total market area of 22 million people.

Valleyfair, located near Minneapolis/ St. Paul, draws from a total population of 8 million people in a multistate market area.

Dorney Park & Wildwater Kingdom is located near Allentown, Pennsylvania; it serves a total market area of 35 million people in the Northeast.

Worlds of Fun/Oceans of Fun, in Kansas City, Missouri draws from a total market area of 7 million people.

Knott's Berry Farm, near Los Angeles, is one of several major year-round theme parks in southern California. It serves a total market area of 20 million people and a large national and international tourist population.

How They Operate

The parks are family-oriented, providing clean and attractive environments with exciting rides and entertainment. Except for Knott's Berry Farm (which is open all year), the operating season is generally from May through September.

The parks charge a basic daily admission price that provides unlimited use of virtually all rides and attractions. Admissions accounted for about 50 percent of revenues in 1999, with food, merchandise, and games contributing 42 percent and accommodations the other 8 percent. Combined in-park guest per capita spending in 1999 continued to rise faster than inflation, increasing 4 percent to a record $34.58, from $33.20 in 1998.

However, combined attendance at Cedar Fair parks was down slightly in 1999, from 10.8 million to 10.6 million guests, reflecting less-than-ideal weather and no new thrill rides at several of the company's parks.

Tax Considerations

Cedar Fair is a publicly traded master limited partnership (MLP). The MLP structure is an attractive business form because it allows the partnership to pay out the majority of its earnings to its owners without first paying significant federal and state income taxes at the entity level, avoiding what is known as the corporate form as double taxation of earnings.

Ownership of Cedar Fair, L. P. units is different from an investment in corporate stock. Cash distributions made by the Partnership are treated as a reduction of basis and are generally not taxable. Instead, unitholders must pay tax only on their pro rata share of the Partnership's taxable income, which is generally lower. The Partnership provides the tax information necessary for filing each unitholder's federal, state, and local tax returns on IRS Schedule K-1 in mid-March each year.

The tax consequences to a particular unitholder will depend on the circumstances of that unitholder; however, income from the Partnership may not be offset by passive tax losses from other investments. Prospective unitholders should consult their tax or financial advisors to determine the federal, state, and local tax consequences of ownership of these limited partnership units.

Ownership of limited partnership units may not be advisable for IRAs, pension and profit-sharing plans and other tax-exempt organizations, nonresident aliens, foreign corporations, and other foreign persons, and regulated investment companies.

Shortcomings to Bear in Mind

- About two-thirds of the company's revenue is derived from the Midwest and Mid-Atlantic regions. Adverse economic conditions in these regions could hurt attendance at Cedar Fair parks. On the other hand, the acquisition of Knott's Berry Farm lessens this risk somewhat.

- When you file your income tax, you may find that Cedar Fair has failed to send you the usual paperwork. In 2000, I didn't get mine till March 20. I had already given my CPA the rest, and he had completed my return before I realized my blunder. Unfortunately, it was back to square one—at my expense. One other thing, since Cedar Fair operates in several states, you may find you have to pay a few of them some tax money. Otherwise, it is a great stock.

- Each of the company's parks faces some direct competition from other parks. For instance, Dorney Park competes with Hershey Park in central Pennsylvania and Six Flags Great Adventure in the New York and New Jersey metropolitan area. Out West, the newly acquired Knott's Berry Farm has to tussle with six parks, all within 50 miles. They include Adventure City, Castle Amusement Park, Disneyland, Six Flags Magic Mountain, Scandia Family Fun Center, and Pacific Park. Cedar Point, the company's biggest park, competes with three nearby parks: Paramount Kings Island in southern Ohio and Sea World and Geauga Lake, both near Cleveland. Valleyfair faces the least competition: Adventureland, 250 miles away in Des Moines, and Camp Snoopy, an indoor park at the Mall of America 15 miles away, now owned by Cedar Fair. Worlds of Fun's competition consists of Silver Dollar City in Branson, Missouri and Six Flags Over Mid America outside St. Louis.

Reasons to Buy

- The company's status as a limited partnership was in doubt until recently, since it was feared Congress would end this favorable business form. To remain a limited partnership, Cedar Fair began paying a tax on its gross profits in 1998. Publicly traded limited partnerships were scheduled to expire at the end of 1997 but were indefinitely extended if the company agreed to a 3.5 percent tax on gross profits.

- Although the Cedar Fair Partnership is relatively young (it was created in April of 1987), it owns four amusement parks with considerable longevity. In 1999, Cedar Point, the flagship park, celebrated it 130th anniversary. That same year, Valleyfair celebrated its 25th season. Dorney Park opened its 117th season in 1999. Finally, Worlds of Fun first opened in 1973 and celebrated its 27th summer in 1999.

- According to one analyst, Cedar Fair's management team "exhibits both strength and depth." The general managers at the five parks have an average tenure of nearly 24 years with the company.

- Cedar Fair operates in an industry with high barriers to entry, with scant likelihood of new competition. The absence of direct competition gives the parks pricing power in their regions, bolstering profit margins.

- The acquisition of Knott's Berry Farm gives Cedar Fair exposure to the faster growing western states. In 1999, the company purchased the Buena Park Hotel, located adjacent to this theme park. The addition of this 320-room hotel should further reduce the cyclical nature of the company's business. Management hopes to duplicate the success it has enjoyed at its Cedar Point resort, which offers numerous amenities typical of a full vacation destination.

- One way of promoting success in the amusement park business is to offer the public new and exciting attractions. Toward this end, Cedar Fair has upgraded its capital expansion program as $110 million worth of improvements are on tap for 2000. In the five years prior to 2000, the company had invested more than $315 million in park improvements.
- The Magnum roller coaster propelled Cedar Point to a record attendance year in 1989. When it was opened in May of that year, Magnum was the tallest, steepest, and fastest roller coaster on earth. A decade later, Magnum is still a major draw to the park and remains the park's most popular roller coaster. In a recent *Amusement Today* poll, it was named the best steel roller coaster on the planet. The same poll ranked Cedar Point as the nation's best amusement park by a wide margin.

- In June of 2000, Knott's Berry Farm opened Soak City U.S.A., a 13-acre water park located adjacent to Knott's Berry Farm's brick-by-brick replica of Independence Hall. Themed around 1950s California beach towns, Soak City U.S.A. features 21 separate water rides and attractions, including 16 high-speed water slides, a wave pool, a lazy river, and a children's activity area, as well as additional food and merchandise shops and a second-story sundeck for public dining and catered events. A separate charge is required for admission to the water park, which is operated seasonally, May through September.

Total assets: $709 million
Current ratio: 0.40
Common shares outstanding: 52 million
Return on 1999 partners' capital: 24.5%

	1999	1998	1997	1996	1995	1994	1993	1992
Revenues (millions)	438	420	264	250	218	198	179	153
Net income (millions)	86	84	68	74	66	61	50	43
Earnings per share	1.63	1.58	1.47	1.59	1.45	1.37	1.13	.98
Dividends per share	1.40	1.29	1.26	1.20	1.14	1.06	.95	.87
Price High	26.1	30.1	28.3	19.5	18.6	18.3	18.3	14.9
Low	18.4	21.8	17.7	16.1	14.1	13.4	13.5	8.9

GROWTH AND INCOME

Chevron Corporation

575 Market Street, Room 3444 ▭ San Francisco, California 94105-2856 ▭ Investor contact: Peter M. Trueblood (415) 894-5690 ▭ Direct dividend reinvestment plan is available: (800) 368-8357 ▭ Web site: www.chevron.com ▭ Listed: NYSE ▭ Ticker symbol: CHV ▭ S&P rating: B+ ▭ Value Line financial strength rating: A++

In 1999, Chevron formed a joint venture with Sasol Ltd. of South Africa to take a technology for converting natural gas to liquids worldwide, a move that could make Chevron one of the oil industry's most aggressive players in this emerging business. Sasol is the world's largest synthetic fuel producer.

Several companies, including Royal Dutch, Exxon, and BP Amoco, are scrambling to develop natural-gas-to-liquid technology, which could make the world's vast, but isolated, natural gas reserves profitable to produce. When natural gas is turned into a form of petroleum, it can be more easily and less expensively transported and sold in world markets. A Chevron spokesman said the two companies anticipate spending billions of dollars on the technology over the next five to 10 years.

Company Profile

Chevron is a worldwide petroleum company with important interests in chemicals and minerals. It is a leading domestic producer of crude oil and natural gas, a marketer of refined products, and is active in foreign exploration and production and overseas refining and marketing.

Supply and Demand

The prices of oil stocks tend to be a reflection of crude oil prices, which are a function of worldwide supply and demand. Demand is determined primarily by weather and economic conditions. Supply, on the other hand, is influenced by inventories and production levels.

In recent years, OPEC (the Organization of Petroleum Exporting Countries) has been able to control—at least to some extent—production by setting quotas that keep crude prices high enough to benefit them but low enough to keep non-OPEC producers from getting too competitive with their exploration and drilling or consumers from finding something else to burn.

A Breakdown of Chevron's Operations

Exploration and Production

Chevron explores for and produces crude oil and natural gas in the United States and 25 other countries. The company is the third-largest domestic natural gas producer.

Major producing regions include the Gulf of Mexico, California, the Rocky Mountains, Texas, China, Canada, the North Sea, Australia, Indonesia, Angola, Nigeria, Kazakhstan, Alaska, Republic of Congo, Papua New Guinea, Colombia, Peru, and Ireland. Exploration areas include the above, as well as Alaska, Azerbaijan, Bahrain, and Qatar.

Refining

CHV converts crude oil into a variety of refined products, including motor gasoline, diesel and aviation fuels, lubricants, asphalt, chemicals, and other products. Chevron is one of the largest refiners in the United States.

The company's principal U.S. locations are El Segundo and Richmond, California, Pascagoula, Mississippi, Salt Lake City, Utah, El Paso, Texas, and Honolulu, Hawaii. The company also refines in Canada (through its Caltex affiliate), Asia, Africa, Australia, and New Zealand.

Marketing

Chevron is one of the leading domestic marketers of refined products, including motor gasoline, diesel and aviation fuels, lubricants, and other products. Retail outlets number 7,900 in the United States, 200 in Canada; Caltex supplies about 9,000 retail outlets worldwide.

Supply and Distribution

The company purchases, sells, trades, and transports—by pipeline, tanker, and barge—crude oil, liquefied natural gas liquids (such as propane and butane), chemicals, and refined products.

Chevron has trading offices in Houston, Walnut Creek, California, London, Singapore, Mexico City, and Moscow. What's more, the company has interests in pipelines throughout the United States and in Africa, Australia, Indonesia, Papua New Guinea, Europe, and the Middle East. Chevron has tanker operations worldwide.

Chemicals

The company's main products are benzene, styrene, polystyrene, paraxylene, ethylene, polyethylene, and normal alpha olefins. Chevron also produces a variety of additives used for fuels and lubricants.

Chevron operates plants in nine states and in France, Brazil, Mexico, Singapore, and Japan. Through affiliates and subsidiaries, the company operates or markets in more than 80 countries.

Shortcomings to Bear in Mind

- The company's operations on the Caspian Sea are speculative. The crux of the problem lies in simple geography—they don't call Kazakhstan Central Asia for nothing. The vast, mostly empty country—one-third the size of the continental United States, with only 16 million people—is equally remote from the world's two main oil importing regions: Western Europe and East Asia. Such distance is not a serious problem in the oil business if it can be covered by ship—an easy enough proposition for producers in West Africa, East Asia, or the Persian Gulf. But the Caspian, though called a sea, is surrounded by land—five different lands, in fact, and none of them easy places to do business. The northern shore is dominated by Russia; the southern edge, by Iran. Azerbaijan is on the west side of the Caspian, Kazakhstan and tiny Turkmenistan on the east side. All of them present tricky problems, not easily solved.

- As a growth stock, Chevron leaves something to be desired. In the 1989–1999 period, earnings per share made modest progress, rising from $2.08 to $3.14, a compound annual growth rate of only 4.2 percent. In the same 10-year period, dividends per share didn't perform much better, advancing from $1.40 to $2.48, a growth rate of 5.9

percent. Meanwhile, the payout ratio is much too high at 79 percent, based on 1999's dividends and earnings per share.

Reasons to Buy

- Tengizchevroil (TCO), a joint venture with Kazakhstan, represents one of Chevron's most promising growth prospects. Production from Kazakhstan's Tengiz Field was up 14 percent in 1999, to 214,000 barrels of oil a day. It is expected to top 700,000 in 2010. Chevron holds a 45-percent interest in TCO.

  The key to unlocking the potential of Tengiz is an export pipeline. In 1999, after years of negotiations, construction began on the Caspian Pipeline Consortium's (CPC) 900-mile pipeline. It's expected to begin transporting oil from the Tengiz Field to the Black Sea port of Novorossiysk in 2001. Chevron is the largest oil company shareholder of CPC, with a 15 percent interest.

- The Kuito Field, Chevron's first deep-water project in Angola, started operations in December of 1999 and is expected to produce 100,000 barrels a day when fully operational. Development studies are underway for the nearby Benguela and Belize fields, both discovered in 1998. Chevron has a 31 percent interest in each. In Angola, one of the company's strongest growth areas, Chevron plans to increase production to 600,000 barrels a day by 2002, up from 460,000 in 1999.

- In Nigeria, another key growth area, Chevron plans to increase production from 1999 levels of 420,000 barrels a day to 600,000 oil-equivalent barrels by 2003. Chevron has a 40 percent interest in the Nigerian fields it operates. Nigeria's oil fields contain large amounts of natural gas, which typically has been flared during oil production. Chevron's long-term gas strategy aims to eliminate flaring and to market clean-burning natural gas, thereby reducing greenhouse gas emissions.

- In 1950, world crude oil reserves were estimated at 76 billion barrels, which was about a 20-year supply at the rate of consumption at that time. In the 45 years since, the world has used 600 billion barrels, and there's an estimated 1 trillion barrels in proved reserves. The world's oil supply now is greater than it has ever been, if we didn't find another drop of oil, we would still have a 50-year supply left.

- In 1999, Chevron and a unit of Atlantic Richfield, ARCO Permian, announced an agreement to exclusively pursue a combination of their oil and gas producing assets in the Permian Basin of West Texas and southeast New Mexico. ARCO and Chevron each own 50 percent of the new company. The new entity develops and produces oil, natural gas, market crude oil, natural gas liquids, and related products in the Permian Basin. Operations consist of more than 7,000 wells and 150 fields, representing 600 million barrels of proved reserves and producing over 170,000 barrels per day of oil equivalents.

- Chevron, making its first foray into Argentina's oil sector, purchased Petrolera Argentina San Jorge SA in late 1999. San Jorge, a closely held exploration and production company, is Argentina's third-largest oil company. It has 180 million barrels of proven oil reserves and more than 400 million barrels of potential reserves of oil equivalent. In addition to its Argentine property, San Jorge has 5 million acres of exploration property in oil basins in Colombia, Ecuador, Peru, Bolivia, and Chile. Chevron, like other integrated oil companies, has said that it is shifting its oil exploration and production efforts to international prospects from more mature North American properties.

- In 2000, Chevron and Phillips Petroleum agreed to combine their chemical operations into one of the world's largest petrochemical companies. The combined business will have revenues of about $5 billion and will generate $150 million in annual cost savings by the end of 2001.

The venture's ethylene annual capacity will climb to 8.2 billion pounds; polyethylene capacity to 5.5 billion pounds; aromatics to 7.4 billion pounds; alpha olefins to 1.6 billion pounds; styrene monomer to 1.7 billion pounds; styrenic polymers to 1.2 billion pounds; and specialty chemicals to over 400 million pounds.

Total assets: 40,668 million
Current ratio: 0.75
Common shares outstanding: 656 million
Return on 1999 shareholders' equity: 11.9%

	1999	1998	1997	1996	1995	1994	1993	1992
Revenues (millions)	36586	30557	35009	36874	31322	30340	32123	37464
Net income (millions)	2070	1339	3180	2651	1962	1693	1819	1593
Earnings per share	3.14	2.04	4.83	4.06	3.01	2.60	2.80	2.35
Dividends per share	2.48	2.44	2.28	2.08	1.93	1.85	1.75	1.65
Price High	113.9	90.2	89.2	68.4	53.6	47.3	49.4	37.7
Low	73.1	67.8	61.8	51.0	43.4	39.9	33.8	30.1

The Chubb Corporation

15 Mountain View Road □ Post Office Box 1615 □ Warren, New Jersey 07061-1615 □ Investor contact: Gail E. Devlin (908) 903-3245 □ Dividend reinvestment plan is available: (800) 317-4445 □ Web site: www.chubb.com □ Listed: NYSE □ Ticker symbol: CB □ S&P rating: B+ □ Value Line financial strength rating: A

Chubb has always been known for its appetite for risk and its innovative approaches to satisfying customers' needs. These traits have enabled the company to grow and prosper over the decades. However, Chubb is also known for financial strength and fairness and speed of paying claims—qualities that are very important to its customers. CEO Dean R. O'Hare points out, "We are committed to protecting this financial strength by accepting only prudent risks and leaving the reckless gambles to our competitors."

Company Profile

In 1882, Thomas Caldecot Chubb and his son Percy opened a marine underwriting business in the seaport district of New York City. The Chubbs were adept at turning risk into success, often by helping policyholders prevent disasters before they occurred. As the twentieth century got underway, Chubb had established strong relationships with the insurance agents and brokers who placed their clients' business with Chubb underwriters.

The Chubb Corporation was formed in 1967 and was listed on the New York Stock Exchange in 1984. Today, Chubb stands among the largest insurers in the United States and the world. Chubb's 10,000 property and casualty employees serve customers from 132 offices throughout North America, Europe, South America, and the Pacific Rim.

Chubb has an excellent reputation for designing specialty property-casualty insurance products and providing high-quality service to its agents and policyholders. In an industry where product and service differentiation is limited, Chubb's specialty lines of property-casualty businesses are a significant franchise. Chubb's strengths include a worldwide branch structure; innovative and targeted product development; a high level of pricing, underwriting, and reserving discipline; and a fair approach to settling claims.

Highlights of 1999

- Chubb made progress all through the year reducing expenses. The company's activity value analysis produced the cost saving that management expected, helping Chubb achieve a full point reduction in its expense ratio to 32.5 percent, from 33.5 percent in 1998.
- Chubb received a license to operate in China, and the company moved closer to entering another potentially huge market as India passed legislation that will open its insurance industry to foreign participation.
- In January 2000, *Fortune* magazine named Chubb to its list of "The 100 Best Companies to Work for in America."
- The repeal of the Glass-Steagall Act is a positive development for the industry. It puts all sectors of the financial services industry on a level playing field, and it enables companies to form alliances with other financial institutions and extend market reach through joint ventures. For example, it enables two institutions to complement the product expertise of one with the distribution network of another.

Shortcomings to Bear in Mind

■ Catastrophe losses were heavy in both 1999 and 1998, but more so in 1999. The company recorded about $100 million in losses from 6,500 victims of Hurricane Floyd; it was the largest number of claims from a single catastrophe in the history of Chubb. And once again, the speed and fairness with which Chubb handled these claims reinforced the company's reputation among customers, brokers, and agents.

In 1999, the company had an underwriting loss of $178.8 million pre-tax. Chubb's combined loss and expense ratio for the year was 102.8 percent, which included 4 percentage points of catastrophe losses. The company's underwriting loss is attributable solely to its standard commercial lines, which had a combined ratio of 123.6 percent. (The combined ratio is the sum of the loss ratio and the expense ratio. A combined ratio below 100 shows profitable results. Thus, the lower the ratio the better.) The combined ratio for personal lines was 89.9 percent, which was remarkable considering that it includes 6.6 percentage points of catastrophe losses. Specialty commercial lines turned in a combined ratio of 93.6 percent.

■ In recent years, some observers have declared the insurance cycle dead. However, as long as the property-casualty industry prices its products before it knows its costs, it will always be cyclical, though the length of the cycle might vary. There are three primary factors that are creating a turnaround in this cycle: cash flows, reserves, and stock prices.

During the first nine or 10 years of the standard commercial price wars, as rates declined costs declined at roughly the same pace because of savings from tort reform and other cost reductions. Then, about two years ago, while rates continued to decline, additional cost reductions were no longer forthcoming. Escalating paid losses and shrinking premiums put a squeeze on cash flow. The company says that cash flow for the industry turned negative in 1999 to the extent that it was not sufficient to cover shareholder dividends. The gravity of this development is emphasized by CEO Dean R. O'Hare, "A cash-negative position in the insurance business is, to put it mildly, not a good place to be. A company can raise quick cash by selling investments—but when you sell under pressure, you don't get the best price—or by cutting rates to gain market share, but this digs the hole even deeper. Fortunately, the industry is beginning to take the responsible actions needed to reverse the hemorrhaging cash flow—by raising rates to fix the underlying problem."

Reasons to Buy

■ According to Mr. O'Hare, "The most challenging effort of 1999 was the battle to fix our standard commercial business, which accounts for about a third of our total premiums. The underwriting loss on these lines in 1999 cost us $1.60 per share of earnings. Until 1999, premium rates in the standard commercial market were in steady decline for 12 years. In the fall of 1998, we decided to put the brakes on the rate slide and began to implement a 'pricing and pruning' strategy. We declined to renew accounts with the worst experience and implemented rate increases on most of the others.

"Most commercial customers accepted the increases in order to remain with Chubb. Through much of 1999, those customers who chose to leave were able to find carriers that were still seeking market share growth, regardless of pricing. But, by the end of the year, most competitors had followed our initiative, and the market showed signs of firming."

- Rate increases early in Chubb's program were relatively small, but they have grown significantly. Since October 1998, when the reversal began, the company has had a 13 percentage-point swing in rate changes—from rate cuts averaging 5 percent to rate increases of 8 percent in February 2000. Chubb is now in the second annual round of renewals, so the company is receiving rate hikes on top of rate hikes. While it's still too early to declare victory over price inadequacy, the rate increases are sticking."

- Fortunately, two-thirds of Chubb's business performed well in 1999. Bolstered by the midyear acquisition of Executive Risk, specialty commercial lines, which accounted for 41 percent of premiums, grew over 9 percent and had a combined ratio of 93.6 percent.

  About half of specialty commercial is the executive protection business, and the rest is mostly property, marine, surety, and financial institutions. Chubb is one of the pioneers of executive protection coverages, and the acquisition of Executive Risk further strengthened the company's leadership position in this market. What's more, this business is among the most profitable of Chubb's specialty commercial lines, producing a combined ratio of 84.3 percent in 1999.

  The process of integrating Executive Risk with Chubb's existing executive protection business was a distraction in the fall of 1999, but the business is once again focused on resuming its historic rapid, profitable growth. Mr. O'Hare says, "Being one of the top two carriers in these lines gives us distinct advantages with our brokers and agents."

- The runaway success story of 1999 was Chubb's personal insurance business, which accounted for 27 percent of the company's premiums. Personal lines not only expanded in double digits but also the rate of growth increased for the fifth consecutive year. Mr. O'Hare says, "This continues to be a superior book of business with premium products and services for which customers are willing to pay a premium price—even in a market that is notorious for positioning the products as commodities and pricing them accordingly."

  The high level of profitability of personal lines in 1999, despite substantial losses from Hurricane Floyd, is a testament to the value of this franchise. Moreover, Chubb emerged from the hurricane with a reinforced reputation among policyholders, agents, and brokers for its broader coverage and superior claim service. The company's Masterpiece policy covers many losses that are not covered by homeowners policies from other companies. Chubb has succeeded in establishing the Masterpiece policy as the gold standard of insurance in the most desirable segment of the market—people with substantial insurable wealth who value quality and have the ability and inclination to pay for it.

- One of Chubb's specialties in personal lines is valuable articles coverage, which insures jewelry, antiques, fine arts, and other collectibles. Increased purchases of jewelry and fine arts resulting from the strong economy in the United States have made valuable articles insurance a growing market for Chubb. Here, too, the company's branded policies offer superior coverage and claim service, and Mr. O'Hare says, "We believe we are the largest underwriter in this profitable market."

- Chubb is among a select segment of insurers with a large stake in overseas business. In the past, foreign property-casualty insurance markets have grown at a faster pace than those in the United States. Chubb looks for one-third of its volume to emanate from abroad by 2005—compared with 17 percent in 1999—even without an acquisition.

Total assets: $23,537 million
Common shares outstanding: 176 million
Return on 1999 shareholders' equity: 9.9%

	1999	1998	1997	1996	1995	1994	1993	1992
Premiums earned (millions)	5524	5304	5157	4569	4147	3776	3505	3163
Net income (millions)	621	707	770	486	697	528	344	617
Earnings per share	3.66	4.19	4.39	2.76	3.93	2.98	1.96	3.48
Dividends per share	1.34	1.24	1.16	1.08	.98	.92	.85	.79
Price High	76.4	88.8	78.5	56.3	50.3	41.6	48.2	45.5
Low	44.0	55.4	51.1	40.9	38.1	34.3	38.0	31.2

AGGRESSIVE GROWTH

Cintas Corporation

Post Office Box 625737 ❑ **Cincinnati, Ohio 45262-5737** ❑ **Investor contact: Karan L. Carnahan (513) 573-4013**
❑ **Dividend reinvestment plan is not available** ❑ **Web site: www.cintas-corp.com** ❑ **Fiscal year ends May 31**
❑ **Listed: Nasdaq** ❑ **Ticker symbol: CTAS** ❑ **S&P rating: A+** ❑ **Value Line financial strength rating: B++**

Many large corporations are re-engineering all aspects of their business, and they are consolidating their source of supply of products and services. They prefer to deal with fewer suppliers to reduce purchasing and administrative costs. They often prefer to do business with Cintas because the company is a complete uniform service, whether the customer wants to rent, lease, or buy their uniforms. In addition, Cintas also provides online ordering, inventory control, and paperless systems.

Company Profile

Cintas designs, manufactures, and implements corporate identity uniform programs, which it rents or sells to customers throughout the United States and Canada. The company also provides ancillary services, including entrance mats, sanitation supplies, first aid products and services, and cleanroom supplies. Cintas provides its award-winning design capability and top quality craftsmanship to the high end of the market—hotels, airlines, cruise ships, and the like. The company delivers the proper uniform to anyone in any job classification from the doorman to the cocktail waitress in a hotel, from the mechanic to the pilot at the airlines, and even people working in the retail sector.

According to Cintas, "Companies like Albertson's use Cintas uniforms to identify their employees to their customers. An employee who wears a clean, crisp, and attractive uniform is always viewed as more professional than someone in ordinary work clothes. Uniforms also complement a company's esprit de corps by building camaraderie and loyalty. Bottom line—we don't just sell uniforms—we sell image, identification, teamwork, morale, pride, and professionalism." Put another way, Cintas believes that when people *look* good, they *feel* good. And when they feel good, they work better. What's more, their improved attitude results in a decline in absenteeism and turnover.

Highlights of 1999

- Achieved 30th consecutive year of uninterrupted growth in sales and profits.
- Net income reached $167 million, an increase of 27 percent.
- In its largest acquisition to date, the company acquired Unitog Company, based in Kansas City.

- Uniform Rental infrastructure expanded:
- 120,000 new customers.
- 15 new uniform rental plants.
- 1,000 additional service routes.
- Began providing Uniform Rental services in 11 new cities.
- Added 110 routes to the company's First Aid distribution network.
- Expanded First Aid service network—now covering 40 of the top 50 domestic markets.
- Boosted dividends 22 percent.
- Recognized in the *Wall Street Journal's* "honor roll" of 32 companies who were ranked on five-year average compound annual total shareholder returns through the end of 1998.
- Recognized as one of the 400 "Best-Performing Big Companies in the U.S." in the inaugural *Forbes* Platinum List.
- Winner of the first annual Bain Award for strategic excellence.
- Recognized as the preferred uniform of NASCAR.

Shortcomings to Bear in Mind

- During 1999 the company's stock slumped from a high of $78.5, falling below $50. This was largely a by-product of the company's acquisition of Unitog. To boost Unitog's margins, Cintas sold some underperforming assets. One unexpected problem involved a high turnover among Unitog's sales force, which made it difficult to obtain new customers.

Reasons to Buy

- When Cintas went public in 1983, it was comparable in size to several other companies in the uniform rental industry. Since then, it has grown much faster than the industry as a whole. It is now more than twice as large as its closest rival.
- A key part of the company's strategy has been growth through acquisitions. One

of the company's foremost achievements in 1999 was its acquisition of Unitog Company, a large player in the uniform rental and direct sale businesses. Although there have been some problems in integrating Unitog into Cintas, the synergy that the company will realize as the consolidation proceeds will be significant. According to management, "We expect to increase the after-tax margin on their sales from the 4 percent that they achieved in the past to the normal Cintas return of approximately 10 percent over the next few years.

"If we can achieve this—and we believe we can—Unitog will prove to be one of the best acquisitions we have ever made. We will completely eliminate their corporate headquarters in Kansas City. We intend to consolidate many of their operations into ours and offer our ancillary services to their 70,000 customers, bringing the revenue per customer in line with Cintas'—a potential increase of 30 percent."

- Another significant acquisition involved Uniforms To You (UTY), the leading company providing uniforms in the hospitality, restaurant, gaming, and transportation industries. With Uniforms To You, the company now has the foremost design team in the business, and that is the reason Cintas has been chosen to provide uniforms to many leading companies such as Marriott, Starwood, Hilton, Hyatt, Fairmont, and the Mirage Resorts.

Since the merger, corporate officials have visited many UTY customers and the trade shows in which they participate, and according to the company, "We have worked with them to improve many aspects of their operation. We are more enthused about the potential in these niche markets of the uniform business than we were when we closed the transaction."

■ Geographic expansion is another top priority for the company as it tries to capitalize on a corporate trend toward consolidation of vendors. In fiscal 1999, Cintas penetrated 11 new cities and gained 120,000 new customers. At year-end it occupied 200 uniform rental locations, serving more than 4 million people who wear Cintas uniforms.

The company's geographic coverage has been an important competitive advantage, especially when calling on regional and national companies. One of the first questions they ask is, "How many of our locations can you service?" Large companies prefer to work with Cintas because it can efficiently serve them from its 200 uniform rental locations throughout the United States and Canada. That is why companies like Firestone hire Cintas to service their 1,500 stores nationwide.

■ The company's frequent contact and its close relationship with its customers "presents us with the opportunity to offer many ancillary products and services. We look for the opportunity to provide services that are very important but are small details that can be easily neglected by our customers—things like entrance mats, hygiene supply services, and first aid services. These small details can be easily delegated to us, since we are already delivering the customer's uniforms weekly anyway," says the company.

■ Over the past 10 years, the uniform rental business has grown at a compound rate of 6.3 percent, compared with Gross Domestic Product growth of 3 percent. In the last five years, moreover, industry growth has averaged 8.6 percent.

■ Cintas recently won twin honors: Recognition by the Staton Institute as one of American's Finest Companies and inclusion in the 1999 Edition of *Moody's Handbook of Dividend Achievers.*

Fewer than 400 of 16,000 publicly traded companies qualified for inclusion in *America's Finest Companies.* The Staton Institute noted that Cintas' record of delivering both higher earnings per share and higher cash dividends for at least 10 years placed the company in the top 1 percent of all U.S. publicly traded companies. Cintas was one of only 38 public companies listed with higher earnings per share for at least 20 consecutive years.

In *Moody's Handbook of Dividend Achievers,* which tracked companies for the 1998 calendar year, Cintas ranked 15th out of 334 companies. Rankings were based on the average annual compound growth rate of a company's regular annual cash dividend. On a compound basis, the company's annual dividend has increased 23.6 percent for the past 10 years.

■ There are 144 million people employed in the United States and Canada. According to the National Association of Uniform Manufacturers and the American Apparel Manufacturers Association, there are 58 million workers who wear a uniform. In addition to these 58 million people, Cintas estimates there are an additional 26 million people who work in occupations that lend themselves to a uniform program. This is especially true for companies who have personnel in the public eye, including courier services, lawn care, and property management personnel.

The potential to put the additional 26 million people in uniform spans a vast number of occupations. For example, special trade contractors, such as the heating and air conditioning industry, currently employ an estimated 3.5 million people, and Cintas believes 3 million of these employees should wear uniforms. Of these employees, about 1 million work for an employer with a uniform program in place. That means in those businesses alone about 2 million employees are potential uniform wearers but currently do not wear uniforms. Thousands of other businesses are in a similar situation, including those in residential services such as appliance repairmen, cable installers, plumbers; people who work in the retail sector like groceries, electronic, and office supply stores; and people who work in the health services industry like research labs, pharmaceutical companies, and outpatient clinics.

The company, despite its success (it's the largest firm in its industry), still has only a 6 percent share of a $31 billion market. Over the past eight years, about two-thirds of the company's new uniform rental business has come from this unserved or potential market.

Total assets: $1,408 million
Current ratio: 3.10
Common shares outstanding: 167 million
Return on 1999 shareholders' equity: 22.1%

		1999	1998	1997	1996	1995	1994	1993	1992
Revenues (millions)		1752	1198	840	730	615	523	453	402
Net income (millions)		167	118	91	75	63	53	45	36
Earnings per share		.99	.76	.64	.53	.45	.38	.32	.26
Dividends per share		.15	.12	.10	.08	.07	.06	.05	.04
Price	High	52.3	47.5	28.3	21.2	16.0	12.1	11.3	10.7
	Low	26.0	26.0	17.0	13.9	11.2	9.9	8.3	7.9

AGGRESSIVE GROWTH

Cisco Systems, Inc.

170 West Tasman Drive ❑ San Jose, California 95134-1706 ❑ Investor contact: M. Thurber (408) 526-8893 ❑ Dividend reinvestment plan is not available ❑ Web site: www.cisco.com ❑ Listed: Nasdaq ❑ Ticker symbol: CSCO ❑ S&P rating: B+ ❑ Value Line financial strength rating: A++

Cisco's strategy for technology excellence is to focus on internal product development and blend that with acquisitions and partnerships. This strategy has allowed Cisco to add more than 65 new products, acquire 11 companies, and develop dozens of partnerships to help the company pursue emerging markets and achieve market share leadership.

Cisco holds the number one market share position in 16 of 20 key markets in which the company competes. It holds the number two position in the remaining four areas. Some of these new emerging market opportunities include broadband access, voice over IP, and optical Internet working.

Company Profile

Cisco Systems was founded in 1984 by a small group of computer scientists from Stanford University seeking an easier way to connect different types of computer systems. The company shipped its first product in 1986. Since then, Cisco has grown into a multinational corporation with more than 20,000 employees in 55 countries.

Cisco Systems is the worldwide leader in networking for the Internet. Cisco's networking solutions connect people, computing devices, and computer networks, allowing people to access or transfer information without regard to differences in time, place, or type of computer system.

Cisco provides end-to-end networking solutions that customers use to build a unified information infrastructure of their own or to connect to someone else's network. An end-to-end networking solution is one that provides a common architecture that delivers consistent network services to all users. The broader the range of network services, the more capabilities a network can provide to users connected to it.

Cisco offers the industry's broadest range of hardware products used to form information networks or give people access to those networks; Cisco IOS software, which provides network services and enables networked applications; expertise in network design and implementation; and technical support and professional services to maintain and optimize network operations. Cisco is unique in its ability to provide all of these elements, either by itself or together with partners.

Cisco serves customers in three target markets:

• Enterprises—Large organizations with complex networking needs, usually spanning multiple locations and types of computer systems. Enterprise customers include corporations, government agencies, utilities, and educational institutions.

• Service Providers—Companies that provide information services, including telecommunications carriers, Internet service providers, cable companies, and wireless communication providers.

• Small/Medium Business—Companies with a need for data networks of their own, as well as connection to the Internet and/or to business partners.

Cisco sells its products in about 116 countries through a direct sales force, distributors, value-added resellers, and system integrators. Cisco has headquarters in San Jose, California. It also has major operations in Research Triangle Park, North Carolina and Chelmsford, Massachusetts, as well as more than 225 sales and support offices in 75 countries.

Shortcomings to Bear in Mind

■ Investors often ask me why I have omitted Cisco Systems from previous editions of The 100 Best Stocks You Can Buy. They stomp their feet in high dudgeon and shout, "How could you possibly leave out the greatest growth company of the century?"

My answer is very simple: I do not subscribe to the strategy that you should buy a growth company regardless of price. So far, I have been wrong about Cisco. It has continued to be a super holding even though its P/E ratio is in the stratosphere. For those investors who want growth at any price, I am belatedly including Cisco in this edition. May it reward you with great riches.

One last word. My feeling that you are destined to suffer the consequences when you invest in high-multiple stocks is shared by a noted author, Jeremy J. Siegel, a professor of finance at the Wharton School. He is also the author of the monumental book, Stocks for the Long Run. According to Dr. Siegel, "History has shown that whenever companies, no matter how great, get priced above 50 to 60 times earnings, buyer beware. A few stocks in the nifty-50 era subsequently outperformed the market, but in that venerated group, no stock that sold above a 50 price-to-earnings ratio was able to match the S&P 500 over the next quarter century. Such great companies as Baxter Labs, Disney, McDonald's, Johnson & Johnson, AMP, and Texas Instruments have trailed the averages."

Jeremy Siegel goes on to say that "Once a firm reaches big-cap status—ranked in the top 50 by market value—its ability to generate long-term double-digit earnings growth slows dramatically."

Finally, Dr. Siegel lists a number of large-cap companies with high P/E ratios in the spring of 2000: Cisco Systems (with a PE of 148.4), AOL/Time Warner (217.4), Oracle (152.9), Nortel Networks (105.6), Sun Microsystems (119.0), EMC (115.4), JDS Uniphase (668.3), Qualcomm (166.8), and Yahoo! (623.2). This is in sharp contrast to a P/E ratio of 28.6 for the S&P 500.

Reasons to Buy

- In its second-largest deal yet, Cisco Systems bought ArrowPoint Communications in a stock swap valued at about $6 billion. ArrowPoint makes "smart" Internet switches—specialized computers that optimize the delivery of content over the Internet. Acquiring ArrowPoint gives Cisco, the leading maker of network equipment, the technology it needs to compete against companies like Alteon Web Systems in the fast-growing segment of the market devoted to what is known as content switching, or load balancing. Analysts applauded the move, saying Cisco had struggled to make a product that would compete with ArrowPoint.

- By providing the systems that make the Internet work, Cisco is helping customers compete in the explosive Internet economy by implementing Internet business models and building New World communications infrastructures that turn change into competitive advantage. As a result, Cisco Systems has grown faster than all of its key competitors. What's more, Cisco has been rewarded with one of the top 10 market capitalizations in the world, and the company has been recognized as the fastest-growing, most profitable company in the history of the computer industry.

- A recent study by the University of Texas found that in 1998 alone, the Internet economy in the United States generated more than $300 billion in revenue and was responsible for more than 1.2 million jobs. In just six years since the introduction of the World Wide Web, the Internet economy already rivals the size of the century-old sectors such as energy, automotive, and telecommunications. Milestones that took up to 100 years to achieve in the Industrial Age are occurring at a staggering pace in this new economy.

- In contrast to many technology companies, Cisco does not take a rigid approach that favors one technology over the alternatives and imposes it on customers as the only answer. Cisco's philosophy is to listen to customer requests, monitor all technological alternatives, and provide customers with a range of options from which to choose. Cisco develops its products and solutions around widely accepted industry standards. In some instances, technologies developed by Cisco have become industry standards themselves.

- In 2000, Cisco unveiled an office telephone system based on Internet technology. The system, which transmits voice calls in the electronic language of the Internet, could push the company to the top of the budding Internet telephone market. Proponents say such systems bring new convenience, efficiency, and cost-savings to corporate communications. While North America's traditional office telephone powerhouses, Lucent Technologies and Nortel Networks of Canada, are also developing Internet phone systems for offices, Cisco may have the early edge.

- Cisco's Home Gateway series introduced a new breed of Internet products. This open platform, which was made available in the fall of 2000, will build high-speed home networks that support New World services such as integrated data, voice, and video. What's more, alliances have been formed with GTE, Sun Microsystems, and Whirlpool to offer consumers a complete package of products and services that transform any domicile into a high-speed, "always on" Internet home with a limitless array of possibilities for Internet home computing, entertainment, and education.

- Behind the bright-eyed charm and soft southern accent of Cisco's CEO, John Chambers, lies one of the shrewdest deal makers in corporate America. Following stints with IBM and Wang Laboratories, the sales veteran joined Cisco in 1991. Chambers, age 51, has rarely let his checkbook rest, buying 40 companies in six years. Few understand the complexities of assessing, purchasing, and assimilating a new company as well as Chambers.

Here are some recent acquisitions that indicate what kind of companies are joining the Cisco camp:

- Growth Networks, Inc., February 16, 2000. Growth Networks is a market leader in Internet switching fabrics, a new category of networking silicon. Growth Networks' technology will allow service providers to deploy advanced systems with switching capacities that scale from tens of gigabits per second (Gbps) to tens of terabits per second (Tbps), meeting customers' critical requirements for scalability, flexibility, multiservice, support, and quality of service.

- Atlantech Technologies Ltd., March 1, 2000. Atlantech is a leading provider of network element management software, which is designed to help configure and monitor network hardware. It provides service providers and ecosystem partners with a single integrated platform for enabling network management functionality across multiple diverse networks.

- Altiga Networks, January 19, 2000. Altiga is a market leader in integrated VPN solutions for remote access applications. Its product suite will complement Cisco's existing family of VPN routers and security appliances. Altiga's integrated VPN client, remote access gateway, and management solutions will extend Cisco's broad VPN portfolio, providing enhanced VPN scalability, manageability, and performance for enterprise edge applications, including service provider-managed remote access.

- Compatible Systems Corporation, January 19, 2000. Compatible is a leading developer of standards-based reliable and scalable VPN solutions for service provider networks. Its industry-leading platform enables service providers to deploy robust IPSec architectures for VPN services.

- E-commerce is ready to expand sharply in Asia. The company will invest 50 billion yen in its operations in Japan over the next three years. To start with, Cisco will establish its first R&D base in Tokyo. The company's work force there is to be tripled, and its distribution facility floor space will be doubled. The goal is to triple annual sales in Japan to 300 billion yen.

Total assets: $14,725 million
Current ratio: 2.04
Common shares outstanding: 6,938 million
Return on 1999 shareholders' equity: 22.3%

	1999	1998	1997	1996	1995	1994	1993	1992
Revenues (millions)	12154	8459	6440	4096	1979	1243	649	340
Net income (millions)	2567	1873	1414	913	479	315	172	84
Earnings per share	.38	.29	.23	.15	.10	.07	.04	.02
Dividends per share	Nil							
Price High	53.6	24.4	10.1	7.7	5.0	2.3	1.8	1.1
Low	22.5	8.6	5.0	3.5	1.8	1.0	1.1	0.4

CONSERVATIVE GROWTH

Citigroup, Incorporated

153 East 53rd Street ⊐ New York, New York 10043 ⊐ Investor contact: Bill Pike (212) 793-8874 ⊐ Dividend reinvestment plan is not available ⊐ Web site: www.citigroup.com ⊐ Listed: NYSE ⊐ Ticker symbol: C ⊐ S&P rating: A ⊐ Value Line financial strength rating: A

In one of the largest corporate mergers in history, Citigroup was formed in late 1998, combining Citicorp (a large bank) with Travelers Group (a major insurance company). Citigroup is now the nation's largest financial services firm.

Melding traditional banking and insurance businesses together on a scale never attempted, the company's goal is to serve the financial needs of the widest possible audience on a global scale. Operations break down as follows:

The Global Consumer Segment

This includes branch and electronic banking, consumer lending services, credit card and charge card services, personalized wealth-management services for high-net-worth clients, and life, auto, and homeowners insurance.

Several specialized units include mortgage banking, which creates mortgages and student loans across North America; cards, which offers products such as MasterCard, VISA, Diners Club, and private-label credit cards. It has some 53 million card-member accounts; consumer finance services, which maintains 980 loan offices in 45 states; and insurance, which offers annuities and various life and long-term-care insurance to individuals and small businesses.

In 1999, total Global Consumer net income amounted to $4,296 million, or 43.5 percent of the company total.

The Global Corporate and Investment Bank Segment

This segment provides investment advice, financial planning and retail brokerage services, banking and other financial services, and commercial insurance products throughout the United states and in 98 foreign countries.

The segment includes Salomon Smith Barney, which offers investment banking services, such as underwriting of fixed-income and equity securities. Specialized units include emerging markets, which offers cash management, short-term loans, trade services, project finance, and fixed-income issuance and trading to countries outside North America, Western Europe, and Japan; global relationship banking, which offers cash management, foreign exchange, securities custody, and structured products to multinational companies; and commercial lines, which provides property and casualty insurance through brokers and independent agencies throughout the United States.

In 1999, this group of operations produced net income of $5,075 million, or 51.4 percent of the company total.

The Asset Management Segment

This segment offers a wide range of products and services to mutual funds, closed-end funds, managed accounts, and unit investment trusts. In 1999, this segment was responsible for 6.1 percent of the company's net income.

Highlights of 1999

- Core income increased 57 percent—making Citigroup the world's most profitable financial-services company. With all the company's business sectors contributing to the upward momentum, it is ahead of its plan to double earnings in the first five years of Citigroup's existence.
- The company had a 22.7 percent return on common equity. With $54.6 billion in total equity capital and trust securities, Citigroup is one of the best-capitalized financial institutions in the world and one of the most efficient users of capital.
- The company achieved its target of $2 billion annualized expense reductions ahead of schedule, while increasing revenues by 16 percent.
- Citigroup returned $4 billion in capital to stockholders through the repurchase of shares on the open market.
- In April of 1999, the board of directors approved a 50 percent common stock dividend, which had the effect of a 3-for-2 stock split, and the quarterly cash dividend was increased to 14 cents per post-split share and then further increased to 16 cents just after the close of 1999.

Shortcomings to Bear in Mind

- Citigroup's Solomon Smith Barney investment bank and its Citibank commercial bank in Europe have been lagging behind their principal Wall Street competitors: Goldman Sachs Group, Morgan Stanley Dean Witter, and Merrill Lynch. The acquisition of Schroders PLC of the United Kingdom is aimed at closing this gap.

However, analysts are not all convinced that the Schroders deal is a panacea for all of Citigroup's concerns in Europe. To be sure, Schroders is strong in corporate finance in Eastern Europe, France, Italy, and the United Kingdom. On the other hand, Schroders ranked only sixteenth in European mergers and acquisitions in 1999.

What's more, some analysts point out that the acquisition may not be easy for Citigroup to digest. Foreign purchases of British investment banks have been notoriously difficult to pull off because the cultures of well-established British banks have been hard for outsiders to penetrate. In fact, Citigroup has had its own travails in merging with Salomon Smith Barney, a former Traveler's unit.

Reasons to Buy

- In the biggest acquisition since Citigroup was formed in 1998, the company purchased the investment-banking operations of Schroders PLC—the last independent investment bank in London—for $2.2 billion. The deal aims to bring Schroders's mergers-and-acquisitions expertise and European client relationships together with Citigroup's sizable European fixed-income business.

The acquisition of Schroders will double the size of Salomon Smith Barney's investment-banking and stock business in Europe. "It puts us two or three years ahead of where we might have been had we not done this," said Citigroup's cochairman, Sanford I. Weill.

Citigroup agreed to pay about $220 million in incentives to retain hundreds of the most important Schroders employees, said Michael Carpenter, chairman and CEO of Salomon Smith Barney. Most of those employees did not own significant amounts of stock in Schroders—the founding family owned 45 percent of its stock.

- Citigroup has established teams of executives worldwide, including six in Japan alone, who are dedicated to finding new purchases in conjunction with the executives in charge of individual businesses there. Further streamlining in Citigroup's regional management structure is also being considered, a move that may make the acquisition process smoother.

Analysts estimate that Citigroup, even after the Schroders acquisition, still has as much as $5 billion in excess capital to spend on future acquisitions, and that's without taking into account its robust stock price, which gives it a strong currency for all-stock deals.

- Citigroup is by far the world's largest card company, with 97 million cards in force worldwide. Cards are the hub of the consumer sector. A credit card is usually among the client's first services purchased from Citigroup, and therefore it becomes the basis for introducing clients to products from the company's other divisions.

Cards are often the first product the consumer business introduces when it enters a new country, as was the case in 1999 with Egypt. In newer Citigroup consumer markets, such as Hungary, Poland, and Turkey, the card business supplies the company's growth and its broadest appeal to customers.

- The Internet will play a significant role in the growth of the cards business. Citibank cards are among those most frequently used for Internet purchases today, and the company's goal is to be the payment vehicle of choice for online shoppers. Citigroup already offers online account management, an Internet-only credit account, an online shopping mall that provides savings exclusively to Citibank cardholders, and CitiWallet for convenient and secure Internet shopping. As consumers grow more comfortable shopping and paying over the Internet, they will be more inclined to use the company's online financial services, such as banking and brokerage.

- In 1999, Citigroup Mortgage provided Salomon Smith Barney Private Client Division customers with more than $675 million in customized mortgages.

- In 1999, more than fifteen thousand Travelers Property Casualty policies were underwritten for Citibank card customers.

- The impact of the merger becomes evident when you examine the synergy. For instance, in 1999 customers of Citibank, Primerica, and SSB Private Client Division purchased more than $2.8 billion in products from Travelers Life & Annuity.

- Citibanking, the company's branch-based banking business, has 28 million accounts in 46 countries and territories and is well on its way to offering one-stop availability of products and services for every stage of one's financial life.

- CitiFinancial, the company's consumer-finance business, serves middle-income families. With the stronger brand identification of its new name, the former Commercial Credit company added 200 offices in the United States and Canada through acquisitions in 1999, and there is still considerable room for expansion to regions not yet covered.

- Already the U.S. market leader in individual term life insurance, Primerica also delivers other Citigroup products and services through direct sales to hundreds of thousands of clients across North America.

The growth of the U.S. franchise continues, benefiting from a stream of new products from other Citigroup companies and the continued expansion of a sales force that now exceeds 100,000 full- and part-time individuals. In 1999, Primerica provided about 500,000 clients with its proprietary financial-needs analysis, a needs-based program especially developed to help individuals and families define and achieve their personal financial goals.

Total assets: $716,937 million
Common shares outstanding: 3,372 million
Return on 1999 shareholders' equity: 22.7%

	1999	1998	1997	1996	1995	1994	1993	1992
Revenues (millions)	57237	48936	47782*					
Net income (millions)	9947	6342	7751					
Earnings per share	2.85	1.77	2.12					
Dividends per share	.54	.12						
Price High	58.3	35.5						
Low	32.7	19.0						

*Because of the merger with Travelers in 1998, no other statistics are available for prior years.

AGGRESSIVE GROWTH

Clayton Homes, Inc.

Post Office Box 15169 ◻ Knoxville, Tennessee 37901 ◻ Investor contact: Carl Koella (423)380-3206 ◻ Web site: www.clayton.net ◻ Dividend reinvestment plan is available: (800)937-5449 ◻ Fiscal year ends June 30 ◻ Listed: NYSE ◻ Ticker symbol: CMH ◻ S&P rating: A- ◻ Value Line financial strength B++

Industry surveys, along with Clayton's own data, confirm that drive-by impressions influence the company's prospects' purchase decisions more than 60 percent of the time. As a result, 1999 was a year to focus on the curb appeal of its sales centers. Clayton upgraded 178 stores with new signage, paving, landscaping, and other visual enhancements designed to make its sales centers more inviting to prospective customers.

What's more, strategic purchasing of sales center real estate permits the company to invest in and retain the prime retail location in most of its markets and insulates it from escalating rents.

Company Profile

Clayton Homes, Inc. is a vertically integrated manufactured housing company headquartered in Knoxville, Tennessee. Employing more than 7,300 people and operating in 31 states, the company builds, sells, finances, and insures manufactured homes. It also owns and operates residential manufactured housing communities.

The company makes a wide variety of single- and multisection manufactured homes. They are factory-built, completely finished, constructed to be transported by trucks, and designed as permanent, primary residences when sited.

The Manufacturing group is a leading producer of manufactured homes, with 19 plants supplying homes to 1,052 independent and company-owned retail centers.

The Retail group sells, installs, and services factory-built homes. At the end of fiscal 1999 there were 306 company-owned retail centers in 22 states.

Financial Services provides financing and insurance for homebuyers of company-owned and selected independent retail sales centers through Vanderbilt Mortgage and Finance, a wholly owned subsidiary.

The Communities group owns and operates 75 manufactured housing communities, with 19,708 home sites in 12 states.

At the beginning of fiscal 1999 (fiscal year ends on June 30), the company set a number of goals. This is how those goals have worked out:

- Have 300 company-owned retail centers in 1999. It surpassed that goal, reaching 306.
- Improve delinquency. The company reduced originated delinquencies from 1.98 percent to 1.84 percent—one of the best results in the industry.
- Improve same-store sales. They climbed 14 percent over 1998.
- Reduce debt. The company repaid its bridge loan for portfolio acquisitions and reduced the debt-to-capital ratio from 22 percent to 9 percent.
- Expand the company's presence in the Southwest. Clayton Homes opened a plant in El Mirage, Arizona in October of 1998. It became profitable in December of the following year.
- Originate $1 billion in mortgages. The company originated slightly more, $1.08 billion in 1999.
- Develop attractive and profitable communities. The company opened two such communities in 1999 and is in the planning stages for two more.
- Develop an interactive Internet wide-area network (WAN). LINK (an automated Internet-based communications system) set up shop in the summer of 1999, providing loan application processing over the Internet—saving time, money, and paper. LINK's communication, real-time management-information systems, and two-way data exchange are reducing costs and shrinkage as well as improving training.
- Recruit, retain, and develop the best people in the industry. The company built a training center for hosting Clayton sales and leadership academies as well as business retreats. These 11 buildings were manufactured at Clayton plants. Together, the buildings can comfortably house 75 guests, and the main facility can accommodate meetings for 100 employees.

Shortcomings to Bear in Mind

- In fiscal 2000, the industry was faced with increased competition and bloated inventory levels. In one two-month period, for instance, 19 industry plants were closed, and retailers began closing satellite locations. On the other hand, such industry problems have historically helped Clayton, presenting the company with opportunities to acquire talent, operating facilities, and loan portfolios.

Reasons to Buy

- Growth among the company's four groups has varied from quarter to quarter and year to year, but the synergies involved in this very-difficult-to-execute concept have enabled the company to consistently achieve records. While one group is undergoing a period of slower growth, another group is enjoying high growth. The challenge of balancing and maintaining the model should not be underestimated—especially since other industry leaders have taken multiple charges to restate their securitization models. On the other hand, Clayton Homes has taken a conservative approach to growth and risk management.
- In 1999, Clayton's plants produced and sold 28,344 homes, representing 42,099 floors—a 6 percent increase over the prior year. Product mix was split 48 percent multisection homes, while 52 percent were single-section homes.

Manufacturing revenues expanded by 9 percent, to $654 million in 1999. Eighteen of the company's plants were profitable. The one exception was a Georgia facility, which sustained severe storm-related damage. The company's newest plant in El Mirage, Arizona was built in seven months and was profitable in the second month of production. El Mirage expanded Clayton's presence in the Southwest, and the company is now serving independent retailers as far west as California. The recently announced site for Clayton's twentieth plant in Hodgenville, Kentucky will allow expansion in the solid manufactured housing states of Michigan, Indiana, and Ohio.

- Material cost reductions, achieved through process improvement, component standardization, and partnership with the company's suppliers, remain a key priority with Clayton Homes. All plants operate with "just in time" inventory management, resulting in an average inventory turn of 26 times in 1999. The company's strong national contract purchasing program with key suppliers (such as GE, Owens Corning, Moen, Weyerhaeuser, Georgia Pacific, Congoleum, and Carriage Carpets to name a few) ensures competitive pricing, unmatched quality, and reliability in every Clayton Home.

- In manufacturing, Clayton's direct customer is the retailer. The company serves 1,052 retailers—671 independent, 306 company-owned sales centers, and 75 company-owned communities—in 31 states.

- The Community group capitalizes on every aspect of profitable vertical integration. Residents may choose a quality home from the company's Manufacturing group, select an attractive home site in the community, and secure their mortgage and insurance from the Clayton Financial Services group.

In 1999, Communities expanded to 75, with a total of 19,708 home sites. The company grew by opening new communities, expanding current ones, and acquiring existing properties. Ground was broken and sales offices opened on two new properties in 1999. Creston Ridge in San Diego, Texas opened in January, with 129 sites available and land for 260 sites. The Stables in Sevierville, Tennessee held its grand opening in June, with 68 sites currently being developed and the potential for 486 total sites. Both communities, as with other Clayton-developed properties, will provide residents with desirable amenities such as pools, walking trails, and a multipurpose clubhouse.

- In 1999, Clayton's Financial Services segment achieved record results in loan originations, servicing, securitizations, and net written insurance premiums. The group originated and secured more than $1 billion in mortgages, raising the total serviced portfolio to $3.47 billion—up 19 percent for the year. The increase in loan volume was achieved while further reducing over-30-day delinquency to 1.84 percent, well below industry norms. Net insurance premiums written totaled a record $61 million for the year—up 19 percent.

- In fiscal 2000, Clayton Homes purchased $95 million in manufactured housing loans originated by Chase Bank. The company expects the transaction to bolster earnings in fiscal 2001, which began July 1, 2000. "This portfolio represents another strategic purchase for Clayton Homes," said Kevin Clayton, President and CEO. "The loans overlay well with our current retail and marketing activities. The company will earn three levels of profit from the transaction, as the loans will be insured, re-sold, and servicing retained."

- Clayton's finance subsidiary, Vanderbilt Mortgage & Finance, enjoys a sterling reputation. As one competitor commented, "It's a class act." Clayton's retail managers—unlike most salespeople—make money not simply by selling homes but by sharing in the profit and losses on the associated loans. If a loan goes bad, the sales manager "eats 40 percent to 50 percent of the loss," according to a company spokesman.

Total assets: $1,417 million
Current ratio: 6.40
Common shares outstanding: 140 million
Return on 1999 shareholders' equity: 16.9%

		1999	1998	1997	1996	1995	1994	1993	1992
Revenues (millions)		1344	1128	1022	929	758	628	476	371
Net income (millions)		155	138	120	107	87	69	54	39
Earnings per share		1.06	.92	.80	.72	.59	.47	.37	.29
Dividends per share		.06	.06	.06	.05	.03			
Price	High	15.4	18.1	15.6	14.5	15.0	11.5	10.6	8.9
	Low	8.3	10.7	10.1	9.9	6.8	6.6	7.1	3.8

AGGRESSIVE GROWTH

The Clorox Company

1221 Broadway ❑ Oakland, California 94612 ❑ Investor contact: Steve Austenfeld (510) 271-7270 ❑ Web site: www.clorox.com ❑ Dividend reinvestment plan is available: (201) 324-1644 ❑ Fiscal year ends June 30 ❑ Listed: NYSE ❑ Ticker symbol: CLX ❑ S&P rating: A ❑ Value Line financial strength rating: A++

Over the years, the name Clorox has become synonymous with household bleach. No wonder. Since the company introduced its first pint of Clorox bleach in the 1920s, The Clorox Company has come to dominate the domestic bleach market with nearly a 70 percent share.

Today, Clorox has evolved into a diversified consumer-products company whose domestic retail products include many of the best-known brands of laundry additives, home cleaning and automotive-appearance products, cat litters, insecticides, charcoal briquets, salad dressings, sauces, and water-filtration systems.

Company Profile

In 1913, a group of Oakland businessmen founded the Electro-Alkaline Company, a forerunner of The Clorox Company. The company originally produced an industrial-strength liquid bleach. It was sold in 5-gallon crockery jugs to industrial customers in the San Francisco Bay area.

A household version of Clorox liquid bleach was developed in 1916 and subsequently was distributed in sample pint bottles. Demand for the product grew, and its distribution was gradually expanded nationally until it became the country's best-selling liquid bleach.

Clorox was a one-product company for its first 56 years, including the 11 years from 1957 through 1968 when it was operated as a division of the Procter & Gamble Company. Following its divestiture by Procter & Gamble in 1969, the company has broadened and diversified its product line and expanded geographically. Today, Clorox manufactures a wide range of products that are marketed to consumers in the United States and internationally. It is also a supplier of products to food service and institutional customers and the janitorial trades. Although the company's growth in the first few years after divestiture came largely through the acquisition of other companies and products, strong emphasis is now being given to the internal development of new products.

The great majority of the company's brands are either number one or number two in their categories. Included in Clorox products are such well-known names as Formula 409, Liquid-Plumr, Pine-Sol, Soft Scrub, S.O.S., Tilex, Armor All, Kingsford charcoal, Match Light, Black Flag insecticides, Fresh Step cat litter, Hidden Valley salad dressing, and Kitchen Bouquet.

Clorox's Professional Products unit is focused on extending many of the company's successful retail equities in cleaning and food products to new channels of distribution, such as institutional and professional markets and the food-service industry.

Internationally, Clorox markets laundry additives, home cleaning products, and insecticides, primarily in developing countries. What's more, Clorox is investing heavily to expand this part of its business. Overall, Clorox products are sold in more than 70 countries and are manufactured in 35 plants at locations in the United States, Puerto Rico, and abroad.

Shortcomings to Bear in Mind

- Because of its consistent success, Clorox often sells at a high multiple.

Reasons to Buy

- You might wonder why anyone would want to be the nation's number one maker of cat litter. Apparently, Clorox likes the idea. The CEO of the company says he wants Clorox to be number two or better in every category in which it competes. In fiscal 1999, Clorox acquired the First Brands Corporation, a firm that makes Glad trash bags, STP car care products, as well as three kinds of cat litter. First Brands gave Clorox a leading share of the market in all three categories. Not least, the cat litter business has very high margins.

The deal added STP to the company's Armor All, the car protectant maker it bought a year earlier. Not only is Clorox now number one in car care products, but it now has a 30 percent stake in plastic bags and plastic wrap with the addition of the Glad lines.

- During fiscal 1999, Clorox advanced from $2.7 billion in sales, with about 6,600 employees, to a $4 billion company with nearly 11,000 employees. Today, the company's products are sold in 110 countries.

What's more, Clorox added four market-leading consumer brands to its portfolio:

- The Glad line of plastic wrap, food storage bags and containers, and trash bags. Glad is the number one brand in this overall category and also leads three key categories: trash bags, plastic wrap, and the disposable container category that Glad created with it innovative GladWare line. Importantly, Glad products are sold in the same stores to the same consumers who buy many other Clorox products. Like other leading CLX brands, Glad products are frequently purchased items that provide important consumer benefits and that lend themselves to continual product and packaging improvements and innovations—things the company does well. Perhaps most critically, Glad is a strong and healthy brand equity that enjoys high consumer awareness and loyalty.

- The STP line of automotive additives. Since the brand was introduced 45 years ago, STP has been trusted by American car owners to prolong and improve their vehicles' performance. It is a strong number one brand with great potential for international expansion. STP products are sold through the same specialty auto and mass distribution channels as the company's Armor All line. Plus, Clorox can combine certain manufacturing processes for the two lines, which provides leverage.

- Scoop Away and Jonny Cat litter brands. Scoop Away created and remains a top brand in the scoopable cat litter segment. Jonny Cat is a well-known brand of regular cat litter that enjoys especially strong regional market shares. Together with the company's Fresh Step cat litter, these brands help consolidate Clorox's number one position in this fast-growing category.

- In a market that Clorox created and which has attracted a host of competitors, the company's Brita water filtration systems business completed another year of record shipments and profits, as well as clear category leadership.

  Growth in this business was propelled by continued household penetration by Brita systems, coupled with strong growth in the sales of replacement filters. What's more, distribution gains have seen a 40 percent increase in the number of stores offering Brita products.

- Clorox continues to expand where the company sees an opportunity to enter a market with a competitive advantage. Once Clorox acquires a business, it expands it by modernizing plants. What's more, the company builds mass through line extensions and strategic acquisitions.

  Clorox also upgrades packaging and leverages marketing expertise gained in the United States by putting it to use in a new country with the company's just-acquired brands. In sum, that's how Clorox built leadership positions in the majority of its worldwide markets.

For example, in Argentina, the company's liquid bleach brand, Ayudin, holds a 70 percent share in the market. Arco Iris and Ayudin Ropa Color, Clorox's brands of color-safe bleach, dominate the competition. The company's two brands in the stain-remover category, Arco Iris and Trenet, have a combined share of over 90 percent, and the company's sponge business, Mortimer, holds nearly one-half of the market.

There are similar success stories in Brazil, Chile, the Republic of Korea, and Malaysia. And, in close step with the company's domestic business, the bulk of its international sales volume is represented by Clorox Company brands that are either number one or two in their respective categories. Today, the company's international business (including exports) accounts for 16 percent of sales, up from 4 percent a few years ago.

- Effective advertising, coupled with expanded distribution into warehouse club stores such as Sam's Club and Costco, catapulted shipment of the full-calorie bottled Hidden Valley dressings and the K. C. Masterpiece barbecue sauces to record levels despite intense competition. Four new flavors of bottled dressings introduced in 1998 also helped volume and sales.

- Clorox's limited international presence is shielding it from economic volatility abroad. Compared with some close competitors, the company derives only a modest volume of sales from foreign operations (about 18 percent in 1999).

- New products and acquisitions have been drivers of growth for CLX. Fiscal 1999 saw a record pace of new product introductions, with 85 new products. Of these new products, 25 were introduced in the United States, including Clorox Advantage liquid bleach, Clorox FreshCare fabric refresher, Fresh Mist Tilex Fresh Shower daily shower cleaner, and Brita faucet-mounted water filters.

Total assets: $4,132 million
Current ratio: .88
Common shares outstanding: 236 million
Return on 1999 shareholders' equity: 24.9%

	1999	1998	1997	1996	1995	1994	1993	1992
Revenues (millions)	4003	2741	2533	2218	1984	1837	1634	1717
Net income (millions)	391	298	249	222	201	180	168	144
Earnings per share	1.63	1.41	1.21	1.07	.95	.84	.77	.66
Dividends per share	.72	.64	.58	.53	.48	.47	.43	.40
Price　High	66.5	58.8	40.2	27.6	19.8	14.9	13.8	13.0
Low	37.5	37.2	24.3	17.5	13.8	11.8	11.0	9.9

CONSERVATIVE GROWTH

The Coca-Cola Company

One Coca-Cola Plaza ❑ P. O. Drawer 1734 ❑ Atlanta, Georgia 30301 ❑ Investor contact: John M. Mongelli (404) 676-1167 ❑ Dividend reinvestment plan is available: (888) 265-3747 ❑ Web site: www.thecoca-colacompany.com ❑ Listed: NYSE ❑ Ticker symbol: KO ❑ S&P rating: A+ ❑ Value Line financial strength rating: A++

Coca-Cola signed a multiyear pact with America Online in May of 2000 to develop online and offline marketing programs, marking Coca-Cola's first worldwide Internet marketing initiative. Under the arrangement, Coca-Cola will make America Online's interactive services and products available to consumers through its distribution channels worldwide, including advertising, merchandising, packaging, and in-store promotions.

For its part, America Online will market Coca-Cola brands online across its interactive brands such as AOL, CompuServe and Netscape.

Company Profile

The Coca-Cola Company is the world's largest producer and distributor of soft-drink syrups and concentrates. Company products are sold through bottlers, fountain wholesalers, and distributors in nearly 200 countries. The company's products represent about 48 percent of total soft-drink unit case volume consumer worldwide. (A unit case is equal to 24 eight-ounce servings.)

Trademark Coca-Cola accounts for about 68 percent of the company's worldwide gallon shipments of beverage products (excluding those distributed by The Minute Maid Company).

The company's allied brands account for the remaining 32 percent of gallon sales. These brands are: Sprite, diet Sprite, TAB, Fanta, Fresca, Mr Pibb, Hi-C, Mello Yello, Barq's, POWERaDE, Fruitopia, and specialty overseas brands.

The company's operations are managed in five operating groups and The Minute Maid Company. Excluding those products distributed by The Minute Maid Company, the company's unit case volume by region is as follows: North America Group, 31 percent; Latin America Group, 25 percent; Greater Europe Group, 21 percent; Middle and Far East Group, 19 percent; and Africa Group, 4 percent.

The Minute Maid Company, headquartered in Houston, Texas, is the world's largest marketer of juice and juice-drink products. Major products of The Minute Maid Company include the following:

• Minute Maid chilled ready-to-serve and frozen concentrated citrus and variety juices, lemonades, and fruit punches.

• Hi-C brand ready-to-serve fruit drinks.

• Bright & Early breakfast beverages.

• Bacardi tropical fruit mixes.

Shortcomings to Bear in Mind

- In many parts of the world, consumers have become pickier, more penny-wise, or a little more nationalistic, and they are spending more of their money on local drinks whose flavors or brand names are not part of the Coca-Cola lineup. The company took an $813 million charge for the costs of carrying poorly performing assets in Russia and the Baltics, and more charges are expected for similar investments in India.

- In late 1999, the company's worldwide bottler system faltered as regional economies fell apart, and many bottlers fumed that Coke was greedily profiting at their expense by raising concentrate prices.

- Carbonated soft-drink sales volume slowed dramatically in 1999, and analysts blamed the nearly flat performance on rising prices and the popularity of alternative beverages like bottled water. Colas, led by Coca-Cola Classic and Pepsi-Cola, continued to account for the majority of sales in the $58 billion domestic cola market. However, they lost market share to Mountain Dew, Sprite, and Dr Pepper. Finally, sales volume rose 0.5 percent in 1999, according to the annual *Beverage Digest*/Maxwell report. That was well below the 3 percent growth in 1998 and was the slowest in at least 15 years, said *Beverage Digest* publisher John Sicher.

  Coca-Cola, the world's biggest soda maker, controlled 44.1 percent of the domestic market in 1999, a drop of 0.4 percent from a year earlier. PepsiCo's market share held steady at 31.4 percent. Coca-Cola Classic remained the number one brand, with a 20.3 percent market share, despite a share decline of 0.3 points. Pepsi-Cola ranked second, declining 0.4 points, to a 13.8 percent share.

- Coca-Cola's plans to buy Orangina faded in April of 1999 when France's highest administrative court refused to overturn a government ruling that had blocked the sale. While Coca-Cola officials sought to put a positive spin on the decision, it was clearly a setback for the company. The transaction dated back to December of 1997 when Coca-Cola announced that it would buy Orangina, a highly popular orange-flavored drink owned by Pernod Richard SA, for $844 million. The French disappointment was the second ruling against Coke's strategy of buying popular international brands.

  On a more positive note, Coke had better luck with Cadbury Schweppes. For $1.1 billion, the company acquired this company's brands sold all over the world, except in the United States. This transaction added far more volume to the Coca-Cola system than the Orangina deal would have. Orangina would have represented about 55 million cases a year; the Cadbury purchase accounts for about 400 million.

Reasons to Buy

- Although the shares of Coca-Cola have lagged of late, they have performed better than analysts might have expected. One reason that Coke has such stamina may be its ownership base. Much of the stock is in the hands of people who either view it as sacrilege to sell or who can't sell. For instance, long-term institutional owners like Berkshire Hathaway, SunTrust, and Fayez Sarofim together own 16 percent of the stock. Then there are S&P 500 index funds, which must own Coke as part of the index and which own 10 percent of the stock. Add to that loyal individuals (that own about 40 percent of the stock), many of whom made a fortune from the company over the years. Add these up and you aren't left with many investors who are eager to unload the shares.

- At Coca-Cola, Robert C. Goizueta remains a legend. His vision transformed

Coke into a global power. After his death, his successor, M. Douglas Ivester, could not make up for a stretch of falling profits and personal blunders even though his credentials were impressive.

Following his resignation after a brief, two-year tour of duty, he was followed on December 6, 1999 by Douglas N. Daft, a cheerful, unassuming Australian who spent 30 years rising through the ranks.

Essentially a stranger in Atlanta because of his overseas postings and constant travel, Mr. Daft wasted no time in putting his stamp on the beleaguered giant. For one thing, Mr. Daft (that's really his name!) announced a plan to shift decision making at the company down to the local level—a plan that included $1.6 billion in charges and the layoff of 6,000 employees—nearly half at Coke headquarters in Atlanta. This reduction in personnel amounted to 20 percent of the company's 30,000 employees throughout the world and was the biggest mass firing in Coke's history.

To improve operations abroad, Mr. Daft said the company would embrace local brands and flavors more than it had in the past. Trying to get everyone to switch to Coke doesn't always work, says the new CEO. The light first came on for Mr. Daft, age 57, when he was assigned to Indonesia in the early Seventies. "I launched Coke and pushed Coke for three years," he recalled. "Then, I launched Fanta," an orange soda, "and the business just tripled and quadrupled." The lesson? "Brand Coke is the core of our company; then you add on to that the volume that you generate by competing in a wider market."

Now that he is Coke's CEO, Mr. Daft says that the company will expand its portfolio of 180 brands and diversify into noncarbonated drinks such as teas and waters, which have become the fastest-growing part of the beverage industry.

Mr. Daft also said that Coke will be doing more to develop new brands in its own laboratories, rather than through acquisitions, as has been its practice in the past.

Mr. Daft is also decentralizing management. To get closer to local markets, he is reassigning hundreds of headquarters people to far-flung outposts. And, rolling back the over-ambitious expansion plans of Mr. Ivester, he is biting the bullet on poorly performing ventures in the Baltics and Japan—which will cost $813 million in writedowns.

The speed at which Coke's new CEO is moving to bring change to Coke is winning him plaudits from observers, analysts, and influential investors in the company. The changes, those around him say, have been needed for years and are only the beginning. "I'm very impressed thus far not only with the quality of the management shifts, but the implications they have for the organization and the message it sends," said one analyst.

■ Coca-Cola popped a new advertising push in early 2000 that will draw on traditional marketing successes as it seeks to reverse a decade of sluggish sales for its flagship Coca-Cola Classic brand. A year and a half in the making, the long-awaited campaign dumped the seven-year-old "Always" tagline for "Enjoy"—a more amiable invitation to consumers to the "total sensory experience" of drinking Coke, said a management spokesman.

"Enjoy" is being recycled after serving as Coke's tagline during several stints over the decades. The ad campaign, with work being developed by six agencies, was introduced January 12, 2000. The new push depicts "a wide range of emotions" and "will show people connecting," said Frank Bifulco, Jr., senior vice president of marketing for Coke's domestic business.

Total assets: $21,623 million
Current ratio: .75
Common shares outstanding: 2,469 million
Return on 1999 shareholders' equity: 27.1%

	1999	1998	1997	1996	1995	1994	1993	1992
Revenues (millions)	19805	18813	18868	18546	18018	16172	13967	13074
Net income (millions)	2431	3533	4130	3492	2986	2554	2188	1884
Earnings per share	.98	1.42	1.64	1.40	1.19	.99	.84	.72
Dividends per share	.64	.60	.56	.50	.44	.39	.34	.28
Price High	70.9	88.9	72.6	54.3	40.2	26.7	22.5	22.7
Low	47.3	53.6	50.0	36.1	24.4	19.4	18.8	17.8

CONSERVATIVE GROWTH

Colgate-Palmolive Company

300 Park Avenue ⊐ New York, New York 10022-7499 ⊐ Investor contact: Kathya R. Guerra (212) 310-3312 ⊐ Dividend reinvestment plan is available: (800) 756-8700 ⊐ Web site: www.colgate.com ⊐ Listed: NYSE ⊐ Ticker symbol: CL ⊐ S&P rating: A- ⊐ Value Line financial strength rating: A++

Colgate's share of the dishwashing market has now climbed to an all-time high of over 40 percent, enhanced by the success of new Palmolive Spring Sensations, a line with sensorial fragrances and vibrant colors.

What's more, strong growth in Personal Care resulted from new Speed Stick clear antiperspirant and Irish Spring soap with aloe, which has a proprietary moisture retention formula. Colgate also increased its market shares in Canada, attaining record shares in dishwashing liquids and toothpaste, along with newly attained leadership positions in deodorants and liquid hand soaps.

Company Profile

Colgate-Palmolive is a leading global consumer products company, marketing its products in 213 countries and territories under such internationally recognized brand names as Colgate toothpaste and brushes, Palmolive, Mennen Speed Stick deodorants, Ajax, Murphy Oil Soap, Fab, and Soupline/Suavitel, as well as Hill's Science Diet and Hill's Prescription Diet.

With two-thirds of its sales and earnings coming from abroad, Colgate is making its greatest gains in overseas markets.

Travelers, for instance, can find Colgate brands in a host of countries:

● They'll find Total toothpaste, with its proprietary antibacterial formula that fights plaque, tarter, and cavities, in more than 70 countries.

● The Care brand of baby products is popular in Asia.

● Colgate Plax makes Colgate number one in mouth rinse outside the United States.

● The Colgate Zig Zag toothbrush, popular in all major world regions outside the United States, helps make Colgate the number one toothbrush company in the world.

● Axion is an economical dishwashing paste popular in Asia, Africa, and Latin America.

Oral Care

Colgate is the global leader in Oral Care, and number one worldwide in toothpaste and toothbrushes. Colgate's Oral Care products include toothbrushes, toothpaste, mouth rinses, and dental floss, as well as pharmaceutical products for dentists and other oral health professionals.

Success in the realm of Oral Care is due in large measure to Colgate's 200 Oral

Care scientists and dentists. Recognized worldwide for leadership in their field, these professionals enable Colgate to provide consumers with advanced Oral Care technologies and products—from patented plaque-fighting toothpaste and mouthrinse formulas to toothbrushes that provide precise cleaning action.

Personal Care

Colgate leads many segments of the Personal Care market, including some of the fastest growing. For instance, Colgate is the market leader in liquid soaps in the United States and globally. It is number two in baby care products and underarm protection worldwide. Strong brands include:

> Irish Spring
> Softsoap
> Palmolive—one of the world's most popular Personal Care names, available as a soap and, in many countries, shampoo and conditioner.
> Colgate also manufactures Mennen deodorants, baby care products, and men's toiletries.

Strong research and development capabilities enable Colgate to support these and other brands with technologically sophisticated products for consumers' Personal Care needs.

Household and Fabric Care

Ajax, Palmolive, and Murphy's Oil Soap are three of the household names through which Colgate markets its wide variety of household cleaning and laundry products. These products include powder and liquid soaps for use in the sink and dishwasher; powder and liquid laundry detergents, including convenient super-concentrates and refills, and the highly regarded Murphy's Oil Soap, North America's leading wood cleaner.

Pet Nutrition

Colgate, through its Hills Pet Nutrition subsidiary, is the world's leader in specialty pet food. Hills markets its pet foods primarily under two well-established brands: Science Diet, which is sold by authorized pet supply retailers, breeders and veterinary hospitals, enables pet owners to provide their dog or cat a nutritionally balanced diet every day.

Prescription Diet, available only through veterinarians, is specially formulated for dogs and cats with disease conditions.

Shortcomings to Bear in Mind

- This stock has two concerns that should be considered: Because of Colgate's excellent record, the stock sells for a high P/E. Secondly, the balance sheet doesn't quite suit me. Common equity is below 50 percent of capitalization.

Reasons to Buy

- In 1999, the company's global market shares increased across key categories, including toothpaste, toothbrushes, shower gels, liquid hand soaps, underarm protection, all-purpose cleaners, bleach, fabric softeners, and pet nutrition. Sales from new products introduced during the past five years contributed over $3.2 billion, or 35 percent of 1999 total sales. Colgate's market-leading positions are being driven by such innovative new products as Colgate Total Fresh Stripe toothpaste, Ajax Fiesta de Flores fragrance cleaner, the Palmolive Botanicals line of shampoo, shower gel, and translucent soap, Speed Stick clear antiperspirant, the Colgate Actibrush battery-powered toothbrush, Soupline Cashmere fabric softener, and Hill's Science Diet Hairball Control for cats.

- In 1999, the company's profitability expanded sharply. Gross margin increased by 150 basis points to 53.7

percent. The operating profit margin, moreover, increased by 130 basis points to 17.2 percent. Colgate's continuing strategy to take costs out of the supply chain helped increase the return on capital to 22.8 percent, up from 20.4 percent in 1998. Cash flow from operations increased to a record $1.3 billion.

- In 1999, Colgate's domestic operation outpaced the market growth of its major categories. Notably, Colgate strengthened its number one position in toothpaste, with the success of Colgate Total Fresh Stripe toothpaste, and added incremental toothbrush share with the premium flexible-head Colgate Navigator toothbrush. Continuing its leadership strategy in Oral Care, the company announced in early 2000 the launch of new Colgate Sensitive Maximum Strength Toothpaste and Toothbrush. Colgate Sensitive Maximum Strength Toothpaste comes in a dual-chamber tube and has a patented, clinically superior formula for reducing sensitivity.

- Colgate entered 1999 just having announced a promising new toothpaste for the large domestic market. Total Fresh Stripe, a striped gel, is the second variant of the Colgate Total line to receive U.S. Food and Drug Administration approval—the only toothpaste cleared to make claims for gingivitis and plaque reduction. Colgate Total was one of *Business Week's* "Best New Products of 1998."

Abdul Gaffar, a Ph.D. chemist who holds more than 100 patents, was part of a Colgate team of 200 scientists that spent 10 years and some $35 million developing Total. Their main challenge: how to embed Triclosan, a highly soluble, broad-spectrum antibiotic used in soaps and deodorants to fight bacteria, into a mint-flavored paste and then make sure it didn't get immediately washed away. Working with dental schools in the United States and Europe, this research team developed polymers capable of binding Triclosan to teeth and gums for 14 hours, thus providing round-the-clock treatment with two daily brushings. Total also contains fluoride to prevent cavities.

Diseases like gingivitis, which cause gums to bleed from a buildup of plaque and tartar, cost some $40 billion per year around the world to treat, estimates Dr. Abdul Gaffar, vice president for advanced technology. Colgate says its treat-as-you-brush strategy is cheaper.

- Adding to region-specific initiatives is the company's vast consumer intelligence. Colgate interviews over 500,000 consumers in more than 30 countries annually to learn more about their habits and usage of the company's product.

- Colgate's global reach lets the company conduct consumer research in countries with diverse economies and cultures to create product ideas with global appeal. The new product development process begins with the company's Global Technology and Business Development groups analyzing consumer insights from various countries to create products that can be sold in the greatest possible number of countries. Creating "universal" products saves time and money by maximizing the return on R&D, manufacturing, and purchasing. To assure the widest possible global appeal, potential new products are test-marketed in lead countries that represent both developing and mature economies.

- A global leader in pet nutrition, Hill's continues to strengthen its ties to veterinarians. Record levels of advertising supported a U.S. campaign for Science Diet, themed, "What Vets Feed Their Pets." New Science Diet products include dry varieties for cats, new canned varieties in chunk and gravy form for cats, and dry varieties for dogs.

Total assets: $ 7,423 million
Current ratio: 1.02
Common shares outstanding: 583 million
Return on 1999 shareholders' equity: 51.1%

	1999	1998	1997	1996	1995	1994	1993	1992
Revenues (millions)	9118	8972	9057	8749	8358	7588	7141	7007
Net income (millions)	937	849	740	635	541	580	548	477
Earnings per share	1.47	1.31	1.14	1.05	.90	.96	.85	.73
Dividends per share	.63	.55	.53	.47	.44	.39	.34	.29
Price High	58.9	49.4	39.3	24.1	19.3	16.3	16.8	15.2
Low	36.6	32.5	22.5	17.2	14.5	12.4	11.7	11.3

AGGRESSIVE GROWTH

Costco Wholesale Corporation

999 Lake Drive □ Issaquah, Washington 98027 □ Investor contact: Richard A. Galanti (425) 313-8203 □ Dividend reinvestment plan is not available □ Web site: www.costco.com □ Listed: Nasdaq □ Fiscal year ends Sunday nearest August 31 □ Ticker symbol: COST □ S&P rating: B- □ Value Line financial strength rating: B++

Costco, the number one domestic warehouse-club chain, knows when a deal is too good to pass up. That's why the company is buying merchandise from Internet retailers. According to Richard Galanti, the firm's chief financial officer, "So many of these e-commerce companies, quite frankly, are using incredible valuations to sell stuff at ridiculous prices. We actually buy some things below cost from some of them."

Meanwhile, Costco has been quietly building up its own Web sales operation and expects to do $60 million of sales online during the 2000 fiscal year. Initially, however, the venture will not be profitable, with a loss of $4 million or so likely during the first year on the Internet.

According to management, at end of calendar 1999 Costco had over one million registered with its Web site www.costco.com. Moreover, that number exceeded two million by the spring of 2000. Finally, Costco's special arrangement with Microsoft for unlimited Internet access via MSN/Costco at a 40 percent discount (currently $11.99 a month paid in three-month intervals) affords Costco "the unique position as a retailer to offer a

high-speed Internet portal site at a great savings to our members," according to Mr. Sinegal. "Costco is committed to capturing the potential of this business, and we will not let this potential bypass us."

Company Profile

Costco is the largest wholesale club operator in the United States (ahead of Wal-Mart's Sam's Club). Costco operates a chain of membership warehouses that sell high quality, nationally branded and selected private label merchandise at low prices to businesses purchasing for commercial use, personal use, or resale. The company also sells to individuals who are members of selected employee groups.

Costco's business is based on achieving high sales volumes and rapid inventory turnover by offering a limited assortment of merchandise in a wide variety of product categories at very competitive prices.

As of December 1999, the company operated a chain of 302 warehouses in 27 states (230 locations), nine Canadian provinces (59 locations), the United Kingdom (seven locations, through a 60-percent-owned subsidiary), Korea (three locations), Taiwan (two locations, through a 55-percent-owned subsidiary), and Japan (one location). The company also operates 17 warehouses in Mexico through a 50-percent joint venture partner.

Costco units offer discount prices on nearly 4,000 products, ranging from alcoholic beverages and computer software to pharmaceuticals, meat, vegetables, books, clothing, and tires. Food and sundries account for 60 percent of sales. Certain club memberships also offer products and services, such as car and home insurance, mortgage services, and small-business loans.

Fiscal 1999 (ended August 29, 1999) was a banner year for Costco in terms of revenues and earnings. The company was able to achieve sales of $27 billion, a 13 percent increase over the prior year. More importantly, warehouses that were open for more than 12 months realized a comparable sales growth rate of 10 percent.

Jeff Brotman, Costco's chairman of the board, believes that this is an accurate indication of the health of its business, "considering that our average sales per warehouse exceeded $94 million per unit for the 292 locations open worldwide in 1999, including $101 million per unit for the 221 warehouses in the United States."

A typical warehouse format averages about 127,000 square feet. Floor plans are designed for economy and efficiency in the use of selling space, in the handling of merchandise, and in the control of inventory.

Merchandise is generally stored on racks above the sales floor and is displayed on pallets containing large quantities of each item, reducing labor required for handling and stocking.

Specific items in each product line are limited to fast-selling models, sizes, and colors. Costco carries only an average of about 3,500 to 4,500 stock keeping units (SKUs) per warehouse. Typically, a discount retailer or supermarket stocks 40,000 to 60,000 SKUs. Many products are offered for sale in case, carton, or multiple-pack quantities only.

Low prices on a limited selection of national brand merchandise and selected private-label products in a wide range of merchandise categories produce high sales volume and rapid inventory turnover. Rapid inventory turnover, combined with operating efficiencies achieved by volume purchasing in a no-frills self-service warehouse facility, enables the company to operate profitably at significantly lower gross margins than traditional retailers, discounters, or supermarkets.

The company buys virtually all of its merchandise from manufacturers for shipment either directly to the warehouse clubs or to a consolidation point (depot) where shipments are combined so as to minimize freight and handling costs.

Shortcomings to Bear in Mind

- The Standard & Poor's financial strength rating is a rather low B-. For its part, Value Line gives the company a B++ rating.
- The wholesale club industry could be vulnerable to an economic slowdown, even though it sells basics, because of its business-membership exposure. What's more, the company's competition has stepped up its presence and is modeling itself more closely to the Costco strategy.
- Insiders, such as officer and board members, have been selling shares of Costco for the past year or so.

Reasons to Buy

- Several factors contributed to the company's recent strong showing. Among them are new store openings and improved margins. What's more, customer traffic and frequency of visits have been climbing thanks to Costco's continued expansion of its ancillary businesses such as gas stations, food courts, hot dog stands, copy centers, print shops, pharmacies, photo labs, and fresh food departments. In all, sales generated by ancillary businesses expanded by close to 36 percent in 1999.

- Costco has a strong balance sheet, with 79 percent of its capitalization in common equity.
- As the new millennium got underway, Costco's CEO, Jim Sinegal, said, "We continue to show robust sales increases in the new markets of Atlanta and Detroit. And our newly opened Chicago warehouses are exceeding our sales expectations. The results in these three markets have encouraged us to open additional units in each of these communities." Mr. Sinegal also pointed out that the company is "proceeding with plans to enter new markets in Texas, Ohio, Pennsylvania, and Missouri during calendar 2000." The company allocated about $1 billion for capital spending for fiscal 2000.
- Costco's gross margins continue to be strong, increasing from 10.28 percent of sales in fiscal 1998 to 10.40 percent in 1999. Mr. Sinegal says that the company's "gross margins have now improved for six consecutive years, despite the fact that we have consistently lowered the prices of our merchandise during the same period. This is

the result of our improved purchasing, performance in shrink control by our merchants and operators."

- What's more, Costco's operating expenses declined as a percent of sales from 8.69 percent in fiscal 1998, to 8.67 percent in the following year. "This is particularly gratifying," says Mr. Sinegal, "after considering the added burden of entering four new markets; opening new regional offices in the Midwest and development expenses for the Executive Membership Program and launch of the American Express Co-Branded Card Program."
- Late in fiscal 1999, Costco announced a major alliance with American Express Company whereby Costco would immediately begin accepting American Express cards in all domestic Costco locations. The company is convinced that American Express "has similar customer philosophies to Costco; a great degree of member/customer loyalty; and overall, an upscale consumer and small business focus. We believe that the card acceptance and co-branded card issuance are the first of many unique and strategic business opportunities that will benefit both Costco and American Express, along with the millions of members and cardholders of our two companies."

Total assets: $7,505 million
Current ratio: 1.16
Common shares outstanding: 442 million
Return on 1999 shareholders' equity: 16.%

	1999	1998	1997	1996	1995	1994	1993	1992
Revenues (millions)	27456	24269	21874	19566	18247	16481	15498	6621
Net income (millions)	397.3	459.8	350.9	248.8	217.2	190.9	223.2	113.3
Earnings per share	1.18	1.02	.82	.61	.53	.44	.50	.47
Dividends per share	Nil							
Price High	46.9	38.1	22.6	13.0	9.8	10.8	12.7	21.4
Low	32.7	20.7	11.9	7.3	6.0	6.3	7.5	10.2

Delphi Automotive Systems Corporation

5725 Delphi Drive ❒ Troy, Michigan 48098-2815 ❒ Investor contact: (877) SEEK-DPH ❒ Direct Dividend reinvestment plan is available: (800) 818-6599 ❒ Web site: www.delphiauto.com ❒ Listed: NYSE ❒ Ticker symbol: DPH ❒ S&P rating: Not rated ❒ Value Line financial strength rating: B

In 2000, Delphi concluded a significant deal with Ericsson Mobile Communications to bring "plug and play" telematics into the vehicle. Plug and play technology makes it possible to cycle in new iterations of computers, phones, and entertainment options as older units grow obsolete.

Electronics will pass through several generations during the typical 10-year life of an automobile. Plug and play makes it possible to add new products just by plugging them into existing interfaces. This deal should strengthen Delphi's market-leading position in telematics.

Company Profile

Delphi Automotive Systems is the world's largest and most diversified supplier of components, integrated systems, and modules to the automotive industry. Delphi's primary mission is providing products directly to automotive manufacturers. A wholly owned subsidiary of General Motors prior to February 1999, Delphi was spun off to GM shareholders in May 1999.

Delphi delivers the broadest range of high-technology solutions worldwide for its customers in the areas of safety, performance, comfort, and aesthetics. It is through the company's approach to new technology and product development that Delphi has established its leadership position while maintaining the tradition of individual product excellence. Today, Delphi's products are organized into three synergistic business sectors, including an aftermarket division (aftermarket refers to products sold for repair and replacement rather than for cars being manufactured):

Electronics and Mobile Communications Sector

As Delphi's fastest-growing sector, Electronics & Mobile Communication designs products to enhance safety, comfort, and security, as well as bring entertainment, information, and connectivity to the vehicle.

Mobile multimedia products include telematics, such as wireless phones, but also the OnStar communications system now being expanded beyond Cadillacs into the entire GM fleet. Equally important are rear seat entertainment systems, including video consoles and DVD players. GM says that about half of the 50 million vehicles produced in 2005 will have significant mobile media content, perhaps $1,000 per vehicle. Delphi believes it has a significant "first mover" advantage, thanks to existing technologies (such as OnStar and Delco) as well as its ability to do business throughout the world.

Safety, Thermal, and Electrical Architecture Sector

This sector offers a comprehensive portfolio of vehicle interior, safety, and occupant-protection products; heating and cooling systems to manage vehicle compartment temperatures; and power and signal distribution systems for advanced electronic management of power, signal, and data communications.

The sector coordinates product development in the rapidly expanding cockpit and interior modules market. The sector's Advanced Safety Interior Systems, Gold Dot Connection Systems, and Advanced Thermal Management Systems are just a few of Delphi's high-tech products.

Among the products in this sector are the following:

To help improve safety, Delphi has developed its Advanced Safety Interior suite of products. This evolving portfolio of technologies is designed to provide protection in front, side, and rear collisions, as well as when a vehicle rolls over. Technologies include anticipatory crash, rollover, and occupant-characteristic sensing systems; head and side airbags; variable airbag inflation; adaptive seatbelt restraints; active knee bolster; adaptive force-limiting pedals; and an energy-absorbing steering column.

Gold Dot Connection Systems are flexible printed materials with shaped planar contacts that simplify high-speed, high-density data connections. The technology can be used in a wide variety of applications, including computer instrumentation and emulation, automotive, and military uses. Current applications include telecommunication applications from cellular phones to network switches and routers.

Dynamics and Propulsion Sector

This sector provides technologies for superior ride and handling performance, including advanced suspension, brake, drive line, and steering products. It also offers complete gas and diesel engine management systems to improve fuel efficiency and increase environmental responsiveness, including air and fuel systems, ignition systems, sensors, and exhaust after treatment.

This sector is rapidly transforming its product portfolio from traditional mechanical systems to electronically enhanced systems. The infusion of electronics and the implementation of lean manufacturing principles in this sector provide great opportunities to enhance the company's margins. "X-by-Wire" Systems, Energen, and MagneRide are just three product systems in this sector.

Aftermarket Division

One exciting area that should double in sales in the next five years is Delphi's

Aftermarket Operation. Launched in 1999, Delphi's newest division is enhancing its brand and sales in the aftermarket. With aftermarket activities on four continents, Delphi is set to deliver the same quality and technological expertise that go into its original equipment products under the new Delphi Aftermarket brand.

Delphi produces a wide variety of aftermarket products, which fall under five key categories: under car (such as shocks/struts), thermal systems (such as air conditioning systems), energy/engine management systems (such as alternators and batteries), electronics (such as audio and security systems), and remanufactured products.

Highlights of 1999

- The company earned a record $1.1 billion on revenue of $29.2 billion, or $1.91 per share.
- Delphi's net margin improved to 3.7 percent in 1999.
- Earnings per share grew by more than 22 percent over the prior year.
- Cash flow was strong, setting a new record of more than $2.5 billion.
- Delphi took advantage of this cash flow to execute 11 strategic acquisitions or joint ventures, the largest of which was the acquisition of Lucas Diesel Systems, which was completed in early 2000.
- During 1999, the company booked $9 billion in new business with non-GM customers to diversify Delphi's customer base.
- Bookings with General Motors were strong, more than $24 billion.

Shortcomings to Bear in Mind

- You will note in the table at the end of this article that the company's history is difficult to assess, since there is no indication what its history of sales and earnings looks like.
- The automotive business is traditionally very cyclical. You can expect years of great prosperity, as well as those when the industry sinks into the doldrums. In

this connection, the company can be vulnerable to higher interest rates since people often buy cars on the installment plan. Lenders are quick to raise their rates when interest rates are boosted, as they were in 2000.

- Competition is formidable and includes Bosch, Siemens, Motorola, and Visteon. On the other hand, analysts point out that Delphi's insider position with GM, as well as GM's growing web of relationships with global OEMs (such as Saab, Suzuki, Isuzu, Subaru, and Fiat) represent a real advantage.

Reasons to Buy

- Delphi had been awarded more than 5,000 patents in the last five years. High-tech products like Forewarn Collision Warning Systems and Gold Dot Connection Systems are now in production. What's more, products like Communiport Mobile MultiMedia Systems, Back-up-Aid, and "X-by-Wire" Systems are expected to be in production soon.
- The acquisition of Lucas Diesel Systems will add 800 technical professionals to Delphi and expand the company's product offerings in the growing diesel systems market.
- Delphi is leading the development and integration of multiple "X-by-Wire" Systems, including steer-, brake-, damp-, roll-, and throttle-by-wire. These advanced systems function through a highly organized network of wires, sensors, and actuators, replacing the traditional system's mechanical hardware connections while improving quality and performance. In the future, "X-by-Wire" technologies are expected to serve as a foundation for total collision avoidance systems.
- The Energen family of energy-management systems offers solutions to powering vehicles with lower emissions, improved fuel economy, and increased consumer features such as electric valve trains, satellite communications, onboard

computers, multi-zoned climate control systems, and electric steering.

- MagneRide represents the first vehicle application of a fluid material technically referred to as "Magnetic Rheological Fluid." This technology enables a vehicle suspension to adjust instantaneously to road conditions, giving the driver precise handling and an exceptionally good ride. It is activated by an onboard sensor that alerts a controller to apply a magnetic field. This increases the mineral oil consistency of the fluid to a peanut-butter thickness within a few milliseconds. The first systems will be appearing on passenger vehicles in 2003.
- Communiport MMM Systems make drive time more productive, convenient, and enjoyable. Center console "smart" receivers integrate radio and audio controls, navigation, cell phone access, and Internet browser functions through advanced user interfaces, such as large full-color flat-panel displays, voice recognition, and text-to-speech technology. Telematics systems combine global positioning satellite functions with cell phone modules. The result: hands-free cell phone use, direct communication with a service center for travel directions, remote vehicle lock/unlock, and emergency service. Rear-seat entertainment systems provide video games, TV, and DVD on large rear displays.
- The company believes it has become a leader in the global automotive parts industry by capitalizing on the extensive experience gained as the principal supplier of automotive parts to General Motors, the world's largest manufacturer of automotive vehicles.
- Analysts believe that Delphi will prove to be a worthwhile investment given the company's lead in technology, its ability to service global customers on all continents, its systems capabilities, and a bedrock of GM business. What's more, this business is increasingly being bolstered by non-GM customers.

Total assets: $18,350 million
Current ratio: 1.46
Common shares outstanding: 562 million
Return on 1999 shareholders' equity: 34%

	1999	1998	1997	1996	1995	1994	1993	1992
Revenues (millions)	29192	28479	*					
Net income (millions)	1083	d						
Earnings per share	1.91	d						
Dividends per share	.14							
Price High	22.3							
Low	14.0							

*Since Delphi was a recent spinoff from General Motors, the usual information is not available for this table.

AGGRESSIVE GROWTH

The Walt Disney Company

500 South Buena Vista Street ❑ Burbank, California 91521-0949 ❑ Investor contact: Winifred Markus Webb (818) 560-5758 ❑ Fiscal year ends September 30 ❑ Direct dividend reinvestment plan is available: (818) 553-7200 ❑ Web site: www.disney.com ❑ Listed: NYSE ❑ Ticker symbol: DIS ❑ S&P rating: B+ ❑ Value Line financial strength rating: A

When Disneyland Paris opened a few years ago, it was anything but magical. It had exorbitant prices, bad American-style food, rides still under construction, and groups of bewildered Europeans sheltering their children from the likes of Goofy, Donald Duck, and Pluto.

Since then, all has changed. Instead of going bankrupt, the park is now booming. In fact, Disneyland Paris (as the company now insists on calling the park commonly referred to as EuroDisney) has now overtaken the Eiffel Tower as the number one tourist spot in France, largely because of some key changes. Among them, lower prices, better food, and the addition of some adult amenities, such as wine with dinner.

Company Profile

The Walt Disney Company is a family entertainment company engaged in animated and live-action film and television production; character merchandise licensing; consumer products retailing, and book, magazine, and music publishing; television and radio broadcasting; cable television programming; and the operation of theme parks and resorts.

In 2000, the company reclassified its businesses into 5 reporting segments:

● Media Networks, which includes broadcasting and cable networks, including ABC, ESPN, and the Disney Channel. Media Networks' revenues rose 2 percent, to $1.79 billion in 1999, and operating income rose 21 percent to $369 million.

● Studio Entertainment, which includes feature-animation and live-action movie, home-video, television, and stage-play productions. Studio Entertainment's revenue declined 18 percent in 1999, to $1.64 billion, reporting an operating loss of $94 million compared with operating income of $192 million in the prior year.

● Theme Parks and Resorts. Revenue from Theme Parks and Resorts rose 2 percent in 1999, to $1.55 billion, and operating income rose 6 percent, to $318 million.

● Consumer Products, which includes merchandise licensing and Disney stores. Consumer Product's revenue declined 8 percent in 1999, to $747 million, and operating income fell 38 percent, to $102 million.

● Internet and Direct Marketing, which includes online activities outside of Infoseek and the Disney catalog. Revenue from Internet and Direct Marketing fell 18 percent, to $47 million, while the operating loss widened, to $50 million, compared with $37 million in 1998.

The Studio Entertainment segment produces live-action and animated motion pictures, television programs, and musical recordings, licenses the company's characters and other intellectual property for use in connection with merchandise and publications, and publishes books and magazines.

The company also produces and acquires live-action motion pictures that are distributed under the banners Walt Disney Pictures, Touchstone Pictures, and Hollywood Pictures. Another subsidiary, Miramax Film Corporation, acquires and produces motion pictures that are primarily distributed under the Miramax and Dimension banners.

The company has book imprints in the United States offering books for children and adults as part of the Buena Vista Publishing Group. Disney also produces several magazines, including *Family Fun, Disney Adventures*, as well as *Discover*, a general science magazine. Finally, the company produces *ESPN The Magazine* as part of a joint venture with ESPN, Inc. and The Hurst Company.

The company operates the ABC Television Network, with 224 primary affiliated stations operating under long-term agreements reaching 99.9 percent of all U.S. television households. Disney also operates the ABC Radio Networks, which reach more than 144 million domestic listeners weekly and consists of over 8,900 program affiliations on more than 4,400 radio stations. The company owns nine very high frequency (VHF) television stations, five of which are located in the top 10 markets in the United States; one ultra high frequency (UHF) television station; 15 standard AM radio stations; and 15 FM radio stations. All of the television stations are affiliated with the ABC Television Network, and most of the 30 radio stations are affiliated with the ABC Radio Networks.

Shortcomings to Bear in Mind

- The last 10 years comprised a spectacular decade for Disney. Unfortunately, in financial terms it ended on a down note, with revenues for 1999 increasing only 2 percent, to $23.4 billion; and operating income declined 21 percent, to $3.2 billion.

  There were two primary reasons for Disney's disappointing performance in 1999: downturns in Home Video and in Consumer Products. Management is now implementing plans designed to return these operations to growth. These are immense businesses, each of which would rank in the Fortune 500 and each of which is the undisputed leader in its field. Of course, given their size, they cannot be turned around on a dime. But when they do turn around, they should be fundamentally pointed in the right direction and headed for renewed long-term success.

- Even as Disney's theme parks and cable properties have been prospering, its primary profit engine, the creative content operation has been under siege. Under the creative content umbrella, which includes the company's film licensing and retail operations, the once-lucrative licensing business has been particularly sour. Sales have been off at Disney's retail stores, and earnings from home videos have been crimped by the company's decision to lengthen the time between the rereleases of titles in its fabled library of animated classics to 10 years instead of seven.

Reasons to Buy

- Because of the expansion that took place during the past decade, Disney entered the new decade as a substantially different company. It now has 7 theme parks (with 4 more in the works), 27 hotels with 36,888 rooms, two cruise ships, 728 Disney Stores, 1 broadcast network, 10 TV stations, 9 international Disney Channels, 42 radio stations, an Internet portal, 5 major Internet Web sites, and interests in 9 U.S. cable networks. Further, in the past decade, the company has enhanced its library with 17 animated films, 265 live-action films, 1,252 animated television episodes, and 6,505 live-action television episodes.

- Part of the Disney legacy is innovation. Walt Disney pioneered the first cartoon with sound, the first color cartoon, the first feature-length animated film, the first use of the multi-plane camera, the first use of stereophonic sound, first 3D cartoon, the first theme park, and the first use of audio-animatronic entertainment.

- Walt Disney, trying to revive its lagging home video sales, said in early 2000 that it would release all future titles on DVD (once known as the digital video disk) at the same time as on videocassette and would revamp the schedule for releasing its animated films into video stores. Slower sales in home video have been one factor behind Disney's slump in earnings.

  Disney has been one of the last Hollywood studios to embrace DVD. But the DVD market is growing faster than even some supporters anticipated, and Disney executives now say that the technology represents an opportunity for the company to resell its animated films to consumers in a new format.

- After Japanese developers signed a deal more than 20 years ago to build a Disney theme park north of Tokyo, they transformed a block of barren, coastal land into an important economic engine for the greater Tokyo area. That is what Hong Kong officials hope they have signed up for in their agreement with

Walt Disney Company to build the company's third overseas theme park on an island near Hong Kong's new airport. With its economy then still in the doldrums as most of Asia had recovered from the prior year's recession, Hong Kong was a city still searching for economic elixirs.

"This world-class development will mark the beginning of a new era for Hong Kong," chief executive Tung Chee Hwa told reporters after the agreement with Disney was signed in November of 1999. Government officials estimate that construction of the Hong Kong Disneyland will create 16,000 jobs and that a further 18,400 jobs will be created once the park opens in 2005. The total cost of the park and related projects is $3.6 billion, of which Disney will contribute only $316 million. For Disney, the park is the first significant beachhead in China, a nation with which it has had a long and occasionally stormy history.

- As disclosed in mid-1999, Disney merged its collection of Internet properties with Infoseek, an Internet search engine operator in which it already owned a 43 percent stake. The combined entity is called go.com. "The assets are so inherently valuable that the stock over time can't remain out of whack," said a media expert. "The value is there, even if near-term earnings aren't."

- While other parts of the Magic Kingdom have foundered, Disney's theme parks have remained a solid growth engine over the past two or three years. What's more, coming years will bring new "gates" in California, Paris, and Tokyo, as well as a new park in Hong Kong. On the other hand, Disney won't have to shell out a lot of its own cash for these ventures abroad.

Total assets: $43,679
Current ratio: 1.47
Common shares outstanding: 2,062 million
Return on 1999 shareholders' equity: 6.2%

	1999	1998	1997	1996	1995	1994	1993	1992
Revenues (millions)	23402	22976	22473	21238	12112	10055	8529	7504
Net income (millions)	1370	1871	1886	1533	1344	1110	889	817
Earnings per share	.66	.90	.92	.74	.84	.68	.54	.51
Dividends per share	.21	.20	.17	.14	.12	.10	.08	.07
Price High	38.7	42.8	33.4	25.8	21.4	16.2	16.0	15.1
Low	23.4	22.5	22.1	17.8	15.0	12.6	12.0	9.5

CONSERVATIVE GROWTH

Dover Corporation

280 Park Avenue ◻ New York, New York 10017-1292 ◻ Investor contact: John F. McNiff (212) 922-1640 ◻ Dividend reinvestment plan not available ◻ Web site: www.dovercorporation.com ◻ Listed: NYSE ◻ Ticker symbol: DOV ◻ S&P rating: A ◻ Value Line financial strength rating: A+

Dover management holds a significant ownership stake in the company. The officers and directors as a group own 7.4 percent of Dover shares.

As a general rule, the top managers pledge not to sell Dover shares obtained through options while employed at the company. In this way, the incentive of the top managers is very much in line with shareholder interests.

Company Profile

Dover Corporation is a diversified manufacturer of a wide range of proprietary products and components for industrial and commercial use. The company is comprised of more than 50 independent operating units, most of which are number one in their niche markets. Dover is an enterprise supplying value-added products and services to thousands of customers in more than 100 countries.

Typical of the company's products: printed circuit board assembly equipment, bearings, precision engineered components, pumps, aerospace products, industrial ink jet printers, garbage trucks, auto service station hydraulic lifts, industrial compressors, and grocery store refrigerator systems.

Over the past 40 years, Dover has consistently applied the same strategic themes, including decentralization, specialty markets, market leadership, customer focus, innovation, and diversity. The result has been steady growth in mature end-markets. Dover's businesses are divided into four segments:

Dover Technologies (the company's largest business, with 1999 revenues of $1,458 million) concentrates on the manufacture of sophisticated automated assembly equipment for the electronics industry, industrial printers for coding and marking, and, to a lesser degree, specialized electronic components. This segment is made up of nine companies, such as Universal Instruments Corporation, Everett Charles Technologies, Inc., and DEK Printing Machines Ltd. (UK).

These companies have a stake in such products as automated assembly equipment for printed circuit boards, spring probes, high-frequency capacitors, Dow-Key coaxial switches, ferrite transformers, and continuous inkjet printers.

Dover Industries (1999 revenues of $1,145 million) makes products for use in waste handling, bulk transport, automotive service, commercial food service, and machine tool industries. Dover Industries is comprised of 12 companies, including Heil Trailer International, Tipper Tie/Technopack, and Texas Hydraulics.

Dover Industries produces such items as liquid and dry bulk tank trailers, refuse-collection vehicles, packaging systems, automotive lifts, welding torches, car wash equipment, commercial refrigeration, benchtop machine tools, and commercial food service cooking equipment.

Dover Diversified (1999 revenues were $1,072 million) builds sophisticated assembly and production machines, heat-transfer equipment and specialized compressors, as well as sophisticated products and control systems for use in the defense, aerospace, and commercial building industries. Dover Diversified is made up of 12 companies, including Hill Phoenix, Waukesha Bearings, and A-C Compressor.

Among the products produced are heat exchangers, transformer radiators, rotary compressors, refrigerated display cases, aircraft fasteners, fluid film bearings, high-performance specialty pistons, autoclaves, and machinery for corrugated boxes.

Dover Resources (revenues in 1999 were $778 million, making this segment the company's smallest) manufactures products primarily for the automotive, fluid handling, petroleum, and chemical industries. This part of the company includes 19 operations, such as OPW Fueling Components, Midland Manufacturing, Tulsa Winch, Petroleum Equipment Group, and Duncan Parking Systems.

Some typical products include key card systems, tank monitors, air-operated double-diaphragm pumps, tank car and barge valves, tank monitoring and control systems, loading arms, toggle clamps, EOA robotic and automation components, industrial gas compressors, peristaltic pumps, filtration systems, quartz-based pressure transducers, worm and planetary gear winches, packings for gas compressors, and progressing cavity pumps.

Shortcomings to Bear in Mind

- Despite its impressive record, Dover might leave some investors cold, since few of the individual businesses have spectacular growth prospects or are extravagantly profitable. Also, analysts have difficulty crafting a compelling story about synergies or significant cost-cutting opportunities and are unable to identify a near-term, time-sensitive event that might stimulate investor interest.

Reasons to Buy

- Dover has a decentralized management structure. Corporate headquarters in New York City consists of about two dozen employees, including Thomas Reece (President and CEO) and nine other key executives. Dover's 50 operating companies are organized within four independent subsidiaries, each headed by a CEO who reports to Mr. Reece. Each of the 50 company presidents operates autonomously. Collectively, they manage over 150 factory locations and more than 140 identifiable product/market businesses. The 50 companies are responsible for their own hiring practices. Some 75 percent of these presidents have been promoted from within the organization. On average, about five presidents are replaced each year. This turnover is the result of poor performance (about one-third fall into this category), retirement (another one-third), and the rest are promoted.

■ Dover has a strong record of earnings increases. In the 1989–1999 period, earnings per share climbed from $.57 to $1.87, a compound annual growth rate of 12.6 percent. In the same span, dividends expanded from $.18 to $.44, a growth rate of 9.4 percent.

■ Dover is a strong cash-flow generator because its companies have above-average operating margins and do not require much additional capital investment. Free cash flow is used to acquire new businesses and for stock repurchases.

■ Under the management of CEO Thomas L. Reece, the company has tended to pursue more bolt-on acquisitions than standalone deals. Generally, Dover's bolt-on acquisitions are smaller and less risky, say analysts, than standalone deals. Importantly, Dover is more likely to have solid knowledge of the business and the ability to patch up problems with bolt-on deals. For these reasons, it seems likely that the bolt-on route will be pursued in the future.

According to analysts, Dover's disciplined acquisition strategy prevents the company from overpaying, and they are convinced that Dover waits patiently for the right opportunities.

Analysts believe that an acquisition should meet most of the these guidelines:

• Strong management that wants to continue to work as part of the Dover family of companies.

• Operates in a niche market.

• High market share, generally number one or two in its sector.

• Manufactures specialty products that are high quality, innovative, and value-adding.

• Makes low-risk/low-technology products that do not require major research investment to maintain market leadership.

• High profit margin.

• Low capital investment needs.

• Financially strong.

In 1999, the company's acquisition policy was typical. Dover set records for new investment by acquisition ($599 million in 18 transactions). These actions were helped by the sale of the company's elevator business early in 1999 for $1.16 billion, netting a profit (after taxes) of $524 million. The balance of these proceeds was used for share repurchases ($672 million for 18.5 million shares at an average price of $36).

The 18 acquisitions added $239 million to sales in 1999 and $44 million to operating income for the varying lengths of their partial year inclusion in Dover's results. Both numbers are expected to double in 2000.

■ In the past, investors have avoided Dover because of concern about the company's exposure to the technology market. The opposite is now the case. In essence, the cycle has bottomed and an upturn is now in full swing.

Total assets: $4,132 million
Current ratio: 1.35
Common shares outstanding: 211 million
Return on 1999 shareholders' equity: 21.7%

	1999	1998	1997	1996	1995	1994	1993	1992
Revenues (millions)	4446	3978	4548	4076	3746	3085	2484	2272
Net income (millions)	405	379	393	340	278	202	158	129
Earnings per share	1.87	1.69	1.74	1.51	1.23	.89	.69	.56
Dividends per share	.44	.40	.36	.32	.28	.25	.23	.22
Price High	47.9	39.9	36.7	27.6	20.8	16.7	15.5	11.9
Low	29.3	25.5	24.1	18.3	12.9	12.4	11.3	9.6

E. I. DuPont de Nemours & Company

1007 Market Street □ Wilmington, Delaware 19898 □ Investor contact: John W. Himes (302) 774-4994 □ Dividend reinvestment plan is available: (888) 98-DUPONT □ Web site: www.dupont.com □ Listed: NYSE □ Ticker symbol: DD □ S&P rating: B+ □ Value Line financial strength rating: A++

For the past two or three years, DuPont was enamored over the prospects for biotechnology and life sciences—a departure from its more traditional chemical business. That idea has since fizzled.

Now DuPont is going back to basics, shifting to the more traditional chemical businesses such as fibers, paints, and plastics. Cost-cutting, productivity programs, and marketing strategies are again reclaiming center stage as life sciences slides into the background, but it is still part of a longer-term strategy.

"I'm absolutely convinced this modern biology is the most powerful technology going into the 21st century," said Charles O. Holliday, DuPont's CEO. "Exactly when it's going to pay off, we can debate forever, but it's not next week."

Company Profile

Although DuPont is the largest domestic chemical company, it is much more. With annual revenues of $27 billion, DuPont links its fortunes to a host of business sectors, including agricultural chemicals, industrial and specialty chemicals, titanium dioxide, fluorocarbons, nylon, polyester, aramid and other fibers, polymer intermediates, films, resins, adhesives, electronic products, automotive paints, coatings, and pharmaceuticals.

The company operates 200 manufacturing and processing facilities in 40 countries. In its fibers segment, DuPont has a diversified mix of specialty fibers produced to serve end uses such as high-strength composites in aerospace, active sportswear, and packaging. Polymers consists of engineering polymers, elastomers, and fluoropolymers. DuPont's diversified businesses include agricultural products, coal, electronics, films, and imaging systems.

In its chemical operations, DD is primarily focused on brand-name downstream materials—rather than commodity items. They include Stainmaster carpet, Lycra, Spandex, and Dacron polyester fiber, Teflon and Silverstone nonstick systems, as well as DuPont automotive paints.

DuPont is also the largest agrochemical producer in the United States and Asia.

Shortcomings to Bear in Mind

- DuPont produces basic chemicals used in the automobile and housing industries, both of which are subject to the vagaries of the economy. In short, DuPont is currently enjoying robust earnings, but it could suffer—along with other cyclical stocks—if another recession is lurking around the corner. On a more positive note, DuPont is much less cyclical than chemical companies that rely on basic chemicals with no brand identity.

- Although DuPont has a solid growth rate, its earnings have not marched ahead every year. In the past 10 years, earnings per share dipped from the prior year five times.

- When Charles "Chad" Holiday became CEO of DuPont two or three years ago, investors hoped for a clear, new direction for the stodgy old chemicals company that would give the stock a shot in the arm. Instead, earnings have remained flat, and the stock hasn't fared well either.

Reasons to Buy

- In 2000, DuPont and Chemdex Corporation announced the formation of Industria Solutions, Inc., a new business-to-business e-commerce company that will streamline the procurement of materials for the $75 billion worldwide fluid processing market. The fluid processing market includes companies that have a broad range of industries, such as chemical, oil and gas, pulp and paper, power generation, and pharmaceuticals. Products that are used in this vertical market are complex and technical in nature, such as pipes, valves, pumps, motors, compressors, and other materials and equipment required for processing fluid for industrial use.

  Industria will leverage the assets and expertise of its founding companies to address supply chain efficiencies in this market. Chemdex brings to the new company its scalable e-commerce technology and expertise in building and operating vertical marketplaces. DuPont, one of the largest purchasers of maintenance and engineering materials in the United States, will contribute substantial buying power to Industria by shifting procurement of these materials to Industria over time.

- Achieving sustained, profitable growth in today's global marketplace requires clear competitive advantage. DuPont defines that advantage as being number one or two in both market position and technology in its chemicals and specialty businesses that are global in scope. About two-thirds of the company's businesses are already positioned as global leaders by this measure. Among them are Lycra, titanium dioxide, agricultural products, fluoroproducts, nonwovens, aramids, and photopolymers. DuPont has some others, such as polyester, finishes, and ethylene copolymers that are very strong regionally. For these, the company is pursuing creative ways to achieve a strong global position.

- Research and development is essential to DuPont's growth strategy, and the company continues to use its technological strength to add superior competitiveness. DD expects R&D to revolutionize the productivity of its manufacturing assets. A third of DuPont's revenue growth is targeted to come from new products. Research programs balance near- and long-term opportunities. The company's agricultural products pipeline includes 14 new crop protection chemicals. In pharmaceuticals, Cozaar is the fastest-growing antihypertension drug introduced in the last decade. Two other promising drugs are in the DuPont Merck research pipeline. Other development programs are focusing on the commercialization of new products and processes from a radical new catalyst system for polyolefins and a series of new technologies for polyester. Both polyesters and polyolefins are large markets that are growing rapidly and represent potential for DuPont based on new technologies.

- Fluorine chemistry is a core DuPont technology. The company buys flurospar, a naturally occurring mineral, and converts it into fluorochemicals, which can also be further upgraded into fluoropolymers. Fluoroproducts are particularly valuable because of their unique inertness, lubricity, and heat-transfer properties.

  The largest and fastest-growing segment is Teflon wire and cable jacketing polymers. They provide flame- and smoke-resistance that allows low-cost plenum installations for the rapidly growing LAN (local area network) market. Teflon, however, is more expensive than polyvinylidine polymers. On the other hand, Teflon can be high-speed, melt extruded as a coating. This eliminates the need for an overlay wrap.

- DuPont has paid dividends annually since 1904.
- A new generation of herbicides is contributing to increased earnings at DuPont's agricultural chemicals division.
- DuPont is the world market share leader in most of its businesses, including nylon, polyester, specialty fibers, titanium dioxide (which serves to make certain substances opaque, such as paint, paper, and plastic), thermoplastics, and other products.
- The company has more than 40 research and development and customer service labs in the United States and more than 35 labs in 11 other countries.
- DuPont is different from most other chemical companies in two ways: its strong brand franchises (such as Stainmaster, Lycra, and Teflon) and its ownership of Conoco, which is 40 percent of overall sales. Thus, DuPont can differentiate itself from the commodity-type chemical companies since most of the company's chemical products are downstream specialties, with 50 percent of sales abroad.

  In addition, the company's business mix has only a tiny portion that can be deemed primary ethylene derivatives, and only about 16 percent of total sales are to construction and automotive markets—with only about half of that being in the more cyclical United States.

  What's more, even within the automotive segment, the largest business is refinish paint, which is fairly insensitive to the OEM auto cycle. In elastomers, DuPont expects 20 percent growth over the next five years from its new joint venture with Dow Chemical. And within the construction market, analysts believe market share gains are being made by the new Stainmaster carpet products, as well as by Corian and Tyvek. DuPont has the number one or two positions in virtually every business it is in.

- In 2000, DuPont and the cereal maker General Mills said they would form a joint venture to develop soy foods in hopes of capitalizing on recent United States Food and Drug Administration (FDA) approval of soy health claims. The FDA said in late 1999 that domestic companies could post health claims on low-fat foods containing at least 6.25 grams of soy protein per serving. "Increased consumer awareness of soy's health benefits is already driving strong market growth for soy-based food products," the companies said in a statement. "Sales for soy foods are expected to top $2.5 billion in 2000 and grow at a 15 to 20 percent compound rate over the next five years."

- For the past few years, DuPont's earnings have been virtually flat. Not content with this lack of progress, the company is bent on shifting out of neutral, with a goal of boosting sales by 6 percent a year, coupled with a 10 percent annual growth in earnings. DuPont says this can be attained by improving productivity, utilizing intellectual capital more effectively, and fully utilizing the company's scientific capability.

  For their part, analysts believe that DuPont's earnings growth will be enhanced by two factors:

  - Global economic growth is on the upswing. Specifically, improvement in the growth rates is evident in key sectors of Asia and Europe. This is important because nearly one-half of DuPont's revenues come from abroad.
  - Analysts also look for benefits from the six-sigma program. DuPont now has 750 black belts—workers trained in the implementation of six-sigma quality methodology—working on an average of three projects.

- In 2000, the company announced that it had signed an agreement with Affymax Technologies, N. V. that will provide DuPont access to Affymax chemical libraries for testing against crop protection targets of interest to DuPont. Affymax, a wholly owned subsidiary of Glaxo Wellcome, is a leader in the field of combinatorial chemistry with a powerful portfolio of technologies that enable efficient synthesis, screening, and optimization of vast numbers of potential new pharmaceuticals. According to a company spokesman, "We are excited about the collaborative agreement with Affymax and the potential to identify novel chemical solutions for helping farmers worldwide meet their pest-control needs."

■ After 194 years of continuous operations, the company has in the past few years achieved one of its greatest transformations—liberating value through productivity and efficiency improvement while

reorganizing to speed decision-making and implementation.

■ DuPont improved its pharmaceutical research effort with the purchase of France's Aventis SA in the spring of 2000. It doubled the company's market presence in Europe and will boost sales of DuPont's drug operation by 15 percent. The Aventis research center—with its 1,000 scientists specializing in antibiotics and treatments for bone diseases such as osteoporosis—has a pipeline of 30 new potential drugs in development. While small, this acquisition boost's the drug unit's R&D spending to almost $800 million and triples the company's drug pipeline.

Total assets: $40,777 million
Current ratio: 1.25
Common shares outstanding: 1,045 million
Return on 1999 shareholders' equity: 18.5%

	1999	1998	1997	1996	1995	1994	1993	1992
Revenues (millions)	26918	24767	45079	43810	42163	39333	37098	37799
Net income (millions)	7690	2860	4087	3636	3293	2777	1667	1697
Earnings per share	6.99	3.90	3.61	3.24	2.91	2.04	1.23	1.25
Dividends per share	1.40	1.37	1.23	1.12	1.02	.91	.88	.87
Price High	75.2	84.4	69.8	49.7	36.5	31.2	26.9	27.4
Low	50.1	51.7	46.4	34.8	26.3	24.1	22.3	21.8

INCOME

Duke Energy Corporation

Post Office Box 1244 ❑ 422 South Church Street ❑ Charlotte, North Carolina 28201-1244 ❑ Listed: NYSE ❑ Investor contact: Sue A. Becht (704) 382-8695 ❑ Direct dividend reinvestment plan is available: (800) 488-3853 ❑ Web site: www.duke-energy.com ❑ Ticker symbol: DUK ❑ S&P rating: A- ❑ Value Line financial strength rating: A+

In a recent two-year period (1998 and 1999), Duke Energy transformed itself from a premier electric utility to one of the master architects in the new energy economy. The company has assembled the assets, resources, people, and market positions that enable it to capture solid returns on its investments.

Under the leadership of its dynamic CEO, Richard B. Priory, Duke Energy

vows to increase its business scope and capital efficiency through a well-designed, growing network of energy businesses. Here is a glimpse of the company's accomplishments in this brief span of two years:

● 911 percent growth in Duke's unregulated power generation portfolio.

● 78 percent growth in natural gas liquids produced.

• 70 percent growth in nonutility domestic power sales.

• 52 percent growth in gas volumes marketed.

• 50 percent growth in volumes of natural gas processed.

• 33 percent growth in operating revenues.

Company Profile

Duke Energy Corporation is an integrated energy and energy-services provider with the ability to offer physical delivery and management of both electricity and natural gas throughout the United States and abroad. Duke Energy provides these and other services through seven business segments:

Energy Operations generates, transmits, distributes, and sells electric energy in central and western North Carolina and the western portion of South Carolina (doing business as Duke Power or Nantahala Power and Light).

Natural Gas Transmission, through its Northeast Pipelines, provides interstate transportation and storage of natural gas for customers primarily in the Mid-Atlantic and New England states.

Field Services gathers, processes, transports, and markets natural gas and produces and markets natural gas liquids (NGL). Field Services operates gathering systems in 10 states that serve major gas-producing regions in the Rocky Mountains, Permian Basin, Mid-Continent, and Gulf Coast regions.

Trading and Marketing markets natural gas, electricity, and other energy-related products across North America. Duke Energy owns a 60 percent interest in Trading and Marketing's operations, with ExxonMobil owning a 40 percent minority interest.

Global Asset Development develops, owns, and operates energy-related facilities worldwide. Global Asset Development conducts its operations primarily through Duke Energy Power Services and Duke Energy International.

Other Energy Services provides engineering, consulting, construction, and integrated energy solutions worldwide, primarily through Duke Engineering & Service, Inc., Duke/Fluor Daniel, and Duke Solutions.

Real Estate Operations conducts its business through Crescent Resources, Inc., which develops high-quality commercial and residential real estate projects and manages forest holdings in the southeastern United States.

Shortcomings to Bear in Mind

■ Public utilities are sensitive to changes in interest rates. This is partly because they often borrow money to finance new plants. Higher interest rates shove up the cost of these funds. High interest rates can also cause investors to sell their shares in order to invest their money where the return is greater.

■ In recent years the industry has been undergoing profound changes, with the specter of competition lurking not far away.

■ A civil engineer by training, Mr. Priory hopes to achieve the company's goals by building new facilities. Duke has 9,200 megawatts of new power plants under construction or development. That's on top of the company's present base of 31,000 megawatts.

Unfortunately, a host of domestic energy companies have given similar blueprints to engineers and builders. Some 170,000 megawatts of new power plant capacity is in the works in the United States—that's a hefty 23 percent of existing capacity. "If only half of that amount gets built, you're going to see a classic boom-bust cycle," says William Grealis, director of strategic planning at Cinergy Corporation, a utility based in Cincinnati, Ohio.

Reasons to Buy

- Duke Energy entered into a major transaction with Phillips Petroleum in 2000. The companies are the nation's two top producers of natural gas liquids (NGL) such as propane and butane. Duke and Phillips combined their gas-gathering and processing operations. Duke owns 70 percent of the new company. Duke says the combination enables the company to release more value from its natural gas operations, which it believes have been undervalued by the market. "It will be more highly valued (in a separate company) than it was as part of our consolidated business," said Richard Priory, Chairman of Duke Energy. Duke said the new venture should help the company meet its goal to increase earnings per share by 8 percent to 10 percent a year.

  For their part, analysts said the natural gas operations of both companies are considered well-run and solid performers that will only increase in value when combined. Those assets include 15 gas-processing plants owned by Phillips in Texas, New Mexico, and Oklahoma, and 52 plants owned by Duke in Wyoming, Colorado, Kansas, Oklahoma, New Mexico, Texas, and Canada.

- Duke Power is uniquely positioned to capitalize on its expertise in designing, building, and operating generating facilities. Duke is one of only a few domestic utilities that has historically designed, built, and operated its own power plants. The expertise Duke gained in those areas over the years has been retained through Duke Engineering & Services, Inc. and Duke/Fluor Daniel (DE&S).

- Duke Power meets its customers' needs for electricity primarily through a combination of nuclear-fueled, fossil-fueled, and hydroelectric generating stations.

  Over the past 20 years, Duke's fossil-fueled generating system has consistently been cited by *Electric Light & Power* magazine as the country's most efficient fossil system as measured by heat rate. Heat rate is a measure of efficiency in converting the energy contained in a fossil fuel such as oil, natural gas, or coal into electricity. A low heat rate means Duke burns less coal to generate a given quantity of electricity, lowering operating costs and helping keep rates competitive.

- Duke Power offers attractive incentive rates for businesses to relocate and expand within its service territory. Duke's Economic Development Rate awards an initial 20 percent discount during the first year for industrial customers who expand their electricity consumption by one megawatt and either hire a minimum of 75 new employees or invest at least $400,000 in capital upgrades. Several dozen companies have qualified for the program.

- Two of the company's coal-fired plants in the Carolinas were ranked the most efficient in the United States in 1998, according to *Electric Light & Power* magazine. For more than a quarter of a century, no company has been able to generate more electricity from a ton of coal than Duke Power.

- Duke Energy North America (DENA) entered the wholesale merchant generation business less than three years ago and is today one of the leading developers, owners, and managers of wholesale merchant generation in the United States. By the end of 1999, DENA's asset portfolio included interest in 4,400 megawatts in operation, 3,300 megawatts under construction, and 9,300 megawatts in advanced stages of development.

- Duke Energy International (DEI) is replicating Duke Energy's North American strategy of integrating natural gas and power assets with energy trading and marketing. DEI manages these energy businesses from within the regions in which it operates, recruiting local talent and brainpower—people who known the markets and have established relationships.

- Asia-Pacific. Duke Energy's primary focus in the region is Australia. In less than a year, DEI became the first energy merchant in Australia, with a portfolio of gas and power assets and a trading and marketing business. No other company has this mix of assets and capabilities. Building upon its initial position in Queensland Gas Pipeline in 1999, DEI acquired 400 megawatts of power and an interest in a pipeline from BHP Power. It followed with a launch of Eastern Gas Pipeline, which will change the competitive landscape in Australia by introducing competition and increasing reliability in time for the 2000 Summer Olympic Games in Sydney.

- Latin America. Some companies are pulling back from Latin America because they lack the skills and capabilities to integrate traditional assets and trading and marketing. These skills are essential in a merchant market. In 1999, DEI established a lead position by building Latin America's first regional power generation and energy trading and marketing business through several significant acquisitions. Duke Energy also withdrew from some noncore assets, leveraging its position into more strategic holdings.

By the end of 1999, DEI had controlling interest in 3,500 gross megawatts of generating capacity in five countries and a trading and marketing business based in Buenos Aires, Argentina. DEI acquired controlling interest in Companhia de Geracao de Energia Electrica Paranapanema, one of Brazil's largest power producers. With a total installed capacity of 2,300 megawatts, Paranapanema is strategically located in Brazil's industrial heartland.

Like Brazil, El Salvador is privatizing energy companies. DEI purchased controlling interest in Generadora Acajutla S.A. de C.V. and Generadora Salvadorena S.A. de C.V., with a combined 275 megawatts of power generation. DEI plans to add generation at this location.

DEI acquired 90 percent interest in EGENOR S.A.A., which owns 525 megawatts of thermal and hydroelectric power generation in northern Peru. DEI's initial interest in EGENOR was acquired from Dominion Resources, Inc. in a broader transaction in which the company agreed to purchase Dominion's controlling interest in a portfolio of hydroelectric, natural gas, and diesel power generation businesses in Argentina, Belize, Bolivia, and Peru, totaling 1,200 gross megawatts.

- Europe. Duke Energy is bringing proven international experience and its core expertise in energy trading and marketing to European markets. The European Union has issued energy market directives that are part of a trend toward liberalization and deregulation. Market reform and region integration will create opportunities for energy arbitrage and for investment and development of energy infrastructure.

Total assets: $ 33,409 million
Current ratio: 1.05
Common shares outstanding: 366 million
Return on 1999 equity: 14.5%

	1999	1998	1997	1996	1995	1994	1993	1992
Revenues (millions)	21742	17610	16309	4758	4677	4279	4282	3962
Net income (millions)	1383	1260	974	730	715	639	626	508
Earnings per share	4.08	3.43	2.51	3.37	3.25	2.88	2.80	2.21
Dividends per share	2.20	2.20	2.16	2.08	2.00	1.92	1.84	1.76
Price High	65.3	71.0	56.6	53.0	47.9	43.0	44.9	37.5
Low	46.8	53.1	41.9	43.4	37.4	32.9	35.4	31.4

CONSERVATIVE GROWTH

Eastman Kodak Company

343 State Street □ Rochester, New York 14650 □ Investor contact: Don Flick (716) 724-4000 □ Direct dividend reinvestment plan is available: (800) 253-6057 □ Web site: www.kodak.com □ Listed: NYSE □ Ticker symbol: EK □ S&P rating: B+ □ Value Line financial strength rating: A

In the fall of 2000, the company introduced a new Kodak Advantix camera that offers Advanced Photo System film users the single most popular benefit of digital picture taking. When you snap the shutter, this new "preview" camera displays your picture on a 1.8-inch color LCD screen. After you view the image, you can choose how many prints you'd like—from zero to nine—and a code on the film will convey the ordering instructions during processing. No more prints you don't want, and no more trips back to the store or mailbox for reprints.

Company Profile

Eastman Kodak has been making cameras for the past 100 years. It was on February 2, exactly 100 years ago, that George Eastman introduced the Brownie camera. Despite its long history, the camera has a bright future. According to a group of Kodak researchers, inventors, and business strategists, the "true power of imaging has barely been tapped—and the advances of this century will vindicate Eastman's dream of making communicating with pictures as easy as 'using a pencil.'"

Of course, Eastman Kodak is still making cameras and film, as well as other consumer and professional photographic products. But it is also expanding and improving its digital imaging products and services here at home. And its well-known cameras and films are also seen in the developing world.

Highlights of 1999

- The company delivered 5 percent revenue growth in 1999, a significant step toward its objective of 8 percent to 12 percent annual growth.
- Diluted earnings per share growth was 15 percent, excluding special charges and gains.
- Total digital sales climbed 46 percent in 1999 and now represent 17 percent of total Kodak revenues.
- As Kodak predicted, sales in emerging markets abroad rebounded, with 6 percent growth in 1999. In China, the largest of these markets, revenues were up 30 percent. Foreign markets now account for more than half of Kodak revenues.
- Kodak exceeded its own goal of taking $1.2 billion in costs out of the company in 1998–1999. At year-end, the cost-reduction for the two-year period totaled $1.25 billion.

- With more than $1 billion in operational free cash flow before dividends, Kodak now has substantial resources for expansion—and the company is actively seeking out such opportunities.

Shortcomings to Bear in Mind

- In recent years Kodak has been defending its lucrative, market-leading, but mature, domestic film business against Japan's feisty Fuji Photo. To fend off this determined, relentless predator, the company has been cutting jobs and selling noncore businesses such as copiers.

  Meanwhile, Eastman Kodak is courting new markets. It has deals that bring pictures to America Online users and to eBay's online auction house. Kodak also provides film and related products to professionals in the health care and entertainment industries.

Reasons to Buy

- In the past five years, Eastman Kodak has been trying to restore luster to its tarnished image. Like many troubled companies, Kodak went outside to find a CEO, in this instance, George M. C. Fisher. However, if you look at earnings per share in the 1994–1999 period, you might not be convinced that Mr. Fisher is another Larry Bossidy, Jack Welch, or Louis V. Gerstner, Jr. Even so, progress has been made. In that five-year span, earnings per share advanced from $2.91 to $5.03, a compound annual growth rate of 11.6 percent.

  In mid-2000, Kodak's new CEO, Daniel A. Carp, told investors that it is building its digital strategy on the strength of its consumer business, which accounts for 57 percent of the company's overall revenue. Digital imaging now accounts for only 11 percent of its consumer revenue; by the end of 2005, that is expected to grow to 42 percent,

he said. Mr. Carp also said he expects Kodak's consumer digital cameras to be a break-even business by 2002.

- In 1999, Kodak helped consumers turn 150 million of their pictures into digital files thanks to the ease and convenience of Kodak Picture CD, Kodak Picture Disk, Kodak PhotoNet online, and the company's "You've Got Pictures" service on America Online. Today, digitalization is as simple as the two seconds it takes to "check the box" on the Kodak envelope when your film is dropped off for processing.

- Kodak has maintained its lead as one of the top three digital camera brands in the world, delivering the user-friendliness and advanced features that people have come to expect from Kodak.

- As digital cameras become more popular (management forecasts 20 percent of U.S. households will own a digital camera by 2005), film usage also continues to grow dramatically. Film sales reached a peak in 1999, achieving double-digit growth in the United States—concurrent with double-digit growth in digital camera sales. This apparent anomaly can be explained in part by the fact that traditional cameras and film are, themselves, making rapid advance in technological sophistication.

- In early 2000, the company formed a joint venture with Hewlett-Packard that offers consumers greater convenience and retailers greater profitability. Kodak and HP are pooling their technical expertise, resources, and marketing strengths to develop commercial inkjet photo-finishing equipment that will print from both film and digital files to a variety of media. With this technology, pictures may also be transmitted from one retail location to another, enabling consumers to share prints easily with friends and family anywhere. The compact, lower-cost unit, available in 2001, will make it possible for retailers with less floor space or customer traffic to offer a wide range of photo-finishing services.

■ In a move that demonstrates why Kodak Document Imaging is known as the market leader in document scanning, the company in the spring of 2000 introduced groundbreaking new high- and mid-volume production systems. Unveiled at AIIM 2000, these innovative new products offer unparalleled image quality and increased throughput, as well as full color functionality in the mid-volume segment.

The company's new high-volume models, the Kodak Digital Science Document Scanner 9520 and Document Scanner 7520, provide a host of standard features at low prices for such robust high-volume systems. They also incorporate Kodak's exclusive Perfect Page Scanning to radically increase productivity and eliminate the need to rescan and reprocess documents. According to Candy Obourn, president, Kodak Document Imaging, "Each year at AIIM, Kodak demonstrates its leadership position in the industry, and this year is no exception. Our excellent line-up of both new and existing products, coupled with our unparalleled service and well-established distribution channel, demonstrates why we provide the market with an unmatched level of quality."

■ In the spring of 2000, Eastman Kodak opened a state-of-the-art facility in Genoa, Italy, in which it plans to invest between $5 million and $10 million over the next few years. It will showcase its cutting-edge health imaging products and catapult customer service and training to a new level. Kodak's Technology and Innovation Center, a 1,500-square-meter product-portfolio showroom and training facility, "expresses our commitment to customers and to growing our business in Europe," said Sharon Crino, Kodak's general manager of its Health Imaging Division for Europe, at the Centre's opening ceremonies. "The Centre will provide customers with a hospital-like setting where they can assess new Kodak equipment and its performance in work-flow management; everything is here, from film radiology and digital capture to full PACS."

■ In April of 2000, Eastman Kodak , SANYO Electric Company Ltd., and ULVAC Japan, Ltd. announced a strategic partnership to jointly develop organic light-emitting diode(OLED) flat panel manufacturing equipment technology. This three-year agreement is the first step toward building a broad manufacturing equipment infrastructure for the production of OLED displays, a revolutionary new flat panel display technology used in advanced electronic applications.

ULVAC, a leading supplier of manufacturing equipment for the semiconductor and flat panel display industries, will use proprietary OLED manufacturing technology from Kodak and SANYO as the framework for the development of flat panel manufacturing equipment. This alliance combines ULVAC's understanding of vacuum deposition equipment used in the manufacture of thin films, Kodak's expertise in OLED technology, and SANYO's experience in manufacturing high-quality flat panel displays.

■ In a keynote address in April of 2000 to a group of leading executives at the Advancing Digital Photography Forum 2000, Kodak CEO, Daniel A. Carp, described how the industry and Wall Street treat digital as a "magic" word, while consumers are far more interested in features and benefits rather than the pixel count of a CCD image sensor.

"We know very well what digital means to us..and to industry analysts . . . and to Wall Street," he said. "But what does it really mean to the public? To consumers, 'digital' does not always mean better. For example, expensive fashion watches are analog; less expensive watches are almost always digital.

"Kodak is convinced that there has never been a better time to be in the picture business. And not just because digital has created some new excitement. What's more intriguing is how digital can change the way people take and use pictures. Suddenly, there are no boundaries to how often you can take pictures, because film cost or availability is no longer an issue. There are no boundaries limiting when you can take pictures,

because digital cameras have conveniently become hooked into everything, from telephones to the new Kodak PalmPix camera that attaches to your Palm organizer."

- Eastman Kodak teamed up with LightSurf Technologies in the spring of 2000, in the latest venture of software entrepreneur Philippe Kahn, to collaborate in wireless and Internet photo services. The alliance is the latest sign of Kodak's desire to become a player in wireless photography. Mr. Kahn and others have been predicting that consumers equipped with modified digital cameras will soon be able to take photos and instantly transmit them through cell phones or other wireless connections and post them on the Web.

Total assets: $14,370 million
Current ratio: 0.95
Common shares outstanding: 316 million
Return on 1999 shareholders' equity: 35.6%

	1999	1998	1997	1996	1995	1994	1993	1992
Revenues (millions)	14089	13406	14538	15968	14980	13557	16364	20183
Net income (millions)	1617	1419	1168	1518	1252	977	840	1056
Earnings per share	5.03	4.33	3.52	4.50	3.67	2.91	2.56	3.26
Dividends per share	1.76	1.76	1.76	1.60	1.60	1.60	2.00	2.00
Price High	80.4	88.9	94.8	85.0	70.4	56.4	64.8	50.8
Low	56.6	57.9	53.3	65.1	47.3	40.8	40.4	37.8

AGGRESSIVE GROWTH

A. G. Edwards, Inc.

One North Jefferson Avenue ❑ St. Louis, Missouri 63103 ❑ Investor Contact: Margaret Welch (314) 955-5912 ❑ Dividend reinvestment plan is not available ❑ Web site: www.agedwards.com ❑ Fiscal year ends February 28th or 29th ❑ Listed: NYSE ❑ Ticker symbol: AGE ❑ S&P rating: A ❑ Value Line financial strength rating: B+

Kiplinger's Personal Finance magazine awarded A. G. Edwards its number one ranking in its "Stocks 2000" survey of full-service investment firms. A. G. Edwards was the only brokerage house to receive a five-star ranking for its overall performance.

Company Profile

A. G. Edwards, Inc. is a holding company whose subsidiaries provide securities and

commodities brokerage, investment banking, trust, asset management and insurance services.

Its principal subsidiary, A. G. Edwards & Sons, Inc., is a financial services company with 670 locations in 49 states and the District of Columbia and an affiliated office in London, England.

A. G. Edwards & Sons provides a full range of financial products to individual and institutional investors and offers investment banking services to corporate, governmental, and municipal clients.

A. G. Edwards continued to expand both the number of its registered investment professionals and its nationwide branch office network in fiscal 2000 (ended February 29, 2000), further strengthening its securities distribution capability.

Shortcomings to Bear in Mind

- Rising interest rates or a falling stock market would have an adverse impact on investors. Since A. G. Edwards is heavily dependent on commission business, its revenues would be hurt by such developments.
- Without a doubt, the brokerage business is more competitive today than ever before. Full-service firms are expanding. Banks are offering brokerage services. Discount brokers are thriving. Mutual funds are marketing directly to investors. And "do-it-yourselfers" are benefiting from the longest bull market in recent history. Despite all these negatives, A. G. Edwards has continued to grow.

Reasons to Buy

- A. G. Edwards ended fiscal year 2000 posting record revenues and earnings. Net earnings increased 31 percent for the year ended February 29, 2000, to a record $383 million on revenue of $2.8 billion. This marked the fifth consecutive year and the 10th time in the last 11 years that the firm has achieved record earnings and revenues.
- In addition to record earnings, the firm continued to broaden its ability to serve more investors by adding 32 branch offices, bringing the national total to more than 670 offices and making AGE the fourth-largest retail branch network in the country. The number of financial consultants (most people call them "brokers") increased by 295, bringing the nationwide total to more than 6,800.

- London was selected as the site of the firm's first overseas affiliate because of its position as the financial hub of Europe. Initially, the subsidiary, A. G. Edwards & Sons (U.K.) Limited, will serve institutional accounts and develop syndicate relationships with European investment banks. Longer term, the subsidiary plans to expand its investment banking and merger and acquisition services to corporations, as well as financial services to high-net-worth clients.
- The company was named the best full-service brokerage firm in the first "Reader's Choice" survey published by *Worth* magazine. The magazine's readers cited several reasons for giving A. G. Edwards high marks, including the firm's "unpretentious, low-pressure approach," its stock-picking abilities, and its focus on serving the clients' best interests.
- For the third consecutive year, *Fortune* magazine named A. G. Edwards to its distinguished list of "The 100 Best Companies to Work for in America." The brokerage house is one of just five companies nationwide to appear on all five versions of the prestigious list, originally published in 1984 by Robert Levering and Milton Moskowitz and now published annually by *Fortune* magazine.
- Over the past 10 years (1990–2000), the company's dividend expanded from $.19 per share to $.60, a compound annual growth rate of 12.2 percent. In the same 10-year span, earnings per share climbed from $.73 to $4.08, a compound annual growth rate of 18.8 percent.
- In the assets-under-management sector, the company had a stellar performance in fiscal 2000. The combined value of assets managed through A. G. Edwards Managed Accounts; A. G. Edwards Trust companies; Private Advisor Service; and the Pathways, Spectrum, Fund Navigator, and Fund Advisor investment advisory programs increased by 47

percent during the year, climbing to $17.4 billion.

- To better serve corporate clients seeking assistance in designing and implementing employee-benefit plans, A. G. Edwards acquired CPI Qualified Plan Consultants, Inc., a pension plan administrator based in Great Bend, Kansas. The acquisition complements the extensive array of services A. G. Edwards provides to closely held businesses, corporations, executives and business owners—including retirement plans, employee-benefit programs, cash management, ownership and management-succession planning, and executive compensation programs.

- The company's Public Finance operation retained its status as the nation's top underwriter of kindergarten through 12th grade tax-exempt negotiated school bonds and ranked 10th nationally for lead-management negotiated long-term municipal underwritings during calendar 1999, with more than $3.8 billion in bonds issued, according to Securities Data Company.

- A. G. Edwards is well prepared to ride out a market correction. The company has one of the strongest balance sheets in the industry—no long-term debt. What's more, with the majority of its costs variable in nature (mostly commissions paid to brokers), the brokerage house can easily ride out the vagaries of a cyclical industry with only moderate impact on margins.

- At A. G. Edwards, the practice is to manage its bond inventory for the primary purpose of meeting client demand for products, rather than to generate profits for the firm's account. Management believes that committing capital to pursue trading profits as an important source of revenue would expose the firm to excessive risk and compromise its commitment to putting its clients' needs ahead of those of the firm.

- The company is known for its practice of keeping its customers' success as its primary focus. One aspect of this philosophy is the company's agency approach. That is, A. G. Edwards does not offer in-house mutual funds or other products; rather, brokers are free to select the best outside products for clients. In addition, registered representatives do not have production quotas.

- The company recently unveiled its *Client Choice* program in response to the proliferation of on-line brokers. The fee-only program allows for unlimited trades while maintaining personal service and other account amenities, such as a debit card. For active investors, analysts think *Client Choice* can be competitive against on-line commissions.

- Alex Bigelow, A. G. Edwards Vice President and Branch Manager, West Palm Beach, Florida, states his belief in the philosophy espoused by the firm:

  What I enjoy most about working for A. G. Edwards is that the culture here allows me to concentrate on being the best branch manager I can be. There are no "products of the month" or monthly sales goals for my branch to contend with. There's much more of an emphasis on people, with the belief that if you hire the right people, the business will naturally follow. A. G. Edwards doesn't offer up-front money to attract new brokers.

  When I recruit new investment brokers, I look for people with character who have a drive to succeed but aren't looking for the shortest route to success. For investment brokers to succeed at A. G. Edwards, they have to care about what they do and care about what's best for the client.

- A. G. Edwards is one of the lowest-risk firms in the volatile brokerage industry because of its extremely strong capital position, solid earnings record, and above-average dividend yield. AGE has avoided the troubles currently afflicting other brokers because investment banking and trading comprise a much smaller part of its total business.

- In the unlikely event that you are not convinced that this is a superior firm, here are some remarks by Louis Harvey, President of DALBAR, Inc., Boston, Massachusetts:

For the last 20 years, my company has conducted nationwide market research on the financial services industry through customer and employee satisfaction surveys and other means. Today, it appears financial services firms are genuinely trying to change to be more customer-driven, rather than product- or profit-driven. The customer orientation is nothing new to A. G. Edwards, which has historically had a client focus and often receives high marks from both clients and its own brokers in DALBAR surveys. In my opinion, one of the things that distinguishes A. G. Edwards is that it doesn't build its own products. If you have your own products, there are pressures to sell your products. Not having them allows A. G. Edwards brokers to focus on clients without the burden of responsibility for products.

Total assets: $5,348 million
Common shares outstanding: 91 million
Return on 2000 shareholders' equity: 22.9%

		2000	1999	1998	1997	1996	1995	1994	1993
Revenues (millions)		2819	2241	2004	1696	1454	1178	1279	1074
Net income (millions)		348	292	269	219	171	124	155	119
Earnings per share		4.08	3.00	2.81	2.29	1.80	1.35	1.75	1.40
Dividends per share		.60	.57	.51	.44	.40	.37	.35	.29
Price	High	41.0	48.8	39.9	35.0	27.0	24.4	25.4	25.7
	Low	24.3	30.9	20.5	22.5	17.5	16.5	18.0	13.8

CONSERVATIVE GROWTH

Emerson Electric Company

8000 W. Florissant Avenue ⊐ St. Louis, Missouri 63136 ⊐ Investor contact: Robert T. Sharp (314) 553-2197 ⊐ Dividend reinvestment plan is available: (888) 213-0970 ⊐ Web site: www.emersonelectric.com ⊐ Listed: NYSE ⊐ Ticker symbol: EMR ⊐ Fiscal year ends September 30 ⊐ S&P rating: A+ ⊐ Value Line financial strength rating: A++

One of the key ways that Emerson is entering more and faster-growing markets is through technology investment. In 1999, engineering and development expenditures exceeded $500 million for the first time. The company's leading areas of technology spending are now electronics, communications, and software.

In the words of CEO Charles F. Knight, "I view this as an important shift, given the opportunities for product differentiation and the increased value proposition for customers that these technologies provide. Customers are responding enthusiastically to the intelligence embedded in our products, as well as to our new software and service offerings. As a result, sales of new products introduced in the past five years reached 35 percent in fiscal 1999, and we fully expect to surpass 40 percent within five years."

Company Profile

Emerson Electric is a leading manufacturer of a broad list of intermediate products such as electrical motors and drives, appliance components, and process-control devices. The company also produces hand and power tools, as well as accessories.

Founded some 107 years ago, Emerson is not a typical high-tech capital goods producer. Rather, the company makes such prosaic things as refrigerator compressors, pressure gauges, and In-Sink Erator garbage disposals—basic products that are essential to industry.

Without question, Emerson Electric is one of the nation's finest companies and should be a core holding in any portfolio devoted to growth of capital. Let's next glance at the company's five segments:

Industrial Automation

Emerson industrial automation products contribute to improved productivity for a variety of industry applications. The company is a global leader in providing application-specific motor and drive solutions. In addition, Emerson produces a variety of industrial valves, electrical equipment, specialty heating, lighting, testing, and ultrasonic welding and cleaning products for use in industrial settings. Well-known brands include Appleton, ASCO, Branson, Browning, Chromalox, Control Techniques, Leroy Some, MORSE, O-Z/Gedney, and USEM. This segment is Emerson's largest, accounting for 24 percent of revenues in fiscal 1999.

Process Control

Emerson is a leading producer of process-control products, including control systems and automation software, measurement devices, analytical instrumentation, and valves. The revolutionary PlantWeb field-based architecture is redefining the way customers manage and connect their businesses by combining intelligent field devices, the innovative DeltaV control system, and advanced software. Leading brands include Daniel, DeltaV, Fisher, Intellution, Micro Motion, Rosemont,

Westinghouse Process Control, and Xomox. In 1999, this segment was responsible for 21 percent of EMR revenues.

Heating, Ventilating, and Air Conditioning

Emerson is a leading producer of compressors, thermostats, temperature controls, hermetic terminals, and valves for heating, ventilating, air conditioning, and refrigeration systems. The Copeland Scroll compressor continues to transform the air conditioning and refrigeration markets with its increased energy efficiency and reliability and quieter operation. This advanced technology also has vast potential in a number of new markets such as transport refrigeration, cryogenics, and air compression. Leading brands include Alco, Copeland, Therm-O-Disc, and White-Rodgers. In 1999, this part of Emerson was responsible for 17 percent of overall company sales.

Electronics and Telecommunications

Emerson provides a broad array of power-related products for the fast growing computer, telecommunications, and Internet infrastructure markets. The company is a global leader in uninterruptible AC and DC power systems, embedded power supplies, environmental control systems, and site-monitoring systems. Emerson also certifies, tests, and services electronic equipment. Key brands include ASCO Switch, Astec, HIROSS, and Liebert. This segment contributed 15 percent of Emerson's revenues in 1999.

Appliance and Tools

Emerson is a leading producer of electric motors for appliances, HVAC equipment, and specialty products. The company also produces a variety of controls, heating elements, and other components for appliances, along with storage products, waste disposers, plumbing tools, benchtop power tools, hand tools, and wet/dry vacuums. Well-known brands include: ClosetMaid, Emerson, In-Sink-Erator, Mallory, METRO, and RIDGID. This operation contributed 23 percent of Emerson's revenues in 1999.

Shortcomings to Bear in Mind

- Long celebrated as a model of stable, consistent earnings growth, Emerson has lost some of its luster on Wall Street. While the company's profits have continued their long-running climb, some critics have complained that the company's risk-averse strategy—the same conservative management style that has allowed Emerson to report higher earnings in each of the past 42 years—has limited growth opportunities.

  For its part, the company disputes such claims. Management asserts that it has spent $600 million on telecommunications and electronics acquisitions in the past two years and that the Jordan transaction will boost that total to more than $1 billion.

- In fiscal 1999, Emerson faced a number of challenges in the industrial automation and process markets that masked outstanding performance in the company's growth initiatives and led to the first year in six that Emerson fell short of double-digit earnings per share growth. Low oil prices, consolidations of customers in the oil and chemical industries, and the continued impact of the Asian economic crisis combined to create some of the weakest market conditions of the past 25 years.

Reasons to Buy

- The company has been active on the acquisition front. For instance, in fiscal 2000 Emerson, moving to rev up its growth prospects, agreed to acquire Jordan Industries Inc.'s telecommunications equipment business. At that time,

Jordan Industries was a privately owned holding company. Jordan makes products used in deploying fiber-optic wires, cable TV components, and a host of products used in the wireless and data-communications infrastructure. At the time of the acquisition, Jordan had annual sales of $381 million, up a hefty 21 percent in the prior 12 months.

- In January of 2000, Emerson announced the $725-million acquisition of Ericsson Energy Systems, a subsidiary of Swedish telecommunications giant, Telefon AB L. M. Ericsson. Ericsson Energy Systems makes power supplies and systems that are used in cellular equipment and other applications. Its substantial presence in Europe and Latin America offers Emerson some big new customers, including Ericsson, Siemens AG of Germany, and Telefonica SA of Spain.

- Fiscal 1999 was another successful year for Emerson. The company achieved its forty-second consecutive year of increased earnings and earnings per share and its forty-third consecutive year of increased dividends per share, a record of consistent, strong performance.

  In the prior five years, moreover, Emerson's stockholders averaged a 19 percent annual return on their investment. Consolidated sales, earnings, and operating cash flow all grew at double-digit rates, while return on total capital improved from 15.4 percent to 16.4 percent.

- The Copeland Scroll compressor continues to transform the air conditioning and refrigeration markets and other industries. Scroll sales grew over 35 percent in fiscal 1999 and are now over $700 million. The company expects Scroll sales to surpass $1 billion in the near future.

- Emerson's PlantWeb process control architecture, made possible by new communications and control technologies and the intelligence the company has embedded in a broad offering of field devices, doubled its sales in 1999. Total control systems and solutions sales in 1999, moreover, approached $700 million. What's more, at the current rate of growth, these revenues will exceed $1 billion within a few years.

- Emerson has enjoyed impressive success in electronics with its focus on telecom. Electronics sales in 1999 increased 32 percent, to over $2 billion. The company is uniquely positioned to power the digital economy and participate in the rapid expansion of the global communications infrastructure. Mr. Knight asserts that "We plan to double this business in the next five years."

- Analysts regard Emerson as being extremely well-positioned over the next several years. Its industrial end-market orientation, focus on manufacturing, global presence in its core activities, and superior financial attributes should serve it in good stead. What's more, analysts are particularly impressed with the concentration on products that allow end users to lower their production costs while at the same time paying heed to environmental concerns.

Total assets: $13,624 million
Current ratio: 1.11
Common shares outstanding: 435 million
Return on 1999 shareholders' equity: 21.9%

		1999	1998	1997	1996	1995	1994	1993	1992
Revenues (millions)		14270	13447	12299	11150	10013	8607	8174	7706
Net income (millions)		1314	1229	1122	1018	908	789	708	667
Earnings per share		3.00	2.77	2.52	2.28	2.03	1.76	1.58	1.49
Dividends per share		1.31	1.18	1.08	.98	.89	.78	.72	.69
Price	High	71.4	67.4	60.4	51.8	40.8	33.0	31.2	29.0
	Low	51.4	54.5	45.0	38.8	30.8	28.2	52.8	23.4

AGGRESSIVE GROWTH

Ethan Allen Interiors, Inc.

Post Office Box 1966 ❏ Danbury, Connecticut 06813-1966 ❏ Investor contact: Margaret (Peg) W. Lupton (203) 743-8234 ❏ Web site: www.ethanallen.com ❏ Dividend reinvestment plan is not available ❏ Fiscal year ends June 30 ❏ Listed: NYSE ❏ Ticker symbol: ETH ❏ S&P rating: Not rated ❏ Value Line financial strength rating: B+

Ethan Allan is now selling its wares over the Internet. In an effort to extend its reach and supplement traditional marketing efforts, the company has expanded and redesigned its Web site to allow for the direct sale of more than 5,000 home-furnishing products.

Analysts believe the company is uniquely positioned to leverage its widely recognized brand name and favorable reputation to swiftly develop a valuable e-commerce endeavor. What's more, Ethan Allen's extensive distribution network and integrated retail structure provides it with a competitive advantage in servicing online customers.

Most other furniture producers have been reluctant to establish an Internet retail presence—such a move would alienate its retail and wholesale customers. For its part, Ethan Allen has no such fears, since its furniture is marketed exclusively through its own network of captive stores.

Company Profile

Ethan Allen, one of the 10 largest manufacturers of household furniture in the United

States, sells a full range of furniture products and decorative accessories through a network of 309 retail stores, of which 73 are company owned. Retail stores are located in the United States, Canada, and Mexico, with 32 located overseas.

The company's stores are scattered across the country, with outlets in nearly every state. However, there are more than a dozen outlets in such states as California, Texas, and Florida. There is also a concentrated cluster of Ethan Allen stores along the Eastern seaboard in such states as New Jersey, Connecticut, and Massachusetts.

The company's 21 manufacturing facilities and 3 sawmills are located in the United States.

Within this fragmented industry, the company has the largest domestic furniture retail network utilizing the gallery concept. Comparable-store sales have benefited from a repositioning of the product mix to appeal to a broader consumer base, a program to renovate or relocate existing stores, coupled with more frequent advertising and promotional campaigns.

Ethan Allen is pursuing an aggressive growth strategy, including investments in technology, employee training, and new stores. Margins have been enhanced by manufacturing efficiencies, lower interest expense, and a strengthening of the upholstery and accessory lines.

With an efficient and flexible vertically integrated structure, a strong, dedicated retail network, an impressive 95 percent brand name recognition and a 67-year reputation for exceptional quality and service, Ethan Allen is uniquely positioned as a dominant force in the home furnishings industry.

As Ethan Allen enters the new millennium, the company's philosophy of design remains the same as it was when it was founded 67 years ago. Styles may have changed from colonial to eclectic, but the company's commitment to exceptional quality, classical design elements,

innovative style, and functionality will continue to position Ethan Allen as a preferred brand for years to come.

In keeping with the way consumers live today, the company has organized its product programs into two broad style categories. "Classic" encompasses more historically inspired styles, from early European and French influences to designs from the eighteenth and nineteenth century masters. "Casual," on the other hand, captures a clean, contemporary line and an updated country aesthetic.

Shortcomings to Bear in Mind

- This stock is labeled "aggressive growth," because it has a high beta coefficient of 1.60. A beta of 1 indicates a stock that fluctuates with the market. High betas are indicative of stocks that can be volatile.

- The stock of Ethan Allen can be sensitive to the cyclical whims of furniture demand. For instance, when interest rates rise, housing starts are hurt, as is the furniture industry.

Reasons to Buy

- The company has been reducing its debt in recent years. In 1995, debt as a percentage of capitalization was 40 percent. In the years since, this figure has declined to 28 percent, 20 percent, and 3 percent (at the end of 1999).

- During the last seven years, Ethan Allen increased its sales by 106.7 percent. In the same period, its plants increased production by 64.6 percent. Interestingly, nearly all of this growth emanated from the same number of stores. What's more, the number of plants declined by seven. During this same span, the company changed more than 90 percent of its products in terms of style and affordability. In addition, the company developed a $68 million annual advertising campaign to project its new identity.

Finally, Ethan Allen renovated 89 percent of its storefronts.

- To enhance marketing, Ethan Allen is developing proprietary products that combine attractive design, quality, and an affordable price. The company is also strengthening its position as a total home furnishings enterprise in both classic and casual styles, with strong programs in wood furniture, upholstery, and decorative accents.
- These efforts are paying off. In fiscal 1999, the company's sales increased by 12.2 percent, to $762.2 million. Net income increased by 13 percent, to $81.3 million. By the end of 1999, the company was virtually debt-free.
- Operating a store in today's environment is a complicated business if management doesn't have the right structure in place. Ethan Allen is convinced that "You need to be able to keep the store beautiful and inspiring, help customers select the right products, train and motivate the sales staff, grow a complicated custom business, make accessory house calls, and anticipate customer service requests—all at the same time."

To respond to these demands, Ethan Allen began testing new ways to staff its stores. For example, at its corporate headquarters in Danbury, Connecticut, management looked at its needs—especially on high-traffic weekends—and created an environment to better support the designers who were working on the front lines.

First, the company established the right sales management structure so that designers were able to obtain the training and direction they needed to build their businesses. Then, Ethan Allen added specialists in the soft goods and accessories areas to help designers sell more of the complicated product programs. In addition, the company also added a merchandise manager to keep the store beautiful and a customer service specialist to address delivery and service issues.

Since this structure has been in place, traffic in the Danbury store increased about 19 percent. During that same period, the store's written business jumped up 35 percent.

- To further increase capacity and improve the company's ability to serve its customers, Ethan Allen is editing its line by about 10 percent and retiring underperforming items. Management is convinced that this strategy will free up capacity immediately while the company begins construction on expansion projects in all four of its manufacturing regions.
- Running a custom business that offers hundred of frames, thousands of fabrics, and endless combination in a challenge in itself. Running it profitably is even harder. At Ethan Allen, the company does it by marrying state-of-the-art technology with smart work processes and trained professionals.

For instance, new technology like the fabric-cutting machine in operation at the company's Maiden, North Carolina facility is changing the way Ethan Allen does business. Using a computerized mapping system and automated cutting mechanism, the machine can cut perfectly matched pieces on a very complicated fabric pattern with precision and accuracy. In addition to eliminating the cost of human error, the machine allows the company to triple its output using fewer people. Plans are underway to install this technology in Ethan Allen's other upholstery plants.

- During the 1999 High Point Furniture Market, The American Society of Furniture Designers (ASFD) honored Ethan Allen for stylish product development. "We have made a concerted effort to create innovative furniture designs far removed from the old image of Ethan Allen," said Farooq Kathwari, CEO of Ethan Allen.

Meanwhile, at the International Home Furnishings Market in High Point, North Carolina, the ASFD presented Ethan Allen with two Pinnacle Awards. "What makes Pinnacle so unique," explained Christine Evan, ASFD executive director, "are that they represent the furniture that consumers actually buy, rather than one-of-a-kind art pieces."

In the four years Pinnacle Awards have been presented, Ethan Allen has received recognition for its Regent's Park Dining Room, Country Colors collection, American Impressions Entertainment Center, and the Home & Garden Spa Series.

- In fiscal 2000, Ethan Allen celebrated the unveiling of its first store in Egypt. The newest location marked the thirty-second store to open abroad.
- During 1999, the shares of Ethan Allen underperformed the market. Apparently, this lackluster action was caused by a rise in interest rates that might hurt the demand for furniture. However, analysts are not convinced. They believe these fears are overblown, as overall economic and demographic trends remain favorable with high housing activity and consumer confidence, a rising stock market, and baby boomers entering their peak years of spending on household furnishings.

Total assets: $480 million
Current ratio: 2.43
Common shares outstanding: 40.8 million
Return on 1999 shareholders' equity: 23.2%

	1999	1998	1997	1996	1995	1994	1993	1992*
Revenues (millions)	762	693	572	510	476	437	384	351
Net income (millions)	81	72	49	28	23	23	def.	def.
Earnings per share	1.92	1.63	1.11	.65	.52	.51	def.	
Dividends per share	.12	.09	.06	.01	nil	nil		
Price High	37.8	44.4	28.6	13.0	8.3	10.7	10.5	
Low	24.7	15.7	12.3	6.5	5.7	6.5	5.4	

*Ethan Allen went public on March 23, 1993, thus this table is incomplete.

GROWTH AND INCOME

ExxonMobil Corporation

5959 Las Colinas Boulevard ◻ Irving, Texas 75039-2298 ◻ Investor contact: Mr. Peter Townsend, V.P. (214) 444-1900 ◻ Direct dividend reinvestment program is available: (800) 252-1800 ◻ Web site: www.exxon.mobil.com ◻ Listed: NYSE ◻ Ticker symbol: XOM ◻ S&P rating: A- ◻ Value Line financial strength rating: A++

At the core of ExxonMobil's prospects are large, highly profitable oil and gas operations in key established regions, including North America, Europe, West Africa, and Asia-Pacific. These operations offer significant near-term growth potential as new opportunities are developed through existing infrastructure.

In addition, ExxonMobil is expanding its strong position in many of the world's rapidly emerging exploration areas, such as deep-water West Africa, South America, the Middle East, the Caspian region, and Eastern Canada. At year-end 1999, 58 major projects were under way in both new and established regions.

Company Profile

Mobil Corporation ceased to exist at the end of November 1999, after government regulators approved the company's $81-billion acquisition by Exxon, reuniting the two largest pieces of the Standard Oil monopoly nearly 90 years after trustbusters split them apart. As a result of this merger, ExxonMobil has passed Royal Dutch Petroleum as the world's largest petroleum company in terms of oil and gas reserves.

The Federal Trade Commission, following an 11-month review, overcame its initial skepticism about the deal and blessed it, having forced the companies to shed as much as $2 billion in service stations and other assets. Commenting on the decision, Exxon's CEO, Lee R. Raymond, said the two companies were creating "the world's premier petroleum and petrochemical company" and estimated that savings from the merger would exceed the $2.8 billion over three years that the companies had originally anticipated.

Merger Requirements of Federal Trade Commission

The companies' chemicals and technology businesses were not affected.

The bulk of the divestitures came in the refining and marketing sectors. In the United States, ExxonMobil was required to sell one refinery; this represented about 2 percent of the company's refining capacity. The remaining worldwide refining networks leads the industry, with 50 refineries and total capacity of 6.4 million barrels a day.

In addition, XOM (prior to the merger, the symbol was XON) was required to divest some 770 company-owned or leased service stations in the United States and to assign contracts to new suppliers. These changes affected more than 1,600 stations owned by branded distributors and others. In Europe, Mobil was required to sell its 30 percent interest in the BP/Mobil joint-venture fuels business and its 28-percent interest in the German joint-venture marketing company, Aral.

These divestitures should be viewed in the context of the more than 45,000 remaining Exxon, Mobil, and Esso stations worldwide. Here at home, despite the refinery and service station divestitures, XOM's combined refining and marketing business is far stronger than either one of the companies had before.

Shortcomings to Bear in Mind

■ Exxon has one of the worst reputations among multinationals, according to a survey of 10,830 people in 1999 by Harris Interactive Inc. and the Reputation Institute, a New York research group. Survey respondents, citing leftover ill will from the Valdez spill and a perception of corporate arrogance, rated Exxon (prior to the merger with Mobil) not much better than Philip Morris, a tobacco company held in contempt by a large part of the public.

While other CEOs court Wall Street, Exxon's Lee Raymond meets with analysts only rarely and routinely castigates at least one analyst per meeting. Contrast Mr. Raymond's reclusiveness, enmity, and lack of charm with the more cordial and affable personalities of the CEOs of Exxon's major rivals: BP p.l.c. and Royal Dutch Petroleum. As their companies have undergone dramatic changes, BP's Sir John Browne and Shell's Mark Moody-Stuart often have spoken on issues such as the environment and corporate responsibility and have not been reluctant to present their respective corporate financial pictures to the investment community.

■ In 1999, ExxonMobil's refining and marketing earnings sagged badly, by 65 percent, to $1.2 billion. Margins were squeezed as crude costs shot up at a faster clip than product prices in an increasingly competitive environment. Capital expenditures were $2.4 billion, down from $3 billion in 1998. Refinery throughput was down 2 percent.

Reasons to Buy

- Originally, management felt that the merger would produce pretax synergies (cost savings and profit-improvement items) of some $2.8 billion per year three years after the merger. After a year of merger planning, the company concluded that near-term merger synergies would be considerably higher. Exxon-Mobil expects synergies directly attributable to the merger itself to amount to $3.8 billion annually on a pretax basis. In addition, management expects cost and margin improvements from its traditional efficiency programs.

- In the important "upstream sector," Mr. Raymond believes that "our exploration and production portfolio of complementary assets is the best in the industry. We are the world's largest private-sector producer of oil and gas combined, and we continue to expand our excellent position in many of the world's most exciting and rapidly emerging oil and gas areas."

  Earnings in the upstream segment in 1999 totaled $5.9 billion, an increase of more than 75 percent over the prior year. Continued focus on expenses, especially during the period of low prices in 1998 and early 1999, led to an expense reduction of $640 million, or about $0.30 per oil-equivalent barrel. Expense reductions strengthened profitability, as crude oil prices improved in the second half of 1999.

- With 17 billion cubic feet of sales a day, ExxonMobil is the world's largest nongovernment marketer of natural gas. These sales, many of which are underpinned by long-term contracts, produce a strong positive cash flow and provide a solid platform for growth. The company markets gas in North and South America, Europe, the Middle East, and Asia-Pacific, with pipeline and LNG (liquid natural gas) sales in more than 25 countries—in some regions for more than 75 years.

  ExxonMobil has access to a diverse portfolio of both mature gas fields and new gas development totaling 57 trillion cubic feet of proved gas reserves and more than 180 trillion cubic feet of discovered resources, providing a solid base for profitable growth. The company is actively pursuing opportunities to develop and bring to market very large resources in areas such as the Middle East, Africa, Russia, Asia, Alaska, Eastern Canada, Bolivia, and Europe. The company's proprietary (LNG), gas-to-liquids, gas pipeline, and power generation technologies, coupled with gas marketing expertise, are key to commercializing large remote gas resources in many areas around the world.

- ExxonMobil has an ownership interest in 50 refineries in 27 countries, with 6.4 million barrels of distillation capacity a day. Seventeen of these refineries have lube base-stock manufacturing facilities with a capacity of 156,000 barrels a day. XOM operates 34 refineries, with the balance operated under joint-venture agreements.

  Significant work continued in 1999 to make ExxonMobil the premier refiner in the industry. This included activities to improve efficiency, achieve full utilization of attractive processing capacity, and improve margins at all refineries.

- ExxonMobil markets gasoline and other fuel products at more than 45,000 branded service stations in 118 countries. Its affiliates serve aviation customers at 700 airports in 80 countries, marine customers at 150 ports in 60 countries, and some one million industrial and wholesale customers in 50 countries. The company markets under three of the best-known brands in the world, Exxon, Mobil, and Esso.

Nearly 4 million domestic motorists are using the ExxonMobil *Speedpass* system, the quick, easy way to buy gasoline without using a credit card or cash. The *Speedpass* system features a miniature radio transponder attached to a motorist's key chain or affixed to a car's rear window. The transponder automatically transmits a secure identification number recognized electronically by the pump. *Speedpass* has also been introduced in Singapore.

■ ExxonMobil Chemical Company brought together complementary product portfolios, strategies, and organization structures, creating a new company that combines the best of Exxon and Mobil. ExxonMobil Chemical had record sales volumes in 1999, up 4 percent from the prior year, as the company capitalized on new capacity to meet growing demand. Global petrochemical demand grew 5 percent because of economic growth in developing nations and improvements in most Asian economies. Earnings surpassed $1 billion for the sixth year in a row.

■ Return on capital employed of 11 percent continued to exceed that of petroleum industry competition, the result of a diverse business portfolio and strong cost management. Investments continued in facilities to meet growth in the Asia-Pacific and Middle East/Africa

regions and to strengthen the company's position in the Americas and Europe.

■ Despite lower coal and copper prices, earnings from ExxonMobil's coal, minerals, and power businesses increased more than 15 percent in 1999 because of operating cost reductions, record coal and copper production, and favorable sales contract revisions.

XOM's share of production from continuing coal mining operations in Colombia, Australia, and the United States reached a record 16.9 million metric tons in 1999. Average unit operating costs were cut by 9 percent. Despite lower coal realizations, earnings from continuing operations reached a new peak.

ExxonMobil concluded an agreement with the Colombian government to extend to 2034 the Association Contract, under which the company conducts its coal mining operations. Also, the company received a cash payment and agreed to increase long-term coal shipments to a major customer of its Illinois coal mine in return for revised contract terms.

In Chile, copper production exceeded the record set in 1998 by 15 percent. Despite the lowest copper prices in 13 years, profitability improved thanks to a 13 percent decline in operating costs.

Total assets: $144,521 million
Current ratio: 0.77
Common shares outstanding: 3,454 million
Return on 1999 shareholders' equity: 12.6%

		1999	1998	1997	1996	1995	1994	1993	1992
Revenues (billions)		165	106	120	117	108	101	100	103
Net income (millions)		8380	6440	8155	6975	6380	4611	5280	4810
Earnings per share		2.38	2.61	3.24	2.80	2.55	1.84	2.11	1.91
Dividends per share		1.67	1.64	1.63	1.56	1.50	1.46	1.44	1.42
Price	High	87.3	77.3	67.3	50.6	43.0	33.6	34.5	32.8
	Low	64.3	56.6	48.3	38.8	30.1	28.1	28.9	26.9

FedEx Corporation

942 South Shady Grove Road ◻ **Memphis, Tennessee 38120** ◻ **Investor contact: Jeff Smith (901) 818-7037**
◻ **Web site: www.fdxcorp.com** ◻ **Direct dividend reinvestment plan is available (800) 446-2617** ◻ **Fiscal year ends May 31** ◻ **Listed: NYSE** ◻ **Ticker symbol: FDX** ◻ **S&P rating: B** ◻ **Value Line financial strength rating: B++**

FedEx Corporation was founded on January 27, 1998 as a holding company comprising Federal Express Corporation and Caliber System, Inc. FedEx, a $16.8-billion global transportation and logistics powerhouse, offers a broad portfolio of services through its network of six principal independent operating companies:

FedEx invented express distribution 26 years ago and remains the industry's global leader, providing rapid, reliable, time-definite delivery to more than 210 countries, connecting markets that comprise more than 90 percent of the world's gross domestic product. Unmatched air route authorities and transportation infrastructure make FedEx the world's largest express transportation company, providing fast and reliable service for more than three million shipments each business day.

RPS, Inc. is North America's second-largest provider of business-to-business ground small-package delivery service. RPS also provides service to Puerto Rico and 28 European countries.

Like FedEx, RPS is a pioneer in applying advanced information technology to meet customer information needs.

Viking Freight, Inc. is the leading regional freight carrier in the western United States, offering premium next- and second-day less-than-truckload freight service to 11 states, along with direct ocean service to Alaska and Hawaii.

Roberts Express, Inc. is the world's largest surface expedited carrier, offering nonstop, time-specific, door-to-door delivery (with a guarantee) of time-critical and special handling shipments with the United States, Canada, and Europe. In keeping with the core competencies of FedEx, Roberts's point-to-point surface and air-charter delivery solutions are driven by sophisticated and proprietary shipment-control technology.

FDX Global Logistics, Inc. designs, develops, and applies integrated logistics and technology solutions that provide a competitive edge for customers worldwide. Services include transportation management, dedicated contract carriage, intermodal transportation, dedicated and shared warehousing, order fulfillment, and value-added services such as kitting, subassembly, and returnable containers management.

Shortcomings to Bear in Mind

- The company's biggest business, the Priority Overnight service, is fairly mature. This segment accounted for about 40 percent of the company's revenues in the most recent fiscal year, down from 43 percent a year earlier. This shrinkage was caused partly by the shift to billing customers according to the distance of the delivery and partly by increased competition from the U.S. Postal Service.
- According to management, "We are a very capital-intensive business. To do what we do takes big wide-bodied planes—and lots of them. It takes trucks and vans and large, costly operating hubs, both across America and abroad. It takes a lot of information and telecommunications devices, whether it be scanners and radios in the trucks or what-have-you."

On the other hand, FedEx's global network is now more or less complete, and that will make a big difference, not least because investors can expect the pace of capital spending to decline sharply.

- The company's e-commerce exposure continues to be misunderstood by investors. Although air freight deliveries for online orders will probably grow at an exponential pace in the years ahead, analysts believe that much of this incremental business will be derived from business-to-business residential deliveries (not FedEx's specialty) rather than the business-to-business segment, which is the company's forte. What's more, there is growing concern that the mushrooming popularity of e-mail may have some impact on FDX's lucrative overnight letter market.

Reasons to Buy

- Increasingly, businesses are seeking strategic, cost-effective ways to manage their supply chains—the series of transportation and information exchanges required to convert parts and raw materials into finished, delivered products. According to management: "Experience tells us that customers prefer one supplier to meet all of their distribution and logistics needs. And FedEx has what it takes: Our unique global network, operational expertise and air route authorities cannot be replicated by the competition. With FedEx, our customers have a strategic competitive weapon to squeeze time, mass, and cost from the supply chain."

- Federal Express, the world's largest express transportation company, and Tianjin-based Datian W. Air Service Corporation announced in mid-2000 the formation of a joint venture in Beijing. According to the company, this is a "joint venture dedicated to providing unparalleled international express services for customers with shipping requirements to and from China. Federal Express-DTW Co. Ltd. represents the first joint venture in FedEx's global network, bringing together two powerhouses in the express transportation industry. With a strong network and a proven track record in the Chinese marketplace, Datian is an ideal partner for FedEx."

- FedEx acquired Tower Group international, an international logistics and trade-related information technology unit in the spring of 2000. Formerly part of McGraw-Hill, Tower Group will provide such services as customs brokerage, trade consulting, and customs clearance using electronic-commerce technology. FedEx thinks it can accelerate Tower's modest growth rate, partly because FedEx's existing customers have been asking the company to provide trade-consulting services. The new subsidiary will expand worldwide from its base in North America.

- Dell Computer Corporation revolutionized the computer industry with a custom-focused direct business model that's lean on inventory and cycle time but long on logistics efficiencies, customization, and customer delight. The company turns inventory in fewer than 8 days, compared with 60 to 90 days through more traditional indirect competitors. To keep its supply chain tight, Dell has FedEx deliver computers and parts from its factory in Malaysia to its largest Asian market—Japan. In North America, Caliber Logistics provides distribution and fleet management services for Dell facilities in Austin, Texas. FedEx, meanwhile, handles the express deliveries of several Dell products, displaying a commitment to velocity, quality, and customer service that mirrors Dell's own uniquely successful approach to business.

- When a large corporation decentralizes shipping, it's like a computer's circuitry firing at random: interesting pyrotechnics, but not very productive. That's why Unisys chose to harness the buying power of hundreds of sales offices, service locations, and manufacturing sites by utilizing the transportation management services of FDX. Unisys employees simply call a toll-free number staffed by Caliber Logistics. Caliber distribution experts rely on FedEx, RPS, Roberts

Express, and Viking Freight to ship everything from critical replacement parts to Unisys enterprise servers directly to the customer site. Each shipping decision reflects the most appropriate and cost-effective delivery solution.

- With 2,000 employees and owner-operators, Roberts Express is the world's largest surface-expedited carrier. For shippers and their customers, Roberts's service guarantee and exceptional on-time performance deliver peace of mind, even in the most time-critical situations.

   To promote ever higher levels of productivity and service, Roberts recently installed a dynamic vehicle-allocation system. As customer orders are received, the system lets dispatchers evaluate at least 20 load and traffic variables to help ensure that delivery vehicles are where they need to be, when they need to be, for optimum customer service and fleet utilization.

- Nearly 1,000 times each business day, Roberts Express's engineers and executives have to come up with time-specific, door-to-door surface and air-charter delivery solutions that solve special handling challenges for FedEx customers within North America and Europe.

   How special? Consider the 60-ton stamping press Roberts recently delivered from Brescia, Italy to Kokomo, Indiana. The largest shipment ever handled by Roberts, the press was delivered quickly and on time, keeping an automaker's assembly plant up and running at peak efficiency and quality levels.

- What the stock market seems to be overlooking right now is that for all the books and computers and corduroy britches consumers buy from today's Internet retailers, someone has to deliver the goods. In millions of instances, that someone is FedEx. This helps explain how FedEx has been able to keep growing.

- FedEx has invested heavily in recent years to develop an international infrastructure. It presently can reach locations accounting for 90 percent of world GDP, with 24- or 48-hour service. International delivery services for documents and freight have been growing faster than domestic business in recent years.

- The company's fastest-growing domestic services are deferred delivery services: FedEx 2Day and Express Saver. Express Saver, launched in July of 1997, provides guaranteed delivery of shipments in most of the United States within three business days.

- Federal Express, which shut down much of its loss-plagued European delivery business in the early 1990s, began a major expansion in the region. Buoyed by improving global economic conditions and the success of its trans-Atlantic delivery service, FedEx rolled out an expanded schedule of intra-European cargo flights in mid-fiscal 2000, offering a new intra-European overnight delivery service called EuroOne. At the same time, the company opened a long-awaited $200 million regional air hub in Paris and continued to add flights and bigger airplanes over the following year.

Total assets: $10,648 million
Current ratio: 1.18
Common shares outstanding: 298 million
Return on 1999 shareholders' equity: 13.5%

	1999	1998	1997	1996	1995	1994	1993	1992
Revenues (millions)	16773	15703	11520	10274	9392	8480	7808	7550
Net income (millions)	531	526	348	308	282	204	110	64
Earnings per share	2.10	1.75	1.51	1.35	1.25	.92	.51	.30
Dividends per share	Nil							
Price High	61.9	46.6	42.3	22.5	21.5	20.2	18.2	14.1
Low	34.9	21.8	21.0	16.7	14.7	13.4	11.1	8.7

GROWTH AND INCOME

Ford Motor Company

The American Road ▢ World Headquarters—Room 1018 ▢ Dearborn, Michigan 48121 ▢ Investor contact: Mel Stephens (313) 323-8220 ▢ Direct dividend reinvestment plan is available: (800) 955-4791 ▢ Web site: www.ford.com ▢ Listed: NYSE ▢ Ticker symbol: F ▢ S&P rating: B ▢ Value Line financial strength rating: B++

When comparing Ford to General Motors, analysts point out that Ford's margins are higher and it has acquired Jaguar, Volvo, and Land Rover. This makes the product line more upscale, and luxury cars are far more profitable than mass-market cars. What's more, says one analyst, "Ford has laid out a credible plan to improve its European business, which has been a mess."

Company Profile

Ford Motor Company is the world's second-largest motor vehicle manufacturer. Ford produces cars and trucks, as well as many of the vehicles' plastic, glass, electronic components, and replacement parts.

Ford has manufacturing facilities in 26 countries on six continents. Manufacturing employment is about two-thirds of the 373,075 people employed at Ford. The company produces passenger cars, trucks, engines, transmissions, castings and forgings, and metal stampings of all kinds at its 112 wholly owned, equity-owned, and joint-venture plants.

Ford owns a 33 percent stake in Mazda Motor Corporation. The company's financial services include Ford Motor Credit (automotive financing and insurance), American Road Insurance Company, Hertz Corporation (which rents cars), and Granite Management. Granite manages a portfolio of real estate loans retained following the 1994 sale of First Nationwide Financial, a savings and loan subsidiary.

In 1999, Ford acquired the automobile operations of AB Volvo for $6.45 billion. More than half of Volvo car buyers are women, with a majority in the important 34- to-53-year-old segment.

Shortcomings to Bear in Mind

- In April of 2000, Ford announced a complex revamping of its ownership structure, including the payment of a $10-billion special dividend—the largest ever by an American company—and issuance of additional stock to the Ford family, cementing its grip on the world's second-largest industrial corporation. The plan was designed to let Ford distribute nearly half of its $24 billion cash hoard while minimizing taxes for its shareholders and giving the Ford family greater financial flexibility, particularly for estate planning. On the other hand, the huge cash distribution could leave the company somewhat more vulnerable in a recession. However, Ford would still have as much cash after the special dividend as General Motor had at that time.

- After the auto industry finished its record-breaking year in 1999, auto executives started girding themselves for a rough-and-tumble 2000. But not because they looked for sales to slump. In fact, some were even predicting strong sales in 2000. Even so, global car makers still build more vehicles for America than Americans are prepared to buy. That translates into a dogfight among the manufacturers. Big spending on marketing, coupled with weaker prices, appear to be the result of the ample supply of cars and trucks in dealers' showrooms.

  Asian and European brands were the big market-share winners in 1999. Asian auto makers gained almost one point of market share in 1999 and now hold 25.8 percent of the U.S. auto market. European brands now control about a 5.7 percent share. The losers: the domestic brands. Overall, domestic auto makers account for 68.5 percent of cars and trucks sold in the United States, down from 70.2 percent in 1998.

Analysts say it's hard to predict how long the automakers will keep up the fight. Incentives—in the form of cash and subsidized interest rates on financing and leases—have been creeping up for several years without huge effects on earnings and because of cost cutting by the manufacturers. But now incentives could get even richer.

- Jacques Nasser's cost-cutting strategy has done little to patch up Ford's woeful overseas operations. Facing mounting losses in South America, Ford announced a $2-billion restructuring of its Brazilian unit late in 1999.

Nor are things much better in Europe, where Ford eked out a narrow profit in 1999. In the past five years, Ford's share of the West Europe market has declined to 9.5 percent from 11.6 percent, putting it number four, behind Volkswagen AG, General Motors' Adam-Opel AG, and Renault SA.

Ford is suffering from self-inflicted wounds and intense competition. Models that were once class leaders have fallen by the wayside, and the brand has lost cachet among drivers, making highly touted new models like the Focus hard to sell. One analyst said that he hoped strong North American results would buy Nasser room "to fix up the rest of the world. But Ford may be running out of time."

Reasons to Buy

- As part of a strategic plan to be involved in all stages of the automobile life cycle, Ford recently acquired Kwik-Fit, Europe's largest vehicle maintenance and light-repair chain. In addition, the company announced plans to open a chain of used auto parts centers. What's more, Ford's goal is to become the global leader in recycled parts, creating a business with $1 billion in annual revenues within a few years.

- Ford is benefiting from higher revenues and lower operating costs. Domestic car sales are strong, led by the premium-branded Jaguar S-TYPE and Volvo S40/V40 models. In addition, unit sales of several year-2000 models, notably the Focus, Excursion, and Lincoln LS, are selling at an impressive pace.

For several quarters the company has been concentrating on whittling the fat off operating expenses. A cost savings on the order of $1 billion was achieved in 1999.

- Ford's new CEO, who took the reins in early 1999, has outlined his plans. In a move to juice up Ford's stodgy executive suite, Jacques Nasser hired several highly regarded managers from rival automakers around the globe. The biggest coup was scooping up former BMW whiz, Wolfgang Reitzle, to take control of Ford's four luxury brands: Jaguar, Volvo, Lincoln, and Aston Martin. Reitzle, who had been BMW's number two executive, has been given the lion's share of the credit for the German company's turnaround during the past decade.

Mr. Nasser has also tapped top consumer-goods makers for marketing and sales talent. According to analysts, Mr. Nasser's new management team is regarded to be among the industry's best.

Mr. Nasser is also bent on building a fire under the stock's price/earnings ratio, which typically hovers below 10, like most car companies. He wants to see it climb to the 30 range—more like a growth stock than a value stock. To reach that goal, Ford's CEO wants the company to move into higher-margin service businesses, such as quick-repair stations.

■ Ford Motor and thousands of its dealers have been teaming up to sell tires as part of its Quality Care service and to expand its Quick-Lane and AutoCare service brands to capture a bigger chunk of the estimated $200-billion auto after-market industry.

"We want to be the McDonald's version of auto service," said Carl Bergman, Ford's customer-service manager.

Ford officials estimate the company controls about 6 percent of the car parts business, about a $100-billion segment of the broader aftermarket industry. Mr. Bergman said Ford's goal is to control about 24 percent of the parts business, or about the same market share as it has in the new-vehicle industry.

■ The challenge to domestic automakers from the federal government in 1993 seems daunting: build a car that gets 80 miles per gallon of fuel without compromising its size, safety, and price. The government's demands may seem unrealistic and out of reach, but industry executives think they surprise skeptics. For its part, Ford has built a test car, the Prodigy, with the space and convenience of a Taurus sedan that gets more than 70 miles per gallon thanks to a long list of high-tech improvements. The car, which was unveiled in January 2000 at the North American International Auto Show in Detroit, "goes a long way toward meeting our goal of an extremely fuel-efficient vehicle," said Neil Ressler, Ford's vice president of research and vehicle technology.

■ Car company fortunes are closely linked to the state of their product portfolio, with good new models lifting volumes, generating dealership floor traffic, improving brand images, and holding back the tide of incentives. For its part, Ford is introducing four brand new models in 2000:

• the Escape SUV

• the Sport Trac midsize SUV with a pickup bed
• the SuperCrew large SUV with a pickup bed
• the retro-styled Thunderbird two-seater

Ford also created new truck segments in 2000 with the SuperCrew and Sport Trac models. According to analysts, this kind of innovation leads the industry and offers pricing strength, as capacity devoted to existing truck models is actually reduced.

■ According to analysts, "the year 2002 will be a blockbuster." Ford will come out with new versions of its Ranger and F-series pickups in 2002, together worth 18 percent of Ford's North American volume, as well as a new Econoline van and a new midsize SUV for Lincoln.

■ Ford is experimenting with new retail concepts. Ford's new Auto-Concierge arranges routine maintenance, sales of new and used vehicles, temporary transportation, and other transportation-related services for owners of any brand vehicle.

Kwik-Fit is the company's recently acquired European quick-service chain. Kwik-Fit has the light-service distribution capability that Ford lacks. Its service model is highly successful, and Ford can support a rapid expansion with its global resources. In addition, analysts believe that the capabilities and expertise that Kwik-Fit brings to Ford are "highly valuable" if implemented throughout the Ford system.

■ Looking to make sport utility vehicles safer, Ford Motor announced in 2000 that buyers of its 2001 sport utility vehicles will have the option of ordering a special air bag package to protect them against rollovers. The system works through special sensors that detect how far an SUV has tilted to one side. Once a vehicle rolls too far, special curtain air bags are deployed downward from the headliner trim on both sides of the vehicle, protecting people in the front and second-row seats. The air bags stay inflated for up to six seconds, the typical time span it takes a vehicle to roll over several times.

■ In a $2.68 billion transaction, Ford acquired the Land Rover line of sport-utility vehicles from Germany's BMW Group in the spring of 2000. The acquisition adds to Ford's stable of premium models, including the Lincoln, Mercury, Volvo, Jaguar, and Aston Martin brands. The Land Rover line, launched in Solihull, England in 1948, includes the Range Rover, Discovery, and Freelander models. Land Rover's products have long been regarded as the world's premium sport-utility vehicles. However, over the past five years, BMW lost $1.25 billion on its Rover investment—it bought the line in 1995 from a British concern. One problem hurting

the company has been the strong British pound. For its part, Ford expects to forge a turnaround and rid Rover of its red ink within two years.

■ In 2000, Ford introduced a new brand, THINK, for cars and bicycles that operate with clean-battery and fuel-cell propulsion technology. Ford officials said they plan to start selling a new version of the Norwegian-made electric THINK City car in the fourth quarter of 2001 through selected Ford electric-vehicle dealerships in certain states, such as California and New York.

Ford Chairman William Clay Ford, Jr. also said that the company intends to build a midsize car with a hybrid electric internal-combustion engine and transmission systems. "To make a significant impact on the environment, we have to sell millions of vehicles" with clean technology, "not just niche vehicles," Ford said.

Total assets: $237,545 million
Current ratio: 1.77
Common shares outstanding: 1137 million
Return on 1999 shareholders' equity: 26.5%

	1999	1998	1997	1996	1995	1994	1993	1992
Revenues (millions)	162558	144416	153627	146991	137137	128429	108521	100132
Net income (millions)	7237	6570	6920	44370	4139	5308	2529	def.
Earnings per share	5.83	5.28	5.62	3.58	3.58	4.97	2.28	def.
Dividends per share	1.88	1.72	1.65	1.47	1.23	.91	.80	.80
Price High	67.9	65.9	50.3	37.3	32.9	35.0	33.1	24.4
Low	46.3	38.8	30.0	27.3	24.8	25.6	21.5	13.9

INCOME

FPL Group, Inc.

700 Universe Boulevard □ P.O. Box 14000 □ Juno Beach, Florida 33408-0420 □ Investor contact: Lisa Kuzel, CFA (561) 694-4697 □ Dividend reinvestment plan is available: (888) 218-4392 □ Web site: www.fplgroup.com □ Listed: NYSE □ Ticker symbol: FPL □ S&P rating: B+ □ Value Line financial strength rating: A

Florida Power & Light (a key component of FPL Group) continued to improve both productivity and reliability in 1999, enabling customers to benefit from better service at lower rates.

● Operating and maintenance costs per kilowatt-hour declined for the ninth consecutive year, from 1.82 cents per kilowatt-hour (kwh) in 1990 to 1.17 cents per kwh—a 36 percent reduction.

• Plant performance remained at exceptionally high levels. The company's fossil fuel (such as oil and coal) availability of 93 percent was among the best in the nation.

• Nuclear plant availability climbed to an all-time high of 94 percent. Both the company's Turkey Point and St. Lucie plants were among the country's top-rated nuclear installations.

• Florida Power & Light's service reliability, which was already well above the national average, continued to improve in 1999. The average number of interruptions per FPL customer was down 19 percent, while the length of interruptions declined 7 percent.

• In customer satisfaction, FPL rated among the nation's top performing utilities in a nationwide survey undertaken in part by J. D. Powers and Associates.

Company Profile

Florida Power & Light was launched in the final days of 1925, with roots tracing back to Thomas Edison and the General Electric Company.

As FPL Group celebrates its 75th anniversary in this millennium year, it has grown significantly from the original patchwork of enterprises that included ice plants, water, gas, fish, telephone, and streetcar companies, and even 35 mules and wagons.

The company, which began its first year with 76,000 customer accounts and total generating capacity of 70 megawatts, today provides electric service to nearly 4 million customer accounts. It is among the largest energy providers in the United States and continues to grow at a rapid pace.

In 1926, FPL embarked upon one of the most ambitious construction programs in the history of the electric utility industry, spending at that time the staggering sum of $50 million on power plants and a transmission network.

Seventy-five years later, FPL is still expanding its system with a $3-billion investment that will add by 2003 nearly two thousand five hundred additional megawatts. This is in addition to its current capacity of more than sixteen thousand megawatts, and will ensure that Floridians continue to enjoy the benefits of safe, reliable, and reasonably priced electricity.

FPL Group, Inc. is the parent of Florida Power & Light Company, one of the largest investor-owned electric utilities in the nation. Other operations include FPL Energy, a leader in producing electricity from clean and renewable fuels. FPL Energy has projects in 13 states, South America, and the United Kingdom.

FPL serves an area covering almost the entire eastern seaboard of Florida and the southern third of the state. Cities served by Florida Power & Light include St. Augustine, Daytona Beach, Melbourne, Stuart, West Palm Beach, Fort Lauderdale, Miami, Bradenton, Sarasota, Fort Myers, and Naples.

The region continues to experience vibrant growth, driven by Florida's attractive climate, natural beauty, and exceptional quality of life.

Throughout the 1990s, FPL Group narrowed the focus of its other businesses to concentrate on the independent power industry outside Florida. It divested several businesses, including insurance, consulting, and real estate, and strengthened its independent power operations. In 1998 the company completed the sale of its citrus subsidiary, Turner Foods. In 1999 the company reached an agreement to sell its cable TV interests. These transactions essentially complete FPL's program of divesting unrelated businesses that were acquired in the 1980s.

During the 1990s FPL Group focused on reducing costs, improving quality and customer satisfaction, and investing outside of Florida in environmentally favored generation technologies. As a consequence, the company is one of the largest, cleanest, most efficient, and financially sound providers of electricity in the country.

Shortcomings to Bear in Mind

■ The stock market in 1999 was not kind to electric power companies. The Standard & Poor's Electric Utilities Index, moreover, returned a negative 19 percent, underperforming the S&P 500 Index by more than 40 percent, the largest margin in history. What's more, FPL Group underperformed the electric utilities index by 8 percentage points. This was due largely to a $350-million-per-year reduction in rates charged by Florida Power & Light, coupled with a writedown taken on FPL Energy's power generating assets in Maine as a result of unexpected changes in federal regulations.

■ Electric utilities are not recommended for growth-oriented investors. According to one analyst, "Earnings growth from the regulated utility will be limited to 2 percent. Thus, if FPL is to realize (after 2000) annual EPS growth of 6 or 7 percent, it will have to come from the growth of the non-regulated operations, primarily through FPL Energy's development and operation of low-cost generation facilities."

■ Until recent years, electric utilities were not unduly concerned with competition. In particular, there was little concern over competition from other electric utilities. By their very nature they were natural monopolies, with each utility serving exclusively its own area, such as a city or part of a state. In fact, since there was no competition, it was necessary to regulate electric companies. Without regulation it was feared that power companies would charge whatever the traffic would bear.

That era may be passing. There seems to be a groundswell in favor of letting large users buy their power from the company with the lowest rates,

regardless of whether it is 10 miles or 1,000 miles away.

Of great importance is the nature of the company's customers. Most of them are residential or commercial. Only a tiny percentage of revenues come from industrial customers: 4 percent. By contrast, a typical utility might obtain one-fourth of its revenues from the industrial sector. It is these large customers who are the most likely to seek lower rates.

Reasons to Buy

■ In the summer of 2000, FPL Group agreed to acquire the Entergy Corporation for about $7 billion in stock in a deal that created the nation's largest electric company. Entergy is based in New Orleans. The new holding company has 6.3 million customers and 48,000 megawatts of power generating capacity. In 1999, Entergy had revenues of $8.77 billion, compared with $6.44 billion for FPL Group. However, FPL had higher net income of $697 million, compared with $595 million for Entergy.

The deal was billed as a $27 billion merger of equals—with neither company's shareholders getting a premium for their stock. Each share of FPL will be converted into one share of a new holding company. Meanwhile, shareholders of Entergy will receive 0.585 of a share of the new company for each share of Entergy. The merger is expected to immediately boost earnings for both companies. The combination must be cleared by stockholders as well has federal regulators. FPL and Entergy said they hope to complete the transaction within 15 months (from the end of July 2000).

■ In 1999 FPL Energy, the company's independent power subsidiary that operates outside Florida, expanded its generating operations and construction projects in 13 states. Its generating capacity grew by nearly 60 percent, to more than three thousand megawatts.

- In January 2000 the company established a new subsidiary, FPL FiberNet, to sell fiber-optic capacity. This subsidiary acquired 1,600 miles of inter-city fiber network from Florida Power & Light and is selling capacity to telephone, cable television, Internet, and other telecommunications companies.

  The company plans to expand the network to major cities throughout Florida and expects to complete construction of 15 metropolitan networks by 2002. First year revenues of the company are expected to be between $30 million and $40 million, and FPL Group believes FiberNet will enhance parent company earnings soon.

- Wind-powered plants totaling 117 megawatts were constructed in Iowa and Texas in 1999, and construction began on a 1,000-megawatt natural gas-fired power plant near Paris, Texas.

- FPL Energy continues to focus on the generation of electricity using "clean" technologies and fuels such as natural gas and renewable sources, including wind, solar, and hydro energy. The company is one of the nation's largest producers of electricity from wind power, and about 75 percent of its power generation is derived from clean fuels.

- FPL uses a diverse energy mix to produce power. This diversity provides operating flexibility and helps lower fuel costs by taking advantage of energy price changes. This means lower bills for FPL customers.

- The Turkey Point plant south of Miami became the first nuclear facility in the country to receive three consecutive "superior" ratings from the Nuclear Regulatory Commission.

- FPL has a long history of offering cost-effective programs that meet the energy conservation-related needs of its customers. In the past two decades, the company successfully reduced demand for energy by more than 2,600 megawatts—meaning that FPL customers aren't paying for six additional power plants.

- FPL Energy's generation portfolio reflects a focus on clean energy: almost 80 percent is either gas-fired or derived from renewables such as wind, hydro, geothermal, and solar energy. FPL Energy is the nation's largest generator of wind energy.

  FPL Energy owns more than 3,000 net megawatts (mw) of generating capacity currently operating. About 97 percent of this capacity is located in the United States. When other projects currently planned or under construction are completed, the company will have close to 4,400 megawatts of capacity.

- The population of Florida has grown dramatically, doubling since 1970 to 15 million residents today. FPL has been part of Florida's growth for more than 70 years, expanding its generation system to keep pace with the substantial increases in customers and average power usage.

Total assets: $13,441 million
Current ratio: 0.73
Common shares outstanding: 171 million
Return on 1999 shareholders' equity: 12.6%

	1999	1998	1997	1996	1995	1994	1993	1992
Revenues (millions)	6438	6661	6369	6037	5593	5423	5316	5193
Net income (millions)	680	679	636	603	553	557	556	511
Earnings per share	3.98	3.85	3.57	3.33	3.16	2.91	2.75	2.65
Dividends per share	2.08	2.00	1.92	1.84	1.76	1.88	2.47	2.43
Price High	61.9	72.6	60.0	48.1	46.5	39.1	41.0	38.4
Low	41.1	56.1	42.6	41.5	34.1	27.4	35.5	32.0

Gannett Company, Inc.

1100 Wilson Blvd. ◻ Arlington, Virginia 22234 ◻ Investor contact: Gracia Martore (703) 284-6918 ◻ Dividend reinvestment plan is available: (800) 778-3299 ◻ Web site: www.gannett.com ◻ Listed: NYSE ◻ Ticker symbol: GCI ◻ S&P rating: A ◻ Value Line financial strength rating: A++

As the Internet continues to be a growing part of people's lives, more Gannett newspapers are jumping onto the World Wide Web. What's more, the online pioneers continue to enhance content and add new products, including those stemming from Gannett's participation in Classified Ventures and CareerPath.com.

As leading information providers for their communities, the company's newspapers are aware that fresh information is essential to success online. *Florida Today's* Space Online (www.spaceonline.com), for instance, covers space shuttle launches, literally as they blast off. Reporters with laptop computers file stories from the beach at Cape Canaveral, supplying live news online within moments of a launch.

Company Profile

Gannett is a diversified news and information company that publishes newspapers and operates broadcasting stations. The company also has a stake in marketing, commercial printing, a newswire service, data services, and news programming. Gannett has operations in 45 states, the District of Columbia, Guam, England, Germany, and Hong Kong.

In terms of circulation, Gannett is the largest domestic newspaper group, with 74 daily newspapers, including *USA Today*, a variety of non-daily publications, and *USA Weekend*, a weekly newspaper magazine. Total average paid daily circulation of Gannett's daily newspapers is about 6.6 million.

Gannett owns and operates 21 television stations in major markets covering 17.4 percent of the United States.

Highlights of 1999

● The business of the Internet was the business of Gannett in 1999. The number of its domestic newspaper Web sites grew to 60 over the year, and the company more than doubled the products it offers online to more than 480. These products include news sites, community-oriented sites, and numerous specialty sites based on the unique characteristics of the individual markets. In 2000, Gannett has been adding more products and is launching the remainder of the small-market newspaper sites.

● As the most visited general news site on the Web, USATODAY.com solidified its position in 1999 as an Internet leader. Over the year, content was enhanced and multimedia coverage was added. Advertising revenue and e-commerce sponsorships exploded in 1999, and USATODAY.com made a profit for the entire year—almost unheard of in the dot.com world.

● The company's broadcast group launched new media activities through Web sites in 13 of its television markets in 1999. Each of the company's major stations has made significant progress in creating a new business around its Web activities, and Gannett plans to have Web sites in all of its TV markets in 2000. Overall, Gannett generated about $40 million in revenue in 1999 from Internet activities, with a minimal loss.

● Readership was up in 1999, proving value should be measured by the number of people who read a newspaper, not solely by the number who buy it. Increasingly, the industry and the advertising world are taking notice, and studies of readership are underway both at Gannett and nationally.

• The company's newspapers had record earnings in 1999, benefiting from strong advertising demand—particularly in classified and national—and newspaper expenses that declined 6 percent for the year. Gannett also enjoyed another year of profit improvement at the *Detroit News*, the company's New Jersey properties, and *USA Weekend*.

• *USA Today* had its best year ever and is the nation's largest-selling daily newspaper with readership at 5.4 million and average circulation of about 2.3 million copies per day. Advertising revenues climbed 17 percent as several of the paper's largest ad categories experienced double-digit growth. Dot-com advertising added to the boom. What's more, *USA Today* led all major print publications in the share of paid dot-com advertising pages.

• *USA Today's Baseball Weekly* had its best year ever, with advertising and circulation revenues at all-time highs. The publication, nine years old in April of 2000, secured new multiyear partnerships with several high-profile advertisers in 1999.

Shortcomings to Bear in Mind

■ The NBC television network and Gannett Broadcasting signed a new arrangement early in 2000, cutting the amount of money NBC will pay Gannett to carry its shows. The move underscores a mounting struggle over the traditional financial relationship between broadcast networks and local television stations.

Those familiar with the five-year pact between the two companies said it dramatically reduces the more than $25 million payment of so-called affiliate compensation that NBC annually pays the broadcaster. By the end of the deal, the network's payments to Gannett are expected to sink to the $10-million level.

For decades the big networks have paid local stations to carry their programming—a practice they are now looking to eliminate. The networks argue that they should end, or at least dramatically reduce, affiliate compensation—longer term they want the affiliates to pay them. For their part, affiliates counter that the networks are risking their strong distribution, and the stage is being set for some tough negotiations in the future.

■ In the words of John J. Curley, CEO of Gannett, "1999 was a challenging year for our television stations. The absence of major special events on our stations—the Super Bowl, Winter Olympics, and strong election spending, all of which bolstered results in 1998—made for difficult comparisons in 1999."

Reasons to Buy

■ Gannett ended 1999 with its eighth consecutive year of record revenues and profits. The company's newspapers led the way, helped by the longest economic expansion in history. Gannett's revenues increased 8 percent to nearly $5.3 billion, and earnings advanced 13 percent to about $886 million. Cash flow increased 12 percent to $1.84 billion, another record.

Behind the success was strong advertising demand at all the papers, an acquisition overseas, and lower newsprint prices. In another realm, *USA Today* had record operating results.

■ In 1999, Gannett bought the British regional newspaper group, Newsquest PLC, for about $1.7 billion in cash.

Newsquest's publications include such major regional newspapers as the *Northern Echo*, based in Darlington, north England, the *Oxford Mail*, the *Evening Argus* in Brighton, south England, and *Westmoreland Gazette*, in the Lake District in north England.

Newsquest had a pretax profit of $204.3 million in 1998 on sales of $483.5 million.

About one-third of Newsquest's newspapers are more than 100 years old. *Berrow's Worcester Journal*, established in 1690, is the oldest continuously published newspaper in the world. While maintaining this fine tradition, Newsquest has been a leader in expanding into new lines of Web-based products and technology. In 1995, Newsquest was the first regional newspaper group in the United Kingdom to launch a Web site. Since then it has continued to build its Web-based strategy, skill base, and knowledge, with every Newsquest newspaper having an Internet presence. In 1999, it pioneered a new e-commerce service called Shoppers World.

Newsquest also publishes lifestyle and business magazines, local information guides, and seasonal publications.

New launches in 1999 included *Limited Edition*, a glossy, high-quality lifestyle magazine, local business news magazines, and a guide to local Web sites.

- In July of 1999 Gannett elected to get out of cable television, selling all of its properties to Cox Communications of Atlanta for $2.7 billion in cash. Gannett President Douglas H. McCorkindale said the company didn't make a strategic decision to get out of the cable business but decided to sell because "someone just offered us a lot of money." The price of cable franchises has been rising rapidly recently, and Gannett was able to get one of the highest per-household price ever paid—$4,500 to $5,100, depending on how the value is calculated—for its 525,000 subscribers. McCorkindale said the sale would have a "positive" effect on Gannett's earnings. Gannett had owned the cable TV operations for only 3½ years.

Total assets: $9,006 million
Current ratio: 1.07
Common shares outstanding: 279 million
Return on 1999 shareholders' equity: 19.8%

	1999	1998	1997	1996	1995	1994	1993	1992
Revenues (millions)	5260	5121	4730	4421	4007	3824	3642	3469
Net income (millions)	919	816	713	531	477	465	398	346
Earnings per share	3.26	2.86	2.50	1.89	1.71	1.62	1.36	1.20
Dividends per share	.82	.78	.74	.71	.68	.67	.64	.63
Price High	83.6	75.1	61.8	39.4	32.4	29.5	29.1	27.0
Low	60.6	47.6	35.7	29.5	24.8	23.1	23.4	20.6

AGGRESSIVE GROWTH

General Electric Company

3135 Easton Turnpike ❑ Fairfield, Connecticut, 06431 ❑ Investor contact: Mark L. Vachon (203) 373-2816 ❑ Direct dividend reinvestment plan is available: (800) 786-2543 ❑ Web site: www.ge.com ❑ Ticker symbol: GE ❑ S&P rating: A+ ❑ Value Line financial strength rating: A++

General Electric, a superbly managed company, has the second-largest market capitalization of any public company. It provides a broad range of industrial products and services. Under the stewardship of the legendary CEO Jack Welch, GE has transformed itself from operating as a maker of diverse industrial equipment to being a provider of a broad range of commercial and consumer services.

In 1980, manufacturing operations generated about 85 percent of operating profits; currently, services operations generate 75 percent of total operating profits. GE Capital (the company's enormous financing arm and the world's largest non-bank financial operation) alone generates nearly 30 percent of operating profits.

Company Profile

General Electric is one of the world's largest corporations, with 1999 revenues of more than $111 billion. Although GE can trace its origins back to Thomas Edison, who invented the light bulb in 1879, the company was actually founded in 1892.

The company's broad diversification is clearly evident if you examine its components. Operations are divided into two groups: product, service, and media businesses and GE Capital Services (GECS).

Product, service, and media includes 11 businesses: aircraft engines, appliances, lighting, medical systems, NBC, plastics, power systems, electrical distribution and control, information services, motors and industrial systems, and transportation systems.

GECS operates 27 financial businesses clustered in equipment management, specialty insurance, consumer services, specialized financing, and mid-market financing.

Shortcomings to Bear in Mind

- With CEO John F. Welch, Jr. set to retire (in April of 2001), there are few more tantalizing questions in corporate America than who will replace the legendary executive. Neither Welch nor the company will discuss succession, and no obvious heir-apparent has surfaced.

  That doesn't mean the race to succeed Jack Welch is not well underway. He has a stable of seasoned lieutenants vying for the job. And over the past two years

Welch has given new tasks to a younger crop of possible heirs and fast-trackers in their forties. His two-pronged strategy: test the front-runners while also developing GE's farm team.

It's a delicate balancing act. If Welch anoints an heir, he could face a brain drain of GE's most seasoned players. With the race still open, however, headhunters say it has been remarkably difficult to lure would-be CEOs away from the giant conglomerate.

- For nearly two decades under Jack Welch, General Electric has dominated businesses through innovation, efficiency, and toughness. In a host of supposedly mature industries, from aircraft engines to power systems, GE has boosted profits, grabbed market share, and nurtured new products. But this success has not been translated to the business that makes the company a household word—appliances. For years the division that makes refrigerators, ovens, and dishwashers has suffered from one wrenching problem after another: sagging retail prices, lackluster innovation, prickly relations with union workers, and intense competition with rivals that have sometimes beaten GE to market with innovative products.

  In one sense, GE Appliances is such a small part of the GE empire that its disappointing fortunes haven't hurt the company overall. The reason: the appliance operation accounts for less than 3 percent of the company's total revenue. Even so, it remains important to GE's brand identity with consumers. People are much more likely to associate GE with ovens, dishwashers, and refrigerators than with aircraft engines, TV programs, or turbine generators.

Reasons to Buy

- The key to GE's business plan is the requirement that businesses be first or second in market share in their industries. Those that fail to achieve this status are divested.

- Jack Welch has developed a defect-reduction program called Six Sigma. Six Sigma contributes mightily to GE's earning growth. Think of sigma as a mark on a bell curve that measures standard deviation. Most companies have between 35,000 and 50,000 defects per million operations, or about 3 sigma. For GE, a defect could be anything from the misbilling of an NBC advertiser to faulty wiring in locomotives. Four years ago engineers determined that the company was averaging 35,000 defects per million operations—or about 3.5 sigma. (The higher the sigma, the fewer the errors.) That was a better-than-average showing, but not enough for Welch's restless mind. He's now maniacal about hitting his goal of reducing defects to the point where errors would be almost nonexistent: 3.4 defects per million, or 6 sigma.

- Six Sigma project work consists of five basic activities: Defining, Measuring, Analyzing, Improving, and then Controlling processes. In the words of management, "These projects usually focus on improving our customers' productivity and reducing their capital outlays, while increasing the quality, speed, and efficiency of our operations."

- GE is strong financially, with 98 percent of its capitalization made up of shareholders' equity. Coverage of total interest, moreover, is a hefty 17 times.

- Despite its huge size, the company continues to demonstrate growth. In the 1989–1999 period, earnings per share climbed from $0.36 to $1.07, a compound annual growth rate of 11.4 percent. (The company, moreover, has had 23 consecutive annual earnings increases.) In the same 10-year span, dividends per share advanced from $0.14 a share to $0.48, a growth rate of 12.8 percent.

- Scientists from GE Plastics and Corporate R&D have developed a new process to improve quality and reduce cycle times in manufacturing Lexan polycarbonate for compact disks.

- NBC has moved aggressively to expand into cable television. The network has stakes in 17 cable networks, including CNBC, Court TV, and the History Channel. NBC has also moved swiftly in recent years to introduce new entertainment and new channels in Europe, Asia, and Latin America.

- In the fall of 1999, the company's NBC television unit bought a 32 percent stake in money-losing Paxson Communications Corporation for $415 million, gaining additional TV stations to air its programs in major markets.

Paxson Chairman Lowell Paxson, who created the Pax network a year earlier to broadcast reruns of *Touched by an Angel* and other family-oriented shows, needed a deep-pocketed partner to cover losses as well as help with marketing and to supply programming.

For its part, NBC wanted to use the Paxson stations to rebroadcast programs such as movies and miniseries and attract more viewers and ad revenue.

The agreement followed a Federal Communications Commission ruling a month earlier that allows one company—for the first time—to own as many as two stations in big U.S. markets. Paxson stations overlap 11 of the 13 markets where NBC owns stations, including Los Angeles, Chicago, Philadelphia, Boston, Miami, and Washington. The extra stations now give NBC the ability to blanket a single city with more of its own programming, which helps it command higher fees from local advertisers.

- GE was an aggressive acquirer of companies in 1999, with acquisitions accounting for nearly half the company's revenue growth during the year. The pace was still growing strong in the fourth quarter of 1999, when GE spent $14 billion on 80 acquisitions, for an annualized revenue rate approaching $55 billion. One analyst said, "I expect this accelerated pace to continue throughout 2000 and to further add to GE revenue and earnings." He predicted that GE would invest between $40 billion and $50 billion for 200 or more companies during 2000, up from $30 billion for more than 150 companies in 1999.

- In the first quarter of 2000, General Electric, the number one maker of appliances for new homes in the United States, said it had agreed to develop standards with the Microsoft Corporation to connect so-called smart appliances with other consumer devices. GE said that it would join Microsoft's Universal Plug and Play Forum (UPC), which includes Sony, IBM, and Intel.

GE made the announcement from the National Association of Home Builders trade show in Dallas, where it was displaying several "smart" appliances for which standards are being developed. They include a microwave that reads Universal Product Codes (UPC) and a refrigerator that could be connected to the World Wide Web, allowing a consumer to monitor home appliances through the Internet.

A consumer, for instance, could get to work and display a Web page to turn off a stove burner that had been left on. The microwave is programmed to read the UPC, display recipe or ingredient information, and start cooking.

- General Electric unveiled two digital imaging systems that it says will transform care in two high-profile medical fields: breast-cancer screening and heart disease. The new products, both 13 years in development, are intended to replace conventional film-based X-ray equipment with digital technology that provides sharper pictures of breast tissue and coronary arteries. But the price of the new machines could temper their acceptance in the market. The mammography machine, called Senographe 2000D, costs between $400,000 and $500,000, compared with about $100,000 for traditional film-based machines. The cardiovascular system, called GE Innova 2000, is priced at $1 million to $1.3 million and is being introduced into a much larger and more profitable market. GE spent $150 million developing the digital X-ray technology that is at the core of both systems.

- In a late-1999 move that substantially beefed up its credit card business, GE's financial arm, GE Capital, bought the credit-card operations of retailer J. C. Penney for close to $4 billion. With the transaction, GE Capital, a provider of private-label and retail credit cards, gained 35 million accounts to add to the roughly 70 million it already had in North America. The Penney transaction came only a few weeks after it had won an agreement to issue the first-ever credit card to be offered by Wal-Mart Stores.

Total assets: $405,200 million
Current ratio: 0.68
Common shares outstanding: 9,855 million
Return on 1999 shareholders' equity: 26.8%

	1999	1998	1997	1996	1995	1994	1993	1992
Revenues (millions)	111630	100469	54515	46119	43013	60109	55701	53051
Net income (millions)	10717	9296	82033	7280	6573	5915	4184	4137
Earnings per share	1.07	.93	.83	.73	.65	.58	.51	.42
Dividends per share	.48	.42	.36	.32	.28	.25	.22	.19
Price High	53.2	34.6	25.5	17.7	12.2	9.1	8.9	7.3
Low	31.4	23.0	16.0	11.6	8.3	7.5	6.7	6.1

General Motors Corporation

3044 West Grand Boulevard ❑ Detroit, Michigan 48202-3091 ❑ Investor contact: (313) 556-2044 ❑ Dividend reinvestment plan is available: (800) 331-9922 ❑ Web site: www.gm.com ❑ Listed: NYSE ❑ Ticker symbol: GM ❑ S&P rating: B ❑ Value Line financial strength rating: B++

General Motors has seen its market share plummet from 44 percent in the early 1980s to 29 percent today. In order to reverse this trend, the company is now building cars that people want. At an auto show in 2000, for instance, the company displayed such concept cars as its Buick Rendezvous, a luxury-car-based sport-utility vehicle aimed at buyers of Toyota's hot-selling Lexus RX300. It will go on sale in early 2001.

For the first time in years, GM cars ranked among the best seen at the year's big auto show, according to a survey of 900 people done by CNW Marketing/Research in 2000.

Company Profile

General Motors Corporation, founded in 1908, is the world's largest vehicle manufacturer. GM designs, manufactures, and markets cars, trucks, automotive systems, heavy-duty transmissions, and locomotives worldwide.

Other substantial business interests include Hughes Electronics Corporation and General Motors Acceptance Corporation.

GM cars and trucks are sold in close to 190 countries, and the company has manufacturing, assembly, or component operations in more than 50 countries.

General Motors' Operations

General Motors North American Operation manufactures vehicles for the following nameplates: Chevrolet, Pontiac, Oldsmobile, Buick, Cadillac, GMC, and Saturn.

General Motors International Operations meet the demands of customers outside North America, with vehicles designed and manufactured for the following nameplates: Opel, Vauxhall, Holden, Isuzu, and Saab.

General Motors Acceptance Corporation provides a broad range of financial services, including consumer vehicle financing, full-service leasing and fleet leasing, dealer financing, car and truck extended-service contracts, residential and commercial mortgage services, and vehicle and homeowners insurance. GMAC's business spans 33 markets around the world.

Hughes Electronics Corporation manufactures advanced technology electronic systems, products, and services for the telecommunications and space, automotive electronics, and aerospace and defense industries on a global scale.

General Motors Locomotive Group manufactures diesel-electric locomotives, medium-speed diesel engines, locomotive components, locomotive services, and light-armored vehicles to a global customer base.

Allison Transmission Division is the world's largest producer of heavy-duty automatic transmissions for commercial-duty trucks and buses, off-highway equipment, and military vehicles.

Shortcomings to Bear in Mind

- In 1999, Ford Motor made its latest incursion into the big sport-utility vehicle market by introducing the biggest SUV yet, the Excursion. General Motors, which has dominated the market for decades with its hulking Chevrolet and GMC Suburban, was not willing to back down without a fight. In March of 1999, the company displayed a prototype of its redesigned 2000 Suburban at the New York International Auto Show. At the same time, GM also displayed its redesigned 2000 GMC Yukon, a slightly smaller SUV whose Chevy twin is called the Tahoe.

The two-and-a-half-ton, nine-seat Suburban is a critical product for General Motors—one of its most profitable and enduring. It was introduced in 1935, predating even the Volkswagen Beetle and making it the longest-running automobile nameplate ever.

According to one analyst, "The Suburban market is one of the few segments where GM can really claim leadership at the moment. But that leadership position is being threatened by a very aggressive Ford innovation."

- For Fiat, General Motors' purchase of 20 percent of its auto business in March of 2000 is just the breather it was seeking. The Italian carmaker—Italy's largest—gets a deep-pocketed partner with a reputation as an easygoing, hands-off minority stakeholder, leaving Fiat's managers in charge. And GM's prize? It gets small Fiat diesel engines and a chance to trim its costs in Europe and Latin America—not to mention the pleasure of thwarting rival DaimlerChrysler's effort to swallow Fiat whole. Yet GM's minority stake gives it little clout to force the tough cost-cutting Fiat needs, and it leaves GM competing fiercely with its new partner in key European auto segments. Laments one large GM institutional investor: "It looks like a huge victory for Fiat, but it doesn't do very much for General Motors."
- Falling behind on new models has cost Saturn and its parent dearly. While just 5.6 percent of GM's sales at its height in 1994, Saturn, with its fresh image and

huge customer following, represented one of the few bright spots on the auto giant's horizon. Since then, however, sales have fallen 20 percent.

Nor have Saturn's prospects improved with the lukewarm reception of the new L-Series midsize car. It was to be Saturn's savior, designed to lure new buyers and bring back its old customers. But when the dealers finally got an ample supply of LS sedans and LW wagons, the crowds never showed up.

- In 1999, United Auto Workers President Stephen Yokich said he strongly opposes GM's plan to slash vehicle production costs by shifting work from assembly plant to suppliers' factories under a strategy known as modular assembly. The union leader also denounced GM's handling of the spinoff of its Delphi Automotive Systems Corp. unit. Mr. Yokich's sharp criticism of General Motors indicates that the nation's leading automaker still has a long way to go to heal the rift with the UAW that sparked 1998's seven-and-a-half-week strike and a series of walkouts prior to that. Mr. Yokich agrees, "People say Ford has a better relationship with the UAW than GM, and Chrysler has a better relationship than GM, and they're right." The UAW represents about 220,000 workers at General Motors, 101,000 at Ford, and 75,000 at Daimler-Chrysler AG.

Reasons to Buy

- According to one automotive writer, "What saves GM is its full-size pickup truck platform. From this chassis, you can get the big pickups and sport-utility vehicles like the Chevy Suburban and Tahoe. The big GM pickups will outsell Ford's big pickup in 2000. Big pickups and SUVs together will account for 1.4 million vehicles in 2000, and most of GM's profits. GM has some strong cars.

The Chevy Impala, the Pontiac Bonneville, and the Saturn SL look like winners. Late in 2000, GM will have the Pontiac Aztek, a crossover vehicle—a car chassis and four-wheel drive. It will cost $28,000 loaded."

- In early 2000, Buick took the wraps off the Rendevous, a vehicle that combines the styling and all-wheel-drive capability of a sport-utility vehicle and the cavernous interior space of a minivan. "GM hasn't had a product that has been as in-tune with the times as this in at least 20 years," said James Hall, a vice president at AutoPacific, Inc., an industry consultant. The Rendevous will arrive in dealer showrooms early in 2001.

- A new CEO took the helm at General Motors in 2000, G. Richard Wagoner, Jr., age 47, previously the president and chief operating officer of the company. He moved into his new office on June 1, 2000. Wall Street applauded the move. "It is good to have younger people moving into positions of importance," commented one analyst. Auto industry veterans echoed the sentiment. "In an organization as traditional and hidebound as General Motors, having a person who doesn't know all the reasons that things *can't* be done can be a benefit," said Robert A. Lutz, former president and vice chairman of Chrysler and now the chief executive of the Exide Corporation, the battery maker.

  Mr. Wagoner has been a star at GM for more than a decade. Just like many past chief executives, he began his career in the company's powerful treasurer's office in New York. He later became treasurer of GM's Brazil operations, then moved to the finance jobs in Canada and Europe. He was then sent back to lead the Brazil operations, which he turned around.

- Competing on a global basis is a priority that is driving the largest international production capacity expansion in the company's history. General Motors has five new manufacturing facilities either under development or up and running in Argentina, China, Brazil, Poland, and Thailand. These plants are the cornerstone of GM's expansion into new markets.

- Chevrolet General Manager Kurt Ritter said the GM marketing division will sell about 2.7 million vehicles in North America in 2000, even if the industry turns down moderately from the pace of 17.5 million units in 1999. Chevrolet said the robust sales figures, which would be up from sales of 2.5 million in 1999, will come primarily from five new products Chevrolet introduced in 1999: the Impala, Monte Carlo, Tracker, Suburban, and Tahoe. Mr. Ritter also said Chevrolet hopes to plug a big hole in its lineup during 2000 with Silverado HD, a heavy-duty work truck that will feature GM's new Duramax diesel engine and an Allison transmission.

  Chevrolet's market share in the highly profitable three-quarter-ton and one-ton work-truck market is 21 percent, a distant second to Ford's 50 percent share. When asked why GM hasn't been able to capitalize on a heavy-truck market that has doubled and a diesel market that has tripled in the past 10 years, Mr. Ritter said GM has been hurt by the lack of a reliable heavy-duty diesel engine and restrained by truck production capacity. He said that Chevrolet hopes to produce about 120,000 Silverado HDs a year and increase its market share to 25 percent, perhaps 30 percent.

- In 2000, General Motors said that it would buy the half of Saab Automobile A.B. that it did not already own. "The brand attracts a very different consumer than we normally see in General Motors showrooms," said G. Richard Wagoner, Jr., then GM's president. "We want to keep that brand very distinctive and very unique."

GM's production unit production costs could decline as a result of the deal. "This is a huge opportunity to do common platforms between GM and Opel and get a lot of cost out," said Harry J. Pearce, the company's vice chairman, referring to the Adam Opel

A. G. subsidiary in Germany. GM is considering broadening Saab's product lineup.

GM Chairman, John F. Smith, Jr., said completing the acquisition will allow the company to add new vehicles to Saab's model lineup faster, boosting its annual sales to 300,000–400,000 units over the next five to seven years. Saab sold 131,500 cars in 1999, 11 percent more than in 1998.

Total assets: $274,730 million
Current ratio: 1.21
Common shares outstanding: 640 million
Return on 1999 shareholders' equity: 29.2%

	1999	1998	1997	1996	1995	1994	1993	1992
Revenues (millions)	176558	161315	153782	164069	168829	154951	138220	132429
Net income (millions)	6002	2956	6698	4668	6932	5659	2466	def.
Earnings per share	8.53	5.21	8.70	5.72	7.28	6.20	2.13	def.
Dividends per share	2.00	2.00	2.00	1.60	1.10	.80	.80	1.40
Price High	94.9	76.7	72.4	59.4	53.1	65.4	57.1	44.4
Low	59.8	47.1	52.3	45.8	37.4	36.1	32.1	28.8

GROWTH AND INCOME

Genuine Parts Company

2999 Circle 75 Parkway ❑ Atlanta, Georgia 30339 ❑ Investor contact: Jerry W. Nix (770) 953-1700 ❑ Dividend reinvestment plan is available: (800) 568-3476 ❑ Web site:www.genpt.com ❑ Ticker symbol: GPC ❑ S&P rating: A+ ❑ Value Line financial strength rating: A++

An automotive aftermarket upturn that began in 1993 is expected to continue. Several factors are contributing to this growth:

• The average age of cars and trucks is increasing. Currently, the average age of the vehicle fleet is over eight years; it is expected to surpass nine years by the year 2000.

• Vehicle usage is up. Miles driven by personal and commercial drivers are increasing at a 3 percent annual pace.

• The vehicle population is climbing steadily at an average annual rate of 2.6 percent since 1970.

• There appears to be significant pent-up demand in discretionary repairs to

add potential sales growth. It is estimated that unperformed maintenance approaches $50 million at retail levels.

• Government regulations will be one of the key drivers in the future growth of the automotive aftermarket. The most widely known initiative has been the IM240 testing programs mandated by the Clean Air Act of 1990. More stringent emissions programs have always benefited the repair business and created additional parts sales. It is believed that governmental agencies will continue to tighten emissions regulations in the future and will provide solid support for aftermarket growth.

Company Profile

Genuine Parts Company, founded in 1928, is a service organization engaged in the distribution of a wide range of products, including automotive replacement parts, industrial replacement parts, office products, and electrical/electronic materials.

The company's products and services are offered through a network of over one thousand seven hundred operations, geographically located across the United States, Canada, and Mexico. Here are the segments that make up the company:

The Automotive Parts Group

The Automotive Parts Group, the largest division of Genuine Parts Company, distributes over two hundred thirty thousand automotive replacement parts, accessory items, and service items. This Group operates 62 NAPA distribution centers, 3 Balkamp distribution centers, 6 Rayloc facilities, and 5 Johnson Industries facilities and serves about five thousand six hundred NAPA Auto Parts stores throughout the United States. This Group also includes UAP Inc., with 16 distribution centers in Canada that serve 652 corporate and associate wholesalers. In addition, this Group has a joint venture with Auto Todo, with 18 distribution centers and 18 company-owned stores in Mexico.

The Automotive Parts Group operates 6 remanufacturing plants that distribute products under the name Rayloc. Also in this Group is Balkamp, Inc., a majority-owned subsidiary that purchases, packages, and distributes service and supply items under the trade name Balkamp to NAPA Distribution Centers.

The NAPA program strives to improve market penetration, reduce costs, and focus on specific customer needs. The great success of the NAPA program has enabled Genuine Parts to become the leading independent distributor of automotive replacement parts and expand in sales and earnings at a faster rate than the industry.

The Industrial Parts Group

The Industrial Parts Group, which operates under the name Motion Industries, distributes over 1.6 million items from 446 operations located around the United States, Canada, and Mexico. Motion's rapid delivery model provides customized product and technical expertise to customers in a just-in-time response, enabling clients to reduce production costs and free working capital. Since 1995, the company has added through acquisition an additional 50 regional branches to the existing distribution network and continues to seek acquisition opportunities that will expand top-line growth.

The Office Products Group

The Office Products Group distributes business products from 48 distribution centers across the nation under S. P. Richards Company to 6,000 independent and national resellers, including a number of the "mega channel" dealers. S. P. Richards serves as an excellent example of GPC's ability to manage its operations at maximum efficiency levels, as the company's operating margins have increased to 10.1 percent from 8.1 percent since the acquisition in 1975.

Electrical/Electronic Materials Group

EIS Supplies and manufactures a full range of critical products for electronic and electrical apparatus. Distribution of more than one hundred thousand items is made from 46 distribution centers nationwide. From insulation and conductive materials to assembly tools, test equipment, and customized parts, EIS serves as an important single source to original equipment manufacturers, repair shops, printed circuit board manufacturers, and the electronic assembly market. EIS acquired three additional companies in 1999 and expects to have future strategic opportunities to "roll up" its markets and consolidate the service base for its customers and suppliers.

Shortcomings to Bear in Mind

- Do-it-yourselfers and professional customers alike have more options than ever when they choose where to buy parts. All of the company's wholesale customers, repair shops, service stations, body shops, and national accounts are also facing more challenges in pleasing their customers. Nor it is merely the do-it-yourself customers who are increasing their demands for quality products and service at a competitive price. The automotive aftermarket is becoming increasingly crowded with retailers who know how to please the retail trade and are now seeking to acquire wholesale customers as well. NAPA, for its part, has designed programs to improve its penetration of each of these markets with the intent to continue to gain market share each year.

- Although Genuine Parts has an impressive record of earnings growth, the pace of this grow is lackluster. In the 1989–1999 period, earnings per share advanced from $1.15 to $2.11, a compound annual growth rate of only 6.3 percent. That's why I have designated the stock for "growth and income." On the other hand, I believe this growth rate could accelerate and be most rewarding to patient investors.

Reasons to Buy

- Over the past two years the company has made 20 acquisitions, and each was funded by stock and cash. About 70 percent of the acquisitions were funded from the company's free cash flow without the need for external financing.

- Genuine Parts is exceptionally strong and is rated A++ for financial strength by Value Line, as well as A+ by the Standard & Poor's *Stock Guide*. It's easy to see why. The company has very little debt, and its ratio of current assets to current liabilities is a solid 3.1 times. Most companies, by contrast, have current ratios below 2.0. Management contends that future expansion will be financed with internally generated funds.

- The Industrial Parts Group supplies plant surveys, inventory management programs, national supply agreements, and technical instruction.

The implementation of programs such as Extra Value Service Process (XVS), Electronic Data Interchange (EDI), and Continuous Service Improvement (CSI) helps to secure the extended quality service that customers expect.

With the advent of an electronic catalog system (ECAT), Motion Industries leads the industry in electronic data retrieval. The electronic catalog provides branches and customers with immediate access to manufacturers' technical and parts information. The Group's state-of-the-art computer system, repenting the first VSAT satellite system in the industry, gives the Industrial Parts Group the edge on technological advancement.

- While consolidation continues throughout all aspects of the office products industry, dealers have increased their efforts to reduce investment and expense by stocking fewer products. S. P. Richards is well-positioned to be the source for those products. Moreover, the company has concentrated its merchandising efforts on bringing new products to market quickly and capitalizing on new growth-market opportunities. Its product offering has been broadened with expansion into the fast growing computer and imaging supply area, janitorial and break-room supplies, and furniture. Further, the company's private label offerings include additional products distributed under the following brand names: Sparco, Nature Saver, and CompuCessory.

- In the words of Larry L. Prince, CEO of Genuine Parts, "We are fortunate in terms of the size of our markets and the resulting opportunities we have. For example, in the auto parts business, it is probably a $70- or $80-billion market at consumer price level. That's a big market, and while our position in that market is a very major one, we still capture only 5 or 6 percent of the market. It is very fragmented, which gives us a great potential for additional penetration."

- In an interview at the end of 1999, Mr. Prince said, "Our goal, as a company, is to grow in double digits, so we decided almost two years ago to step up our acquisition activity and bring our growth rate up somewhat. We have managed to do that and in the past 12 months, we have added about $1.3 billion to our revenue base through acquisitions."

- Genuine Parts supplies hard-to-get parts as well a fast-moving parts that are needed to serve the market. The company's coverage is broader than any of its major retail competitors, with over two hundred thousand items available today in its automotive group. Mr. Prince says, "This is a key service advantage."

- NAPA is committed to extending its leading automotive aftermarket presence to the Internet in 2000.

Total assets: $3,930 million
Current ratio: 3.10
Common shares outstanding: 178 million
Return on 1999 shareholders' equity: 18.4%

	1999	1998	1997	1996	1995	1994	1993	1992
Revenues (millions)	7982	6614	6005	5720	5262	4858	4384	4017
Net income (millions)	378	356	342	330	309	289	258	237
Earnings per share	2.11	1.98	1.91	1.82	1.68	1.55	1.39	1.28
Dividends per share	1.04	1.00	.96	.88	.84	.77	.70	.67
Price High	35.8	38.3	35.8	31.7	28.0	26.3	26.0	23.2
Low	22.2	28.3	28.7	26.7	23.7	22.4	21.9	19.3

CONSERVATIVE GROWTH

W. W. Grainger, Inc.

100 Grainger Parkway ◻ Lake Forest, Illinois 60045-5201 ◻ Investor contact: Nancy A. Hobor (847) 535-0065 ◻ Dividend reinvestment plan is not available ◻ Web site: www.grainger.com ◻ Listed: NYSE ◻ Ticker symbol: GWW ◻ S&P rating: A ◻ Value Line financial strength rating: A++

With 1999 sales of $4.5 billion, W. W. Grainger is the North American leader in the distribution of maintenance, repair, and operating (MRO) supplies and related information. The company does business in the commercial, industrial, contractor, and institutional markets. W. W. Grainger regards itself as a service business.

The company does not engage in research and development. Rather, new items are added regularly to its product line on the basis of market information as well as on recommendations of its employees, customers, and suppliers, coupled with other factors.

Company Profile

The company distributes motors, HVAC (heating, ventilation, and air conditioning) equipment, lighting, hand and power tools, pumps, electrical equipment, along with thousands of other items. In another sphere, W. W. Grainger provides support functions and coordination of benefits, data systems and data processing, employee development, finance, government regulations, human resources, industrial relations, insurance and risk management, internal audit, legal, planning, real estate and construction services, security and safety, taxes and treasury services.

Grainger sells primarily to contractors, service shops, industrial and commercial maintenance departments, manufacturers and hotels, and health care and educational facilities.

The company purchases from more than 1,000 suppliers for its General Catalog, most of whom are manufacturers and numerous other suppliers in support of Grainger Integrated Supply Operations (GISCO).

Grainger offers its line of products at competitive prices through a network of stores in the United States and Mexico (373 at December 31, 1999).

Shortcomings to Bear in Mind

- In the 1989–1999 span, earnings per share advanced from $1.10 to $1.92, a growth rate of only 5.8 percent. This growth rate was hurt by a decline in earnings in 1999, a dip from $2.44 to $1.92.

  Most of the hit to earnings took place in the fourth quarter of the year and was caused by an inventory adjustment and higher operating expenses. Grainger said the negative adjustment to inventory was related to the installation of its new Enterprise Resource Planning system. Installation problems led to system slowdowns and outages, and a physical inventory count showed inventory shrinkage was greater than expected.

  The installation demands and physical inventory count pushed employee compensation higher, Grainger said. The company also said the higher operating costs were also related to its Internet initiatives.

Reasons to Buy

- The company's decision to move to an ERP (Enterprise Resource Planning system) represents a fundamental change in the way it manages its IS (information services). Prior to 1999, the majority of Grainger's systems were written internally. In recent years, the company was spending almost all of its IS budget merely to maintain those systems. As Y2K approached, Grainger elected not to patch up the old system used in the field but to select a new approach, one that would enable the company to devote more of its IS resources to systems development.

  After extensive analysis, the company selected SAP R/3 to be the backbone of its new system, and in 18 months installed the new system at 373 branches and six zone distribution centers. "That was not an easy task," said Richard L. Keyser, the company's CEO. "The new system will let us capture more customer data, which we will use to make better customer decisions. It will also allow us to be more productive. These benefits were not realized in 1999, but we expect to see productivity gains beginning in 2000."

- In 1999, the company announced that it was extending its commitment to digital commerce as it formed an alliance with SAP AG, the world's leading provider of enterprise business solutions. Grainger is integrating its online catalog into the SAP Business-to-Business Procurement solution (SAP B2B), providing direct access to Grainger products and product information through one standardized Internet procurement solution. This access allows users seamless electronic commerce transactions between both supplier and buyer Internet sites for reduced overall purchasing costs and improved efficiency. The alliance with SAP represents greatly expanded customer access to grainger.com.

- Grainger's industry expertise enables it to build market share by enhancing product availability in unique markets. For example, at Boston's "Big Dig" construction project, the business introduced a mobile branch, complete with wireless computer links to Grainger's order entry systems. In Manhattan, the company replaced large branches with a number of small branches in convenient locations. Frequent replenishment of these small units maintains Grainger's commitment to availability while leveraging its investment in inventory.

- In 1998 and 1999, *Fortune* magazine selected Grainger as one of "The 100 Best Companies to Work for in America."

- Grainger offers to customers services that reduce the hidden costs of MRO (maintenance, repair, and operating) supplies. In many cases, these costs can exceed the cost of the product itself. They include the customer's procurement process, the costs associated with possessing and maintaining inventory, the interface with multiple suppliers, and the use of MRO supplies.

- Small businesses represent over 1.1 million of Grainger's customers. Strong relationships with these customers are best achieved using direct marketing methods. Many customers cite a preference for this form of contact. With relatively simple operations and little MRO inventory, small businesses can reduce their total cost of MRO supplies with easy-to-use product information and selection assistance, one-stop service, and inventory nearby. The company's industry-leading General Catalog, broad product line, and network of local stores are a good solution for these customers.

- Large businesses represent about 210,000 of Grainger's customers but constitute over two-thirds of the revenues. The Grainger direct sales force is the key relationship builder with this customer group. Customers served by the direct sales force range from medium-sized manufacturing plants to Fortune 500 companies. The common thread for these customers is their desire to reduce the total cost of MRO supplies.

  Larger businesses generally have more sophisticated purchasing processes, more MRO suppliers, and more inventory. While product price is always important, the keys to reducing total MRO costs are improving the purchasing process, reducing the interface with multiple suppliers, and applying better inventory management methods. The company's network of leading manufacturers, product availability, order processing systems, and customer inventory management tools form a powerful solution.

- The company increased its 1999 dividend for the 27th consecutive year. Over the past 10 years, the dividend climbed from $.25 to $.63, a compound annual growth rate of 9.7 percent.

- Lab Safety Supply is the leading direct marketer of safety products and other industrial supplies to American business. Located in Janesville, Wisconsin, Lab Safety Supply reaches its customers through its aware-winning General Catalog, targeted catalogs, and other marketing materials throughout the year.

Customers select Lab Safety Supply for its extensive product depth (over four hundred thousand products in the 1999 General Catalog), its superior technical knowledge, and its industry-leading service. It is a primary supplier for many small- and medium-sized companies and a critical back-up supplier for many larger companies.

■ Some analysts regard W. W. Grainger as rather boring since it sells such lackluster items as electric motors, pumps, cleaners, light bulbs, and mops. Behind this drab image is a company that targets people in the factory supply office. Of late, however, these office toilers are being wooed through the Internet. Over the past four or five years, Grainger's online business has quietly become one of the highest-volume business-to-business sites on the Internet. Sales at grainger.com totaled about $100 million in 1999, up from $13.5 million the prior year. In 2000, the company looks for this business to mushroom to $160 million. No other company, except high-tech giants Cisco Systems, Dell Computer, and IBM, can come even close to Grainger's Web-sales volume, according to Anthony J. Paoni, a professor at Northwestern University's Kellogg Graduate School of Management.

Most of Grainger's customers have yet to switch to its Web site—but those using grainger.com appear to love it. According to Grainger, its Web customers are spending 20 percent more annually than they did before. Here's why. To find what they needed, Grainger's customers used to have just one option—page through a gigantic, red, 4,000-page, seven-pound catalog listing 70,000 products. On the Web site, customers can search through even more products (220,000) in a fraction of the time, get up-to-date prices (discounted for certain customers), and know immediately whether the items are in stock. "It's hard to imagine a world where more than 50 percent of our orders aren't flowing through the digital space," says Don Bielinsky, W. W. Grainger's group president. "The Internet is clearly the best vehicle for our customers."

For the third year in a row, Grainger.com was named among the top business-to-business Internet sites in the world by *Advertising Age's Business Marketing Magazine*.

■ Grainger's auction site is an early player in the online business-to-business auction market, which is expected to reach more than $50 billion by 2002. This site gives customers an opportunity to place real-time bids on surplus products from a variety of product categories. Grainger's auction site serves as another channel for generating revenue and developing the online community of Grainger's customers.

Total assets: $2,565 million
Current ratio: 1.75
Common shares outstanding: 93 million
Return on 1999 shareholders' equity: 13.1%

	1999	1998	1997	1996	1995	1994	1993	1992
Revenues (millions)	4534	4341	4137	3537	3277	3023	2628	2364
Net income (millions)	181	238	232	209	187	178	149	137
Earnings per share	1.92	2.44	2.27	2.02	1.82	1.74	1.44	1.29
Dividends per share	.63	.59	.53	.49	.45	.39	.35	.33
Price High	58.1	54.7	49.9	40.8	33.8	34.6	33.4	30.5
Low	36.9	36.4	35.3	31.3	27.8	25.8	25.8	19.5

Hewlett-Packard Company

3000 Hanover Street ◻ Palo Alto, California 94304 ◻ Investor contact: Steve Pavlovich (415) 857-2387 ◻ Dividend reinvestment plan is available: (800) 286-5977 ◻ Web site: www.hp.com/go/financials ◻ Fiscal year ends October 31 ◻ Ticker symbol: HWP ◻ S&P rating: A+ ◻ Value Line financial strength rating: A++

Hewlett-Packard, long a laggard behind Sun Microsystems and IBM in computer systems for electronic commerce, took a step forward toward strengthening its Internet presence with the announcement in late 1999 of a deal with the Oracle Corporation to collaborate on developing and selling Oracle's electronic commerce software on Hewlett-Packard computers.

Oracle said it would make HP-UX, Hewlett-Packard's version of the Unix operating system, a "strategic development platform" for all of Oracle's e-business software applications. In practical terms, this should ensure that each new version of Oracle's software runs as well on Hewlett-Packard's computers as it does on machines made by Sun, Hewlett-Packard's archrival in the network and Internet server market.

According to analysts, the endorsement of Oracle, the clear leader in software for electronic commerce, is key to Hewlett-Packard's Internet products. They said that the deal helped Hewlett-Packard at the expense of Sun, which every year sells billions of dollars worth of servers running Oracle's database software.

Company Profile

Since the spin-off of Hewlett-Packard's test and measurement business (Agilent Technologies, which made up about 15 percent of Hewlett-Packard's revenues) in 1999, the company is now comprised of its computing and imaging businesses. These operations include personal computers (PCs), servers, workstations, and printers, including service and support. The company's servers and workstations run Hewlett-Packard's (HP) version of the UNIX operating system and Windows NT.

Hewlett-Packard's computer lines include workstations (including its Kayak line) and multi-user systems for both technical and commercial users, the HP Vectra and Brio series of corporate PCs, and the Pavilion PC line for consumers.

The company's 9000 family of workstations and servers run the 64-bit PA-8000 Precision Architecture reduced instruction set computing (PA-RISC) chips. Hewlett-Packard is also developing Intel's next generation 64-bit Merced chip.

Hewlett-Packard is well-known for its position in the printer market with its popular HP LaserJet and DeskJet families. There has been aggressive pricing from Lexmark in the printer market, but Hewlett-Packard still dominates and has launched a series of new products.

Hewlett-Packard's PC products include the checkbook-size 200LX palmtop PC with built-in Pocket Quicken and the HP OmniBook family of notebook PCs for mobile professionals.

Hewlett-Packard's products are used by people in industry, business, engineering, science, medicine, and education.

HWP is one of the 19 largest industrial companies in the United States and one of the world's largest computer companies. The company had revenues of $42.4 billion in its fiscal 1999 year (ended October 31, 1999). This is down from the prior year because of the spin-off of Agilent, which had annual revenues of about $8 billion.

Nearly 60 percent of Hewlett-Packard's business is generated abroad; two-thirds of that is in Europe. Other principal markets include Japan, Canada, Australia, the Far East, and Latin America. HP is one of the top eight U.S. exporters.

Hewlett-Packard's domestic manufacturing plants are situated in 28 cities, mostly in California, Colorado, the Northeast, and the Pacific Northwest. The company also has research and manufacturing plants in Europe, Asia-Pacific, Latin America, and Canada.

HWP sells its products and services through some 600 sales and support offices and distributorships in more than 130 countries.

Shortcomings to Bear in Mind

- Analysts believe that Hewlett-Packard's competition has increased in the past two or three years. More companies are selling low-cost printers, while Sun Microsystems competes fiercely in the market for Unix-based computers. HWP is a leader in computers that use the Unix operating systems.

According to some observers, Hewlett-Packard suffers from turf battles, complacency, and slow growth. The company also seems to analyze decisions endlessly and sends no clear message to a fast-moving market.

Reasons to Buy

- On a more positive note, the company has staked its future on a new CEO, 45-year-old Carleton S. Fiorina (a former Lucent Technologies executive hired in mid-1999). Known usually as "Carly," Ms. Fiorina (who is the first woman ever to head one of the 30 companies that make up the Dow Jones Industrial Average) is intent on shaking up Silicon Valley's largest company. Nor does she pull any punches as to what kind of company she has inherited.

"Take a deeper look at HP," she says, "and you will see something sick and endangered."

The star executive, who spent 19 years with AT&T and Lucent Technologies, appears to be just the person to bring out the best at Hewlett-Packard. Just as the computer giant needs to shed its lumbering ways, so too did Lucent—AT&T's slow-moving communications-equipment business. Carly Fiorina managed the highly successful spin-off of Lucent in 1996. She then launched a bold, $90-million brand-building campaign that helped transform the company from a humdrum maker of phone equipment into an Internet player supplying the gear for the New Economy. And in 1998, after being promoted to president of Lucent's $19-billion global service-provider business, she helped to reinvigorate product development by the long-coddled Bell Labs engineers. "She has it all," said Vodafone AirTouch PLC Chairman Sam Ginn, an HP director who headed the search committee. Incredible as it may seem, the search committee looked at 300 potential candidates before settling on Carly Fiorina.

- Late in 1999, the new HP CEO said the company would relaunch its brand and adopt a new logo, coupled with a $200-million advertising campaign as part of her effort to revitalize the company. The campaign marks the first time Hewlett-Packard has tried to emphasize its brand on a companywide basis. Rather, its diversified units have tended to focus their ad spending on roughly 100 individual product lines, such as the company's Pavilion personal computers or its LaserJet printers, as opposed to creating an overarching image.

While Hewlett-Packard's brand is still well-recognized—thanks in no small part to its successful consumer PC and printer businesses—Ms. Fiorina argues that the company as a whole would benefit from taking a much higher profile. In so doing, she hopes to focus attention on the company's core strengths and efforts to help customers instead of merely on its products.

- In 1999, Hewlett-Packard unveiled several partnerships and a software technology dubbed e-speak that helps manage service requests among different Web sites, part of an ambitious effort to position itself as a leader in Internet-based services. E-speak is a software architecture designed to allow electronic services to communicate in a dynamic, automated way with each other over the Internet. That is difficult to do today because there is no standard way for services to recognize each other. For instance, an Internet travel service using e-speak could put out requests for airline tickets, hotel reservations, and automobile rentals over the Internet on behalf of a client and let individual Web sites offering such services "bid" for the business automatically.

  The announcement is the latest sign of the company's intention to challenge dynamic rivals such as Sun Microsystems and IBM. Both have made major pushes to sell the equipment and software needed to run Web sites and offer Internet-based services.

- In 1999, Hewlett-Packard said that it planned to unveil a strategy to sell personal computers and other products directly to corporate customers, stepping into an arena that has plunged some competitors into chaos. The company said that it will extend to corporate customers the ability to buy most of its product line through its Web site. HP sells its entire customer line of PCs, printers, scanners, and supplies over the Internet but has been slower to take the same route for corporate sales where the

company has traditionally been more dependent on its network of third-party dealers.

Instead of cutting its dealers out of its sales process, HP plans to give them an opportunity to compete for the company's online business. For instance, a corporate customer that wants to buy 10 laser printers could either order them directly from a Hewlett-Packard Web page or follow a link from that page to a list of recommended local dealers that could sell the printers and assist with installation. The company's strategy is explained by a company official, "We just want to serve those who would otherwise go to Dell Gigabuys for a solution."

- In an unusual alliance between two rivals in the digital-imaging field, Eastman Kodak and Hewlett-Packard formed a joint venture in 2000 to manufacture digital photo-processing machines for use by retailers. The machines, which the companies likened to digital versions of minilabs found at drug stores and photo shops, will use high-end inkjet printers made by Hewlett-Packard and paper made by Kodak. The machines are expected to cost less than the $70,000 to $100,000 price tag for traditional minilabs. That lower price should prompt more retailers to offer on-site processing. The company will be owned equally by EK and HWP and could generate as much as $1 billion in annual sales by 2005.

- In 1999, Hewlett-Packard announced a new line of midrange servers, plugging a gap in its product line and putting it back into competition with Sun Microsystems Inc. and IBM. Analysts said that the company's N-Class servers, priced starting at $48,000, should help Hewlett-Packard catch up to its competitors in the market for servers—powerful computers that increasingly run everything from corporate networks to Internet-based electronic commerce. The new machines are designed to pick up the slack from the company's aging K-Class line, whose sales started to wane in 1998.

■ The company's new HP LaserJet 4000 printers produce 1,200 dots per inch print equivalent at full engine speed—

an important innovation over competitors who must cut engine speed by half to achieve the highest quality output possible on their printers. The HP LaserJet 4000 is the first product to incorporate HP's new JetSend technology, which allows printers, scanners, and other devices to exchange information directly without a PC.

Total assets: $35,297 million
Current ratio: 1.74
Common shares outstanding: 1,019 million
Return on 1999 shareholders' equity: 17.1%

	1999	1998	1997	1996	1995	1994	1993	1992
Revenues (millions)	42370	47061	42895	38420	31519	24991	20317	16410
Net income (millions)	3126	3065	3119	2675	2433	1599	1177	881
Earnings per share	2.99	2.88	2.95	2.54	2.32	1.54	1.16	.87
Dividends per share	.64	.60	.56	.42	.35	.26	.23	.18
Price High	118.4	82.4	72.9	57.7	48.3	25.6	22.3	21.3
Low	63.4	47.1	48.1	36.8	24.5	18.0	16.1	12.6

AGGRESSIVE GROWTH

The Home Depot, Incorporated

2455 Paces Ferry Road, NW ❑ Atlanta, Georgia 30339-4024 ❑ Investor contact: Kim Schreckengost (770) 384-2666 ❑ Direct dividend reinvestment plan is available (800) 577-0177 ❑ Web site: www.homedepot.com ❑ Fiscal year ends Sunday closest to January 31 of following year ❑ Listed: NYSE ❑ Ticker symbol: HD ❑ S&P rating: A+ ❑ Value Line financial strength rating: A++

Arthur Blank, the company's 58-year-old chief executive and cofounder, takes nothing for granted. "We're in the relationship business, not the transaction business," he says. "People can buy this merchandise somewhere else. The challenge is always remembering to walk in the customer's footsteps, not our own."

Customers, in fact, are responsible for 70 percent of Home Depot's 50,000 items. Among them: precut Venetian blinds, tool rentals, Christmas trees, pretzels, and now large appliances. After a two-year test, Home Depot decided to start selling washers, dryers, and refrigerators in all of its stores. Maximizing its gross profit bang per invested buck, Home Depot decided to

stock only 60 percent of the appliance line. It struck a deal with GE to ship the other 40 percent directly to the home.

Company Profile

Founded in 1978, The Home Depot—or Big Orange—is the world's largest home improvement retailer, currently operating 930 stores, including 854 Home Depot stores, 15 EXPO Design Centers, and two Villager's Hardware stores in the United States, 53 Home Depot stores in Canada, two Home Depot stores in Puerto Rico, and four in Chile.

The Home Depot is credited as being the innovator in the home improvement retail industry by combining the economies of scale inherent in a warehouse format with a level of customer service unprecedented among warehouse-style retailers.

Home Depot stores cater to do-it-yourselfers as well as home improvement, construction, and building maintenance professionals.

Each Home Depot store stocks about 40,000 to 50,000 different kinds of building materials, home improvement supplies, and lawn and garden products. New Home Depot stores in the United States and Canada range from 105,000 to 115,000 square feet with an additional 15,000 to 25,000 square foot garden center.

The stores have a design center staffed by professional designers who offer free in-store consultation for home improvement projects ranging from lighting to computer-assisted design for kitchens and bathrooms.

Home Depot offers installation services of select products, ranging from single-items such as carpet to more extensive projects such as kitchen cabinets. The company is also testing the At-Home Services program that will offer complete installation of roofing, siding, and window products in limited markets.

Home Depot expects to be operating more than 1,900 stores in the Americas by the year 2003.

Home Depot has been publicly held since 1981 and is included in the Standard & Poor's 500. The company has been named America's most admired specialty retailer by *Fortune* magazine for six consecutive years.

Shortcomings to Bear in Mind

- According to analysts, the only possible threat to Home Depot's dominance in hardware retailing is Lowe's Companies of Wilkesboro, North Carolina. Lowe's is half the size of Home Depot in sales and store count (556 units compared to Home Depot's 900). On the other hand, don't forget that Big Orange has already obliterated its share of competitive chains, not to mention scads of mom-and-pop hardware emporiums.

Reasons to Buy

- The U. S. home improvement industry continues to grow as new and existing home sales reach record levels, home ownership rates increase, and existing houses and their owners age. In addition, the quality of home life has become more important to many homeowners, prompting them to make improvements or enhancements to kitchens, bathrooms, and other frequently used rooms. All of these factors spell opportunity for Home Depot.

  The company intends to capture these opportunities in new and existing Home Depot stores, which will continue to drive consistent sales and earning growth for the foreseeable future. Longer term, increasing the company's sales in other segments of the industry will become progressively more important to supporting a consistent growth pattern.

- Home Depot has increased its average customer ticket and sales-per-square-foot 3.8 percent a year since 1989. The average sale rung up at Home Depot stores rose 6.9 percent in 1999 to $48.75, up from $45.62 a year earlier. That rise demonstrates that Big Orange is inducing consumers to buy more upscale items, ranging from professional-strength power tools to fancy ceiling fans and Ralph Lauren paint.

- Despite its significant market presence, Home Depot holds relatively low share—20 percent of the combined do-it-yourself and repair/remodel market and 3 percent of the professional market. With Home Depot having market share penetration opportunities in essentially all markets in the United States, the company is poised for continued growth through expansion of its store base and greater productivity of existing stores.

- Analysts believe that Home Depot is showing prudence in its rollout of new concepts, refining store concepts for several years before launching, testing new launches before adopting a more widespread rollout, and requiring a strict profitability hurdle for all store formats.
- After spending years refining the EXPO concept, the company is now accelerating the rollout. In 1999, HD announced expansion into four new markets, including Boston, San Francisco, New Jersey, and Detroit, which feature 11 stores. The company operates 12 EXPO Design Centers with an additional three stores built in 1999 and 11 planned for 2000 for a total of 26 stores. Analysts look for the concept to expand to 200 units by 2005.

  According to management, "There's no other retailing concept that comes close to matching its product and service offerings, or capturing its look, feel, and excitement. EXPO will allow us to gain a larger share of the home decor market and provide an alternative to Home Depot shoppers whose remodeling preferences sometimes go beyond a Home Depot store."

- The company is taking steps to increase its share of the professional business customer market. In some respects, this has been a balancing act for Home Depot since do-it-yourself customers are still the company's most important customers, and the company is committed to continuing to serve their needs. However, Home Depot is also focusing on gaining more sales from the pros already shopping in its stores. According to management, "As we refine the tests we are conducting today to expand our

professional programs to more stores, we expect this customer segment will drive incremental sales."

- Home Depot's profit margins have been increasing of late. Flexing its buying power, the company continues to call in suppliers to demand better terms and more attractive merchandise. It is also buying more goods directly from foreign suppliers, shutting out middlemen. In addition, the company says it is reducing losses from shoplifting and has expanded a tool-rental program.
- Until recently, appliance sales have been only a sideline for Home Depot. Late in 1999, however, the powerful 900-store retail chain announced plans for a major push to expand such sales. At the time, Home Depot said it intended to offer products from two suppliers, Whirlpool and General Electric. In early 2000, however, the company stopped ordering appliances from Whirlpool, at least temporarily. Whirlpool is one of a number of big U.S. companies that encountered transient—but costly—snags after implementing complex "enterprise resource planning" software.

  Home Depot buys in huge quantities and is known as a demanding customer. Meanwhile, a Home Depot spokesman said the retailer is looking at other potential appliance suppliers. But he declined to identify them. One analyst believes Maytag will be added as a supplier.

- Recently, Big Orange disclosed a few more details about its longstanding plans for online sales of merchandise, which began in the first half of 2000. People who want to buy merchandise via the company's Web site must key in their zip codes. Online prices and merchandise offerings are the same as those in stores near the customer's home. Home Depot officials said that online sales won't immediately be available nationally but will be rolled out region by region.

- The company's long-term plans are also addressing alternative methods of distribution to attract more customers, enhance their shopping experiences, and obtain a larger share of the total market. Through the company's acquisition of Maintenance Warehouse, Home Depot has learned how to serve the property maintenance and repair market through direct mail distribution. The company is now beginning to leverage Maintenance Warehouse's business expertise with The Home Depot brand and capabilities. This is resulting in more aggressive sales growth at Maintenance Warehouse, the pursuit of new target markets, and steps toward a more seamless integration of the two companies.

- The Home Depot is testing a concept called Villager's Hardware, with test stores being opened in 1999. The Villager's Hardware format will test the best products and methods for gaining market share in the $50-billion hardware convenience market, a home improvement segment whose customers tend to be doing smaller fix-it projects and prefer convenient store locations with quick in-and-out service.

Total assets: $17,081 million
Current ratio: 1.75
Common shares outstanding: 2,302 million
Return on 1999 shareholders' equity: 18.8%

	1999	1998	1997	1996	1995	1994	1993	1992
Revenues (millions)	38434	30219	24156	19536	15470	12477	9239	7148
Net income (millions)	2320	1614	1160	938	732	604	457	363
Earnings per share	1.00	.71	.52	.43	.34	.29	.22	.18
Dividends per share	.11	.08	.06	.05	.04	.03	.02	.02
Price High	69.8	41.3	20.2	13.2	11.1	10.7	11.3	11.4
Low	34.6	18.4	10.6	9.2	8.1	8.1	7.9	6.6

AGGRESSIVE GROWTH

Honeywell International Incorporated

101 Columbia Road ◻ P.O. Box 2245 ◻ Morristown, New Jersey 07962-2245 ◻ Investor contact: James V. Gelly (973) 455-2222 ◻ Dividend reinvestment program is available: (800) 647-7147 ◻ Web site: www.honeywell.com ◻ Ticker symbol: HON ◻ S&P rating: B ◻ Value Line financial strength rating: A++

The new CEO of Honeywell has a tough act to follow. In December of 1999, AlliedSignal completed the $14-billion acquisition of Honeywell Inc., putting the 58-year-old Michael R. Bonsignore in charge of one of the nation's largest industrial conglomerates. Mr. Bonsignore had been at the helm of Honeywell at the time of the AlliedSignal takeover. He replaced the former CEO of AlliedSignal, Lawrence A. Bossidy, then age 64, who remains as chairman of the company.

When Larry Bossidy became chairman and CEO of AlliedSignal in 1991, he set out to make it "a premier company, distinctive and successful in everything we do." During the Bossidy years, AlliedSignal built itself from a disparate collection of 50 businesses to a cohesive portfolio with triple the margins. The company's earnings grew

227 percent, a compound average of 14 percent a year. Net sales grew from $12 billion to $15 billion pre-merger, and to nearly $24 billion after the closing. AlliedSignal's market value grew 819 percent and, with dividends reinvested, an investment of $1,000 when Larry Bossidy became CEO had grown to $10,180 on December 31, 1999.

With a new leader at the helm, Honeywell is likely to continue seeking acquisitions. Mr. Bonsignore expects that acquisition-related cost savings to help drive earnings per share at the new Honeywell up 20 percent in 2000, with an average annual increase in per-share profit of 18 percent during the next three years.

The Purchase of Honeywell

In June of 1999, AlliedSignal agreed to acquire Honeywell Inc. in a stock transaction valued at $13.8 billion, creating an aerospace parts-and-electronics powerhouse that also would be one of the country's largest industrial conglomerates. The friendly deal resolved the question of who would succeed the company's high-profile CEO, Lawrence A. Bossidy.

The deal also accomplished several of Mr. Bossidy's long-running aims: broadening AlliedSignal's operations, damping the cyclical ups and downs of the business, and boosting the company's revenues to more than $20 billion a year. In fact, it will do even more. The combined company had revenues of nearly $24 billion in 1999, putting it in the same league as top diversified manufacturers such as United Technologies.

The combined company was renamed Honeywell but is still based in Morristown, New Jersey. Honeywell is a leading maker of control systems and components for buildings, homes, industry, aerospace, and aviation. Its home- and building-control products include building-automation systems, energy-management equipment, and fire-protection and security-control devices. Honeywell's industrial products division makes automation and control products and field instrumentation. The space and aviation unit manufactures equipment for companies in the aviation industry.

The New Honeywell

To describe the new Honeywell would take several pages, but in brief, this gives you a glimpse of its businesses:

Automation and Asset Management

Major segments include Home and Building Control and Industrial Control.

Performance Materials

Major segments include Electronic Materials, Performance Polymers, and Specialty Chemicals.

Aerospace Solutions

Major segments include Engines and Systems, Aerospace Electronic Systems, Aerospace Services, Aircraft Landing Systems, and Federal Manufacturing and Technologies.

Power and Transportation Products

Major segments include Consumer Products Group (automotive), Friction Materials, Transportation, and Power Systems.

Highlights of 1999

- Signed exclusive agreement with Continental Airlines for repair of its fleet of auxiliary power units.
- Received certification of Honeywell avionics on the Boeing 717-200 and Bombardier Global Express business jet.
- Completed largest avionics retrofit program to date, with extensive Honeywell cockpit upgrade for FedEx MD-10.
- Acquired Johnson Matthey Electronics, a leading electronic materials company.

This transformed Honeywell into one of the top five providers of integrated materials and technology solutions to the electronics industry.

- Awarded contract to provide communications management unit and airborne satellite communications system for the U.S. Air Force global air traffic management system.
- Selected as member of Lockheed Martin team by U.S. Air Force for the $450-million C-5 Avionics Modernization program.
- Selected to provide front disc brake pads on several popular vehicles, including DaimlerChrysler minivans and midsize Volvo cars.
- Bendix Import Quiet (IQ) brake pads chosen by *Popular Mechanics* magazine as the recipient of its 1999 Editor's Choice Award for outstanding achievement in design and innovation.
- Introduced the Extra Life III Air Filter with Triad Filter Technology, the largest new technology launch in FRAM history.

Shortcomings to Bear in Mind

- The Performance Materials business is suffering from a poor price-cost environment. This unit has been facing high raw materials costs and low pricing for its polymer products. The company has taken action to turn the business around: instituted a 5–15 percent price increase, cut capital expenditures, and reduced capacity. As a result, analysts look for this unit to increase revenues in 2000 by 5 percent and widen its operating margin.
- Some analysts are concerned about whether the new management teams will be able to execute their strategic plans as well as the old management at AlliedSignal. Part of the anxiety comes from a perceived culture difference between the two companies. In the words of one analyst, "Back at the old

Honeywell, there was a culture that took care of the employees and the community, but shareholders seemed further back in the pecking order." And since the new company is being run by a combination of executives from both companies, "you have a perception issue associated with this company."

Still another observer points out that there may be concern about the style of Mr. Bonsignore, who will become chairman when Mr. Bossidy steps aside. "Bonsignore seems a little more laid back, not as forceful. But that doesn't mean he's going to fail."

Reasons to Buy

- Mr. Bonsignore said Honeywell will continue an aggressive buying spree, adding companies to its portfolio even as it works to integrate its global operations. He said Honeywell will have billions in cash to fund acquisitions.
- The new Honeywell wasted no time in pushing forward on the acquisition front. In December of 1999 the company signed a definitive agreement to acquire Pittway Corporation in an all-cash deal valued at about $2 billion. Pittway makes security and fire systems and other low-voltage products for homes and buildings. The company markets its products under such names as Ademco, Notifier, System Sensor, ADI, and Northern Computers.

The deal boosts Honeywell's home and building control business by expanding its product offerings in the fire and security-system industries.

The acquisition could transform Honeywell's $3.4-billion home- and building-control unit into a $5-billion global player. The unit already offers a vast array of products, including controls for heating, ventilation, humidification, and air-conditioning equipment; home-automation systems, and energy-efficient lighting controls.

The Honeywell division has struggled in the past, mainly due to weak margins and revenue growth in building controls. "These businesses are seasonal, dependent on weather conditions," said Kevin Gilligan, president of the unit. Given that the fire and security industries are growing at twice the rate of the temperature-control market, Mr. Gilligan said the Pittway acquisition could transform home and building controls into "a major growth engine for Honeywell."

- Meanwhile, Mr. Bossidy is still part of the action. His main chore in 2000 is weeding out redundancies and streamlining operations. He said he expects the combination to result in cost savings of $750 million by 2002.

- Although acquisitions are in prospect, it is likely that some businesses will be sold. Since the merger is being accounted for as a pooling of interests, in general the new company can't dispose of anything until two years after the merger is completed. But Mr. Bonsignore sees potentially expendable assets in the new Honeywell portfolio, including Honeywell's home-comfort retail business, the channel through which air cleaners and heaters are sold

to consumers. "It's gotten to be a very tough business," Mr. Bonsignore said.

Another possible target for divestiture is the car-care business, which accounts for just under a third of the new Honeywell's transportation division revenue. Analysts point out that the auto aftermarket business hasn't delivered the growth prospects and return on investment AlliedSignal expected.

- Those familiar with Mr. Bonsignore's record at the old Honeywell have no doubts about his ability to do the job. They say some of the speculation about Mr. Bonsignore, who was profiled along with six others in a 1999 book, *Comeback: How Seven Straight-Shooting CEOs Turned Around Troubled Companies*, could be because he is simply a new, partly unknown quantity to some highly vocal fans of the former AlliedSignal. "I think Bonsignore is underrated as a CEO, says Robert Spremulli, managing director of global research at TIAA-CREF, the big teachers' pension fund that holds 14.7 million Honeywell shares. At the old Honeywell, "he was able to meet commitments to the analysts, able to develop revenue sources, and change the businesses in order to position them better."

Total assets: $23,527 million
Current ratio: 1.23
Common shares outstanding: 795 million
Return on 1999 shareholders' equity: 26.2%

	1999	1998	1997	1996	1995	1994	1993	1992
Revenues (millions)	23735	15128	14472	13971	14346	12817	11827	12042
Net income (millions)	2165	1331	1138	1020	875	759	659	541
Earnings per share	2.68	2.32	2.02	1.81	1.55	1.34	1.16	.96
Dividends per share	.68	.60	.52	.45	.39	.32	.29	.25
Price High	68.6	47.6	47.1	37.2	24.9	20.3	20.0	15.5
Low	37.8	32.6	31.6	23.6	16.7	15.2	14.4	10.2

Houghton Mifflin Company

222 Berkeley Street ◻ Boston, Massachusetts 02116 ◻ Investor contact: Susan E. Hardy (617) 351-5114
◻ Dividend reinvestment plan is available: (800) 730-4001 ◻ Web site: www.hmco.com ◻ Listed: NYSE
◻ Ticker symbol: HTN ◻ S&P rating: B+ ◻ Value Line financial strength rating: B++

There are a number of macro industry factors that favor educational publishing. For one thing, the current period is, according to management, "the best funding environment we have seen in many years." The purchase of educational books are primarily funded by state and local governments; very little comes from the federal government (only 6 or 7 percent).

Compared with the early 1990s, the economic picture has improved dramatically, including many states having budget surpluses. What's more, education is currently a key priority throughout the country. Businesses, parents, and other groups have made education a key issue for government spending. Of course, employing more and better teachers is a part of this picture, but better books is also important.

Still another factor is demographic—the number of students is growing at a steady 1 or 2 percent pace.

Company Profile

Houghton Mifflin is a leading publisher of books for schools and colleges. Textbooks and related educational products provided 90 percent of 1999 revenues. Houghton Mifflin also publishes trade books, such as *The American Heritage Dictionary*, scholarly biographies, and novels.

In the mid-1990s, HTN embarked on a strategy to reach revenues of $1 billion by the year 2000 and is well on its way to reaching that goal. It began with the 1994 acquisition of McDougal Littell, followed by D. C. Heath (then part of Raytheon) a year later.

Added products and staff from D. C. Heath significantly strengthened three divisions while yielding $30 million in cost savings. The College division is now a leader in mathematics, history, modern languages, chemistry, English, and political science.

The Secondary School division, bolstered by McDougal Littell, has strong positions in modern languages, social studies, literature, and mathematics.

The School division (kindergarten through eighth grade) has broadened its offerings in mathematics and reading. The acquisitions also contributed to HTN's successful entry into the supplemental-materials market.

Houghton Mifflin is actively developing integrated multimedia programs in all subject areas. It offers computer-assisted and computer-managed instructional programs for all education levels, computer tools and operating systems for the college market, and a computer-based career and college guidance information system in versions for junior and senior high school students.

The company's Riverside Publishing Company unit provides educational and psychological test and measurement materials to schools and colleges, in addition to providing guidance information and products.

In 1998 the company acquired Computer Adaptive Technologies, a developer of computer-based testing solutions. It also widened Riverside's product offerings and Houghton's role in the testing market.

In the nonschool sector, which operates under General Publishing, the company's products include fiction, nonfiction, children's books, dictionaries, and reference materials in a variety of formats and media.

Houghton Mifflin Interactive, a unit of the Trade and Reference division, develops CD-ROM titles for sale in the multimedia consumer product markets. Trade and reference works are largely sold to retail stores.

Shortcomings to Bear in Mind

■ Creating textbooks is complicated by the adoption process. Some 21 states are referred to as "adoption states," which means that the company's proposed textbook must be approved by state officials before it can be sold to specific schools within the state. Among the major states that have this approach are California, Texas, and Florida.

The problem is further complicated because one state may approve the publisher's book, but that same book may not appeal to another major state. Obviously, it doesn't pay to print separate books for both states. However, there are times when changes can be made if the state is a major one such as Texas or California.

As noted, not all states are "adoption states" that require books be approved by a central authority. A total of 29 states leave purchasing and decision-making up to local school districts. These states are referred to as "open territories." In an adoption state, an approved list is published after the book and other parts of the program have been examined. However, once a publisher gets on an approved list, the sales process from that point forward is the same as it is in an open territory. In other words, in order to make sales, the marketing team still has to convince each school board that their program is the best.

In 1998, adoption opportunities were "quite limited," according to management. Even so, earnings held up well. On a more positive note, the future looks much better since this is a cyclical business. Most states adopt every five to seven years. In the meantime, they continue to use the old books. The years 2000 through 2002 are expected to bring a solid batch of adoption opportunities. This is a major factor in favor of investing in a textbook company such as Houghton Mifflin.

Reasons to Buy

■ The company is ably led by CEO Nader Darehshori, who has been chairman since 1990, when the company was much less profitable. At that time, HTN relied primarily on producing reading materials for primary schools. If it was a good year for reading, it was a good year for Houghton Mifflin—otherwise earnings suffered. Mr. Darehshori has spent his entire tenure divesting unprofitable operations and building the performing assets, as well as making key acquisitions. Now the company has a much broader base, with participation in grade school, high school, and college. This has led to greater stability.

■ Houghton Mifflin has only a few major competitors, notably McGraw-Hill, Pearson (owned by Pearson PLC, a British concern), Harcourt General, and Scholastic. Assuming you like educational publishing, Houghton Mifflin is the clear choice since about 90 percent of the company's revenues come from textbooks and related material. The other companies are all involved in other ventures. In other words, HTN is essentially a "pure play."

- A new edition of the division's outstanding literature series, *The Language of Literature*, has been completed and is being marketed throughout the country. The series introduces students in grades 6–12 to the finest literature, connecting the selections to their own lives. It includes print and technology components and resources on the World Wide Web. According to management, *The Language of Literature* is "expected to be an extremely strong competitor in the many literature adoption opportunities in 2000–2002."

- The company's School Division's new *Math Steps* program, which is doing extremely well in the California interim adoption, has roused strong interest in many other parts of the country. What's more, the School Division remains the nation's leading publisher in reading intervention; it developed intervention products and teacher training seminars in response to a clear market need. In 2000, this division launched a mathematics intervention line. Since acquiring the elementary school science program, *DiscoveryWorks*, at the end of 1998, it has had great success in the science market in which there are many opportunities in the next few years. In the online universe, the Education Place Web site averages more than 450,000 visits per month, and a new fee-based service has been recently piloted on the site.

- Using up-to-the-minute electronic development and protection techniques, McDougal Littell launched five new programs in 1999 in preparing for a number of upcoming adoptions. The second edition of its market-leading *The Language of Literature* is being "very well received by customers," according to CEO Nader Darehshori. *The Language Network*, McDougal Littell's new program in grammar and composition, is designed to bring writing into the information age.

- Sales at The Great Source Education Group increased at double-digit rates in 1999, as they have each year since the division was established in 1996. According to Mr. Darehshori, "Its success is based on a deep understanding of the supplemental school materials market, a flexible customer-oriented outlook, and a very efficient publishing process."

  Taking advantage of the popularity of its Write Source line of language arts handbooks, Great Source is extending the concept to other formats and disciplines. It has published new handbooks for mathematics and social studies as well as *Daybooks of Critical Reading and Writing* and *Reading and Writing Sourcebooks*.

- In the last several years, The Riverside Publishing Company has become one of the leading publishers of customized texts in the country. In 1999, Riverside won the Michigan contract to develop mathematics tests and published the *Tests of New York State Standards*.

- The Trade and Reference Division had three titles on the *New York Times* bestseller list in 1999, *The Best American Short Stories of the Century*, edited by John Updike; *River-Horse* by William Least Heat-Moon; and *Woman* by Natalie Angier. A new edition of *The American Heritage Dictionary* was published in the fall of 2000 in electronic and print versions. Houghton Mifflin now controls all electronic licensing rights to the dictionary and will take advantage of opportunities offered by emerging technology. The dictionary will be embedded in more than 100 digital products.

otal assets: $1,039 million
Current ratio: 1.46
Common shares outstanding: 30 million
Return on 1999 shareholders equity: 11.5%

	1999	1998	1997	1996	1995	1994	1993	1992
Revenues (millions)	920	862	797	718	529	483	463	455
Net income (millions)	49	41	43	31	19	34	38	27
Earnings per share	1.67	1.40	1.48	1.11	.70	1.22	1.37	.96
Dividends per share	.51	.50	.49	.48	.47	.44	.42	.40
Price High	52.5	47.3	40.3	28.4	27.4	26.5	25.2	9.9
Low	34.9	26.8	26.3	20.2	19.8	18.1	18.2	13.3

AGGRESSIVE GROWTH

International Business Machines Corporation

New Orchard Road ◻ Armonk, New York 10504 ◻ Investor contact: Hervey C. Parke (914) 499-5008 ◻ Direct dividend reinvestment plan is available: (888) IBM-6700 ◻ Web site: www.ibm.com/investor ◻ Listed: NYSE ◻ Ticker symbol: IBM ◻ S&P rating: B ◻ Value Line financial strength rating: A++

IBM is the largest manufacturer of data processing equipment and systems. Its products run the gamut from personal computers to mainframes.

There's good reason to believe that IBM has more upside potential. For one thing, IBM owns some big, fast-growing businesses that don't always make the headlines. Its disk-drive unit, barely visible a few years ago, now generates an estimated $3 billion in revenue, putting it at the top ranks of the industry. What's more, sales of IBM software actually exceed those of Microsoft. And IBM's tech-services unit has been growing 23 percent a year—it passed EDS in 1997 as the leader in the field. The company also generates over $5 billion in free cash each year, a big chunk of which is earmarked for a huge stock buy-back plan.

Company Profile

IBM is the world's largest supplier of advanced information processing technology and communications systems and services and program products. The company's revenue breakdown in 1999 was: Hardware, 42 percent; Global Services, 37 percent; Software, 14 percent; Global Financing, 4 percent; Enterprise Investment/Other, 3 percent. Foreign business accounted for 58 percent of 1999 revenues.

Shortcomings to Bear in Mind

■ About seven years ago, Louis V. Gerstner, Jr. signed on to a job nobody else wanted. Since then he has done things nobody thought could be done. Doubters derided the new CEO from RJR Nabisco as a "biscuit salesman" and said he had no vision for how to turn around a technology company. Then they watched him add $20 billion in annual revenue to IBM, restore profits to record levels, and lift the stock price more than 900 percent.

But one big thing has eluded Gerstner's rebuilt IBM—robust growth. Despite a rock-solid balance sheet and a rebirth in the laboratory, IBM falls further behind every year. In Unix servers, the backbone of the Web, IBM's sales rose only 3 percent in 1998, a far cry from the sales racked up by Sun Microsystems—an astounding 29 percent. In PCs, IBM's sales slid 2.4 percent the same year. That doesn't look very impressive against the 53-percent sales gain racked up by Dell Computer, or the 23 percent turned in by Microsoft.

- IBM has long had the dubious distinction of running the biggest software business that nobody ever heard of. Late in 1999, the company was determined to change that with a major marketing and advertising campaign. The effort is intended not only to raise the profile of the company's $12-billion-a-year software business, but also to highlight the striking changes IBM has made in its software division recently and to accelerate its growth. The company has much at stake. Software is one of three businesses that Mr. Gerstner has singled out as engines of IBM's growth in the future, along with services and the sale of technology to other companies. The software business has been the laggard of the three until recently. Indeed, the company's software sales declined from $12.7 billion in 1995 to $11.2 billion in 1997 before rising a modest 6 percent the following year.

Reasons to Buy

- In early 2000, IBM announced that it would sell data-storage products and flat-panel screens through Bell Microproducts Inc., bringing in as much as $2 billion. Bell Microproducts, which distributes more than 100 computer-related product lines, also signed a four-year pact with Big Blue to package IBM products such as tape systems and hard drives and resell them to computer dealers and installers.

- Just before the new millennium dawned, IBM unveiled a $100 million plan to build the world's fastest supercomputer; it would be used to understand how proteins fold—this is considered important to understanding diseases and finding cures. The ambitious plan envisions a new RS/6000 computer named "Blue Gene," capable of more than one quadrillion operations per second, or 1,000 times more powerful than the Deep Blue machine that beat world chess champion Garry Kasparov in 1997. Blue Gene will consist of more than one million processors, each capable of one billion operations per second. That would make it 2 million times more powerful than today's top personal computers. Researchers believe they can achieve that level of performance in about five years, when the computer would be put to work on complex genetic mysteries.

- In the first quarter of 2000, IBM, the biggest computer services company, announced that it would design and run an Internet site for customers of Vodafone AirTouch PLC who want to use cellular phones and other wireless devices to connect to the World Wide Web. The site has customized browsers that can link customers to the online broker Charles Schwab or to the Travelocity.com unit of Sabre Holdings. IBM and Vodafone (the world's largest cellular operator) opened the site in July 2000 in North America, Europe, and Australia.

- In late 1999, Japanese camera maker Olympus and the Japanese unit of IBM came out with a prototype of a new computer—a pocketbook-sized box with two buttons. It is a "Wearable PC." The two companies jointly developed the machine for those who can't be bothered to carry laptops around and want to wear their computers instead. The 13-ounce computer has an Intel Pentium processor, 64 megabytes of memory, and runs the Microsoft Windows operating system. The tiny screen flips out from a headset and covers one eye, projecting the image of a much larger monitor.

- IBM, i2 Technologies and Ariba agreed to form an alliance in 2000 to service the hot business-to-business sector. The companies will sell an integrated technology to meet the needs of businesses that seek to capture a part of the B2B e-commerce marketplace, which is estimated to total $1.3 trillion to $1.4 trillion by 2003.

  IBM Global Services, IBM's consulting arm, brings its existing e-business technology to the table while i2 provides its TradeMatrix software that links suppliers and manufacturers. For its part, Ariba provides software that processes orders on the Internet.

- IBM is seeking a role in the communications industry. In late 1999, the company introduced a new line of semiconductors for network equipment, the creation of a communications research center, and an alliance intended to encourage the spread of industry-standard software in telecommunications. According to analysts, IBM's plan for the Internet-era communications market seems sound. It is an extension of its accelerating effort to exploit its industry-leading computer expertise in disk drives, chips, and flat-panel display screens by selling those parts to other companies. In 1999, IBM announced parts-sale deals totaling $30 billion over the subsequent seven years with companies such as Dell Computer, Acer, EMC, and Cisco.

  IBM's renowned research laboratories, analysts believe, could give it an edge in supplying the communications market. In the prior two years, IBM had come up with a series of advances in semiconductor development and manufacturing that enable it to make chips that consume less power and run at higher speeds. Both are major potential advantages.

- In late 1999, IBM announced that it would provide computer installation and repair services to buyers of Dell Computer Corporation's equipment, expanding an earlier agreement between the two computer makers. IBM and Dell estimated that Big Blue could provide $6 billion or more in services to Dell customers during the next seven years. The partnership was the latest in a string of agreements IBM has announced to sell services and computer parts to competitors. Earlier, the company reached a similar service deal with Cisco Systems, Inc. and signed original equipment manufacturer agreements to supply products to rivals, including EMC Corporation and Dell.

- In early 2000, IBM announced that all of its powerful network computers will be able to run on the Linux operating system, embracing the fast-growing rival to offer Unix formats and Microsoft's Windows as the best platform for Internet commerce. IBM, the leading manufacturer of computer servers, said that all four of its product lines will now be compatible with Linux, a Unix-based operating system that has grown popular among independent software developers since its Finnish creator started giving it away for free.

- IBM's services business is growing rapidly. The company's global reach helps it to win outsourcing contracts from companies with worldwide operations.

- In late 1999, IBM announced a new generation of computer processors known as the Power4, challenging a competing chip being developed by the Intel Corporation and the Hewlett-Packard Company. Both Intel's and IBM's advanced designs are intended to meet the demands for a new class of commercial computer brought on by the rapid growth of the Internet. E-commerce has created a seemingly insatiable demand for computers that can process millions of transactions a second and achieve reliability once demanded only by banking and other specialized applications. To build the Power4, IBM relies on its most advanced chipmaking technology, making it possible to squeeze as many has 170 million transistors onto the chip. According to Keith Deifendorff, a computer designer and an editor at *Microprocessor Design*, an industry newsletter, "This is a phenomenal piece of engineering."

- IBM's expertise in networking is a plus in gaining contracts from the many businesses that are trying to tie together their vast computer resources.
- In a move to expand its ability to manage Web sites and software applications for corporate customers, IBM in 2000 formed a multibillion-dollar deal with Qwest Communications International Inc. The pact calls for IBM to build and help operate Internet data centers for Qwest across North America. One of the fastest-growing segments of the electronic economy is the so-called hosting business, in which information technology companies manage computer systems that run Web sites or internal software programs for corporate customers. The idea is that by allowing an outside concern to act as host for those computers, rather than managing them internally, companies can focus on their core business while receiving expert technical support.
- In 1999, IBM unveiled a more powerful model of its supercomputer in a move to help revive slumping computer hardware sales. The Power3 processor, the heart of the newest RS/6000 SP, per-

forms up to 2 billion operations per second. That's twice as fast as the computer chip that ran Deep Blue, the machine that beat chess grandmaster Garry Kasparov in 1997. According to one analyst, "The RS/6000 was not getting enough attention. This product should give IBM a boost." IBM is also counting on the RS/6000's traditional strength with scientific and technical customers. The University of Utah in Salt Lake City, for instance, is using an early version of the computer to simulate drug effects.

- Competing against everyone from Electronic Data Systems to Big Four accounting firms to boutique shops offering only Web services, IBM has emerged as the world's largest purveyor of technology services, according to *Business Week*. It counsels customers on technology strategy, helps them prepare for mishaps, runs all their computer operations, develops their applications, procures their supplies, trains their employees, and even gets them into the dot-com realm.
- IBM launched a security system that it expects will set the industry standard for protecting confidential documents such as those used in the growing sector of electronic commerce. Unlike previous security measures that rely on software "fireballs" that filter out unauthorized users of information, IBM has developed a security chip embedded within the computer hardware, which adds additional levels of security. "People from outside your organization can get at your software," said Anne Gardner, general manager of desktop systems for IBM. "People from the outside can't get to your hardware."

Total assets: $87,495 million
Current ratio: 1.13
Common shares outstanding: 1,802 million
Return on 1999 shareholders' equity: 37.6%

	1999	1998	1997	1996	1995	1994	1993	1992
Revenues (millions)	87548	81667	78508	75947	71940	64052	62716	64523
Net income (millions)	7712	6328	6093	5429	6334	2965	13	1435
Earnings per share	4.12	3.29	3.01	2.76	2.76	1.23	def.	.62
Dividends per share	.47	.44	.39	.33	.25	.25	.40	1.21
Price High	139.2	95.0	56.8	41.5	28.7	19.1	15.0	25.1
Low	80.9	47.8	31.8	20.8	17.6	12.8	10.2	12.2

CONSERVATIVE GROWTH

Illinois Tool Works, Inc.

3600 West Lake Avenue □ Glenview, Illinois 60025-5811 □ Investor contact: John L. Brooklier (847) 657-4104 □ Dividend reinvestment plan is available: (888) 829-7424 □ Web site: www.itwinc.com □ Listed: NYSE □ Ticker symbol: ITW □ S&P rating: A+ □ Value Line financial strength rating: A

Illinois Tool Works is not a household name since it does not produce products that are familiar to the average investor such as Coca-Cola, Rubbermaid, Goodyear Tires, or Hewlett-Packard calculators.

Nonetheless, ITW is a classic growth stock with a long history of increasing earnings and dividends. What's more, it is still small enough (only $9 billion in sales) so that it should continue to expand for many years to come—often enhanced by acquisitions. By contrast, all of the "household names" listed above are vastly larger.

Company Profile

Illinois Tool Works is a multinational manufacturer of highly engineered fasteners, components, assemblies, and systems. ITW's businesses are small and focused so they can work more effectively in a decentralized structure to add value to customers' products.

The company has subsidiaries and affiliates in 40 countries on six continents. More than 500 ITW operating units are divided into six business segments:

Engineered Products—North America
Businesses in this segment are located in North America and manufacture

short-lead-time components and fasteners and specialty products such as adhesives, resealable packaging, and electronic component packaging. In 1999, these units primarily served automotive (27 percent), construction (48 percent), and general industrial (11 percent) markets.

Engineered Products—International
Businesses in this segment are located outside North America and manufacture short-lead-time components and fasteners and specialty products such as electronic component packaging and adhesives. In 1999, these operations primarily served the automotive (34 percent), construction (38 percent), and general industrial (11 percent) markets.

Specialty Systems—North America
Businesses in this segment operate in North America and produce longer-lead-time machinery and related consumables and specialty equipment for applications such as industrial spray coating, quality measurement, and static control. In 1999, these companies concentrated their efforts in such sectors as general industrial (19 percent), food retail and service (34 percent) construction (9 percent), food and

beverage (9 percent), and automotive (12 percent).

Specialty Systems—International

Operations in this segment do business outside North America. They have stakes in longer-lead-time machinery and related consumables and specialty equipment for industrial spray coating and other applications. In 1999, these units served such markets as food retail and service (32 percent), general industrial (24 percent), and food and beverage (9 percent).

Consumer Products

Businesses in this segment are located primarily in North America and manufacture household products that are used by consumers, including small electric appliances, physical fitness equipment, and ceramic tile. In 1999, this segment served the consumer durables (67 percent) and construction (33 percent) markets.

Leasing and Investments

This segment makes investments in mortgage-related assets; leveraged and direct-financing leases of equipment, properties, and property developments; and affordable housing.

How Illinois Tool Works got Started

Founded in 1912, Illinois Tool Works's earliest products included milling cutters and hobs used to cut gears. Today ITW is a multinational manufacturer of highly engineered components and systems.

In 1923 the company developed the Shakeproof fastener, a patented twisted tooth lock washer. This product's success enabled ITW to become the leader in a new industry segment—engineered metal fasteners.

Illinois Tool Works soon expanded the Shakeproof line to include thread-cutting screws, pre-assembled screws and other metal fasteners.

By the late 1940s the line grew to include plastic and metal/plastic combination fasteners. Today, ITW units produce fasteners for appliance, automotive, construction, general industrial, and other applications.

After World War II the company also expanded into electrical controls and instruments, culminating in the formation of the Licon division in the late 1950s. Today, ITW units provide a wide range of switch components and panel assemblies used in appliance, electronic, and industrial markets.

In the early 1960s the newly formed Hi-Cone operating unit developed the plastic multipack carrier that revolutionized the packaging industry. Hi-Cone multipacks today are used to package beverage and food products as well as a variety of other products.

Also in the 1960s the company formed Buildex to market existing Shakeproof fasteners as well as a line of masonry fasteners to the construction industry. Buildex today manufactures fasteners for drywall, general construction, and roofing applications.

In the mid-1980s ITW acquired Ramset, Phillips Drill (Red Head), and SPIT, manufacturers of concrete anchoring, epoxy anchoring, and powder actuated systems; and Paslode, maker of pneumatic and cordless nailers, staplers, and systems for wood construction applications. Today, the construction industry is the largest market served by Illinois Tool Works.

In the 1970s ITW purchased Devcon Corporation, a producer of adhesives, sealants, and related specialty chemicals. Today the company's engineered polymers businesses offer a variety of products with home, construction, and industrial applications.

In 1986 Illinois Tool Works acquired Signode Packaging Systems, a multinational manufacturer of metal and plastic strapping stretch film, industrial tape, application equipment, and related products. Today ITW offers a wide range of industrial packaging systems, including Dynatec hot-melt adhesive application equipment.

In 1989 Illinois Tool Works acquired Ransburg Corporation, a leading producer of finishing equipment. ITW expanded its capabilities in industrial finishing with the purchase of DeVilbiss Industrial/Commercial division in 1990. Today DeVilbiss and Ransburg manufacture conventional and liquid electrostatic equipment, while Gema Volstatic (acquired with the Ransburg and DeVilbiss purchases) produces electrostatic powder coating systems.

The company acquired the Miller Group in 1993. Miller is a leading manufacturer of arc welding equipment and related systems. Miller's emphasis on new product development and innovative design fits well with ITW's engineering and manufacturing strategies.

In the latter part of 1999 the company made its biggest purchase yet—Premark International Inc.—a $2.7-billion conglomerate making everything from industrial food equipment to gym equipment to residential flooring and appliances.

Shortcomings to Bear in Mind

- The stock has historically traded at a premium to the market, but based on its exceptional performance over the years it would appear to be warranted. With some 500 businesses, Illinois Tool Works offers investors wide diversification by product line, geographic region, and industry. This helps insulate the company from weakness in any one sector. Over the years this has resulted in consistent performance despite the cyclical nature of the automotive and construction sectors.

Reasons to Buy

- Acquisitions are likely to remain a key component of the company's growth strategy. ITW has grown steadily over the years largely by taking underperforming businesses and turning them into solid performers. This strategy was again employed in 1999.

Specifically, the company completed 31 "bottom-up" acquisitions—companies that are directly related to or integrated into an existing product line or market. These transactions, representing more than $900 million in combined revenues, are typically initiated by operating management for both North American and international businesses. According to management, "Looking ahead, our pipeline of potential acquisitions remains full."

A second type of acquisition, which the company undertakes far less frequently, is a major, or "top-down," proposition. These transactions are identified by senior management and represent entirely new businesses for ITW. Illinois Tool Workscompleted the largest transaction of this type in its history when ITW merged with Premark in late 1999.

This merger brings the company nearly 80 decentralized businesses with products marketed in more than 100 countries. Two principal lines of business—commercial food equipment and laminate product used in construction—represent about $2.5 billion in revenues. Their products have strong brand names (Hobart, Wilsonart, Traulsen, Vulcan, and Wittco), established market positions, good distribution channels, and benefit from value-added engineering—all the things ITW looks for in a successful acquisition.

- Illinois Tool Works' record of sustained quality earnings is the result of a very practical view of the world. The company relies on market penetration—rather than price increases—to fuel operating income growth. What's more, the company's conservative accounting practices serve as a reliable yardstick of financial performance. These results then generate the cash needed to fund ITW's growth—through both investing in core businesses and acquisitions.

- Illinois Tool Works has an exceptional record of growth. In the 1989–1999 period, earnings per share climbed from $0.77 to $2.99, an annual compound growth rate of 14.5 percent. In the same 10-year stretch, dividends advanced from $0.14 to $0.63, for a growth rate of 16.2 percent.

Total assets: $9,060 million
Current ratio: 1.54
Common shares outstanding: 251 million
Return on 1999 shareholders' equity: 20.1%

	1999	1998	1997	1996	1995	1994	1993	1992
Revenues (millions)	9333	5648	5220	4997	4152	3461	3159	2812
Net income (millions)	841	810	587	486	388	278	207	192
Earnings per share	2.99	2.67	2.33	1.97	1.65	1.23	.92	.36
Dividends per share	.63	.54	.46	.36	.31	.28	.25	.23
Price High	82.0	73.2	60.1	48.7	32.8	22.8	20.3	18.2
Low	58.0	45.2	37.4	26.0	19.9	18.5	16.3	14.3

AGGRESSIVE GROWTH

Intel Corporation

2200 Mission College Boulevard ☐ Santa Clara, California 95052-8119 ☐ Investor contact: Alex Lenke (408) 765-1773 ☐ Dividend reinvestment plan is available: (800) 298-0146 ☐ Web sites: www.intc.com and www.intel.com ☐ Listed: Nasdaq ☐ Ticker symbol: INTC ☐ S&P rating: A- ☐ Value Line financial strength rating: A++

It has been more than 25 years since Intel introduced the world's first microprocessor, making technology history. The computer revolution that this technology spawned has changed the world. Today Intel supplies the computing industry with the chips, boards, systems, and software that are the "ingredients" of computer architecture. These products are used by industry members to create advanced computing systems.

Company Profile

Processor Products

- *Microprocessors* (also called central processing units—CPUs or chips) are frequently described as the "brains" of a computer because they control the central processing of data in personal computers, servers, workstations, and other computers.

- *Motherboards* combine Intel microprocessors and chipsets to form the basic subsystem of a PC or server.

Computer Enhancement Products

- *Chipsets* perform essential logic functions surrounding the CPU in computers, based on Intel architecture processors.

- *Flash memory* provides easily reprogrammable memory for computers, mobile phones, and many other products. Flash memory has the advantage of retaining data when the unit's power is turned off.

● *Embedded control chips* are designed to perform specific functions in products such as automobile engines and braking systems, hard disk drives, laser printers, input/output control modules, cellular phones, and home appliances.

Networking and
Communications Products

These products enhance the capabilities of PC systems and networks and make them easier to use and manage. They are sold through reseller, retail, and original equipment manufacturer (OEM) channels.

Major Customers

● Original equipment manufacturers of computer systems and peripherals.

● PC users who buy Intel's PC enhancements, business communications products and networking products through reseller, retail, and OEM channels.

● Other manufacturers, including makers of a wide range of industrial and telecommunications equipment.

Shortcomings to Bear in Mind

■ In the past, when Intel brought out new chips, they went into desktop systems priced well above what had been the top of the line. However, when it introduced the Pentium III in early 1999 it was a different story. This time the company was faced with a softening consumer market and competition from the likes of Advanced Micro Devices with its new K6-III. In trying to persuade customers to upgrade to the Pentium III, Intel and the computer manufacturers faced a tough dual challenge. First they had to sell people on the need for more speed. Then they had to convince them that the Pentium III delivers.

■ Though Intel's profits have held up well so far, many analysts believe that the rise of the Internet will inevitably erode its margins. Consumers are increasingly expected to use simpler, lower-cost devices—from handheld machines to television set-top boxes—to access the Internet. The proliferation of these so-called Internet appliances, they note, will not replace personal computers by any means. But the Internet will fuel more diverse computing technologies and other access devices.

Reasons to Buy

■ In the fall of 2000 Intel introduced the world's fastest computer chip, running at 1.5 gigahertz, in its latest bet that consumers and businesses increasingly will feel the need for speed. Intel has been locked in a race with its main rival, Advanced Micro Devices, to produce the fastest chip. The new chip, code-named "Willamette," far outpaces the processing power of AMD's latest product, the Athlon chip, running at 1 gigahertz, or one billion bits of information per second.

Intel's processors provide brainpower for about 90 percent of the world's computers. But critics say the company's newest chips have far more processing power than the average consumer needs for popular computer uses such as word processing, using spreadsheets, and playing games. While developers are likely to write software that demands more powerful chips, doubts persist over how many customers will bite.

For its part, Intel says that the increasing popularity of the Internet—for everything from video streaming to electronic commerce to ever-more realistic 3-D games—will require greater computing power.

■ In mid-2000 Intel began mass production of its next-generation microprocessor, code-name Merced. The new microprocessor is Intel's first chip that processes 64 bits of data at a time, rather than 32 bits, which significantly boosts its power when using specially designed software.

- In the fall of 1999 Intel announced its intention to move into the Internet realm. In its most radical diversification ever, Intel spent more than $3 billion in 1999 to become as big a player in communications as it is in personal computers. The PC powerhouse is still a novice in the field, but Chairman Andrew Grove sees a historic opportunity. The principle is the same as in the personal-computer movement, which caught fire when a cheaper, general-purpose chip replaced many specialized chips. For the Internet, "the driving force is the combination of data and voice over the same network," Mr. Grove said.

  Revealing the first major weapon in its campaign, Intel introduced its "network processor" that can replace the higher-cost custom chips used in the switches and routers that form the backbone of the Web. Initial customers for the chip include the communications behemoth Cisco Systems, network equipment maker Newbridge Networks and cable television-equipment maker Broadband Access Systems. The processor is based on the StrongArm chip architecture that Intel acquired from Digital Equipment Corporation.

- In early 2000 Intel said it would spend $2 billion to build its first chip plant that will use larger dinner-plate-sized silicon wafers. Prior to construction of the new facility there were 8,150 Intel employees in Chandler, Arizona, where the new plant is being built. Construction of the new plant will create about 1,000 new jobs during the next five to eight years and will include technicians, engineers, and support personnel.

The chip industry is gradually moving to the larger wafers, which are 300 millimeters, or about 12 inches, in diameter from the then-prevalent salad-plate-sized wafers, which are 200 millimeters, or about 8 inches across. The company said that using the larger silicon wafers—the raw material from which computer chips are made—allows for the production of more than three times as many individual chips and cuts costs by more than 30 percent.

- Intel landed a contract in 2000 to supply Sweden's Telefon AB L. M. Ericsson with $1.5 billion in flash-memory chips over a three-year period. The contract was one of the first major deals in the company's effort to tap into the fast-growing market for cellular phones. It ensures a steady supply of chips for Ericsson at a time when flash-memory use is rising at a swift pace. Once used primarily in computers, flash-memory is becoming an increasingly important component of mobile phones, hand-held organizers, digital cameras, and music players that download songs from the Internet.

- Intel acquired Danish chipmaker Giga AS in 2000 for $1.25 billion in a recent foray into the fast-growing market for high-speed communications chips. Giga makes semiconductors that route vast streams of data traffic through the core of heavy-duty optical networks. Mark Christensen, general manager of Intel's network-communications group, said Giga's customers include many of the world's largest communications-gear providers, including Cisco Systems, Nortel Networks, and Alcatel SA of France. Giga's newest 10 gigabit-per-second chips are just beginning to appear in routers and switches, he said.

- Few investors have ever heard of the thousands of fledgling technology companies. But at least one very important investor has, Leslie L. Vadasz, who is head of corporate investments at Intel. In 1999 alone he invested $1.2 billion in 246 start-ups, mostly Internet companies, but also desktop and server computing operations. To be sure, some of these outfits will not make it past first base, but the ones that cross home plate will more than make up for the rookies that strike out. In the past couple of years Intel has scored blockbuster gains with investments in CMGI Inc., Red Hat Software, Inc., Broadcom Corporation, Broadcast.com Inc., Geocities Inc., Inktomi Corporation, Covad Communications Inc., and iVillage Inc.

Mr. Vadasz and Intel represent the new breed of venture investor: the successful multinational, often in the technology business itself, that views investing in start-ups as a strategic mission with an added fillip—the prospect of staggering profits. Intel's portfolio alone consists of 350 companies valued at $8.2 billion at the end of 1999, compared with just 50 companies valued at $500 million two years earlier. Intel's investment "track record is among the best anywhere," said Stephen Smith, a managing director of Broadview Investments, an investment bank.

■ Intel has accelerated the pace of acquisitions. In late 1999 Intel acquired DSP Communications, a leader in digital cellular communications products, for $1.6 billion. With the addition of the DSP technology, Intel has a bigger arsenal of tools as a supplier to the cellphone market. It already makes microprocessors known by the brand name StrongArm that can act as the brains of cell phones, as well as flash-memory chips used to store programs and data. Buying DSP fits Intel's broader strategy of minimizing its exposure to falling prices in the PC market by expanding into the fast-growing communications sector.

Also during 1999 the company bought networking chip maker Level One Communications for $2.2 billion in stock. These acquisitions augmented Intel's earlier purchase of Shiva Corporation, a networking equipment supplier of remote access solutions and virtual private networks. Networking products include hubs, switches, routers, adapters, and communications silicon components.

■ In 1999 company officials said that Intel and computer makers resolved a dispute over the future technical specifications for moving data within a computer. The dispute over the so-called next-generation input-output technology in the computer, commonly known as a "bus," ends a fractious debate that pitted Intel and ally Dell Computer Corporation against three companies that came up with a rival technology: Compaq Computer Corporation, Hewlett-Packard Company, and IBM. "Cooler heads prevailed and, while we have a lot of work to do, we should see the technology arrive in 2001," said Craig Barrett, Intel's CEO.

■ Intel's research arm continues to churn out new products. The company introduced a slew of new products in 1999, such as the Pentium III processor, running at 600 megahertz and higher, enabling fast personal computers for home and business applications; three new Pentium III Xeon processors at megahertz that support four-way and greater server and workstation configurations, as well as the Profusion chipset for eight-way servers; Intel Celeron processor at 500 megahertz, Intel's fastest desktop PC processor for the value segment; mobile Intel Celeron processors at 466 and 433 megahertz; and Pentium III processors at 600 and 533 megahertz that support a higher speed 133-megahertz system bus.

Total assets: $43,849 million
Current ratio: 2.80
Common shares outstanding: 6,668 million
Return on 1999 shareholders equity: 26.2%

		1999	1998	1997	1996	1995	1994	1993	1992
Revenues (millions)		29389	26273	25070	20847	16202	11521	8782	5844
Net income (millions)		7314	6178	6945	5157	3491	2562	2277	1077
Earnings per share		1.17	.89	.97	.73	.50	.37	.33	.16
Dividends per share		.05	.04	.03	.03	.02	.02	.02	.01
Price	High	44.8	31.6	15.5	17.7	9.8	4.6	4.7	2.9
	Low	25.1	16.4	15.7	6.3	4.0	3.5	2.7	1.5

GROWTH AND INCOME

International Paper Company

Two Manhattanville Road ❑ **Purchase, New York 10577** ❑ **Investor contact: Carol Tutundgy (914) 397-1625**
❑ **Direct dividend reinvestment plan is available: (800) 678-8715** ❑ **Web site: www.internationalpaper.com**
❑ **Listed: NYSE** ❑ **Ticker symbol: IP** ❑ **S&P rating: B-** ❑ **Value Line financial strength rating: B++**

For the past four years the paper industry has been in the doldrums. The price for pulp—the mush of wood chips that forms the raw material for most paper products—peaked at $925 per metric ton in 1995, convincing companies to start putting up new plants. As demand softened, and a glut of new supply hit the market, pulp prices plunged, retreating to as low as $460 early in 1999.

Now, however, demand is on the rise—magazine ad pages were up 3.7 percent in 1999—and prices are starting to recover.

In the first quarter of 2000, open market coated paper pricing increased 4.4 percent, and pulp prices moved up 6 percent. What's more, analysts look for pulp to reach $700 by mid-2000. These price increases have been enhanced by demand growth in the United States, Europe, and Asia.

As Asian demand for paper and pulp increased, the flood of imports to Europe from Asia dried up, and the paper industry has entered a period of very little capacity expansion. In fact, capacity over the next two years will most likely be at its lowest ebb in a decade. This minimal expansion, coupled with rising demand, may even create spot shortages of some grades.

Company Profile

International Paper is a global forest products, paper, and packaging company that is complemented by an extensive distribution system with primary markets and manufacturing operations in the United States, Europe, and the Pacific Rim.

A Glance at International Paper's Operations

• International Paper manufactures the broadest line of office papers for advanced digital imaging printers, as well as more traditional office equipment. In addition, IP offers printing papers for offset printing and opaques for books, direct mail, and advertising materials. Hammermill and Springhill brands are produced in the United States. In Europe, the company is the leading supplier of office papers with its EverRey, Duo, Presentation, and Tecnis brands. In New Zealand, Carter Holt Harvey produces reprographic and fine papers at the Mataura mill.

• The company's converting and specialty group provides papers for specialized applications such as envelopes, tablets, security papers, and release backings. This business group has had extensive success in developing new products with higher returns, using its diverse technical and product-development capabilities.

• International Paper manufactures coated papers and bristols in the United States and Germany. The company's improved Miraweb II and new Accolade coated papers target high-end magazines and catalogs. Publication Gloss and Hudson Web are also used for catalogs, magazines, and newspaper coupon inserts. Zanders Ikono remains the preferred coated freesheet paper for premium printing applications.

• The company's Springhill and Carolina coated bristols are used for book covers and commercial printing. Its uncoated Springhill bristols are used for commercial printing and converting applications such as file folders, tags, tickets, and index cards.

• International Paper is a major producer of market pulp in the United States, France, Poland, and New Zealand. Its grades range from high-purity pulp for acetate and fabrics to fluff pulp for hygiene products and paper pulp for the production of paper and paperboard.

• The company manufactures 3 million tons of containerboard annually at seven manufacturing facilities in the United States, Europe, and New Zealand. Its facilities are among the most efficient in the world. What's more, aggressive cost-management efforts are targeted at continuously improving the company's competitive cost position. In addition, International Paper manufactures one of the industry's widest product ranges, including visual-appeal grades such as ColorBrite and WhiteTop linerboard.

• In specialty panels, the company designs and produces engineered products based on wood and paper. Its Masonite subsidiary molds wood fiber into a broad line of door facings with many different designs and sizes. The company's customers fabricate these facings into doors that bring style, functionality, durability, and economy to both new construction and remodeling. Today, Masonite is the world leader with its CraftMaster brand. It also manufactures a broad line of hardboard exterior siding and industrial hardboard and softboard.

• International Paper owns or manages about 6.3 million acres of forest lands in the United States, mostly in the South where loblolly pine trees thrive. The company's forest lands are managed to strike a balance between the public's need for forest products, the sustainability of the forests, and the health and well-being of the forest environment. In the United States, the company has developed advanced land-management techniques that enable it to harvest trees while providing water-shed protection, wildlife habitat preservation, and recreational opportunities.

Shortcomings to Bear in Mind

■ If you are looking for a classic growth company, International Paper doesn't fit the bill. The paper industry—like chemicals, automobiles, metals, and machinery—is cyclical and tends to have earnings that bounce up and down with the economy. For its part, International Paper has a history of earnings volatility.

■ The industry is still reeling from the price gyrations that ravaged the industry in the mid-1990s. The price of newsprint, for instance, climbed above $750 a ton in the fourth quarter of 1995 then slumped to about $515 a ton a year later. Analysts say prices must reach above $600 a ton for producers to earn their cost of capital.

In another sector the pattern is similar. In the past 10 years, for instance, linerboard (the outer layer of corrugated board) has fluctuated in price between

$310 and $530 a ton. During many of those years, moreover, the price plunged below $400, spewing red ink on the industry's financial performance.

Reasons to Buy

- International Paper succeeded in its bid to take over Champion International in May of 2000. The deal, which was for $7.3 billion in cash and stock, strengthens IP's position as the world's number one paper producer. It also put papermaking capacity in fewer hands, enabling big companies to better manage supplies and, indirectly, prices. The acquisition of Champion has a big impact in two major markets. In office paper, the deal gives IP roughly 33 percent of North American capacity, up from 23 percent, and (including Champion's Brazilian operations) about 13 percent of the world's capacity, up from about 9 percent.

- Not even the paper industry is immune to the dot-com revolution. Despite dire predictions that the Internet could depress demand for paper. In fact, it's producing the opposite effect. Sales of newsprint and coated stock are climbing as newspapers and magazines swell with advertising from e-businesses. Demand for computer paper is up because so many Web pages get printed out. And all that merchandise sold by e-tailers such as Amazon.com or CDNOW is shipped in paper cartons. "Every time someone buys from a dot.com, that means more paper, more packaging is used," said John V. Faraci, chief financial officer of International Paper Company. "Those predictions 10 to 15 years ago of a paperless office just didn't play out."

- When International Paper's scientists at the company's Southlands Experiment Forest in Bainbridge, Georgia built their "field of dreams," they attracted top researchers from throughout the southern United States and the U.S. Department of Energy to "play ball" with them. Southlands' field of dreams is not a game, however. Instead, it is a laboratory for fast-growing loblolly pine and sweetgum trees. Southlands' scientists and research partners have the goal of growing trees 50 feet tall and 10 inches in diameter in 10 years. Using treatments like fertilization and irrigation, plus pest and disease protection, researchers are determining the upper limits of the trees' growth. Field of dreams results will give company foresters a benchmark for operational plantations and potential environmental and pest impacts, providing valuable information that will continue to advance the success of IP's forest productivity initiatives

- The art and science of papermaking is advancing at a rapid rate, and International Paper is at the forefront of that progress. At the same time, it is critical to keep all of the company's employees abreast of the latest technical advances. Advanced training at the company's new Manufacturing Technology Center (MTC) in Cincinnati, Ohio is ensuring that IP's pulp and paper mill process area employees have an in-depth understanding of new problem-solving techniques. The MTC offers management skills courses for both hourly operators and supervisors. Students are taught by a faculty made up of seasoned technical employees from across the company. To make the course interactive, students are required to bring a specific problem from their mill to discuss in class and then return home with solutions.

- In the spring of 1999 the company acquired Union Camp, a major paper company, for about 110 million shares of IP plus the assumption of about $1.6 billion in debt. In the words of CEO John Dillon, "By all measures, the merger with Union Camp is shaping up to be a tremendous success. The complementary product lines and land holdings have allowed us to increase our focus in our key areas of paper, packaging, and forest products. We generated over $130 million in annualized merger benefits in 1999 and are ahead of schedule to meet our goal of at least $425 million in annualized merger benefits by the end of 2000. A significant portion of our $1.8 billion in profit improvement by 2002 will be a direct result of the Union Camp merger."

- Less than a year after completing the acquisition of Union Camp, IP acquired Shorewood Packaging for about $875 million, including the assumption of $275 million of debt. Consolidation with Shorewood, a leading producer of folding cartons, significantly enhances the company's presence in the premium segments of the paperboard packaging markets.

- International Paper and Motorola agreed to a groundbreaking deal to put microchips in IP's boxes, a big step toward eliminating bar codes and ultimately bringing the entire manufacturing supply chain online. The "smart packages," the first of which are scheduled to roll out by the end of 2000, will allow manufacturers to track individual packages as they move from the assembly line to delivery trucks to store shelves to checkout counters.

Unlike bar codes, the chips can be read from any angle, don't need to be in a reader's line of sight, hold much more information, and allow the information to be changed en route.

Smart packages "will bring massive efficiencies to the global supply chain," said Kevin Ashton, director of the Massachusetts Institute of Technology's Auto-ID Center, a project aimed at coming up with standards to replace bar codes.

Total assets: $30,268 million
Current ratio: 1.56
Common shares outstanding: 414 million
Return on 1999 shareholders' equity: 5.3%

	1999	1998	1997	1996	1995	1994	1993	1992
Revenues (millions)	24573	19541	20096	20143	19797	14966	13685	13598
Net income (millions)	551	308	310	434	1153	432	314	405
Earnings per share	1.33	1.00	1.03	1.49	4.50	1.73	1.27	1.67
Dividends per share	1.00	1.00	1.00	1.00	.92	.84	.84	.84
Price High	59.5	61.8	61.0	44.6	45.7	40.3	34.9	39.3
Low	39.5	35.5	38.6	35.6	34.1	30.3	28.3	29.3

GROWTH AND INCOME

Jefferson-Pilot Corporation

P.O. Box 21008 ◻ Greensboro, North Carolina 27420 ◻ Investor contact: John T. Still, III (336) 691-3382 ◻ Dividend reinvestment plan is available: (800) 829-8432 ◻ Web site: www.jpfinancial.com ◻ Listed: NYSE ◻ Ticker symbol: JP ◻ S&P rating: A+ ◻ Value Line financial strength rating: A+

Jefferson-Pilot views the Internet as a very substantial opportunity. With a surging percentage of domestic households now possessing Internet connections, and with online banking established as a viable consumer product, there is no question as to its potential as a medium.

According to management, "Certain of our product may achieve direct distribution via the Internet, but the real opportunity, we believe, is to upgrade our service levels and strengthen our relationship with our clients."

Company Profile

Jefferson-Pilot has two business segments: insurance and communications. Within the insurance segment, JP offers individual life insurance products, annuity and investment products, and group insurance products through three principal subsidiaries: Jefferson-Pilot Life, Jefferson-Pilot Financial Insurance Company, and Alexander Hamilton Life Insurance Company of America (AH Life).

Within the communications segment, JP operates television broadcasting stations (three), radio broadcasting stations (17), and provides sports and entertainment programming. These operations are conducted through Jefferson-Pilot Communications Company (JPCC).

Highlights of 1999

- Net income per share grew 13 percent, to $4.42.
- Earnings before realized investment gains increased 13 percent, to $3.80.
- Return on equity expanded again, to 16.8 percent, from 16.4 percent.
- The company acquired The Guarantee Life Companies in a transaction that adds a significant block of universal life insurance to Jefferson Pilot's business in force and will strengthen JP as a competitor in the employee benefits market.

   Founded in 1901, Guarantee Life Insurance Company markets group life and long-term disability insurance products to employers and other groups. Guarantee brought Jefferson Pilot a major block of universal life insurance that fits well with the company's individual life business, adding $1.2 billion of reserves and $125 million of life pre-

miums. Moreover, as a strategic growth opportunity, Jefferson-Pilot is impressed with the potential that Guarantee brings to the company in the employee benefits market. After getting out of the group medical insurance business, JP has continued to seek growth in its nonmedical employee-benefit business—life and long-term disability insurance. Guarantee is an excellent addition, with sales of employee benefit products—primarily life insurance and long-term disability coverages—that have grown 30 percent annually over five years, reaching $79 million in 1999.

Shortcomings to Bear in Mind

- According to one analyst, "the surrender rate has remained uncomfortably high (nearly 16 percent of beginning fund balances in 1999), and is continuing to restrict asset growth. Higher crediting rates and strong sales of new products, however, should help to improve the flow of funds going forward."

Reasons to Buy

- Jefferson-Pilot is now established as a market leader in life insurance and annuity products. Over the past five years the company has recorded steadily rising life insurance sales, with new premiums growing at a compound annual rate of 39 percent, from $35 million to $180 million. The company's life insurance distribution arm in that span has mushroomed from 2,400 to nearly forty thousand agents. Annuity sales have grown at a compound annual rate of 33 percent, from $228 million to $939 million. Total corporate assets reached $26 billion in 1999, up from $6 billion five years ago.
- Today, Jefferson-Pilot is a focused provider of financial products and services to increasingly upscale markets. JP

manufactures and administers a portfolio of competitive financial products in centralized, very efficient operations and distributes them via diversified sales channels.

■ Jefferson-Pilot is focused on the high end of the financial services market. The company is using its capability in variable universal life, as well as its broker dealer, Jefferson-Pilot Securities Corporation, to service agents and clients in the estate planning and well-preservation market. This is reflected in the average size of JP's life sale, which ranks the company among the top-tier life companies serving the affluent market. Demographic projections indicate strong growth over the next two decades in both the over-65 population and the 45-to-54 age cohort, providing tremendous potential for retirement-planning and wealth-preservation products and services in that target market.

■ Jefferson-Pilot Financial's fixed annuity receipts grew by 128 percent during 1999. The market for fixed annuities was enhanced by the growing population sector of preretirees and retirees and greater diversity in the products that are available.

■ Jefferson-Pilot's annuity management capitalized on the favorable market conditions by adding new products, including popular multiyear rate guaranteed contracts, by responding quickly and aggressively to changing interest rates, and by focusing more effectively on all of the elements necessary to be a performance leader in the dynamic annuity marketplace.

■ The company has a strong offering of products and services:

● A leadership position in universal life insurance as the third-largest underwriter in the nation.

● A rapidly growing variable life insurance business, a product line the company acquired about three years ago as part of the acquisition of Chubb Life. With that acquisition, JP became the 16th-ranked variable universal life (VUL) writer, a position the company has subsequently improved to number 12. Variable universal life provided more than one-third of the company's life sales in 1999, and VUL sales were up almost 20 percent from the prior year.

● A strong franchise in fixed annuities, where Jefferson-Pilot enjoyed a doubling of sales in 1999, due to a new and innovative product line.

● A growing presence in variable annuities, marketed as a companion line to the company's variable life products.

● One of the largest independent broker dealers, a huge asset as the company builds its presence in the upscale market.

● A new line of products that came to market in 2000. Jefferson-Pilot introduced 13 new life and annuity products during 2000, including five new universal life products and three new variable life products.

■ Jefferson-Pilot is a leader in low-cost manufacturing. Its expenses as a percentage of premiums in the individual life business are now less than 9 percent, compared to an industry average of 15 percent. JP's annuity expenses as a percentage of average assets total 0.31 percent, against an industry average of about 0.50 percent. Management views this capability as a key strategic advantage, and one that it continuously seeks to improve.

■ Jefferson-Pilot appears strategically positioned for a changing world. The financial services industry, and in particular the life insurance industry, is changing at a pace that will quicken further.

Jefferson-Pilot sees four key issues that will impact the life insurance business in the next several years. All involve the issue of industry consolidation, which JP management expects to continue and accelerate:

- Business and product lines focus are increasingly important to well-managed companies. That will drive rationalization and consolidation.
- Market demands for better return on equity will force efficiencies. For many companies, the most direct way to achieve efficiency will be consolidation.
- Demutualization is here. Of the 12 major mutual life insurance companies, two-thirds have either begun the process or publicly committed to it. Mutuals as a group have an excellent opportunity for efficiency improvement. Some of that will come from internal cost-cutting, and some will come via consolidation.
- Financial deregulation will happen. The melding of the insurance, banking, and securities industries will, no doubt, take unexpected turns and may follow an unpredictable schedule, but it will happen.

- In addition to JP's growth in financial services, the company has built a premier media company. Jefferson-Pilot Communications Company has been a part of Jefferson-Pilot since the 1930s, JP Communications has grown steadily through acquisitions and through participation in the growth of the excellent markets in which it operates.

The company's radio operations, the dominant part of JP Communications today, consists of 17 stations in five very attractive markets—Atlanta, Charlotte, Denver, Miami, and San Diego. The television business consists of three network affiliates, also in excellent growth markets—Charlotte, Richmond, and Charleston, South Carolina.

Total assets: $26,446 million
Common shares outstanding: 103 million
Return on 1999 shareholders' equity: 16.8%

		1999	1998	1997	1996	1995	1994	1993	1992
Premium income (millions)		903	1049	1135	994	810	655	670	658
Total income (millions)		2460	2610	2578	2125	1569	1334	1247	1202
Earnings per share		4.42	3.91	3.47	2.73	2.37	2.10	1.94	1.77
Dividends per share		1.29	1.16	1.04	.93	.83	.75	.69	.58
Price	High	79.6	78.4	57.8	39.8	32.2	24.5	25.7	22.0
	Low	61.2	48.7	34.3	22.4	19.3	20.2	14.8	10.2

CONSERVATIVE GROWTH

Johnson & Johnson

One Johnson & Johnson Plaza WH1235 ◻ New Brunswick, New Jersey 08933 ◻ Investor contact: Helen E. Short (800) 950-5089 ◻ Dividend reinvestment plan is available: (800) 328-9033 ◻ Web site: www.jnj.com ◻ Listed: NYSE ◻ Ticker symbol: JNJ ◻ S&P rating: A+ ◻ Value Line financial strength rating: A++

The biggest news for Johnson & Johnson in 1999 was its largest merger ever, the $4.9-billion stock-for-stock transaction with Centocor Inc., a leader in monoclonal antibody technology and immunology and acute vascular-care products. In the words of CEO Ralph S. Larsen, "With Centocor and our Ortho Biotech affiliate, Johnson & Johnson has now become a world leader in biotechnology."

Company Profile

Johnson & Johnson is the largest and most comprehensive health care company in the world, with 1999 sales of $27.5 billion.

JNJ offers a broad line of consumer products, ethical and over-the-counter drugs, as well as various other medical devices and diagnostic equipment.

The company has a stake in a wide variety of endeavors: anti-infectives, biotechnology, cardiology and circulatory diseases, the central nervous system, diagnostics, gastrointestinals, minimally invasive therapies, nutraceuticals, orthopaedics, pain management, skin care, vision care, women's health, and wound care.

Johnson & Johnson has 190 operating companies in 51 countries, selling some 50,000 products in more than 175 countries.

One of Johnson & Johnson's premier assets is its well-entrenched brand names, which are widely known in the United States as well as abroad. As a marketer, moreover, JNJ's reputation for quality has enabled it to build strong ties to health care providers.

Its international presence includes not only marketing but also production and distribution capability in a vast array of regions outside the United States.

One advantage of JNJ's worldwide organization: Markets such as China, Latin America, and Africa offer growth potential for mature product lines.

The company's well-known trade names include Band-Aid adhesive bandages, Tylenol, Stayfree, Carefree, and Sure & Natural feminine hygiene products, Mylanta, Pepcid AC, Neutrogena, Johnson's baby powder, shampoo, and oil, and Reach toothbrushes.

The company's professional items include ligatures and sutures, mechanical wound closure products, diagnostic products, medical equipment and devices, surgical dressings, surgical apparel and accessories, and disposable contact lenses.

Shortcomings to Bear in Mind

- In 2000 the Food & Drug Administration (FDA) strengthened its warnings for JNJ's popular heartburn drug, Propulsid. The FDA said 70 deaths and 200 other episodes of irregular heartbeats have been linked to the drug since it was approved for marketing in 1993. However, about 85 percent of the events occurred in patients with conditions known to put them at risk if they took the drug, according to the FDA.

  The fatalities and other events have continued to occur even though the FDA has ordered changes in the product's labeling four previous times since 1993. Propulsid already carries a so-called black-box warning—used in instances where approved medicines can be especially risky for some patients—highlighting its association with potentially fatal heart arrhythmia.

  "Propulsid has been a major source of growth for J&J's pharmaceutical business," said one analyst. "There's no question there is going to be a negative effect." He estimated that the drug's sales in 1999 were about $1.1 billion, including $600 million in the American market.

  In late March of 2000, JNJ said it would cease marketing Propulsid in the United States. However, there are no plans to curtail marketing in Europe and other international markets where the drug generally is prescribed for other digestive afflictions at lower doses and where the incidence of life-threatening heart problems is much lower.

- Five years ago Johnson & Johnson sparked a revolution in the treatment of coronary-artery disease with a medical innovation called a stent. Few devices have yielded such an immediate eye-popping bonanza for their manufacturer. Doctors rushed to use the tiny metal scaffold to prop open obstructed heart vessels. In just 37 months, Johnson & Johnson tallied more than $1 billion in stent sales and garnered more than 90 percent of this lucrative market.

All was well until Guidant Corporation entered the scene, introducing a competitive stent. According to a Guidant spokesman, "Within 45 days, we had gained a 70 percent market position." Meanwhile, other rivals have joined the fray, including Arterial Vascular Engineering Inc. and Boston Scientific Corporation. By the end of 1998, JNJ's share of the stent business had withered to less than 10 percent.

Reasons to Buy

- A new contact lens made by Johnson & Johnson promises to clear the fuzzy vision of aging Americans who would rather squint that be caught wearing bifocals. The Acuvue Bifocal disposable contact lenses are being heavily marketed by the company to the 80 million people who have presbyopia, a vision problem that usually begins shortly after the fortieth birthday. Caused by a loss of flexibility in the eye, presbyopia makes it hard to thread a needle, read a newspaper, or focus on a computer screen. The lenses are paper-thin and can be worn continuously for seven days or during waking hours for two weeks. Designed with five invisible concentric rings that bring distant and near objects into focus, they allow wearers to shift back and forth easily. They cost about $13 to $14 a pair.
- The company has a consistent record of growth. Earnings per share advanced from $0.81 per share in 1989 to $2.97 in 1999, a compound annual growth rate of 13.9 percent. In the same 10-year span, dividends per share climbed from $0.28 to $1.12, a growth rate of 14.9 percent.

  Here is some additional evidence confirming the company's past record of growth:

- 66 consecutive years of sales increases.
- 55 continuous years of dividend payments.
- 36 consecutive years of dividend increases.

- Johnson & Johnson markets more than 100 prescription drugs sold in 150 countries. Of these, 33 had annual 1999 revenues in excess of $50 million—and 20 had revenues in excess of $100 million.
- The company can boast of impressive world leadership:
  - It is the largest medical-device company.
  - It is the eighth-largest pharmaceutical company.
  - JNJ has the largest:
    - Over-the-counter pharmaceutical business
    - Disposable contact lens business
    - Minimally-invasive surgical-equipment business
    - Surgical suture business
    - Blood glucose monitoring business
- Johnson & Johnson and its biotech ally, Genset SA of France, have unearthed a novel "candidate gene" associated with schizophrenia, a discovery that nudges them close to victory in one of the most competitive races of the genetic revolution. However, Genset scientists warn that the final step—moving from candidate gene to confirmed discovery—could be delayed until late in 2000. And even if the gene ultimately is confirmed, it could take a few years before a drug based on the discovery reaches the market.

  Even so, the breakthrough has generated excitement among schizophrenia specialists who remain baffled by the disease, which afflicts tens of millions of people around the world and costs governments and health care providers billions of dollars a year. What's more, confirmation of the gene's role in schizophrenia would be one of the most successful applications yet of a gene-hunting technique pioneered by Genset.

For its part, Johnson & Johnson has been at the forefront of schizophrenia research for decades with its drugs Haldol and Risperdal. There is plenty of room for improvement, because existing drugs alleviate only symptoms. Scientists hope that gene discoveries will lead to a cure.

- Cardiology—and more broadly, the management of circulatory diseases—is an important growth platform for JNJ. Through its Cordis affiliate, the company is well positioned for a profitable future in cardiology and the treatment of circulatory diseases. To be sure, this business is intensely competitive. However, Cordis is moving forward with a substantial pipeline of new stent, balloon, and endovascular products. Management is particularly pleased with the merger of Biosense, Inc. into Cordis for its patented medical sensor technologies to facilitate a wide range of diagnostic and therapeutic procedures, particularly in the realm of correcting heart rhythm problems.

- Skin care is the largest consumer market in which Johnson & Johnson participates—some $47 billion at retail. What's more, JNJ believes that it has the fastest-growing skin portfolio in the world. Its presence extends from its well-known heritage in baby products to consumer toiletries to prescription pharmaceuticals. Four of the company's five key skin care brands—Neutrogena, RoC, Clean & Clear, and Johnson's pH5.5—have been growing at double-digit rates.

- A 1999 alliance between Johnson & Johnson and Integra LifeSciences Corporation gave the company exclusive marketing and distribution rights to Integra Artificial Skin—the leading tissue-engineered skin substitute. The agreement also serves as a foundation for expanding indications and developing skin repair and regeneration products.

- In mid-1999 JNJ acquired Centocor, one of the nation's largest biotechnology companies, for $4.9 billion in stock. According to one analyst, "All of the drug companies are looking to invigorate their research and development efforts through biotech companies. Johnson & Johnson is a leader in biotechnology anyway." While some analysts said that the company might have paid too much for Centocor, few objected to the benefits of the deal. In the past, analysts have been critical of JNJ's weak pipeline of new drugs. On the other hand, they are quick to agree that Centocor should quickly remedy this shortcoming.

  The transaction gives Johnson & Johnson an attractive array of products that could benefit from the company's marketing muscle, including Remicade, which is approved for treating Crohn's disease and rheumatoid arthritis. Centocor's ReoPro anticlotting medication gives JNJ its first major foothold in the lucrative market for heart-disease drugs. "The thing that really excited us was the complementary nature of the two companies," said William Weldon, worldwide chairman of Johnson & Johnson's pharmaceutical group. "If you look at Remicade or ReoPro, both are billion-dollar opportunities."

- In 1999, the company's worldwide pharmaceutical sales growth reflected strong performance of Procrit/Eprex (Epoetin alfa) for the treatment of anemia; Risperdal (risperidone), an antipsychotic medication; Duragesic (fentanyl), a transdermal patch for chronic pain; Levaquin (levofloracin), an anti-infective; Ultram (tramadol hydrochloride), an analgesic; and the oral contraceptive line of products.

- In the worldwide consumer segment, the company said that sales were led by continued strength in the skin franchise, which includes Neutrogena, RoC, and Clean & Clear product lines, as well as solid results from McNeil Consumer Healthcare, which markets product lines that include the Tylenol acetaminophen family of products, cholesterol-lowering Benecol spread, and Nizoral A-D Shampoo. Benecol, launched in the United States in 1999, is a low-fat margarine spread that contains the dietary ingredient stanol ester, which is patented for use in reducing cholesterol. Johnson & Johnson has a licensing agreement with Raisio Group of Finland for the worldwide marketing rights (excluding Finland) to Benecol products.

Total assets: $29,163 million
Current ratio: 1.85
Common shares outstanding: 1,391 million
Return on 1999 shareholders' equity: 27.5%

	1999	1998	1997	1996	1995	1994	1993	1992
Revenues (millions)	27471	23657	22629	21620	18842	15734	14138	13753
Net income (millions)	4209	3669	3303	2887	2403	2006	1787	1525
Earnings per share	2.97	2.67	2.41	2.17	1.86	1.56	1.37	1.23
Dividends per share	1.12	.97	.85	.74	.64	.57	.51	.45
Price High	106.9	89.8	67.3	54.0	46.2	28.3	25.2	29.3
Low	77.0	63.4	48.6	41.6	26.8	18.0	17.8	21.5

GROWTH AND INCOME

Kimberly-Clark Corporation

P.O. Box 619100 ◻ Dallas, Texas 75261-9100 ◻ Investor contact: Michael D. Masseth (972) 281-1478 ◻ Dividend reinvestment plan is available: (800) 730-4001 ◻ Web site: www.Kimberly-Clark.com ◻ Ticker symbol: KMB ◻ S&P rating: A- ◻ Value Line financial strength rating: A++

In the last year or two, Kimberly-Clark has surprised Wall Street skeptics with robust earnings. For the most part, it is a batch of new products that have helped the company turn the corner after a difficult stretch following the company's acquisition of Scott Paper.

Some of these new products are refinements of old brands, such as Kotex feminine pads with an added "safety zone" and a new kind of Depend men's diapers. Kimberly-Clark invented Depend—and the adult-diaper category—20 years ago. Later modifications to the product included Velcro adjustable straps and breathable liners. A women's line called Poise followed.

However, nothing matched the clamor when Kimberly rolled out Depend "protective underwear" in late 1998. With an elastic waistband and stretch panels, the new model resembles regular (if somewhat bulky) briefs. The adult-care category is growing at a near double-digit rate, and demographics are on the company's side as an aging population increasingly requires incontinence-protection products.

Company Profile

Kimberly-Clark is a worldwide manufacturer of a wide range of products for personal, business, and industrial uses. Most of the products are made from natural and synthetic fibers, using advanced technologies in absorbency, fibers, and nonwovens.

The company has manufacturing facilities in 40 countries and sales in more than one hundred and fifty. Kimberly-Clark has been one of *Fortune* magazine's "Most Admired" corporations since 1983.

The company's well-known brands include Kleenex facial and bathroom tissue, Huggies diapers and baby-wipes, Pull-Ups training pants, GoodNites underpants, Kotex and New Freedom feminine care products, Depend and Poise incontinence care products, Hi-Dri household towels, Kimguard sterile wrap, Kimwipes industrial wipers, and Classic premium business and correspondence papers.

Shortcomings to Bear in Mind

- In an effort to increase the company's health care business, Kimberly-Clark acquired Safeskin Corporation in late 1999. The deal pushed the company's health care segment to nearly $1 billion. Even so, this pales beside its giant $6.7-billion tissue segment and its $4.6-billion personal-care operation.

  But that's not the whole story. Prior to the takeover of Safeskin, the shares of the latex-glove maker had been depressed when the company warned investors that it wouldn't meet analysts' estimates—and by a wide margin. As a result of the announcement, shareholders filed securities-fraud suits, alleging Safeskin had "stuffed" distribution channels in 1998 to improperly inflate its sales and financial results. What's more, Safeskin was also named in suits brought by health care workers, alleging the company sold defective products and failed to warn consumers about the risk of developing allergies from their products.

  Responding to this litigation, a Kimberly-Clark spokesman said the company was aware of all the suits. He countered that the suits were without merit and that Kimberly-Clark had thoroughly evaluated the product liability suits and that "we're comfortable that we're well-prepared to manage that issue."

- If Kimberly-Clark is to succeed, it must continually battle against the relentless, determined Procter & Gamble, one of the most innovative and skillful companies in the world.

- Growth in earnings has been rather pedestrian of late. In the 1989–1999 period, earnings per share advanced from $1.32 to $3.09, a compound annual growth rate of 8.9 percent. In the same 10-year stretch, dividends expanded from $.55 a share to $1.03, a growth rate of 6.5 percent. This lackluster growth rate prompted me to keep the stock in the growth and income category.

Reasons to Buy

- The acquisition of Safeskin Corporation in late 1999 provides Kimberly-Clark an entry into the $3-billion latex synthetic-glove market, boosting its overall presence in health care. KMB makes surgical gowns and drapes and sterile headwear and footwear.

  A Safeskin spokesman said his company recently had begun to make a surgical glove and would now be able to market it through Kimberly's distribution channels to hospital operating rooms, where KMB already has a strong presence.

- In the fall of 1999, Kimberly-Clark bought Ballard Medical Products, a maker of disposable operating-room products. This deal followed the company's acquisition of Tecnol Medical Products, a producer of disposable face masks, ice packs, and blood-pressure cuffs. This group of new businesses clearly indicates that Kimberly-Clark is making a concerted move to enhance its presence in health care.

■ The cornerstone of Kimberly-Clark, according to management, is "brands and technology. Let's take our successful re-launch of Kleenex Cottonelle bathroom tissue. It's a great example of how we're now applying to tissue the same formula that's worked so well for us in personal care and health care—that is, employing technology to deliver superior-performing products that win in the marketplace."

Using a patented process first commercialized at the company's mill in Villey-Saint-Etienne, France, KMB has produced a tissue with superior bulk, strength, softness, and absorbency—while reducing manufacturing costs. As a result, Kleenex Cottonelle has achieved record profits for the company's premium bathroom tissue business in North America. In 1999, Kimberly-Clark expanded distribution of this product across the United States.

What's more, the company has begun applying this and other patented tissue technologies to improve the quality and reduce the manufacturing cost of many other Kimberly-Clark products.

These include a significantly improved Kleenex Scottfold towel for commercial users introduced in late 1998 and a new Scott household towel that became available in domestic stores in 1999. Still another introduction in 1999 was an even better Andrex bathroom tissue, which is already one of the best-selling nonfood grocery brands in the United Kingdom.

■ As the world's foremost producer of nonwoven fabrics, Kimberly-Clark also brings sophisticated technology and cost advantages to bear on its health care products, which include sterile wrap, surgical drapes and gowns, and other protective apparel. In fact, the company holds an impressive 25 percent of the hundreds of patents granted in the nonwoven field since 1995. In the opinion of KMB management, "health care is a business that continues to exceed expectations and offers enormous potential for further growth."

■ In 1999, the company announced plans for additional facility consolidations, the charge for which was taken in 1998. With these moves Kimberly-Clark has completed a three-year process of redesigning and rationalizing its asset base—eliminating excess, high-cost capacity and consolidating its operations into fewer, larger, and more-efficient facilities. The company has realized significant savings from this process, with more savings to come.

■ In the realm of professional health care products, the company has been achieving impressive results, much of it emanating from innovative surgical gowns, drapes, and wraps. The same is true of the performance of KMB's nonwoven materials segment, which supplies versatile fabrics to its consumer-products operations and other businesses at a cost advantage compared with its competition.

■ One of Kimberly-Clark's strengths stems from the leadership position it holds in three core technologies—fibers, absorbency, and nonwovens. It also comes from the company's capacity in high-speed manufacturing and from its constant emphasis on innovation, productivity, and cost reduction.

■ Looking at Kimberly-Clark as it is now constituted, it is a much more balanced company. Before the Scott Paper merger and other acquisitions, the company derived almost half of its revenues from diapers and other personal care products. That portion is now one-third. Consumer tissue also accounts for about one-third of revenues, with the balance coming from a combination of away-from-home and other products.

- The company's Huggies Utratrim diapers now feature hook-and-loop fasteners from suppliers such as Velcro USA Inc. KMB also added a breathable outer cover to its Huggies Supreme brand.

- In Central and Eastern Europe, Kimberly-Clark extended its line of consumer products in Russia with the introduction of economy-priced diapers and feminine care products. The company also acquired Zisoft-Bobi, a Czech diaper and incontinence care products manufacturer, making Kimberly-Clark the largest personal care products company in that country. This presence provides a platform for offering products throughout Central and Eastern Europe. KMB has already introduced Kleenex and Scottex tissue products throughout the region and markets Huggies diapers in Russia, Romania, Croatia, Slovenia, and the Baltic states.

- In KMB's diaper business, Huggies remains the leading brand in North America. As part of the company's strategy to continuously improve the product, it has added hook-and-loop fasteners to Huggies Ultratrim and a leakage barrier at the waist to Huggies Supreme diapers.

- Kimberly-Clark has dominance in many of its brands throughout the world. In country after country, the company's position in its product is either number one or two. In Australia, for instance, its Snugglers diapers and Thick & Thirsty paper towels fall into this group. The same holds true in such countries as Bolivia with Bebito diapers, Intima feminine pads, Sanex paper towels, and a host of other products. Similarly, in Brazil this distinction includes Monica diapers, Chiffon paper towels, and Neve bathroom tissue; in China, it's Comfort & Beauty feminine pads; in the Netherlands, Page bathroom tissue and paper towels; in Mexico, Kleen Bebe diapers and Petalo bathroom tissue; in Spain, Monbebe diapers; in Germany, Camelia feminine pads and Tampona tampons; in Israel, Titulim diapers, Lily feminine pads, Molett bathroom tissue and paper towels, and Iris paper napkins. The list goes on and on.

Total assets: $12,816 million
Current ratio: 0.93
Common shares outstanding: 541 million
Return on 1999 shareholders' equity: 31.6%

	1999	1998	1997	1996	1995	1994	1993	1992
Revenues (millions)	13007	12298	12547	13149	13789	7364	6973	7091
Net income (millions)	1609	1353	1403	1404	1104	535	511	517
Earnings per share	2.98	2.45	2.44	2.49	1.98	1.67	1.59	1.61
Dividends per share	1.03	.99	.95	.92	.90	.88	.85	.82
Price High	69.6	59.4	56.9	49.8	41.5	30.0	31.0	31.6
Low	44.8	35.9	43.3	34.3	23.6	23.5	22.3	23.1

INCOME

Kimco Realty Corporation

3333 New Hyde Park Road ▢ Suite 100 ▢ Post Office Box 5020 ▢ New Hyde Park, New York 11042-0020 ▢ Investor contact: Scott G. Onufrey (516) 869-7190 ▢ Dividend reinvestment plan is available: (800) 733-5001 ▢ Web site: www.kimcorealty.com ▢ Listed: NYSE ▢ Ticker symbol: KIM ▢ S&P rating: Not rated ▢ Value Line financial strength rating: B++

Milton Cooper, Kimco's CEO, calls the REIT Modernization Act the "Emancipation Proclamation" of the REIT sector. He believes the Act will give REITs the ability to retain a greater percentage of their earnings as the taxable subsidiaries will be treated as separate businesses with the ability to retain cash flow. In addition, he noted that this act should give REITs the ability to compete more effectively with other real estate companies and be more entrepreneurial and aggressive in their expansion and operating strategies.

The law, which becomes effective January 1, 2001, will allow REITs to own a taxable REIT subsidiary (TRS). The law permits a REIT to own up to 100 percent of the stock of a TRS that can provide services to tenants and others without jeopardizing a REIT's ability to avoid paying federal income taxes at the corporate level. To ensure that a REIT remains focused on core real estate operations, the bill contains a size limit on TRSs. Specifically, TRS securities may not exceed 20 percent of a REIT's assets, and income received from a TRS may not exceed 75 percent of a REIT's gross revenues.

Company Profile

Kimco Realty Corporation, a publicly traded real estate investment trust (REIT), owns and operates the nation's largest portfolio of neighborhood and community shopping centers (measured by gross leasable area) with interests in 473 properties comprising about 62 million square feet of leasable area in 41 states.

Since incorporating in 1966, Kimco has specialized in the acquisition, development,

and management of well-located centers with strong growth potential. Self-administered and self-managed, the company's focus is to increase the cash flow and enhance the value of its shopping center properties through strategic retenanting, redevelopment, renovation, and expansion, and to make selective acquisitions of neighborhood and community shopping centers that have below market-rate leases or other cash flow growth potential.

A substantial portion of KIM's income consists of rent received under long-term leases, most of which provide for the payment of fixed-base rents and a pro rata share of various expenses. About 41 percent of the leases also provide for the payment of additional rent as a percentage of gross sales.

KIM's neighborhood and community shopping center properties are designed to attract local area customers and typically are anchored by a supermarket, discount department store, or drugstore, offering day-to-day necessities rather than high-priced luxury items. Among the company's major tenants are Kmart, Wal-Mart, Kohl's, and TJX Companies.

Kimco's core strategy is to acquire older shopping centers carrying below-market rents. This space is then released at much higher rates. A simple way to understand upside releasing is to compare the company's average base rent of $6.31 per square foot to what it believes current market rents are—about $9. Taking this spread, $2.69, and applying it to Kimco's 34 million square foot portfolio (excluding the Price REIT portfolio) infers that Kimco will receive $91.5 million, or $1.63 per share, as rents are bumped up to market. Such gains will not be realized at once, but they demonstrate the amount of built-in growth potential within the company's holdings.

What is an equity REIT?
Equity REITs make their money by owning properties, as opposed to mortgage REITs, which lend money to property owners. Equity REITs allow you to invest in a diversified collection of apartment buildings, hospitals, shopping centers, hotels, warehouses, and office buildings.

Like mutual funds, REITs are not taxed themselves, providing they pay out at least 95 percent of their taxable income. That translates into fat dividends for shareholders, as REITs pass along the rents and other income they collect. Dividend yields are typically 6 percent or more. "Put it all together, and you are looking at a double-digit total return. Over the long haul, the return should be lower than traditional stocks, but higher than bonds," says Chris Mayer, a real-estate professor at the University of Pennsylvania's Wharton School.

Kevin Bernzott, an investment adviser in Camarillo, California, views REITs as a stock-bond hybrid. "If you select quality REITs, they kick off a highly predictable stream of income, and eventually you may get some price appreciation. We plug them into the bond portion of the portfolio. They're almost like a bond with an equity kicker."

Shortcomings to Bear in Mind
- Real estate, like many industries, is cyclical. KIM's performance will be, to some degree, dependent on the health of the economy in its markets. Kimco's prospects will also be dependent upon the balance between supply and demand for shopping center space in each of its markets.

- Like the other shopping center REITs, Kimco has been hurt by concerns that its tenants will see their businesses undercut by Internet sales. Although sales remain strong at most Kimco strip malls, Milton Cooper admits the Internet isn't good news. "In my mind, the Internet is deflationary. You can comparison shop anywhere, anytime, and the middleman is under attack. It will not help retail rents."

On the other hand, he says, "If there's an overreaction, and everybody is concerned about everybody going broke, it will create buying opportunities."

- According to an analyst with J.P. Morgan Securities: "We remain concerned on the current oversupply of retail real estate and the risk of property obsolescence." Conversely, this same analyst says that "The company has distinguished itself as a leader through the efforts of one of the most experienced management teams in the business. KIM continues to maintain a solid development pipeline in strong sub-markets."

Reasons to Buy
- Kimco is active on the acquisition front. In 1999, the company acquired 34 properties totaling 3.4 million square feet for an aggregate cost of $229.4 million. In the fourth quarter, for instance, Kimco acquired 13 cites totaling 1.5 million square feet. Many of the properties acquired have tenants with below-market rents or expansion areas that will provide potential for future growth.

- In 1999, the company executed a joint venture agreement with the New York State Comptroller H. Carl McCall, as sole trustee of the New York State Common Retirement Fund (NYSCRF), to launch the Kimco Income REIT (KIR), an investment vehicle designed to acquire high-quality retail properties, financed primarily through the use of individual non-recourse mortgages. Under the agreement, Kimco contributed 19 properties to the venture with an aggregate equity value of about $105 million and has agreed to contribute an additional $12 million. NYSCRF has also subscribed for up to $117 million of equity in the venture, of which $70 million has been used to fund the venture's recent acquisition of four additional properties.

As a result of the contributions, the KIR portfolio is comprised of 23 shopping centers with a value of about $430 million, comprising nearly 4 million square feet of gross leasable area located in 13 states. The portfolio is 98 percent leased and includes anchor tenants such as Home Depot, Target, Kmart, and others.

Milton Cooper, Kimco's CEO, said, "This is only the first phase in the development of Kimco Income REIT. In fact, discussions are currently underway with other investors for an additional 20 percent equity interest, or about $58 million.

"In addition to proceeds from non-recourse mortgage financing, this new equity, as well as the remaining commitments from NYSCRF and Kimco, will provide the necessary capital to expand the asset base."

Comptroller McCall said, "This investment complements the Common Retirement Fund's diversified portfolio. Given Kimco's expertise in retail properties, we look forward to excellent returns over the long term."

- Since Milton Cooper took Kimco Realty public in November 1991, Kimco has been one of the stars of the REIT universe, averaging a total annual return of 18.8 percent. That's more than double the 9.1 percent return, including dividends, of the average real estate investment trust during that span.

- Kimco's success comes not by accident but as the careful product of business principles that have remained firmly in place since the company was founded in the 1950s. The company invests in properties that are undervalued assets where management knows it will be able to capitalize on the margin between the price at which it can buy the property and the price at which it can lease it. The average rent on properties in Kimco's portfolio remains below the market, providing the company with significant upside potential.

- Known for its history of pursuing creative transactions and delivering value-added growth, Kimco's management depth, according to one analyst, is "unparalleled among its peers. The Price REIT transaction has increased this depth even further, particularly with respect to the development and leasing of 'big box' retailers."

- Management is clearly aligned with shareholders as indicated by their collective 21.2 percent ownership stake in the company.

- Kimco has had a knack for opportunistic buys. In 1998, it did a sale-leaseback to take control of some 10 million square feet of space of Venture Stores' real estate. It seemed like a risky move because Venture Stores was tottering. When the retailer eventually went belly-up, Kimco quickly leased the Venture units to new tenants at even higher rates.

In a more recent move into the bankruptcy realm, Kimco was awarded asset designation rights for 34 former Hechinger Stores and Builders Square locations at the end of 1999. The rights enable Kimco to direct the disposition of the positions held by the bankrupt estate. Separately, Kimco acquired fee title to seven Hechinger locations and one ground lease position.

Total assets: $ 3,007 million
Current ratio: NA
Common shares outstanding: 61 million
Return on 1999 equity: 11%

	1999	1998	1997	1996	1995	1994	1993	1992
Rental income (millions)	434	339	199	168	143	125	99	79
Net income (millions)	177	122	86	74	52	41	32	19
Earnings per share	2.46	1.93	1.78	1.61	1.33	1.17	1.05	.83
Funds from operations	3.61	3.03	2.63	2.37	2.16	1.98	1.77	1.61
Dividends per share	2.43	1.97	1.72	1.56	1.44	1.33	1.25	.99
Price High	40.8	41.6	36.2	34.9	28.1	25.9	26.2	20.8
Low	30.9	33.4	30.3	25.3	23.6	22.1	20.3	14.1

CONSERVATIVE GROWTH

Leggett & Platt, Incorporated

No. 1 Leggett Road □ Carthage, Missouri 64836 □ Investor contact: J. Richard Calhoon (417) 358-8131 □ Dividend reinvestment plan is not available □ Web site: www.leggett.com □ Listed: NYSE □ Ticker symbol: LEG □ S&P rating: A □ Value Line financial strength rating: A

Since 1967, acquisitions have been a key part of Leggett's growth strategy. Traditionally, the company pursues friendly acquisitions—those that fit with existing operations either in marketing, technology, or both.

Normally, Leggett's acquisitions broaden the company's product lines, providing entry into additional markets or secure sources of select raw materials.

The company uses cash, stock, or combinations of the two in making acquisitions. In 1999, the company made 29 acquisitions, adding annualized sales of $480 million.

Company Profile

Founded in 1883, Leggett & Platt is a leading manufacturer of engineered products serving several major markets, including residential furnishings, commercial furnishings, aluminum products, industrial materials, and specialized products.

Products include components for bedding and furniture, retail store fixtures, displays, die castings, custom tooling and dies, drawn steel wire, welded steel tubing, control cable systems, and automotive seating suspension.

Standard & Poor's added Leggett & Platt to the S&P 500 Index in October of 1999. The S&P 500 is widely regarded as one of the most important standards for measuring U.S. stock market performance. The index includes a cross section of large-capitalization companies in a host of industries. As a component of the S&P 500, Leggett should gain increasing recognition throughout the investment community.

Here is a glimpse of LEG's businesses:

Residential Furnishings

Leggett & Platt is the world's leading supplier of a broad line of components, many of which are proprietary, for bedding and residential furniture. Manufacturers of mattresses and box springs can buy almost all of their component requirements from Leggett. Product lines have been expanded to include a wide range of components for stationary and motion upholstered furniture as well.

In addition, the company designs and produces select lines of finished home furnishings and consumer products. Customers include manufacturers, retailers, distributors, and institutions.

Commercial Furnishings

Leggett's rapidly expanding lines of commercial furnishings include creatively designed store fixtures, point-of-purchase displays, and storage and material handling systems. A multitude of retailers, brand-name packagers of consumer products, as well as companies in the food service, health care, and other industries are increasingly looking to Leggett as a one-stop-one-shop resource. Manufacturers of office and institutional furnishings and additional commercial products also can buy Leggett components designed and produced to meet their requirements. The company's components add significant value, comfort, and distinctive features to chairs and other office furniture.

Aluminum Products

The Leggett companies in its aluminum group are North America's leading independent suppliers of aluminum die castings, primarily for nonaluminum applications. Major customers include manufacturers of consumer products, telecommunications and electrical equipment, plus other industrial products that incorporate aluminum and zinc die cast components. Leggett's aluminum smelting and refining operations produce raw materials for internal use in die casting plants, and for sale to other manufacturers of aluminum products.

Industrial Materials

Several Leggett companies produce industrial materials for a wide range of customers, including other Leggett operations. Drawn steel wire and welded steel tubing are produced in various strategic locations. Additional operations produce specialty wire products, such as rolled, flattened, and shaped wire, proprietary bale ties, tying heads, and other parts for automatic baling equipment.

Shortcomings to Bear in Mind

- The market is concerned about a future slowdown in the economy and the potential impact on the furniture business. To an extent, Leggett's business is tied to home-buying and new housing starts. The two years after a home is purchased are normally years of heavy furniture purchases.

Reasons to Buy

- According to a U.S. Department of Labor study, the age group that spends the most amount on furniture is the 45-to-54-year-old bracket. The second-highest amount is spent by those 35 to 44. The Census Bureau says the number of consumers in the 45-to-54 age group expanded 14.1 percent from 1994 to 1999. The 35 to 44 age group advanced 7.3 percent. At the same time, the general population increased only 4.7 percent.

There are a number of reasons why middle-aged people spend more money on furniture:

- Their income is high during this span of their lives.
- They are more likely to be homeowners than are younger people.
- These more mature couples have sold their starter homes. Their new homes, moreover, are larger and may need a whole new set of more expensive furniture. In 1993, the average home had 2,100 square feet of living space, up 5 percent from 1988. According to surveys, the average home has now increased to 2,200 square feet. Larger homes require much more furniture than smaller ones. For instance, a home with 3,000 square feet needs 2.5 times as much as one with 2,000 square feet.

- In 1999, *Fortune* magazine ranked Leggett & Platt in the top 5 percent of "America's Most Admired Companies." More than ten thousand executives, directors, and securities analysts judged companies on innovativeness, quality of management, employee talent, quality of products/services, long-term investment value, financial soundness, social responsibility, and use of corporate assets.

- Leggett & Platt boasts a remarkable record of growth. In the 1989–1999 period, earnings per share climbed from $0.33 to $1.45, a compound annual rate of 16 percent. In the same 10-year stretch, dividends per share expanded from $0.09 to $0.35, a growth rate of 14.5 percent. What's more, Leggett & Platt has increased its dividend for 29 consecutive years. Over that span the dividend increased 60-fold, or 15.2 percent per year compounded.

- Leggett's commitment to research and development has kept pace with company growth. LEG has R&D facilities at both centralized and divisional locations. At those locations, engineers and technicians design and build new and improved products in all major lines and machinery. They also perform extensive tests for durability and function. Leggett's experience and accumulation of data in this highly specialized area of R&D is unmatched.

- There are no comparable companies to Leggett & Platt in the public sector. However, since the company is, in part, a supplier to the furnishings industry, the market tends to view LEG as a furniture company. This is not a correct perception. Here is why I believe this to be so:
  - Residential furniture (whether a finished product or a component) represents less than 30 percent of Leggett's revenue base. What's more, bedding components, a much more stable product line, accounts for nearly 30 percent of revenue. This is a replacement business with just a minor decline in shipments during the last recession. The balance is composed of office, institutional and commercial furnishings and fixtures (components and finished products), and the company's diversified non-furnishings products.
  - The risk/reward parameters of Leggett's business are quite different from that of a furniture manufacturer. Keep in mind that LEG's components go into making the "insides" of furniture (springs, frames, motion mechanisms, and construction fabric), thus making Leggett immune to the fashion risk inherent in the furniture business. Since most manufacturers buy components from Leggett, there is little, if any, fashion risk related to Leggett's products. This risk is borne by the manufacturer and the way the finished product is differentiated with style or fabric.
  - Leggett has opportunities to grow even if overall demand does not grow. This is accomplished through internal growth, driven by market share gains and aggressive new product development, plus an aggressive acquisition program—responsible for two-thirds of the company's growth over the past 15 years.
  - Leggett & Platt has a proven strategy in place to expand its position in existing markets and selectively approach a larger portion of the total market for furniture and bedding components. A strong financial position also provides substantial capital resources and flexibility to pursue future growth opportunities, both internally and through selective acquisitions.
  - Through its leadership role in new product development, new

manufacturing techniques, and technological improvements, analysts believe Leggett can gain market share at the expense of its smaller, less-well-financed competitors.

- Participation in such diverse furnishings categories as bedding and residential, office, and contract furniture gives Leggett & Platt the opportunity to spread new product developments into several sectors at all price points while limiting its exposure to any one sector.

- Leggett & Platt has created a reputation for both innovation and confidentiality, often working with several larger manufacturers to develop exclusive components, giving each a competitive edge while utilizing Leggett & Platt's massive manufacturing capabilities. Consequently, LEG can manufacture a broad range of distinctive, cost-effective components for any customer, whether large or small.

Total assets: $2,978 million
Current ratio: 2.91
Common shares outstanding: 196 million
Return on 1999 shareholders' equity: 18.8%

	1999	1998	1997	1996	1995	1994	1993	1992
Revenues (millions)	3779	3370	2909	2466	2110	1858	1527	1170
Net income (millions)	290	248	208	153	135	115	86	62
Earnings per share	1.45	1.24	1.08	.93	.80	.70	.52	.41
Dividends per share	.35	.32	.27	.23	.19	.155	.135	.115
Price High	28.3	28.8	23.9	17.4	13.4	12.4	12.5	8.8
Low	18.6	16.9	15.8	10.3	8.5	8.3	8.2	4.7

AGGRESSIVE GROWTH

Eli Lilly and Company

Lilly Corporate Center ▫ **Indianapolis, Indiana 46285** ▫ **Investor contact: Patricia A. Martin (317) 276-2506** ▫ **Direct dividend reinvestment plan is available: (800) 451-2134** ▫ **Web site: www.lilly.com** ▫ **Listed: NYSE** ▫ **Ticker symbol: LLY** ▫ **S&P rating: A-** ▫ **Value Line financial strength rating: A++**

Investors have been concerned about Eli Lilly's dependence on Prozac. However, other drugs are beginning to play important roles. In 1999, for instance, results were helped by such drugs as Zyprexa, Gemzar, Evista, and ReoPro.

"As our product line continues to become more diversified, we have become less dependent on Prozac's performance," said Sidney Taurel, Eli Lilly's CEO. "Major products introduced in the last five years accounted for fully one-third of our sales in 1999 and had a combined growth rate of 41 percent during the year."

Mr. Taurel went on to say, "The addition of innovative products from our pipeline and from our partnerships, combined with continuing strong sales growth from newer products, will help drive improved top-line performance and overall strong earnings growth in the coming years."

Company Profile

Eli Lilly is one of the world's foremost health care companies. With a solid dedication to R&D, Eli Lilly is a leader in the development of ethical drugs—those available on prescription.

It is well-known for such drugs as Prozac (to treat depression), Ceclor (an antibiotic), insulin, and other diabetic care items. Some of its other important drugs include Keflex, Kefzol, Lorabid, Mandol, Nebcin, Vancocin HCL, Tazidime, Darvon, Nalfon, and Axid. Lilly also has a stake in animal health and agricultural products.

Like most drug companies, Lilly is active abroad and does business in 120 countries.

Shortcomings to Bear in Mind

- Eli Lilly is concerned that economic turbulence will slow the availability of modern medical care, including the company's medicines, to people in many developing nations. Meanwhile, affluent countries are experiencing higher health care costs that are prompting concerns about the affordability of new medicines.
- The cost of developing new drugs— which was already high—is getting even higher. More emphasis is being placed on generic drugs by cost-conscious health care providers.
- There is some concern about the sale of Lilly's blockbuster drug Prozac, which was introduced to the domestic market for the treatment of depression in 1988 and has since been approved in the United States for the treatment of obsessive-compulsive disorder and bulimia. In 1999, however, Prozac sales fell 7 percent, to $2.6 billion, as it was hurt by competition from Effexor XR, sold by the American Home Products Corporation, and from Celexa, developed by H. Lundbeck and introduced in the United States in 1998 by Forest Laboratories and the Warner-Lambert Company. Still another concern for Prozac is its patent, which expires in late 2003 and could lead to cheaper generic competition soon thereafter.

In the company's 1999 annual report, management comments on the coming expiration of Prozac's patent. "We're accelerating the development of a number of pipeline compounds with strong commercial opportunity. For example, tomoxetine for attention-deficit hyperactivity disorder, Protein Kinase C-beta inhibitor for diabetes complications, recombinant human Activated Protein C for sepsis, and other new molecules now may launch prior to Prozac losing U. S. marketing exclusivity."

Reasons to Buy

- In the spring of 2000, Eli Lilly filed an application with the FDA to sell a new formulation of Prozac that can be taken once a week. Prozac is normally taken once or twice a day. If the new version is approved, it will be the only once-weekly depression medication on the market. That might help Lilly shore up sales for Prozac, which has been on the market for 12 years and has been losing out to newer pills with fewer side effects
- Eli Lilly is emerging as an industry leader in forging productive alliances. The company is engaged in more than 100 R&D agreements, involving everything from new gene discoveries to new delivery technologies to late-stage drug candidates.
- Depression is a more serious and widespread illness than many realize. In the United States alone, one in five people will experience clinical depression at some time in their lives. Left untreated, depression can be dangerous. Discovered and developed by Lilly scientists, Prozac represented an important new treatment option—the first widely available product in a class of drugs called SSRIs (for selected serotonin reuptake inhibitors). In simple terms, SSRIs help the brain to maintain higher levels of an

important natural substance called serotonin by selectively reducing its absorption or "reuptake."

- Lilly's own research into the brain and central nervous system (CNS) has led to the discovery and launch of additional important drugs, including Permax for the treatment of Parkinson's disease and Zyprexa, the company's new product for the treatment of schizophrenia. Furthermore, Eli Lilly is testing investigational compounds that may aid patients with Alzheimer's disease, migraine headaches, sleep disorders, epilepsy, and urinary incontinence.

- Lilly is leveraging its research and development resources by focusing them more sharply within five broad disease categories—those that match Lilly's strengths: central nervous system diseases, endocrine diseases, infectious diseases, cancer, and cardiovascular diseases. What's more, the company is seeking to be the world leader in each of those five categories.

- Diabetes, within the endocrine category, is a good example. As the developer of the first insulin product and one of the world's major suppliers of insulin, Lilly has long been a global leader in the field. But diabetes, which affects more than 100 million people worldwide, continues to cause severe long-term complications, suffering, lost productivity, and death.

For many patients with this disease, diabetes is also inconvenient. Diabetics have to check their blood glucose several times a day. They may have to give themselves one or more shots of insulin. And they must take insulin at least 30 minutes before a meal or risk severe complications.

Lilly believes that it has an answer that gives patients with diabetes a better quality of life—and a good deal more convenience. Humalog acts faster than traditional insulin to control blood-glucose

levels. Patients take it right before a meal, compared with 30 to 45 minutes before with current products. Humalog provides them with more freedom, better health, and fewer complications.

- The Food & Drug Administration (FDA) gave Lilly approval to sell Zyprexa for the treatment of manic depression, also known as bipolar disorder. In the past, Zyprexa was used primarily to treat schizophrenia. "The market for mania is almost as big as the market for schizophrenia," said Dr. John M. Davis, a psychiatry professor at the University of Illinois at Chicago. Prior to the new FDA ruling in late 1999, Zyprexa was already generating sales at an annual rate of about $2 billion a year. In the past, lithium and older antipsychotic drugs were the leading medicines used in bipolar disease.

- Gemzar is the world's third best-selling oncolytic agent. In 1999, the company reached several Gemzar milestones: approval for non-small-cell lung cancer in Japan; approval for bladder cancer in Denmark, France, and Mexico; and submission for bladder cancer in the United States. Lilly is also studying its use with other anticancer compounds for additional indications, including breast and ovarian cancers.

- Evista is the company's fastest-growing drug. More than 1 million women in more than 50 countries have already used the product for the prevention or treatment of osteoporosis. And more good news might be on the horizon. Early data suggest Evista many reduce the incidence of breast cancer and benefit the heart in postmenopausal women.

- In 1999, Lilly helped successfully launch Takeda's oral antidiabetes agent, Actos, in the United States; launch plans are under way for 70 additional countries. What's more, Lilly continues to expand its core insulin business by introducing novel products and delivery devices. Sales of the company's newest insulin, Humalog, grew 73 percent in 1999.

- With more than a half-dozen potentially new antidepressants in Lilly's pipeline, the company is capitalizing on its experience in the realm of depression. Researchers are intrigued with duloxeline, a potent compound in Phase II clinical trials that may work better and faster than current therapies. The company is also encouraged by the combination of Prozac and Zyprexa, now in Phase II clinical trials for treatment-resistant depression.
- Diabetes is the leading cause of adult blindness, a condition for which no satisfactory treatments are currently available. Lilly is conducting studies of

Protein Kinase C-beta inhibitor, a promising compound being investigated for the prevention of diabetes-related blindness and other complications of chronic diabetes.

- Lilly is rapidly winning international recognition for outstanding results in recruiting, developing, and retaining world-class talent. The long list of people-related awards the company received in 1999 includes being honored by *Fortune* magazine as one of the 100 Best Companies to Work for in America; by *Working Mother* magazine as one of the top 10 companies for women; and by the U. S. Department of Labor, which gave Lilly its highest honor, the Opportunity 2000 Award.

Total assets: $12,825 million
Current ratio: 2.07
Common shares outstanding: 1,090 million
Return on 1999 shareholders' equity: 53.9%

	1999	1998	1997	1996	1995	1994	1993	1992
Revenues (millions)	10003	9237	8518	7346	6764	5712	6452	6167
Net income (millions)	2721	2098	1774	1524	1307	1269	1347	1393
Earnings per share	2.50	1.91	1.57	1.33	1.15	1.09	1.15	1.22
Dividends per share	.92	.80	.74	.69	.66	.63	.61	.55
Price High	97.8	91.3	70.4	40.2	28.5	16.6	15.5	21.9
Low	60.6	57.7	35.6	24.7	15.6	11.8	10.9	14.4

INCOME

The Lubrizol Corporation

29400 Lakeland Boulevard ❑ Wickliffe, Ohio 44092-2298 ❑ Investor contact: Greg D. Taylor (440) 943-4200 ❑ Direct dividend reinvestment plan is available: (877) 573-3998 ❑ Web site: www.lubrizol.com ❑ Listed: NYSE ❑ Ticker symbol: LZ ❑ S&P rating: B+ ❑ Value Line financial strength rating: B+

Lubrizol was founded by six men with an idea that set the stage for every Lubrizol product that followed. From the beginning, the company recognized a problem, used technology to solve it, and developed a product that was better than anything else available.

Next, Lubrizol found a way to make it easy for its customers to use the product. The result of that first idea was a product

called Lubri-Graph. Designed to eliminate the squeak caused by the leaf springs in early model cars, it was sold with a 10-gallon pressurized drum dispenser that made it easy to apply.

Company Profile

Lubrizol is a fluid technology company concentrating on high-performance chemicals, systems, and services for transportation and industry. LZ develops, produces, and sells specialty additive packages and related equipment used in transportation and industrial finished lubricants. The company creates its products through the application of advanced chemical and mechanical technologies to enhance the performance, quality, and value of the customer products in which they are used.

Lubrizol groups its product lines into two operating segments: chemicals for transportation and chemicals for industry. Chemicals for transportation made up about 83 percent of consolidated revenues and 87 percent of segment pretax operating profit in 1999.

Lubrizol products can be found in a variety of markets, including coatings, inks, compressor lubricants, and metalworking fluids. The company is also combining the expertise of its equipment-related businesses with chemicals for transportation and industry to provide integrated solutions for lubrication or environmental problems.

Highlights of 1999

- In 1999, Lubrizol achieved substantial improvement in the operational and financial performance of its business. Earnings per share, before special items, increased 48 percent; cash flow from operating activities increased from $155 million in 1998 to $289 million; and return on shareholders's equity, before special items, expanded from 10.9 percent to 16.1 percent in 1999. Lubrizol's revenues advanced 8 percent, reaching a record $1.75 billion. And the company's product shipments increased 5 percent for the year when acquisitions are excluded. Finally, net income in 1999, excluding unusual items, was $125.3 million, or $2.30 per share.
- The company implemented a new commercial organization, value proposition, and operating model for its chemicals

for transportation business to be better able to serve its customers.

- Lubrizol's acquisition of Adibis was completely integrated into the company's operation ahead of plan and under budget.
- The company successfully introduced advanced new heavy-duty diesel engine oil technology.
- LZ's chemicals for industry business delivered strong performance in several areas, including AMPS Monomer, surfactants, and compressor lubricants.
- In 1999, the company defined and implemented new performance systems initiatives, announcing an alliance with General Electric Transportation Systems to market Lubrizol's FluiPak technology for fluid management in locomotive and mining applications.
- Lubrizol also announced a relationship with Caterpillar, Inc. for the testing and endorsement of the company's new PuriNOx low emission, water blend fuel product.
- Lubrizol's position in Asia-Pacific continued to grow in 1999, as the company worked to establish a joint venture in China. Shipments to that region increased 16 percent in 1999. What's more, in 2000 the company has been expanding its new globally integrated management information system into Asia-Pacific, which follows successful implementation of this system in Europe in 1999.
- The first phase of the company's cost-reduction initiative was completed in 1999, and further reductions were announced which will be completed by the end of 2000. Total operating expenses in 1999 increased only 3 percent, and all of the increase was attributable to acquisitions.

Shortcomings to Bear in Mind

- In the 1989–1999 period, earnings per share made modest progress, moving ahead from $1.26 to $2.30, a compound annual growth rate of only 6.2 percent—hardly a record that would lead you to regard Lubrizol as a growth company. In the same 10-year period, dividends per share inched ahead, from $0.69 to $1.04, a growth rate of 4.2 percent. However, the dividend yield is far above most other stocks, which leads me to think this stock should be considered suitable for investors seeking dependable income.

- Management believes that the global growth rate for lubricant additives is about 1 percent per year. Due to changing industry market forces, such as improved engine design and longer drain intervals, the company does not expect the annual growth rate to exceed 1 percent in the future. On a more positive note, 1999 shipment volume increased by 9 percent over the prior year, augmented by acquisitions made during 1998, coupled with improvement in the economies in the Asia-Pacific region and new business in North America.

- Lubrizol has been hurt by increased costs of raw materials. Cost of sales for 1999, including acquisitions, increased 5 percent, reflecting higher shipment levels, partially offset by lower average raw material cost compared with 1998. However, the company experienced a 4 percent increase in average raw material cost during the third quarter of 1999 and an additional 2 percent increase during the fourth quarter as a result of higher crude oil prices. To offset the higher raw material prices, management announced a global price increase to take effect December 15 1999. It was successful, and management believes it will result in an average increase of 4 percent or more during 2000.

The company began to see the impact on revenues in the first quarter of 2000 and felt the full impact by the end of the second quarter of 2000. However, Lubrizol is still feeling the pressure of material cost increases, and it is likely that further price increases will be necessary to maintain margins.

Reasons to Buy

- Lubrizol chemical products all have one thing in common. They do their work in the molecular world, wherever surfaces interact. It doesn't matter whether the surfaces are the parts of a diesel engine or paint on a wall. Lubrizol chemicals are designed to slip between them, helping things to work better. Lubrizol chemicals enhance performance. They improve the operating efficiency of equipment and extend its useful life. For the company's customers, that means lower maintenance costs and a reduction in scheduled downtime.

- Improving performance and extending equipment life is one part of the equation. The other is the increased demand placed on chemical manufacturers by environmental regulations and worker health and safety. These are top priorities in all of the company's markets, so they are top priorities for Lubrizol. In addition to improving operating efficiency, Lubrizol chemicals also reduce harmful emissions. They extend the useful life of performance fluids, which results in less waste fluid for disposal. The company's antimist technologies, with applications in metalworking, coatings, and inks and the transportation industry, help keep work environments cleaner and safer and save energy and maintenance costs.

- Lubrizol's e-business offers the company the opportunity to improve the way it reacts with its customers while reducing its cost to serve. In 1999, Lubrizol became the first company in the additive industry to use Internet technology to provide North American customers with online ordering capability.

While this service is still in its early stages, management anticipates that it will continue to expand, becoming a vital part of the way Lubrizol does business. As the company's initiatives to streamline its operations begin to take hold, other service opportunities are becoming obvious. For example, Lubrizol is experimenting with offering its manufacturing, testing, and research expertise to the marketplace on a fee-per-project basis.

- In 2000, Lubrizol announced that it had purchased Alox Metalworking Additive Business from RPM, Inc. Alox Corporation is a leading supplier of additives for corrosion prevention in metalworking products. The acquisition further supports Lubrizol's growth strategy for metalworking additives; it follows two previous metalworking acquisitions in 1997 and 1998.

Total assets: $1,682 million
Current ratio: 2.51
Common shares outstanding: 54 million
Return on 1999 shareholders equity: 16%

	1999	1998	1997	1996	1995	1994	1993	1992
Revenues (millions)	1743	1615	1669	1593	1658	1593	1518	1544
Net income (millions)	125	87	155	135	133	149	114	119
Earnings per share	2.30	1.55	2.68	2.23	2.08	2.26	1.67	1.73
Dividends per share	1.04	1.04	1.01	.97	.93	.89	.85	.81
Price High	31.4	40.2	46.9	32.4	37.4	38.6	36.4	35.3
Low	18.0	22.4	30.4	26.5	25.5	28.5	26.6	23.4

AGGRESSIVE GROWTH

Lucent Technologies

600 Mountain Avenue ❏ **Room 3C-446** ❏ **Murray Hill, New Jersey 07974-0636** ❏ **Investor contact: Jeffrey A. Baum (908) 582-7635** ❏ **Direct dividend reinvestment plan is available: (888) 582-3686** ❏ **Web site: www.lucent.com** ❏ **Listed: NYSE** ❏ **Fiscal year ends September 30** ❏ **Ticker symbol: LU** ❏ **S&P rating: Not rated** ❏ **Value Line financial strength rating: A+**

Lucent, the world's leading provider of telecommunications equipment, sells the hardware, software, and service that long-distance carriers, Baby Bells, and smaller companies need to ensure their customers' phone calls get through.

Embedded within Lucent is the brain power few companies can rival: It is home to Bell Labs, which has produced inventions such as the transistor and the laser.

Lucent was formed from the systems and technology units that were formerly part of AT&T Corporation, including the research and development capabilities of Bell Laboratories. Prior to February 1, 1996, AT&T conducted Lucent's original business through various divisions and subsidiaries.

On February 1, 1996, AT&T began executing its decision to separate Lucent into a standalone company by transferring to Lucent the assets and liabilities related to its business. In April 1996, Lucent completed the initial public offering of its common stock, and on September 30, 1996 became independent of AT&T.

Company Profile

Systems for Network Operators includes switching and transmission systems for voice and data; data networking routing switches and servers; wireless network infrastructure; optical networking systems; optical fiber products; communications software; Internet telephony servers. Lucent has a number one market share in optical networking, U.S. switching systems, and wireless infrastructure equipment.

Business Communications Systems includes private branch exchange and key telephone systems; wireless systems; support services for voice, data, and video networks; network cabling within and between buildings; messaging systems and servers (offered through Lucent's Octel Messaging Division); call center offerings; conferencing systems; Internet-based products and network management software.

Lucent has a number one market share in messaging, in-building wiring systems, call centers in the United States, and in-building wireless systems.

Microelectronics Products include integrated circuits for wireless and wired communications, computer modems, and networks; optoelectronic components for communications systems; and power systems. Lucent has a number one market share in communications integrated circuits (ICs), transmission, modem ICs in personal computers, optoelectronic components for optical transmission systems, and power equipment.

The company has a number two market share in local area network ICs and digital signal processors.

Richard A. McGinn, CEO

When Richard A. McGinn took over the CEO post at Lucent Technologies in October of 1997, he was following the footsteps of Henry B. Schacht, one of the nation's most respected corporate executives. Schacht, the former Cummins Engine Company CEO brought in to head Lucent when the company was spun off from AT&T in 1996, had just guided Lucent to a spectacular first year.

But McGinn, age 52, didn't miss a beat after Schacht stepped down at age 63. His success may be related to his competitive spirit. He has a keen interest in golf and deep-sea fishing—and will do anything to win. In the world of business, this competitive drive makes it imperative that he take market share from the likes of Motorola and Northern Telecom. In 1998, Lucent won a host of marquee deals, including contracts from wireless-service provider PrimeCo Personal Communications and Baby Bell SBC Communications.

Despite a sunny disposition and an easy laugh, McGinn is not one to be taken lightly. He starts his day at 5 A.M. by working out on his treadmill and catching up on news from Asia and arrives at his office at 7. On the way to work, a 30-minute commute, McGinn is on his cell phone with other top executives.

Always a man in a rush, McGinn spent 1998 pushing Lucent into a host of new markets, including acquisitions in the fast-growing market for data gear. He's also aggressively expanding abroad.

Shortcomings to Bear in Mind

■ Lucent continues to face significant competition and expects the level of competition on pricing and product offerings will intensify. The company expects that new competitors will enter its markets as a result of the trend toward global expansion by foreign and domestic competitors, as well as continued changes in technology and public policy.

These competitors may include entrants from the telecommunications, software, data networking, and semiconductor industries. Such competitors may include Cisco Systems, Nortel Networks, Ericsson, Alcatel Alsthom, and Siemens.

- Lucent is less adept at packet switching than some competitors, and it must play catch-up. Thus, notes one analyst, "It will be extremely difficult for earnings to grow faster than those of the overall market. As the market moves from circuit to packet switching, Lucent's sales will grow, at best, at the expense of circuit switchers, and, at worst, won't grow at all."

Reasons to Buy

- Lucent, considered an ugly-duckling hardware business when it was spun off by AT&T in 1996, has emerged as a high-technology powerhouse and one of the decade's hottest stocks, defying predictions that the Internet would overwhelm the traditional telephone gear it makes.

  In fact, the Net, by fueling demand for phone lines, has propelled sales of Lucent's bread-and-butter product, the circuit switches that route billions of phone calls a day over local and long-distance networks around the globe.

  Lucent is convinced, however, that the future belongs not to the circuit switch but to the fancy packet networks sold by companies like Ascend Communications, maker of Internet switching equipment. In 1999, conceding it had fallen behind in its efforts to devise similar products, Lucent agreed to acquire Ascend for $20 billion.

  The new generation of networking equipment made by Ascend and such rivals as Cisco Systems and 3Com sends information across phone lines more efficiently by breaking the data into bits, called packets. The technology allows a single phone line to carry many messages simultaneously, promising savings for phone companies that now must allocate a separate line to each caller.

- In mid-2000, Lucent acquired Ortel for about $3 billion. Based in Alhambra,

California, Ortel is a developer of optoelectronic components for cable television networks. Lucent said that Ortel would enable it to develop cable television's capabilities as a two-way interactive medium.

- Late in 1999, the company bought Excel Switching Corporation for $1.7 billion in stock. "They are a premier company in programmable switching, with more than eleven years of experience and have one of the largest communities of application developers in the industry," said Dan Stanzione, Lucent's chief operating officer. Excel, which employs about 460 people, targets its switches at new telecom service providers and established providers entering new markets.

- Lucent Technologies expanded its presence in the growing field of designing and consulting on high-speed data networks by acquiring International Network Services for about $3.6 billion. Chairman Rich McGinn said the merger "will offer customers the industry's deepest portfolio of network planning, design, integration, maintenance, and management solutions." According to one analyst, "Lucent made a huge coup in the market, because INS, frankly, was thought to be unattainable."

- Lucent entered a new market in 1999—the cable TV market—with a product portfolio that includes the company's breakthrough PathStar Access Server. Part of Lucent's CableConnect Solutions portfolio, PathStar helps transform a cable operator from a video supplier to a full-service supplier of video, high-speed data, and telephony. Cable TV operators in the United States, a big market for Lucent, are expected to spend $18 billion over the next five years to upgrade their networks for broadband services.

- Lucent is a leader in optical networking, having delivered some 4,000 systems to customers worldwide. For instance, the company's high-speed products will help EuroTunnel expand its communications network between Paris and London.

- The global Bell Laboratories R&D community supports every Lucent business group from its centers in 20 different countries. The company earns more than three patents every business day, creating a remarkable stream of ideas for innovation and next-generation technology that sets Lucent's businesses apart from all others.

  Bell Labs is focused on the leading-edge technologies that are transforming communications as thoroughly as earlier milestones like the laser, transistor, and cell phone. Today, researchers are engaged in both the practical application and long-term development of breakthroughs such as the all-plastic transistor and high-capacity optical fiber. Bell Labs' innovation in areas like photonics, digital signal processing, software, data networking, wireless, and semiconductors is constant and productive.

- In a move to sharpen its focus on selling hot high-technology gear to telephone companies, Lucent spun off certain slow-growing operations in the spring of 2000. They included Lucent's PBX business, which provides switching services for corporate phone systems, the Systimax business, which sells cabling systems for offices, and the local-area network business. Analysts said that by spinning off these businesses, Lucent should trade at a higher multiple, similar to such companies as Cisco Systems and Nortel Networks.

- Lucent Technologies announced in 1999 that it had developed a computer chip for phones that will help small and mid-size businesses use their companies' computer networks to deliver voice calls. The chip will help lower the cost of Internet phones from about $250 to $150 by decreasing the number of chips in a phone from five to one. The market for these Internet telephone sets is expected to average annual growth of more than 250 percent for the next three years.

- The 30,000 people employed by the Business Communications Systems Group, the company's second-largest segment, provide more than 1.5 million business locations around the world and U.S. government customers with voice-related and computer telephony integrated products. Leaders in many business communication areas, they design, manufacture, and sell solutions for sales and service operations, conferencing and collaboration, mobility and distributed workforce, messaging and intelligent networking. Offerings include the *Definity* family of private branch exchanges (PBXs), key telephone systems, call centers, structured cabling systems, voice processing and Octel Messaging Division solutions, wireless systems, multimedia, and Internet capabilities.

Total assets: $38,775 million
Current ratio: 1.86
Common shares outstanding: 3,142 million
Return on 1999 shareholders' equity: 28.2%

	1999	1998	1997	1996	1995	1994	1993	1992
Revenues (millions)	38303	30147	26360	23286	21413	19765	*	
Net income (millions)	3833	2287	1507	1054	806	482		
Earnings per share	1.22	.87	.59	.41	.39	.19		
Dividends per share	.08	.08	.08	.04				
Price High	84.2	56.9	22.7	13.3				
Low	47.0	18.4	11.2	7.4				

*This table is incomplete since Lucent was not a public company until recently.

GROWTH AND INCOME

Marsh & McLennan Companies, Incorporated

1166 Avenue of the Americas ◻ New York, New York 10036 ◻ Investor contact: J. M. Bischoff (212) 345-5000 ◻ Dividend reinvestment program is available: (212) 815-2560 ◻ Web site: www.mmc.com ◻ Listed: NYSE ◻ Ticker symbol: MMC ◻ S&P rating: A ◻ Value Line financial strength rating: A+

A number of developments are benefiting the industry and Marsh & McLennan in particular. Large organizations are increasingly global, conducting more of their business outside their home countries. Deregulation and the liberalization of markets are creating new opportunities. More open markets have coincided with the continuing wave of privatization and investments in major infrastructure projects. The fact that global property-casualty insurance premium volume now totals $750 billion illustrates the important role of commercial insurance in the worldwide economy.

Company Profile

Marsh & McLennan is a global professional-services firm, with annual revenues exceeding $9 billion. It is the parent company of Marsh, the world's leading risk and insurance services firm, Putnam Investments, one of the largest investment management companies in the United States, and Mercer Consulting Group, a major global provider of consulting services. More than fifty thousand employees provide analysis, advice, and transactional capabilities to clients in more than 100 countries.

Risk and Insurance Services
Marsh Inc. is the world leader in delivering risk and insurance services and solutions to clients. Insurance brokering is conducted under the Marsh name and includes the total range of services to identify, value, control, transfer, and finance risk for business, public-entity, and professional-services organizations.

Worldwide reinsurance brokering advice and services for insurance and reinsurance companies are provided through Guy Carpenter & Company, Inc. The company structures and places reinsurance coverage and other risk-transfer financing with reinsurance firms and capital markets worldwide.

Insurance program management services are provided through Seabury & Smith, Inc., which designs, markets, and administers specialized insurance programs for employees of large corporations, small businesses, associations and their members, and private clients.

The company also provides wholesale brokering services to the U.S. and London markets and underwriting management services in North America and the United Kingdom to insurers, primarily for professional liability coverages.

Marsh & McLennan Securities Corporation serves clients with investment banking and capital markets solutions, transaction structuring, and execution services

Marsh & McLennan Capital, Inc. is a global private equity firm with over $2.5 billion in assets under management that invests in industries where MMC possesses specialized knowledge and proprietary deal flow.

Investment Management
Putnam Investments, Inc., one of the oldest and largest money-management organizations in the United States, offers a full range of both equity and fixed-income products, invested domestically and globally, for individual and institutional

investors. Putnam, which manages more than one hundred ten mutual funds, has over six hundred institutional clients and twelve million individual shareholder accounts. It had $391 billion in assets under management at the end of 1999.

Consulting
Mercer Consulting Group, Inc., one of the world's largest consulting firms, provides advice and services, primarily to business organizations. William M. Mercer Companies LLC is the global leader in human resource, employee benefit, and compensation consulting. Mercer Management Consulting, Inc., one of the world's premier corporate strategy firms, helps clients achieve sustained shareholder value growth through the development and implementation of innovative business designs. National Economic Research Associates, Inc. (NERA), the leading firm of consulting economists, specializes in providing solutions to problems involving competition, regulation, finance, and public policy.

Highlights of 1999

■ Marsh & McLennan had another year of record results. Revenues climbed 27 percent, to $9.2 billion. Net income rose 20 percent, to $959 million, and earnings per share advanced 17 percent, to $3.48, before special charges related to the acquisition of Sedgwick Group.

■ MMC's operating companies performed well:
  ● Marsh's revenues were $4.5 billion, up from $3.4 billion in 1998. Operating income reached $806 million, an increase of 31 percent.
  ● Putnam Investments' assets under management rose to $391 billion at year-end 1999, up from $294 billion the prior year. Revenues increased 17 percent, and operating income climbed 24 percent.

● Mercer Consulting Group reported revenue gains of 26 percent, and operating income growth of 29 percent.

● Marsh & McLennan Capital, MMC's equity investment firm, attracted $1.4 billion in capital commitments for investment in Trident II, the fund it organized in 1999 for investment in global insurance, reinsurance, and related industries.

Shortcomings to Bear in Mind

■ Some investors are fretting that MMC would be hurt if the stock market were to lose its luster. Such a decline would convince some people to shun mutual funds, which would have a negative impact on Putnam Group.

■ Some analysts are concerned that persistent pricing pressures in its commercial lines "may impair growth trends" in the core insurance brokerage segment. However, they concede that "the company's market dominance should afford it some degree of pricing power."

Reasons to Buy

■ Marsh & McLennan has a consistent record of growth. In the 1989–1999 period, earnings per share advanced from $1.37 to $3.48, a compound annual growth rate of 9.8 percent. What's more, there were no dips along the way. In the same 10-year stretch, dividends expanded from $.83 to $1.80, a growth rate of 8.0 percent.

■ Over the last three years, the company has completed mergers with Johnson & Higgins and Sedgwick, with results that have exceeded expectations. Johnson & Higgins brought together two complementary cultures, strengthened the company's professional staff, and produced significant consolidation savings.

Sedgwick promises to be a similar success. When the company announced the merger in August of 1998, Marsh & McLennan estimated net consolidation savings of $110 million. Integration efforts have gone well, and the company now expects net savings that will approach $160 million over a three-year period, including $30 million in 1999. Although integration work remains to be done, the company is realizing substantial operating efficiencies and has a unified organization in place. Finally, Sedgwick strengthened MMC's position in Europe and Asia-Pacific and provided an important addition to the company's domestic business.

■ By any measure, Putnam had an exceptional year in 1999—strong growth in assets under management, increased profitability, and exceptional performance. Putnam is one of the fastest-growing money managers in the nation. Its assets under management shot up 33 percent, reflecting excellent gains in its mutual fund, defined benefit, defined contribution, and international business. During 1999, Putnam broadened its product range through its venture with Thomas H. Lee Partners, a leading private equity firm.

■ In 1999, Mercer strengthened its position as a global firm consulting on all aspects of management and produced solid results. With revenues approaching $2 billion, and earnings reaching $260 million, it achieved strong professional and financial performance across its human resource and management consulting practices.

■ The distribution of the company's $4.5 billion of revenues in 1999 demonstrates Marsh's international scope and client service focus. About 60 percent is generated in specific geographic regions such as the United States, Europe, Asia-Pacific, and Latin America. The company derives roughly 20 percent from practices that operate globally and specialize in more than 20 industries, ranging from aviation to technology and finance.

Insurance programs for individuals through affinity groups, the workplace, or the company's private client services represent more than 10 percent of revenues. These activities are conducted through several business units, the largest being Seabury & Smith. Global insurance brokering, provided by Guy Carpenter, accounts for 10 percent of revenues.

■ Marsh's revenues have more than doubled over the past five years to achieve a compound annual growth rate of 19 percent. During the period, MMC acquired Johnson & Higgins and Sedgwick, but organic growth has averaged about 4 percent since 1995 and the company sees significant opportunities to increase that growth rate going forward.

Total assets: $13,021 million
Current ratio: 0.96
Common shares outstanding: 267 million
Return on 1999 shareholders' equity: 17.4%

	1999	1998	1997	1996	1995	1994	1993	1992
Revenues (millions)	9157	7190	6008	4150	3770	3435	3163	2937
Net income (millions)	947	796	592	459	403	382	332	304
Earnings per share	3.48	2.98	2.36	2.11	1.84	1.73	1.51	1.40
Dividends per share	1.80	1.46	1.26	1.10	.99	.95	.90	.88
Price High	96.8	64.3	53.3	38.3	30.0	29.6	32.5	31.5
Low	57.1	43.4	34.2	28.1	25.4	23.8	25.7	23.8

McCormick & Company, Incorporated

18 Loveton Circle ▢ Sparks, Maryland 21152-6000 ▢ Investor contact: Joyce L. Brooks (410) 771-7244 ▢ Direct dividend reinvestment plan is available: (800) 424-5855 ▢ Fiscal year ends November 30 ▢ Web site: www.mccormick.com ▢ Listed: NYSE ▢ Ticker symbol: MKC ▢ S&P rating: A- ▢ Value Line financial strength rating: B++

The market environment for McCormick's consumer products—spices, herbs, extracts, propriety seasoning blends, sauces, and marinades—varies worldwide. In the United States, for instance, usage is up, and consumers are seeking new and bolder tastes.

Although many people use prepared foods and eat out, a *Parade* magazine survey published in November of 1999 reports that 75 percent of families polled eat dinner together at least four nights a week. A study conducted by *National Panel Diary* indicates that 70 percent of all meals are prepared at home, and a Canned Food Association Survey reports that 51 percent of women 18 to 64 actually "scratch-cook" meals six times a week.

Company Profile

McCormick, the world's foremost maker of spices and seasonings, is committed to the development of tasty, easy-to-use new products to satisfy consumer demand. To this end, the company launched a new line of zesty new products in 1999, designed to add excitement to meals while being user-friendly. Flavor Medleys are four liquid sauces that can be used to bake, broil, grill, or saute. Spice Blends, a companion line of shake-on blends with zesty tastes and lively names, includes "Santa Fe Style," which is featured on the cover of the 1999 annual report. Since the introduction of these products in mid-1999, more than 95 percent of McCormick's customers have placed all seven products in the spice section of their stores.

When investors hear the name McCormick, they think of the spices they use every day. Indeed, McCormick is the world's largest spice company. Yet the company is also the leader in the manufacture, marketing, and distribution of such products as seasonings and flavors to the entire food industry. These customers include foodservice and food-processing businesses, as well as retail outlets.

McCormick also has a stake in packaging. This group manufactures specialty plastic bottles and tubes for food, personal care, and other industries. Founded in 1889, McCormick distributes its products in about 100 countries.

McCormick's U.S. Consumer business, its oldest and largest, is dedicated to the manufacture and sale of consumer spices, herbs, extracts, proprietary seasoning blends, sauces, and marinades. They are sold under such brand names as McCormick, Schilling, Produce Partners, Golden Dipt, Old Bay, and Mojave.

Many of the spices and herbs purchased by the company are imported into the United States from the country of origin. However, significant quantities of some materials, such as paprika, dehydrated vegetables, onion and garlic, and food ingredients other than spices and herbs originate in the United States.

McCormick is a direct importer of certain raw materials, mainly black pepper, vanilla beans, cinnamon, herbs, and seeds from the countries of origin.

The raw materials most important to the company are onion, garlic, and capsicums (paprika and chili peppers), which are produced in the United States; black pepper, most of which originates in India, Indonesia, Malaysia, and Brazil; and vanilla beans, a large portion of which the company obtains from the Malagasy Republic and Indonesia.

Shortcomings to Bear in Mind

- The company purchases certain raw materials that are subject to price volatility caused by weather and other unpredictable factors. While future movements of raw material costs are uncertain, a variety of programs, including periodic raw material purchases and customer price adjustments, help McCormick address this risk. Generally, the company does not use derivatives to manage the volatility related to this risk.
- The company's packaging business has not been a stellar performer. After a challenging year in 1998, this segment made only a modest improvement in 1999. According to management, "While the plastic container market remains soft, we achieved a 7 percent sales growth in 1999. We continue to focus on improving efficiencies and controlling costs."
- The company does not have a strong balance sheet, since only 59 percent of capitalization is in common equity. However, coverage of bond interest is more than adequate, at 8.8 times.

Reasons to Buy

- McCormick has paid dividends every year since 1925, and dividends have increased by 300 percent during the past 10 years. In December of 1999, the board of directors boosted the dividend by 12 percent, as an indication of management's confidence in the future.
- A major contributor to 1999's success was the outstanding performance of the company's consumer business. Extensive advertising and promotional programs helped drive this growth. These marketing efforts were directed primarily at convenient, value-added products, such

as McCormick's Grill Mates line of grilling seasonings and marinades.

- Foreign operations, which constitute well over 20 percent of revenues, are doing well. In Canada, for instance, expanded distribution, increased consumer advertising, and innovative new products spurred sales growth in 1999. A line of convenient, flavorful seasonings called One Step Seasonings was expanded in 1999 and gained nearly 100 percent acceptance by the company's customers.

In the United Kingdom, the company continued to build volume with the Schwartz Make It Fresh! Line launched in 1998. The line gained more than five share points in its category in 1999 and has been one of the company's most successful product launches ever. In Australia, 25 new products were introduced in 1999, including a line of barbeque and grilling items.

McCormick launched a number of new products abroad in 1999. Based on the success of "Italiano" and "Tex Mex" One Step Seasonings in Canada, the company introduced eight new flavors, including "Parmesan and Herbs" and "Garlic Plus." Within five weeks of launching these items, the company had achieved distribution of all eight items in nearly 90 percent of the Canadian retail trade. South of the border, moreover, the company's El Salvador operation launched "Delicia De Loroco," a mayonnaise combined with a developed flavor from the Salvadoran loroco flower.

- The company's second-largest segment, its industrial business, had an extremely strong year in 1999. McCormick's product research and development expertise and ability to provide technically advanced flavor solutions to its customers are key ingredients in this success. According to the 1999 annual report, "We are the cinnamon in your cereal, the sauce on your lunchtime sandwich, or the seasoning in your dinner entree at a favorite restaurant. Every day, no matter where you eat or what you eat, you are likely to taste something flavored by McCormick."

Several very successful new products, using flavors developed by McCormick, were launched by key industrial customers in 1999. The company's focus on the value-added compound flavor in adding new distribution in the warehouse club segment. And, as foodservice distributors consolidate, the company benefits from its reputation as a dependable supplier of high-quality products for the restaurant industry.

- Contributions from the company's joint ventures improved significantly in 1999. In particular, McCormick's Mexican partnership benefited from stronger operations and a stable currency.
- Worldwide, the retail grocery industry continues to consolidate, creating larger customers. What's more, in many of McCormick's markets, the company has multiyear contracts with customers to secure the shelf space for its products. McCormick's capabilities in category management and electronic data interchange, along with its high-quality products and service, also forge a link to its increasingly larger customers.
- The company's past successes and future potential are rooted in the strength of the McCormick name. As a consequence, the company is now experiencing a 95 percent brand-awareness rating in the United States. This leadership role in the food industry ensures that consumers will enjoy a McCormick product at nearly every eating occasion. Grocery store aisles present more than 700 well-known products from major processors that rely on McCormick for seasoning or flavor.

- McCormick's record of growth is impressive. Earnings per share expanded from $.58 per share in 1989 to $1.69 in 1999, a compound annual growth rate of 11.3 percent. In the same 10-year span, dividends per share climbed from $.17 to $.68, a growth rate of 14.9 percent.
- In the United States, McCormick continues to roll out the Quest program (which was launched in 1997). Quest seeks to increase volume by encouraging retailers to reduce their prices on McCormick items. Quest prices most of the company's best-selling spice items and all of its seasoning mixes to the customer, net of discounts and allowances; the objective is to increase consumer sales. Using McCormick's category-management capabilities, the company is working with its customers to provide a wide variety of products at attractive prices. This benefits its customers with higher volumes sold, and gives the consumer a better value, as well. At the end of 1999, nearly 75 percent of sales to domestic customers were invoiced under the Quest program.

Total assets: $1,189 million
Current ratio: 0.95
Common shares outstanding: 9 million voting, 62 million nonvoting
Return on 1999 shareholders' equity: 30.5%

	1999	1998	1997	1996	1995	1994	1993	1992
Revenues (millions)	2007	1881	1801	1732	1859	1695	1557	1471
Net income (millions)	122	106	998	83	98	108	100	93
Earnings per share	1.69	1.43	1.30	1.03	1.20	1.32	1.22	1.14
Dividends per share	.68	.64	.60	.56	.52	.48	.44	.38
Price High	34.6	36.4	28.4	25.4	26.6	24.8	29.8	30.3
Low	26.6	27.1	22.6	18.9	18.1	17.8	20.0	20.5

McDonald's Corporation

McDonald's Plaza □ Oak Brook, Illinois 60523 □ Investor contact: Lynn Irwin Camp (630) 623-8432
□ Direct dividend reinvestment plan is available: (800) 228-9623 □ Web site: www.mcdonalds.com
□ Ticker symbol: MCD □ S&P rating: A+ □ Value Line financial strength rating: A++

McDonald's, which boasts one of the world's most valuable brand names, is the world's number one fast-food chain. The company operates nearly twenty seven thousand restaurants worldwide, and its more than twelve thousand four hundred and fifty domestic outlets command a 42 percent share of the nation's fast-food hamburger business.

Most McDonald's outlets are the familiar freestanding variety, with a heavy emphasis on playgrounds to attract its devoted audience: kids.

McDonald's is building mini-units with simplified menus at such alternative locations as Wal-Marts. Nearly 80 percent of the company's restaurants are franchised. Restaurants abroad account for about 60 percent of the company's sales and profits.

Every day, McDonald's serves more than forty million people in some twenty seven thousand restaurants in 115 countries around the world. Annually, that's nearly fifteen million people served. Yet, on any given day, that amounts to less than 1 percent of the world's population. Obviously, the proliferation of McDonald's outlets is far from saturation.

Company Profile

The company develops, operates, franchises, and services a worldwide system of restaurants that prepare, assemble, package, and sell a limited menu of value-priced foods. These restaurants are operated by McDonald's or, under the terms of franchise arrangements, by franchisees who are independent third parties,

or by affiliates operating under joint-venture agreements between the company and local businesspeople.

The company's franchising program is designed to assure consistency and quality. What's more, McDonald's is selective in granting franchises and is not in the practice of franchising to investor groups or passive investors.

McDonald's restaurants offer a substantially uniform menu consisting of hamburgers and cheeseburgers, including the Big Mac and Quarter Pounder with Cheese, the Filet-O-Fish, several chicken sandwiches, French fries, Chicken McNuggets, salads, milk shakes, McFlurries, sundaes and cones, pies, cookies, and soft drinks and other beverages.

McDonald's restaurants operating in the United States and certain international markets are open during breakfast hours and offer a full or limited breakfast menu, including the Egg McMuffin and the Sausage McMuffin with Egg sandwiches, hotcakes and sausages, three varieties of biscuit sandwiches, and Apple-Bran muffins. The company believes in testing new products and introducing those that pass muster.

The company, its franchisees, and affiliates purchase food products and packaging from numerous independent suppliers. Quality specifications for both raw and cooked food products are established and strictly enforced.

The Beginning

The McDonald brothers' first restaurant, founded in 1937 in a parking lot just east of Pasadena, California, didn't serve hamburgers. Nor did it have a playground. The most popular item on the menu was the hot dog, and most people ate it sitting on an outdoor stool or in their cars while being served by teenage carhops.

For about a decade that embryonic version of McDonald's was a big success. Then America's tastes began to change—and the Golden Arches changed, as well. As automobiles lost some of their romance, indoor restaurants took over. In the 1960s, however, some customers became bored with the menu and drifted away. Alert to what was happening, McDonald responded by creating the Big Mac—and customers came flocking back. Later, beef was not always enough to keep and draw in enough customers. Once again, the company was ready for the challenge, as it introduced bite-size chunks of chicken in the early 80s. And within four years, the company was the nation's second-largest poultry vendor.

Highlights of 1999

- Return on average assets increased to 16.6 percent, from 16.4 percent in 1998. Return on average equity increased to 20.8 percent, from 19.5 percent the prior year.
- Diluted earnings per share increased 10 percent in 1999 and grew at an 11 percent compound annual rate over the past 10 years.
- McDonald's sales reached $38.5 billion, a 10-year compound annual growth rate of 8 percent.
- Operating income exceeded $3.3 billion in 1999, a 10 percent increase in constant currencies.
- Free cash flow exceeded $1.14 billion in 1999, a 29 percent increase over 1998.
- The company purchased 24.2 million shares of common stock for $933 million during the year.

Shortcomings to Bear in Mind

- Outside the United States, McDonald's is gaining huge chunks of business every week—much faster than rival Burger King. But on McDonald's $18-billion home turf, the numbers the company sees are not so rosy. One day—maybe not next year or in five years, but eventually—the Big Mac will flatline in the United States. The evidence: In the past four years, McDonald's has averaged only 1 percent annual same-store sales growth, trailing the 4 percent average for its main burger competitors, Burger King, Wendy's, and Jack-in-the-Box.

  The main reason is that McDonald's menu is stale. The last successful new product it introduced was Chicken McNuggets, in 1983. Nearly every new menu offering since then, such as the McDLT, the McLean, the Arch Deluxe, and McPizza, came and went with only a burp to remember them by.

Reasons to Buy

- The company's two largest geographic segments, the United States and Europe, generated constant currency operating income increases of 11 percent and 13 percent, respectively, in 1999.
- McDonald's added two new brands in 1999—Donatos Pizza in the United States and Aroma Cafe in the United Kingdom. These new concepts now join Chipotle Mexican Grill as trailblazers in the company's strategic effort to capture an ever-increasing percentage of the total meals-away-from-home market.
- The company added 1,790 McDonald's restaurants in 1999, more than 90 percent of them outside the United States. In 2000, the company continued to open restaurants at the remarkable pace of five per day.
- A behind-the-scenes transformation is underway at McDonald's. The

company's relatively new chief executive, Jack M. Greenberg, is leading an overhaul of the long-insular restaurant company that has made both franchisees and investors more optimistic than they have been in years. In a break with tradition, Mr. Greenberg has turned to outsiders to fill key posts. As of early 1999, he had cut 23 percent of headquarters staff, the first layoff in company history. What's more, franchisees and corporate managers stationed in the field now make more of the decisions about when to discount and what food to test.

The result: McDonald's has found modest success with new products, including a bagel breakfast sandwich and the McFlurry sundae, coupled with regional discounts. Those were big reasons why average store sales climbed in 1998, and overall company revenues advanced 9 percent. In the words of one analyst, "Greenberg has done a fantastic job bringing a new sense of urgency and getting rid of their corporate arrogance."

- During 1999, McDonald's began upgrading its kitchens in a program dubbed, "Made for You." In this $500 million transformation, instead of keeping food in taste-killing warming bins, the new system uses computers to project customer traffic and an assembly line to keep lettuce cold and burgers hot. Meanwhile, custom orders are available, as they are at such rivals as Burger King.

- McDonald's has long been popular with children because of its elaborate playground facilities and the frequent promotional tie-ins with major motion picture characters.

- McDonald's, selected by *Fortune* magazine as the most admired food service company in the world, has clung fast to its long-term strategy. While its domestic operations have struggled with

sluggish growth and management blunders, the company's international business has prospered. Jim Cantalupo, president and chief executive officer of McDonald's International, credits the fast-food chain's infrastructure as the key to the company's continued global success. "We are second to none in sourcing our products," Cantalupo brags. He may just be right. McDonald's in Singapore typically imports its chicken from the United States. But within days of Thailand's currency devaluation, McDonald's Singapore restaurants were buying foul from Thailand.

McDonald's has found other ways to take advantage of wild swings in exchange rates. For example, to build its 80 restaurants in Indonesia, it took out millions in construction loans in the local currency. After the rupiah crashed in 1998, McDonald's was able to pay off those loans at 20 cents to the dollar. "Our assets were devalued, but so was our debt," Cantalupo said. He also moved to shore up troubled franchises in exchange for a greater equity stake in their restaurants.

- According to one analyst, "McDonald's has plenty going for it. The company plans to roll out a number of new key product offerings in 1999, including The Big Extra, which is aimed at the crowd that prefers Burger King's successful flame-broiled Whopper. Other new products include the Big McBacon cheeseburger and the McBagel breakfast sandwich."

- In a move that is part of its domestic growth plan, McDonald's acquired the Boston Market, including 751 restaurants and franchise rights for 108 more stores. Boston Market restaurants are located in 33 states and the District of Columbia; the majority of the sites are in the Eastern and Midwestern states.

Boston Market specializes in homestyle entrees, fresh vegetables, sandwiches, salads, and side dishes. The deal closed in mid-2000.

A spokesman for McDonald's said the company would keep Boston Market in operation but would convert some of the restaurants to the company's Chipotle Mexican Grill or Donatos Pizza restaurants. McDonald's acquired Donatos and a minority stake in Chipotle, also as part of its domestic growth plan.

- McDonald's has never been an income stock, since its dividend yield is below 1 percent. However, like most public companies, McDonald's has traditionally paid a quarterly dividend—but no more. Beginning in 2000, its dividend will be paid only once a year. The last dividend was 4.875 cents, paid in December of 1999. The new annual dividend is $0.20. Thus, if you own 100 shares, you will receive $20 every December—unless, of course, the dividend is increased, which is likely.

Total assets: $20,983 million
Current ratio: 0.59
Common shares outstanding: 1,354 million
Return on 1999 shareholders' equity: 20.8%

	1999	1998	1997	1996	1995	1994	1993	1992
Revenues (millions)	13259	12421	11409	10687	9794	8321	7408	7133
Net income (millions)	1948	1769	1642	1573	1427	1224	1082	959
Earnings per share	1.39	1.26	1.15	1.11	.99	.84	.73	.65
Dividends per share	.20	.18	.16	.15	.13	.12	.11	.10
Price High	49.6	39.8	27.4	27.1	24.0	15.8	14.8	12.6
Low	35.9	22.3	21.1	20.5	14.3	12.8	11.4	9.6

CONSERVATIVE GROWTH

The McGraw-Hill Companies

1221 Avenue of the Americas ◻ New York, New York 10020-1095 ◻ Investor contact: Donald S. Rubin (212) 512-4321 ◻ Direct dividend reinvestment program is available: (888) 201-5538 ◻ Web site: www.mcgraw-hill.com ◻ Listed: NYSE ◻ Ticker symbol: MHP ◻ S&P rating: not rated ◻ Value Line financial strength rating: A+

The company started out 2000 with surprisingly strong operating results, beating analysts' estimates by 71 percent, before a one-time gain. Financial services are benefiting from healthy demand, global expansion, continued growth in nontraditional rating services, and new products.

What's more, educational publishing is also off to a strong start, benefiting from demographic trends and a favorable adoption schedule. (See Houghton-Mifflin for an explanation of "adoption schedule.")

Information and media services revenues is likely to be bolstered by strong demand for advertising and by higher advertising rates.

Overall profitability is being helped by revenue growth and efficiency measures, although the improvement will be limited by the cost of investments in new products and services.

Company Profile

The McGraw-Hill Companies is a multimedia information provider. The company publishes textbooks, technical and popular books, periodicals (Business Week, Aviation Week, ENR, and others).

McGraw-Hill holds leadership positions in each of the markets it serves:

Financial Services

• Standard & Poor's Ratings Services is the number one rating service in the world and is applying its leadership to rating and evaluating a growing array of nontraditional financial instrument.

• Standard & Poor's Indexes, led by the S&P 500, are the world's benchmark measures of equity market performance.

• Standard & Poor's *Compustat* is the leading source of financial databases and advanced PC-based software for financial analysis.

• Standard & Poor's *MMS* supplies the world with real-time fundamental and technical analysis in the global money, bond, foreign exchange, and equity markets.

• Standard & Poor's *Platt's* is the key provider of price assessments with the petroleum, petrochemical, and power markets.

• Standard & Poor's *J. J. Kenny* produces the most comprehensive evaluating pricing information for the fixed-income investment community.

• Standard & Poor's *DRI* is the leading supplier of economics-driven information to corporate and government clients.

Educational and Professional Publishing

• The McGraw-Hill School Division stands number one in providing educational materials to elementary schools.

• Glencoe/McGraw-Hill tops the grade 6–12 segment.

• CTB/McGraw-Hill is the preeminent publisher of nationally standardized tests for the U.S. K-12 market.

• Irwin/McGraw-Hill is the premier publisher of higher educational materials in business, economics, and information technology.

• The Professional Book Group is the leading publisher of business, computing, and reference books serving the needs of professionals and consumer worldwide.

Information and Media Services

• *Business Week* is the world's most widely read business publication, with a global audience of 6.3 million.

• F. W. Dodge is the leading provider of information to construction professionals.

• Sweet's Group is the premier supplier of building products information, in print and electronically.

• *Architectural Record* stands atop its industry as the official publication of the American Institute of Architects.

• *Aviation Week & Space Technology* is the world's most authoritative aerospace magazine.

• Tower Group International is the leading provider of customs brokerage and freight forwarding services.

Shortcomings to Bear in Mind

■ McGraw-Hill is an exceptional company and typically sells for a premium price.

Reasons to Buy

■ McGraw-Hill's educational products are known for exemplary scholarship in technology. The company's Versatile Learning System, to cite one example, provides students and teachers with balanced, easy-to-use multimedia learning materials integrating textbooks, software, laser disks, audio, and video components.

■ Every business day, Standard & Poor's indexes are cited as key benchmarks of stockmarket performance. The worldwide reputation of the S&P 500 has nurtured a growing international family of indexes.

■ S&P indexes are the foundation for a growing array of investment funds and exchange-traded products that continue to generate new revenue. The company receives fees based on assets and trading activity. In addition, the recent volatility of the stock market has increased the revenue stream. Currently, more than $700 billion is invested in mutual funds tied to the S&P indexes.

- SPDRs (S&P depository receipts), linked to and directly tracking S&P indexes, consistently top the American Stock Exchange's most active list. Similarly, trading volume on the Chicago Mercantile Exchange of futures and options linked to S&P indexes is also high. Both exchanges introduced new trading instruments in 1998 tied to S&P indexes.

- Europe contributes almost half of McGraw-Hill's international revenue, growing at a double-digit rate. With a push from the new Monetary Union, the European market will be a springboard for growth in many of the company's key businesses. Here are some expectations:

  - European companies that once financed their growth mainly by borrowing from banks are shifting to the issuance of corporate bonds instead, while nontraditional financial instruments also boom. Those are both large opportunities for Standard & Poor's Rating Services, which has built the world's largest network of ratings professionals.

  - Increases in investments by Europeans building retirement funds—the result of a transition to privately funded pension plans—will accelerate demand for global financial information. These are pluses for Standard & Poor's Financial Information Services.

  - The continued growth of English in business communications and as a second language in everyday use widens. These will benefit the company's educational products and the European edition of *Business Week*.

  - The promise of the global economy depends on educational training. This is a plus for McGraw-Hill's global publishing activities—most notably the company's business, finance, engineering, information technology, and English instruction products.

- In Asia, economic problems have slowed growth but have not seriously affected the company's operations or diminished the region's long-term opportunities. McGraw-Hill's brands are strong in Asia. In a survey of 6,000 executives representing 11 Asian countries, MHP was chosen as one of Asia's 200 leading companies.

- In the construction industry, The McGraw-Hill Construction Information Group (MH-CIG) is the foremost source of information crucial to new construction projects and planning. MH-CIG has increasingly turned to the Internet and other electronic tools to gather and distribute information. By the end of 2000, nearly half of its revenue will derive from electronic products.

  Dodge Plans is the latest of several MH-CIG electronic products stemming from print media. It provides access—online or by CD-ROM twice weekly—to the plans, specifications, and bidding requirements for more than 60,000 new construction and renovation projects.

- Growing enrollments are a worldwide phenomenon and will keep the education market growing here and abroad for the next several years. In the United States, the combination of more students, the best funding picture in a generation, and a robust adoption schedule is expected to produce steady growth in the education market for the foreseeable future.

- The digital economy and e-commerce have the capacity to transform McGraw-Hill, adding a completely new dimension to its products and services. More than 90 percent of the company's information is already in digital form, and in each of the company's major business units there are major efforts to create and deliver a host of new electronic services.

- In 1999, *Business Week* leveraged its strong brand name by introducing special editions aimed at specific groups within the readership:
  - *E.biz,* a technology-focused special report, was launched in 1999 and delivered to the full North American print run. A companion Web site, accessed through *Business Week Online,* offers additional features.
  - *Frontier* is a monthly report for small business owners and entrepreneurs. It is delivered to 225,000 subscribers. *Frontier Online,* a companion Web site, provides expanded content and tools.
- The McGraw-Hill Professional Book Group publishes nearly 800 titles per year in computing, business, science, technical, medical, and reference markets.

The group continues to expand by creating publishing alliances with partners such as Oracle and Global Knowledge, transforming key reference titles into Internet-based services. In addition, the Professional Book Group offers electronic products, ranging from Internet subscription services to CD-ROMs, and is building its capabilities in on-demand publishing.

In 1999, the 22-volume *McGraw-Hill Encyclopedia of Science & Technology* was launched as an Internet subscription service. *AccessScience.com* features 7,000 articles from the *Encyclopedia* and 15,000 definitions from McGraw-Hill's *Dictionary of Science and Technical Terms,* as well as article updates, current science news, and biographies of scientists whose work relates to articles in the *Encyclopedia.*

Total assets: $4,089 million
Current ratio: 1.05
Common shares outstanding: 196 million
Return on 1999 shareholders' equity: 26.3%

	1999	1998	1997	1996	1995	1994	1993	1992
Revenues (millions)	3992	3729	3534	3075	2935	2761	2196	2050
Net income (millions)	402	342	291	250	227	203	172	153
Earnings per share	2.02	1.71	1.46	1.25	1.14	1.03	.88	.78
Dividends per share	.86	.78	.72	.66	.60	.58	.57	.56
Price High	63.1	51.7	37.7	24.6	21.9	19.3	18.8	16.6
Low	47.1	34.3	22.4	18.6	15.9	15.6	13.8	13.3

INCOME

MDU Resources Group, Inc.

Post Office Box 5650 ◻ Bismarck, North Dakota 58506-5650 ◻ Investor contact: Warren L. Robinson
(800) 437-8000 ◻ Dividend reinvestment plan is available: (800) 813-3324 ◻ Web site: www.mdu.com
◻ Listed: NYSE ◻ Ticker symbol: MDU ◻ S&P rating: B+ ◻ Value Line financial strength rating: A

Analysts believe that MDU has been overlooked by many investors. According to a Merrill Lynch analyst, "It is no longer a utility (60 percent of 1999 earnings per share came from non-regulated and growing businesses)." The analyst goes on to say, "we believe this is one of the best-managed companies in our universe (of utilities)."

Company Profile

MDU Resources Group, Inc. is a natural resource company. The company's diversified operations, such as oil and gas and construction materials, should help MDU Resources grow at a better rate than electric utilities that depend entirely on their electric business.

MDU Resources Group has a number of operations:

Electric and Natural Gas Distribution

Montana-Dakota Utilities Company generates, transmits, and distributes electricity; distributes natural gas; and supplies related value-added products and services in the northern Great Plains.

Utility Services

Utility Services, Inc. is a full-service engineering, design, and building company; it operates in the western United States. It specializes in construction and maintenance of power and natural gas distribution and transmission lines as well as communication and fiber optic facilities.

Pipeline and Energy Services

WBI Holdings, Inc. provides natural gas transportation, underground storage, and gathering services through regulated and nonregulated pipeline systems and provides energy marketing and management throughout the United States.

Oil and Natural Gas Production

Fidelity Exploration & Production Company is engaged in oil and natural gas acquisition, exploration, and production throughout the United States and in the Gulf of Mexico.

Construction Materials and Mining

Knife River Corporation mines and markets aggregates and related value-added construction materials products and services in the western United States, including Alaska and Hawaii. It also operates lignite and coal mines in Montana and North Dakota.

The Economy of the Region

The company's traditional four-state service area is expected to experience moderate growth. The notable development of information processing and telecommunication operations, along with the population migration from small communities to metropolitan centers, are anticipated to result in continued growth in Montana-Dakota's customer base. The company's construction materials operation can expect continuation of the healthy regional growth experienced in Oregon and Alaska and improving economies in northern California and Hawaii.

Highlights of 1999

Financial Performance

Consolidated earnings for the year reached a record $83.3 million, or $1.52 per share, diluted, compared with $33.3 million, or $.66 per share in 1998. The record earnings reflect gains made at the company's existing businesses, combined with profits from newly acquired businesses. Revenues for 1999 exceeded $1 billion for the first time, totaling nearly $1.3 billion, a 43 percent increase from the prior year.

Financial results for the year reflect the consolidation of the company's oil and natural gas production operations into one operating segment. In the past, financial results from these operations were reflected in two separate operating segments. This is also the first time that utility services is being shown separately from the electric utility.

Electric

Electric earnings increased 15 percent in 1999, to $16 million, largely due to increased wholesale electric sales at higher margins combined with lower retail fuel and purchased power costs.

Natural Gas Distribution

Weather that was 5 percent warmer than a year ago and 11 percent warmer than normal hurt natural gas sales and was largely responsible for the 9 percent decrease in natural gas distribution earnings, to $3.2 million.

Utility Services

Earnings from utility services companies were $6.5 million, virtually double those of the prior year. The improvement was the result of higher earnings from existing operations and earnings from companies acquired since the comparable period of 1998.

Pipeline and Energy Services

Pipeline and energy services operations benefited from three positive outcomes in 1999 related to outstanding regulatory issues and the resolution of certain state tax matters. These benefits added $6.9 million after-tax, net of a $3.1 million after-tax reversal in 1998 of reserves for certain contingencies. Earnings from this segment totaled $21 million.

Oil and Natural Gas Production

Earnings at the oil and natural gas production unit were $16.2 million, an increase of $6.8 million, when excluding the effects of $39.9 million in noncash after-tax writedowns of oil and natural gas properties taken in 1998. This significant increase was due to higher realized oil and natural gas prices, higher natural gas production, and lower depreciation, depletion, and amortization in 1999.

Construction Materials and Mining

At the construction materials and mining operations, earnings decreased to $20.4 million. The earnings decrease was largely due to $5.6 million in after-tax charges and lower than average coal prices. Both are outcomes of the resolution of the coal contract arbitration proceedings. Earnings from the construction materials business increased by $4 million, compared with a year earlier.

Shortcomings to Bear in Mind

- You should not ignore the increasingly competitive nature of the utility business. In this regard, MDU should fare better than utilities situated in more populated regions.

In 1997, the Montana State legislature passed an industry restructuring bill that provides for full customer choice by 2002, as well as full stranded-cost recovery and securitization. Based on other provisions of the legislation, however, MDU should be exempt from competition at least until 2002.

In North Dakota and South Dakota, all of MDU's electric customers with loads of 10 megawatts or more are under special contracts of five years or more. In Montana, all new customers with these loads should be under similar special contracts. Currently, no significant deregulatory efforts are occurring in the other states in which the company operates. One significant plus factor: The company's rates are well below the national average, making inroads from competitors less likely. In addition, only 11.5 percent of MDU's electric utility retail revenue comes from industrial customers—industrial customers are considered to be the most likely to demand lower rates. Because of these factors, analysts consider MDU to be a utility with some of the lowest competitive risks in the United States.

Reasons to Buy

- Demand in the electric wholesale markets continued to show strength in 1999, with wholesale volumes improving by 61 percent compared to the previous year. Control system upgrades and lower fuel costs at electric generating stations helped the company reduce its per-unit retail electricity production costs by nearly 6 percent. Meanwhile, customer growth continues in the company's natural gas service territory.

- Unlike most public utilities, MDU Resources is active in the acquisition realm. The company made these moves in 1999 and early 2000:

- Late in 1999, the company acquired MTN Utility Construction and Design, a full-service electric, natural gas, and telecommunications contractor headquartered in Montana.

- Earlier in the year, the company acquired Loy Clark Pipeline Company of Beaverton, Oregon.

- The company acquired a pipeline gathering system that connects its existing pipeline system to developing coal bed methane production in Wyoming's Powder River Basin. Coal bed methane holds promise to be a valuable new natural gas supply source for the company's pipeline system.

- During the fourth quarter, the company completed the acquisition of 80 percent of American Resources Offshore, Inc.'s offshore properties that increased both oil and natural gas reserves and production.

- In early 2000, the company continued this aggressive trend with the acquisition of the Connolly-Pacific Company, a southern California aggregate mining and marine construction company. As is often the case with MDU's acquisitions, the existing management team of CPC is expected to remain in place after the completion of the acquisition. Connolly-Pacific is vertically integrated and specializes in furnishing and placing rock to construct multilift dikes, enclose new landfills, and repair existing breakwaters and levees.

- The construction materials and mining company had a large backlog of construction work at the beginning of 2000. In 1999, the company set new sales volume records in several categories. When compared with 1998 levels, aggregate sales increased by 26 percent, asphalt by 67 percent, and concrete by 16 percent.

Total assets: $1,766 million
Current ratio: 1.88
Common shares outstanding: 57 million
Return on 1999 shareholders' equity: 13.9%

	1999	1998	1997	1996	1995	1994	1993	1992
Revenues (millions)	1280	897	608	515	464	450	440	352
Net income (millions)	84	74	55	46	42	40	39	35
Earnings per share	1.52	1.44	1.24	1.05	.95	.91	.89	.81
Dividends per share	.82	.78	.75	.73	.72	.70	.67	.65
Price High	27.2	28.9	22.3	15.7	15.4	14.3	14.7	11.9
Low	18.8	18.8	14.0	13.3	11.5	11.3	11.5	9.7

AGGRESSIVE GROWTH

Medtronic, Inc

7000 Central Avenue NE ▫ Minneapolis, Minnesota 55432-3576 ▫ Investor contact: Rachael Scherer (612) 514-4971 ▫ Dividend reinvestment plan is available: (800) 468-9716 ▫ Web site: www.medtronic.com ▫ Listed: NYSE ▫ Ticker symbol: MDT ▫ Fiscal year ends April 30 ▫ S&P rating: A ▫ Value Line financial strength rating: A+

One of medicine's frontiers is the brain, and among the greatest challenges are discovering how the debilitating effects of cerebral palsy, Parkinson's disease, epilepsy, ALS (Lou Gehrig's disease), and other chronic, degenerative illnesses can be reduced or eliminated. Equally important is the search for more effective pain treatment and efforts to address the spinal disorders affecting so many of the world's population. Because treatments involving neurostimulation and drug delivery are growing—and both are long-standing Medtronic strengths—the company is today the world leader in neurological stimulation and implantable drug-delivery therapies. In addition, these same technologic strengths in neurostimulation are being successfully applied to meet unmet needs of incontinence and other disorders.

Company Profile

Medtronic is the world's leading medical-technology company. Over the past 50 years, Medtronic has pioneered in the development of sophisticated instruments that help restore health, extend life, and alleviate pain.

Medtronic's devices help regulate erratic heartbeats, tremors, and incontinence. About one-half of the company's revenues come from the sale of defibrillators and pacing devices, including products for slow, irregular, and rapid heartbeats.

Medtronic also has a stake in spinal implant devices, mechanical and tissue heart valves, as well as implantable neurostimulation and drug-delivery systems, catheters, stents, and guide wires used in angioplasties.

Fiscal 1999 marked the company's 14th consecutive year of increased revenues. Net sales of $4.13 billion represented a 23.7 percent increase over the $3.34 billion in the prior year (after restatement to reflect the fiscal 1999 mergers with several companies). Results in 1999 were led by the performance of core product lines. Finally, growth in 1999 was accelerated by the five major mergers and acquisitions that were completed during the year.

50 Years of History

Medtronic recently celebrated the 50th anniversary of its founding by Earl Bakken and his brother-in-law Palmer Hermundslie on April 29, 1949. Medtronic began in the humblest of circumstances in a garage in northeast Minneapolis. Bakken's close relationships with physicians at the University of Minnesota gave him a chance to invent the first battery-powered, external cardiac pacemaker and see it used successfully. The young company was strapped for cash, but no banker would bet on Medtronic, especially when market research pegged the maximum number of pacemakers ever needed at a mere 10,000.

These dire predictions failed to stop Bakken. From two employees and $8 in revenues in the first month, the company has grown to more than $4 billion in revenues and 22,000 employees serving 120 countries around the world.

Earl Bakken invented the pacemaker when the only treatments for failing hearts were marginally effective drugs—or no therapy at all. The pacemaker—the most ubiquitous implantable product in history—gave patients renewed hope to live healthier, longer lives.

With the invention of the pacemaker, Medtronic created a whole new industry based on medical technology. What's more, it spawned nearly 300 companies.

For 50 years, Medtronic has collaborated with physicians around the world to change the course of human disease and improve the lives of millions of people. Thanks to the pioneering efforts of Medtronic, people suffering from slow heartbeat, arrhythmias of the heart, arteriosclerosis, defective heart valves, spinal injury, chronic pain, cerebral palsy, Parkinson's disease, and incontinence have new life and new hope.

Shortcomings to Bear in Mind

- Like most great growth companies, Medtronic typically sells at a lofty price-earnings ratio.

Reasons to Buy

- Building on Medtronic's strong historic base of cardiac rhythm management and neurological therapy, the company nearly doubled its size in less than eight months during fiscal 1999 with strategic mergers involving five major companies—all with leading product lines worldwide:

- Sofamor Danek, of Memphis, Tennessee, is a global leader in spinal and cranial surgery and an innovator in the new frontier of surgical navigation.
- Arterial Vascular Engineering (AVE), based in Santa Rosa, California, is a prominent player in the world's coronary stent business because of innovation and its commitment to customer responsiveness.
- Physio-Control, of Redmond, Washington, leads in external defibrillators, the crucial devices that give more people a chance of surviving sudden cardiac arrest.
- Avecor, of Minneapolis, Minnesota, produces the world's best operating room oxygenator and other products used for blood circulation during heart surgery.
- Midas Rex, of Fort Worth, Texas, makes the world's leading high-speed drills essential to neurological surgery.

■ At the same time these mergers signaled a new chapter, major product introductions during Medtronic's fiftieth year underscored its research and development vitality. Brand new products designed to treat life-threatening heart rhythm disorders include:

- The Medtronic.Kappa 700 pacemaker series that constantly monitors a patient's heart and automatically adapts to precisely what the patient needs at any moment.
- The Gem platform of implantable defibrillators featuring the GEM II DR—the smallest, most powerful dual-chamber defibrillator available today. It has twice the number of transistors of a Pentium II computer

chip, is no bigger than a small pager, and protects a patient from unnecessary shocks.

- The InSync stimulator for the most effective, life-restoring treatment of heart failure available today.

■ To maintain this ambitious product development pace, Medtronic invested nearly $500 million in R&D during fiscal 2000 and nearly $3.6 billion over the past five years. This investment is borne out in performance: the U.S. Patent and Trademark Office ranks Medtronic first in the world, based on the number of patents issued for medical devices from 1969 through 1998.

■ Since its origin, Medtronic has held a clear market leadership in cardiac pacing, chiefly with pacemakers designed to treat bradycardia (hearts that beat irregularly or too slowly) and more recently, tachyarrhythmia (hearts that beat too fast or quiver uncontrollably, called tachycardia and fibrillation). Today, more than half the cardiac rhythm devices and leads implanted throughout the world come from Medtronic.

■ Medtronic's recent merger with Sofamor Danek, the preeminent company in technologies used by spine surgeons, enhances this leadership. Sofamor Danek is best known for its internal fixation devices for delicate spine surgeries, systems used to surgically remove damaged discs, image-guided surgical navigation products, and "biologics," such as bone proteins, that enhance healing following surgery.

Together with PS Medical—the world leader in neurosurgery products for the treatment of hydrocephalus, interventional neurological monitoring, and critical care products—and Midas Rex, the maker of the world's leading high-speed drills used in neurological surgery, Medtronic brings life-enhancing relief to patients.

- The worldwide coronary vascular market is estimated at $4 billion and is expected to grow because it serves significant unmet medical needs. Medtronic's coronary vascular products include several types of catheters used to unblock coronary arteries, stents that support the walls of an artery and prevent more blockage, and products used in minimally invasive vascular procedures for coronary heart disease, the chief cause of heart attack and angina.

  Medtronic merged with Arterial Vascular Engineering (AVE) in early 1999. AVE, founded through a collaboration of engineers and cardiologists in 1991, is a leader in the $2 billion worldwide coronary stent market. Along with its recent acquisition of USCI/Bard, this significantly expands Medtronic's balloon catheter, guide catheter, guide wire, and stent graft product lines.

- Medtronic's cardiac surgery group offers superior products to support cardiac surgeons, including tissue heart valves that are best represented by the Freestyle stentless valve, the Mosaic stented tissue valve, and the Hall mechanical valve. In addition, the company is expanding its leadership in cardiac cannulae used to connect a patient's circulatory system to external perfusion systems used in conventional and minimally invasive surgeries.

  The recent acquisition of Avecor adds to Medtronic's well-established line of perfusion systems designed to sustain patients during open-heart surgery. These systems include market-leading oxygenators, blood pumps, arterial filters, and autotransfusion and monitoring products that are used to circulate and oxygenate the blood and regulate body temperature during procedures when the heart must be stopped while repairs are made.

  Finally, Medtronic is leading the way in developing products to make cardiac surgery less invasive and, ultimately, reduce pain, patient recovery time, and medical costs. One new product that addresses these needs is the Octopus2 tissue-stabilization system that allows the cardiac surgeon to repair blocked blood vessels while the heart is still beating.

Total assets: $4,870 million
Current ratio: 2.44
Common shares outstanding: 1,174 million
Return on 1999 shareholders' equity: 23.5%

	1999	1998	1997	1996	1995	1994	1993	1992
Revenues (millions)	4134	2605	2438	2169	1742	1391	1328	1177
Net income (millions)	905	595	530	438	294	232	198	162
Earnings per share	.77	.63	.56	.47	.32	.25	.21	.17
Dividends per share	.12	.11	.10	.07	.05	.04	.04	.03
Price High	44.6	38.4	26.4	17.5	15.0	7.0	6.0	6.5
Low	29.9	22.7	14.4	11.1	6.5	4.3	3.2	4.0

CONSERVATIVE GROWTH

Merck & Co., Inc.

One Merck Drive ⊐ P.O. Box 100 ⊐ Whitehouse Station, New Jersey 08889-0100 ⊐ Investor contact: Laura Jordan (908) 423-5185 ⊐ Direct dividend reinvestment plan is available: (888) 291-3713 ⊐ Web site: www.merck.com ⊐ Listed: NYSE ⊐ Ticker symbol: MRK ⊐ S&P rating: A+ ⊐ Value Line financial strength rating: A++

In the first quarter of 2000, Merck reported strong sales of five of its newer drugs—Vioxx, Zocor, Cozaar-Hyzaar, Fosamax, and Singulair. These now account for half of the company's total pharmaceutical sales, a clear sign that the company is moving away from its reliance on older drugs, four of which are destined to lose patent protection over the next two years.

"The concern that Merck would roll over and play dead may be alleviated," said Mara Goldstein, an analyst at CIBC World Markets.

Company Profile

Merck is a leading research-driven pharmaceutical products and services company. Directly and through its joint ventures, the company discovers, develops, manufactures, and markets a broad range of innovative products to improve human and animal health. Merck also provides pharmaceutical and benefit services through Merck-Medco Managed Care.

Human Health Products

Human health products include therapeutic and preventative drugs, generally sold by prescription, for the treatment of human disorders. Among these are elevated-cholesterol products, which include Zocor and Mevacor; hypertensive/heart failure products include Vasotec, the largest-selling product among this group, Cozaar, Hyzaar, Prinivil and Vaseretic; anti-ulcerants, of which Pepcid is the largest-selling; antibiotics, of which Primaxin and Noroxin are the largest-selling; ophthalmologicals, of which Timoptic, Timoptic-XE, and Trusopt are the largest-selling; vaccines/biologicals, of which Recombivax HB (hepatitis B vaccine recombinant), M-M-R II, a pediatric vaccine for measles, mumps, and rubella, and Varivax, a live virus vaccine for the prevention of chickenpox, are the largest-selling; HIV, comprised of Crixivan, a protease inhibitor for the treatment of human immunodeficiency viral infection in adults that was launched in the United States in 1996; and osteoporosis, which includes Fosamax, for the treatment and prevention in postmenopausal women.

Animal Health Products

Animal health products include medicinals used to control and alleviate disease in livestock, small animals, and poultry. Crop protection includes products for the control of crop pests and fungal disease. In July 1997, the company sold its crop-protection business to Novartis. In August 1997, Merck and Rhone-Poulenc combined their animal health and poultry genetics businesses to form Merial Limited.

Merck-Medco

Merck-Medco primarily includes Merck-Medco sales of non-Merck products and Merck-Medco pharmaceutical benefit services, primarily managed prescription drug programs and programs to manage health and drug utilization.

Marketing

Merck sells its human health products to drug wholesalers, retailers, hospitals, clinics, government agencies, and managed-health care providers, such as health-maintenance organizations and other institutions. The company's professional representatives communicate the effectiveness, safety, and value of the company's products to health care professionals in private practice, group practices, and managed-care organizations.

Shortcomings to Bear in Mind

- Product patents for Vasotec, Vaseretic, Mevacor, Prinivil, Prinzide, Pepcid, and Prilosec (which Merck manufactures and supplies to Astra for the U.S. market) will go off-patent in 2000 and 2001. On the other hand, Merck contends that its newer products "will keep us competitive." Increasingly greater percentages of the company's overall sales derive from the 14 new drugs and vaccines it has introduced since 1995. These important medicines accounted for 22 percent of worldwide human health sales in 1998, up from 2 percent just three years ago. What's more, the five newest products are at the early stages of their life cycles. As the company expands its marketing in Europe and the rest of the world in 1999, they will contribute even further to Merck's growth.

- Competitive pressures will inhibit the growth of some of Merck's key products. For instance, Warner-Lambert's Lipitor has been gaining market share in the rapidly expanding market for cholesterol-lowering drugs, at the expense of Merck's Zocor and Mevacor. What's more, the company's Fosamax faces a formidable challenge from Eli Lilly's Evista. In addition, the protease inhibitor market is becoming ever-more crowded—Agouron's Viracept has been showing solid growth. Finally,

Bristol-Myers' Avapro will probably take some market share away from Merck's Cozaar.

- The markets in which the company's business is conducted are highly competitive and, in many ways, highly regulated. Global efforts toward health care cost containment continue to exert pressure on product pricing.

In the United States, government efforts to slow the increase of health care costs and the demand for price discounts from managed-care groups have limited the company's ability to mitigate the effect of inflation on costs and expenses through pricing.

Outside of the United States, government mandated cost-containment programs have required the company to similarly limit selling prices. Additionally, government actions have significantly reduced the sales growth of certain products by decreasing the patient reimbursement cost of the drug, restricting the volume of drugs that physicians can prescribe, and increasing the use of generic products. It is anticipated that the worldwide trend for cost containment and competitive pricing will continue and result in continued pricing pressures.

Reasons to Buy

- In 1999, Merck received FDA approval for Vioxx, a new drug for arthritis and acute pain. Its principal claim is that is doesn't cause stomach ulcers, whereas most anti-inflammatory drugs may. Drugs now being used include aspirin, Relafen, Lodine XL, and Advil. An estimated 16,000 people a year die from deadly ulcers caused by conventional painkillers. Forty million people suffer from arthritis in the United States alone. Vioxx competes with Monsanto's Celebrex (which is also marketed by Pfizer—which paid Monsanto

$240 million for this pact) arthritis medication, the first drug in the new Cox-2 class to get FDA approval. Celebrex, which was introduced in January of 1999, has enjoyed one of the fastest new-drug launches in industry history. Now, Merck will try to steal market share away from Celebrex as well as older drugs that still make up the majority of the market. Vioxx has one major advantage going for it: the FDA approval was for such afflictions as osteoarthritis and acute short-term pain (such as menstrual cramps and pain following dental and orthopedic surgery). These uses are much broader than the FDA approval for Celebrex. Merck's drug has another advantage: it needs to be taken only once a day, regardless of the affliction being treated. Celebrex must be taken once or twice a day for osteoarthritis and twice a day for rheumatoid arthritis.

- Growth in earnings per share has been impressive. For instance, in the 1989–1999 period, earnings per share climbed from .63 to $2.45, a compound annual growth rate of 14.6 percent. In the same 10-year span, dividends advanced from $.27 cents to $1.10, a growth rate of 15.1 percent.

- Women taking a once-daily pill made by Merck to prevent the bone-thinning disease osteoporosis may soon be able to take a higher dose of the same medicine (Fosamax) just once a week, according to a new medical research study released in November of 1999. Fosamax helps prevent the loss of bone-mineral density in the spine and hip. In the study, researchers tested a once-a-week 70-milligram tablet of Fosamax. The scientists compared the new formulation's effectiveness against the traditional 10-milligram version that must be taken every day.

Analysts believe that the once-weekly regimen is likely to boost Fosamax sales. This is because, while Fosamax is becoming an increasingly popular medication, getting women to comply with the once-daily dosage has been a marketing challenge. That's because Fosamax in the usual dosage can cause problems for women with digestive illnesses, and the drug must be taken with plenty of water on an empty stomach in the morning before breakfast. Even so, Fosamax is already generating significant revenues for Merck, on the order of $1 billion a year in 1999. Merck developed the newer formulation to fend off competition. Procter & Gamble has a similar-acting drug called Actonel, but it must be taken once a day.

- Late in 1999, Merck and CVS Corporation (the nation's second-largest drug-store chain, in terms of sales) jumped into the race to grab drugstore customers on the Internet by forming an alliance that connects their Internet sites and combines the strengths of the largest pharmacy-benefits manager (Merck-Medco) and the nation's second-largest drugstore chain (CVS).

Under the new pact, the Merck-Medco site contains a CVS site, selling the same 7,000 over-the-counter products that CVS sells through its Internet drugstore. Those products include private-label, nonprescription medications, as well as health and beauty items.

- Merck has introduced 15 major products since 1995. These drugs were responsible for 30 percent of the company's sales in the fourth quarter. Among these 15 were four drugs that will lose patent soon, representing 25 percent of the total. On the other hand, this is a smaller percentage than a year earlier—and much smaller than five years ago. According to one analyst, "This is a confirmation that what the company has been arguing all along is actually playing out. That's why they keep saying they don't need to do a deal." Merck's chairman, Raymond V. Gilmartin, has assured investors that the company isn't interested in jumping into the drug industry's merger frenzy. In his words, "In examining the history of the industry, companies that have expanded through internal R&D have grown faster—and created more shareholder value—than those depending on mergers."

Mr. Gilmartin also said that Merck is on a steady course to deliver solid earnings growth in 2000. He pointed out that the strong sales of its Cox-2 anti-inflammatory drug, Vioxx, and the asthma drug Singulair are helping account for the rosy earnings estimate for 2000. Sales of the osteoporosis drug Fosamax, moreover, climbed 44 percent in 1999.

Total assets: $35,635 million
Current ratio: 1.59
Common shares outstanding: 2,346 million
Return on 1999 equity: 44.5%

	1999	1998	1997	1996	1995	1994	1993	1992
Revenues (millions)	32714	26898	23637	19829	16681	14970	10498	9662
Net income (millions)	5890	5248	4614	3881	3335	2997	2687	2447
Earnings per share	2.45	2.15	1.92	1.60	1.35	1.19	1.17	1.06
Dividends per share	1.10	.95	.85	.71	.62	.57	.52	.46
Price High	87.4	80.9	54.1	42.1	33.6	19.8	22.1	28.3
Low	60.9	50.7	39.0	28.3	18.2	14.1	14.3	20.3

AGGRESSIVE GROWTH

Microsoft Corporation

One Microsoft Way ❑ **Redmond, Washington 98052-6399** ❑ **Investor contact: Carla Lewis (425) 936-3703** ❑ **Dividend reinvestment plan is not available** ❑ **Web site: www.microsoft.com** ❑ **Fiscal year ends June 30** ❑ **Listed: Nasdaq** ❑ **Ticker symbol: MSFT** ❑ **S&P rating: A-** ❑ **Value Line financial strength rating: A++**

After a long and acrimonious trial, the Justice Department and 17 states proposed the most sweeping antitrust action in a quarter century against one of history's most successful enterprises. In late April 2000, U.S. District Judge Thomas Penfield Jackson ordered the breakup of Microsoft into two separate entities, with one company devoted to Office software applications and the other built around its core Windows operating systems business.

In a subsequent court filing, Microsoft said that if the government's breakup plan were adopted, its employees might "leave the company in droves."

In the weeks that followed, the stock plummeted from a high of just under $120 to about half that value.

To predict the ultimate outcome of this tussle is not easy, but suffice it to say that it may be two or three years before the legal strife is over. For one thing, Microsoft may fare better at the appellate level.

In a move to seek some sort of compromise, Microsoft said that it would be willing to:

● Stop displaying the desktop icon in Windows that leads users to its Web browser, Internet Explorer.

● Allow computer makers to prominently feature any software, including software from rivals, on the Windows desktop.

● Offer equal contracts to computer makers, regardless of their support of competitors's software.

• Provide equal access to technology that would allow any software maker to easily write programs for Windows.

Company Profile

Microsoft is the dominant player in the PC software market. It climbed to prominence on the popularity of its operating systems software and now rules the business-applications software market. Microsoft, moreover, has set its sights on becoming the leading provider of software services for the Internet.

By virtue of it size, market positioning, and financial strength, Microsoft is a formidable competitor in any market it seeks to enter. Earnings have shown explosive growth in recent years, enhanced by a strong PC market in general, along with new product introductions and market share gains.

Microsoft is best known for its operating systems software programs, which run on close to 90 percent of the PCs currently in use. Its original DOS operating system, of course, gave way to Windows, a graphical user interface program run in conjunction with DOS, which made using a PC easier.

The company entered the business-applications market in the early 1990s via a line-up of strong offerings combined with aggressive and innovative marketing and sales strategies. The company's Office 97 Suite, which includes the popular Word (word processing), Excel (spreadsheet), and PowerPoint (graphics) software programs, is now by far the best-selling applications software package.

Shortcomings to Bear in Mind

■ At times, Microsoft resembles a stumbling giant. In the federal antitrust case, for instance, the company's courtroom strategy was often described as inept.
■ Most of Microsoft's new wares merely match those introduced months—or

even years ago—by competitors. Comparative shopping, for instance, which enables Netizens to check prices and products from a variety of vendors in one place, was introduced by Yahoo! Inc. in 1997. Microsoft's version of the service didn't come out until late in 1999.

■ The browser war may be a memory, but executives of Microsoft concede that the company now faces an even greater challenge in the next phase of the Internet revolution as the role of traditional desktop software recedes and the power center of computing shifts from the operating system to the World Wide Web.

Software is increasingly becoming a Web-based service whose main goal is to hasten the spread of electronic commerce over the Internet. Microsoft, of course, controls the dominant software standard in the personal computer industry with its Windows operating system, which runs on 90 percent of PCs sold today. In the past, outside software developers had little choice but to write their programs to run on Microsoft's technology. However, the basic technology standards on the Web are openly available and not controlled by any single company. As a consequence, Microsoft has a much tougher job on its hands in trying to persuade software developers to use its software for Web applications and Internet commerce services.

Reasons to Buy

■ In the spring of 2000, Microsoft made converts out of skeptical game developers with eye-popping demonstrations of its new X-Box entertainment console. Microsoft CEO Bill Gates put his company's challenge succinctly in a speech at the Game Developers Conference in San Jose, California. "One key element that is crucial is making it fun, making sure that people are entertained by what they do." According to analysts, the X-Box promises to deliver on that challenge, as Microsoft moves to capture a chunk of the $11-billion gaming industry from Sony, Sega, and Nintendo.

The X-Box, which will be out in time for the holiday shopping season in 2001, will have an Intel Pentium III chip running at speeds of at least 600 megahertz, a DVD-ROM drive, and at least 64 megabytes of memory—the equivalent of today's midrange personal computers.

Unlike other consoles, it also will have a hard drive that can store games or act as a "virtual memory" system to hold data for upcoming use. Even more impressive, a proprietary graphics chip made by NVidia will process a trillion operations a second, as much as three times faster than the current leader, Sony's PlayStation2.

- One of the company's game plans is to beef up the Microsoft Network (MSN) into a more potent Web portal by adding an unparalleled menu of software products and services. Among other things, Microsoft will update its low-cost commerce software to enable online merchants to create more personalized Web stores. The key part of its initiative is BizTalk, a business-to-business tool that lets companies that operate on different systems do business with one another over the Net, even if they have never done business together before.

Microsoft believes that by offering the soup-to-nuts e-commerce system it will leapfrog the likes of Netscape/America Online. The reason: By controlling the operating system, software, services, and portal, the company can create seamless links between the different technologies and offer the whole package at a low price.

- Microsoft has always had a reputation as an aggressive competitor. Now it is making a name for itself as an aggressive deal maker. The company said it completed 90 investments or acquisitions valued at $9.88 billion in 1999, including 71 equity investments, 14 acquisitions, and 5 joint ventures.

- Microsoft, battered in previous attempts to extend its sway over the personal computer to home electronics and hand-held computers, is making a fresh assault. During 2000, the company introduced a range of new initiatives aimed at securing a foothold in the nascent markets for non-PC computing devices that can be used to access the Internet, manage home-entertainment systems, and control the flow of information through the home and functions such as light and heating.

Among the new products Microsoft plans is a new generation of hand-held computers that will enable users to more easily access the Internet as well as software aimed at managing digital music and video entertainment. Microsoft has long had its eye on the market for non-PC devices, but, until recently, had not made much headway. Its current operating system for handheld devices, Windows CE, has lagged behind in the hand-held market, compared with devices made by 3Com. On the other hand, it has enjoyed better success in the market for TV set-top boxes.

- In 1999, the company announced availability of Microsoft Office 2000 beta 2 and the largest ever early evaluation for Office. Responding to customer demand, the Office 2000 evaluation program has been expanded to an expected 700,000 customers participating in 43 countries, making it 10 times larger than all previous Office evaluation programs put together.

- Microsoft has recently expanded into the market for new consumer platforms. MSFT provides software for consumer devices, including hand-held PCs, palm-sized PCs, wireless-communication devices, and Internet access devices. The company develops Windows CE, an operating system for communications, entertainment, and mobile computing devices.

- After investing more than $1 billion, Microsoft launched Windows 2000—both Professional and several versions of Windows 2000 server—in the spring of 2000. Windows 2000 Professional is an operating system targeted for business desktop and laptop users. The company claims that this new 32-bit operating system is "utterly reliable." It has safeguards that are geared to reduce the scenarios in which the user is required to reboot the system. Moreover, with 64 megabytes or more of memory, the operating system is able to operate 25 percent faster than either Windows 95 or 98. Windows 2000 server is designed to operate networks with improved features for the Internet and e-commerce server applications. The 2000 models, augmented with improved reliability and communications capabilities, could help Microsoft capture market share from such competitors as Sun Microsystems, Novell, and product offerings based upon the Linux operating system.

- Late in 1999, Microsoft bought Visio Corporation, a maker of diagraming and technical drawing software. This $1.3-billion deal helps Microsoft fill a gap in its line of business products. Visio's products let professionals like corporate administrators and designers make flow and organizational charts as well as more technical drawings. The deal strengthened the company's grip on a market for business productivity software, which it already dominates with its Office suite of word processing, spreadsheet, and presentation products.

Visio, founded in 1990, says its technical drawing software is used by 3 million customers.

Visio, whose Seattle offices are about a half-hour from Microsoft's in the suburb of Redmond, had been struggling with the transition from sales of software through retail stores and distributors to direct sales to corporations through its own sales force. Microsoft's powerful marketing machine should accelerate that process and add to the earnings of the business's new parent quickly.

- Just before the end of 1999, Ericsson of Sweden and Microsoft created a joint-venture company to market and deliver mobile e-mail and other Internet services for wireless network operators. Ericsson is the world's third-largest mobile phone maker. Analysts said the deal should help Ericsson regain market share lost to Motorola and to Nokia of Finland. For Microsoft, it represents another significant step in the company's efforts to be a major competitor in wireless networking. Microsoft has entered into a similar joint venture with Qualcomm, called Wireless Knowledge, and has made a number of acquisitions of companies with wireless technology or software.

For Microsoft, the link with Ericsson provides credibility in winning deals with major wireless carriers. According to Andrew Seybold, an industry consultant, "Microsoft, in order to be competitive in the wireless arena, has to get into the carriers' back-end infrastructure some way because that's where all the smarts are. Ericsson is a trusted back-end supplier."

- With impressive new software for hand-held computers, Microsoft in the spring of 2000 mounted what industry analysts regard as the first serious challenge to Palm Inc., the leader in the fast-growing market for pocket-size machines. Microsoft's new version of its Pocket PC software can play music in the popular MP3 audio format, display electronic books in the first major introduction of the company's Cleartype software, and play video clips. However, analysts say that Microsoft faces an uphill struggle in trying to catch Palm. In 1999, according to International Data Corporation, Palm machines accounted for nearly 85 percent of the market, compared with 10 percent for hand-held machines running the Microsoft software.

Total assets: $5,363 million
Current ratio: 2.10
Common shares outstanding: 5,205 million
Return on 1999 shareholders' equity: 26.8%

	1999	1998	1997	1996	1995	1994	1993	1992
Revenues (millions)	19747	14484	11358	8671	5937	4649	3753	2759
Net income (millions)	7625	4786	3454	2176	1453	1210	953	708
Earnings per share	1.39	.89	.66	.43	.29	.25	.20	.15
Dividends per share	Nil							
Price High	119.9	72.0	37.7	21.5	13.7	8.1	6.1	5.9
Low	68.0	31.1	20.2	10.0	7.3	4.9	4.4	4.1

GROWTH AND INCOME

Minnesota Mining & Manufacturing Company

3M Center, 225-1S-15 □ St. Paul, Minnesota 55144-1000 □ Investor contact: Jon Greer (651) 736-1915 □ Web site: www.3M.com/about3M □ Listed: NYSE □ Dividend reinvestment plan is available: (800) 401-1952 □ Ticker symbol: MMM □ S&P rating: A □ Value Line financial strength rating: A++

Pedestrians, bicyclists, and motorists have a new safety edge with 3M Scotchlite Diamond Grade Reflective Sheeting. The company's eye-catching fluorescent yellow-green sheeting was approved in 1998 for signs near schools, playgrounds, bike paths, and other areas where driver awareness is critical.

Another product in the line, Diamond Grade fluorescent orange sheeting, rapidly is becoming the standard in many states for signs in construction work zones. 3M's durable fluorescent sheetings are the first to include a warranty for fluorescent-color retention. The company's Diamond Grade sheeting, which also makes large vehicles highly visible at night, draws on many 3M technologies and extends the company's leadership in reflective materials for transportation safety.

Company Profile

Minnesota Mining & Manufacturing Company is an international manufacturer with a vast array of products (more than fifty thousand). The company has a stake in such items as tapes, adhesives, electronic components, sealants, coatings, fasteners, floor coverings, cleaning agents, roofing granules, fire-fighting agents, graphic arts, dental products, medical products, specialty chemicals, and reflective sheeting.

The company's Industrial and Consumer Sector is the world's largest supplier of tapes, producing more than 900 varieties. It is also a leader in coated abrasives, specialty chemicals, repositionable notes, home cleaning sponges and pads, electronic circuits, and other important products.

The Life Sciences Sector is a global leader in reflective materials for transportation safety, respirators for worker safety, closures for disposable diapers, and high-quality graphics used indoors and out. This sector also holds leading positions in medical and surgical supplies, drug-delivery systems, and dental products.

3M has a decentralized organization with a large number of relatively small profit centers aimed at creating an entrepreneurial atmosphere.

Minnesota Mining & Manufacturing is a highly diversified manufacturer of industrial, commercial, consumer, and health care products that share similar technological, manufacturing, and marketing resources. Its business initially developed from its research and technology in coating and bonding.

MMM has many strengths:

• Leading market positions. Minnesota Mining is a leader in most of its businesses, often number one or number two in market share. In fact, 3M has created many markets, frequently by developing products that people didn't even realize they needed.

• Strong technology base. The company draws on more than 30 core technologies—from adhesives and nonwovens to specialty chemicals and microreplication.

• Healthy mix of businesses. 3M serves an extremely broad array of markets—from automotive and health care to office supply and telecommunications. This diversity gives the company many avenues for growth, while also cushioning the company from disruption in any single market.

• Flexible, self-reliant business units. 3M's success in developing a steady stream of new products and entering new markets stems from its deep-rooted corporate structure. It's an environment in which 3M people listen to customers, act on their own initiative, and share technologies and other expertise widely and freely.

• Worldwide presence. Minnesota Mining has companies in more than 60 countries around the world. It sells its products in nearly 200 countries.

• Efficient manufacturing and distribution. 3M is a low-cost supplier in many of its product lines. This is increasingly important in today's value-conscious and competitive world.

• Strong financial position. 3M is one of a small number of domestic companies whose debt carries the highest rating for credit quality.

Highlights of 1999

■ The company achieved record sales, net income, and earnings per share in 1999, along with high returns on invested capital. Excluding nonrecurring items, net income totaled $1.71 billion, or $4.21 per share, up more than 12 percent over the prior year. Sales, at $15.7 billion, increased 4.3 percent.

■ Operating income in 1999 was 18.2 percent of sales, up from 16.9 percent in 1998. Return on invested capital was 18.6 percent, up from 15.9 percent, and about 8.6 percentage points above the company's cost of capital. What's more, all six of 3M's business segments enjoyed solid profitability.

■ 3M posted its strongest sales and profit growth in the Asia-Pacific. In 1999, Asia-Pacific volume rose 13 percent, and profit margins returned to their traditional levels.

■ Across the globe, new products were a primary driver of 3M growth. The company, moreover, generated 34 percent of sales—$5.3 billion—from products new to the market within the past four years.

Shortcomings to Bear in Mind

■ Over the past 10 years, the company's growth, although steady, has not been dynamic. In the 1989–1999 period, earnings per share increased from $2.80 to $4.21, an annual compound growth rate of only 4.2 percent. In the same 10-year stretch, dividends expanded from $1.30 to $2.24, a growth rate of 5.6 percent.

Reasons to Buy

- To sustain a strong flow of new product, 3M continues to make substantial investments—about $1 billion a year—in research and development.
- Minnesota Mining is a global leader in industrial, consumer, office, health care, safety, and other markets. The company draws on many strengths, including a rich pool of technology, innovative products, strong customer service, and efficient manufacturing.
- The unrelenting drive toward smaller, lighter, more powerful, and more economical electronic products creates strong demand for leading-edge 3M Microflex Circuits. Minnesota Mining is the world's number one supplier of adhesive-less flexible circuitry. 3M microflex circuits connect components in many of the world's ink-jet printers. They also link integrated circuits to printed circuit boards efficiently and reliably, making it possible to develop even smaller cellular phones, portable computers, pagers, and other electronic devices.
- 3M supplies a wide variety of products to the automotive market, including high-performance tape attachment systems; structural adhesives; catalytic converter mounts; decorative, functional, and protective films; and trim and identification products.
- The Life Sciences Sector produces innovative products that improve health and safety for people around the world. In consumer and professional health care, 3M has captured a significant share of the first-aid market with a superior line of bandages. 3M Active Strips Flexible Foam Bandages adhere better to skin—even when wet—and 3M Comfort Strips Ultra Comfortable Bandages set new standards for wearing comfort. Under development are tapes, specialty dressings, and skin treatments that will reinforce and broaden the company's leading market positions and accelerate sales growth.

- In pharmaceuticals, 3M is a global leader in technologies for delivering medications that are inhaled or absorbed through the skin, and the company is expanding its horizons in new molecule discovery.
- Hostile conditions lie under any vehicle's hood, but 3M's Dyneon Fluoropolymers withstand the heat. Found in seals, gaskets, O-rings, and hoses in automotive and airplane engines, the company's fluoropolymers outperform the competition when high temperatures and chemicals cross paths. And 3M technology isn't merely under the hood. Minnesota Mining also makes products for the vehicle's body and cabin that identify, insulate, protect, and bond—such as dimensional graphics, Thinsulate Acoustic Insulation, cabin filters, and super-strong adhesives and tapes that replace screws and rivets. The company is also developing window films that help keep the cabin cool by absorbing ultraviolet light and reflecting infrared light.
- In 1999, the company experienced sharp increases in demand for optical films that make displays brighter for computers, electronic organizers, cell phones, and other electronic devices that require displays.
- In 1999, 3M achieved strong growth in automotive products due to record vehicle production and higher 3M sales penetration per vehicle.

- The company's Health Information Systems acquired the health care operations of Hyatt, Imler, Ott and Blount, Inc. at the end of 1999. Founded in 1981, Hyatt, Imler, Ott and Blount is an international leader in clinical information management, with products ranging from medical records coding to a comprehensive computer-based patient record system. The company provides high-level health care consulting services to over two thousand health care organizations in over forty states.

- Post-it Notes were named one of the twentieth century's best products by *Fortune* magazine, and Scotch Tape was listed among the century's 100 best innovations by *Business Week* magazine. Also, 3M ranked as the world's most respected consumer-goods company and fifteenth overall in a survey published by the *Financial Times of London*. Finally, 3M has received Achieved Vendor of the Year status from four leaders in the office-supply industry.

Total assets: $13,896 million
Current ratio: 1.70
Common shares outstanding: 401 million
Return on 1999 shareholder's equity: 27.2%

	1999	1998	1997	1996	1995	1994	1993	1992
Revenues (millions)	15659	15021	15070	14236	13460	15079	14020	13883
Net income (millions)	1711	1526	1626	1516	1359	1345	1263	1229
Earnings per share	4.21	3.74	3.88	3.63	3.23	3.18	2.91	2.82
Dividends per share	2.24	2.20	2.12	1.92	1.88	1.76	1.66	1.60
Price High	103.4	97.9	105.5	85.9	69.9	57.1	58.5	53.5
Low	69.3	65.6	80.0	61.3	50.8	46.4	48.6	42.8

GROWTH AND INCOME

J. P. Morgan & Company, Inc.

60 Wall Street ◻ **New York, New York 10260** ◻ **Investor contact: Ann B. Patton (212) 648-9446**
◻ **Dividend reinvestment plan is available: (800) 519-3111** ◻ **Web site: www.jpmorgan.com** ◻ **Listed: NYSE**
◻ **Ticker symbol: JPM** ◻ **S&P rating: B+** ◻ **Value Line financial strength rating: A+**

In 2000, J. P. Morgan unveiled an online version of its private-banking wealth-management service that uses specialized software to generate computerized analysis and advice. The bank's online service, priced at $2,500 a year, is likely to attract far more customers than the 15,000 clients served by the company's private-banking business.

Not only does it offer 24 free online stock trades each year, charging $30 per trade thereafter, it also enables users to track daily fluctuations in individual securities and mutual funds from different fund managers and offers advice on saving for tuition and retirement, estate planning, and asset allocation.

Company Profile

J. P. Morgan, which is the parent of Morgan Guaranty Trust Company of New York, is a broad-based financial services firm, providing corporate finance, advisory, investment management, trading, and risk management, as well as other financial services to corporations, governments, and financial institutions throughout the world. J. P. Morgan has a substantial stake in overseas ventures—more than half of its revenues and profits come from abroad.

J. P. Morgan is a much different company than it was two or three years ago. Earnings are more diversified, with increased emphasis on asset management, equities, and investment banking. What's more, with less reliance on proprietary trading, the overall risk profile has been reduced, dampening the impact of global market volatility. J. P. Morgan is now allocating its capital based on prospects for risk-adjusted returns.

Near term, J. P. Morgan's private-banking initiative could be a temporary drain on earnings, but if the bank can entice enough people away from their discount brokers to the more personal services of Morgan, this very lucrative business is likely to further diversify and stabilize the company's traditionally volatile earnings stream.

According to an analyst at Argus Research Corporation, "We believe that JPM is well-positioned for global growth this decade and should continue to gain market share from its peers."

Highlights of 1999

J. P. Morgan made solid progress in 1999, as the bank focused on generated revenues, risk reduction, and productivity. Here are some highlights:

- Net income of $2.055 billion was a record.
- Firm-wide after-tax economic value added of $86.3 million was up $1.1 billion before special items.
- Return on average common equity was 18.4 percent.
- Risk in the bank's credit portfolio was down 50 percent from the level of 1997.
- Revenues climbed 31 percent.
- Operating expenses before performance-driven compensation were down about $400 million.

Shortcomings to Bear in Mind

- Whenever a company encounters problems or setbacks, it often uses the word "challenging." Here is what J. P. Morgan had to say about one of its operations: "1999 was a challenging year for Proprietary Investing and Trading—a period of strategic change in which we significantly shifted our focus. Results across our portfolios were mixed—significant losses in our U.S. investment portfolio and Asian trading portfolio, but strong returns from newer, more diversified global trading activities.

  "In 1999, the substantial decline in reported revenues and in total return revenues—the most meaningful measure for these activities—was related to two factors: a decrease in the value of longer-term mortgage-backed security positions in our U.S. investment securities portfolio, and losses in Asia, following an extremely strong 1998. These risk positions, which were part of our historical, longer-term strategies, have been substantially reduced."

Reasons to Buy

- J. P. Morgan was involved in a number of high-profile deals in 2000. It handled the $2.2-billion secondary stock sale of Network Solutions Inc., a company that registers Internet site names. It also jointly managed with Goldman Sachs Group the sale of $2.3 billion in stock of Corning Inc. Its mergers and acquisitions team also managed the sale of Network Solutions to VeriSign Inc., a company that provides online security services, in a deal valued at $21.1 billion.
- Investors have been increasing their allocations to alternative asset classes, such as private equity and real estate. J. P. Morgan is one of the leading managers in this market and believes it can continue to grow by capturing a greater share of existing clients' assets. In 1999,

the bank raised almost $3 billion in two private equity funds. Morgan was also awarded its single largest mandate ever when the Teamsters' Central States Southeast and Southwest Areas Pension Funds appointed the bank as fiduciary, overseeing more than $10 billion in assets.

- J. P. Morgan's partnership with American Century has achieved its primary objective: the bank's Retirement Plan Services joint venture has become a leading provider of defined contribution services. Assets under management increased by 39 percent in 1999, to $31 billion. The company's strategy has been to leverage its long-standing defined benefit corporate relationships: the bank won business from Champion International Corporation and Navistar International Corporation among others. As of year-end 1999, J. P. Morgan was managing 248 bundled service plans with more than 350,000 participants.

- J. P. Morgan has three interrelated areas of focus in e-business: First, the company will embrace electronic media to improve service and reach greater numbers of clients. To advance the bank's client strategy and raise market share, JPM will be developing portals aimed at markets that have not traditionally been part of J. P. Morgan's client base. The expansion of the company's private bank to reach affluent households by leveraging Internet and phone-based service channels is a major initiative in this regard. The bank will also develop market-specific e-commerce sites, such as the European government-bond hub, J. P. Morgan eXpress, and invest in platforms that appear best positioned for success.

- J. P. Morgan's private bank is a major growth opportunity for the company. It already has leadership position among high-net-worth individuals and families, based on the bank's integration of liquidity management, investment management, brokerage, trust and estate planning, combined with J. P. Morgan's capabilities as a premier investment bank.

The aim of the company is to extend this offering to still more affluent households. In the United States, for example, the number of households with net worth of $1 million or more has doubled in the last five years and now exceeds 7 million. J. P. Morgan's long experience in advising individuals on optimizing their after-tax wealth places JPM in an ideal position to meet the needs of this growing affluent population. Recognizing that the bank must provide choices and flexibility, it is building service options that meet the needs of the market and use, in particular, the power of the Internet and phone-based delivery channels to deliver service to investors when and as they choose.

In 1999, J. P. Morgan spent $71 million on developing these distribution channels.

- As industries rationalize and established companies seek scale and relevance, they demand an integral approach from their advisors. This was true in the $42.7-billion merger of Germany's VIAG AG and VEBA AG, which created Europe's largest investor-owned energy utility. Because of the complex conglomerate structure of both companies, J. P. Morgan's advisory work for VIAG required a wide range of expertise—in the energy, chemical, industrial, real estate, and telecommunications industries as well as in German and European regulatory issues.

Likewise, J. P. Morgan's versatility came to the fore after the bank advised Lyondell Chemical Company on its successful 1998 acquisition of ARCO Chemical. The company sought a creative restructuring of its balance sheet. In response, in May of 1999 JPM priced a $2.4-billion high-yield bond offering, the fourth-largest ever completed; arranged a $1-billion leveraged loan; and executed a $765-million secondary equity offering.

- J. P. Morgan demonstrated its strength in serving clients' most complex cross-border needs in the three-way, $1.9-billion strategic partnership of AT&T Corporation, British Telecom, and Japan Telecom, which was announced in mid-1999. By advising AT&T on backing Japan Telecom's bid to enhance its competitiveness in a rapidly consolidating market, the bank helped bolster its client's presence in that market and completed the largest foreign investment ever made in Japanese telecommunications.

- In 1999, J. P. Morgan maintained or built upon selected leadership positions in credit markets. Once again, Morgan was the number one trader of emerging market debt in 1999, with a market share of 24 percent. The bank was named the number one debt originator in Latin America and emerging Asia. Notable emerging market transactions included the $3.9-billion debt exchange for the Republic of Argentina and the $2-billion Brady bond exchange for the Republic of Brazil. The bank also led the first straight corporate bond issuance in Latin America since the 1998 crisis, for Embotelladora Arica S. A.

- In structured finance and credit derivatives, J. P. Morgan had a record year in 1999 as a result of improved credit markets, increased usage of securitization markets by issuers as a means of funding, greater investor appetite for structured transactions, and new product innovation. Morgan was named Best Overall Credit Derivatives House by *Institutional Investor* and other

leading publications. Among the most innovative transactions of 1999 was a $345-million collateralized debt obligation of other collateralized debt obligations for Zais Investment Grade Ltd., which was selected as derivatives deal of the year by *Institutional Investor.*

- The company's debt underwriting activities had a good year in 1999 as the bank expanded into more profitable, higher-growth areas. An increase in lead manager roles and acquisition financings created strong results in high-grade origination. The company was the lead manager in such major transactions as Packaging Corporation of America and Lyondell Petrochemical Company.

- J. P. Morgan Capital Corporation (JPMCC) is an experienced global private equity investor, with a current portfolio of more than one hundred twenty companies in 23 countries. The bank's strategy is to create a portfolio that is diversified both globally and by industry while favoring those regions and sectors that JPM believes will provide the greatest risk-adjusted returns. The bank makes the majority of its investments in private companies— those not available to the public on Nasdaq or stock exchanges. JPMCC also serves as general partner to $2.5 billion in private equity funds focused on the real estate and financial service industries.

JPMCC comes to the business with a number of competitive advantages that differentiates it in a bustling private equity marketplace. First is J. P. Morgan's broad network for deal sourcing. The company's investment banking, equity research, private banking, and corporate technology teams provide the bank with ideas and opportunities, particularly in rapidly expanding industries such as telecommunications and e-commerce.

Total assets: $261 billion
Common shares outstanding: 165 million
Return on 1999 shareholders' equity: 18%

	1999	1998	1997	1996	1995	1994	1993	1992
Net interest income (millions)	1541	1281	1872	1702	2003	1981	1772	1708
Net income (millions)	2055	1067	1465	1574	1296	1215	1723	1382
Earnings per share	10.39	5.22	7.17	7.63	6.42	6.02	8.48	6.92
Dividends per share	3.97	3.84	3.59	3.31	3.06	2.79	2.48	2.24
Price High	147.8	148.8	125.8	100.7	82.5	72.0	79.4	70.5
Low	97.3	72.1	93.1	73.5	56.1	55.1	59.4	51.5

AGGRESSIVE GROWTH

Motorola, Incorporated

1303 East Algonquin Road ◻ Schaumburg, Illinois 60196-1079 ◻ Investor contact: Tim Callard
(847) 576-4995 ◻ Dividend reinvestment plan available: (800) 704-4098 ◻ Web site: www.motorola.com
◻ Listed: NYSE ◻ Ticker symbol: MOT ◻ S&P rating: A ◻ Value Line financial strength rating: A

Although Motorola manufactures a wide variety of electronic products, it is best known for its wireless communications products. What's more, as the number of worldwide users of cellular telephones and pagers has mushroomed, Motorola has emerged as a leading supplier to the rapidly expanding wireless industry.

Company Profile

The Personal Communications segment focuses on delivering integrated voice, video, and data communications solutions to consumers. This segment manufactures cellular telephone subscriber units as well as messaging and paging products and consumer two-way radio products.

The company manufactures cellular products based on all three of the major digital standards: GSM, TDMA, and CDMA. This segment of Motorola accounts for about one-third of the company's revenues.

The Network Systems unit (about one-quarter of annual revenues) manufactures cellular and satellite communications infrastructure. During 1999, Motorola entered into a 10-year agreement with Sun Microsystems, enabling Motorola to deliver Internet protocol-based network servers, base station controllers, and base stations for wireless networks based on Sun's software.

The Commercial, Government, and Industrial Systems unit (14 percent of sales) provides total system solutions, including infrastructure and non-consumer two-way radio products.

The Other Products segment (10 percent of sales) is comprised of the Integrated Electronics Systems Sector, the Internet and Networking Group, and the Network Management Group.

Shortcomings to Bear in Mind

■ Lamella Rutherford has been shopping for a mobile phone at Carphone Warehouse in London's financial district. She likes some Nokia and Siemens models but is not impressed with one made by Motorola. Motorola is trying to change that image.

According to analysts, Europe leads the United States in wireless technology. Three year ago, Motorola introduced a fresh line of more powerful phones, began adding another 2,000 factory jobs in Europe, and even hired fashion models to promote its products. So far, the company's market share has not budged, but the company is convinced its efforts will soon pay off. In 1999, Motorola lost a further 2.1 percent share to competition.

In the words of one analyst, "For every Motorola product you look at, there will be another that is more desirable, whether from a design aspect or a brand perception." He estimates that Motorola mobile-phone share in Europe slipped to 14 percent in 1999, from 16.1 percent the prior year.

Europe is a crucial battleground for every mobile-phone maker. Western Europe bought a record 93 million mobile phones in 1999, compared with 48.3 million sold in the United States. What's more, Europe is also everyone's favorite testing ground: If you can sell a cellular phone to a finicky European, you can probably sell it to anyone else.

- Motorola's reputation as a technology leader has taken a hit over Iridium, the high-profile satellite-phone project whose principal backers include Motorola. In 1999, Iridium filed for bankruptcy-court protection. However, Motorola has continued to defend the $5-billion project, even as Iridium's problems have continued to pile up.

In the fourth quarter of 1999, Motorola announced that it would take a charge of $500 million, a move that essentially wrote off the company's entire exposure to Iridium. Moreover, the charge brought the total to more than $2.3 billion—eclipsing even the huge corporate misstep that the Quaker Oats Company made a few years ago with its acquisition of Snapple, the beverage maker, which ultimately cost Quaker Oats $1.4 billion.

In March of 2000, after its search for new investors failed, Iridium moved to shut off the innovative phone and messaging service it designed to reach the remotest regions of the world.

Iridium told Judge Arthur Gonzalez of the federal bankruptcy court in the Southern District of New York that it wanted to end commercial service to its remaining customers and start the tricky process of destroying its constellation of 74 satellites. Lawyers for Iridium said it would take up to $50 million and the rest of 2000 to program the destruction of the network of satellites Iridium spent billions to create.

- Motorola's recent purchase of General Instrument for $17 billion will dilute earnings by about $.15 per share in 2000. The shares of Motorola dropped 8.5 percent on the day the deal became known in the fall of 1999. One long-time stockholder grumbled, "This is one of the worst ideas I've ever seen."

Reasons to Buy

- In February 2000, Motorola announced that it had formed a new unit in its semiconductor products sector that will focus on "emerging" accounts, smaller customers such as start-ups that need technology to get their businesses growing. The new unit, called the Standard Embedded Solutions Group, will free up other divisions to focus on the bigger original equipment manufacturers. At the same time, it will give Motorola access to some smaller businesses that may one day be giants, said Mario Rivas, who was named to head the new unit. "Clearly, the strategy is customer intimacy." he said. "There are a lot of start-up companies. It is to our advantage that we service them early in the game. When they get purchased by large OEM customers, Motorola's technology will already be in use, and the OEMs will need Motorola as a supplier."

■ In late 1999, Motorola announced that it had received contracts totaling $228 million from two Chinese communications networks to upgrade and enhance their mobile systems, including cellular phones and pagers. China Unicom awarded five contracts, totaling $163 million, to Motorola's Network Solutions Sector for the expansion of mobile communications systems in the provinces of Jiangsu, Guangdong, Fujian, Shandong, and Xinjiang, according to Motorola.

Motorola installed additional microcellular and macro-cellular base stations that increased the capacity of the networks by 1.65 million subscribers. China Unicom serves 4.7 million subscribers. China Mobile also awarded a contract to Motorola worth $65 million to increase capacity of its network in Sichuan province, China's most populous, by 700,000 subscribers. The work for both companies was completed in mid-2000.

■ In the first quarter of 2000, Motorola acquired General Instrument Corporation, the leading maker of cable set-top boxes, with a 72 percent share of the North American market. The number of set-top boxes in North American homes is expected to skyrocket from 20 million to 113 million over the next five years, according to Allied Business Intelligence, a technology research company.

Most analysts said the merger was a good fit, since it teamed General Instrument, a cable-equipment powerhouse with little brand-name recognition, with Motorola, a global technology leader whose name is linked to everything from the first car radios to the latest cellular phones.

"A major focus for them is broadband technology," Mona Eraiba, an analyst at Gruntal & Company, said of the Motorola-General Instrument deal. "There are going to be set-top boxes with cable modems and satellite technology. This is really a chance to deploy the technology." Motorola is already the leading maker of cable modems, which can deliver cable programming into the personal computer. Now the company can combine that technology and its ability to feed data into a set-top box and cable infrastructure devised by General Instrument that delivers everything from interactive video to electronic commerce capacities.

Wall Street analysts say that leading telecommunications, cable, and media companies are scrambling to find partners in the expectation that many of the technologies will converge. Wireless phones, televisions, video games, and other devices will no longer have distinct voice, data, and video applications. They will be one—or at least linked through cable and wireless ports—that can deliver high-quality video and audio.

■ In the latter part of 1999, Motorola announced a new chip design that is meant to support a wide range of cellular telephone standards while offering more computer-like features. The new Motorola system, which is known as the DSP56690 baseband processor, comes with both a microprocessor and a specialized digital signal processor capable of handling a variety of cellular telephone technical formats. Unlike Japan and Europe, which mainly have single cellular telephone standards, the United States remains a hodgepodge of competing cellular formats.

The new chip is part of Motorola's effort to move its chip production beyond supplying the company's own cell-phone business and toward competing directly in the cellular market with chip makers like Texas Instruments, Royal Philips Electronics, and Qualcomm. In 1999, 225 million cellular phones were sold worldwide, accounting for the sale of

$10.7 billion worth of semiconductors, according to researchers at International Data Corporation, a market research firm in Mountain View, California.

Motorola said its new chips, which became available in the first quarter of 2000, make it possible for a telephone designer to build a single device capable of working with a variety of cell phone standards. But the company said it expected the new processor's "universal" architecture to enable a manufacture to use the same basic design for a variety of phone models that would each be intended for use with a specific transmission format.

The new chips have a variety of data-oriented features, including the ability to run Web browsers and the Java programming language widely used on the World Wide Web, as well as allowing for connections to display screens and the USB serial ports by which a variety of devices can be connected to personal computers.

■ Fully-fledged wireless Internet edged closer in early 2000 when British palmtop computer group Psion Plc said it and Motorola were developing mobile devices for launch in the first half of 2001. "The intention is to put the Internet in the user's pocket," said Psion's CEO David Levin. "This will be full web browsing as we understand it."

Full remote access at present requires a laptop computer linked to a cell phone at best, while some wireless handsets can deliver a low-tech version of the Internet.

Mr. Levin predicted Psion's new format with integrated voice and data capabilities being developed with U.S. wireless telephone handset maker and communications group Motorola would quickly become a major global mass market. "In a number of years' time, everybody will have a pocket Internet terminal. Inasmuch as the PC has spread and then the mobile phone has spread, so the pocket Internet terminal will go the same way," he said.

Total assets: $28,728 million
Current ratio: 1.35
Common shares outstanding: 2,145 million
Return on 1999 shareholders equity: 7.9%

		1999	1998	1997	1996	1995	1994	1993	1992
Revenues (millions)		30931	29398	29794	27973	27037	22245	16963	13303
Net income (millions)		1297	347	1338	1239	1781	1560	1022	576
Earnings per share		.69	.19	.73	.68	.98	.88	.59	.36
Dividends per share		.16	.16	.16	.15	.13	.10	.07	.07
Price	High	49.8	22.0	30.0	22.8	27.5	20.4	17.9	8.9
	Low	20.3	12.8	18.0	14.7	17.2	14.0	8.1	3.0

INCOME

National City Corporation

P.O. Box 5756, Dept. 2101 ◻ **Cleveland, Ohio 44101-0756** ◻ **Investor contact: Jeffrey C. Douglas (800) 622-4204** ◻ **Dividend reinvestment plan is available: (800) 622-6757** ◻ **Web site: www.national-city.com** ◻ **Listed: NYSE** ◻ **Ticker symbol: NCC** ◻ **S&P rating: A-** ◻ **Value Line financial strength rating: A**

Based on the changing preferences of consumers, National City is changing the way it delivers financial products and services.

More than a third of traditional branches will be converted by the end of 2000 to the "Bank Express" model, improving the customer service environment and efficiency of National City's 13,000 retail professionals. Many consumers also like the convenient hours and locations of some 100 branches in grocery stores and other retail sites.

Company Profile

National City provides broad-based banking and financial Services to about 8.5 million consumers in Ohio, Pennsylvania, Kentucky, Michigan, Illinois, and Indiana. Services are delivered through more than 1,200 branch office, more than 1,800 ATMs, and 3 telephone banking centers handling a monthly average of 4.5 million calls.

A growing number of customers choose the convenience of National City's online banking service at www.national-city.com. Enhancements planned for 2000 will increase the Web site's versatility, functionality, ease of use, and interconnectivity.

Since David A. Daberko was named chairman and chief executive officer of National City Corporation in mid-1995, the company, once known only to Ohioans, has more than doubled in size through acquisitions.

National City subsidiaries provide financial services that meet a wide range of customer needs, including commercial and retail banking, trust and investment services, item processing, mortgage banking, and credit card processing.

Retail Banking

The retail banking business includes the deposit-gathering branch franchise, along with lending to individuals and small businesses. Lending activities include residential mortgages, indirect and direct consumer installment loans, leasing, credit cards, and student lending.

Fee-Based Businesses

The fee-based businesses include institutional trust, mortgage banking, and item processing.

• Institutional trust includes employee benefit administration, mutual fund management, charitable and endowment services, and custodial services.

• Mortgage banking includes the origination of mortgages through retail offices and broker networks and mortgage servicing.

• Item processing is conducted by National City's majority-owned subsidiary, National Processing, Inc. (NYSE:NAP) and includes merchant credit card processing, airline ticket processing, check guarantee services, and receivables and payables processing services.

Customer Needs and Preferences

To gain insight into customer preferences, National City has been making substantial investments in data warehouse technology to more effectively capture and manage customer information. This capability has already resulted in more effective cross-selling and has given the bank tools to better understand and predict customer needs and preferences.

The bank is well aware that customer demand for financial services transcends traditional time –and place limitations. To that end, the company initiated a multiyear plan to reconfigure its branch delivery system—reducing traditional full-service branches while expanding nontraditional alternatives. This includes in-store locations, limited-service facilities, and off-site ATMs—which, along with better call-center capability, makes it easier and more convenient for customers to do business with National City.

Shortcomings to Bear in Mind

■ National City has a lackluster record of growth. In the 1989–1999 period, earnings per share expanded from $1.09 to $2.22, a compound annual growth rate of 7.4 percent. In the same 10-year span, however, dividends per share outperformed EPS growth, climbing from $.43 to $1.09, a growth rate of 9.7 percent.

- In recent years, banks have been finding it increasingly difficult to expand revenues. Those with the broadest product mix are more likely to have an easier time registering top-line growth. In addition, savings from cost-cutting efforts, which have propelled earnings for many large banks in recent years, are becoming more difficult to come by, placing greater emphasis on top-line growth. Loan growth also remains a regional phenomenon, with strength in areas of the Southeast and Midwest where economies continue to grow at a rate above the national average.

- Although loan demand remains strong in the company's economically healthy Midwestern market, the growth in low-cost deposit balances hasn't kept pace. To support the robust loan growth, National City has been relying more on short-term borrowed funds, which have become more expensive as interest rates have risen. Competition is also squeezing spreads on commercial loans. As a consequence, net interest income has been slipping from year-earlier levels.

Reasons to Buy

- In corporate banking, National City's second-largest business, the bank has worked hard to retain its position as the number one middle-market lender in its region. The bank's markets have been economically vibrant, as evidenced by low rates of unemployment and significant growth in small and medium-size businesses over the past several years. The bank's decentralized system of credit approval permits quick responsiveness to customer needs. At the same time, the company's product capability is second to none. For example, NCC introduced an innovative lending product, Corporate Select, that utilizes built-in interest rate protection options inside a conventional loan. This helps companies manage risk in a seamless, straightforward manner. Corporate Select offers a competitive advantage in winning and strengthening customer relationships. There is no comparable product currently available in the market. Through initiatives such as these and a strong team of relationship managers, National City has been able to maintain or increase market share in virtually all of its markets. What's more, the company has been particularly successful in western Pennsylvania, which it entered through the merger with Integra Financial Corporation.

- In 1999, National City acquired First Franklin Financial Companies, a leading wholesale originator of nonconforming home mortgages. This acquisition, combined with Altegra, the existing nonconforming mortgage lender, placed National City in the top 10 nationally in this type of financing.

- National City is one of the five top originators of federally guaranteed student loans in the country. What's more, in dealer finance, the company is ranked as the fifth-largest noncaptive originator of retail loans and leases. National City offers competitive credit card products and indirect consumer installment loans and leases for automotive, marine, recreational vehicle, heavy equipment, and property improvement.

- National City provides professional investment services to individuals, families, and businesses. Through an integrated structure encompassing personal trust, investment management, private banking, and brokerage, National City offers a single-source solution for clients to manage their personal and family wealth. Clients maintain relationships with skilled financial professionals, and state-of-the-art technology enables efficient access to trust, investment, and brokerage services.

National City's primary objective is to produce sustainable, above-average investment performance. Offering 39 mutual funds, National City covers the full spectrum of investment styles. In 1999, seven mutual funds in the Armada and Parkstone fund families earned impressive four-star or five-star ratings (the two best ratings) from Morningstar, an industry rating service, for their relative performance over the previous five-year period.

National City also provides professional investment services for businesses. The PlanWorks online reporting service allows 401(k) participants to check their balances, fund performance, and elections in a secure Internet-based environment. In a survey of stock transfer clients conducted by Group Five, Inc., National City's stock transfer

service was recognized as the industry leader in customer service and satisfaction in each of the last two years.

- In 1999, National City expanded its presence in the Chicago and Detroit metropolitan areas and opened an office serving corporate clients in the Philadelphia market. There are some 150 relationship managers covering these markets, up from 70 in 1998, and more are being added in 2000. These markets provide significant opportunity for growth, given their high concentration of small- and middle-market businesses, as well as Fortune 1000 corporations.

- In early 2000, National City's stock was selling in the low 20s, down from a 1998 high of $39. Thus, the dividend provided a well-covered yield of more than 5 percent. When you read this book, the yield may not be as attractive. But if it is—and you are looking for a dependable income stock—National City would be a solid long-term holding.

Total assets: $87,121 million
Return on Assets in 1999: 1.67%
Common shares outstanding: 617 million
Return on 1999 shareholders' equity: 22.6%

		1999	1998	1997	1996	1995	1994	1993	1992
Loans (millions)		60204	58011	39573	35830	25732	22566	20843	18354
Net income (millions)		1404	1333	807	733	465	429	404	347
Earnings per share		2.22	2.00	1.83	1.64	1.48	1.32	1.21	1.05
Dividends per share		1.09	.97	.86	.94	.65	.59	.53	.47
Price	High	37.8	38.8	33.8	23.6	16.9	14.5	14.0	12.4
	Low	22.1	28.5	21.3	15.3	12.6	11.9	11.6	9.0

INCOME

New Plan Excel Realty Trust, Inc.

1120 Avenue of the Americas ▢ New York, New York 10036 ▢ Investor contact: Ms. Stacy Lipschitz (212) 869-3000 Ext. 3359 ▢ Dividend reinvestment plan is available: (212) 869-3000 ▢ Web site: www.newplanexcel.com ▢ Listed: NYSE ▢ Ticker symbol: NXL ▢ S&P rating: not rated ▢ Value Line financial strength rating: A

Real estate investment trusts are, by their vary nature, less risky than other sectors and the stock market as a whole. In good

times and bad, REIT performance across all real estate sectors traditionally is less volatile than the Standard & Poor's 500, moving at about half the rate of the popular index.

For stockholders, the predictable performance of REITs offers a safer haven in times of turmoil. Because income is generated from rent on leased space, REITs have a fairly steady revenue stream, says one analyst.

Shares of REITs trade like the stock of other public companies, but they have a hybrid nature—part bond, part common stock—which many investors don't fully understand. REITs can avoid paying corporate income tax if they pass on nearly all of their net income to shareholders in the form of dividends. These dividends create a steady stream of income—typically 5 percent or more—that is similar to yield investments such as bonds. But, unlike bonds, shares of REITs can increase in value if the underlying property appreciates and if the REIT can raise rents.

Company Profile

New Plan Excel Realty Trust is one of the nation's largest real estate companies, focusing on the ownership, management, acquisition, development, and redevelopment of community and neighborhood shopping centers and garden apartment communities. New Plan is also one of the oldest real estate companies in the nation, incorporated in 1926. It became a REIT in 1972.

The company operates as a self-administered and self-managed REIT, with a national portfolio of 357 properties and total assets of about $3 billion. The company is a blue-chip REIT, with an investment grade rating of A from Standard & Poor's and A2 from Moody's. What's more, it has an exceptional—or incredible—track record of 83 consecutive quarters of dividend increases.

Its properties are strategically situated across 31 states and include 297 retail centers, with a total of about 37 million square feet of gross leasable area; 53 garden apartment communities containing 12,560 units; and 7 miscellaneous commercial properties.

Community shopping centers range from 100,000 to 600,000 square feet. They are typically anchored by a supermarket and/or a drug store. Other merchants might include a dry cleaner, a stationer, apparel shops, restaurants, and so on. Among the tenants in these malls are Wal-Mart, Kmart, J.C. Penney, Winn Dixie, Food Lion, CVS Drug Stores, Ames department stores, Kroger, Rite Aid, Office Max, and Marshalls.

Community centers tend to be recession-resistant because most goods and services sold by tenants are considered consumer necessities. Also, these merchants are not likely to compete with those that deal on the Internet.

Garden apartments are two-story apartments with landscaped common areas and amenities such as tennis courts and swimming pools. In the past, New Plan's acquisition strategy has focused on buying middle-income properties away from metropolitan areas for less than replacement cost. Management believes that tenants in these buildings move less frequently, and that below-market rents provide room for future rent hikes.

Shortcomings to Bear in Mind

- According to Glenn J. Rufrano, CEO of New Plan, "1999 was a challenging year for the company, as we worked to assimilate the Excel Realty Trust portfolio. We believe this integration is now behind us, and we have started the process of building a foundation to move our company forward."

Reasons to Buy

- The company is beginning to realize returns on the renovation of its garden apartments. At the end of 1999, these units were 91 percent leased (this excludes three properties then under renovation). For example, renovation began in the first quarter of 1999 at Turtle Creek in Greenville, South Carolina and at Ashford Place in Clarksville, Tennessee. By year-end, as a result of this work, occupancy at these properties increased from 82 percent to 92 percent, and from 84 percent to 95 percent, respectively.

- The company has cultivated sophisticated problem-solving skills, enabling it to execute a strategy of acquiring undermanaged properties and then managing, renovating, and repositioning the properties to drive growth and property cash flows. Substantial upside value is created for the company's real estate assets by optimizing tenant mix, increasing occupancy, rolling leases, adding space, and implementing renovations. Once profitability has been maximized, properties are disposed of and funds redeployed at higher yields.

- As a result of these strategies, the company has built a high-quality portfolio of real estate assets that is well-diversified by both geography and tenant mix. The company's retail centers are usually anchored by brand-name supermarkets or discount drug store chains. These properties are strategically situated in 31 states, and the 10 largest tenants account for 17.1 percent of total annualized base rent. This approach moderates exposure to regional economic cycles while at the same time enhancing the company's pricing power. The garden apartments are located in middle-income suburban areas where residents are less transient.

- With a strong, low-leverage balance sheet, coupled with investment-grade bond ratings from Standard & Poor's and Moody's, the company has access to the capital markets at a relatively low cost.

- In early 2000, the company announced the appointment of Glenn J. Rufrano, then age 50, to serve as its chief executive. He succeeded Arnold Laubich, who retired after 50 years of service.

Mr. Rufrano has been a partner for over 17 years at The O'Connor Group, a diversified real estate investment firm. He acted as both chief financial officer and chief operating officer during this period. He brings to New Plan Excel Realty Trust a solid knowledge of corporate finance and property fundamentals, as well as established relationships with real estate investors, including public and private pension funds, insurance companies, foundations, and endowments.

- The REIT industry has proven itself to be a particularly successful form of ownership. The reasons for that starts out with the 1960 Act of Congress that enabled the REIT industry to get started. What it did was to provide a structure that is free of income tax, similar to the mutual fund industry. It is a pass-through type of structure, which means that by law REITs are to distribute 95 percent of their taxable earnings to their shareholders. The main reason for their existence was that Congress felt that REITs would enable the small investor to participate in the benefits of real estate ownership.

- One of the drawbacks of real estate has always been the lack of liquidity. With a REIT, you have complete and instant liquidity. Another point is that syndicators require large individual investments from participants. With REITs, you can buy one share or a million shares, so you have an ability to buy into the largest pieces of property with the smallest amount of money.

- The majority of the company's leases contain provisions to mitigate the adverse impact of inflation. Such provisions include clauses enabling the company to receive percentage rents, which generally increase as prices rise, and/or escalation clauses, which are typically related to increases in the consumer price index or similar inflation indexes.

In addition, the company believes that many of its existing lease rates are below current market levels for comparable space and that upon renewal or rerental such rates may be increased to current market rates. This belief is based upon an analysis of relevant market conditions, including a comparison of comparable rental rates and upon the fact that many of such leases have been in place for a number of years and may not contain escalation clauses sufficient to match the increase in market rental rates over such time.

Most of the company's leases require the tenant to pay its share of operating expenses, including common area maintenance, real estate taxes, and insurance, thereby reducing the company's exposure to increases in costs and operating expenses resulting from inflation.

■ New Plan is actively managing its properties, adding new ones as they become available and selling those with less promise. For instance, in the final quarter of 1999, the company completed

the acquisition of Westland Crossing, a 147,000-square-foot shopping center situated in Westland, Michigan, for about $10 million. Anchor tenants—a key ingredient in shopping malls—include Office Depot, Michaels Stores, and Frank's Nursery & Crafts. In total, five properties were acquired in 1999 for an aggregate of about $40 million. These properties include four shopping centers with a combined square footage of 453,000 and one garden apartment community with 176 units. In January the company acquired Dover Park Plaza, a 60,000-square-foot center situated in Yardville, New Jersey, for about $3 million. The property is anchored by Acme Markets and CVS, a major drug store chain. It is 100 percent leased.

Conversely, the company sold several properties in 1999. During the fourth quarter, for instance, New Plan completed the sale of three properties for an aggregate of about $25 million. In total, seven properties were sold in 1999 for an aggregate of about $37 million, including five shopping centers and two garden apartment communities.

At the end of 1999, the company's retail and commercial properties were 92 percent leased.

Total assets: $2,954 million
Common shares outstanding: 89 million
Return on 1999 shareholders' equity: 8.7%

	1999	1998	1997	1996	1995	1994	1993	1992
Total revenues (millions)	438	419	202	163	126	96	65	48
Net income (millions)	150	154	77	70	63	51	42	39
Funds from operations	2.18	2.06	1.74	1.60	1.47	1.27	1.02	.97
Earnings per share	1.43	1.49	1.31	1.25	1.19	1.04	.87	.86
Dividends per share	1.64	1.62	1.44	1.40	1.36	1.32	1.28	1.21
Price High	22.6	26.1	26.0	25.6	23.0	24.4	26.4	26.1
Low	14.8	17.9	21.4	19.9	19.6	18.8	21.5	19.6

Nicor Inc.

P.O. Box 3014 □ Naperville, Illinois 60566-7014 □ Investor contact: Mark Knox (630) 305-9500, ext. 2529 □ Dividend reinvestment plan is available: (630) 305-9500 □ Web site: www.nicorinc.com □ Listed: NYSE □ Ticker symbol: GAS □ S&P rating: A- □ Value Line financial strength rating: A+

Nicor Gas, Nicor's principal subsidiary, has an enviable service territory, one of the lowest cost structures in the industry, a strategic location in the domestic supply grid, valuable assets, solid customer relations, and a reputable brand name.

In addition, Tropical Shipping gives the company an element of profitable diversification that many other utilities are seeking. Finally, as was the case in the deregulation of the telecommunications industry, regulatory changes in the energy industry have opened up several growth opportunities.

Company Profile

Nicor is a holding company. Its principal business is Nicor Gas (previously Northern Illinois Gas), the nation's fifth-largest gas distribution company. Nicor Gas delivers natural gas to more than 1.9 million customers, including transportation service, gas storage, and gas supply backup to about 40,000 commercial and industrial customers who purchase their own gas supplies.

The Nicor Gas subsidiary operates in a 17,000-square-mile territory, covering 544 communities in northern Illinois, excluding Chicago.

The company operates seven underground gas storage facilities. On an annual basis, GAS—the company's ticker symbol—cycles about 130 billion cubic feet (Bcf) in and out of storage. Having ample storage is particularly important during cold winter months when there is a huge demand on the pipelines. Nicor has one of the most extensive storage facilities in the industry.

Nicor Gas' service territory has a stable economic base that provides strong and balanced demand among residential, commercial, and industrial natural gas users. Residential customers account for about 40 percent of deliveries, while industrial and commercial customers account for about 35 percent and 25 percent of deliveries, respectively.

Nicor also owns Tropical Shipping, which transports containerized freight between the Port of Palm Beach, Florida and 23 ports in the Caribbean and Central America. Tropical Shipping is recognized as a dependable, on-time carrier in its operating region.

Tropical Shipping is one of the largest carriers of containerized cargo in the region. The company has a reputation for providing quality, on-time service and has established dominant market shares in many of the ports it serves. Markets include the Bahamas, the Cayman Islands, the Dominican Republic, the Virgin Islands, and the Eastern Caribbean.

To improve profitability, Tropical plans to increase vessel utilization and reduce costs. Future growth is anticipated, mostly from higher-margin services to existing and new markets. Tropical Shipping accounts for 11 percent of Nicor's operating income.

Shortcomings to Bear in Mind

- By their very nature, public utilities are for conservative investors who are seeking above-average yield. However, growth is modest. In the 1989–1999 period, for instance, Nicor—like most utilities—did not enjoy explosive growth. In that stretch, earnings per share advanced from $1.99 to $2.58, a compound annual growth rate of 2.6

percent. In the same 10-year period, dividends per share advanced from $1.00 to $1.54, a compound growth rate of 4.4 percent.

■ All public utilities are vulnerable to shifts in interest rates. In fact, interest-rate changes are the most potent factor affecting the action of utility stocks. There are two reasons: for one thing, utilities borrow a lot of money, and higher interest rates can hurt. Secondly, many investors buy utilities for income. If they are convinced that they can do better elsewhere, they may be tempted to sell their utility shares, thus depressing them to lower levels.

■ The weather has an impact on electric as well as natural gas utilities. Electric companies like hot summers so they can sell more air conditioning. They like cold winters so they can sell more space heating. For their part, natural gas utilities don't worry much about the summer, since they typically lose money during those months. But in the winter, they want plenty of cold weather. If they don't get it, their profits are hit hard.

■ From 1993 through 1998, Tropical Shipping's operating income grew at a compound annual rate of 12 percent. However, shipping operating income declined to $22.5 million in 1999, from $27.6 million in 1998, as the positive impact of an increase in volumes shipped was more than offset by lower prices, higher operating expenses, and reduced charter revenues. The pricing declines resulted primarily from Tropical Shipping's need to respond to increased competition in the Eastern Caribbean. In addition, heavy hurricane activity in the fall of 1999 hampered normal business activities, particularly in the tourism sector.

In the first quarter of 2000, results for Tropical Shipping began to show improvement, helped by increased volumes and firmer prices.

■ In 1999, Nicor stock was down more than 20 percent. However, it was in good company, since many other gas and electric utilities declined as well. According to analysts, a number of factors were at work. For one thing, the winter was warmer than normal across much of the country. Rising interest rates also hurt. Finally, it was a year when investors were enamored with high-tech stocks, not stodgy income stocks.

Reasons to Buy

■ Nicor Gas typically accounts for about 90 percent of Nicor Inc.'s consolidated operating income. The company is widely regarded as one of the best companies in the natural gas distribution industry, and it consistently ranks at or near the top of its industry in terms of operating efficiency and financial returns.

■ In the company's gas distribution business, a performance-based plan went into effect January 1, 2000. The plan establishes economic incentives for Nicor Gas to further reduce already low gas costs. Nicor also purchased weather insurance to mitigate the impact of extremely warm weather on Nicor Gas's financial results in 2000. The company's earnings will still fluctuate with variations in weather patterns, but results will be less susceptible to the impact of unusually warm weather.

■ In the company's energy-related ventures, there have been several important developments:

● Nicor Energy is off to an excellent start in retail energy services. The company is one of the leading retail natural gas marketers in the Midwest, and in 1999 it began marketing electricity.

● Through Nicor Enerchange, the company is building a niche wholesale natural gas marketing business.

- Nicor recently agreed to become an equal partner with Natural Gas Pipeline Company of America in the proposed Horizon Pipeline, a project to provide additional gas service to northern Illinois.
- Nicor remains one of the largest operators of underground natural gas storage in the United States, and industry developments are providing the company with opportunities to significantly increase the value these assets can bring to the company.

■ Changes in the energy industry made it possible for Nicor to enter the market for energy services, and as those changes continue, other opportunities have emerged. One of those opportunities is in the market for electric power generation. The company believes power generation is a logical extension of Nicor's strategic focus as it establishes Nicor as a total energy provider, increases deliveries in its regulated gas distribution business, and builds on the knowledge it has developed from cogeneration projects over the years.

■ Public utilities generally rely on a greater amount of debt in their balance sheets than industrial companies. For its part, Nicor is exceptionally strong, with 64 percent of capitalization in the form of shareholders' equity. At the other extreme, some utilities have only 35 percent in equity.

- One of the reasons Nicor Gas has been able to increase gas deliveries in recent years is the upward trend in diversified uses of natural gas. The company continues to make steady inroads in such markets as electric power generation, cogeneration, and large-tonnage gas air conditioning.

■ At Nicor Gas, earnings growth will come from a combination of customer additions, increases in gas deliveries to existing customers, and efforts to minimize costs.

Beyond the company's traditional gas distribution business, Nicor has developed several new sources of revenue. Examples include utilization of its transmission network and storage facilities to provide services to pipelines, gas distribution companies, and gas marketers. The company has also established several unregulated businesses that provide value-added services to Nicor's customers.

■ Nicor has a flexible supply position. Nicor Gas has interconnects with five interstate pipelines, providing access to most major gas-producing areas in North America. This allows for a diverse supply portfolio that helps assure reliability and competitive pricing.

■ Largely because of its location on the nation's pipeline grid, Nicor Gas has been able to use its transmission and storage assets in nontraditional ways through operation of the Chicago Hub and by providing transportation and storage services for others.

Total assets: $2,452 million
Current ratio: 0.59
Common shares outstanding: 47 million
Return on 1999 shareholders' equity: 15.9%

		1999	1998	1997	1996	1995	1994	1993	1992
Revenues (millions)		1547	1465	1993	1851	1480	1609	1674	1547
Net income (millions)		124	116	128	121	100	110	109	95
Earnings per share		2.58	2.31	2.55	2.42	1.96	2.07	1.97	1.67
Dividends per share		1.54	1.48	1.40	1.31	1.28	1.26	1.22	1.18
Price	High	42.9	44.4	42.9	37.1	28.5	29.3	31.6	25.8
	Low	31.2	37.1	30.0	25.4	21.8	21.9	24.1	19.0

Nordson Corporation

28601 Clemens Road ◻ Westlake, Ohio 44145-1119 ◻ Investor contact: Barbara T. Price (440) 414-5344 ◻ Dividend reinvestment plan is available: (800) 622-6757 ◻ Web site: www.nordson.com ◻ Fiscal year ends Sunday closest to October 31 ◻ Listed: Nasdaq ◻ Ticker symbol: NDSN ◻ S&P rating: A- ◻ Value Line financial strength rating: B++

Nordson Corporation designs, manufactures, and markets systems that apply adhesives, sealants, and coatings to a broad range of consumer and industrial products during manufacturing operations.

Nordson's high value-added product line includes customized electronic-control technology for the precise application of materials to meet customers' productivity, quality, and environmental management targets.

Nordson products are used around the world in the appliance, automotive, construction, container, converting, electronics, food and beverage, furniture, graphic arts, metal finishing, nonwovens, packaging, and other diverse industries.

Nordson markets its products through four international sales divisions—North America, Europe, Japan, and Pacific South. These organizations are supported by a network of direct operations in 32 countries. Consistent with this strategy, more than 50 percent of the company's revenues are generated outside the United States.

Nordson has manufacturing facilities in Ohio, Georgia, Alabama, California, Connecticut, Germany, the Netherlands, Sweden, and the United Kingdom.

Company Profile

The U.S. Automatic Company, the parent of Nordson, was founded in Amherst, Ohio in 1909. Initially, the company specialized in high-volume, low-cost screw machine parts for the burgeoning automotive industry.

In the years following World War II, Walter Nord, along with sons Eric and Evan, searched for a proprietary product to serve as a basis for future growth. This resulted in the acquisition of patents covering the "hot airless" method of spraying paint and other coating materials. The company later expanded its product line to include air-spray equipment and incorporated the highly efficient electrostatic process in both airless and air-spray painting systems.

Beginning in the late 1960s, Nordson pioneered the technology and equipment for applying powder coatings with the development of the compact and efficient cartridge-type recovery/recycle systems. Nordson has steadily refined its cartridge-booth technology and is an innovator in all aspects of the powder coating process for both organic and porcelain enamel applications. Today, Nordson is the acknowledged industry leader in powder coatings systems.

Each year, the worldwide appliance industry transforms millions of square feet of prefinished sheet steel into consumer durables, including refrigerators, ranges, washers, and dryers. Before appliances are assembled, manufacturers use Nordson flatline powder coating systems to apply flexible porcelain enamel "powder paint" that quickly turns steel into gleaming panels of white, almond, and black metal that can be bent and wrapped to achieve new model designs. The benefit to manufacturers is increased line speed, higher quality, and lower operating costs. Consumers benefit, too: these uniformly coated appliances are more attractive and less prone to corrosion.

Shortcomings to Bear in Mind

- The company's record of growth leaves something to be desired. In the 1989–1999 period, earnings per share advanced from $1.77 to $2.96, which amounts to a compound annual growth rate of only 5.3 percent. In the same 10-year span, dividends performed much better, climbing from $0.32 in 1989 to $0.96 in 1999, a growth rate of 11.6 percent. What's more, the all-important payout ratio is still a conservative 32 percent.

Reasons to Buy

- Nordson's finishing businesses have always set a high priority on new product developments that enhance customer productivity. As industry continues to demand increased efficiencies and cost controls, these developments are paying off handsomely for the powder coating, liquid finishing, and container businesses.

    While powder coating offers distinct advantages over liquid finishing in applying paint to many types of products, liquid technologies have held the lead in quick color change. Now, Nordson's newest powder coating system introduces a technology that makes color changes possible in as little as 15 minutes. "Fast color changes makes Nordson a market winner in powder coating," says Mark Gacka, vice president. "These new offerings allow manufacturers to change colors faster than ever before. And it makes powder coating economical for a wider range of industrial uses."

- To further support the company's growth programs, Nordson completed four acquisitions in 1999, expanding total sales in the fast-growing, high-technology segments of industry. The addition of Advanced Plasma Systems, Inc. and March Instruments, Inc., for example, enabled Nordson to enter the plasma treatment systems business, which complements existing company operations that serve electronics and general industrial markets.

    Other acquisitions added to Nordson's capability to manufacture ultraviolet lamps domestically and significantly strengthen the company's position as a supplier of cold adhesive equipment.

    In addition, the late 1998 acquisition of JM Laboratories, a major producer of nonwoven fiber systems, continues to meet Nordson's expectations. JM Laboratories's sales are growing at double-digit rates, and management has continued optimism for this business—supported by newly developed technologies and strong demand from growing markets.

- "Finishers of consumer and industrial products come to Nordson for the most efficient methods to apply liquid paints and powder coatings," says Sam Dawson, vice president of Nordson. "Spraying coating materials is the easy part . . . our ability to control their precise application is where we deliver real value to our customers."

    Nordson markets complete material application systems that help manufacturers improve product quality while lowering material usage.

    "Today, finishers want to reduce the environmental impact of their operations," says Dawson. "That's why Nordson focuses on providing systems that apply solvent-free powder coatings and low-solvent liquid paints. Finishers who convert to these finishes can meet environmental goals and reduce waste-disposal costs without sacrificing quality.

    "Proactive involvement in the industries we serve, through memberships in professional associations and relationships with coatings suppliers, is key to understanding our customers' needs," Dawson adds. "This involvement, combined with our experience base, gives Nordson two competitive advantages— the best equipment available and the fastest new-product cycle time."

- Nordson technology delivers precise applications of both hot and melt adhesive and cold glue—simultaneously—to tightly seal cases of agricultural products, beverages, and consumer packaged goods. The hot-melt adhesive delivers an instant bond to seal the cases. At the same time, the slower-setting cold glue permeates the paper fiber to ensure that packages remain intact regardless of the environmental conditions. This dual-gluing process ensures that shipments won't be rejected due to carton failure during transit—a substantial customer benefit.

- At the end of fiscal 1999, Nordson announced Action 2000, a company-wide initiative to accelerate growth and improve operational effectiveness. This far-reaching program combines both growth and cost-reduction initiatives, all geared to achieve specific performance targets.

A major component of Action 2000 is the realignment of the company's global adhesive systems businesses under the leadership of senior vice president Don McLane. Historically, Nordson organized its operations geographically. But as customers restructured globally and the challenges of Nordson's businesses became more diverse, management began to focus on lines of business across geographic areas. Action 2000 recognizes this need to serve global customers by realigning its adhesive systems businesses.

The restructuring of Nordson's adhesive systems businesses provides a platform to pursue a number of opportunities to improve and expand while delivering even better customer service. With six engineering design centers and nine manufacturing locations, opportunities exist to globalize regional product lines, consolidate operations, and speed time to market.

- Action 2000 also kicks off a company-wide e-commerce initiative that will accelerate Nordson's Web-based technologies. While the company already utilizes the World Wide Web extensively to communicate with and support customers, management believes the Internet will fundamentally change industrial commerce to a far greater degree and at a faster pace than it has seen thus far. Company officials will exploit these opportunities and make Nordson a prime example of how capital goods companies can use electronic media to grow and strengthen their businesses. The company's use of Web technology will reduce costs for both customers and itself, while strengthening the depth and texture of the company's customer relations.

- Nordson's strategy is to participate in the higher-growth segments of the global economy by expanding its expertise to electronic assembly and printed circuit board coating. In the future, as electronic parts become smaller, labor rates continue to increase in emerging countries, and electronics assembly become more complex, we will continue to see more highly automated electronic assembly processes. Management is convinced that Nordson will be a major participant in the market for electronics assembly equipment with internally developed products and acquired businesses.

- After years of preparation and thousands of work hours, Nordson's automotive systems group earned QS-9000 certification with TE supplement—the auto industry's version of the international ISO 9000 quality standard. And with it, Nordson has positioned itself as a supplier of choice with the Big Three auto manufacturers. Suppliers with QS-9000 certification are preferred because they reduce customers' auditing requirements and assure high-quality production. "Obtaining QS-9000 TE status reflects our commitment to the auto industry," says Robert A Dunn, Jr., vice president. "It's a standard that car makers will soon require of all suppliers and, at present, gives us a competitive edge."

Total assets: $592 million
Current ratio: 1.35
Common shares outstanding: 16 million
Return on 1999 shareholders' equity: 23%

	1999	1998	1997	1996	1995	1994	1993	1992
Revenues (millions)	700	661	637	609	581	507	462	426
Net income (millions)	50	47	50	53	53	47	41	40
Earnings per share	2.96	2.86	2.85	2.92	2.84	2.45	2.13	2.03
Dividends per share	.96	.88	.80	.72	.64	.56	.48	.44
Price High	65.9	52.4	65.0	65.0	61.0	63.0	54.8	57.0
Low	43.0	42.3	47.1	45.5	53.8	52.0	38.3	43.0

INCOME

PACCAR Inc.

777 106th Avenue NE ❑ Bellevue, WA 98004 ❑ Investor Contact: Ron E. Ranheim (425) 468-7425 ❑ Dividend reinvestment plan is not available ❑ Web site: www.paccar.com ❑ Listed: Nasdaq ❑ Ticker symbol: PCAR ❑ S&P rating: A- ❑ Value Line financial strength rating: A

Making heavy-duty trucks is clearly an industry with a reputation for feast or famine. The domestic heavy truck industry hit bottom in 1991 with 98,600 units. From that nadir, industry sales climbed through the 1990s, peaking at a record 263,000 units in 1999. For the moment at least, it looks like a peak, with sales in 2000 clearly ebbing.

With about twelve heavy truck makers, the world is awash in truck-making over-capacity. As a result, the industry is consolidating. The latest merger activity involves a Volvo mid-2000 agreement to buy Renault's Mack truck division, which will make Volvo number two in the world.

Despite the cyclicality of the industry, PACCAR has avoided red ink for more than a half century. Every year since 1939, in boom times and recessions, PACCAR has made money. The company has also paid a dividend every year since 1941.

Thanks to a family-dominated corporate culture that emphasizes lean operations, PACCAR is likely to continue its winning ways, in good times and bad. "They're probably one of the best-run truck companies in North America, if not the world," says Gary F. McManus, an analyst with J. P. Morgan Securities.

Company Profile

PACCAR is the world's number three truck maker, behind DaimlerChrysler and the Freightliner division of Navistar.

As a diversified, multinational company, PACCAR manufactures heavy-duty, on- and off-road Class 8 trucks sold around the world under the Kenworth, Peterbilt, DAF and Foden nameplates. The company competes in the North American Class 6-7 market with its medium-duty models assembled in North America and sold under the Peterbilt and Kenworth nameplates.

In addition, DAF manufactures Class 6-7 trucks in the Netherlands and Belgium for sale throughout Europe, the Middle East, and Africa and is the exclusive distributor in Europe for Class 4-5 trucks assembled by Leyland Trucks (UK).

PACCAR also manufactures and markets industrial winches, and competes in the truck parts aftermarket through its dealer network. Its plants are situated in the United States, Canada, Australia, Mexico, the United Kingdom, and the Netherlands.

Finance and leasing subsidiaries facilitate the sale of PACCAR products in many countries worldwide. Significant company assets are employed in financial services activities.

PACCAR maintains exceptionally high standards of quality for all its products: they are well-engineered, are highly customized for specific applications and sell in the premium segment of their markets, where they have a reputation for superior performance and pride of ownership.

A Look at PACCAR's History

In 1905, William Pigott, Sr. founded Seattle Car Manufacturing Company to produce railway and logging equipment at its plant in West Seattle. The company later merged with Twohy Brothers of Portland to become Pacific Car and Foundry Company, a name it retained for the next 55 years.

The company entered the heavy-duty truck market in 1945 with its first major acquisition, Kenworth Motor Truck Company of Seattle. Pacific Car and Foundry greatly expanded its heavy-duty truck capability with the purchase of Peterbilt Motors Company in 1958.

The acquisition of DAF Trucks N.V. in 1996 and Leyland Trucks in 1998 solidified PACCAR's position as one of the major truck manufacturers of the world. DAF Trucks, based in the Netherlands, has production facilities in Eindhoven, the Netherlands and Westerlo, Belgium. Leyland manufactures trucks at its plant in Lancashire, England.

Shortcomings to Bear in Mind

- U.S. sales of heavy-duty trucks are expected to decline 12 percent in 2000, to 231,500. For its part, PACCAR announced three rounds of layoffs in its domestic plants that build its Peterbilt and Kenworth models.

- Higher fuel costs and interest rates are keeping many truck buyers on the sidelines. But the company's biggest concern is the generous trade-in terms that its rivals are granting, in an effort to increase market share. Dealer lots are clogged with used trucks, and prices are sagging.

  On the other hand, PACCAR should fare better than most. Whereas a typical vehicle factory teems with robots and automated equipment, PACCAR's plants are manned by people. When times are slack, layoffs can cut costs. This works better than having to idle expensive equipment and machinery.

- In mid-2000, PACCAR had an attractive dividend yield. That's the good news. Unlike most companies, PACCAR does not maintain an ever-increasing dividend. Instead, it adjusts the payout, depending on its current earnings. For the most part, the dividend is about one-half of its earnings. This can mean that the payout will be cut back sharply during years when business is sagging. In 1990, for instance, the dividend dropped to $.43, compared with $1.09 the prior year. What's more, it remained below a dollar for four straight years (1990-1993).

Reasons to Buy

- PACCAR may be in a cyclical industry, but its record of earnings growth is impressive, nonetheless. In the 1989-1999 period, earnings per share advanced from $2.35 to $7.18, a compound annual growth rate of 11.8 percent. In the same 10-year stretch, dividends climbed from $1.09 to $2.40, a growth rate of 8.2 percent. Not bad numbers for a stock I am classifying in the income category.

- Peterbilt stays lean by purchasing 75 percent of every Peterbilt and Kenworth truck from outside vendors. The company builds none of its own engines or transmissions. Rather, PACCAR focuses on assembly, marketing, and design.

- In recent years, PACCAR has increased its operation abroad. Nearly a third of its business comes from outside North America. In Europe, solid business is helping to offset slack at home. As a result, the company has been increasing its capacity in that region.

- ePACCAR, a division of PACCAR Inc., announced that it had formed a venture with InfoMove in mid-2000. The joint venture delivers personalized, real time, location-specific traffic navigation to truck drivers in PACCAR's commercial vehicles. Through the partnership, Info-Move supplies ePACCAR with a suite of wireless applications to enhance truck operators' productivity. Using these applications, ePACCAR's systems alert truck drivers of traffic congestion along planned routes, plus recommended alternative routes and turn-by-turn driving directions.

"This partnership will allow PACCAR to provide its customers with the dynamic InfoMove traffic information they need to navigate their routes with safety and ease," said Peter Holland, president and CEO of InfoMove. "PACCAR is taking the lead in providing functional wireless Internet applications to its customers on the road."

- PACCAR's innovative and leading-edge use of information technology earned the company the number one ranking in *PC Week* magazine's 1999 Fast-Track 500, which ranks 500 companies from a spectrum of industries based on their use of technologies applied to their business framework. PACCAR earned the top ranking for launching company-wide initiatives in business-to-business e-commerce, enterprise resource planning, virtual private networks, data warehousing, web-based collaboration software and specialized Intranet applications.

- PACCAR won the prestigious 1999 Leadership and Excellence in the Application and Development of Integrated Manufacturing (LEAD) award from the Society of Manufacturing Engineers (SME) for "innovative and leading edge manufacturing techniques." This award recognized PACCAR's implementation of computer and automated robotics systems in the assembly of the Kenworth T2000 and the Peterbilt 387 at its Chillicothe, Ohio and Denton, Texas facilities.

- PACCAR recently confirmed its commitment to advanced engine technology when it became the first manufacturer in Europe to introduce its 12.6-liter Euro 3 engine, which delivers 530 horsepower while meeting emissions specifications two years before the legislation is effective. In addition, PACCAR expanded its medium-duty product line with the introduction of a new Peterbilt model 270 and the Kenworth K300, Class 5 through 7 cab-over-engine trucks based on the highly successful DAF 45/55 Series. Other recent PACCAR product introductions include Peterbilt's new aerodynamic Class 8 model 387, which began production in the third quarter of 1999.

- Although the company business is almost entirely based on the manufacture of trucks, it is making an effort to add a little luster to its image. It's even dabbling in high-tech investments, pumping $40 million into wireless telecom and computer technologies with transportation applications. CEO Mark C. Pigott boasts that within 25 to 30 years, perhaps half of PACCAR's profits will come from businesses other than trucks. "We're not in a Rust Belt here. We're a high-tech growth company," says Mr. Pigott.

- "PACCAR's 16 manufacturing facilities and 13 parts distribution centers around the world are aggressively moving from traditional business models to 'click and mortar' e-business. We already have the world-class facilities; now we are extending their reach and impact up and down the logistical value chain," says management.

"Every customer, dealer and supplier is benefiting from our ability to electronically transact business—everything from automatic part restocking at dealer and fleet locations to locating emergency road repair service for our customers."

PACCAR has invested more than $300 million in its facilities and systems over the past several years to increase capacity and efficiency. PACCAR's newly opened world-class $85-million truck plant in Saint Therese, Quebec, Canada, is an example of PACCAR's seamless integration of information technology into nearly every phase of the facility's operation.

Total assets: $7,933 million
Current ratio: 1.73
Common shares outstanding: 77 million
Return on 1999 shareholders' equity: 26.8%

	1999	1998	1997	1996	1995	1994	1993	1992
Revenues (millions)	9021	7895	6752	4600	4848	4490	3542	2735
Net income (millions)	566	417	310	201	253	204	142	65
Earnings per share	7.18	5.30	3.96	2.59	3.25	2.63	1.83	.84
Dividends per share	2.40	2.20	2.10	1.25	2.00	1.50	.89	.57
Price High	63.0	66.8	59.5	36.6	27.3	30.9	30.5	27.4
Low	39.5	37.0	30.3	20.9	19.6	20.0	23.3	20.8

AGGRESSIVE GROWTH

Pfizer Inc.

235 East 42nd Street ◻ New York, New York 10017-5755 ◻ Investor contact: Ronald C. Aldridge
(212) 573-3685 ◻ Direct dividend reinvestment plan is available: (800) 733-9393 ◻ Web site: www.pfizer.com
◻ Listed: NYSE ◻ Ticker symbol: PFE ◻ S&P rating: A+ ◻ Value Line financial strength rating: A++

When Pfizer acquired Warner-Lambert Company in the spring of 2000, analysts focused primarily on how much Lipitor, the cholesterol-lowering drug, would bolster Pfizer's profit margins. However, Wall Street may have overlooked an equally impressive part of the deal— Warner-Lambert's biotechnology unit,

Agouron Pharmaceuticals, a leader in computer-aided drug design. Instead of tediously screening thousands of substances to discover a new drug, Agouron scientists employ 3D computer visualization techniques to create molecules that precisely knock out invaders bent on inflicting damage to the human body.

Today, Agouron's pipeline is well stocked with potential wonder drugs that Pfizer can now latch onto to maintain its growth rate. For instance, the once-obscure Agouron is among the leaders developing a prescription drug targeted specifically against the virus that causes the common cold. It also has two promising AIDS drugs in development.

Company Profile

Pfizer traces its history back to 1849 when it was founded by Charles Pfizer and Charles Erhart. In those early days, Pfizer was a chemical firm. Today, it is a leading global pharmaceutical manufacturer, creating and marketing a wide range of prescription drugs.

PFE also has an important stake in hospital products, animal health items, and consumer products.

Pfizer's growth over the past half century was paced by strategic acquisitions, new drug discoveries, and vigorous foreign expansion. Its most recent move involved the giant acquisition of Warner-Lambert in 2000, making it the second-largest in the world. The largest is Glaxo SmithKline, the company created by Glaxo Wellcome and SmithKline Beecham, which announced intentions to merge in 2000.

Shortcomings to Bear in Mind

- Like most stocks with bright prospects, Pfizer often sells at an elevated price-earnings ratio.
- Viagra took off faster than any drug in history when it was launched in April 1998, including an unprecedented

3 million prescriptions in the first three months. In 1999, the drug had worldwide sales of $1 billion. But Viagra is vulnerable, and a host of new rivals will challenge it in the next few years. For one thing, Viagra doesn't work for at least a third of the men who try it. What's more, it can take an hour to kick in, or as long as two hours if taken after a meal. The side effects, though usually mild, can be disconcerting, such as headaches, flushing, indigestion, and a bluish haze in vision.

Worst of all, Viagra can lead to death if taken by patients who are on nitrates or nitroglycerin, drugs used to treat some three million men with heart problems, many of whom also have erectile dysfunction. Even cardiac patients not on nitrate drugs can risk a heart attack on Viagra if they have sex and are badly out of condition. Some 700 men have died after taking Viagra, according to the Food & Drug Administration. On the other hand, the market is huge. Pfizer says 6 million men in the United States have tried Viagra, and some four million are regular users. Even so, up to thirty million men age 40 or older have some degree of erectile dysfunction. And that doesn't count the men abroad who suffer the same affliction. Meanwhile, several other drug companies are working on products to serve this same group of men, including TAP, Zonagen, Lilly, Bayer, and Bristol-Myers.

- In 1999, the FDA asked Pfizer to revise its label on Trovan, an antibiotic, to include a warning about rare cases of serious liver damage. Some 140 cases of liver problems have been reported among patients who have taken Trovan since February 1998. Most of those cases were resolved after the patients stopped taking the drug. One analyst said that these warnings may significantly slow growth of new Trovan prescriptions in the United States, and they also could delay or prevent approval in countries where Trovan is not yet marketed.

In October of 1999, Pfizer lost a trademark-infringement lawsuit against Britain's Trovan Ltd. The award was for $143 million. Trovan Ltd., a maker of electronic tracking devices, based on the Isle of Man, claimed that Pfizer had not only infringed on its trademark name but had also devalued it. The verdict represents the second half of a double whammy for the antibiotic Trovan, which Pfizer once expected would be a blockbuster profit producer. As a result of these developments in 1999, the drug's use is being sharply limited to serious hospital-based infections that don't respond to any other antibiotics.

- The odds of discovering a new drug are staggering. Out of every 7 million compounds screened, only 1,000 hold promise. Of that 1,000, only 12 compounds actually become candidates for development. And of those 12, only one makes it to market.

Reasons to Buy

- In late 1999, Pfizer announced that it would buy genetic information from Celera Genomics Group, a gene-mapping company that is a unit of the PE Corporation, and collaborate on research under a five-year agreement. Under the pact, Pfizer gained access to Celera's genetic databases until 2005. The databases include 3 billion base pairs of human DNA, or about 75 percent of all human genetic information. Celera and Pfizer will also collaborate to discover gene-based therapies.
- Pfizer also stuck a deal with ArQule, of Medford, Mass., valued at more than $100 million, to create drug leads using an automated method known as combinatorial chemistry. Neurogen Corporation of Branford, Conn., will provide

computerized design tools to optimize these leads. In addition, Aurora Biosciences Corporation of San Diego and Evotec BioSystems AG of Hamburg, Germany will provide Pfizer with robotic equipment that performs speedy drug tests using microscopic amounts of material.

George Milne, Pfizer's research director, said this set of tools will permit "high-speed empiricism" and eventually could make a huge difference in Pfizer's output. "We've seen isolated examples that we are on the threshold of a leap up," he said. Instead of producing a handful of new drugs each year, Dr. Milne said he hopes the company eventually will be able to launch dozens of drugs in the same period, including ones tailored to the varied genetic make-up of individual patients, a scenario that could lead to an era of so-called "personalized medicine."

- After a protracted struggle, Pfizer won out in its effort to purchase Warner-Lambert (a hostile takeover). The final deal was for $92 billion. The merger makes the new firm the world's second-largest and fastest-growing drug company. The combined company has a wide range of medications, including the blood-pressure control drug Norvasc and the antidepressant Zoloft, the blockbuster cholesterol drug Lipitor, as well as consumer products like Bubblicious Gum, Certs mints, Lubriderm, Sudafed, Rolaids, Trident, Zantac 75, Visine, Ben Gay, Schick razors, and Listerine mouthwash.

Behind Pfizer's three-month tussle to take over Warner-Lambert—the biggest hostile takeover fight in U.S. history—was a powerful and little-known motive. To the general public, the company looked like an invincible drug-industry star. Underneath that stalwart facade, Pfizer had been experiencing some serious setbacks—which it failed to reveal during the struggle— including problems with Trovan. In addition, an experimental drug for diabetic nerve damage had been terminated. And development of once-promising migraine and schizophrenia drugs had been delayed. On a more positive note, the combined behemoth plans to use its greater size to negotiate better deals with HMOs and other large drug buyers.

- Building on the strength of Pfizer's in-line products, the company is forging ahead with an ambitious R&D program, with more than 170 research projects in discovery and development—more than at any time in its history.
- In 1998, Pfizer acquired the rights to help develop and market a new arthritis drug being developed by Monsanto, setting up a race among Merck, Johnson & Johnson, and Pfizer to market the first new class of prescription pain killers in more than two decades. These new drugs, called Cox-2 inhibitors, are expected to relieve pain without causing stomach distress and other problems associated with existing anti-inflammatory drugs. In addition to treating arthritis, the new drugs have potential to prevent certain cancers and even Alzheimer's disease.
- Selling drugs is more complicated than selling, say, soap. You need to interest consumers, but first you must win over doctors. Though it ranks only fourth in worldwide drug sales, Pfizer deploys the largest sales force in the industry—five thousand four hundred marketers pushing free samples. Their ranks are filled with former military men and women urged to ever greater effort with the carrot-and-stick of hefty bonuses and multiple quotas.
- Pfizer's Consumer Health Care Group (CHC) is a worldwide marketer of leading over-the-counter (OTC) health care products. Among the category-leading

domestic OTC brands are Visine in eye care, Cortizone anti-itch medicines, BenGay topical analgesics, Desitin diaper rash treatments, Unisom sleep aids, and Rid for killing lice.

In recent years, Pfizer has launched three prescription drugs for over-the-counter use—OcuHist, an antihistamine eyedrop; Zyrtec, an antihistamine for allergies, called Reactine in Canada; and Diflucan, a one-pill treatment (sold in the United Kingdom) for vaginal yeast infections.

- Pfizer's Animal Health Group (AHG) in not only one of the largest in the world, but it is also noteworthy for the breadth of its product lines and its geographic coverage. Innovative marketing has become an AHG hallmark in its efforts to succeed in a highly competitive market. An independent survey of U.S. veterinarians, for example, named the Pfizer sales force the best in the industry.
- Pfizer had a solid year in 1999, as five of its drugs each had sales of $1 billion or more: Norvasc (a calcium-channel blocker), Zoloft (an antidepressant), Zithromax (a broad-spectrum quinolone antibiotic), Viagra, and Diflucan (an antifungal preparation). Their combined sales advanced at an impressive 18 percent rate. What's more, copromoted products, Aricept (to treat Alzheimer's disease), Lipitor, and Celebrex (for arthritis), did even better, shooting up 139 percent over the 1998 level.
- The company has a number of key compounds in the pipeline, including Tikosyn for atrial fibrillation, Zeldox for psychosis, Relpax for migraine, inhaled insulin for diabetes, Alond for diabetic kidney and heart damage, voriconazole for fungal infections, darifenacin for urinary urge incontinence, ezlopitant for chemotherapy-induced nausea, and droloxifene for the prevention of osteoporosis, breast cancer, and heart disease.

Total assets: $18,302 million
Current ratio: 1.22
Common shares outstanding: 3,847 million
Return on 1999 shareholders' equity: 38.2%

	1999	1998	1997	1996	1995	1994	1993	1992
Revenues (millions)	16204	13544	12504	11306	10021	8281	7478	7230
Net income (millions)	3360	2627	2213	1929	1554	1298	1180	1094
Earnings per share	.87	.67	.57	.50	.41	.35	.31	.27
Dividends per share	.31	.25	.23	.20	.17	.16	.14	.12
Price High	50.0	43.0	26.7	15.2	11.1	6.6	6.3	7.3
Low	31.5	23.7	13.4	10.0	6.2	4.4	4.4	5.4

INCOME

Philip Morris Companies Inc.

120 Park Avenue ◻ **New York, New York 10017-5592** ◻ **Investor contact: Nicholas M. Rolli**
(917) 663-5000 ◻ **Dividend reinvestment plan is available: (800) 442-0077** ◻ **Listed: NYSE**
◻ **Web site: www.philipmorris.com** ◻ **Ticker symbol: MO** ◻ **S&P rating: A** ◻ **Value Line financial strength rating: A**

In addition to the continued strength of the company's business fundamentals, the litigation environment improved in significant ways in 1999. CEO Geoffrey C. Bible remains "confident in our ability to successfully manage the challenges we face over time. The following are some of the reasons why he says this:

• Trial courts in all jurisdictions approved the Master Settlement Agreement with the states. This removed a significant source of litigation risk to the company.

• In addition to numerous dismissals at the trial court level, five federal district courts of appeal rejected lawsuits brought by third-party payers of health care costs. These decisions rendered in 1999, and continuing into 2000, further bolster "our position that these cases are illegitimate attempts at end-runs around established legal principles."

• A jury returned a unanimous verdict in the company's favor in the Iron Workers case in Ohio, the only third-party payer case to proceed to a jury verdict to date.

• Following two losses early in 1999 on the West Coast—both of which are now on appeal—juries returned defense verdicts in all of the six subsequent individual smoking and health lawsuits that went to trial against the industry in 1999.

• The industry continues to solidify its position on class actions, as there were no decisions in 1999 certifying such smoking and health claims. With several exceptions, the courts are making it increasingly clear that class actions are not appropriate vehicles for litigating smoking and health claims. To date, state and federal courts have rejected attempts by plaintiffs to have smoking and health cases certified as class actions in 21 cases.

• The first lawsuit brought by a foreign country (Guatemala) in the United States seeking reimbursement of health care expenditures was dismissed by a federal court. Mr. Bible says, "We believe the rationale underlying that decision should be applied to all other such cases filed in the United States."

Company Profile

Operating in nearly 200 countries, Philip Morris is the largest consumer packaged-goods company in the world. Philip Morris is the largest domestic cigarette manufacturer, with total cigarette shipments in the United States amounting to 208.2 billion units in 1999, down 8.5 percent from the prior year. Philip Morris is also the nation's largest food processor (Kraft). It accounted for 22.3 percent of total company sales in 1999, and 21.3 percent of its operating profits. Finally, Miller Brewing is the nation's second-largest brewer.

In 1999, a total of 76 Philip Morris brands generated annual revenues of more than $100 million each, an increase from 73 the prior year. What's more, 14 of these brands could boast of revenues that exceeded $1 billion.

In 1999, the company's business was largely tobacco (60 percent of revenues), followed by food (34 percent), brewing (5.5 percent), and financial services (0.5 percent).

International operations accounted for about 47 percent of sales and 41 percent of operating profits in 1999.

As noted, Philip Morris is primarily a tobacco company, with such major brands as Marlboro (the top-selling brand in the United States), Merit, Virginia Slims (the best-selling women's cigarette), Benson & Hedges, and Parliament. Philip Morris has a 49.4 percent share of the domestic tobacco market. Outside the United States, the company also has well-known brands, such as L & M and Lark.

The company's other large operation is food, as a result of prior acquisitions of General Foods (1984) and Kraft (1988). Some well-known names include Jell-O, Shake 'n Bake, Lender's Bagels, Philadelphia Cream Cheese, Post cereals, Velveeta, Kool-Aid, Miracle Whip, Oscar Mayer, Cracker Barrel cheese, Tang, and Maxwell House coffee.

Ranking third is the company's beer business, featuring such brands as Miller Lite, Miller Genuine Draft, Miller, Icehouse, Red Dog, Lowenbrau, Meister Brau, and Milwaukee's Best. During 1997, Miller sold its equity interest in Molson Breweries in Canada and 49 percent of its ownership of Molson USA, which holds the rights to import, market, and distribute the Molson and Foster's brands in the United States. Currently, Miller holds a 21 percent share of the domestic beer market.

Finally, MO also has a stake in financial services (Philip Morris Capital Corp.), with assets of $6.5 billion.

Highlights of 1999

- The company's tobacco business performed well in the face of its challenges in 1999. As expected, volume declined sharply, but market share increased to a record level of nearly 50 percent. And in a year when one might have expected some erosion in the company's premium-brand business, actual shipments of these high-margin cigarettes as a percentage of total shipments actually grew by 1.6 points, to 88 percent. That includes Marlboro, which set a new record for shipment share. Finally, Philip Morris solidified its position as market leader.

- Philip Morris's international tobacco business had slightly higher income of $5 billion, though overall volume declined 6.8 percent. This volume decline was largely due to weaker business conditions in the lower-margin markets of Russia and the rest of Eastern Europe and Brazil, as well as lower worldwide duty-free shipments. However, income was bolstered by the company's strong performance in the key profitable markets of Western Europe and Japan, which account for 60 percent of the company's international tobacco income—and where total volume expanded by close to 5 percent.

- The company's Kraft North American food business generated impressive results. Income, volume, and margins made solid gains again. Volumes were up for most of the key brands, with the beverage and frozen pizza businesses continuing their robust growth. Kraft is making substantial progress toward its goal of being recognized as the undisputed leader of the food industry.

■ The international food business showed signs of recovery, with underlying income up 1.8 percent, to $1.1 billion. In particular, the company's European and Asian food businesses, which account for nearly 90 percent of MO's total international food business, showed income growth of 7.5 percent.

■ Finally, Philip Morris's beer operation, led by a dynamic new management team, recorded strong income growth of 19.7 percent, driven by a contract-management agreement with Pabst, the acquisition of four new brands, and higher prices. And most encouraging was the 2 percent volume gain for Miller Lite.

Shortcomings to Bear in Mind

■ As most investors are aware, Philip Morris is being besieged by the many pressures facing the U.S. tobacco industry: public smoking restrictions, possible excise tax hikes, congressional hearings, negative media coverage, and litigation. Still, we should remember that the company's tobacco segment has faced similar threats before and has overcome them. Finally, it's important to note that over the past 40 years, the tobacco industry has rarely lost or paid to settle a smoking-health product liability case.

More recently, however, that seems to be changing. In early 1999, a jury in San Francisco awarded $1.5 million in damages to compensate a former smoker with lung cancer, the largest such award against the tobacco industry and the first against Philip Morris. The verdict, following a month-long Superior Court

trial, served abrupt notice to the tobacco industry that it remains vulnerable to suits brought by individual smokers, despite a $206-billion settlement with states in 1998 that ended their efforts to recoup health outlays linked to smoking-related illnesses.

■ Unprecedented in its scope and complexity, the historic settlement between the major domestic tobacco companies and 46 state attorneys general and representatives of other U.S. jurisdictions—added to previous settlements with four states—essentially puts an end to many of the claims made or threatened against the company's domestic operations by the states.

According to CEO Geoffrey C. Bible, "Obviously, the 1998 settlement is a costly, bitter pill to swallow. And obviously, we still have some considerable hurdles to overcome as we seek to create a more stable and predictable business environment and find common ground with our critics."

Reasons to Buy

■ In mid-2000, Philip Morris acquired Nabisco Holdings Corporation for $18.9 billion. The company plans to combine Nabisco with its Kraft Foods, to create a huge and profitable food company to help offset its tobacco liabilities. The merger created a mammoth food company that combines such dominant brands as Oreo cookies, Ritz crackers, Planters nuts, and Life Savers candies, with the Philip Morris brands of Kraft, Jell-O, Maxwell House, and Oscar Meyer. More than 90 percent of Nabisco's domestic brands are leaders in their respective categories. Based on 1999 financial figures, the combined Philip Morris and Nabisco companies would have had revenue of $88.6 billion and operating income of $16.3 billion. Kraft and Nabisco would have had combined revenue of $34.9 billion and operating income of $5.5 billion in 1999.

- According to Mr. Bible, "Our brands do not just grow by momentum: We build them and protect them with world-class marketing and expertise."
- Philip Morris's outstanding brands, marketing, and infrastructure have made the company the market leader in tobacco in the United States and in 30 other major markets around the world. They have also won the company first place positions in 18 of its 20 most profitable food categories in North America and in more than 40 of its major coffee, confectionery, cheese, and powdered soft drink businesses.
- Despite the never-ending strife against antismoking forces, Philip Morris has been a most successful company. Unlike many other huge companies, Philip Morris is growing at a consistent and impressive pace. In the 1989–1999 period, earnings per share climbed from $1.01 to $3.30, a compound annual

growth rate of 12.6 percent. Similarly, dividends per share expanded from $.42 to $1.84, a growth rate of 15.9 percent.

- Miller acquired four new brands in 1999: Olde English 800 and Hamm's from the Pabst Brewing Company, and Mickey's Malt Liquor and Henry Weinhard's from Stroh Brewery Company. In addition, Miller acquired a Pabst brewery in Tumwater, Washington and began operations there in the fall of 1999.
- Kraft is one of the largest coffee companies in the United States. Major brands include Maxwell House, Yuban, Sanka, Maxim, and General Foods International Coffees. In 1999, the company's coffee business gained both volume and market share in a highly competitive environment. This performance was attributable to the success of Kraft's licensing agreement to roll out Starbuck's coffee to grocery customers, as well as the introduction of Maxwell House Slow Roast coffee.

Total assets: $61,381 million
Current ratio: 1.21
Common shares outstanding: 2,378 million
Return on 1999 shareholders' equity: 48.5%

		1999	1998	1997	1996	1995	1994	1993	1992
Revenues (millions)		78286	74391	72055	69204	66071	65125	60901	59131
Net income (millions)		7926	5372	6310	6303	5478	4725	3568	4939
Earnings per share		3.30	2.20	2.58	2.56	2.17	1.82	1.35	1.82
Dividends per share		1.84	1.68	1.60	1.47	1.22	1.01	.87	.78
Price	High	55.6	59.5	48.1	39.7	31.5	21.5	25.9	28.9
	Low	21.3	34.8	36.0	28.5	18.6	15.8	15.0	23.4

INCOME

Piedmont Natural Gas Company

P.O. Box 33068 ◻ Charlotte, North Carolina 28233 ◻ Investor contact: Headen B. Thomas (704) 364-3483 Ext. 6438 ◻ Dividend reinvestment program is available: (800) 937-5449 ◻ Fiscal year ends October 31 ◻ Listed NYSE ◻ Web site: www.piedmontng.com ◻ Ticker symbol: PNY ◻ S&P rating: A- ◻ Value Line financial strength rating: B++

One of the highlights of 1999 was the addition of 34,700 new gas utility customers, a record for the company, which

reflects a growth rate of over three and a half times the national average for natural gas distribution companies.

Over the past five years, moreover, Piedmont Natural Gas has added 159,000 new customers. An equally impressive achievement over that five-year stretch is the 26.7 percent reduction in the capital costs of connecting customers. This reduction equates to $59.6 million of capital savings over the five years.

Company Profile

Incorporated in 1950, Piedmont Natural Gas is an energy services company, primarily engaged in the transportation, distribution, and sale of natural gas and the sale of propane to over 710,000 residential, commercial, and industrial customers in North Carolina, South Carolina, and Tennessee.

The company is the second-largest natural gas utility in the Southeast, serving over 660,000 natural gas customers. Piedmont Natural Gas and its nonutility subsidiaries and divisions are also engaged in acquiring, marketing, transporting, and storing natural gas for large-volume customers, in retailing residential and commercial gas appliances, and the sale of propane to over 48,000 customers in the company's three-state service area.

An unregulated subsidiary of the company is an equity participant in a venture that is marketing natural gas to an additional 476,000 customers in Georgia, the first state in the venture's eight-state southeastern market to open to retail competition for natural gas.

Other business interests in which the company is engaged that are not subject to state utility regulation include the sale of propane and investments in a natural gas pipeline and an interstate LNG (liquefied natural gas) storage facility and marketing natural gas and other energy products and services to deregulated markets.

The company markets propane and related appliances to residential, commercial, agricultural, and industrial customers in and near its natural gas service area in the Carolinas and Tennessee. The combined operations of the company's six propane divisions rank eighteenth in the nation in terms of gallons sold.

Shortcomings to Bear in Mind

- Public utilities are often affected by weather. Natural gas utilities, for instance, don't do well when the winter is unseasonably mild. In 1999, the three-state service area of the company had a winter that was 6.4 percent warmer than the prior year and 13 percent warmer than normal. As a result, net income for the year declined 3.5 percent from the prior year's record level. Although weather was a factor, the major cause of the decline came from startup costs of the company's South-Star joint venture in the newly deregulated Georgia market. These costs were incurred in 1999 as the two-year planned phase-in of opening the state to unregulated marketers moved forward more rapidly than anticipated and was completed by October 1999 rather than November 2000.

  SouthStar, doing business in Georgia as Georgia Natural Gas Services, is now serving over 476,000 residential, commercial, and industrial customers, or 33 percent of the market in that state. The costs associated with gaining these customers, including promotional and advertising expenses, adversely affected net income and earnings per share in 1999 by $5.2 million and $.17, respectively. It is anticipated that SouthStar will contribute to Piedmont's earnings in 2000.

- With capital expenditures required to meet the company's growing service area needs, cost reductions were not sufficient to maintain an adequate rate of return on the company's investments. As a result, in December of 1999 the company filed a $10.7-million rate increase request with the Tennessee Regulatory Authority. In early 2000, the company made a similar filing with the North Carolina Utilities Commission. In other state regulatory activity, Piedmont is proceeding with construction to provide natural gas service to three previously unserved counties in northwestern North Carolina. About 83 percent of the funding for this project will come from expansion funds made available from interstate pipeline funds.

Reasons to Buy

- Piedmont Natural Gas enjoys an economically robust and diverse service area that is among the fastest growing in the nation. The company's three-state service area consists of the Piedmont region of the Carolinas—Charlotte, Salisbury, Greensboro, Winston-Salem, High Point, Burlington, and Hickory in North Carolina and Anderson, Greenville, and Spartanburg in South Carolina—and the metropolitan area of Nashville, Tennessee. Both *Plant Sites and Parks* and *Site Selection* magazines continue to rank the Carolinas and Tennessee among the best in the nation for business relocation and expansion and business climate.

    The center of the Piedmont Carolinas area is the Greater Charlotte urban region—sixth largest in the nation—with over six million people within a 100-mile radius. Charlotte is the nation's second-largest financial center. It is the headquarters city for Bank of America, the nation's largest bank, and for First Union National bank, the sixth largest. Wachovia Corporation, the nation's sixteenth-largest bank, is headquartered in Winston-Salem.

    Charlotte/Douglas International Airport, with over 500 flights per day and 23 million passengers annually, is US Airways' largest hub and the twentieth busiest airport in the world.

    The Nashville region is a diverse center of a retail trading area of over two million people, where health care is the largest industry. It is also home to major transportation, publishing, printing, financial, insurance, and communications companies as well as 20 colleges and universities.

- In 1999, the company raised its dividend for the 21st consecutive year. In the past 10 years, the dividend has been boosted from $.79 to $1.36, a compound annual growth of 5.6 percent, or better than the rate of inflation. The company's payout ratio is conservative, which means it is retaining a good portion for future investment. By contrast, many utilities pay out nearly all of their earnings, which means they must obtain expansion funds from the issuance of debt or more common stock.

- The Pine Needle LNG facility began operations in May of 1999. A subsidiary, Piedmont Interstate Pipeline Company, owns a 35 percent equity interest in this $107-million, 4 Bcf (billion cubic feet) interstate storage facility. It is one of the largest above-ground peaking facilities (used on extremely cold days to supplement gas from pipelines) in the nation. The company has subscribed to 2 Bcf of the storage capacity and 200,000 Mcf (thousand cubic feet) per day of vaporization capacity, which are required to meet customer growth.

- For the third consecutive year, no rate increase applications were filed with the company's three state commissions. This was achieved by continuing efforts to eliminate or reduce costs at every level of the organization. For the second successive year, operations and maintenance expenses were lower than the previous year.

- In November of 1999, Cardinal Pipeline Company, L.L.C., a North Carolina limited-liability company, placed its pipeline extension project into service. The pipeline transports additional natural gas supplies to serve the growing demand for natural gas by the company's customers and by those of two other natural gas distributors in North Carolina. Piedmont Interstate Pipeline Company, a wholly owned subsidiary of the company, owns a 16.45 percent equity interest in the pipeline.

  The $98-million project, which has a total capacity of 270,000 dekatherms per day, extends the existing 37-mile, 24-inch diameter pipeline by an additional 67 miles from Burlington to a point southeast of Raleigh. The original Cardinal Pipeline originates in Rockingham County and extends to a point southeast of Burlington.

- Analysts expect that 1999's subpar results will not continue in 2000. There are several factors to back up this assertion. For one thing, the warm weather of 1999 may not continue, though, of course, predicting the weather is more difficult that predicting interest rates or the stock market.

  In addition, absence of SouthStar Energy's startup costs, which were heavily front-loaded in the company's first year, should help bolster earnings. Analysts say that SouthStar could add $.02 a share to earnings. Finally, the company will continue to cut costs, as they have in recent years. Put it all together and an increase in earnings of 12 percent seems a good possibility in 2000.

- Piedmont Natural Gas has a strong balance sheet. In fiscal 1999, shareholders' equity was 53.8 percent of total capitalization. This compares favorably to the other 22 companies in this sector of Value Line: 49.2 percent.

Total assets: $1,289 million
Current ratio: 0.67
Common shares outstanding: 31 million
Return on 1999 shareholders' equity: 11.8%

	1999	1998	1997	1996	1995	1994	1993	1992
Revenues (millions)	686	765	776	685	505	575	553	460
Net income (millions)	58	60	55	49	40	36	38	35
Earnings per share	1.86	1.96	1.85	1.67	1.45	1.35	1.45	1.40
Dividends per share	1.36	1.28	1.21	1.15	1.09	1.01	.95	.91
Price High	36.6	36.1	36.4	25.8	24.9	23.4	26.4	20.4
Low	28.6	27.9	22.0	20.5	18.3	18.0	18.8	15.4

GROWTH AND INCOME

Pitney Bowes Inc.

1 Elmcroft Road ❑ **Stamford, Connecticut 06926-0700** ❑ **Investor contact: Charles F. McBride (203) 351-6349** ❑ **Dividend reinvestment plan is available: (800) 648-8170** ❑ **Web site: www.pitneybowes.com** ❑ **Listed: NYSE** ❑ **Ticker symbol: PBI** ❑ **S&P rating: A+** ❑ **Value Line financial strength rating: A**

Although Pitney Bowes officials say they expect Internet-related products to ultimately bring in 30 percent of revenues, e-commerce is still a modest part of Pitney Bowes sales. The bulk of revenues revolves around postage meter rentals, financing, bulk mailing systems, and services such as running mail rooms and handling direct marketing.

Analysts say investors have been wary of PBI's shares because of concerns that the Internet will make inroads into basic mailing products. But Pitney Bowe's Wall Street fans—and they are legion—say such worries are unfounded. "The Street psychology may be negative, but their fundamentals are outstanding," comments an analyst with Salomon Smith Barney.

What's more, the electronic markets that Pitney Bowes are pursuing are potential blockbusters. To be sure, older meters require a trip to the post office to buy refill postage. On the other hand, today's sophisticated meters can be reloaded by telephone. In both instances, the post office, not Pitney, sells the postage. However, the company charges higher rentals for newer digital meters, which it says are more convenient to use. And the company will offer, for a fee, to buy the postage for customers and reload the meters remotely.

Company Profile

A pioneer and world leader in mailing systems, Pitney Bowes is a multinational manufacturing and marketing company that provides mailing, shipping, dictating, copying, and facsimile systems; item identification and tracking systems and supplies; mailroom, reprographics and related management services; and product financing.

The key to Pitney Bowes will probably continue to be consistency rather than spectacular growth, in view of the maturity of its highly profitable postage meter rental business and the moderate growth of some of its other annuity revenues, such as service.

On the other hand, analysts believe that the stock has limited downside risk; it should appeal largely to long-term investors.

Pitney Bowes is best known as the worldwide leader in mailing systems. It markets a full line of mailing systems,

shipping and weighing systems, addressing systems, production mail systems, folding and inserting systems, as well as mailing software.

Pitney Bowes Software Systems, a division of Mailing Systems located in Illinois, offers a full range of advanced software and services for business communications, and marketing and mailing applications to Fortune 1000 companies.

Shipping and Weighing Systems (SWS) provides parcel and freight information and automation systems for the shipping and transportation management functions of the logistics market.

SWS's products are marketed through Mailing Systems's worldwide distribution channels, with particular emphasis on North America. Service is provided by specially trained service representatives and a National Remote Diagnostic Center.

Pitney Bowes Transportation Software, a division of Pitney Bowes located in Minnesota, markets and develops logistics management solutions and provides consulting services.

Other Businesses of Pitney Bowes
The company's other businesses are also important. A brief description of each follows.

Pitney Bowes Management Services (PBMS) is a leading provider of facilities management services for the business support functions of creating, processing, storage, retrieval, distribution, and tracking of information, messages, documents, and packages.

Using the latest available technology, PBMS manages mail centers, copy and reprographic centers, facsimile services, electronic printing, and imaging services and records management services for customers across the United States, as well as in Canada and the United Kingdom.

Pitney Bowes Facsimile Systems is a leading supplier of high-quality facsimile equipment to the business market. It is the only facsimile system supplier in the United States that markets solely through its own direct sales force nationwide.

Pitney Bowes Copier Systems concentrates on serving larger corporations with multi-unit installations of its full line of equipment.

Pitney Bowes Financial Services provides lease financing programs for customers who use products marketed by Pitney Bowes companies.

Shortcomings to Bear in Mind

- Several small newcomers are racing to develop a computer-generated stamp that would replace the old, expensive system of stamping inky, eagle-adorned postmarks onto envelopes. The new "stamps" would include a bold, black bar code below the traditional postmark. Instead of going to the post office to purchase postage in bulk, users would save time by simply ordering and downloading stamps off the Internet and printing them onto envelopes.

  On the other hand, Pitney postage meters still dominate the domestic market, despite aggressive competition from digitally savvy companies like Neopost and Francotyp-Postalia AG of Germany. And analysts expect Pitney Bowes to garner 30 percent of the international postage meter market by 2004, up from about 14 percent at present.

Reasons to Buy

- Some observers are concerned that the volume of mail may be declining, as people rely more on the telephone and their connection with the Internet.

  Pitney Bowes's CEO, Michael Critelli, responds to this concern, "Outside experts confirm our internal findings that mail volumes worldwide will continue to increase for the next 10 years. Lots of paper-based communication is going away, but it is more than being offset by growth engines."

According to Mr. Critelli, there is explosive growth in direct mail marketing. To be sure, individual mailings are falling a couple of percent each year. On the other hand, direct mail is climbing at a far faster pace, between 6 and 8 percent a year. As a result, says the Pitney Bowes CEO, the overall volume of mail is going up each year. What's more, the same trend is visible in other developed markets. In the developing world, moreover, the growth of mail is even more explosive. China, for example, is registering increases of 25 percent a year.

- Pitney Bowes has a consistent record of earnings growth. In the 1989–1999 period, earnings per share mounted from $0.80 to $2.31, an annual compound growth rate of 11.2 percent. In the same 10-year span, dividends per share climbed from $0.26 to $1.02, a growth rate of 14.6 percent.

- As the largest business unit of Pitney Bowes, Mailing Systems is the world leader in helping customers manage their messages through mailing solutions. These systems are marketed to businesses of all sizes—from the smallest office to Fortune 500 companies. With over 2 million customers worldwide, Pitney Bowes Mailing Systems is focused on keeping business messages moving and its customers ahead of the curve.

  With products such as the DocuMatch Integrated Mail System, Paragon II Mail Processor, and the AddressRight System, large mailers are provided the tools they need to drive their businesses and enhance competitiveness. The Galaxy Mailing System and Series 3 Folder and Inserter address similar needs in midsize organizations. With DirectNet, a hybrid mailing service, the company is able to assist customers of all sizes with value-added capabilities to improve the efficiency and impact of their messaging applications.

- The company's fastest-growing division, Pitney Bowes Business Services, provides customers with on-site and off-site business support services, including mail, reprographics, facsimile, records, electronic document management, and mortgage financing services. The Management Services subsidiary is the outsourcing leader in the legal market and a leading provider to Fortune 500 companies.

■ Still another development revolves around infrastructure. Along with the much-desired provisions of telephones, gas, water, or electricity come less-welcome bills for these services. This makes Michael Critelli respond enthusiastically, "The number of telephones in emerging markets is going to double over the next five years. We love the monthly billings."

■ Deregulation is another growth engine for Pitney Bowes. When governments sell off their ownership of businesses, private businesses step in and mail soars. Critelli points to Thailand, where government deregulation of the insurance market three years ago produced "astronomical" increases in the number of newly issued insurance policies, all involving regular billing.

■ Operating profits at Pitney Bowes's largest business, mail systems, should benefit from a host of new products along with greater operating efficiencies. New software-driven equipment and systems utilize advanced digital technology, which, in turn, is derived from both its own research program and joint ventures with various partners, including IBM.

■ Pitney Bowes has a number of businesses that lag the economic cycle, but they should also resist a downturn. About two-thirds of total revenues come from annuity sources such as postage meter rentals, rentals of other mailing and business equipment, facilities management, rental, finance, service, and supply revenues.

■ Pitney Bowes took major steps in 1999 to reposition itself as a strong partner for the one-to-one marketing initiatives critical to its customers' business success. PBI acquired Automated Mailing and Office Systems Inc. (AMOS), a producer of high-quality systems for the direct mail document factory environment. Pitney's DocuMatch integrated mail processor, which creates customized, personalized mail, enjoyed its best year ever in 1999, supporting departmental marketing applications that had previously been outside PBI's reach. The digital technology introduced for printing both addresses and postal payment evidence gives a more professional look to marketing mail, increasing the likelihood that recipients will open it.

■ Patents and other intellectual property will be more valuable than ever in the Internet era. Pitney Bowes has been ranked in the top 200 of U.S. patents issued for 13 years in a row. The company holds more than three thousand active patents worldwide—200 on Internet concepts alone.

Total assets: $8,223 million
Current ratio: 1.16
Common shares outstanding: 265 million
Return on 1999 shareholders' equity: 38%

	1999	1998	1997	1996	1995	1994	1993	1992
Revenues (millions)	4433	4221	4100	3859	3555	3271	3543	3434
Net income (millions)	630	568	526	469	408	348	369	312
Earnings per share	2.31	2.03	1.80	1.56	1.34	1.11	1.16	.98
Dividends per share	1.02	.90	.80	.69	.60	.52	.45	.39
Price High	73.3	66.4	45.8	30.7	24.1	23.2	20.5	16.4
Low	40.9	42.2	26.8	20.9	15.0	14.6	18.1	14.0

PPG Industries, Inc.

One PPG Place □ Pittsburgh, Pennsylvania 15272 □ Investor contact: Douglas B. Atkinson (412) 434-3312 □ Direct dividend reinvestment plan is available: (800) 648-8160 □ Web site: www.ppg.com □ Listed: NYSE □ Ticker symbol: PPG □ S&P rating: A- □ Value Line financial strength rating: A

Over the past several years, PPG has positioned itself to make its earnings less cyclical. What's more, the company has evolved into more of a global player than it was a decade or two ago, making it is less dependent on markets here at home. This strategy—largely fueled by acquisitions—has paid handsome dividends. For instance, in the mid-1980s, domestic housing starts and auto manufacturing were sluggish, yet PPG's earnings did not feel much of an impact.

Company Profile

PPG Industries, a diversified global manufacturer, is a leading supplier of products for manufacturing, building, automotive, processing, and numerous other world industries.

Established in 1883, the Pittsburgh-based company makes decorative and protective coatings, flat glass and fabricated glass products, continuous-strand fiber glass, and industrial and specialty chemicals.

PPG is a leading worldwide producer of chlorine and caustic soda, vinyl chloride monomer, and chlorinated solvents. Specialty chemicals include silica compounds, surfactants, photochromic lenses, and fine chemicals, such as optical resins, pool and water-treatment chemicals, phosgene derivatives, and flame retardants.

PPG operates 110 major manufacturing facilities in Australia, Brazil, Canada, China, France, Germany, Ireland, Italy, Mexico, the Netherlands, Portugal, Spain, Taiwan, Turkey, the United Kingdom, and the United States.

To benefit its customers through leadership in technology, the company conducts research and development at 10 facilities throughout the world.

Competitive Position
- Among the world's leading suppliers of automotive and industrial coatings.
- Major supplier of architectural and packaging coatings.
- World's second-largest producer of continuous-strand fiberglass.
- Among the leading producers of float glass.
- Major global supplier of automotive transparencies.
- World's leading supplier of aircraft transparencies.
- World's third-largest producer of chlorine and caustic soda.
- World's leading producer of optical monomers.
- World's leading maker of changeable-tint lenses, through Transitions Optical, Inc.
- World's leading producer of amorphous precipitated silicas.

Shortcomings to Bear in Mind

- PPG is not a classic growth stock, with steadily increasing earnings. For instance, earnings fell from the prior year three times in the last 10 years (in 1989, 1991, and 1999).
- PPG has paid uninterrupted dividends since 1899. What's more, the company has increased its dividend for 30 consecutive years—certainly an impressive

298 THE 100 BEST STOCKS YOU CAN BUY, 2001

record. In the 1989-1999 period, however, dividends per share climbed from $.74 to $1.52, a compound annual growth rate of only 7.5 percent. In the same 10-year span, moreover, earnings per share advanced from $2.09 to $3.68, a lackluster growth rate of only 5.8 percent.

- In the past decade, investors have seen examples of remarkable improvements in turnaround situations (such as AlliedSignal, IBM, AT&T, Sears, Roebuck, Union Carbide, and Goodyear), when companies cut costs, sold poorly performing businesses, eliminated levels of bureaucracy, and sent thousands of employees packing. These actions often produced dramatic reversals in earnings per share. By contrast, PPG has been well run for a long time, so there is no apparent need nor opportunity for a drastic restructuring, with the resultant escalation of earnings. Cost reductions are expected to continue in most PPG units, however, analysts expect these cost savings to be similar to the overall industry. Thus, cost reductions will help PPG stay competitive rather than significantly improve profitability.

Reasons to Buy

- Industrial coatings expanded its presence in Europe with two key acquisitions in 1999. PPG purchased ICI's German-based unit that supplies original equipment specialty coatings used by large-scale manufacturers of buses and trucks, as well as for rail car, military, and industrial applications. However, the transaction did not include manufacturing facilities.

  Meanwhile, PPG purchased a 60-percent interest in Bellaria of Felizzano, Italy, a maker of powder coatings. Powders, the fastest-growing segment of the industrial coatings industry, are applied in the form of a spray or are over-fused on products as diverse as appliances,

motor vehicle parts, lawn equipment, and metal furniture.

- In 1999, architectural coatings expanded the distribution of its Porter Paints brand with the acquisition of the retail business of Wattyl Paint Corporation. Most of the 20 stores acquired are in cities in Southeastern towns in which Porter has one or more stores. Porter, which PPG acquired in late 1998, makes a broad range of paints and stains sold mostly to painting contractors.

- In 1999, the Automotive refinish segment added to its European presence with the acquisition of the commercial transport refinish business of Sigma Coatings. PPG acquired the portion of Sigma's business involving fleet finishes in Belgium, the Netherlands, and the United Kingdom. The transaction, however, did not include manufacturing facilities.

- Meanwhile, the company's automotive refinish, automotive coatings, and industrial coatings segments extended their geographic reach when PPG and AECI Ltd. of Johannesburg, South Africa agreed to join forces in a new unit—AECI Coatings Ltd.

- In 1999, PPG bolstered its position as a global player in automotive refinish coatings with the acquisition of ICI's automotive refinish and industrial coatings businesses. As a result, PPG can generate about one-half of its refinish sales outside North America. And the addition of ICI Autocolor, one of the most respected brand names in the refinish industry, strengthens PPG's ability to serve the needs of high-end customers. In addition to finish coatings, PPG acquired ICI's Asian and Latin American industrial powder and liquid coatings units. Also part of the transaction, PPG obtained Grow Automotive, which supplies a variety of North American industrial customers with flushing solvents, which are used to clean paint-spray equipment and reducing solvents to complete final paint formulation. Grow Automotive helps the automotive coatings segment's ability to provide assembly plant total fluids management.

- The acquisition of PRC-DeSoto International positions PPG to provide more total value to the aircraft industry while complementing the company's strengths in the manufacture of glass and coatings. Already a world leader in the manufacture of aircraft transparencies, PPG is now a leading supplier of coatings and sealants for the world's commercial, general, and military aircraft. Sealants ensure that fuel tanks, windows, cabins, aircraft doors and other components remain tightly sealed and withstand the rigors of flight.

    PRC-DeSoto coatings, meanwhile, cover virtually every model of Boeing and Airbus airliner and numerous military aircraft, including the U.S. Navy F-18 "Super Hornet" and European "Eurofighter Typhoon" fighter jets.

    PRC-DeSoto also makes a wide array of application systems, including dispensing guns, mixers, cartridges, nozzles, and syringes.

- According to analysts, acceleration of PPG sales and growth is likely to be driven by acquisitions in coatings and specialty chemicals, PPG's top-priority businesses. Fortunately, there are plenty of consolidation opportunities in this fragmented market. Analysts look for the company to make aggressive moves in acquiring European-based paint businesses, as well as improving profitability through leveraging the company's existing customer base with PPG products. In the past, the company has demonstrated the ability to accomplish that goal. What's more, PPG has a strong balance sheet, which should enhance its ability to make a large acquisition, such as $2 billion or more.

- Through the Value Focus process, PPG has been able to drive down production costs. This activity aims for breakthrough improvements in such areas as production yields, cycle times, and in-process inventory. Highlighting activities in automotive replacement glass, PPG opened a second advanced-technology call center to accommodate the growth in LYNX Services from PPG. With this addition, LYNX Services will handle more than 20 percent of the insurance industry's auto glass claims yearly, making the company a national leader in managing automotive claims for insurance companies.

- At the company's joint-venture plant in Taiwan, PPG began construction of a third large melting furnace. When completed in 2001, the unit will increase capacity by 50 percent. Virtually all of the new production will be used for printed circuit boards, which are growing in demand for computers, cell phones, automotive components, and other electronic items.

- PPG's emphasis on chemicals centers are shifting toward specialty products. This includes strengthening its leadership in changeable-tint optical lenses, expanding the company's presence in pharmaceutical intermediates, and developing new, high-value-added products.

- Within fine chemicals, a key strategy involves strengthening relationships with major customers for the company's pharmaceutical intermediates. Reinforcing this strategy was the acquisition of Sipsy Chimie Fine, which supplies intermediates and related products. Based in France, the firm has expanded PPG's array of technologies and its presence in France.

- At the La Porte, Texas complex, construction began on a full-scale certified facility for producing pharmaceutical intermediates. This operation, which went on stream in 2000, represents the second expansion in the past two years.

Total assets: $8,914 million
Current ratio: 1.28
Common shares outstanding: 174 million
Return on 1999 shareholders' equity: 19.3%

		1999	1998	1997	1996	1995	1994	1993	1992
Revenues (millions)		7757	7510	7379	7218	7058	6331	5754	5814
Net income (millions)		646	738	729	744	748	566	377	342
Earnings per share		3.68	4.13	4.06	3.96	3.70	2.67	1.78	1.61
Dividends per share		1.52	1.42	1.33	1.26	1.18	1.12	1.04	.94
Price	High	70.8	76.6	67.5	62.3	47.9	42.1	38.1	34.2
	Low	47.9	49.1	48.6	42.9	34.9	33.8	29.7	25.0

CONSERVATIVE GROWTH

Praxair, Inc.

39 Old Ridgebury Road ☐ **Danbury, Connecticut 06810-5113** ☐ **Investor contact: Scott S. Cunningham**
(203) 837-2073 ☐ **Dividend reinvestment plan is available: (800) 432-0140** ☐ **Web site: www.praxair.com**
☐ **Listed: NYSE** ☐ **Ticker symbol: PX** ☐ **S&P rating: Not rated** ☐ **Value Line financial strength rating: B++**

The sparkle in soft drinks, the freshness of pastries, the crunch in an apple—chances are Praxair carbon dioxide or nitrogen had something to do with it. At Praxair's Food Technology Laboratory—the only one of its kind in the industry—technologies and equipment are developed and tested to assist bakers, meat processors, and specialty foods producers deliver products that retain their taste and freshness.

Company Profile

Of course, Praxair's expertise in the realm of industrial gases extends far beyond the food and beverage industries. The company serves a diverse group of industries through the production, sale, and distribution of industrial gases and high-performance surface coatings, along with related services, materials, and systems.

Praxair, which was spun off to Union Carbide shareholders in June 1992, is the largest producer of industrial gases in North and South America; it is the third-largest company of its kind in the world.

Praxair's major customers include aerospace, chemicals, electronics, food processing, health care, glass, metal fabrication, petroleum, primary metals, as well as pulp and paper companies.

As a pioneer in the industrial gases industry, Praxair has been a leader in developing a wide range of proprietary and patented applications and supply-system technology.

The company's primary industrial gases products are atmospheric gases (oxygen, nitrogen, argon, and rare gases) and process gases (helium, hydrogen, electronics gases, and acetylene). Praxair also designs, engineers, and supervises construction of cryogenic and noncryogenic supply systems.

Praxair Surface Technologies provides metallic and ceramic coatings and powders used on metal surfaces to resist wear, high temperatures, and corrosion. Aircraft engines are its primary market, but it serves others, including the printing, textile, chemical, and primary metals markets and provides aircraft engine and airframe component overhaul services.

The company was founded in the United States in 1907 as Linde Air Products Company.

Shortcomings to Bear in Mind

- Analysts are concerned that higher energy costs will put a damper on the stock's performance, as they have during late 1999 and early 2000.

Reasons to Buy

- Praxair has been investing its resources to help its customers improve their operations, with special emphasis on those industry segments that represent the highest long-term growth potential for Praxair. Resource allocations are being made in favor of segments such as food and beverage and certain health care markets, which are less prone to economic swings. What's more, the company has been investing in Praxair Surface Technologies, which continues to exhibit solid growth and earnings potential. It earned top supplier recognition from American Airlines and Delta Air Lines.

  At the same time, the company is being more selective about geographic markets. Praxair has found that it generates the highest return where the company has a leading market share, a balanced distribution mix (on-site, merchant, packaged gases), and high operating rates. The company's investment program supports growth in already profitable markets in North America, southern Europe, and South America. Meanwhile, the company has been consolidating its position in established Asian markets, such as Korea and Thailand, while strengthening its presence in China and India.

- The addition of carbon dioxide to Praxair's portfolio opens up new avenues for growth in relatively noncyclical markets: food preservation, beverage carbonation, and water treatment. Looking ahead, increased demand for beverage carbonation and water treatment, particularly in emerging South American and Asian markets, promises to generate continued growth. Supplying global beverage-carbonation customers also leads to opportunities in new markets for other Praxair products and technology. Use of carbon dioxide in new food preservation markets, such as bakery goods and dairy products, also is on the verge of rapid growth.

- In recent years, Praxair has developed noncryogenic air-separation technology, which allows lower-cost delivery to customers who have smaller volume needs. By sacrificing a small amount of purity, these customers can purchase a gas that meets customer needs at a discount to the cost of traditional supplies of product in cryogenic liquid form. This product is less expensive for Praxair to produce—and thus higher-margined relative to "cryo" liquid. Not least, demand is growing dramatically.

- The company has refocused strategies for the electronics market, which allows Praxair to capitalize on growth opportunities. Its packaged-gases strategies and geographic expansion enhance the company's ability to provide high-quality, total gas-management services to the worldwide electronics market.

- New developments in combustion and oxidation processes—with emphasis on steel, chemicals, glass, and pulp and paper markets—promise to increase the use of oxygen, much of which can be supplied through Praxair's state-of-the-art noncryogenic supply systems.

- Producers of wine bottles, light bulbs, and construction glass use Praxair's oxygen. Praxair's argon, krypton, neon, and xenon also are used in the production of light bulbs.

- Metal fabricators use Praxair's blended shielding gases to increase productivity and decrease fume levels. Based on argon, helium, or hydrogen, these blends are used to produce a wide range of products, from ships and chemical plants to milk containers and motor cycles.

- Profitable solutions to environmental challenges are the key to many Praxair offerings across various markets. The company's patented CoJet gas injection technology raises productivity at steel mills while reducing harmful emissions to the air. Other combustion technologies reduce nitrogen oxide emissions for glass makers, and a patented system helps semiconductor producers recover and reuse by-product gases. Water treatment—industrial and municipal—is yet another way Praxair is making a difference on planet earth.

- For something so small, the production of a semiconductor chip is incredibly complex. Praxair's Point One fab integration services can simplify it. The company streamlines construction of semiconductor tabs by consolidating requirements for not only gases and chemicals but also design, engineering, construction, installation, startup, and ongoing on-site technical support.

- Metal-bending—for motorcycles, pipelines, buildings, bridges, ships, rail cars, appliances, and furniture—has come a long way. Laser, plasma, and robotic technologies use Praxair's sophisticated blends of gases and advanced welding techniques to boost product quality and process efficiency.

- In addition to respiratory therapy, laboratory gases, and magnetic resonance imaging cryogens, health care organizations are increasingly relying on Praxair for site support services and expertise in asset, inventory, transaction, and distribution management. Nurses and doctors save precious seconds with Praxair's new Grab 'n Go portable medical oxygen system, just the latest in the company's one-stop health care shop.

- Jet engine fan blades last longer under tremendous heat, pressure, and corrosive operating conditions with the help of Praxair Surface Technologies's high-performance surface coatings. Aircraft engines are the subsidiary's primary market, but it also serves the printing, textile, chemical, computer, and primary metals markets.

- In a strategic alliance, Merck KGaA Electronic Chemicals and Praxair announced a global alliance and also agreed to jointly develop new semiconductor process materials, the first collaboration of its kind in the industry.

- The company sees opportunities to differentiate its offering in the food and beverage segment, based on the need for higher standards of food safety. Praxair is bringing the potential to save more than 15 billion gallons of water and $70 million each year to the U.S. poultry processing industry through a water recycling system that helps increase production and reduce water consumption without compromising food safety.

- Several oil refining customers in North America are using Praxair's new rapid-response hydrogen supply service, which, in most cases, can be installed at the customer's site within 48 hours and does not require a long-term contract. To meet the projected 20 percent growth in hydrogen demand, two major projects expanded Praxair's Gulf Coast hydrogen pipeline capacity by more than 20 percent in 1999.

- Over the past five years, Praxair Surface Technologies has made 18 acquisitions and experienced double-digit growth rates. Among its acquisitions in 1999 was TAFA Group, an international supplier of thermal spray technologies, equipment, and products to the aircraft, automotive, and general industrial markets.

    The subsidiary also acquired from Sony Corporation of America the assets of Materials Research Corporation, a supplier of materials used in making semiconductor devices.

Total assets: $8,096 million
Current ratio: 1.28
Common shares outstanding: 159 million
Return on 1999 shareholders' equity: 19%

	1999	1998	1997	1996	1995	1994	1993	1992
Revenues (millions)	4639	4833	4735	4449	3146	2711	2438	2604
Net income (millions)	441	425	416	335	262	203	143	124
Earnings per share	2.69	2.60	2.53	2.11	1.82	1.45	1.06	.64
Dividends per share	.56	.50	.44	.38	.32	.28	.25	.125
Price High	58.1	53.9	58.0	50.1	34.1	24.5	18.6	17.5
Low	32.0	30.7	39.3	31.5	19.8	16.3	14.1	13.6

CONSERVATIVE GROWTH

The Procter & Gamble Company

Post Office Box 599 ◻ Cincinnati, Ohio 45201-0599 ◻ Investor contact: Tom Hills (513) 983-2414 ◻ Direct dividend reinvestment plan is available: (800) 764-7483 ◻ Web site: www.pg.com/investor ◻ Listed: NYSE ◻ Fiscal year ends June 30 ◻ Ticker symbol: PG ◻ S&P rating: A ◻ Value Line financial strength rating: A++

Procter & Gamble (P&G) believes in product quality. One of the reasons given for the company's problems in 2000 (when the stock plummeted from a high of $104 to the mid-50s) is its refusal to get into the lower-quality, lower-cost private-label business. That just goes against the grain.

P&G believes that the consumer will reward even minor product advantages, and it will not launch a brand if it does not have a competitive advantage. Then, it will continually improve its products and make every effort to maintain that advantage. Tide, for example, has been improved more than 70 times over the years.

Company Profile

Procter & Gamble is a uniquely diversified consumer-products company with a strong global presence. Established in 1837, P&G today markets its broad line of products to nearly 5 billion consumers in more than one hundred and forty countries.

Procter & Gamble is a recognized leader in the development, manufacturing, and marketing of superior quality laundry, cleaning, paper, personal care, food, beverage, and health care products, including prescription pharmaceuticals.

Among the company's more than three hundred brands are Tide, Always, Whisper, Didronel, Pro-V, Oil of Olay, Pringles, Ariel, Crest, Pampers, Pantene, Crisco, Vicks, Bold, Dawn, Head & Shoulders, Cascade, Zest, Bounty, Comet, Scope, Old Spice, Folgers, Charmin, Tampax, Downy, Crisco, Cheer, and Prell.

In fiscal 1999, laundry and cleaning products contributed 30 percent of P&G's sales; paper 30 percent; beauty care 19 percent; food and beverage 12 percent; health care 7 percent; and corporate and other 2 percent.

Based in Cincinnati, the company has operations in more than seventy countries and employs 110,000.

Procter & Gamble is a huge company, with 1999 sales of $38.1 billion. In the same fiscal year (which ended June 30, 1999), earnings per share advanced from $2.56 to $2.85. Dividends also climbed—as they have for many years—from $1.01 to $1.14.

Such outstanding results tend to dispel the notion that large companies are only for widows and orphans. In my estimation, Procter & Gamble is a "core holding," a term used by my profession to indicate a stock you must own.

Shortcomings to Bear in Mind

- Though the fat substitute olestra is approved for use only in potato chips and other salty snacks, the company's ultimate goal has been to turn olestra (sold under the trade name Olean) into a staple, just as Crisco was a generation earlier. Procter & Gamble confidently projected $1 billion in worldwide sales by the end of 1999. Olestra did rack up decent sales in 1998, but the company grossly miscalculated the size of the market. Part of the problem was that regulatory approval was so long in coming that the fickle cycle of consumer taste had edged away from low-fat food. P&G never overcame olestra's image problem—backed up by numerous complaints that it causes stomach upset in some people. What this adds up to is that with luck, sales may hit half that $1 billion target. P&G admits that olestra, an amber-colored fake fat, probably will not be the liquid gold that management once envisioned.

- Procter & Gamble, a bluechip stock with great credentials, fell from grace in early 2000 when the company announced that earnings would be disappointing. It lowered its forecasts, based on higher raw-material costs, inventory problems in Europe, shrinking profit margins in several Latin American countries, a delayed payment for a new osteoporosis drug that awaits regulatory approval, and competition in its snacks and beverage businesses in North America. What's more, P&G also said that it had spent heavily early in the fiscal year on new products and marketing programs.

Reasons to Buy

- In January of 2000, Procter & Gamble rolled out Fit Fruit and Vegetable Wash, which promises to get apples and greens "squeaky clean," according to a company spokesman. The rollout, which includes products for home and professional use, brings to fruition a six-year test period at P&G and creates a distinct product line.

  Initially, the product was the butt of jokes among analysts, who thought consumer demand for the antiseptic-sounding Fit was hardly ripe. But the heightened awareness of pesticides and food-borne illness "has increased the need for a product like Fit," said Steve Bullock, a P&G global product-development manager. The company cites research claiming 61 percent of consumers believe their produce is "never as clean as they want."

- Procter & Gamble is consistently recognized as one of the best-managed companies in the world.

- In 1999, about 50 percent of the company's net sales came from outside North America. P&G has built a strong global presence by continuously improving some of the world's most-recognized brands, including Pampers, Pringles, Oil of Olay, and Pantene. Procter has the number one global market share in seven consumer product categories, including laundry, diapers, hair care, and feminine protection. What's more, P&G has the number one or two brand in over thirty product categories in North America.

- Innovation enables Procter & Gamble to deliver the best possible products to the world's consumers. The company files for nearly 2,000 patent applications every year, ranking P&G among the most innovative companies in the world. More than 7,000 scientists, from nearly 600 colleges and universities, work at P&G's 18 research centers around the world.

In 1999, the company invested 4.5 percent of net sales into research and development efforts, making it the 21st largest domestic and the 52nd largest global investor in R&D. As a result, Procter has more new ideas in its product pipeline than at anytime in the company's history.

- Historically, Procter & Gamble has delivered consistent earnings per share growth (15 percent since 1994) and expanded its operating margins (over 100 basis points annual improvement during the last five years). Furthermore, return on equity has improved from 27 percent in fiscal 1994 to more than 34 percent in 1999.

- The company has split its stock eight times since 1950. The most recent was a two-for-one split in 1997.

- Today, about half of P&G's sales come from North America, yet 95 percent of the world's population lives *outside* that region.

According to recently retired CEO John Pepper, "If we can achieve these levels of success around the world in just our existing businesses, we'll more than double our current sales and profits."

"This tremendous potential for growth exists in category after category," states Procter & Gamble's annual report. Capitalizing on this potential will not be easy, but the company will pursue it by staying focused on the company's key value and globalization strategies, while placing particular emphasis on three fundamental areas:

- Better products at more competitive prices.
- Deeper, broader cost control.
- Faster, more effective globalization.

- Procter & Gamble is entering new categories and introducing new brands throughout the world. From new categories like fine fragrances to new brands such as Olay Body Wash and Olay Bath

Bar, new P&G businesses are building a foundation for future growth.

- In an effort to loosen its stiff corporate culture and free more cash for product development, P&G said in June 1999 that it would cut 15,000 jobs worldwide—about 13 percent of its work force—close 10 plants, and take nearly $2 billion in charges linked to the reorganization. The company said the reorganization would spur future growth and save about $900 million a year by 2004.

What's more, management said that it is determined to overhaul how products are developed, tested, and introduced. That includes lengthy research and development and market testing of products in the United States before those products are turned over for redevelopment by overseas marketing groups. Now, all products will be developed by seven global brand groups and tested simultaneously around the world to shorten time to market.

- From the start, Febreze—the fabric spray that permanently removes odors from clothes and household fabrics—was a product with something to prove. Consumers who tried it said Febreze was a big idea. But conventional wisdom said it was a niche product. Febreze had trouble meeting early sales goals, but the Febreze group refused to give up. Driven by their passion, they went back to consumers and listened to their feedback about the variety of uses they were finding. As a result, the Febreze advertising began to reflect how consumers felt about Febreze and how it fit into their lives. Febreze is sold in Japan, Korea, Australia, New Zealand, the United States, and more than 15 European countries. In the United States alone, over 35 million households depend on Febreze.

- In August of 1999, the company announced the $2.3 billion acquisition of The Iams Company, a worldwide leader in pet nutrition. Iams is a popular maker of premium pet foods known for its tiny paw-print logo and higher-priced meals for finicky cats and dogs. Founded in 1946 by animal nutritionist Paul Iams, the Dayton, Ohio company has catered to doting pet owners and has allowed its products to be sold by a select group of veterinarians. Over the years it has groomed legions of faithful customers.

This was the largest acquisition in P&G's history. Through the purchase of Iams, Procter & Gamble entered the $25 billion global pet nutrition market with two outstanding brands of dog and cat food: Eukanuba and Iams.

According to management, "It's a great fit for P&G and Iams. Iams's products are based on superior science, just like our brands. In fact, we see major opportunities to apply our expertise in nutrition, bone and tooth health, hygiene, and hair and skin care. We can leverage our global scale and distribution capability to expand Eukanuba and Iams around the world. Today, only about 30 percent of Iams's sales come from outside the United States."

- Procter & Gamble, looking to tap into the neurosis of people who really believe in such a thing as bad-hair days, took on beauty salons in fiscal 2000 by launching its first new hair-care brand in more than a decade: the "Physique" line costing as much as $10 a bottle. The 24-product line for men and women was sent to supermarkets and department stores in January 2000, along with an innovative marketing approach. Shoppers entering the stores find specially trained stylists who show them how to use the products in much the same way that a high-priced salon shows clients how to mold their hair.

Total assets: $32,113 million
Current ratio: 0.93
Common shares outstanding: 1,314 million
Return on 1999 shareholders' equity: 34.4%

	1999	1998	1997	1996	1995	1994	1993	1992
Revenues (millions)	38125	37154	35764	35284	33434	30296	30433	29362
Net income (millions)	4148	3780	3415	3046	2645	2211	2015	1872
Earnings per share	2.85	2.56	2.28	2.15	1.86	1.55	1.41	1.31
Dividends per share	1.14	1.01	.90	.80	.70	.62	.55	.52
Price High	115.6	94.8	83.4	55.5	44.8	32.3	29.4	27.9
Low	82.0	65.1	51.8	39.7	30.3	25.6	22.6	22.6

INCOME

Royal Dutch Petroleum Company

Carel van Bylandtlaan 30 ❐ 2596 HR The Hague ❐ The Netherlands ❐ Investor contact: J. C. Grapsi (212) 261-5660 ❐ Dividend reinvestment plan is not available ❐ Web site: www.shell.com/investors ❐ Ticker symbol: RD ❐ S&P rating: A- ❐ Value Line financial strength rating: A++

Royal Dutch has great and growing competitive strength:

• In exploration and production— unrivaled operational experience, leadership in deep waters, the largest private gas reserves, and the industry's lowest finding and development costs.

• In downstream gas and power—the lowest cost for building and operating liquefied natural gas (LNG) facilities and a leading position, through InterGen, in developing independent power plants.

- In oil products—the best-known and most preferred brand, selling to 20 million customers a day through 46,000 service stations in 90 countries.
- In chemicals—world-scale chemical plants and leadership in various products.

Company Profile

Operating in more than one hundred thirty five countries around the world, the companies of the Royal Dutch/Shell Group are engaged in the core businesses of Exploration and Production, Oil Products, Chemicals, Downstream Gas, and Power and Renewables.

Royal Dutch Petroleum Company is a holding company that, in conjunction with The Shell Transport and Trading Company, PLC—an English company— owns either directly or indirectly investments in the numerous companies of the Royal Dutch/Shell Group. Royal Dutch has an interest of 60 percent in the Group and Shell Transport an interest of 40 percent.

Exploration and Production
Searching for oil and gas fields by means of seismic survey and exploration wells; developing economically viable fields by drilling wells; and building the infrastructure of pipelines and treatment facilities necessary for delivering the hydrocarbons to market.

Crude oil prices remain unpredictable. Nevertheless, overall world demand is likely to continue growing, driven by the economic recovery of several Asia-Pacific countries and the continuing strength of the U.S. economy. Technological advances—particularly in drilling—will drive down industry costs.

In 1999, the asset portfolio was upgraded by divestments (mainly in the United States and Canada) and certain dilutions (most notably in the Philippines). The go-ahead was given for projects in Nigeria (the offshore EA and Bonga fields), in the United States (the deep-water Brutus field), and in Canada (the Athabasca oil sands). Plans to redevelop a pair of oil fields in Iran were announced. Important new licenses were acquired in Malaysia, Norway, China, and in Brazilian deep waters.

Oil Products
Refining and processing crude oil and other feedstocks into transportation fuels, lubricants, heating and fuel oils, liquefied petroleum, and gas and bitumen; distributing and marketing them—together with complementary services—to meet customer needs.

Oil demand is forecast to increase by some 2 million barrels a day in 2000, driven by economic growth. European and U.S. Gulf Coast refinery margins are expected to remain under pressure until demand reduces excess stocks of distillates. Asia-Pacific margins are likely to remain weak because of the surplus capacity in the region. Pressures on gross fuels margins will continue. But if oil prices are stable or falling, gross marketing margins may rise from 1999 levels.

The Group's exposure to low refining margins continued to be reduced in 1999. The Shell Haven refinery in the United Kingdom ceased operations; the closure of the Sola refinery in Norway was set for 2000; and an Equilon refinery in the United States was sold. Refinery capacity and retail assets were swapped with other oil companies in Europe. Fuels tailored to specific consumer needs were introduced in seven markets, and various e-commerce initiatives were launched around the world.

Chemicals
Transforming hydrocarbon feedstocks into base chemical products, petrochemical

building blocks, and polyolefins, and marketing them globally to create customer value.

Chemicals trading conditions improved in the fourth quarter of 1999 from earlier in the year as confidence returned to the Asia-Pacific region and feedstock price rises throughout the year were increasingly reflected in the finished product prices. No significant change in trading conditions is anticipated in the short term.

Performance improvements through cost leadership programs, improved plant reliability, and capacity additions were achieved in 1999. Additionally, in keeping with the divestment program announced in 1998, Shell companies sold several chemicals businesses (such as general purpose rubber, polystyrene, and polyvinyl chloride). Negotiations on other divestments continued into 2000. Finally, an agreement with BASF to create a global polyolefins business was reached.

Downstream Gas and Power
Marketing and trading natural gas; commercializing natural gas through investments in processing and transportation infrastructure; wholesaling and retailing of natural gas and electricity to industrial and domestic customers; developing and operating independent electric power plants.

Gas and electricity demand is expected to continue to grow strongly. But liberalization of the gas market is likely to challenge the Group's strong position in Europe. Future success will depend on integrating the energy requirements of consumers and on optimizing the entire gas-to-power value-added chain, from wellhead to burner and to electricity meter.

In 1999, long-term sales contracts of liquefied natural gas (LNG) to India were won, and decisions were taken to invest further in Nigeria LNG and Malaysia LNG. An additional 5 percent interest was acquired in Comgas, the largest gas

distribution company in Brazil. Financing was secured for five power plants. The U.S. portfolio was restructured, with the sale of Oklahoma pipeline assets and the establishment of a joint venture to handle the natural gas liquids business.

Renewables
Bringing renewable resources to everyday life by developing viable businesses; manufacturing and marketing solar energy systems; implementing rural electrification projects in developing countries; sustainably growing and marketing wood; converting wood fuel into marketable energy; developing wind energy projects.

Renewable energy can be competitive in niche markets. Outside these markets—and in the short term—it will need governmental support. Yet its cost will continue to decline as more experience is gained. And as it becomes more competitive, it will supply a significant proportion of the world's energy. Paper and pulp prices, having suffered a cyclical downturn, are now strengthening as demand tracks economic growth.

Shortcomings to Bear in Mind

- In the 1989–1999 period, earnings per share gains were not that of a growth stock. EPS advanced from $2.06 to $2.11. In the same 10-year stretch, dividends expanded from $0.84 to $1.59, a compound annual growth rate of 6.6 percent. What's more, the payout ratio is too high: 75.4 percent. On the other hand, this is a large and well-managed company and should be suitable for investors seeking income.

Reasons to Buy

- A high-capacity, modern warehouse was recently opened in Dubai's Jebel Ali Free Zone, a designated economic development area. It will play a key role in the distribution of polyurethane polyols and solvent products (used in the manufacture of paints, cleaners, agrochemicals, furniture, and mattresses) to a growing number of customers in the Middle East and surrounding regions.

- Two energy marketing and trading businesses—one in the United Kingdom and one in the United States—are set to grow on the strength of their relationships with industrial and commercial customers. Shell Gas Direct of the United Kingdom, which is now selling not only natural gas but also electricity, continues to be ranked highly in terms of its customer service in independent market surveys. U.S.-based Coral Energy is offering its customers both gas and electricity directly from regional trading hubs and, through a robust financial products business, allows them to tailor the cost of their energy to meet specific objectives.

- Shell Aviation was presented with the first-ever award for an airport refueling business by the UK-based Institute of Transport Management. This award is based on an evaluation of a company's customer orientation, pricing, services offered, innovation, and safety awareness.

- A computerized energy management system enables Coral Site Advantage (CSA), a unit of Shell subsidiary Coral Energy, to keep a finger on the energy pulse of the Continental Tire factory in Mt. Vernon, Illinois. On the basis of such diagnostic information, CSA can recommend the best mix of energy sources and pricing structures to minimize both costs and risks.

- Shell Technology Ventures is in the process of commercializing a novel device for extracting liquids from natural gas, which they have dubbed Twister. Elegant by virtue of its simplicity, Twister forces the gas to reach supersonic speeds, causing water or hydrocarbon vapors to condense into droplets. The droplets are than separated from the gas by an induced swirling motion that flings the liquid outward. Devoid of both chemicals and moving parts, the device reduces emissions into the atmosphere and offers significant space and weight savings.

- The recently opened Shell Renewables solar-cell plant in Gelsenkirchen, Germany houses the world's first fully automated, high-throughput, solar-cell production line. The factory building, which has a striking architectural form, has solar roof panels that provide part of the facility's annual electricity requirements.

Total assets: $56,171 million
Current ratio: 0.91
Common shares outstanding: 2,144 million
Return on 1999 shareholders' equity: 13.4%

	1999	1998	1997	1996	1995	1994	1993	1992
Revenues (millions)	105366	93692	128155	128313	109872	96919	93631	93544
Net income (millions)	7534	5146	8031	8126	7492	5440	4434	5209
Earnings per share	2.11	1.55	2.40	2.48	2.20	1.67	1.63	1.53
Dividends per share	1.59	1.58	1.51	1.45	1.37	1.21	1.18	1.16
Price High	67.4	60.4	59.4	43.5	35.4	29.2	27.0	22.9
Low	39.6	39.8	42.0	33.4	26.8	24.2	19.7	18.4

SBC Communications Incorporated

175 East Houston, Room 8-A-60 □ San Antonio, Texas 78205 □ Investor contact: Sandy Wagner
(210) 351-3327 □ Direct dividend reinvestment plan is available: (800) 351-7221 □ Web site: www.sbc.com
□ Listed: NYSE □ Ticker symbol: SBC □ S&P rating: A- □ Value Line financial strength rating: A+

For many decades, American Telephone & Telegraph was the essence of the telephone industry. Although there were many other telephone companies—hundreds, in fact—Ma Bell was what came to mind when you dialed your telephone.

That all ended in 1984 when the federal government decreed that AT&T could keep its Bell Labs and long-distance service but had to divest the Bell companies that provided local telephone service. At the stroke of a pen, this brought forth seven Regional Bell Operating Companies, often known as Baby Bells. The term hardly fits these huge companies, since none had less than $10 billion in annual revenues.

With the passage of time, there are no longer seven. In 1997, Southwestern Bell (now SBC Communications) acquired Pacific Bell, with local service in California. In 1998, SBC acquired an independent company, Southern New England Telecommunications, for $4.4 billion in stock. In still another Baby Bell elimination, Bell Atlantic acquired NYNEX, with operations in New York and New England. Of the seven Regional Bell Operating Companies spawned in 1984, only four are left standing: SBC Communications, Bell Atlantic (now Verizon), BellSouth, and US West.

In October of 1999, SBC acquired still another Baby Bell, Ameritech, for $62 billion in stock. Based in Chicago, Ameritech provides local phone service in five Midwestern states: Illinois, Michigan, Ohio, Indiana, and Wisconsin. SBC shareholders now own 56 percent of the combined company, while former Ameritech shareholders hold 44 percent.

Company Profile

SBC Communications now ranks first among U.S. telecommunications providers, with 59 million access lines, and third with 10.1 million domestic wireless subscribers.

As of late 1999, SBC Communications became one of the 30 stocks in the Dow Jones Industrial Average. As you might surmise, SBC is *not* an industrial company—it's clearly a public utility—and might more properly have been included in the Dow Jones Utility Average. Moreover, the same thing could be said of AT&T, which has been a component of the Industrial Average since 1939 when it replaced IBM. To atone for their egregious pre-war blunder, some kindly souls let IBM back into the Average in 1979.

As now constituted, SBC Communications serves 59.5 access lines in high-growth regions. It also reaches more than 113 million potential domestic wireless customers and has equity stakes in international telecommunications businesses reaching more than 375 million potential customer.

International operations include a 10 percent interest in Telefonos de Mexico, cable and telecommunications operations in the United Kingdom and Chile, and wireless operations in France, South Korea, and South Africa. SBC also has a long-distance alliance and cable television operations in Israel. Additional ventures were formed in 1997 with Switzerland, South Korea, and Taiwan. What's more, the company has joined with 13 other international companies to build a trans-Pacific fiber-optic cable for long-distance traffic between the United States and China, which is expected to be completed in 2000. Finally, in late 1998 the company and 11 partners agreed to build an undersea communications pipeline between the United States and Japan for operation in mid-2000.

Shortcomings to Bear in Mind

- As the Bells slowly push into the long-distance market, they also appear to be stampeding the likes of AT&T and MCI WorldCom to expand their local phone offerings, providing more options for consumers. For instance, it was not until Bell Atlantic's long-distance application for New York appeared close to approval in the fall of 1999 that AT&T started marketing its own local service broadly in New York.

Reasons to Buy

- In April of 2000, SBC Communications and BellSouth said they planned to combine their domestic cell phone operations to form the nation's second-largest wireless telecommunications carrier. The venture will have about 16.2 million subscribers, rivaling Verizon Wireless, the joint venture between Bell Atlantic and Britain's Vodafone AirTouch p.l.c. The partnership allows BellSouth and SBC to expand their geographic reach without the cost of building new wireless networks. The companies can also save money by avoiding costly roaming fees paid to transmit their customers' calls over rival wireless networks.
- In late 1999, SBC Communications said that it would transfer all of its residential Internet customers to the Prodigy Communications Corporation, the online service that has long been overshadowed by America Online, in return

for a 43-percent stake in Prodigy. SBC said Prodigy would assume day-to-day management of SBC's 650,000 residential and small-business Internet customers. The deal made Prodigy SBC's Internet service provider for consumers and small business.

Just prior to the pact with Prodigy, SBC said it would spend $6 billion to deploy high-speed Internet systems throughout its service region, which covers more than one-third of the United States population. SBC intends to deploy a technology called digital subscriber line, or DSL, which uses standard telephone wires to transmit digital data at speeds many times that of those using normal modems. The DSL announcement reflected the company's confidence that it could profit from the exploding demand for Internet access, particularly at high speeds.

- In early 2000, SBC Communications made its first big push to deliver telecommunications outside its 13-state home territory through an alliance with Network Access Solutions Corporation, a provider of high-speed Internet access.

In 1998, SBC promised federal regulators that it would provide competitive phone services in 30 markets outside its core local-phone territory, which stretches from California to Connecticut. The company indicated it would serve such cities as Boston, Miami, and Seattle but provided little additional detail. The alliance with Network Access, which operates on the East Coast, will help SBC eventually reach all of the 30 new markets it promised to serve.

Stephen McGaw, managing director of corporate development for SBC, said the alliance with Network Access Solutions is the latest step in the regional Bell's effort to remake itself as a national provider of high-speed, or broadband, services. In 1999, the company announced "Project Pronto," a $6-billion upgrade of its in-region networks to deliver broadband services.

"Project Pronto is our big digital subscriber line deployment, but one obvious gap has been our offering outside our region." Mr. McGaw said. "This alliance fills that gap."

- In the biggest move by a major local phone company into the torrid electronic-commerce business, SBC acquired Sterling Commerce for $3.9 billion in 2000. Based in Dallas, Texas, Sterling provides software that enables businesses to electronically transmit orders, invoices, and payment data to suppliers.

Sterling, which had revenues of $561 million in fiscal 1999, provides electronic-commerce systems to over forty five thousand customers worldwide, including many large corporations such as Wal-Mart, Johnson & Johnson, and Sony. Sterling's revenue growth in 2000 is targeted at 20 percent, with 27 percent forecast for 2001.

SBC's CEO, Edward E. Whitacre, Jr., is betting that the move into high-margin e-biz services will help convince customers and investors that his company is more than a fuddy-duddy Baby Bell stuck in slow-growing traditional telephone markets.

- In the breathless atmosphere of cutting-edge investments and next-generation opportunities, the phone companies don't rate—or at least no one seems to think so. Think again. The Baby Bells are a critical link in the value chain of the enabling technologies necessary for the Internet to be commercially successful.

And unlike most of the stocks that make up the Internet realm, their prices are reasonable—their P/E ratios are typically below average. What's more, their earnings are rising, and their survival and growth are not in doubt. For the price of a single share of Yahoo, you could buy a share in each of the companies remaining from the breakup of AT&T. In addition, look at the contrast in annual revenues: Yahoo had $540 million in 1999; the Bell companies had a combined total of $90 billion.

"All the attention is being paid to the smaller upstart communications companies, " said Ian Link, portfolio manager of the Franklin Global Communications Fund. Since the upstarts have no earnings, investors have adopted a "totally different metric and a totally different mind-set" that doesn't quite compute when confronted with such strangeness as dividends. "There's a disconnect," Link said.

The Bells are the largest Internet service providers in the country and the largest cellular providers, yet they "are being completely ignored." But Link said he's been buying the stocks because he believes they are still cheap. He noted that their earnings are growing— from 8 to 10 percent annually to 12 to 14 percent.

- SBC has made impressive progress in its national expansion into 30 new metropolitan area markets. As part of the expansion launched in concert with the acquisition of Ameritech, SBC expects to introduce service in nine new markets in 2000, and another 21 during the following two years.

- SBC's broad international portfolio continues to be a powerful contributor to earnings growth. For instance, in the fourth quarter of 1999, pretax income from the company's international investments increased 22.8 percent from the year-earlier quarter. What's more, the publically traded companies in SBC's international portfolio saw their market share value increase 38 percent during 1999. Finally, the company's international portfolio has an estimated value of more than $25 billion.

- SBC's data services had a banner year in 1999, as revenues increase 42.9 percent, to $5.7 billion. Based on market expansion and SBC's growth initiatives, the company expects its data revenue stream to continue to grow strongly. The company, moreover, expects 40 percent of its top-line growth over the next three years will come from data services.

    SBC's largest data initiative, Project Pronto, is being deployed after being launched in the fourth quarter of 1999. Project Pronto is designed to enable SBC to deliver DSL broadband Internet access to more than 80 percent of its local telephone customers by the end of 2002. Finally, the company projects that the initiative will generate $3.5 billion in new annual revenues by 2004.

- During 1999, SBC significantly expanded its domestic wireless market coverage. In addition to more than 21 million total population (POPs) acquired from Ameritech, the company added Comcast's wireless operations covering Philadelphia and surrounding areas as well as Cellular Communications of

Puerto Rico. And in the fourth quarter, SBC announced plans to acquire Radiofone, which covers about 2.4 million POPs in Michigan and Louisiana, including New Orleans. At year-end, the company had 11.2 million domestic subscribers. Its markets include 23 of the nation's 35 largest metropolitan areas.

- Cisco Systems, the data networking company, announced in April of 2000 that it had entered into a multibillion-dollar alliance with SBC Communications. Under the agreement, SBC will be among the biggest buyers of Cisco's routers and switches that are used to build the Internet's infrastructure. It is one of the first times that Cisco has closely aligned itself with a traditional phone company. It will provide equipment to send information over five different networking platforms, including digital subscriber lines, which are faster than dial-up modems and other services that can transmit data, voice, and video. The two companies hope to develop products to make it easier for Internet users to switch between different Internet service providers, as well as a local area network.

Total assets: $83,215 million
Current ratio: 0.60
Common shares outstanding: 3,458 million
Return on 1999 shareholders' equity: 30.5%

	1999	1998	1997	1996	1995	1994	1993	1992
Revenues (millions)	48960	45323	25044	13898	12670	11619	10690	10015
Net income (millions)	8159	7690	3364	2101	1889	1649	1435	1302
Earnings per share	2.36	2.08	1.84	1.73	1.55	1.37	1.20	1.09
Dividends per share	.97	.94	.89	.86	.83	.79	.76	.73
Price High	59.9	54.9	38.1	30.1	29.3	22.1	23.5	18.7
Low	44.1	35.0	24.6	23.0	19.8	18.4	17.1	14.2

Stryker Corporation

Post Office Box 4085 ▫ Kalamazoo, Michigan 49003-4085 ▫ Investor contact: David J. Simpson
(616) 385-6000 ▫ Web site: www.stryker.com ▫ Listed: NYSE ▫ Dividend reinvestment plan is not available
▫ Ticker symbol: SYK ▫ S&P rating: B+ ▫ Value Line financial strength rating: A

In 1999, the company continued its pioneering work in high-technology bearing surfaces, aimed at reducing wear. The prior year, Stryker became the first company authorized by the U.S. Food & Drug Administration (FDA) to market highly cross-linked polyethylene, shown to reduce wear by about 90 percent.

By the end of the year, one-quarter of the company's acetabular inserts were lined with Crossfire, Stryker's brand of this material. This proportion is expected to climb to 50 percent in 2000, as the company applies Crossfire to more hip systems.

Company Profile

Stryker Corporation was founded in 1941 by Dr. Homer H. Stryker, a leading orthopedic surgeon and the inventor of several orthopedic products. The company now ranks as a dominant player in a $12-billion global orthopedics industry. SYK has a significant market share in such sectors as artificial hips, prosthetic knees, and trauma products.

Stryker develops, manufactures, and markets specialty surgical and medical products worldwide. These products include orthopedic implants, trauma systems, powered surgical instruments, endoscopic systems, and patient care and handling equipment. Stryker also provides outpatient rehabilitative health services in the United States and is engaged in testing of the bone growth factor, osteogenic protein-I.

Stryker Products and Sales Divisions

Orthopedic Implants
- Howmedica Osteonics—Orthopedic reconstructive products, including hip, knee, and shoulder implants.

- Stryker Spine—Spinal implant products.

Trauma Systems
- Stryker Trauma—Trauma-related products, including nailing, plating, and external fixation systems.
- Stryker Leibinger—Plating systems, instruments, and related products for craniomaxillofacial surgery; systems for image-guided surgery.

Surgical Instruments and Equipment
- Stryker Instruments—Powered surgical instruments and other products, such as lavage systems and cement injection systems.
- Stryker Endoscopy—Medical video-imaging equipment and instruments for arthroscopy and general surgery.

Biotechnology
- Stryker Biotech—Osteogenic protein-I (OP-I) bone growth factor.

Medical Equipment
- Stryker Medical—Specialty hospital beds and stretchers, general patient-room beds, and EMS cots.

Rehabilitative Medical Services
- Physiotherapy Associates—Outpatient rehabilitation services, with a focus on physical and occupational therapy.

Shortcomings to Bear in Mind

- Weakness in the European currency could put pressure on sales. During the fourth quarter of 1999, for instance, weakness in the euro lowered revenues by nearly $4 million.

- At the end of 1998, the company acquired Howmedica, formerly the orthopedic division of Pfizer, to become a stronger competitor in the global medical marketplace. In order to do this, Stryker took on considerable additional debt. As a consequence, its balance sheet (which previously had very little debt), is now very leveraged. Common equity is only 32 percent of total capitalization. I generally regard anything less than 75 percent as a negative factor.

Reasons to Buy

- Analysts look for gross margins to approximate 63 percent in 2000, as the product mix continues to shift toward higher-margined reconstructive products and as inventory revaluation issues abate.

- Stryker has a well-deserved reputation for growth. At the end of 1998, when the company deliberately assumed debt to acquire Howmedica, management was acting on a long-term strategy for growth that reflected the new realities of the medical marketplace. In the United States, the dual forces of expansion and consolidation have created larger hospitals and buying groups. These organizations, together with governments worldwide, have exerted more pricing pressure than ever on their medical-products suppliers. Only market leaders—companies that match first-class products with scale and efficiency—will succeed in winning their business.

For its part, Stryker is committed to forging its destiny in this new environment by offering to the world marketplace broad and deep lines of diversified products around an orthopedic core. The combined market force of Stryker and Howmedica provides the company with the means to promote long-term growth for Stryker and its shareholders.

- Throughout the acquisition of Howmedica, Stryker knew that retention of the orthopedic sales force—from both Stryker and Howmedica—would be critical to the success of the merger. Fortunately, all but a fraction of a percent of the members of the combined sales forces worldwide have elected to remain with the company. In all likelihood, they were motivated by the comprehensive range of products, the company's rewarding compensation structure, as well as a conviction that Stryker has a bright future.

The newly merged company now has an orthopedic sales force of some 2,200 professionals who are bent on earning the trust of physicians and hospital personnel around the globe.

- With the acquisition of Howmedica, Stryker seized the opportunity to grow and expand its presence in the global orthopedic marketplace. Propelled by aging populations, increased longevity, rising living standards, and higher patient expectations around the world, this market now stands at close to $12 billion.

At the same time, hospitals and buying groups, spurred on by governments and private payers alike, are demanding higher quality medical products at lower costs. These pressures create challenges that only the largest and most efficient companies can surmount. Since its founding, Stryker has won wide respect for the quality of its products. Now, the company has the capacity to serve the medical marketplace more effectively.

- Howmedica's Osteonics's hip implants offer a range of solutions in joint replacement and revision, meeting different types of patient needs and physician preferences. In 1999, for example, the company experienced exceptional sales in two contrasting and well-established hip implants. The cemented Exeter stem, with a 30-year record of success in the Howmedica line, doubled its sales.

At the same time, the cementless Osteonics stems that are coated with hydroxylapatite (HA), a calcium phosphate, enjoyed their third consecutive year of more than 20 percent growth and reached the 10-year clinical milestone. New products were also launched, notably the EON hip implant, a cemented stem that is the latest generation of the Osteonics Omnifit System, and the Restoration PS and Restoration T-3 hip revision systems. Finally, having supported hip implantation for 40 years, the company's Surgical Simplex bone cement remains the leading product of its kind throughout the world.

- In the realm of upper extremities, the Solar Total Shoulder System continues to be favored by surgeons, not only for its unique head design, which expands range of motion, but also for its performance, size options, and for its instrumentation, which is designed to provide greater access to the surgical site. The company also introduced the Solar Bipolar Shoulder System, an implant created specially to treat tears of the rotator cuff.
- The union of Howmedica and Osteonics has made Stryker a formidable competitor in the knee market, with an emphasis on rapid development of global products that are both easier to use and less costly to manufacture. The company's leading knee implants— Duracon from the Howmedica line and Scorpio from the Osteonics line—cover the major areas of surgeon preference in total knee arthroplasty.

The Duracon line, which is entering its ninth year of clinical success with more than 360,000 implanted, was significantly augmented in 1999 with the launch of the Duracon Total Stabilizer. This complete revision system incorporates new technology that offers the potential for knee revisions that are even more reliable.

The Scorpio Cruciate Retaining Knee System, introduced in 1996, is one of the fastest-growing products in its market segment. The Scorpio Cruciate Retaining Knee System, which followed in 1998, had been employed in nearly 60,000 implantations by the end of 1999.

- In 1999, the company organized the development of its spinal implant products as a global business unit. This initiative enables Stryker to take maximum advantage of the $1-billion worldwide spine market, the most rapidly growing in orthopedics. Accordingly, the company will continue to expand its spine sales force in key markets throughout the world.

Total assets: $2,580 million
Current ratio: 1.77
Common shares outstanding: 97 million
Return on 1999 shareholder's equity: NM

	1999	1998	1997	1996	1995	1994	1993	1992
Revenues (millions)	2104	1103	980	910	872	682	557	477
Net income (millions)	161	150	125	101	87	72	60	48
Earnings per share	1.62	1.53	1.28	1.04	.90	.75	.63	.50
Dividends per share	.13	.12	.11	.10	.05	.04	.04	.03
Price High	73.3	55.8	45.3	32.1	29.3	18.8	19.9	26.1
Low	44.4	31.0	24.3	19.9	18.1	11.9	10.5	13.1

Sysco Corporation

1390 Enclave Parkway ◻ Houston, Texas 77077-2099 ◻ Investor contact: Ms. Toni R. Spigelmyer
(281) 584-1458 ◻ Web site: www.sysco.com ◻ Dividend reinvestment plan is available: (800) 730-4001
◻ Fiscal year ends the Saturday closest to June 30 ◻ Listed: NYSE ◻ Ticker symbol: SYY ◻ S&P rating: A+
◻ Value Line financial strength rating: A+

As they go about their lives, many people encounter the familiar Sysco trucks, bearing giant blue lettering, delivering products to customers. Few are aware, however, of Sysco's far-reaching influence on meals served daily throughout North America. As the continent's largest marketer and distributor of food-service products, Sysco operates 78 distribution facilities serving more than 325,000 restaurants, hotels, schools, hospitals, retirement homes, and other locations where food is prepared to be eaten on the premises or taken away and enjoyed in the comfort of the diner's chosen environment. The company's distribution network extends throughout the continental United States, as well as portions of Alaska and Canada.

Sysco is by far the largest company in the foodservice distribution industry. In sales, Sysco dwarfs its two chief competitors, $6.2-billion US Foodservice and $2.1-billion Performance Food Group.

The company's operations break down as follows: restaurants (64 percent of 1999 sales), hospitals and nursing homes (10 percent), schools and colleges (7 percent), hotels and motels (5 percent), other (14 percent).

With annual sales in 1999 of $17.4 billion, Sysco distributes a wide variety of fresh and frozen meats, seafood, poultry, fruits and vegetables, plus bakery products, canned and dry foods, paper and disposables, sanitation items, dairy foods, beverages, kitchen and tabletop equipment, as well as medical and surgical supplies.

Sysco's innovations in food technology, packaging, and transportation provide customers with quality products, delivered on time, in excellent condition and at reasonable prices.

Shortcomings to Bear in Mind

- I am having trouble finding anything wrong with Sysco. However, the balance sheet is more leveraged than I would like. Common stock as a percentage of capitalization is only 59 percent. I would prefer a figure closer to 75 percent. On the other hand, coverage of bond interest is more than adequate, at 10.3 times.

- The stock has performed well in recent years and often sells at a healthy P/E multiple of 30 or more.

Reasons to Buy

- Sysco keeps margins high by selling products under its own label, a strategy it began a year after its founding. It saves on national advertising and passes some of the savings along to its customers. Its private-label business carries an estimated 24 percent gross margin, or 10 percent more than it earns on national brands.

- Sysco's industry-leading sales are indicative of the overall health and prosperity of the foodservice industry. During Sysco's fiscal year 1999, the foodservice industry grew at a real rate of 4 percent (after adjusting for inflation), according to industry sources, while Sysco achieved a real growth of more than twice that rate. This was primarily attributed to the company's dedication to providing innovative products and unequaled service to all customers in an effort to assist them in fulfilling the needs of their patrons. After adjusting sales for the effects of very moderate food cost inflation of 0.98 percent and acquisitions of 1.14 percent, Sysco's real sales growth was 11.6 percent for the 53-week fiscal year. As the year progressed, Sysco continued to increase its rate of growth, ending the fiscal year with an exceptionally strong fourth quarter.

- The SYGMA Network, Inc., Sysco's subsidiary that focuses on chain restaurant distribution, increased sales 44 percent in fiscal 1999, to a record $2 billion. This figure represents 11.5 percent of overall Sysco sales and includes about $600 million annualized in new business from 1,700 additional Wendy's International locations across the United States. To accommodate these new outlets, SYGMA added three distribution facilities in 1999, increasing to 15 the number of SYGMA facilities nationwide.

- The company also expanded geographically in 1999 through several acquisitions. The merger with Doughtie's Foods, (Portsmouth, Virginia), was completed in August of 1999. Sysco also acquired two precision custom-cut meat companies, Newport Meat Company (Irvine, California) and the Buckhead Beef Company (Atlanta, Georgia). Combined, the three acquisitions represent about $387 million in annualized revenues.

In 2000, the company acquired FreshPoint Holdings, Inc., one of the largest foodservice and wholesale produce distribution companies in North America. Current annualized sales of FreshPoint Holdings are about $750 million, approaching the $1 billion in produce sales generated by Sysco during 1999. FreshPoint distributes a product mix of 60 percent fresh vegetables, 25 percent fresh fruit, and 15 percent other produce and refrigerated products. Its customer base of more than twenty thousand includes foodservice establishments such as restaurants, hotels, cruise ships, government facilities, and other institutional customers.

Bill M. Lindig, Sysco's chairman of the board, said management was surprised by how little customer duplication exists between the two companies. "We've often said this great North American foodservice distribution market of $165 billion in calendar 1998 had plenty of opportunity for growth, and Sysco holds only about a 10 percent market share. With our current produce sales of about 6 percent of total sales, this acquisition will give us the ability to grow by providing just-in-time and more frequent produce deliveries to customers that require these superior service levels."

- While Sysco does not manufacture or process any products, the company is dedicated to procuring products of the most consistent quality for America's diners. This ideal is reinforced by a team of more than one hundred eight quality-assurance professionals unparalleled in the industry. Continually, they consult with 1,500-plus worldwide growers and manufacturers of Sysco Brand products, developing product specifications, monitoring production processes, and enforcing Sysco's stringent standards.

- Sysco has a solid record of growth. In the past 10 years (1989–1999), earnings per share advanced from 30 cents to $1.08 (with no dips along the way), a compound annual growth rate of 13.7 percent. In the same span, dividends per share climbed from 4 cents to 38 cents, a growth rate of 25.2 percent. Growth was still in evidence in the first quarter of 2000, as earnings per share shot up 23 percent.

- Although acquisitions played a vital role in establishing geographic footholds in Sysco's early years, the company's sustained growth in market share primarily reflects internally generated sales increases within each market served.
- As the largest distributor of foodservice products in North America, Sysco assists customers in creating a vast array of dining choices. Menus have greatly improved since a French chef named Boulanger offered a choice of soups, or "restorative" to patrons who paused at his inn to refresh themselves as they traveled during the 1700s. The sign in French read "restaurant," and his establishment may have been the first to offer a menu.

  Today's diverse menu choices could not have been imagined then—raspberries from Australia served fresh in Wisconsin in January; gourmet pesto sauce rich with garlic, fresh basil, and pine nuts delivered to a Vancouver chef's doorstep; or artfully prepared hearts of lettuce served in an Arizona college's cafeterias each day. Providing choices from soup to nuts, and everything in between, Sysco leads the way in helping chefs in restaurants, schools, business cafeterias, health care locations, lodging, and other facilities increase the variety and quality of food choices in North America.
- Whether dining in an upscale restaurant or picking up pasta as the entree for a meal at home, people spend less time on food preparation than ever before. They want variety and flavor in the foods they choose to eat, yet their time to prepare meals is constantly in competition with work and leisure activities. More than ever, people are turning to meals prepared away from home for greater convenience, quality, and, most of all, choice.

  It is a trend that started in World War II, as women began to work outside the home. Business cafeterias, coffee shops, school lunchrooms, and restaurants broadened the range of dining choices for people who were used to much simpler fare. Twenty-five years ago not many consumers could identify kiwi fruit. During the past three decades, foodservice offerings have moved from fruit cocktail with a cherry on top to kiwi and other exotic fare; from steak and potatoes to fajitas with all the trimmings.
- Each day, the drivers of Sysco's nearly 5,800 delivery vehicles crisscross the cities and counties of North America to deliver more than 2 million cases of product. From the back alley door of a small deli in Los Angeles to the loading dock of a major hospital in St. Louis, Sysco distributes a range of 275,000 products system-wide that have been transported by rail, trucked, or flown from points near and far around the globe to Sysco warehouses. That foods are shipped daily so reliably and accurately is possible only because of advances in computer technology, transportation, refrigeration, and warehousing.

  In the 1970s, the typical fleet unit was a 12- to 16-foot truck with modest refrigeration capabilities. Frozen and dry goods were the primary commodities of the foodservice industry. Today's 28- to 36-foot, single-axle trucks typically have three separate food storage compartments with the most reliable mechanical refrigeration systems available.

Total assets: $4,097 million
Current ratio: 1.69
Common shares outstanding: 330 million
Return on 1999 shareholders' equity: 26%

	1999	1998	1997	1996	1995	1994	1993	1992
Revenues (millions)	17423	15328	14455	13395	12118	10942	10022	8893
Net income (millions)	362	325	302	277	252	217	202	172
Earnings per share	1.08	.95	.86	.76	.69	.59	.54	.47
Dividends per share	.38	.33	.29	.25	.20	.16	.14	.10
Price High	39.2	28.7	23.6	18.1	16.3	14.6	15.5	13.9
Low	24.9	19.9	14.6	13.8	12.4	10.6	11.1	10.3

AGGRESSIVE GROWTH

Texas Instruments Incorporated

8505 Forest Lane, MS 8657 ◻ **Dallas, Texas 75243** ◻ **Investor contact: Ron Slaymaker (972) 480-6388** ◻ **Dividend reinvestment plan is not available** ◻ **Web site: www.ti.com** ◻ **Listed: NYSE** ◻ **Ticker symbol: TXN** ◻ **S&P rating: B** ◻ **Value Line financial strength rating: A+**

Texas Instruments' digital light processor, a novel chip that uses microscopic mirrors instead of electric circuits, is nearly ready for prime time. The first big-screen TVs featuring the odd-shaped computer chips are supposed to be out late in 2000.

TI developers have spent years—and hundreds of millions of dollars—trying to get the technology and the pricing right. The company still isn't there. But in late 1999 the company announced ventures with Japan's Hitachi Ltd. and Mitsubishi Electric Corporation to develop tubeless televisions based on the technology. TI's big-screen projection TVs promise to show pictures more clearly than most current TV models.

Company Profile

Texas Instruments is a global semiconductor company and the world's leading designer and supplier of digital signal processors (DSPs) and analog technologies, the engines driving the digitalization of electronics. The company's businesses also include materials and controls, educational and productivity solutions, and digital imaging. Texas Instruments has manufacturing or sales operations in more than 25 countries.

Semiconductors

The worldwide leader and pioneer in digital signal processing solutions since 1982, Texas Instruments provides innovative DSP and mixed-signal/analog technologies to more than 30,000 customers in the computer, wireless communications, networking, Internet, consumer, digital motor control, and mass storage markets worldwide.

To help customers get to market faster, TI offers easy-to-use development tools and extensive software and hardware support, enhanced by its extensive network of third-party DSP solutions providers that produce more than 1,000 products using TI technology.

Materials and Controls

Materials and Controls is a leader in engineering and control devices for the transportation, appliance, HVAC (heating, ventilating, and air conditioning), industrial/commercial, and electronic/communication markets. This division also provides innovative custom solutions in materials and controls and sensors, including TIRIS, a radio frequency-based identification technology.

Educational and Productivity Solutions

TI is a recognized leader in hand-held educational technology, with a exceptional strength in the graphing calculator market. By working closely with teachers to develop learning tools and educator programs, TI can develop the best products to meet their needs.

Digital Imaging

Digital Light Processing uses more than 500,000 microscopic mirrors on a chip to reflect images on screen. This Emmy award-winning technology displays information digitally and creates bright, clear, and vivid images.

Highlights of 1999

- The world's two largest digital wireless phone makers, Nokia and Ericsson, selected the company's DSP-based Open Multimedia Application Platform for their third-generation (3G) phones.
- Eight of the top 10 wireless network providers selected TI DSPs for their 3G base stations.
- TI introduced the industry's fastest DSP, the C6203, which runs at 300 megahertz and executes 2,400 million instructions per second.
- TI and Cisco announced they will jointly develop a complete end-to-end cable modem chip solution that will provide data, voice, and video convergence for all cable standards.
- Twelve major central office and personal computer manufacturers announced they would use TI DSPs for their Digital Subscriber Line products.
- TI introduced eXpressDSP Real-Time Software Technology, a complete, open software environment that cuts development time in half, enabling an expected 10-fold increase in DSP applications.
- The number of programmers on TI DSPs grew to more than fifty thousand.

- TI broadened its wireless expertise to include short-distance wireless technology with the acquisition of Butterfly, a pioneer in the field. TI also acquired radio frequency engineering expertise with the purchase of ATL Research A/S.
- The company significantly expanded its capabilities in broadband with the acquisitions of Libit Signal Processing Ltd., a technology leader for the cable-access equipment market, and Telogy Networks, Inc., a world leader in the fast-growing market for voice over Internet. Combined with the 1998 acquisition of Amati Communications Corporation and TI's existing technology expertise, these acquisitions position the company as the technology leader in the broadband market for both DSL and cable modems. TI already is the industry leader in voice over DSL, with four out of five equipment suppliers selecting TI DSPs, and also in the voice over cable market where 90 percent of voice-enabled cable modems have designed in TI DSPs.
- TI and Microsoft announced a collaboration for Internet audio, combining TI's programmable DSP and software upgradability with Microsoft Windows Media Format.

Shortcomings to Bear in Mind

- According to management, "The hard disk drive market is expected to remain weak, as drive manufacturers work through inventories and component pricing continues to be under pressure."
- Like most stocks with bright prospects, Texas Instruments often sells for a lofty P/E ratio—far above the general market.
- The company's growth record has not been a smooth one. In 1990 and 1991, for instance, it recorded red ink. Earnings per share also fell sharply in 1996, to $.19 from $.71 the prior year.

Reasons to Buy

- When CEO Jerry Junkins was stricken with a fatal heart attack in the spring of 1996, the stock of Texas Instruments plummeted 25 percent. That's when Tom Engibous, then head of the company's semiconductor division, took the reins. Rather than respond to Junkins's death with paralysis, Engibous galvanized the company. Accelerating changes that Junkins had set in motion, he transformed Texas Instruments from a large, unfocused colossus with a reputation for arrogance to a linchpin of the digital communications revolution. "This is a company that has completely reinvented itself. It is unlike anything I have ever seen before in the technology arena," said Drew Peck, an analyst with S. G. Cowen Securities.

  At the time of Junkins's death, the company had been dabbling in everything from military electronics and notebook computers to memory chips and printers. Today, after selling off 14 businesses and acquiring 15 others, it is focused on being number one in digital signal processors (DSPs) and analog chips, two of the semiconductor industry's fastest-growing segments. Under Tom Engibous, a husky, ruddy-cheeked former hockey player at Purdue University, the company's market capitalization has exploded from $10 billion to more than $70 billion. What's more, TI's digital signal processors now provide the power for two out of three digital cell phones, as well as most high-performance disk drives and a third of all modems.

- "DSPs are the idiot savants of the semiconductor world," says Drew Peck. Unlike a microprocessor, which performs many tasks reasonably well, a digital signal processor can be programed to do a few things extraordinarily well—at a fraction of the power consumption and cost of a microprocessor. DSPs can manipulate sounds, images, and data ten times faster than the most powerful microprocessors and are now used in everything from digital cameras to automobiles to cell phones. DSPs, moreover, are especially good at performing fast real-time calculations. DSPs are an ideal device when you want to compress, decompress, encrypt, or filter signals and images.

  Texas Instruments owns about half of the $4-billion-a-year market for digital signal processors. And it is also the number one supplier of analog chips, with an 11 percent share of a $21-billion-a-year market. Tom Engibous's strategy revolves around keeping his company number one in DSPs and analog chips, as the market for both mushroom. Demand for DSPs is expanding at more than 25 percent a year, in part because they are ideally suited for mobile communications and in part because they are programmable. Thus, they appeal to companies developing products for new, fast-changing niches.

- To continue its winning ways, the company invested $1.3 billion in R&D in 1999, a hefty 15 percent of sales. In 2000, research expenditures are forecast at $1.5 billion, primarily for DSP and analog. Texas Instruments is seeking to come up with new uses for its DSP chips in such niche markets as digital cameras, Internet audio devices, and laser printers—even for the search for life in outer space.

- TI is the world leader in digital signaling processing, with 47 percent market share, the only DSP vendor to gain share during the past six years in a row.

- The company is the world leader in analog technology and is the only major supplier to gain market share in each of the last four years.

- Texas Instruments has more than six thousand patents worldwide.
- The company has an 80 percent market share of the graphing calculator market in North America.

- In 1999, the company acquired Unitrode Corporation, a major designer and supplier of power management components, the fastest-growing segment of the analog semiconductor market.

Total assets: $15,028 million
Current ratio: 2.25
Common shares outstanding: 1,584 million
Return on 1999 shareholders' equity: 15.2%

	1999	1998	1997	1996	1995	1994	1993	1992
Revenues (millions)	9468	8460	9750	9940	13128	10315	8523	7049
Net income (millions)	1406	716	809	281	1088	722	460	254
Earnings per share	.88	.45	.51	.19	.71	.48	.31	.16
Dividends per share	.09	.07	.09	.09	.08	.06	.05	.05
Price High	55.8	22.6	17.8	8.6	10.5	5.6	5.3	3.3
Low	21.3	10.1	7.8	5.1	4.3	3.8	2.9	1.9

AGGRESSIVE GROWTH

United Parcel Service, Incorporated

55 Glenlake Parkway N. E. ◻ Atlanta, Georgia 30328 ◻ Investor contact: Norman Black (404) 828-7593 ◻ Dividend reinvestment plan is not available ◻ Web site: www.ups.com ◻ Listed: NYSE ◻ Ticker symbol: UPS ◻ S&P rating: Not rated ◻ Value Line financial strength rating: A+

After resisting the sale of its stock to the public for almost a century, United Parcel Services, the world's biggest package-delivery company, finally offered a few of its shares to enthusiastic investors late in 1999. The underwriting raised $5.47 billion—the biggest initial public offering in U.S. history. Known for its fleet of chocolate-brown trucks and uniforms, UPS sold 109.4 million shares for $50 each. As anticipated, the stock took off and climbed to a peak of nearly $77.

The stock's initial popularity reflects a deep well of investors who were looking to own a piece of a venerable, reliable company with a long history of consistent profit—and one with a solid future, as the Internet is now hosting and exploding the number of online retailers who in many instances deliver their goods via UPS. According to the company, it moves 6 percent of the gross domestic product. Even

more impressive, UPS ships half of all Christmas gifts purchased electronically.

Company Profile

United Parcel—known as Big Brown—is one of the largest employee-owned companies in the nation. With a fleet of 149,000 vehicles and 536 airplanes, UPS delivers 12.5 million packages and documents each day, or more than 3 billion a year.

The company's primary business is the delivery of packages and documents throughout the United States and in over 200 other countries and territories. In addition, UPS provides logistic services, including comprehensive management of supply chains, for major companies worldwide.

United Parcel has built a strong brand equity by being a leader in quality service and product innovation in its industry. UPS has been rated the second-strongest business-to-business brand in the United States in a recent Image Power survey and has been *Fortune* magazine's Most Admired Transportation Company in the mail, package, and freight category for 16 consecutive years.

The UPS shares sold in late 1999 represent about 10 percent of the company's total ownership. The rest is still owned by about 125,000 of its managers, supervisors, hourly workers, retirees, foundations, and descendants of the company's early leaders. The company sold only Class B shares to the public. Each share has one vote, compared with the Class A stock, which has 10 votes per share.

Shortcomings to Bear in Mind

- By going public after all these years there could be a downside to bear in mind. For one thing, UPS is worried that the new attention will dramatically reshape its culture, built on promoting line workers from within and opening distribution centers in college towns. "It will be a shock to its insular culture," said Benn Konsynki, a professor at Emory University's Goizueta Business School who has served as a consultant to United Parcel.
- The company was hurt in 2000 by the high price of fuel. Oil prices tripled to more than $30 a barrel as OPEC was able to cut down its output while demand was rising.

Reasons to Buy

- The sale of company stock was not done to replenish empty coffers. Even before the public offering, UPS had more than $3 billion in cash reserves. Rather, UPS wanted to have a publicly traded stock to use as an alternative currency for acquiring other companies. UPS will use part of the money to buy back about $4 billion of its Class A voting shares from employees. It will also embark on

aggressive expansion—in Europe and in the burgeoning business-to-business market, which represents about 20 percent of the company's business.

- The company's CEO, James P. Kelly, age 56, has repositioned the UPS delivery folks as foot soldiers of the dot-com revolution. "We're a 92-year-old company that's reinvented itself several times, and we're doing it again," he said. Kelly has lived through many of these reinventions since he started as a UPS relief driver for the 1963 holiday season. Working his way through night school at Rutgers University, Kelly decided to become a full-time driver when he realized it paid double what he was making as an accountant. From there, he climbed up the management ladder, handling labor relations and other divisions before becoming CEO in 1997.

The recast United Parcel is more than just a cargo hauler. Kelly has organized the company to manage an array of logistics systems for its dot-com customers, from managing inventory to performing customer service functions. Some six years ago, Kelly saw the power of the Internet as a sales channel and made it a key focus. Kelly's big bets are paying off. Already UPS handles 55 percent of all Internet purchases. By contrast, the U.S. Postal Service accounts for 32 percent, with 10 percent left for Federal Express.

- The company has poured a stunning $11 billion into technology in the last decade—mainframes, PCs, hand-held computers, wireless modems, cellular networks, and 4,000 programmers and technicians. UPS used to be a trucking company with technology. Now it's a technology company with trucks.
- Since UPS began shuttling parcels from Seattle department stores with a Model-T Ford and a few motorcycles in the early 1900s, it has become an almost invisible

hand in the domestic economy. Even as it has evolved, the company has rigorously adhered to its successful business model. Its legendary operational drill entails everything from training drivers to hold their keys on a pinky finger so they don't waste time fumbling for them in pockets to asking employees to clean off desks at day's end so they can be clear for takeoff the next morning. UPS drivers are taught 340 precise methods of how to correctly deliver a package. Regimented? Absolutely. On the other hand, UPS credits its uniformity and efficiency with laying the foundation for a high-tech future. And those UPS drivers average a tidy $60,000 or $70,000 a year for their diligent toil. It seems to be paying off, since UPS has an employee retention rate of over 90 percent, a tremendous benefit when it comes to operational execution. Tenures at the company typically span decades, with many executives getting their start as drivers or loaders.

■ United Parcel Service, in trying to adapt its rigid culture to the freewheeling Internet economy, formed a subsidiary, eVentures, in early 2000 that will test and launch new businesses aimed at boosting the company's presence in electronic commerce. Already, eVentures is working on its first incubation project in Atlanta, which would significantly expand the potential reach of UPS's fast-growing logistics division by targeting small and medium-size companies.

If the initial test of the logistics project is successful, UPS plans to expand the service gradually across the country. Such a move would increasingly pit UPS against a crowded field of competitors, including Federal Express, which also run warehouses and fill orders for companies that don't want to handle those complicated tasks on their own. One major advantage for UPS, however, is that no logistics rival can match UPS's ubiquitous fleet of chocolate-brown delivery vans.

The eVentures unit plans to eventually work on several different projects at a time, launching and running each new business until it is declared financially sound or liquidated. The new subsidiary also expects to invest in Internet start-up companies working on longer-term ideas that could help UPS further develop its electronic-commerce capabilities.

■ In a test aimed at appealing to new kinds of customers, UPS is opening stores that will help people pack and ship packages, competing with such firms as Mail Boxes Etc. The UPS stores will also hold packages for customer pickup, sell office supplies, and provide copying service and rental mailboxes.

The launch of the pack-and-ship stores reflects a push inside UPS to increase access to its well-established delivery network while using the company's strong brand name to help generate revenue in businesses not tied directly to package delivery. In particular, the package-and-ship concept is aimed at small businesses that need basic mailroom services or find the existing network of shipping-only offices at UPS to be inconvenient.

The plans at UPS are sending shivers through the mailing-service industry, made up of about 11,000 pack-and-send stores that steer shipments to UPS or rivals such as Federal Express.

Total assets: $17,067 million
Current ratio: 1.13
Common shares outstanding: 1,164 million
Return on 1999 shareholders' equity: 26.5%

	1999	1998	1997	1996	1995	1994	1993	1992
Revenues (millions)	27052	24788	22458	*				
Net income (millions)	2325	1741	909					
Earnings per share	2.04	1.57	.82					
Dividends per share	.58	.43	.35					
Price High	76.9							
Low	61.0							

*United Parcel was a private company prior to 1999, and thus no additional statistics are available.

CONSERVATIVE GROWTH

United Technologies Corporation

One Financial Plaza ◻ Hartford, Connecticut 06103 ◻ Investor contact: Angelo J. Messina (860)-728-7000
◻ Dividend reinvestment plan is available: (800) 519-3111 ◻ Web site: www.utc.com ◻ Listed: NYSE
◻ Ticker symbol: UTX ◻ S&P rating: B+ ◻ Value Line financial strength rating: A++

Otis Elevator is taking elevator design to a new level. In early 2000, the company unveiled a innovative model that uses rubber belts to hoist elevator cars. This is notable because for the past century most elevators have been lifted by steel ropes. The Gen2, short for Generation 2, is a gearless machine pulled up and down by a device that resembles a belt for trousers. The product marks Otis's entry into the "machine-room-less" elevator market, so called because the systems eliminate the need for a separate machine room above the shaft. The Gen2 also provides a quieter, smoother ride.

Gen2 is designed for buildings with two to 20 floors. That segment, which includes apartment buildings and hotels, is one of the hottest segments of the industry, accounting for about 75 percent of the new elevators sold each year.

Elevators without machine rooms are appealing because they can save developers money and give building owners more rentable space. "An elevator machine room can cost anywhere from $10,000 to $20,000, depending on the type of building," says Ray Moncini, vice president for Otis North America. "The guys who build buildings work on very small margins." He also noted that the system is less expensive to install and is energy-efficient because it uses smaller motors that can be mounted inside the shaft.

Company Profile

United Technologies provides high-technology products to the aerospace and building systems industries throughout the world. Its companies are industry leaders and include Pratt & Whitney, Carrier, Otis, Sikorsky, International Fuel Cells, and Hamilton Sundstrand. Sikorsky and Hamilton Sundstrand make up the Flight Systems segment.

United Technologies posted strong revenue and earnings performance in 1999. Diluted earnings per share jumped 19 percent. Net income increased 22 percent. Revenue, however, expanded by a less impressive 6 percent, to $24.13 billion.

The commercial businesses—Carrier (air conditioning) and Otis (elevators)—

generated 53 percent of total segment revenues, and international revenues contributed 54 percent of total segment revenues.

Pratt & Whitney

- Products and services: Large and small commercial and military jet engines, spare parts and product support, specialized engine maintenance, and overhaul and repair services for airlines, air forces, and corporate fleets; rocket engines and space propulsion systems; industrial gas turbines.
- Primary customers: Commercial airlines and aircraft-leasing companies; commercial and corporate aircraft manufacturers; the U.S. government, including NASA and the miliary services; regional and commuter airlines.
- Financial results in 1999: Revenues were $7.67 billion, down 3 percent from the prior year. Operating profit was $634 million, including restructuring and other charges of $534 million. Acquisition spending in 1999 of about $220 million focused primarily on expansion of the aftermarket business.

Carrier

- Products and services: Heating, ventilating, and air conditioning (HVAC) equipment for commercial, industrial, and residential buildings; HVAC replacement parts and services; building controls; commercial, industrial, and transport refrigeration equipment.
- Carrier emphasizes energy-efficiency, quiet operation, and environmental stewardship in its new residential and commercial products. The new WeatherMaker residential air conditioner using Puron, a non-ozone-depleting refrigerant, provides the domestic market with low operating costs and sound levels—about the same as a refrigerator's. The Puron unit gives Carrier a healthy lead over competitors, as chlorine-free refrigerants become the standard.
- Primary customers: Mechanical and building contractors; homeowners, building owners, developers, and retailers; architects and building consultants; transportation and refrigeration companies; shipping operations.
- Financial results in 1999: Revenues were $7.35 billion, up 6 percent over 1998. Operating profit was $459 million, including restructuring and other charges of $196 million. Carrier acquisition activity in 1999 included International Comfort Products, with 1998 revenues of $734 million, to augment Carrier's residential and light commercial products business.

Otis

- Products and services: Elevators, escalators, moving walks and shuttle systems, and related installation, maintenance, and repair services; modernization products and service for elevators and escalators.
- Primary customers: Mechanical and building contractors; building owners and developers; home owners; architects and building consultants.
- Financial results in 1999: Revenues were $5.65 billion, up 1 percent over the prior year. Operating profit was $493 million, including restructuring and other charges of $186 million. Acquisition spending in 1999 of more than $700 million included the purchase of 80 percent of the elevator business of LG Industrial Systems.

Flight Systems

- Products and services: Aircraft electrical and power distribution systems; engine and flight controls; propulsion systems; environmental controls for aircraft, spacecraft, and submarines; auxiliary power units; space life support systems; industrial products including mechanical power transmissions, compressors, metering devices, and fluid handling equipment; military and commercial helicopters, spare parts, civil helicopter operations; and maintenance services for helicopters and fixed-wing aircraft.

- Primary customers: The U.S. government, including NASA, FAA, and the military services; non-U.S. governments; aerospace and defense prime contractors; commercial airlines; aircraft and jet engine manufacturers; oil and gas exploration companies; mining and water companies; construction companies; hospitals and charters.
- Financial results in 1999: Revenues were $3.81 billion, up from $2.89 billion in 1998. Operating profit was $247 million, including restructuring charges of $161 million. This segment expanded significantly in 1999 with the acquisition of Sundstrand for $4.3 billion.

Shortcomings to Bear in Mind

- Analysts say that Pratt & Whitney and Flight Systems could be under pressure. They look for P&W to build its aftermarket business in response to weak military and commercial engine shipments in 1999. However, the company's installed base of JT8D and JT9D engines are being retired, which will hurt spare parts sales.

Reasons to Buy

- In 2000, Sikorsky launched its S-92 commercial helicopter, its first new helicopter since the Black Hawk and the S-76 in the 1970s.
- Pratt & Whitney's PW6000 engine for narrow-body aircraft is now firmly launched with Airbus's 100 passenger A318, with seven of eight airlines selecting the PW6000 over a competitor's engine. Without a placement on the popular 737, Pratt & Whitney has been at a disadvantage in the higher-volume narrow-body segment; the PW6000 fixes this emphatically.

- The Frankfurt Auto Show saw a United Technologies fuel cell in operation for 15 hours daily over the show's two-week duration. Virtually silent and environmentally benign, the company's APU (auxiliary power unit) powered without interruption every electrical accessory in a BMW 7-series vehicle.
- UTX is going aggressively after Web-enabled changes in its businesses and processes and was recognized for this by *Bloomberg* magazine, *Barron's*, and other media. According to the 1999 annual report, "In some instances, we have been presciently early, notably as the founding client for FreeMarkets, the on-line industrial auction site. Pratt & Whitney began Web-based shipping releases from suppliers as early as 1995. Today its Supplier Delivery System coordinates almost 400,000 such shipments annually, covering 97 percent of production material requirements."
- Three major acquisitions, a joint venture, and a divestiture changed the company's portfolio of businesses in 1999. The divestiture was of UT Automotive for $2.3 billion in cash, which generated a $650 million capital gain.

The acquisitions were in the company's core businesses, augmenting UTX's already industry-leading positions. Sundstrand joined Hamilton Standard to more than double the size of the company's aerospace systems activities and presence. International Comfort Products brings $750 million of residential product sales to Carrier's North American comfort cooling and heating businesses. LG Industrial Systems's elevator business adds more than $500 million to Otis's sales, mostly in Korea where LG is the leading elevator company. With the completion of a joint venture agreement incorporating Toshiba's air conditioning business, Carrier strengthened its position in Japan and its industry-leading range of products.

- Through internal growth and acquisition, Carrier's commercial refrigeration business has become a leader in the highly fragmented $17-billion global industry. Carrier's acquisition of Electrolux Commercial Refrigeration will broaden its offerings to supermarkets, convenience stores, and food and beverage markets, particularly in Europe. A new transport refrigeration unit, the Vector, can cool a trailer from 30°C to -20°C twice as fast as a conventional unit can. By the end of 1999, more than one thousand Vector units were sold for use from the United Kingdom to Saudi Arabia.

- In 1999, the company took major steps to reduce its cost structure with a massive restructuring plan, eliminating jobs and reducing manufacturing space. These actions were expected to save $750 million a year beginning in 2000.

Total assets: $24,366 million
Current ratio: 1.15
Common shares outstanding: 481 million
Return on 1999 equity: 24.6%

		1999	1998	1997	1996	1995	1994	1993	1992
Revenues (millions)		24127	25715	24713	23512	22802	21197	21081	21641
Net income (millions)		1531	1255	1072	906	750	616	487	486
Earnings per share		3.01	2.53	2.11	1.73	1.43	1.16	.83	.90
Dividends per share		.76	.70	.62	.55	.52	.48	.45	.45
Price	High	78.0	56.2	44.5	35.2	24.5	18.0	16.6	14.5
	Low	51.6	33.5	32.6	22.7	15.6	13.8	11.0	10.4

CONSERVATIVE GROWTH

Varian Medical Systems, Inc.

3100 Hansen Way ▫ Palo Alto, California 94304-1038 ▫ Investor contact: Elisha W. Finney (650) 424-6803 ▫ Dividend reinvestment plan is not available ▫ Web site: www.varian.com ▫ Fiscal year ends on Friday nearest September 30 ▫ Ticker symbol: VAR ▫ S&P rating: B+ ▫ Value Line financial strength rating: B++

The company's oncology (the treatment of cancer) business, which comprises 78 percent of its sales, drove Varian's growth in sales and orders in fiscal 1999. Oncology Systems generated $459 million in sales, up 13 percent from fiscal 1998, and $504 million in net orders, up an impressive 22 percent from the prior year.

Through this business, Varian Medical Systems is supplying hospitals and clinics around the world with the most advanced systems for radiotherapy, including the very promising high-resolution IMRT (intensity modulated radiation therapy).

Company Profile

Varian Medical Systems is the world's leading manufacturer of integrated radiotherapy systems for treating cancer and other diseases; it is also a leading supplier of X-ray tubes for imaging in medical, scientific, and industrial applications. Established in 1948, the company has manufacturing sites in North America and Europe and has 40 sales and support offices worldwide.

In the spring of 1999, the company (formerly Varian Associates, Inc.) reorganized itself into three separate publicly traded companies by spinning off two of its businesses to stockholders via a tax-free distribution.

Since then, the company has significantly broadened its product and business offerings, acquired new businesses, and set records for sales and net orders. More importantly, Varian put itself at the forefront of a radiotherapy revolution that is making a dramatic difference in the struggle against cancer.

About three out of every ten people will be afflicted with some form of cancer. The good news is that their chances of surviving, of beating cancer, have greatly improved thanks to recent advances in radiation therapy—many of which have been led by Varian Medical Systems.

Results in 1999

Varian Medical Systems reported a record $590 million in sales of products and services in 1999, pushing sales up 9 percent over the prior year. Net orders reached a record $638 million, up 17 percent. What's more, backlog finished the year at a near-record $400 million, up 14 percent over 1998.

The company has three segments:

Oncology Systems

Varian Oncology Systems is the world's largest supplier of radiotherapy systems for treating cancer. Its integrated medical systems include sales and service to linear accelerators, ancillary accessories, and software for treatment planning, delivery, quality assurance, and patient record administration.

Thousands of patients around the world are treated daily on Varian systems. Oncology Systems works closely with health care professionals in clinics, hospitals, and universities worldwide, addressing their requirements for continually improving treatment efficacy and cost containment.

X-Ray Products

X-Ray Products is the world's premier independent supplier of X-ray-generating tubes. It serves major original-equipment manufacturers in the diagnostic-imaging industry and replacement tube distributors around the world.

This business provides the industry's broadest selection of X-ray tubes expressly designed for the most advanced CT scanning, radiographic, mammographic, and other diagnostic applications.

These products are continuously evolving to meet more and more stringent requirements for high-resolution imaging, rapid examination, patient throughput, long tube life, compact design, and cost-efficiency. X-Ray Products also manages the emerging business of amorphous silicon solid-state images.

Ginzton Technology Center

The Ginzton Technology Center acts as Varian Medical Systems' research and development facility for breakthrough technologies and operates a brachytherapy business for the delivery of internal radiation to treat cancer. In addition to brachytherapy, current efforts are focused on emerging biotechnologies that shrink tumors by triggering therapeutic gene activity with radiation beams. This business also conducts externally funded contract research related to medical technology, which leads to long-term partnerships and new business opportunities.

Shortcomings to Bear in Mind

- In 1999, the X-Ray Products business maintained gross margins and contributed to the operating profits of the company. However, sales and orders for its X-ray tubes declined. Sales and net orders each totaled $123 million, down 6 percent and 4 percent respectively. Consolidation among original equipment manufacturers led to the declines. On a more positive note, the company believes "several new products should begin to put this business back into a modest growth track."

Reasons to Buy

■ In 1999, Varian announced the addition of several powerful new elements to its Generation 6 system of equipment and software that operates off a single shared database for planning, delivering, and verifying treatment.

Some key additions include the company's Millennium MLC-120 multi-leaf collimator for finely shaping and targeting beams of radiation, its Helios inverse treatment planning software that cuts treatment planning from hours to minutes, and the company's PortalVision amorphous silicon imaging system for verifying the accuracy of treatments as they are delivered. These new tools give clinicians (doctors who treat patients) the ability to deliver high-resolution IMRT with which they can precisely target tumors—minimizing healthy tissue exposure—and significantly step up radiation doses to improve the possibility of a cure.

According to Dr. Roger Macklis, Chairman of Radiation Oncology at the Cleveland Clinic, "Intensity modulated radiation therapy is a paradigm shift in the way that radiotherapy is performed. In terms of the delivery dose, IMRT is the fulfillment of the original promise of the merger of computer technology and advanced imaging."

■ During 1999, the X-Ray Products segment began shipping the world's most powerful tube for high-speed CT scanning. Shipments also began on two products with high growth potential: Varian Medical Systems' proprietary cost-reduced, air-cooled X-ray tube and the company's amorphous-silicon-based imaging systems.

■ The odds of conquering some forms of cancer have improved dramatically in recent years thanks to new techniques in radiotherapy, specifically 3D conformal radiotherapy and high-resolution IMRT, which control tumors locally before the disease can spread.

Today, clinicians can shape a beam to deliver a precise radiation dose to the tumor while significantly reducing the exposure of healthy organs and tissue. This has enabled radiation oncologists to increase the cancer-killing radiation dose directed at tumors while reducing the adverse complications.

Dose escalation studies at leading institutions show that cure rates in some cancer patients are being dramatically improved with the use of advanced techniques. For example, with prostate cancer patients at Memorial Sloan-Kettering Cancer Center in New York, raising the radiation dose from traditional dose levels of 64.8-70.2 Gy to 81 Gy increase the control rate defined by biopsies of the prostate from 55 percent to 94 percent—an almost 71 percent improvement. Using IMRT techniques, doctors were able to deliver these high doses while actually reducing the rate of normal tissue complications from 10 percent to 2 percent.

■ Varian Medical Systems has helped to drive the evolution of this technology, from developing the first isocentric linear accelerator to launching today's SmartBeam system for high-resolution IMRT introduced in fiscal 2000. Varian's SmartBeam technology provides physicians with the most advanced treatment equipment and software for the highest-resolution IMRT ever. For the first time, treatments can be digitally matched to diagnostic images that reveal disease activity within the cells.

- Varian Medical Systems' new high-power CT scanning tube, which is capable of performing at almost twice the sustained output of any other tube in the medical imaging industry, makes possible improved images in the next generation of half-second CT scanning.

Tubes made by VMS X-Ray Products are now used in nearly one-half of the mammography systems and in nearly one-fourth of the CT scanners worldwide, accounting for more than 2.2 billion diagnostic medical exposures a year.

Total assets: $539 million
Current ratio: 1.38
Common shares outstanding: 30 million
Return on 1999 shareholders' equity: 22.5%

	1999	1998	1997	1996	1995	1994	1993	1992
Revenues (millions)	590	1422	1426	1599	1576	1552	1311	1288
Net income (millions)	39	74	82	122	106	79	46	39
Earnings per share	1.28	2.43	2.74	3.81	3.01	2.22	1.26	1.02
Dividends per share	.20	.39	.35	.31	.27	.23	.20	.18
Price High	43.0	58.4	67.0	62.9	57.4	39.3	30.0	22.4
Low	16.3	31.6	45.9	40.5	34.5	28.3	19.0	16.8

GROWTH AND INCOME

Vulcan Materials Company

1200 Urban Center Drive □ Birmingham, Alabama 35242 □ Investor contact: E. Starke Sydnor (205) 298-3202 □ Dividend reinvestment plan is available: (800) 519-3111 □ Web site: www.vulcanmaterials.com □ Listed: NYSE □ Ticker symbol: VMC □ S&P rating: A □ Value Line financial strength rating: A

For the third year in a row, *Industry Week* magazine named Vulcan one of the 100 best-managed industrial companies in the world. What's more, the company's Construction Materials segment received numerous awards from the National Stone Association for quarry beautification, environmental stewardship, employee safety, and community relations.

Company Profile

Vulcan Materials is the largest domestic producer of construction aggregates (a product category that includes crushed stone, sand, and gravel). The company does not materially depend upon sales to any one customer or group of customers. Typically, its products are sold to private industry. However, most of VMC's construction materials are ultimately used in public projects.

From 330 aggregates plants and other production and distribution facilities, Vulcan provides a diversified line of aggregates, other construction materials, and related services to all parts of the construction industry in 22 states. Vulcan's principal product, crushed stone, is used in virtually all forms of construction.

Vulcan's Chemicals segment is a significant producer of basic industrial and specialty chemicals. Through its Chloralkali Business Unit, it produces chlorine, caustic soda, hydrochloric acid, potassium chemicals, and chlorinated organic chemicals. The food and pharmaceutical markets provide stable demand for several of Chloralkali's chemical products.

Through its Performance Systems Business Unit, it provides process aids for the pulp and paper and textile industries and chemicals and services to the municipal, industrial, and environmental water-management markets. It also has a stake in the custom manufacture of a variety of specialty chemicals.

A Look at the Industry

Aggregates account for about 95 percent of the weight of each ton of asphalt that is used to pave highways and parking lots. Aggregates account for 85 percent of the weight of ready-mix concrete used for such projects as dams, highways, and foundations.

Vulcan quarries and processes the stone to various sizes so that it conforms to specific engineering standards. Independent truckers or customer trucks haul the stone to the construction site—rarely more than 20 or 30 miles away.

There are two major exceptions to this rule. The first exception is the Reed quarry, which ships a large portion of its production great distances, mainly by barge on the Mississippi River system. A much smaller portion is shipped by rail.

The company's so-called Crescent Market Project is the second exception to the local-market rule of thumb. Because aggregates deposits along the Gulf Coast are limited, most aggregates are supplied from inland sources 70 or more miles away. Consequently, transportation costs increase the product's delivery prices substantially.

Vulcan participates in a venture that produces crushed limestone at a quarry near Cancun, Mexico, ships the product to the U.S. Gulf Coast, and markets the stone in a number of cities, including Houston, Galveston, New Orleans, Mobile, and Tampa.

The economics of the project work because ocean shipping costs much less than truck or rail transportation, even though the distance is much greater.

The largest end-use for aggregates is highway construction and maintenance. Crushed stone is used as a highway base material and as the major portion of the asphaltic concrete and ready-mixed concrete used as a surface material.

Crushed stone is the company's largest product; it accounts for three-fourths of Construction Materials' sales. Vulcan also produces sand and gravel, asphaltic and ready-mix concrete, and numerous other less-significant products.

Shortcomings to Bear in Mind

- The company's Chloralkali unit is part of its commodity chemicals business. A commodity differs from a proprietary product in that it is not differentiated from the products of its competitors. In order to survive in a commodity business you should be a low-cost producer or offer a unique service, such as quick delivery.
- Demand for aggregates is both cyclical and mature.
- Caustic soda prices tend to be volatile. For instance, prices peaked in April 1991 at nearly $300 per ton; then they plummeted to $61 in March of 1994. In the spring of 1997 the price was about $130 per ton—or well below earlier levels. The reason for the decline was too much of the chemical in the marketplace. Vulcan sells nearly all of the caustic soda it produces. As a consequence, any price change can impact earnings significantly.

Reasons to Buy

- In June of 1998, the Transportation Equity Act for the 21st Century (TEA-21) was signed into law. This $216-billion, six-year transportation authorization is expected to increase demand significantly. Most of this impact still lies ahead due to long lead times for large projects.

- Earnings per share have moved ahead steadily in recent years, with only one significant drop (in 1991 EPS slumped to $.46 from $1.03). In the 1989–1999 period, earnings per share expanded from $1.10 to $2.35, a compound annual growth rate of 7.9 percent. In the same 10-year stretch, dividends per share climbed from $0.37 to $0.78, a growth rate of 7.7 percent.

- The aggregates industry has undergone significant ownership and concentration changes in recent years. In 1985, the top 10 producers in the United States accounted for about 13 percent of total domestic sales.

    Ten years later, the top 10 producers shipped about 22 percent of the U.S. market. Vulcan, the industry leader with an estimated 6.3 percent of the U.S. aggregates market and an estimated 10.4 percent of the crushed stone market, currently serves geographic markets with about 25 percent of the U.S. population. Notwithstanding the recent consolidation, the aggregates industry remains highly fragmented and contains significant growth opportunities.

- Historically, Construction Materials enjoys good results when housing starts are strong. Conversely, Chemicals enjoys its best results when caustic soda prices are high. The inverse relationship between changes in housing starts and caustic prices has been almost perfect for the last 25 years.

    The relationship occurs because the demand for chlorine is heavily dependent upon economic activity, especially construction. Demand for caustic is much less cyclical because of the diverse nature of its end-use markets. Hence, when economic activity is strong, chlorine demand increases sharply, putting caustic in an oversupply situation.

However, when the economy is slack, chlorine production is curtailed, thus reducing caustic production and creating a shortage of caustic.

- Vulcan manufactures sodium chlorite at a world-class facility at the company's Wichita, Kansas chemical complex. Vulcan is the largest North American producer of sodium chlorite and the world's second-largest. Sodium chlorite is used in a variety of applications, including drinking and industrial water treatment, air scrubbing, and paper, textile, and electronics manufacturing.

- Early in 2000, Vulcan Materials acquired the assets of Garves W. Yates & Sons, Inc. of Abilene, Texas. These assets include six quarry sites, four portable aggregate production plants, a portable asphalt plant, and a fleet of trucks used to transport stone and asphalt products. Commenting on the acquisition, CEO Donald M. James said, "This acquisition will expand significantly the reach, scope, and flexibility of our operations in Texas, particularly in the Abilene and Brownwood areas, along the Interstate 10 corridor west of San Antonio and along the Interstate 20 corridor west of Fort Worth. Moreover, the Yates business represents a valuable addition to Vulcan's limestone reserves in Texas, especially in Abilene. The state of Texas is receiving approximately a 61 percent increase in transportation funding under the TEA-21 legislation, and the Yates Acquisition positions Vulcan to participate more fully in the increased highway construction in Texas expected over the next five years."

- Within the company's Construction Materials segment, where it now employs over 80 percent of its capital, Vulcan integrated CalMat Company in 1999. CalMat is the leading aggregates company on the West Coast and is the largest acquisition in Vulcan's history.

Also during the year, Vulcan acquired another 20 quarries and opened four greenfield (a fancy term for new) aggregates plants and further strengthened the company's distribution network.

- The Chemicals segment made significant progress in construction of the facilities for the company's joint venture with Mitsui & Company, Ltd. The joint venture expands ethylene dichloride (EDC) production and adds a new chloralkali plant at Vulcan's Geismar, Louisiana site. The company structured the joint venture to take advantage of Vulcan's manufacturing and domestic marketing capabilities and Matsui's access to global EDC markets. Mitsui, the world's leading EDC trader, will purchase all of the EDC output at Geismar. The project is structured to provide attractive and relatively stable returns over chloralkali business cycles and its life span.

- In early 2000, CEO Donald M. James said, "Our Chemicals segment is poised for recovery in 2000. Prices for our chloralkali products have increased in recent months, and industry analysts expect this trend to continue. Based on our current outlook, our chemicals segment's earnings could approach the earnings achieved in 1998."

- Vulcan Materials Company was added to the Standard & Poor's 500 Stock Index in 1999, which means the stock must be purchased by index funds that track the S&P 500, such as the Vanguard 500 Index Fund.

- Pursuant to the company's long-standing stock purchase program, Vulcan purchased 336,400 shares of its common stock in 1999 at an average price of $37.18. Since the inception of the program in 1985, the company has purchased 42,511,981 shares (30.6 percent of shares outstanding) at an average price of $14.31. These purchases reflect management's confidence in Vulcan Materials and its commitment to delivering shareholder value.

Total assets: $2,839 million
Current ratio: 1.62
Common shares outstanding: 101 million
Return on 1999 shareholders' equity: 19.4%

	1999	1998	1997	1996	1995	1994	1993	1992
Revenues (millions)	2356	1776	1679	1569	1461	1253	1134	1078
Net income (millions)	240	248	209	189	166	98	88	91
Earnings per share	2.35	2.44	2.03	1.79	1.54	.89	.80	.80
Dividends per share	.78	.69	.63	.56	.49	.44	.42	.40
Price High	51.3	44.7	34.6	22.2	20.1	18.8	18.7	16.5
Low	34.3	31.3	18.4	17.7	16.0	14.7	13.4	12.0

GROWTH AND INCOME

Wachovia Corporation

100 North Main Street ◻ Winston-Salem, North Carolina 27150 ◻ Investor contact: Marsha L. Hunt
(336) 732-5788 ◻ Dividend reinvestment plan is available: (800) 633-4236 ◻ Web site: www.wachovia.com
◻ Listed: NYSE ◻ Ticker symbol: WB ◻ S&P rating: A ◻ Value Line financial strength rating: A+

For years, Wachovia has enjoyed a reputation as a "banker's bank." It consistently generates a high return on equity.

Its discipline in keeping overhead costs low puts it among the elite of efficient banking institutions. What's more,

Wachovia's conservative stance when granting credit helped it sidestep the loan losses that bedeviled rivals in the past.

Company Profile

Wachovia Corporation is an interstate bank holding company. It has dual headquarters in Atlanta, Georgia and Winston-Salem, North Carolina. The company's properties are situated in the Southeast and include operations headquartered in Atlanta, Winston-Salem, Columbia, South Carolina, and Wilmington, Delaware.

At the end of 1999, Wachovia had assets of $67.4 billion, making it the 16th-largest banking company in the United States.

Wachovia's Heritage

Wachovia traces its roots deep into the European continent. Wachovia originates from the German word "Wachau," which is the name given by Moravians, a European Protestant sect, to land they settled in the Piedmont region of North Carolina. The Moravians chose the name because their new land reminded them of the Wachau Valley along the Danube River, the ancestral home of their benefactor in Germany. As the settlers made the new area their home, "Wachau" was Anglicized into Wachovia (pronounced wah-KO-vee-yah).

The Moravians were the entrepreneurs of their day, organizing the First National Bank of Salem in 1866 to supply the growing need for financial services in the town of Salem. When nearby Winston experienced industrial growth, they moved the bank and renamed it Wachovia National Bank in 1879.

Wachovia's Operations

Major corporate and institutional relationships are managed by Wachovia Corporate Services, Inc. through banking offices in Georgia, North Carolina, and South Carolina and through representative offices in Chicago, London, New York City, and Tokyo. The corporation maintains foreign branches at Grand Cayman, through its banking subsidiaries, and an Edge Act subsidiary in New York City.

Wachovia Trust Services, Inc. provides fiduciary, investment management, and related financial services for corporate, institutional, and individual clients.

Discount brokerage and investment advisory services are provided by Wachovia Investments, Inc., to customers primarily in Georgia, North Carolina, and South Carolina.

Wachovia Operational Services Corporation provides information processing and systems development for Wachovia's subsidiaries. Finally, WB is involved in other financial services activities including residential mortgage origination, state and local government securities underwriting, sales and trading, foreign exchange, corporate finance, and other money market services.

Highlights of 1999

- Wachovia has been active on the merger and acquisitions front. In 1999, it completed the following transactions:
  - Interstate/Johnson Lane, a leading Southeastern full-service broker-dealer and investment banking firm based in Charlotte, North Carolina.
  - OFFITBANK, a New York-based wealth-management company serving high-net-worth individuals and institutional clients.
  - Barry, Evans, Josephs & Snipes, a national insurance broker based in Charlotte with expertise in wealth-management strategies for affluent clients.
  - In October of 1999, Wachovia announced plans to acquire B C Bankshares, parent company of the Bank of Canton, with eight branches in the Atlanta area. The transaction was completed in 2000.

- Late in 1999, Wachovia announced plans to purchase the $2-billion credit card portfolio of Partners First Holdings. The transaction was completed early in 2000.
- In December of 1999, Wachovia said that it had agreed to buy the United States credit card unit of Bank of Montreal, Canada's third-largest bank. The acquisition puts Wachovia among the top 10 bank card issuers in the United States. Wachovia said it wants to increase its credit card business because consumers are increasingly using them for everyday spending, especially on the Internet.
- Wachovia was named one of the best Internet banks in the nation by a number of professional journals and rating agencies, including *Smart Money* magazine, CNN and *Money Line*. Wachovia's commitment to the Internet as a vital customer delivery channel is reflected in the January 2000 formation of an eBusiness Division that will provide centralized, strategic leadership and support for initiatives across all lines of business.

Shortcomings to Bear in Mind

- As its in-state competitors have expanded aggressively through mergers, Wachovia has lost some ground. At one time, Wachovia was the largest bank in North Carolina as measured by deposit share, but it now ranks second.
- The year 1999 was challenging for banking companies. After posting remarkable performance in every year since 1994, the shares of many traded well below yearly highs. This is discouraging but can be understood. The world is in transition from the old economy to the new. Investors are thinking about the future.

Ironically, a number of banks reported solid earnings in 1999, on track with market expectations. And yet, in the eyes of investors, banks have lost a degree of luster in the face of perceived bonanzas dangling from the Internet.

In truth, investors may be justified in reacting nervously to the uncertainty of future earnings growth. They are questioning the value proposition banks offer to customers. They are worried about risk.

Reasons to Buy

- The bank's stripes have been changing under the leadership of its CEO, Leslie "Bud" Baker, Jr. Since the 56-year-old president, who has been with Wachovia since 1969, took the reins in 1994, he has launched a quiet revolution, which some analysts contend is beginning to bear fruit.

According to one analyst, "When Bud Baker came in, he was really faced with a pretty monumental task. He had to spend hundreds of millions of dollars to bring technology up to par."

Mr. Baker carefully examined every part of the bank's operations and has been taking steps to discover the best way to proceed. For one thing, Wachovia is closing as many as 10 percent of its branches and reorganizing its trust operation.

Mr. Baker says he believes that Wachovia will be able to exceed its historical target of 10 to 12 percent a year growth in earnings per share. The bank also plans to boost fee income to 50 percent of total revenue, up from only 32 percent, by introducing fee-based products and raising current charges.

- WB has a fine record of growth, which means dividends are likely to move smartly ahead over the years. In the 1989–1999 period, earnings per share expanded from $1.94 to $4.97, with no dips during those years. The compound annual growth rate for earnings per share is a solid 9.86 percent. Dividends, moreover, climbed at an even better clip in this 10-year stretch, rising from $0.70 to $2.06, a compound growth rate of 11.4 percent.

- Wachovia is one of the leaders in addressing the growing issue of check fraud. WB's check fraud task force, with representatives from operations, product management, legal, and security, is helping bring industry associations together to focus on common loss prevention initiatives, conducting seminars to educate companies on risks and prevention measures, and seeking ways to leverage image processing and other technology capabilities to combat the problem.

- "In many ways, Wachovia is uniquely equipped to extend its leadership as a wealth-management provider," says Robert S. Kniejski, executive vice president for Wachovia Asset and Wealth Management. He cites a combination of factors, some as old as the company itself, others reflecting recent innovations. Among them: Wachovia's strong relationship heritage, corporate culture, advantageous geographic location, and proven ability to serve high-wealth clients.

Wachovia already has relationships with a large percentage of affluent households in its home states—Georgia, North Carolina, South Carolina, Virginia, and Florida. These states are among the most prosperous and fastest-growing in the nation; Wachovia's markets are projected to grow more than 50 percent faster than the national average from 1999 to 2004.

As one of the first providers of trust services in the nation, Wachovia's reputation for product innovation and service excellence spans 121 years and encompasses a broad range of wealth-management and related financial services.

- As noted earlier, Wachovia acquired OFFITBANK in 1999. OFFITBANK, a premier wealth-management bank with offices in New York, San Francisco, and Miami, serves clients in 36 states, Latin America, Europe, and Asia. About 60 percent of the company's relationships have $30 million or more in managed assets with the firm. OFFITBANK's expertise in fixed-income investment management complements Wachovia's capabilities in specialized lending, philanthropy management, personal trust, and equity investment management. These four areas add immediate value to OFFITBANK's high-net-worth client base. At the same time, that client base brings important relationships to Wachovia.

- Barry, Evans, Josephs & Snipes (BEJS), also acquired in 1999, represents an ideal complement to the merger with OFFITBANK. A leading national life insurance broker, the firm specializes in designing and implementing wealth-transfer strategies for affluent families and benefit plans for corporate executives. BEJS serves a national client base that includes many executives from Fortune 500 companies.

Total assets: $67,353 million
Return on average assets: 1.55%
Common shares outstanding: 203 million
Return on 1999 shareholders' equity: 18.6%

		1999	1998	1997	1996	1995	1994	1993	1992
Loans (millions)		49621	45719	44194	31283	29261	25891	22416	19642
Net income (millions)		1024	930	800	645	602	539	492	433
Earnings per share		4.97	4.45	3.96	3.81	3.50	3.13	2.83	2.51
Dividends per share		2.06	1.86	1.68	1.52	1.38	1.23	1.11	1.00
Price	High	92.3	96.8	83.9	60.3	48.3	35.4	40.5	34.8
	Low	65.4	72.8	53.5	39.6	32.0	30.1	31.9	28.3

Wal-Mart Stores, Inc.

702 SW Eighth Street □ **Bentonville, Arkansas 72716-8611** □ **Investor contact: Steve Hunter (501) 273-8446** □ **Direct dividend reinvestment plan is available: (800) 438-6278** □ **Web site: www.wal-mart.com** □ **Listed: NYSE** □ **Fiscal year ends January 31** □ **Ticker symbol: WMT** □ **S&P rating: A+** □ **Value Line financial strength rating: A++**

In 1999, Wal-Mart made a major international move with the $10.7-billion purchase of Britain's third-largest supermarket chain, Asda Group PLC. This acquisition doubled the company's international sales to $25 billion—some 17 percent of annual revenues.

What's more, the Asda purchase gave Wal-Mart a second leg on which to build a continent-wide business, adding to the two German chains it acquired in the last two years. The company wants a third of its growth over the next five years to come from international operations.

Company Profile

Wal-Mart is the world's number one retailer—larger than Sears, Kmart, and J. C. Penney combined. At the end of fiscal 2000 (January 31, 2000), the company operated 1,801 domestic Wal-Mart stores, 721 domestic Supercenters, 463 Sam's Clubs, and 1,004 international units.

Most of the company's outlets are in the United States, but it is moving abroad aggressively and has a presence in Canada, Latin America, Asia, and Europe.

In fiscal 2000, Wal-Mart completed its best year ever, with sales of over $165 billion, up 20 percent, which is over $27 billion more than the prior year. What's more, earnings per share shot up 26 percent.

Shortcomings to Bear in Mind

- In the spring of 2000, Wal-Mart said it would close meat-cutting operations in 180 stores in six states, including a store in Jacksonville, Texas where 10 meat workers voted to unionize two weeks prior to the company's announcement.

In defense of this move, management said the decision was the result of a successful year-long pilot program to stock prepackaged meat at its stores. "Case-ready meat is the way the entire industry is going," said a company official. "It increases quality control, helps overall appearance of the product, and helps us keep better track of our stock."

Needless to say, union people are upset and are not likely to let the matter lay. "The law says Wal-Mart has to bargain in good faith with their employees over any change in the workplace," said Greg Denier, director of communications for the United Food and Commercial Workers International Union. "Wal-Mart is sending a clear message to its workers that joining the union is the only way to have a voice in the workplace decision making."

- At 192,000 square feet, Wal-Mart Supercenters are about the size of four football fields. Wal-Mart quickly found that some customers have trouble navigating them. According to one shopper, "The stores are too big. It takes too long to get around." On the other hand, the store's "really good prices" keep them coming back, but warns, "We've just about decided we'll go somewhere else and pay more not to have to go through all the hassle."

Reasons to Buy

- Higher interest rates are often feared by investors. In the case of Wal-Mart, that fear may be overblown. Some analysts believe that Wal-Mart could actually benefit from a boost in interest rates. Who better to benefit from consumers watching the bottom line than a chain famous for its low prices? What's more, while rising wages and fuel prices are tough on businesses, Wal-Mart is better prepared than its rivals. "Wal-Mart can spread out fuel and labor costs over a dense volume of merchandise because it is more efficient," said Burt Flickinger III, managing director of Reach Marketing, a marketing consulting firm. "It could be a critical competitive advantage."

■ Over the years, naysayers have scoffed at Wal-Mart's international aspirations, claiming that the company's culture and business practices would never translate beyond U.S. borders. Skeptics even doubted that Wal-Mart could succeed in Canada. But six years in Canada have proven the critics wrong. Wal-Mart now has 166 discount stores in Canada, and the company's operations there are considered a model for Wal-Mart's expansion into other international markets. When acquired, the 122-store Canadian Woolco chain was losing millions of dollars annually, but operations became profitable within three years. Today, Canadian operations are among the most profitable in the company. So far, Wal-Mart has captured more than 35 percent of the Canadian discount-and-department-store retail market and has become the largest retailer in Canada, the United States, and Mexico.

■ Two or three years ago, Sam's Club experienced some challenges but has bounced back of late. Sam's Club is a concept that was started back in 1983. The company entered the business because it was the retail innovation with the lowest-cost method of distributing merchandise. Unfortunately, according to Don Soderquist, senior vice chairman, "Over the years, the industry and Sam's as well, has lost some of its merchandising focus. The Sam's team

used the last two years or so to reinvigorate the clubs and put some fun back into the operation, and with their new president, Tom Grimm, continue to improve the merchandise offering. I believe this is obvious by the acceleration in the sales increases as well as the number of new members and the renewal rates of existing members."

■ Some 10 years ago, Wal-Mart began experimenting with a retail concept called a "Hypermarket," which the company translated into its Supercenter. This concept took the idea of retailing both general merchandise and food in the same building and created the convenience of one-stop shopping.

According to the CEO of Wal-Mart, David Glass, "It has become our key domestic growth vehicle and will remain so for at least the next 10 years.

"Supercenters effectively serve a large trade area, but we think there may be some business that we are not getting purely because they may be as close to the customer or convenient for small shopping trips. That's where we think there may be an opportunity for the small grocery/drug store format where we are testing the Neighborhood Market."

Already, Wal-Mart's push into groceries is pressuring giants like Kroger Company and Safeway Inc. to cut costs and boost service. And the pressures aren't coming merely from the Supercenters: Add food and other grocery items sold through the Wal-Mart discount and Sam's Clubs units and one retail analyst estimates that groceries now account for more than $30 billion of Wal-Mart's total sales. According to still another analyst, "Wal-Mart is totally flanking the grocery industry. It is terribly threatening." He predicts that in 10 years Wal-Mart and Safeway will be the two largest food retailers in the

United States, leaving such rivals as Kroger and Albertson's in the dust.

■ Wal-Mart makes a concerted effort to find out precisely what its customers want. To do this, the company relies on information technology. It does this by collecting and analyzing internally developed information, which it calls data-mining. It has been doing this since 1990.

The result is an enormous database of purchasing information that enables management to place the right item in the right store at the right time. The company's computer system receives 8.4 million updates every minute on the items that customers take home—and the relationship between the items in each basket.

Many retailers talk a good game when it comes to mining data at cash registers as a way to build sales. Wal-Mart, since it has been doing this for the past 10 years, is sitting on an information trove so vast and detailed that it far exceeds what many manufacturers know about their own products. What's more, Wal-Mart's database is second in size only to that of the U.S. government, says one analyst. Wal-Mart also collects "market-basket data" from customer receipts at all of its stores, so it knows what products are likely to be purchased together. The company receives about 100,000 queries a week from suppliers and its own buyers looking for purchase patterns or checking a product.

Wal-Mart plans to use the data in its new Neighborhood Markets. Equipped with a drive-through pharmacy and selling both dry goods and perishables, the stores are a little smaller than typical suburban supermarkets. They are much smaller than Wal-Mart's Supercenters,

the massive grocery-discount store combinations that Wal-Mart began opening in 1987.

This kind of information has significant value in and of itself. According to management, "Consider Wal-Mart's ability to keep the shelves stocked with exactly what customers want most, but still be able to keep inventories under tight control. Consider the common banana—so common, in fact, that the grocery carts of America contain bananas more often than any other single item. So why not make it easy for a shopper to remember bananas? In Wal-Mart grocery departments, bananas can be found not just in the produce section, but in the cereal and dairy aisles too."

■ Wal-Mart has taken its time in getting into electronic retailing but has finally unveiled its revamped online store, promising to introduce the Internet to the "have-nots." Since July of 1996, the company has operated only a bare-bones site with minimal advertising. Now it has an alliance with America Online. "People may believe we were slow coming to market," said Glenn Habern, Wal-Mart's senior vice president for new business. But Wal-Mart didn't want to devote extensive resources to the Internet until it could bring its core shoppers online. During recent months, the company has lined up a host of companies to support the site, including the Fingerhut unit of Federated Department Stores. Now that it is in full swing, the company's new online shop, which includes about 600,000 items from clothing to shampoo to computers to garden supplies, also offers services such as airline, hotel, and car-rental booking.

Total assets: $70,349 million
Current ratio: 0.93
Common shares outstanding: 4,454 million
Return on 1999 shareholders' equity: 22.9%

	1999	1998	1997	1996	1995	1994	1993	1992
Revenues (millions)	165013	137634	117958	104859	93627	82494	67345	55484
Net income (millions)	5377	4430	3526	3056	2740	2681	2333	1995
Earnings per share	1.21	.99	.78	.67	.60	.59	.51	.44
Dividends per share	.20	.16	.14	.11	.10	.09	.07	.05
Price High	70.3	41.4	21.0	14.2	13.8	14.6	17.0	16.4
Low	38.7	18.8	11.0	9.6	10.2	10.6	11.5	12.6

INCOME

Washington Gas Light Company

1100 H Street, N.W. ◻ Washington, D. C. 20080 ◻ Investor contact: Craig W. Gilbert (202)624-6410
◻ Dividend reinvestment program is available (888) 269-8845 ◻ Fiscal years end September 30th ◻ Listed NYSE
◻ Web site: www.washgas.com ◻ Ticker symbol: WGL ◻ S&P rating: A- ◻ Value Line financial strength rating: A

Washington Gas Light is expanding its customer base by working closely with area builders and developers. Today, more than 95 percent of the new homes sold by top builders in the Washington area use natural gas. The company has focused its marketing and development efforts on increasing the number of gas appliances installed in these new homes. Results have been impressive. Over the past five years, the number of new homes in its service territory featuring gas fireplaces or lot sets has more than doubled. What's more, the number of new homes with gas ranges has risen by 25 percent.

Company Profile

Washington Gas Light Company often omits the word "Light" from its official name—probably because people sometimes mistakenly think WGL is an electric utility. In any event, Washington Gas is the energy company of choice in the Washington, D. C. metropolitan area and surrounding region.

Meter growth on the Washington Gas system averaged 3.1 percent annually during the past five years—significantly higher than the rate for the gas industry.

Firm customers, both residential and commercial, provide a stable financial base, accounting for 92 percent of the company's regulated gas sales during fiscal 1999.

The D. C. area, since it is the nation's capital, has a stable economy, often shielded from the ups and downs of more industrial cities.

Washington Gas has service agreements with eight interstate pipelines and connects directly to four. The company purchases gas from nearly seventy suppliers. This portfolio approach enables the company to benefit from competition among gas suppliers.

Washington Gas dates back to 1848. It has paid dividends for 148 consecutive years, a record matched by few companies on the New York Stock Exchange.

Washington Gas Light's service territory encompasses 6,648 square miles in and around the nation's capital. The franchise has a population of 4.4 million. It has been growing at an average annual rate of 1.3 percent over the past five years, driven by the expansion of such industries as the region's telecommunications, biotechnology, and information services.

Most of the growth has taken place in the suburban areas around Washington, D.C., generating high levels of new home construction. What's more, WGL has been able to capture a majority share of all new single-family homes built within its service territory.

Highlights of 1999

■ Net utility revenues for the 12 months ended September 30, 1999, rose $6.8 million (1.6 percent) from the prior year.

■ By the end of the fiscal year, more than 100,000 of Washington Gas's residential and commercial customers in the District of Columbia, Maryland and Virginia were shopping for competitively priced natural gas.

■ Washington Gas Energy Services, the leading natural gas marketer in the Washington metropolitan region, topped the $100 million revenue mark and increased its sales volume by 29 percent.

■ Washington Gas Energy Systems and American Combustion Industries, Inc. grew revenues to $31.2 million in fiscal year 1999 by providing heating, ventilating and air conditioning services to commercial customers.

■ Washington Gas's Board of Directors authorized the company to obtain the necessary approvals to create a holding company structure over Washington Gas and its subsidiaries. The holding company will be known as WGL Holdings, Inc. Under the new structure, Washington Gas, as the regulated utility, and the subsidiaries it currently holds, will each operate as separate subsidiaries of WGL Holdings, Inc.

James H. DeGraffenreidt, Jr., the company's CEO, noted that the creation of the holding company strengthens the company's ability to succeed in deregulating energy markets. "This new structure supports the vitality of our utility business while providing the financial and regulatory flexibility necessary to respond quickly and effectively to changing industry and economic conditions," Mr. DeGraffenreidt said. "It enables us to take full advantage of growth opportunities in and beyond our regulated business that provide superior value for our shareholders and expanded services for customers."

Shortcomings to Bear in Mind

■ Over the past 10 years (1989-1999), earnings per share inched ahead from $1.22 to $1.47, for a compound annual growth rate of only 1.9 percent. In the same period, dividends per share made only modest progress, rising from $0.97 to $1.22, for a compound growth rate of 2.3 percent. These figures may not be as disconcerting as they seem. The weather comes into the picture. In fiscal 1999, the weather was unusually warm during the winter, thus reducing revenues from space heating.

Reasons to Buy

■ Washington Gas is positioning itself to succeed in a changing energy market through service innovations and improvements. When fully deployed, a new computer-aided dispatch system will automate the managing, scheduling, and dispatching of work orders to field personnel and significantly improve responsiveness. Upgraded in 1999 to include state-of-the-art laptop computers using sophisticated software, the new system will feature a scheduling package that ties into the company's existing customer order system. The system will schedule the job, identify the type of technician required, and take into account the approximate travel and work time. Customers will be able to get status reports on their orders from customer service representatives, resulting in greater convenience and time savings.

- Washington Gas Energy Services, the company's unregulated marketing subsidiary, is the leading non-regulated gas supplier in the Washington metropolitan area. Its reach extends into the Baltimore area—and even as far as Delaware. Established about four years ago, the affiliate's performance has exceeded all expectations. In 1999, Washington Gas Energy Services surpassed the $100-million mark in annual revenues, achieving 29 percent sales growth.

  Initially, Washington Gas Energy Services supplied gas primarily to commercial customers. In 1999, it focused marketing efforts on obtaining new residential business, supplying natural gas to households in all the jurisdictions Washington Gas serves, including the District of Columbia, Virginia, and Maryland. The results were dramatic—Washington Gas Energy Services provides natural gas to five times the number of residential customers it did a year ago.

- The company's franchise area possesses a significant number of conversion opportunities for Washington Gas Light to pursue. Conversion takes place when owners of older homes that use some other energy source (typically electricity or fuel oil) for their space heating are persuaded to convert to natural gas. The company now has about two-thirds of the business in existing structures in its service territory.

  The conversion potential is a legacy of events that took place during the 1970s. This was when natural gas was perceived to be in short supply. To "cure" the problem, WGL's regulators imposed a moratorium on new gas hook-ups. This ruling prohibited

Washington Gas from investing in facilities to serve new customers. With natural gas denied to them, home owners turned to electricity. Electric heat pumps became a popular alternative for heating new homes built during the mid- to late-1970s. As a consequence, a thick ring, composed of thousands of electrically heated homes, sprung up around the company's service territory. Washington Gas calls this an "electric doughnut."

When the moratorium was lifted in 1980, WGL had to make large capital investments to extend its gas line beyond the doughnut, so that it could provide service to new customers in the growing parts of its franchise area. Meanwhile, the electric heat pumps are now nearing the end of their useful lives. Consequently, with the favorable economics and greater effectiveness of natural gas heating, coupled with the presence of natural gas mains crossing through the area, the aging electric doughnut provides Washington Gas with a significant opportunity to tap into these lines to recapture this business from the electric company.

- Washington Gas enjoys the stability of a customer base that is made up of 92 percent of residential customers, with 95 percent of these using natural gas for space heating. Of the remaining 8 percent, most are small commercial accounts that also use natural gas for space heating. Lacking are the industrial customers that can make the territory sensitive to the ups and downs of the economy.

  On the other hand, since WGL sells most of its gas for space heating, it is particularly sensitive to changes in the weather. To offset this weather sensitivity, the company features declining rate blocks. Translated, this means that successively higher levels of usage each month are charged lower incremental rates. In addition, there are other temperature-shielding rate mechanisms. Even so, the weather still makes earnings quite volatile.

To be sure, the vagaries of the weather also help or hurt other natural gas companies. Some of them have found a way to mitigate this volatility by making a deal with the regulators to set up a weather normalization scheme. Under this arrangement, the utility adds an extra charge during a warm winter and gives back a little when the heating season is abnormally cold. However, Washington Gas Light has rejected this idea, fearing that the various state commissions would lower their allowed rate of return as an offset.

Total assets: $1,767 million
Current ratio: 0.88
Common shares outstanding: 46 million
Return on 1999 shareholders' equity: 10.4%

		1999	1998	1997	1996	1995	1994	1993	1992
Revenues (millions)		972	1040	1056	970	829	915	894	746
Net income (millions)		67	69	82	82	63	60	55	52
Earnings per share		1.47	1.54	1.85	1.85	1.45	1.42	1.31	1.27
Dividends per share		1.22	1.20	1.17	1.14	1.12	1.11	1.09	1.07
Price	High	29.4	30.8	31.4	25.0	22.4	21.3	22.9	19.6
	Low	21.0	23.1	20.9	19.1	16.1	16.0	18.1	15.6

INCOME

Washington Real Estate Investment Trust (WRIT)

6110 Executive Boulevard ◻ Rockville, Maryland 20852-3927 ◻ Investor contact: Larry E. Finger (301) 255-0820 ◻ Listed: NYSE ◻ Dividend reinvestment plan is available: (800) 278-4353 ◻ Web site: www.washreit.com ◻ Ticker symbol: WRE ◻ S&P rating: Not rated ◻ Value Line Financial Strength B++

Washington Real Estate Investment Trust (WRIT) has had an enviable record. Over the past 27 years, WRIT shareholders earned a compound annual rate of return of 18.1 percent. This compares favorably to the total returns (stock appreciation plus dividends) of 14.6 percent for the Standard & Poor's 500 and 12.8 percent for the real estate investment trust industry over the same period.

What's more, the company's record is consistent: WRIT has produced positive earnings every year since its inception. The company's streak of 33 consecutive years of increased earnings per share (EPS) is matched by only 10 other publicly traded companies in the United States. Also, the dividend had been raised for 29 straight years. Finally, its streak of 27 consecutive years of increased Funds From Operations (FFO) per share is nearly three times as long as any other in the real estate investment trust industry. FFO is often used by the REIT industry instead of earnings per share.

Company Profile

Washington Real Estate Investment Trust, founded in 1960, invests in a diversified range of income-producing properties. Management's purpose is to acquire and manage real estate investments in markets it knows well and to protect the company's assets from the risk of owning a single property type, such as apartments, industrial parks, or shopping centers. WRIT achieves its objectives by owning properties in four different categories.

The trust's properties are primarily situated within a two-hour radius of Washington, D. C. that stretches from Philadelphia in the north to Richmond, Virginia in the south. Its diversified portfolio consists of 20 office buildings, 12 shopping centers, 8 apartment complexes, and 16 industrial distribution centers. WRIT's real estate investment portfolio, at cost, consists of properties located in Maryland, Washington, D. C., and Virginia:

	December 31	
	1999	1998
	(In thousands)	
Office buildings	$352,145	$323,152
Retail centers	97,004	95,017
Apartment buildings	99,125	83,163
Industrial distribution/flex prop	113,596	97,542
	$661,870	$598,874

Shortcomings to Bear in Mind

- Some investors might fret that Washington Real Estate Investment Trust lacks geographic diversification since its properties are confined to the region around Washington. While this fear might seem valid, it is my belief that Washington's economy is less sensitive to economic fluctuations than most other large cities because of its close link to the federal government. What's more, the company's diversified holdings tend to offset its lack of geographic diversification since it does not rely on one type of property that might be out of favor for a period. If office buildings are not doing well, for instance, apartments or shopping centers may be thriving.

Reasons to Buy

- In 1999, WRIT achieved FFO growth of 12.0 percent, or 40 percent greater than the REIT industry average. This solid performance was enhanced by the strong Washington-Baltimore real estate

market and tight cost controls. The results of operating in such strong markets have been dramatic. In 1996, the company's average commercial rent increase was a minimal 0.2 percent. This rate jumped to 10 percent in 1997 and has risen 50 percent since then. These extraordinary rates of growth are occurring at a time of low inflation coupled with high demand and insufficient supply.

- WRIT's focus on increasing rents and occupancies is accompanied by a similar focus on cost containment. The company's core portfolio operating expenses increased by only 2.4 percent in 1999. At the same time, general and administrative (G&A) expenses *decreased* by 5 percent. As a result, WRIT has been able to continue its trend of lowering total expenses as a percentage of revenues.

- While rents have been increasing, Washington Real Estate Investment Trust has also been able to dramatically increase occupancy levels to an extraordinarily high 96.4 percent in 1999. As with rental rates, 1997 occupancy levels reflected the beginning of the current strong market. In 1996, WRIT's overall portfolio occupancy level was 92.6 percent. This occupancy level increased by over two full percentage points in 1997 and has increased by nearly a full percentage point in 1998 and 1999.

- The Greater Washington-Baltimore region, the fourth-largest domestic metropolitan area, with a population of 7.4 million, is ranked first in the United States in median household income and percentage of population with education at the undergraduate and graduate level.

What's more, the region is an economic machine driven by the federal government at its center and the growth that results from the number one high-tech center in the nation. The technology/biotechnology sector has surpassed the federal government as the largest employer in the region. The Washington region itself now ranks number one in the nation in number of high-technology firms and employees.

While federal employment as a percentage of regional employment has decreased from 22 percent in 1970 to 11 percent in 1999, federal procurement (purchase of goods and services) has continued to grow in the region. Federal procurement in the Washington region totaled $25.7 billion in 1999, making the region number one in the nation, exceeding the combined total of the number two and number three metro areas (Los Angeles and St. Louis). Though the region may not be recession proof, this federal procurement makes it substantially better positioned than most others to withstand an economic downturn.

- MAE East, situated in Tysons Corner, Virginia, is one of only two Internet convergence centers in the United States. The presence of MAE East and the thousands of high-tech firms in the area has spawned a concentration of data centers in the region where large Internet and other high-tech firms process tremendous amounts of data. As a result, it is estimated that up to 60 percent of the world's Internet traffic flows through Northern Virginia.

This concentration of high-tech companies has served to attract even more high-tech firms. Amazon.com, Cisco Systems, and Global Crossing have all set up shop in the Washington-Baltimore market.

The region's real estate markets are the beneficiary of this growth. Vacancies are extremely low, and rental rate growth is very strong. At the end of 1999, regional vacancy rates stood at 1.1 percent in apartments, 2.7 percent in

grocery-anchored shopping centers, and 5.7 percent in office buildings. The industrial sector, at 9.2 percent, is the only sector with vacancy that is close to a normal level. This 9.2 percent vacancy rate, however, is somewhat overstated because a percentage of this industrial vacancy is the result of obsolescence.

The apartment vacancy rate of 1.1 percent at year-end 1999 was the area's lowest since World War II. The office vacancy rate of 5.7 percent was the third lowest among major metropolitan areas. More importantly, the cities ranked number one and number two had vacancy rates only slightly lower than Washington's. On the other hand, fourth-ranked New York City had a vacancy rate of 8.8 percent.

- Prior to acquiring a property, WRIT performs extensive inspections, tests, and financial analyzes to gain confidence about the property's future operating performance, as well as any required near-term improvements and long-term capital expenditures. Upon completion of this evaluation, the company develops well-informed operating projections for the property. Accordingly, when the company announces an acquisition and its anticipated return on investment, it is confident that the property will meet or exceed its projections.

- Washington Real Estate Investment Trust has always recognized the value of capital improvements to remain competitive, increase revenues, reduce operating costs, and maintain and increase the value of its properties.

During 1999, WRIT successfully completed one expansion and one major renovation: 7900 Westpark Drive. In 1999, the company completed the 49,000-square-foot addition to 7900 Westpark Drive. This $7.5-million addition was 100 percent leased and occupied upon completion, producing a 13.6 percent cash return on investment.

Bradlee Shopping Center. This major renovation coincided with the retenanting of the expired G. C. Murphy leased space and the conversion of the Roy Rogers to a newly completed, free-standing McDonald's. The renovation is complete, the McDonald's is open for business, and WRIT has leased the 26,640-square-foot former G. C. Murphy space. The $3.1-million renovation has not merely been aesthetically successful—it is producing a 15 percent cash return on investment.

Total assets: $608 million
Current ratio: not relevant
Common shares outstanding: 36 million
Return on 1999 equity: 14.0%

	1999	1998	1997	1996	1995	1994	1993	1992
Revenues (millions)	119	104	79	66	53	46	39	34
Net income (millions)	44	41	30	28	26	23	22	20
Funds from Operations	1.57	1.39	1.23	1.13	1.05	.96	.93	.89
Earnings per share	1.02	.96	.90	.88	.88	.82	.80	.76
Dividends per share	1.16	1.11	1.07	1.03	.99	.92	.89	.84
Price High	18.8	18.8	19.6	17.5	16.6	21.1	24.8	21.3
Low	13.8	15.1	15.5	15.3	13.9	14.9	18.6	14.9

INCOME

Weingarten Realty Investors

2600 Citadel Plaza Drive ❑ Post Office Box 924133 ❑ Houston, Texas 77292-4133 ❑ Investor contact: M. Candace DuFour (713) 866-6000 ❑ Direct dividend reinvestment program is available: (888) 887-2966 ❑ Web site: www.weingarten.com ❑ Listed: NYSE ❑ Ticker symbol: WRI ❑ S&P rating: not rated ❑ Value Line financial strength rating: B++

As a long-term owner of its properties, WRI maintains a program for renovating, remerchandising, and/or recycling its existing centers in order to keep each competitive within its trade area.

For instance, Wyoming Mall located in Albuquerque, New Mexico was acquired by the company in 1995 and renovated in 1998. The half-million-dollar redevelopment included additional landscaping, increased lighting, and a 36,600-square-foot Stein Mart.

Company Profile

Weingarten Realty Investors is an equity-based real estate investment trust (REIT). The company focuses primarily on the development, acquisition, and long-term ownership of anchored neighborhood and community shopping centers and, to a lesser degree, industrial properties.

At the end of 1999, its portfolio included 239 income-producing properties totaling 27.8 million square feet in 14 states. Except for Maine and Tennessee, the company's properties are west of the Mississippi. The other states are Nevada, Colorado, Arizona, New Mexico, Kansas, Oklahoma, Texas, Florida, Arkansas, Louisiana, Missouri, and Illinois.

By far the largest concentration of WRI's properties are in Texas, particularly Houston and Harris counties. Of the company's 239 properties, a total of 179 are in Texas.

Founded in 1948, Weingarten restructured itself into a real estate investment trust and listed on the New York Stock Exchange in 1985. Its performance as a public company has been among the best in the industry. This is a product of 50 years of real estate experience (in both growth and recessionary cycles), combined with a seasoned management team focused on specific segments of real estate. In addition to developing and acquiring properties, Weingarten adds value to them through consistent, high-quality operations that incorporate renovation, retailer recycling, and ongoing asset management.

Some History

Weingarten Realty Investors was founded in 1948 with two part-time employees, $60,000 in cash, and a portfolio of supermarket buildings totaling 51,000 square feet. The company was created to develop free-standing stores for J. Weingarten, Inc., a fast-growing grocery chain that was owned by the Weingarten family.

In addition to developing the stores, the company was charged with the responsibility to acquire raw land for future development and expansion. As a result, management was in an ideal position to take advantage of the trend to develop clusters of stores as the evolution of the shopping center began to take shape in the early 1950s.

As Weingarten began its new course, it focused on the neighborhood and community shopping center that ranged in size from 100,000 to 400,000 square feet and was anchored primarily by supermarkets. This practice is still continued today, with the company also focusing on certain industrial properties as well.

In 1980, the J. Weingarten supermarket chain was sold, and the realty company began to diversify and expand its relationships with other grocers and general retailers throughout the United States.

Today, it boasts a diversified tenant roster of over 2,900 different tenants, many with multiple locations.

During the 50 years of Weingarten's existence, the company has emerged as one of the largest REITs listed on the NYSE. Its portfolio has expanded from four properties to 239 at year-end 1999. The company's square footage has increased from 51,000 to nearly 28 million, and the company has expanded its holdings from one city and one state to more than 55 cities in 14 states. Likewise, Weingarten's revenue, funds from operations, and dividends have increased significantly over the 13 years of being a REIT. From the $60,000 that it began with, its total market capitalization today is over $1.9 billion.

Funds from Operations—a Definition

Investors in common stock use net income as a key measure of profitability. However, in measuring a REIT, most investors prefer the term funds from operations, or FFO. This is because earnings and expenses of a real estate investment trust must be looked at differently.

The Securities and Exchange Commission has a blanket requirement that all publicly traded companies file audited financial statements. On a financial statement, the term net income has a meaning clearly defined under generally accepted accounting principles. Since a REIT falls under the classification of a publicly traded company, net income therefore appears on a REIT's audited financial statement.

For a REIT, on the other hand, this figure is less meaningful as a measure of operating success than it is for other types of corporations. The reason is that, in accounting, real estate depreciation is always treated as an expense. In the real world, most well-maintained quality properties have *retained* their value over the years. This is because of rising land values.

In other words, it is because of steadily rising rental income, property upgrades, or higher costs for new construction for competing properties. Whatever the reason, a REIT's net income, since it suffers from a large depreciation expense, is a less-than-meaningful measure of how a REIT's operations have actually fared. It is because of this reasoning that FFO is often a better way to judge a real estate investment trust than traditional net income. You will note that I have used this alternative term in the table at the end of the article.

Shortcomings to Bear in Mind

- Weingarten Realty Investors is primarily an income stock, which often yields 6 percent or more. In terms of growth, however, it is not exciting. In the 1989–1999 period, funds from operations advanced from $2.14 to $3.93, a compound annual growth rate of only 6.3 percent. Similarly, dividends during this 10-year span advanced from $1.76 to $2.84, a growth rate of 4.9 percent.
- There is no way to avoid risk completely. Real estate ownership and management, like any other business, is subject to all sorts of risks. Mall REITs, for instance, are subject to the changing tastes and lifestyles of consumers.
- Although the company operates in 14 states, it is predominantly situated in Texas and thus lacks effective geographic diversification.

Reasons to Buy

- In 1999, the company had several significant accomplishments. Acquisitions, new developments, and the performance of the company's existing portfolio all contributed to the outstanding results of 1999. Highlights include:
  - Funds from operations on a diluted per-share basis, increased 9.2 percent, to $3.93 from $3.60 the prior year.
  - Net income increased 59.2 percent, to $96.1 million, from $60.4 million in 1998, due primarily to the sale of certain properties that resulted in a gain of $20.6 million.
  - Rental revenues increased 15.7 percent, to $225.2 million, up from $194.6 million in 1998.
  - Rental rates on new leases and renewals increased 9.5 percent on a same-space basis.
  - Total capital invested in acquisitions and new developments exceeded $193 million.
- Overall, 1999 was another outstanding year for the company's acquisition program, with purchases of five shopping centers and two industrial facilities. Additionally, Weingarten purchased a 98,000-square-foot building adjacent to one of its existing shopping centers and its joint venture partner's interest in a New Mexico shopping center. Total acquisitions in 1999 represented an investment of over $150 million. However, competition and prices for the company's product type remained high. Even so, the company's comprehensive, detailed approach to underwriting all of its acquisitions ensures that each asset it purchases will produce the risk-adjusted returns necessary to generate an appropriate spread over its long-term cost of capital. Finally, management remains focused on specific property types: the supermarket-anchored community shopping centers and industrial facilities located in markets where the company can intensely manage its assets.
- From a geographic perspective, Weingarten made great strides in 1999 in continuing to build critical mass in cities where the company already owned other properties. In Houston, the company purchased the Champions Village Shopping Center. This 408,000-square-foot shopping center is anchored by a

Randall's Flagship supermarket, Barnes & Noble, Stein Mart, and Walgreens and is located in one of the more affluent and densely populated areas of the city.

Also in Houston, WRI purchased the Claywood Industrial Park. This 330,000-square-foot building was vacant when purchased. After completing certain capital improvements, the company was able to lease the entire facility to one user. Included with the building purchase was 20 acres of undeveloped land on which Weingarten plans to develop additional facilities.

- The company's primary focus is on neighborhood and community shopping centers. Almost all of the centers are anchored by supermarkets, drug stores, discount stores, and other "necessity" type retailers that have wide consumer appeal through all economic cycles.

Total assets: $1,309 million
Current ratio: NM
Common shares outstanding: 26 million
Return on 1999 shareholders' equity: 12%

	1999	1998	1997	1996	1995	1994	1993	1992
Rental income (millions)	223	195	169	145	125	112	94	83
Net income (millions)	96.3	61.8	55.0	53.9	44.8	43.8	36.2	21.2
FFO per share	3.93	3.60	3.32	3.09	2.82	2.71	2.40	2.36
Dividends per share	2.84	2.68	2.56	2.48	2.40	2.28	2.16	2.04
Price High	45.6	46.9	45.6	40.8	38.5	40.5	45.3	38.0
Low	37.0	35.9	38.8	34.3	33.4	32.8	36.5	29.5

CONSERVATIVE GROWTH

Wells Fargo & Company

420 Montgomery Street ▫ San Francisco, California 94163 ▫ Investor contact: Bob Strickland (415) 396-0523 ▫ Direct dividend reinvestment plan is available: (800) 813-3324 ▫ Web site: www.wellsfargo.com ▫ Listed: NYSE ▫ Ticker symbol: WFC ▫ S&P rating: A ▫ Value Line financial strength rating: A

The giant Wells Fargo got even larger in April of 2000 when it acquired First Security Corporation, Utah's biggest bank, for stock valued at $2.89 billion. The deal came after Zions Bancorp spurned a chance to buy First Security—voted down by shareholders. The troubled deal was originally worth $5.9 billion in stock but later fell to $3.4 billion after First Security's fortunes were hurt by a slowdown in mortgage banking revenues.

First Security has $23 billion in assets and 333 branches. "It's obviously a small transaction for Wells," said Lori Appelbaum, an analyst at Goldman Sachs. "The important thing is the position it gives the company in fast-growing markets." In Utah, for example, Wells Fargo will jump from the ninth-largest bank chain to the top position. In Idaho, it leapt from sixth to first.

Company Profile

Wells Fargo & Company, the nation's seventh-largest bank holding company, is the result of a 1998 merger of Norwest Corporation, a bank in Minnesota, and Wells Fargo, a major bank based in San Francisco. Wells Fargo has $218 billion in assets and has banking operations in 22 states.

Wells Fargo & Company was founded on the American frontier 148 years ago to satisfy a fundamental human need—to connect one market to another and one customer to another by transporting goods, services, and funds fast and securely across great distances.

Today, Wells Fargo is a diversified financial services company, providing banking, insurance, investments, mortgage, and consumer finance from 5,310 stores (translated, branches), the industry's leading Internet site, and other distribution channels across North America. Wells Fargo is the product of more than one thousand five hundred mergers in 148 years, including the merger of equals involving Norwest Corporation and Wells Fargo & Company. By most standards, Wells Fargo ranks high on the list of major banks:

- Assets: $218 billion
- Rank in size among U.S. peers: seventh
- Market value of stock at the end of 1999: $65.7 billion
- Rank by market cap among U.S. peers: third
- Rank by market cap among global peers: seventh
- Team members: 103,053 (employees)

Highlights of 1999

- Net income in 1999 was $3,747 million, compared with $1,950 million the prior year, an increase of 92 percent. Diluted earnings per share were $2.23, compared with $1.17 in 1998, an increase of 91 percent.
- Return on average assets (ROA) was 1.85 percent, and return on average common equity (ROE) was 17.66 percent in 1999, compared with 1.04 and 9.86 percent, respectively in 1998.
- Diluted earnings before the amortization of goodwill and nonqualifying core deposit intangible (CDI or "cash" earnings) were $2.56 per share in 1999, compared with $1.50 per share in 1998. On the same basis, ROA was 2.22 percent,

and ROE was 34.08 percent in 1999, compared with 1.39 percent and 23.15 percent, respectively, in 1998.

- Net interest income on a taxable-equivalent basis was $9,419 million in 1999, compared with $9,049 million a year earlier. The company's net interest margin was 5.66 percent for 1999, compared with 5.79 percent the prior year.
- Noninterest income increased to $7,420 million in 1999, from $6,427 million in 1998, an increase of 15 percent. The increase was primarily due to higher net venture capital gains, partly offset by a loss on the sale of investment securities.
- Noninterest expense totaled $9,782 in 1999, compared with $10,579 million the prior year. The decrease was primarily due to fourth quarter 1998 merger-related and other charges.
- The provision for loan losses was $1,045 million in 1999, compared with $1,545 million in 1998. During 1999, net charge-offs were $1,049, or .94 percent of average total loans, compared with $1,617 million, or 1.52 percent during 1998. The allowance for loan losses was $3,170 million, or 2.65 percent of total loans, at year-end 1999, compared with $3,134 million, or 2.90 percent at the end of 1998.

Shortcomings to Bear in Mind

- When the Federal Reserve raises interest rates, as it did in 2000, banks have a tougher time earning money off the difference between their own borrowing costs and loan prices.
- In 1999, Congress repealed a Depression-era law that had built a wall between commercial banking and investment banking. Congress enacted a new law that allows banking, insurance, and investment firms to enter fully into each other's businesses.

The evolution of this industry has coincided with another phenomenon:

the explosive growth of the Internet. The result is an unprecedented number of new players in this huge, intensely competitive, and very-fast-growing industry. There are fewer banks in the United States, but there also are more and more companies offering financial services—from retailers to manufacturers to Internet portals.

It seems everyone these days wants to be in the money business. Never before have so many companies competed through so many different channels to lend money, accept deposits, sell insurance, mortgages, stocks, process payments, finance equipment, or invest in business. Brokerage companies want to be your bank. Banks want to be your broker. Banks want to sell you insurance. Insurance companies want to be your bank and broker and real estate developer. And that's just the tip of the iceberg.

Reasons to Buy

- On a more positive note, Wells Fargo has been preparing for the next stage for a long time. According to management, "We've built one of America's most diversified financial service companies. We have market leadership in major categories, including community banking, mortgage lending, Internet banking, commercial real estate, education finance, small business lending, commercial banking for middle market and larger corporations, agricultural lending, and supermarket banking.

"Our vision is not the vision of just a bank, a brokerage firm, a mortgage company, or an insurance agency. Our vision is to bring all these products to our customers through all our channels, satisfy our customers's financial needs, offer sound financial advice, and help them succeed financially."

- During the 1989–1999 period, earnings per share advanced from $0.63 to $2.23, a compound annual return of 13.5 percent. In the same 10-year span, dividends per share climbed from $0.19 to $0.79, a compound growth rate of 15.3 percent.

- Richard Kovacevich, chief executive of Wells Fargo, is the banking industry's king of cross-selling. He has made a career out of selling more and more financial products to the same people, and now he's doing it on a grand scale. Wells Fargo, which merged with Minneapolis-based Norwest in 1998, wants each of its 15 million customers to take eight products, up from three now. The industry norm is two.

Plenty of other huge financial institutions have taken a crack at cross-selling—mostly with little success. But Wells Fargo, the nation's third-largest bank in market capitalization, has something special going for it: Kovacevich. "He's a huge believer in cross-selling. He wakes up every morning thinking about it," said Ken Charles Feinberg, portfolio manager of Davis Selected Advisers.

Mr. Kovacevich admits the company still has "a long way to go. We have 48 systems conversions scheduled for 2000, including 19 banking states, acquisitions, and new products. Later in 2000, both Norwest Mortgage and Norwest Financial (consumer finance) will adopt the Wells Fargo name so they can take full advantage of cross-sell opportunities with our banking businesses.

"Our average banking household has 3.4 products with us. We want to get to eight. To do that, we must offer customers a package of products all at once, not one at a time. In Lewiston, Montana, our first test site, our bankers sold an average of 2.39 products to new customers in 1999, up 62 percent from a year earlier."

Kovacevich, age 56, got his start in marketing at General Mills, then moved to Citibank, managing its new York City branches in the 1970s and launching its pioneering automated teller machine system. In 1986, he went with Norwest and turned it into one of the nation's most admired banks. Then, in 1998, Norwest acquired Wells Fargo for $32 billion. Rather than retaining the Norwest name, Mr. Kovacevich elected to stick with the better-known Wells Fargo stagecoach logo, along with its San Francisco home office.

Total assets: $218 billion
Common shares outstanding: 1,627 million
Return on 1999 shareholders' equity: 17.7%

	1999	1998	1997	1996	1995	1994	1993	1992
Net interest income (millions)	9355	8990	4033	3701	3269	2804	2376	2009
Net income (millions)	3747	2906	1351	1154	956	800	654	518
Earnings per share	2.23	1.75	1.75	1.54	1.37	1.21	1.05	.86
Dividends per share	.79	.70	.62	.53	.45	.38	.32	.27
Price High	49.9	43.9	39.5	23.4	17.4	14.1	14.5	11.1
Low	32.2	27.5	21.4	15.3	11.3	10.5	10.3	8.3

GROWTH AND INCOME

Weyerhaeuser Company

Post Office Box 2999 ◻ Tacoma, Washington 98477-2999 ◻ Investor contact: Richard J. Taggart (253) 924-2058 ◻ Dividend reinvestment plan is available: (800) 561-4405 ◻ Web site: www.weyerhaeuser.com ◻ Listed: NYSE ◻ Ticker symbol: WY ◻ S&P rating: B+ ◻ Value Line financial strength rating: B++

A century ago, Weyerhaeuser was a fledgling enterprise in the woods of Washington. When the company was founded on January 18, 1900, few could have foreseen how the industry would develop. The concept of timber as a renewable resource, for instance, was unthinkable in 1900. Today it is the guiding principle of the industry.

Or who would have guessed that wood would eventually be used in everything from aspirin to apparel, in addition to lumber and paper? And who would have thought that Weyerhaeuser would be making engineered wood products that have the benefits of wood and the strength of steel?

Finally, could Frederick Weyerhaeuser and the company's other founders have envisioned what their company would become in the year 2000? Here is how it looks today:

● The world's largest owner of softwood timber and the world's largest producer of softwood market pulp and softwood lumber.

● One of the largest producers of containerboard packaging and fine paper.

● The world's second-largest producer of oriented strand board (OSB).

● The world's largest producer and distributor of engineered wood products.

● One of the largest producers of hardwood lumber.

● A company that serves customers in more than sixty countries.

Company Background
Weyerhaeuser is primarily engaged in the growing and harvesting of timber and the manufacture, distribution, and sale of forest products. It is also in real estate development and construction.

The company's wood products businesses produce and sell softwood lumber, plywood, and veneer; composite panels;

oriented strand board; hardboard; hardwood lumber and plywood; doors; treated products; logs; chips and timber.

These products are sold primarily through the company's own sales organizations. Building materials are sold to wholesalers, retailers, and industrial users.

Weyerhaeuser's pulp, paper, and packaging businesses include:

- Pulp—manufactures chemical wood pulp for world markets.
- Newsprint—manufactures newsprint at the company's North Pacific Paper Corporation mill and markets it to West Coast and Japanese newspaper publishers.
- Paper—manufactures and markets a range of both coated and uncoated fine papers through paper merchants and printers.
- Containerboard Packaging—manufactures linerboard and corrugating medium, which is primarily used in the production of corrugated shipping containers, and manufactures and markets corrugated shipping containers for industrial and agricultural packaging.
- Paperboard—manufactures bleached paperboard that is used for production of liquid containers and is marketed to West Coast and Pacific Rim customers.
- Recycling—operates an extensive wastepaper collection system and markets it to company mills and worldwide customers.
- Chemicals—produces chlorine, caustic, and tall oil, which is used principally by the company's pulp, paper, and packaging operations.

Highlights of 1999

- The acquisition and integration of MacMillan Bloedel Limited attracted the most attention. This merger enabled the company to:
  - Acquire facilities that provide an excellent match with the company's existing Containerboard Packaging business.
  - Expand Weyerhaeuser's OSB facilities by more than 50 percent, enabling the company to more efficiently serve new and existing markets in the eastern part of North America.
  - Extend the geographic reach of the company's Building Materials Distribution network of customer service centers.
  - Add high-value cedar and clear whitewood lumber from coastal British Columbia to its product line.
  - Assume a 49 percent ownership in Trus Joist and build upon the company's existing strategic alliance with Trus Joist in the fast-growing engineered wood products segment. Trus Joist makes home-building products out of wood strands and sheets of veneer. Early in 2000, the company assumed full ownership of Trus Joist by acquiring TJ International, the holding company that had owned the remaining 51 percent of Trus Joist.
  - Achieve a potential $200 million in annual savings through synergies from MacMillan Bloedel and Trus Joist over the next three years.

Shortcomings to Bear in Mind

- The major markets, both domestic and foreign, in which the company sells its products are highly competitive, with numerous strong sellers competing in each realm.

Many of Weyerhaeuser's products compete with substitutes for wood and wood fiber products. The real estate and financial services subsidiaries, moreover, also compete in highly competitive markets, competing with numerous regional and national firms in real estate development and construction and in financial services.

- In the past 10 years (1989–1999), earnings per share made only minimal progress, rising from $2.83 to $3.31. During that period, moreover, earnings declined five times. Nor have dividends done much better; they advanced from $1.20 to $1.60.

Reasons to Buy

- In 2000, pulp and paper markets have been tight. Rising demand and a lack of any significant new capacity—at least through 2001—enabled the company to increase prices three times in a recent 12-month period.
- Weyerhaeuser is uniquely positioned in its industry. It manages more privately owned timber than any other company.

  Likewise, Weyerhaeuser leads the industry in private forestry, having launched—nearly a generation ago—a program to maximize timber yield on every acre of planted forest land.
- To build on the timber asset and increase shareholder value, Weyerhaeuser is following a strategy that contains three elements:
  - Sell or dispose of nonstrategic assets
  - Work assiduously to upgrade the company's portfolio of land, mills, and other facilities
  - Ally strategically with domestic and international partners
  - Emphasize value-added products
  - Continually improve product quality and the cost efficiency of production
- The company is improving its returns on its Pulp, Paper, and Packaging sector by reducing its exposure to commodity grades, improving process reliability, and maintaining tight controls on capital spending.
- As a leader in the use of advanced silviculture practices, Weyerhaeuser is getting the most out of the trees on the millions of acres of land the company owns or manages. Because of these practices, the company will greatly increase how much timber it harvests over the next 10 years. This increased harvest level comes at a time when private, managed woodlands such as Weyerhaeuser's are being called upon to play an even bigger role in meeting society's demand for softwood sawtimber. The company has also selectively pruned many of its trees to produce knot-free lumber and other higher-value products that command higher market values and maximize the value the company gets from its timber harvest.
- The company believes that it has good prospects in the Southern hemisphere—especially New Zealand and South America. Weyerhaeuser owns a 51 percent interest in 193,000 acres of managed forest land and related assets in New Zealand. As the majority owner, the company is responsible for the management and marketing activities of the joint venture.

  In 1998, the company also made additional investments through its partnership with institutional investors known as the World Timberfund. This partnership currently holds a 97 percent interest in a venture that has acquired 234,000 acres of private agricultural land in Uruguay that is being converted into plantation forests.
- Weyerhaeuser has been narrowing its business focus since 1990. The company divested its milk carton, personal care products, insurance, nursery products, and gypsum wallboard businesses. What's more, WY reduced its investments by selling selected real estate assets.
- Extensive restructuring carried out by former CEO John W. Creighton, Jr. since he took the reins in 1991 has transformed Weyerhaeuser—a one-time laggard—into one of the industry's most

profitable players. In years past, investors scorned Weyerhaeuser as unwieldy and paternalistic. It was loaded down with outdated mills. What's more, it was hobbled by a host of noncore subsidiaries making everything from milk cartons to disposable diapers. Besides jettisoning these businesses, Creighton led his managers through an 18-month re-engineering in which each mill and tree farm had to redesign the way it worked. Creighton's goal: to add $700 million to operating earnings by 1995—a goal he achieved a year earlier than planned.

■ Weyerhaeuser owns or manages an enormous expanse of highly productive forest land in North America. Thirty years ago, the company had the foresight to pioneer the High Yield Forestry programs. As a result, the company will see a dramatic increase in its timber harvest over the next 20 years. By the year 2020, the timber harvest from the land WY owns and manages in the United States will increase by about 70 percent from 1995 levels and significantly enhance cash flow from this source. Meanwhile, Weyerhaeuser's manufacturing facilities are operating more efficiently and producing higher quality products than ever before.

■ The company is also differentiating other parts of its product line. For instance, Weyerhaeuser's Containerboard Packaging business began exploring new packaging solutions for customers. What's more, its Pulp operation is working on new absorbency fibers. Both efforts will help the company develop higher-value products capable of producing new growth opportunities and higher margins. New absorbency fibers, for instance, improve product function and provide manufacturers with greater flexibility and speed in commercializing their product upgrades. Management is convinced this will allow providers to develop a greater range of products and increase demand for its own products.

■ In the spring of 2000, Weyerhaeuser, Georgia-Pacific, and International Paper announced plans to develop a global online business-to-business marketplace for paper and forest products. The three companies have equal stakes in the venture, which operates as an independent entity with its own directors and management. More partners are expected to join later.

Total assets: $18,339 million
Current ratio: 1.55
Common shares outstanding: 226 million
Return on 1999 shareholders' equity: 9.5%

	1999	1998	1997	1996	1995	1994	1993	1992
Revenues (millions)	12262	10766	11210	11114	11788	10398	9545	9219
Net income (millions)	681	339	351	463	983	589	463	372
Earnings per share	3.31	1.70	1.76	2.34	4.83	2.86	2.26	1.83
Dividends per share	1.60	1.60	1.60	1.60	1.50	1.20	1.20	1.20
Price High	73.9	62.0	63.9	49.9	50.4	51.3	46.5	39.3
Low	49.6	36.8	42.6	39.5	36.9	35.8	36.3	26.6

Williams-Sonoma, Inc.

3250 Van Ness Avenue ▫ San Francisco, California 94109 ▫ Investor contact: John W. Tate (415) 616-8775 ▫ Dividend reinvestment plan is not available ▫ Fiscal year ends Sunday closest to January 31 ▫ Web site: www.williams-sonoma.com ▫ Listed: NYSE ▫ Ticker symbol: WSM ▫ S&P rating: B ▫ Value Line financial strength rating: B++

Some observers are convinced that Williams-Sonoma is *the* preeminent home furnishings play on the Internet. Unlike toys, books, or pets, there is no dominant pure play Internet home furnishings company with which to compete.

One analyst said, "Williams-Sonoma, in our opinion, is head and shoulders above the crowd. Without a penny hit to earnings, the company has developed a complex bridal and gift registry and comprehensive site." What's more, Internet sales are more profitable than catalog sales since they don't require the cost of developing and mailing catalogs.

Company Profile

Williams-Sonoma is the leading specialty retailer of home-related products, operating 336 stores, four mail-order catalogs, and an e-commerce site. The company houses the following four dominant brand names: Williams-Sonoma, Pottery Barn, Hold Everything, and Chambers.

The Williams-Sonoma concept, marketed through 185 retail stores and a catalog, is the nation's premier marketer of cookware and kitchen accessories and boasts a loyal customer following.

Pottery Barn, which operates 110 retail stores and two catalogs (Pottery Barn and Pottery Barn Kids), offers middle-income households fashionable tabletop products and home furnishings.

The company markets two additional catalogs: Chambers (high-end bathroom and bedroom accessories) and Hold Everything (organizational products, in 33 retail locations).

Still the largest player in the $25-billion home accessories industries, the company appears to be poised to capitalize on the reinvigorated franchise value of its concepts as well as the consumer's heightened demand for home-related products.

Analysts, moreover, are looking for earnings growth in the years ahead of 30 percent. On the other hand, they hedge their bets by warning that there could be bumps along the way, such as a recession, merchandising errors, sourcing interruptions, and increased competition.

Some History

The company was founded in 1956 in Sonoma, California by Charles E. Williams, currently vice chairman and a director. Williams-Sonoma was one of the first retailers of fine quality cookware in the United States. Two years later, the Sonoma store was moved to San Francisco. In 1972, the company began to offer its Williams-Sonoma kitchen products through mail order catalogs. WSM expanded into areas of the home-centered business beyond kitchen products by acquiring:

• Gardeners Eden, a mail order merchandiser of home gardening and outdoor-related products (in 1982). In early 1999, the company sold Gardeners Eden to Brookstone in order to deploy resources to its businesses with higher growth potential, including Pottery Barn Kids and emerging Internet projects.

• Pottery Barn, a retailer of home furnishings, accessories and housewares (in 1986).

Internally, the company developed Hold Everything, a retail and mail order merchandiser of innovative household storage products, and Chambers, a mail order merchandiser of high-quality bed and bath products.

Shortcomings to Bear in Mind

- Alas, nothing is perfect. Investors are enthusiastic over the prospects for Williams-Sonoma and have pushed the share price up to lofty levels. This creates extra risk.
- The specialty retail business is highly competitive. The company's specialty retail stores and mail order catalogs compete with other retail stores, including specialty stores and department stores and other mail order catalogs. The substantial sales growth in the mail order catalog industry within the last decade has encouraged the entry of many new competitors and an increase in competition from established companies. On the other hand, WSM competes in the marketplace on the basis of the quality of its merchandise, service to customers, and its proprietary customer list.

Reasons to Buy

- On November 1, 1999, the company launched www.williams-sonoma.com, its e-commerce Internet site. The new venture offers over 2,000 of the company's most popular products and has enhanced features that make online shopping easier. According to management, "As a company with mutually supportive channels—retail stores, catalogs, and the Internet—we believe our brands are in a particularly good position to dominate the market."
- Aging baby boomers are spending more time at home and are more focused on fashion for the home. Williams-Sonoma is well-positioned to exploit this trend.

- Analysts see solid potential on the Internet. The company's extensive database of Net-savvy customers should lead to lower customer acquisition costs. In addition, the company's 27 years of direct-to-consumer marketing experience provides competitive advantages.
- Williams-Sonoma recently launched a magazine named *Williams-Sonoma Food.* This upscale publication is for sale at newsstands. It focuses on food preparation. Analysts believe the new magazine will act as a brand-building and traffic driver to the stores, catalogs, and online sites.
- The vast majority of Pottery Barn products are, in the words of management, "Exclusively ours. Our in-house design team keeps the contemporary urban home in mind while drawing inspiration from time-honored models." On the other hand, not everything is created in-house. "Today, we shop the world for our customers—if there's a better crepe maker to be had or a richer Italian olive oil, we find it."
- Williams-Sonoma has been the store for serious cooks for over 40 years. The company offers everything the discerning home cook could want—from stainless steel cookware to dipping sauce bowls, as well as small electric appliances, gourmet foods, and the nation's best-selling series of cookbooks.
- With a database of 19 million households, Williams-Sonoma is now one of the largest consumer catalog companies in the country, and the largest catalog company focusing on the upscale home market. The Pottery Barn catalog, for instance, is now sent to about 6 million homes each month, a circulation larger than the circulation of the five largest upscale home magazines combined.

In January of 1999, the company circulated its first Pottery Barn Kids catalog, which was well received and appears to hold great potential. What's more, Pottery Barn Kids retail stores are slated to open in the fall of 2000. The company plans to open units with 6,000 to 7,000 square feet of floor space. Ideally, the company plans to open stores in the same malls as Pottery Barn and strategically situate them close to complementary retailers, such as Gap Kids. If the initial four to six units are successful, analysts expect there could be 20 or 30 units operating in 2001.

About 60 percent of the company's Pottery Barn catalogs are circulated in the retail store trading areas. This enables each channel to leverage the other, creating even greater brand awareness.

- The home furnishings sector should benefit from demographic trends, including the aging baby boomer segment of the population, coupled with increasing home ownership and the trend toward larger homes. Remodeling and redecorating is also on the rise. Studies show that one in three homeowners have completed a major project on their home in the past two years, and 51 percent expect to be doing one in the next year or two. Studies also show that spending on home furnishings will coincide with the fastest-growing population segment. In addition, the company should benefit from such factors as healthy consumer economic indicators, including increased consumer confidence, high employment, economic growth, and the strong stock market.

- In the fall of 2001, the company plans to launch a new value-oriented home furnishings format called Elm Street. The 15,000-to-20,000-square-foot stores will be situated primarily in strip malls and aimed at the middle market. The concept is modeled after the Gap's Old Navy division, a fast-growing specialty store. The new format will offer a merchandise mix for the entire home—including tabletop, home accessories, home furnishings, furniture, bed and bath, and kids. The concept will be oriented toward home furnishings and won't emphasize kitchen goods.

Total assets: $576 million
Current ratio: 1.90
Common shares outstanding: 56 million
Return on 1999 shareholders' equity: 17.1%

	1999	1998	1997	1996	1995	1994	1993	1992
Revenues (millions)	1384	1104	933	812	645	538	410	345
Net income (millions)	66	55	41	23	2	20	13	2
Earnings per share	1.12	.96	.74	.44	.05	.38	.26	.04
Dividends per share	Nil							
Price High	60.3	40.8	25.0	18.2	15.2	17.6	9.4	4.1
Low	25.3	17.4	12.3	6.3	7.8	7.9	2.2	1.9

Index

About the Author

John Slatter, a consultant with First Financial Investment Managment, has a varied investment background and has served as a stockbroker, securities analyst, and portfolio strategist.

John Slatter has written hundreds of articles for such publications as *Barron's*, *Physician's Management*, *Ophthalmology Times*, and *Better Investing*, as well as for brokerage firms he has worked for, including Hugh Johnson & Company and Everen Securities. His books include: *Safe Investing*, *Straight Talk About Stock Investing* and four prior editions of *The 100 Best Stocks You Can Buy*.

John Slatter has been quoted in such periodicals as the *Cleveland Plain Dealer*, the *New York Times*, the *Gannett News Service*, the *Burlington Free Press*, the *Wall Street Journal*, the *Cincinnati Enquirer*, the *Toledo Blade*, the *Christian Science Monitor*, *Money* magazine, the *Dayton Daily News*, and the *Buffalo News*. He has also been quoted in a number of books, including *The Dividend Investor* and *Stocks for the Long Run*.

In August of 1988, John Slatter was featured in the *Wall Street Journal* concerning his innovative investment strategy that calls for investing in the 10 highest-yielding stocks in the Dow Jones Industrial Average. This approach to stock selection is sometimes referred to as "the dogs of the Dow," a pejorative reference that he does not believe is justified, since the stocks with high yields typically include such blue chips as Merck, IBM, 3M, General Electric, AT&T, Caterpillar, DuPont, ExxonMobil, J. P. Morgan, and Philip Morris.

John Slatter may be reached by calling (802) 879-4154, Fax (802) 878-1171 or by writing him at 70 Beech Street, Essex Junction, Vermont 05452. His e-mail address is: bluechip@together.net

FIND MORE ON THIS TOPIC BY VISITING
BusinessTown.com
The Web's big site for growing businesses!

- ☑ Separate channels on all aspects of starting and running a business

- ☑ Lots of info on how to do business online

- ☑ 1,000+ pages of savvy business advice

- ☑ Complete web guide to thousands of useful business sites

- ☑ Free e-mail newsletter

- ☑ Question and answer forums, and more!

Accounting
Basic, Credit & Collections, Projections, Purchasing/Cost Control

Advertising
Magazine, Newspaper, Radio, Television, Yellow Pages

Business Opportunities
Ideas for New Businesses, Business for Sale, Franchises

Business Plans
Creating Plans & Business Strategies

Finance
Getting Money, Money Problem Solutions

Letters & Forms
Looking Professional, Sample Letters & Forms

Getting Started
Incorporating, Choosing a Legal Structure

Hiring & Firing
Finding the Right People, Legal Issues

Home Business
Home Business Ideas, Getting Started

Internet
Getting Online, Put Your Catalog on the Web

Legal Issues
Contracts, Copyrights, Patents, Trademark

Managing a Small Business
Growth, Boosting Profits, Mistakes to Avoid, Competing with the Giants

Managing People
Communications, Compensation, Motivation, Reviews, Problem Employees

Marketing
Direct Mail, Marketing Plans, Strategies, Publicity, Trade Shows

Office Setup
Leasing, Equipment, Supplies

Presentations
Know Your Audience, Good Impression

Sales
Face to Face, Independent Reps, Telemarketing

Selling a Business
Finding Buyers, Setting a Price, Legal Issues

Taxes
Employee, Income, Sales, Property, Use

Time Management
Can You Really Manage Time?

Travel & Maps
Making Business Travel Fun